PROFESSIONAL
BAKING

SEVENTH EDITION

PROFESSIONAL

BAKING

WAYNE GISSLEN

Photography by **J. GERARD SMITH**

WILEY

Library of Congress Cataloging-in-Publication Data:

Names: Gisslen, Wayne, 1946– author.
Title: Professional baking / Wayne Gisslen ; photography by J. Gerard Smith.
Description: Seventh edition. | Hoboken, New Jersey : John Wiley & Sons,
  2016. | Includes bibliographical references and index.
Identifiers: LCCN 2016011013 (print) | LCCN 2016011537 (ebook) | ISBN
  978-1-119-14844-9 (hardback) | ISBN 978-1-119-19537-5 (pdf) | ISBN 978-1-119-19532-0 (epub)
Subjects: LCSH: Baking. | Food presentation. | BISAC: COOKING / Methods / Baking.
Classification: LCC TX763 .G47 2016 (print) | LCC TX763 (ebook) | DDC 641.81/5—dc23
LC record available at http://lccn.loc.gov/2016011013

ISBN: 978-1-119-14844-9

Printed in the United States of America

V10010257_051619

This book is dedicated to the memory of
Anne Smith

Contents

1 The Baking Profession 3

2 Basic Professional Skills: Bakeshop Math and Food Safety 15

3 Baking and Pastry Equipment 41

26 Baking for Special Diets 683

Recipe Contents

13 Pies

14 Pastry Basics

15 Tarts and Special Pastries

16 Cake Mixing and Baking

17 Assembling and Decorating Cakes

18 Cookies

19 Custards, Puddings, Mousses, and Soufflés

Preface

Professional Baking has been a widely used resource and teaching tool for tens of thousands of students since it was first published. During that time, the baking industry has evolved as interest in artisan baking has blossomed, and **Professional Baking** has changed with each new edition to keep pace with new demands. At the same time, the art and science of teaching has also evolved rapidly as new technological resources have become available to instructors and students.

Electronic media, including WileyPLUS, Wiley's online teaching and learning environment, and CulinarE-Companion™ recipe management software, provide a wealth of resources and tools to make the latest **Professional Baking** the best learning and teaching text yet. This new 7th edition of the text has been reorganized to fully integrate the print book with its electronic resources. (This wealth of resources is described in more detail later in this preface.)

Even with these developments, however, the focus of the text remains, as it always has, on a solid grounding in the basics, presented in a straightforward and easy-to-grasp style.

The goal of **Professional Baking** is to provide students and working chefs with a solid theoretical and practical foundation in baking practices, including selection of ingredients, proper mixing and baking techniques, careful makeup and assembly, and skilled and imaginative decoration and presentation. It is designed as a primary text for use in colleges and culinary schools, baking courses within broader food-service curricula, and on-the-job training programs, as well as providing a solid reference for professional bakers and pastry chefs.

Professional Baking focuses on both *understanding* and *performing*. The practical material is supported by a systematic presentation of basic theory and ingredient information, to ensure that students learn not only what techniques work but also why they work. Procedures for basic bread and pastry doughs, cake mixes, creams, and icings form the core of the material. Much of the text is devoted to step-by-step procedures and production techniques. The discussion of techniques is reinforced with straightforward formulas that allow students to develop their skills while working with large or small quantities.

Organization of the Text

Two factors strongly influence the arrangement and organization of **Professional Baking**. First is the aforementioned dual emphasis of the book, on both understanding and performing. It is not enough to present readers with a collection of formulas; nor is it sufficient to give them a freestanding summary of baking theory and principles. These must be presented together, and the connections between them made clear. In this way, when students practice preparing specific items, their study of theory helps them understand what they are doing, why they are doing it, and how to achieve the best results. At the same time, each formula they prepare helps reinforce their understanding of the basic principles. Knowledge builds upon knowledge.

The second factor revolves around the fact that most of a baker's activities fall naturally into two categories: (1) mixing, baking, and/or cooking doughs, batters, fillings, creams, and icings, and (2) assembling these elements (for example, baked cake layers, fillings, and icings) into finished pieces. The first category of tasks requires careful selection of ingredients, accurate measurement, and close attention to mixing and baking procedures. Naturally, most of the detailed guidelines and procedures in this book are devoted to these kinds of tasks. The second category, the assembly of prepared components, is less a matter of scientific accuracy than of manual skills and artistic abilities.

The Formulas

Nearly 900 formulas and recipes are given for the most popular breads, cakes, pastries, and desserts. These formulas have not been selected at random, merely for the sake of having formulas in the book. Rather, they are carefully chosen, developed, and tested to teach and reinforce the techniques students are learning, and to strengthen their understanding of basic principles. The goal is for students to understand and use not only the formulas in this book, but any formula they encounter.

The formulas in this book are instructional; their purpose is not only to give directions for producing baked goods but also to provide an opportunity to practice, with specific ingredients, the general principles being studied. Directions within formulas are often abbreviated. For example, instead of spelling out the straight dough method for breads in detail for each dough mixed in this way, the book refers the student to the preceding discussion of the procedure. By thinking and reviewing in this way, students derive a stronger learning experience from their lab work.

Many formulas are followed by variations. These are actually whole formulas given in abbreviated terms. This feature encourages students to see the similarities and differences among preparations. For example, there seems little point in giving a formula for cream pie filling in the pie chapter, a formula for custard filling for éclairs and napoleons in the pastry chapter, and separate formulas for each flavor of cream pudding in the pudding chapter, without pointing out that these are all basically the same preparation. Skill as a baker depends on knowledge, and being able to exercise judgment based on that knowledge, not just on following recipes. The ability to exercise judgment is essential in all branches of cookery but especially so in baking, where the smallest variation in procedure can produce significant changes in the finished product. The formulas in this text will help students develop good judgment by requiring them to think about the relationships between general procedures and specific products.

Media and Supplements

WileyPLUS Learning Space to Accompany Professional Baking

A place where students can define their strengths and nurture their skills, WileyPLUS Learning Space transforms course content into an online learning community. WileyPLUS Learning Space invites students to experience learning activities, work through self-assessment, ask questions, and share insights. As students interact with the course content, each other, and their instructor, WileyPLUS Learning Space creates a personalized study guide for each student. Through collaboration, students make deeper connections to the subject matter and feel part of a community.

Through a flexible course design, instructors can quickly organize learning activities, manage student collaboration, and customize your course—having full control over content as well as the amount of interactivity between students.

WileyPLUS Learning Space lets the instructor:

- Assign activities and add your own materials.
- Guide your students through what's important in the interactive e-textbook by easily assigning specific content.
- Set up and monitor group learning.
- Assess student engagement.
- Gain immediate insights to help inform teaching.

Defining a clear path to action, the visual reports in WileyPLUS Learning Space help both you and your students gauge problem areas and act on what's most important.

Technique Videos

Detailed, engaging technique videos are available as part of the WileyPLUS course with *Professional Baking*. These video clips clearly demonstrate the essential skills and procedures students must master to succeed in the professional bakeshop, and they enhance, in an engaging manner, the textbook's approach to teaching these basic skills. They can be used for study and review purposes to prepare for kitchen time or as a step-by-step presentation of these techniques.

Math Tutor

Math Tutor whiteboard-type exercises and review are available as part of the WileyPLUS course. These video-like segments are brief examples of common math problems used in the bakeshop. These videos are intended to demonstrate and reinforce bakeshop math principles cited by instructors as the #1 issue students struggle with in this course. These tutorials allow students to see a variety of math exercises explained and calculated. Further, practice exercises are included for students to use to apply and reinforce these calculations as well.

CulinarE-Companion™ Recipe Management Software

CulinarE-Companion™ is a web-based database of recipes from *Professional Baking*. You can set up an account and have instant access to the software, *viewable from any device's browser, whether a laptop, desktop, tablet, or mobile device*.

In addition to the recipes from the book and additional bonus recipes, the software includes a range of useful features. The registration code included with each copy of *Professional Baking, Seventh Edition*, allows you to access this valuable asset at no additional cost—and your account does not expire so it can be used throughout your professional career.

Feature Highlights

- **Enhanced recipe management tools:** Edit, scale, view nutritional information, convert from U.S. to metric measures and vice versa; print and share recipes. Users can also add their own recipes and create and revise shopping lists.
- **Search recipes** by main ingredient, primary cooking method, and cuisine type.
- **Calculate nutritional analyses** and update if an ingredient is changed.
- **My files:** Organize your recipes, your images, and your videos in one location.
- **Audio pronunciations:** Within the extensive glossary, *CulinarE-Companion™* has over 1,000 terms with audio pronunciations to make learning a snap.
- **Food costing:** Calculate food costs based on each ingredient's individual cost.
- **Unit conversions:** Scale recipes and units of measures are converted to the next logical unit.
- **Adding new ingredients:** Add new ingredients that do not exist in *CulinarE-Companion™* and they are automatically added into the ingredient database.
- **Nutritional analysis:** Add ingredients to a recipe that does not have nutritional information and select from an existing list of ingredients with possible USDA matches so nutritional analysis is complete.

Method Cards

As a handy reference in the kitchen, a set of six laminated Method Cards accompanies this book. They detail mixing methods for quick breads, cakes, cookies, and yeast doughs, as well as preparation methods for pies and pastry basics.

Additional Student and Instructor Resources

To enhance mastery of the material in *Professional Baking, Seventh Edition,* the following student and instructor supplements are available:

The Student Study Guide (ISBN 978-1-119-14848-7) contains review materials, practice problems, and exercises. (Answers to questions are included in the Instructor's Manual.)

The Instructor's Manual with Study Guide Solutions (available online) includes teaching suggestions and test questions.

A newly updated and revised website contains information for the student and instructor, and is available at www.wiley.com/college/gisslen.

PowerPoint slides are also available electronically to provide additional support in delivering course material.

Acknowledgments

I could not have written this book without the help of a great many people, to whom I would like to express my gratitude. Foremost among them are the many instructors and chefs who have corresponded with me or with my publisher over the years since the first edition first appeared, offering criticism and suggestions that have helped me improve the book. Many of them are among the reviewers listed at the end of these acknowledgments. No doubt I have inadvertently omitted some names, and to address this oversight, I would like to thank every instructor who has talked or written to me about this book and given me ideas for its improvement.

In addition, I would like to offer special thanks to Jim Smith, whose photography has been such an important part of these texts since the first edition, and to Chefs Andy Chlebana, Rick Forpahl, David Eisenreich, Julie Walsh, and Laurent Duchêne, whose artistry and creativity are evident in many of the photos in this book.

The technique videos available in WileyPLUS could not have been accomplished so successfully without the on-air talent of Chef Ambarush Lulay, Chef Klaus Tenbergen, Chef Melina Kelson, Chef Lisa Brefere, and most especially, Chef Andy Chelbana. Andy's role in scripting, planning, executing, and ensuring each video meets the professional kitchen standards is incalculable. Many thanks as well to Kendall College and the College of DuPage for the gracious use of their kitchens in the filming of many of the technique videos.

Finally, I would like to thank everyone at John Wiley and Sons who has worked so hard on this project: James Metzger, Wendy Ashenberg, Beth Tripmacher, Gabrielle Carrasco, Melissa Edwards, Lynne Marsala Basche, and especially my editors, JoAnna Turtletaub and Andrea Brescia.

Reviewers

I would like to acknowledge the following instructors who contributed to this book over seven editions by suggesting revisions and additions.

ROBERT L. ANDERSON
Des Moines Area Community College
Ankeny, Iowa

ANNE BALDZIKOWSKI
Cabrillo College
Aptos, California

MARY BARTON
Bunker Hill Community College
Boston, Massachusetts

THOMAS BECKMAN
The Cooking and Hospitality Institute of Chicago
Chicago, Illinois

KARLA V. BOETEL
Des Moines Area Community College
Ankeny, Iowa

ERIC BRECKOFF
J. Sargeant Reynolds Community College
Richmond, Virginia

BELINDA BROOKS
Kendall College
Chicago, Illinois

ANDY CHLEBANA
Joliet Junior College
Joliet, Illinois

JOANNE CLOUGHLY
SUNY Cobleskill
Cobleskill, New York

MARK S. COLE
Del Mar College
Corpus Christi, Texas

MARTHA CRAWFORD
Johnson & Wales University
Providence, Rhode Island

CHRIS CROSTHWAITE
Lane Community College
Eugene, Oregon

RICHARD EXLEY
Le Cordon Bleu College of Culinary Arts in Scottsdale
Scottsdale, Arizona

JOHN R. FARRIS
Lansing Community College
Lansing, Michigan

SUSAN FEEST
Milwaukee Area Technical College
Milwaukee, Wisconsin

DOUGLAS FLICK
Johnson County Community College
Overland Park, Kansas

JOSEPH D. FORD
New York Food and Hotel Management
New York, New York

CARRIE FRANZEN
Le Cordon Bleu–Minneapolis
Minneapolis, Minnesota

ROBERT J. GALLOWAY
Dunwoody Industrial Institute
Minneapolis, Minnesota

DAVID GIBSON
Niagara College of Applied Arts and Technology
Niagara Falls, Ontario, Canada

KATHRYN GORDON
Art Institute of New York City
New York, New York

KRISTEN GRISSOM
Dayton State College
Daytona Beach, Florida

JEAN HASSELL
Youngstown State University
Youngstown, Ohio

IRIS A. HELVESTON
State Department of Education
Tallahassee, Florida

NANCY A. HIGGIN
Art Institute of Atlanta
Atlanta, Georgia

ROGER HOLDEN
Oakland Community College
Bloomfield Hills, Michigan

CARALYN HOUSE
Wake Technical Community College
Raleigh, North Carolina

GEORGE JACK
The Cooking and Hospitality Institute of Chicago
Chicago, Illinois

JOANNE JACUS
New York City College of Technology
Brooklyn, New York

MIKE JUNG
Hennepin Technical College
Brooklyn Park, Minnesota

GERRINE SCHRECK KIRBY
Southeast Community College
Lincoln, Nebraska

FREDERICK GLEN KNIGHT
The Southeast Institute of Culinary Arts
St. Augustine, Florida

PAUL KREBS
Schenectady County Community College
Schenectady, New York

JEFFREY C. LABARGE
Central Piedmont Community College
Charlotte, North Carolina

MARY LASORELLA
Cincinnati State University
Cincinnati, Ohio

FRED LEMEISZ
St. Petersburg Vocational Technical Institute
St. Petersburg, Florida

LAUREL LESLIE
Kapiolani Community College
Honolulu, Hawaii

JANET LIGHTIZER
Newbury College
Brookline, Massachusetts

VALERIA S. MASON
State Department of Education
Gainesville, Florida

ELIZABETH McGEEHAN
Central New Mexico Community
College
Albuquerque, New Mexico

JOHN OECHSNER
Art Institute of Atlanta
Atlanta, Georgia

PHILIP PANZARINO
New York City Technical College
Brooklyn, New York

JAYNE PEARSON
Manchester Community College
Manchester, Connecticut

KENNETH PERRY
Le Cordon Bleu
Minneapolis, Minnesota

RICHARD PETRELLO
Withlacoochee Vocational–Technical
Center
Inverness, Florida

WILLIAM H. PIFER
Bellingham Technical College
Bellingham, Washington

GUNTER REHM
Orange Coast College
Costa Mesa, California

KENT R. RIGBY
Baltimore International
College
Baltimore, Maryland

LOU SACKETT
Dauphin Country Technical
School
Harrisburg, Pennsylvania

ANTHONY SARDINA
Valencia Community College
Orlando, Florida

KIMBERLY SCHENK
Diablo Valley College
Pleasant Hill, California

PETER SCHOLTES
George Brown College
Toronto, Ontario, Canada

GEORGE L. SOUTHWICK
Ozarks Technical
Community College
Springfield, Missouri

SIMON STEVENSON
Connecticut Culinary Institute
Suffield, Connecticut

PATRICK SWEENEY
Johnson County
Community College
Overland Park, Kansas

CHRIS THIELMAN
College of DuPage
Glen Ellyn, Illinois

ANDREA TUTUNJIAN
Institute of Culinary Education
New York, New York

DAVID VAGASKY
Culinary Institute of Charleston at
Trident Technical College
Charleston, South Carolina

HOPE WALBURN
The Art Institutes of Minnesota
Minneapolis, Minnesota

F. H. WASKEY
University of Houston
Houston, Texas

J. WILLIAM WHITE
Pinellas County School System
St. Petersburg, Florida

RONALD ZABKIEWICZ
South Technical Education
Center
Boynton Beach, Florida

Culinary Media Library Reviewers

MARCO ADORNETTO
Zane State College
Zanesville, Ohio

CHARLTON ALVARES
George Brown College
Toronto, Ontario, Canada

ALAN BROWN
George Brown College
Toronto, Ontario, Canada

DEANE COBLER
Columbus State Community College
Columbus, Ohio

RODNEY DONNE
George Brown College
Toronto, Ontario, Canada

COLLEN ENGLE
Miami Culinary Institute
Miami, Florida

ALBERT I. M. IMMING
Joliet Junior College
Joliet, Illinois

JOANNE JACUS
New York City College of Technology
Brooklyn, New York

WILLIAM JOLLY
Clover Park Technical College
Lakewood, Washington

JOHN KAPUSTA
Indiana University of Pennsylvania
Indiana, Pennsylvania

AMEDE LAMARCHE
George Brown College
Toronto, Ontario, Canada

ROBYNNE MAII
Kingsborough Community College
Brooklyn, New York

ELAINA RAVO
Liaison College
Hamilton, Ontario, Canada

CHRIS THIELMAN
College of DuPage
Glen Ellyn, Illinois

JEAN YVES VENDEVILLE
Savannah Technical College
Savannah, Georgia

CHRISTINE WALKER
George Brown College
Toronto, Ontario, Canada

Wiley CulinarE-Companion™ Recipe Management Software

Supporting chefs throughout their careers, **CulinarE-Companion** includes all recipes from **Professional Baking, Seventh Edition**, plus *bonus recipes, audio pronunciations,* and *illustrated procedures.* Create shopping lists, resize recipes, perform metric conversions, and analyze nutritional content of ingredients and recipes. You can also add your own recipes, photos, and videos, and create your own cookbooks.

CulinarE-Companion™ is a web-based database of recipes from **Professional Baking**. You can set up an account and have instant access to the software, *viewable from any device's browser, whether a laptop, desktop, tablet, or mobile device.* The registration code included with each copy of **Professional Baking, Seventh Edition** allows you to access this valuable asset at no additional cost—and your account does not expire so it can be used throughout your professional career.

THE HOME PAGE

▶ View recipes by clicking on the Professional Baking cover.

▶ Search by recipe name, partial name, or by variation.

▶ View recipes and procedures, which are organized by kitchen skill, by clicking in the "Skills" tab.

▶ Click "Glossary" tab to access definitions from **Professional Baking's** glossary plus hundreds of additional defined terms and audio pronunciations.

RECIPE SCREEN

▶ Resize recipes, perform metric conversions, show recipe notes, variations, and more!

▶ Easily access referenced procedures and recipes by clicking the referenced link.

▶ View photos of plated dishes and techniques: click the "Images" tab. You can also upload your own photos and videos.

RECIPE LIST

▶ Refine your search by course, cuisine, main ingredient, primary cooking method, or dietary considerations.

▶ Add recipes to your shopping list, as well as export and print recipes.

NUTRITIONAL INFORMATION

▶ View important nutritional information for ingredients and recipes.

▶ Nutritional information calculates automatically for all recipes, including recipes you add.

WileyPLUS with ORION

A personalized, adaptive learning experience.

WileyPLUS with ORION delivers easy-to-use analytics that help educators and students see strengths and weaknesses to give learners the best chance of succeeding in the course.

Photo credit: Monkey Business Images/Shutterstock

Identify which students are struggling early in the semester.

Educators assess the real-time engagement and performance of each student to inform teaching decisions. Students always know what they need to work on.

Help students organize their learning and get the practice they need.

With ORION's adaptive practice, students quickly understand what they know and don't know. They can then decide to study or practice based on their proficiency.

Measure outcomes to promote continuous improvement.

With visual reports, it's easy for both students and educators to gauge problem areas and act on what's most important.

PROFESSIONAL

BAKING

1

THE BAKING PROFESSION

1. Describe the major events in the history of baking, from prehistoric times to the present.
2. Describe various types of baking and pastry careers and the attitudes needed to be successful in them.

BAKING IS ONE of the oldest occupations of the human race. Since early prehistoric human beings made the transition from nomadic hunters to settled gatherers and farmers, grains have been the most important foods to sustain human life, often nearly the only foods. The profession that today includes baking artisan sourdough breads and assembling elegant pastries and desserts began thousands of years ago with the harvesting of wild grass seeds and the grinding of those seeds between stones.

Today, the professions of baker and pastry chef are growing quickly and changing rapidly. Thousands of skilled people are needed every year. Baking offers ambitious men and women the opportunity to find satisfying work in an industry that is both challenging and rewarding.

Before you start your practical studies, which are covered in this book, it is good to first learn a little about the profession you are entering. Therefore, this chapter gives you a brief overview of baking professions, including how they got to where they are today.

BAKING: HISTORICAL BACKGROUND

GRAINS HAVE BEEN the most important staple foods in the human diet since prehistoric times, so it is only a slight exaggeration to say that baking is almost as old as the human race.

The First Grain Foods

Before human beings learned to plant, they gathered wild foods. The seeds of various wild grasses, the ancestors of modern grains, were rich in nutrients and valued by prehistoric peoples as important foods. These seeds, unlike modern grains, had husks that clung tightly to them. People learned that by toasting the seeds, probably on hot rocks, they could loosen the husks and then remove them by beating the seeds with wooden tools.

The early development of grain foods took place mostly in the eastern Mediterranean regions, where, it seems, wild grains were especially abundant.

Few cooking utensils were in use at this point in human history, so it is probable that the earliest grain preparation involved toasting dry grains, pounding them to a meal with rocks, and mixing the meal to a paste with water. The grains had already been cooked by toasting them, to remove the husks, so the paste needed no further cooking. Later, it was discovered that some of this paste, if laid on a hot stone next to a fire, turned into a flatbread that was a little more appetizing than the plain paste. Unleavened flatbreads, such as tortillas, are still important foods in many cultures. Unleavened flatbreads made from grain pastes are the first stage in the development of breads as we know them.

To understand how breads evolved, you must also understand a little about how grains developed. As you will learn in Chapter 4, modern yeast breads depend on a combination of certain proteins to give them their structure. For all practical purposes, only wheat and its relatives contain enough of these proteins, which form an elastic substance called *gluten*. A few other grains also contain gluten proteins, but they do not form as strong a structure as wheat gluten.

Further, the proteins must be raw in order to form gluten. Because the earliest wild grains had to be heated to free them from their husks, they could be used only to make grain pastes or porridges, not true breads. Over time, prehistoric people learned to plant seeds; eventually, they planted only seeds of plants whose seeds were easiest to process. As a result, hybrid varieties emerged whose husks could be removed without heating the grains. Without this advancement, modern breads could not have come about.

Ancient Leavened Breads

A grain paste left to stand for a time sooner or later collects wild yeasts (microscopic organisms that produce carbon dioxide gas) from the air, and begins to ferment. This was, no doubt, the beginning of leavened (or raised) bread, although for most of human history the presence of yeast was mostly accidental. Eventually, people learned they could save a small part of the current day's dough to leaven the next day's batch.

Small flat or mounded cakes made of a grain paste, whether leavened or unleavened, could be cooked on a hot rock or other hot, flat surface, or they could be covered and set near a fire or in the embers of a fire. The ancient Egyptians developed the art of cooking leavened doughs in molds—the first loaf pans. The molds were heated and then filled with dough, covered, and stacked in a heated chamber. These were perhaps the first mass-produced breads. Breads made from wheat flour were costly and so affordable for only the wealthy. Most people ate bread made from barley and other grains.

By the time of the ancient Greeks, about 500 or 600 BCE, true enclosed ovens were in use. These ovens were preheated by building a fire inside them. They had a door in the front that could be closed, so they could be loaded and unloaded without losing much heat.

Still, for the most part, the breads baked in these ovens were nothing more than cakes of baked grain pastes mixed with a little of the paste from the day before to supply wild yeasts for leavening. Such flat or slightly mounded breads were called *maza*. Maza, especially those made of barley, were the staple food of the time. In fact, in ancient Greece, all foods were divided into two categories, maza and *opson*, meaning things eaten with maza. Opson included vegetables, cheese, fish, meat, or anything else except bread. Often the opson was placed on top of the flat bread, forming the ancestors of modern pizzas.

Writings from ancient Greece describe as many as 80 kinds of bread and other baked grain products originated by professional bakers. Some of these could be called true breads, rather than flatbreads or maza, because they were made with kneaded doughs containing wheat flour, which provided gluten proteins.

Several centuries later, the ancient Romans were slow to develop breads. Not until master bakers arrived from Greece did grain foods advance much beyond porridges and simple flat-breads. By the latter period of the Roman Empire, however, baking was an important industry. Bakeshops were often run by immigrant Greeks.

An important innovation in Roman baking was introduced by the Gauls, a European people who had been conquered by the Romans. The Gauls, the ancestors of the modern French, had invented beer making. They discovered that adding the froth from beer to bread dough made especially light, well-leavened breads. The froth contained yeast from beer fermentation, so this process marked the beginning of the use of a controlled yeast source for making bread doughs.

Many of the products made by Roman bakers contained quantities of honey and oil, so these foods might more properly be called pastries rather than breads. That the primary fat available was oil placed a limit on the kinds of pastries that could be made, however. Only a solid fat such as butter enables the pastry maker to produce the kinds of stiff doughs we are familiar with today, such as pie doughs and short pastries.

Baking in the Middle Ages

After the collapse of the Roman Empire, baking as a profession almost disappeared. Not until the latter part of the Middle Ages did baking and pastry making begin to reappear as important professions in the service of the nobility. Bread baking continued to be performed by professional bakers, not homemakers, because it required ovens that needed almost constant tending. And because of the risk of fire, baking ovens were usually separated from other buildings, and often outside city walls.

In much of Europe, tending ovens and making bread dough were separate operations. The oven tender maintained the oven, heated it properly, and supervised the baking of the loaves that were brought to him. In early years, the oven may not have been near the workshops of the bakers, and one oven typically served the needs of several bakers. It is interesting to note that in many bakeries today, especially in the larger ones, this division of labor still exists. The chef who tends the ovens bakes the proofed breads and other products that are brought to him or her and may not have any part in the mixing and makeup of these products.

Throughout the Middle Ages, one of the bread maker's tasks was sifting, or *bolting*, the whole-grain flour that was brought to him by customers. Sifting with coarse sieves removed only part of the bran, while sifting with finer sieves removed most or all of the bran and made whiter flour. More of the grain is removed to make white flour, so the yield was lower and, thus, white bread was more expensive, putting it out of reach of ordinary people. Not until around 1650 CE did bakers start buying sifted flour from mills.

Because bread was the most important food of the time, many laws were passed during this period to regulate production factors such as bolting yields, bread ingredients, and loaf sizes. It was also in the Middle Ages that bakers and pastry chefs in France formed guilds to protect and advance their art. Regulations prohibited all but certified bakers from baking bread for sale, and the guilds had the power to limit certification to their own members. The guilds, as well as the apprenticeship system, which was well established by the sixteenth century, also provided a way to pass the knowledge of the baker's trade from generation to generation.

To become master bakers, workers had to go through a course of apprenticeship and obtain a certificate stating they had gained the necessary skills. Certified master bakers could then set up their own shops. Master bakers were assisted by apprentices, who were learning the trade and so were not paid, and by journeymen, who were paid servants and who may have completed an apprenticeship but had not gained a master baker's certificate.

Sugar and Pastry Making

Bakers also made cakes from doughs or batters containing honey or other sweet ingredients, such as dried fruits. Many of these items had religious significance and were baked only for special occasions, such as the Twelfth Night cakes baked after Christmas. Such products nearly always had a dense texture, unlike the light confections we call cakes today. Nonsweetened pastry doughs were also made for such products as meat pies.

In the 1400s, pastry chefs in France formed their own corporations and took control over pastry making from bakers. From this point on, the profession of pastry making developed rapidly, and bakers invented many new kinds of pastry products.

Honey was the most important sweetener at the time because, for Europeans, sugar was a rare and expensive luxury item. Sugarcane, the source of refined sugar, was native to India and grown in southern regions of Asia. To be brought to Europe, sugar had to pass through many countries, and each overland stop added taxes and tolls to its already high price.

The European arrival in the Americas in 1492 sparked a revolution in pastry making. The Caribbean islands proved ideal for growing sugar, which led to increased supply and lower prices. Cocoa and chocolate, native to the New World, also became available in the Old World for the first time. Once these new ingredients became widely accessible, baking and pastry became more and more sophisticated, and many new recipes were developed. By the seventeenth and eighteenth centuries, many of the basic pastries we know today, including laminated or layered doughs like puff pastry and Danish dough, were being made. Also in the eighteenth century, processors learned how to refine sugar from sugar beets. At last, Europeans could grow sugar locally.

From the First Restaurants to Carême

Modern food service is said to have begun shortly after the middle of the eighteenth century. Just as bakers and pastry cooks had to be licensed, and became members of guilds, which controlled production, so too did caterers, roasters, pork butchers, and other food workers become licensed members of guilds. For an innkeeper to be able to serve meals to guests, for example, he had to buy the various menu items from those operations that were licensed to provide them. Guests had little or no choice. They simply ate what was offered for that meal.

Portrait of Marie-Antoine Carême, from M.A. Carême. *L'art de la cuisine française au dix-neuvième siècle. Traité élémentaire et pratique*, **1833.**

Division of Rare and Manuscript Collections, Cornell University Library.

In 1765, a Parisian named *A. Boulanger* (whose name, incidentally, means "bread baker") began advertising on his shop sign that he served soups, which he called "restaurants," or "restoratives." (The word "restaurant" comes from the French *restaurer*, "to restore.") According to the story, one of the dishes he served was sheep's feet in a cream sauce. The guild of stew makers challenged him in court, but Boulanger won by claiming he didn't stew the feet *in* the sauce but served them *with* the sauce. In challenging the rules of the guilds, Boulanger changed the course of food service history.

For the bread baker, two important events during this period were the publication of the first major books on bread making: *L'art du meunier, du boulanger et du vermicellier* (*The Art of the Miller, the Bread Baker, and the Pasta Maker*) by Paul-Jacques Malouin in 1775, and *Le parfait boulanger* (*The Perfect Bread Baker*) by Antoine-Augustin Parmentier in 1778.

The nineteenth century saw not just a revolution in food service but also in the development of modern baking as we know it. After the French Revolution in 1789, many bakers and pastry cooks who had been servants in the houses of the nobility started independent businesses. Artisans competed for customers with the quality of their products, and the general public—not just aristocrats and the well-to-do—were able to buy fine pastries. Some of the pastry shops started during this time are still serving Parisians today.

An invention in the eighteenth century forever changed the organization of the commercial kitchen, which to date had been centered round an open cooking fire. This invention was the stove, which provided a more controllable heat source. In time, commercial kitchens were divided into three departments, each based on a piece of equipment: the stove, run by the cook, or *cuisinier*; the rotisserie, run by the meat chef, or *rôtisseur*; and the oven, run by the pastry chef, or *pâtissier*. The pastry chef and the meat chef reported to the cuisinier, who was also known as *chef de cuisine*, which means "head of the kitchen." Although the stovetop was a new feature of this reorganized kitchen, the baker's oven was still the wood-fired brick oven that had long been in use.

The most famous chef of the early nineteenth century was *Marie-Antoine Carême*, also known as Antonin Carême, who lived from 1784 to 1833. His spectacular constructions of sugar and pastry earned him great fame, and he elevated the professions of cook and pastry chef to respected positions. Carême's book, *Le pâtissier royal*, was one of the first systematic explanations of the pastry chef's art.

Ironically, most of Carême's career was spent in the service of the nobility and royalty, in an era when the products of the bakers' and pastry chefs' craft were becoming more widely available to average citizens. Carême had little to do with the commercial and retail aspects of baking.

In spite of his achievements and fame as a pastry chef, Carême was not primarily a baker, but a chef de cuisine. As a young man, he learned all the branches of cooking quickly, and he dedicated his career to refining and organizing culinary techniques. His many books contain the first systematic account of cooking principles, recipes, and menu making.

Modern Baking and Modern Technology

The nineteenth century was a time of great technical progress in the baking profession. Automated processes enabled bakers to do many tasks with machines that once required a great deal of manual labor. The most important of these technological advances was the development of *roller milling*. Prior to this time, flour was milled by grinding grain between two stones. The resulting flour then had to be sifted, or bolted, often numerous times, to separate the bran. The process was slow. Roller milling, described in Chapter 4 (see page 55), proved to be much faster and more efficient. This was a tremendous boost to the baking industry.

Another important development of the period was the availability of new flours from the wheat-growing regions of North America. These wheat varieties were higher in protein than those that could be grown in northern Europe, and their export to Europe promoted the large-scale production of white bread.

In the twentieth century, advances in technology, from refrigeration to sophisticated ovens to air transportation that can carry fresh ingredients around the world, contributed immeasurably to baking and pastry making. Similarly, preservation techniques have helped make available and affordable some ingredients that were once rare and expensive. Also, thanks to modern food preservation technology, it is now possible to do some or most of the preparation and processing of foods before shipping, rather than in the bakeshop or food service operation itself. Thus, convenience foods have come into being. Today, it is feasible to avoid many labor-intensive processes, such as making puff pastry, by purchasing convenience products.

Modern equipment, too, has helped advance production techniques and schedules. For example, dough sheeters speed the production of laminated doughs, such as Danish dough, while at the same time producing a more uniform product. Retarder-proofers hold yeast doughs overnight and then proof them so they are ready to bake in the morning. It is now possible to prepare some foods farther in advance and in larger quantities, maintaining them in good condition until ready for finishing and serving.

Modern Styles

All these developments have led to changes in cooking styles and eating habits. The evolution in cooking and baking, which has been going on for hundreds of years, continues to this day. It is helpful to explore the shifts in restaurant cooking styles, because those in baking and pastry have followed a similar course.

A generation after *Escoffier*, the most influential chef in the middle of the twentieth century was Fernand Point (1897–1955). Working quietly and steadily in his restaurant, La Pyramide, in Vienne, France, Point simplified and lightened classical cuisine. His influence extended well beyond his own lifetime.

Many of Point's apprentices, such as Paul Bocuse, Jean and Pierre Troisgros, and Alain Chapel, went on to become some of the greatest stars of modern cooking. They, along with other chefs of their generation, became best known in the 1960s and early 1970s for a style of cooking called *nouvelle cuisine*. They took Point's lighter approach even further, by urging the use of simpler, more natural flavors and preparations, with lighter sauces and seasonings and shorter cooking times. In traditional classical cuisine, many dishes were plated in the dining room by waiters. Nouvelle cuisine, in contrast, emphasized artful plating presentations done by the chef in the kitchen. In the pastry chef's department, this practice marked the beginning of the modern plated dessert.

GEORGES-AUGUST ESCOFFIER

Georges-August Escoffier (1847–1935), the greatest chef of his time, is still revered by chefs and gourmets as the father of twentieth-century cookery. His main contributions were: (1) the simplification of the classical menu; (2) the systematizing of cooking methods; and (3) the reorganization of the kitchen.

Escoffier's books and recipes remain important reference works for professional chefs. The basic cooking methods and preparations we study today are based on his principles. Escoffier's *Le guide culinaire*, which is still widely used, arranges recipes in a system based on the main ingredient and cooking method, greatly simplifying the more complex system handed down from Carême. Learning classical cooking, according to Escoffier, begins with mastering a relatively few basic procedures and understanding essential ingredients.

Although Escoffier didn't work as a bread baker, he applied the same systems to the production of desserts that he did to savory food. Several of the desserts he invented, such as peach Melba, are still served today.

Georges-August Escoffier.

Courtesy of Getty Images.

A landmark event in the history of modern North American cooking was the opening of Alice Waters's restaurant, Chez Panisse, in Berkeley, California, in 1971. Waters's philosophy is that good food depends on good ingredients, so she set about finding dependable sources of the highest-quality vegetables, fruits, and meats, and preparing them in the simplest ways. Over the next decades, many chefs and restaurateurs followed her lead, seeking the best seasonal, locally grown, organically raised food products.

During the latter part of the twentieth century, as travel became easier, and more immigrants began arriving in Europe and North America from around the world, awareness of and taste for regional dishes grew. To satisfy these expanding tastes, chefs became more knowledgeable, not only about the traditional cuisines of other parts of Europe but also of Asia, Latin America, and elsewhere. Many of the most creative chefs today are inspired by these cuisines and use some of their techniques and ingredients. Master pastry chefs such as Gaston Lenôtre have revitalized the art of fine pastry and inspired and taught a generation of professionals.

Alice Waters of Chez Panisse.

Courtesy of David Liittschwager

The use of ingredients and techniques from more than one regional cuisine in a single dish has become known as *fusion cuisine*. Fusion cuisine can, however, produce poor results because it is not true to any one culture and becomes too mixed up. This was especially true in the 1980s, when the idea of fusion cuisine was new. Cooks often mixed ingredients and techniques without a true understanding for how everything worked together. The result was sometimes a jumbled confusion of tastes. Fortunately, since the early days of fusion, those chefs who have taken the time to study in depth the cuisines and cultures they borrow from have brought new excitement to cooking and restaurant menus. In the pastry department specifically, ingredients such as passion fruit, mangoes, and lemongrass, once thought strange and exotic, are now commonly found.

The discussion of modern styles must include a mention of trends, fad, and fashions. An interest in what's new has always been a concern of professional cooks, but with the speed of modern communication and the widespread use of social media, trends seem to come and go more quickly than ever. An example is the recent popularity of cupcakes, which were suddenly in such demand that bakeshops selling nothing but a large variety of cupcakes sprang up in many neighborhoods. By the time large chain stores had added cupcakes to their product offerings, the fashion faded and many of the original cupcake bakeries had closed. New shops offering dozens of varieties of doughnuts had taken their place to take advantage of the next trend.

The interest in gluten-free diets, even among those who have no medical reasons to avoid gluten, is another example. To satisfy demand, bakers must learn new techniques, develop new formulas, and even set aside part of their production areas as gluten-free environments. Fads and trends offer both opportunity and challenge to modern bakers. To adapt to trends quickly and take advantage of new demands, bakers need to have a solid foundation in basic baking techniques and procedures so that they can produce goods of the highest quality and, at the same time, be ready to move on when fashions change.

The Evolution of Modern Bread

The progression of bread baking since the nineteenth century is an interesting example of how technology has affected our food production. Two developments changed how bread was made, and for the first time made possible the mass production of bread: the widespread use of mixers and the development of modern yeast. Mixing machines, though invented decades earlier, didn't really become popular until the 1920s. Within a few years, stronger commercial yeasts became available, meaning that bakers no longer had to depend on slow-fermenting sponges and sour-dough starters to leaven their breads. Now, large quantities of breads could be mixed, fermented, and baked in just a few hours.

By the 1950s and 1960s, most bread was being mass produced. Unfortunately, most of it was boring and flavorless. To compensate for the rapid mixing and production processes, bakers had to add dough conditioners and other additives to their products. But much of the flavor of good bread comes from long yeast fermentation, so the new mixing and leavening procedures meant sacrificing flavor for speed. As a result, bread became little more than a vehicle to hold sandwich fillings or to convey butter and jelly to the mouth. Even in France, the baguette had become bland and uninteresting.

Perhaps the most important figure in the bread revolution of the twentieth century was a professor of baking from Paris, France, Raymond Calvel. Calvel did extensive research on flour composition, fermentation, and other aspects of bread making for the purpose of restoring character and flavor to bread and to produce bread with only natural ingredients. His work stimulated a return to older-style flours and more traditional mixing techniques. More than this, he developed new techniques, such as autolyse (explained on page 159), that enabled bakers to produce flavorful artisanal breads without resulting in a return to the 12- to 16-hour days of heavy labor required of bakers in earlier times. (More information on the bread revolution launched by Calvel is detailed in the Bread Mixing: A Historical Perspective sidebar in Chapter 7 on page 119.) Calvel's book *Le Goût du Pain* (translated as *The Taste of Bread*) is today one of the most important reference books for artisan bakers.

This effort to recapture in bread lost flavors of times gone by has carried over to other baked goods, including pastries and desserts of all kinds. The same artisan bakeries selling flavorful old-style breads are also now enticing customers with higher-quality Danish, brioche, and croissants, made with many of these rediscovered techniques. On restaurant dessert menus, this trend can be seen in the home-style desserts made with the best ingredients, which sit comfortably side by side with ultramodern pastry presentations.

KEY POINTS TO REVIEW

▪ Why is wheat the most important grain in the development of baked goods?

▪ How have new technologies changed the baking industry since the nineteenth century?

LIONEL POILÂNE

A generation younger than Raymond Calvel, the Parisian baker Lionel Poilâne expanded the baking business he inherited from his father into one of the world's most famous boulangeries, shipping his signature 2-kg round sourdough loaves around the world. Except for the use of mixing machines, he relied on traditional techniques and ingredients—such as stone-ground flour, wood-burning ovens, and sourdough fermentation—to produce his intensely flavorful breads. Sadly, Poilâne was tragically killed in a helicopter crash in 2002, but his daughter Apollonia carries on the business today.

BAKING AND PASTRY CAREERS

SINCE THE BEGINNING of the twenty-first century, the popularity of fine breads and pastries has been growing faster than new chefs can be trained to support it. Those entering careers in baking or pastry making today will find opportunities in many areas, from small bakeshops and neighborhood restaurants to large hotels and wholesale bakeries.

Restaurant and Hotel Food Service

As you learned earlier in this chapter, one of Escoffier's important achievements was the reorganization of the kitchen. He divided the kitchen into departments, or stations, based on the kinds of foods they produced. A station chef was placed in charge of each department. This system, with many variations, is still in use today, especially in large hotels offering traditional kinds of food service. In a small operation, the station chef may be the only worker in the department. But in a large kitchen, each station chef might have several assistants.

Station chefs in large kitchens include the sauce chef (*saucier*), who is responsible for sauces and sautéed items; the fish chef (*poissonier*); the roast chef (*rôtisseur*); and the pantry chef (*chef garde manger*). Desserts and pastries are prepared by the pastry chef (*pâtissier*). Station chefs report to the executive chef, or *chef de cuisine*, who is in charge of food production. In the largest kitchens, the duties of the executive chef are mostly managerial. The executive chef may, in fact, do little or no cooking personally. The *sous chef* assists the executive chef and is directly in charge of the cooking during production.

The pastry department is usually separated physically from the hot kitchen, for at least two important reasons. First, and most obvious, is that many desserts and confections must be prepared in a cool environment. Second, the division helps prevent creams, icings, and batters from absorbing the aromas of roasted, grilled, and sautéed foods.

In a small to medium-size restaurant, the pastry chef may work alone, preparing all the dessert items. Often he or she works early in the morning and finishes before the dinner service starts. Another cook or the dining room staff then assembles and plates the desserts during service.

In large restaurants and hotels, the chef in charge of baking and desserts is the executive pastry chef. This is a management position comparable to the executive chef in the hot kitchen. The executive pastry chef supervises workers in the department, including specialists such as the bread baker (*boulanger*), who prepares yeast goods including such breakfast items as brioche, croissants, and Danish pastry; the ice cream maker (*glacier*), who makes frozen desserts; the confectioner or candy maker (*confiseur*); and the decorator (*décorateur*), who prepares showpieces, sugar work, and decorated cakes.

In hotels, the work of the baking and pastry department can be extensive, including preparing not only desserts and breads for all the on-premise restaurants, cafés, and room service, but also breakfast breads and pastries and all baked goods, including specialty cakes and decorative work, for the banquet and catering departments. Such large operations provide many opportunities for the baker wishing to gain a wide range of experience.

Caterers, institutional volume-feeding operations (e.g., schools, hospitals, employee lunchrooms), executive dining rooms, and private clubs may also require the services of bakers and pastry chefs. The required skills vary from one establishment to another. Some prepare all their baked goods in-house, while others rely on convenience products and finished wholesale bakery foods.

Courtesy of Shutterstock Images, LLC; copyright areashot.

Bakeries

Retail bakeries include independent bakeshops as well as in-store bakery departments in grocery stores and supermarkets. High-end supermarkets, in particular, have opened many new opportunities for creative bakers and pastry chefs. A few grocery stores have even installed wood-burning hearth ovens for baking handcrafted artisan breads.

The **head baker** is the professional in charge of the production in a retail bakery. He or she is in charge of a staff that may range from a few bakers who share most tasks to, in a larger bakery, many specialists who work in different departments, such as breads and yeast goods, cakes, and decorated items. Even bread-making tasks may be divided among different workers, with some mixing, proofing, and making up the doughs, and others baking the items and managing the ovens.

Although most independent bakeshops offer a full range of products, from breads to cakes and pastries, some make their reputations on one or two specialty items, such as cupcakes or artisan breads, and concentrate on those products. More specialized yet are shops whose entire business consists of preparing and decorating celebration cakes, such as for weddings, birthdays, and the like.

Wholesale bakeries accomplish the same tasks as retail bakeries, but their production facilities may be more automated and industrialized. In them, equipment such as mixers and ovens handle large volumes of doughs and baked goods. In addition to finished items, wholesale bakeries may produce unfinished products such as cake layers, cookie dough, and puff pastry dough for sale to restaurants, hotels, caterers, supermarkets, and other food service operations.

Professional Requirements

What does it take to be a qualified baker or pastry chef?

The emphasis of a food service education, whether in baking and pastry or in the hot kitchen, is on learning a set of skills. But in many ways, *attitudes* are more important than skills because a good attitude will help you not only learn skills but also to persevere and overcome the difficulties you may face in your career.

Mastery of skills is, of course, essential to success. There are, in addition, a number of general personal qualities that are equally important for the new pastry chef or baker just graduated from school who wants to advance in the industry. The following sections describe a few of these important characteristics.

Eagerness to Work

Baking professionally is demanding, both physically and mentally. By the time students graduate, they realize that those of their fellow students who have been the hardest working—especially those who sought extra work and additional opportunities to learn—are the most successful. Once they have graduated, bakers and chefs who continue to give the greatest effort are the ones who advance the fastest.

One of the most discouraging discoveries for new culinarians is how repetitive the work is. They must do many of the same tasks over and over, day in and day out, whether it's making up hundreds of dinner rolls a day or thousands of cookies for holiday sales. Successful bakers and chefs approach repetition as an opportunity for building skills. Only by doing a cooking task over and over can you really master it—really understand every nuance and variable.

Stress is another issue caused by repetitive hard work. Overcoming stress requires a sense of responsibility and a dedication to your profession, to your coworkers, and to your customers or clients. Dedication also means staying with a job, resisting the urge to hop from kitchen to kitchen every few months. Sticking with a job for at least a year or two shows prospective employers you are serious about your work and can be relied on.

Commitment to Learning

A strong work ethic is empowered by knowledge, so it is important that you, as a baking professional, make a commitment to your ongoing education: The baking and food service industries are constantly changing, as new products and techniques are developed and new technology is introduced. Therefore, continual learning is necessary for success. Read. Study. Experiment. Network with other chefs. Share information. Join the alumni association of your school and stay in touch with your fellow graduates. Take continuing education courses offered by schools and trade associations. Enter competitions to hone your skills and to learn from your competitors. Learn management and business skills and master the latest computer software in your field. Remember that learning to bake and cook and manage a kitchen or bakery is a lifelong process.

An effective way to foster your own learning is through professional associations like the American Culinary Federation (ACF), the Canadian Culinary Federation—Fédération Culinaire Canadienne (CCFCC), and the Retail Bakers of America. These organizations provide a way to network with other professions in local chapters and at regional and national trade shows. In addition, they sponsor certification programs that document your skill level and encourage ongoing study.

In return, help others learn. Share your knowledge. Be a mentor to a student. Teach a class. Help a coworker. Judge a competition. Contribute to professional workshops and seminars. Do what you can to raise the skill level of the profession.

Dedication to Service

Food service, as its name implies, is about serving others. Baking and cooking professionally mean bringing enjoyment and a sense of well-being to your guests. Providing good service requires sourcing high-quality ingredients and handling them with care and respect; guarding the health of guests and coworkers, paying full attention to food safety and sanitation; treating others with respect; making guests feel welcome and coworkers feel valued; and maintaining a clean, attractive work environment. Look after others, and your own success will follow.

Professional Pride

Professionals take pride in their work, and want to make sure it is something they can be proud of. A professional cook maintains a positive attitude, works efficiently, neatly, and safely, and always aims for high quality. Although it might sound like a contradiction, professional pride should be balanced with a strong dose of humility, for it is humility that leads chefs to dedicate themselves to hard work, perpetual learning, and commitment to service. A professional who takes pride in his or her work recognizes the talent of others in the field and is inspired and stimulated by their achievements. A good baker or pastry chef also demonstrates pride by, in turn, setting a good example for others.

KEY POINTS TO REVIEW

- What are the major baking and pastry career positions in food service? In retail and wholesale bakeries?

- What are the personal characteristics that are important to the success of bakers and pastry chefs?

TERMS FOR REVIEW

A. Boulanger	Marie-Antoine Carême	saucier	glacier
cuisinier	roller milling	poissonier	confiseur
rôtisseur	Georges-August Escoffier	chef garde manger	décorateur
pâtissier	nouvelle cuisine	sous chef	head baker
chef de cuisine	fusion cuisine	boulanger	

QUESTIONS FOR REVIEW

1. What characteristic of modern wheat flour makes it possible to produce an elastic, yeast-fermented dough? Why was it not possible for prehistoric people to make such doughs from the earliest wild grains?

2. What historical event did the most to make sugar widely available? How so?

3. What contribution did beer production make to the process of bread making?

4. Briefly describe how commercial kitchens were organized after the invention of the stove in the eighteenth century.

5. What is nouvelle cuisine? How did nouvelle cuisine affect the style of desserts served in restaurants?

6. Describe the organization of a large, modern hotel kitchen. Name and describe specialty positions that may be found in large bakeries.

2

BASIC PROFESSIONAL SKILLS:

Bakeshop Math and Food Safety

AFTER READING THIS CHAPTER, YOU SHOULD BE ABLE TO:

1. Describe the structure, uses, and limitations of baking formulas.
2. Measure ingredients correctly.
3. Calculate ingredient weights based on baker's percentages, and convert formulas correctly.
4. Calculate formula costs.
5. Describe the steps to prevent foodborne diseases in the areas of personal hygiene and food-handling techniques.

RECIPES AND FORMULAS are fundamental tools of the kitchen and bakeshop. They indicate ingredients to be purchased and stored. They give measuring and preparation instructions for the items to be produced. And they are the focus of other management tools and techniques, including modifying quantities and determining costs.

In this chapter, you are introduced to basic bakeshop production through a discussion of the kinds of measurements and mathematical calculations necessary for baking and of the basic processes common to nearly all baked goods.

The final portion of this chapter gives you a brief overview of another critically important issue in running a successful bakeshop: sanitation.

USING FORMULAS

A SET OF instructions for producing a certain dish is called a *recipe*. In order to duplicate a desired preparation, it is necessary to have a precise record of the ingredients, their amounts, and the way in which they are combined and cooked. This is the purpose of a recipe.

FORMULAS AND MOPS

Strictly speaking, the term *formula* refers only to the list of ingredients and quantities. The directions for using those ingredients, referred to in this book as the *procedure*, are known by many chefs as the *method of preparation*, or MOP. There are relatively few MOPs, or basic procedures, and these are applied to nearly all the products of the bakeshop. To a trained baker, these MOPs are so well understood that they need not be repeated with every formula, as explained in the text.

One of the major purposes of this book is to familiarize you with the principal procedures used in the bakeshop so you too can make use of professional formulas.

Bakers generally talk about *formulas* rather than recipes. If this sounds to you more like the lingo of a chemistry lab than a food production facility, it is with good reason. The bakeshop is very much like a chemistry laboratory, both in terms of the scientific accuracy required of the procedures and of the complex reactions that take place during mixing and baking.

Note there are no exact rules for using the word *formula* in the context of baking (see the Formulas and MOPs sidebar). Some bakers use the term to refer to flour goods only, while using the word *recipe* when talking about such items as pastry cream, fruit fillings, and dessert mousses. Other bakers are in the habit of calling all recipes *formulas*. Still others consistently use the word *recipe*. In this book, we use the word *formula* for most products, although you will also see the word *recipe* used occasionally.

The primary function of a formula is, of course, to give a set of ingredients and quantities for making a product. But a formula is also useful for related purposes. A written formula provides a means of modifying quantities and yields and determining costs. These functions require the use of math. Procedures for working with formula math are the main focus of the next three sections.

Uses and Limitations of Formulas and Recipes

In spite of their importance, written formulas and recipes have many limitations. No matter how detailed a formula is, it assumes you already have certain knowledge—that you understand the terminology it uses, for example, and that you know how to measure ingredients.

Before talking specifically about baking formulas, let's briefly consider recipes in general. Many people believe that learning how to cook simply means learning recipes. A professional cook, on the other hand, learns to work by mastering a set of basic procedures. A recipe is a way of applying basic techniques to specific ingredients.

The main purpose of learning basic cooking principles is not to be able to cook without recipes but rather to understand the recipes you use. As we just said, every recipe assumes you have certain knowledge, so you can understand the instructions and follow them correctly.

If you have leafed through this book, you know it is made up of more than formulas and recipes. Although it does contain hundreds of formulas, they make up only part of its contents. Its main concern is to teach you the basic techniques and procedures so that you can apply them to any formula.

Bakers use a relatively small number of basic mixing techniques to prepare doughs and batters. For this reason, a baker's formula may consist only of a list of ingredients and quantities and the name of the mixing method. A trained baker can produce a finished product with this information alone. In fact, often the name of the mixing method isn't even necessary because the baker can tell from the ingredients and their proportions which mixing method is needed. To accustom you to this way of working, and to emphasize the importance of learning basic mixing methods well, most of the formulas in this book indicate the name of the required mixing method without repeating the steps for each formula. In each case, you should review the basic procedures as needed before using a formula.

Some recipes supply very little information; others supply a great deal. But no matter how detailed it is, a written recipe can't tell you everything, and some judgment by the cook is always required. This is especially true in the hot kitchen, where cooks must always make adjustments for ingredient product variation—some carrots are sweeter than others, for example, some oysters are saltier than others, and so on.

In the bakeshop, there is less product variation. Specifically, flour, yeast, sugar, butter, and other basic ingredients are pretty consistent, especially when purchased from the same source. Nevertheless, many other factors can't be accounted for when writing a recipe. To name just two:

- Equipment varies from bakeshop to bakeshop. For example, different mixers as well as different-size mixers process dough differently, and ovens vary in their baking properties.
- It is impossible to give exact instructions for many processes. For example, a bread formula may indicate a mixing time, but the exact time needed for a particular batch will vary. The baker must be able to judge by the feel and texture of the dough when it has developed properly.

Standardized Recipes and Formulas

A *standardized formula* or *recipe* is a set of instructions describing the way a particular establishment prepares a particular item. In other words, it is a customized recipe developed by an operation for the use of its own cooks, pastry chefs, and bakers, using its own equipment, to be sold or served to its own patrons.

Standardized formula formats differ from operation to operation, but nearly all of them try to include as much precise information as possible. The following details may be listed:

- Name of the recipe
- Yield, including total yield, number of portions, and exact portion size
- Ingredients and exact amounts, listed in order of use
- Equipment needed, including measuring equipment, pan sizes, portioning equipment, and so on
- Directions for preparing the dish—kept as simple as possible
- Preparation and cooking times
- Directions for holding the product between preparation and service
- Directions for portioning, plating, and garnishing
- Directions for storing leftovers

As you can tell, some of these points apply more to the pastry or dessert station in a restaurant than they do to retail bakeries. Bread recipes don't require instructions for plating and garnishing, for example. Nevertheless, the basic principles apply to bakeries, as well as to restaurant kitchens.

Functions of Standardized Formulas

An operation's own recipes are used to control production. They do this in two ways:

- *They control quality.* Standardized formulas and recipes are detailed and specific. This is to ensure the product is the same every time it is made and served, no matter who cooks it.
- *They control quantity.* First, they indicate precise quantities for every ingredient and how to measure that quantity. Second, they indicate exact yields and portion sizes and how to measure and serve those portions.

Limitations of Standardized Formulas

Standardized formulas have the same problems as all recipes—those discussed earlier regarding variations in ingredients, equipment, and vagueness of instructions. These problems can be minimized by writing the recipe carefully, but they cannot be eliminated. Even if an operation uses proven, standardized recipes, a new employee making a dish for the first time usually requires some supervision to make sure he or she interprets the instructions the same way as the rest of the staff. These limitations don't invalidate standardized recipes. If anything, they make exact directions even more important. But they do show that experience and knowledge are still very important.

Instructional Recipes and Formulas

The formulas in this book are *not* standardized. Remember that a standardized formula is custom-made for a particular operation. The formulas in this book, obviously, can't be.

The purpose of a standardized formula is to direct and control the production of a particular food item. Directions must be as complete and exact as possible. In contrast, the purpose of the instructional formulas in this book is to teach basic baking and cooking techniques. They provide an opportunity for you to practice, with specific ingredients, the general procedures you have learned.

If you glance at any of the formulas in this book, you will see they do not contain all the features of standardized formulas, as described in the previous section. In particular, you will see the following differences:

1. **Instructions for preparation.** In most cases, formulas in this book follow a discussion of a basic procedure. The formulas are examples of the general procedure, to give you experience in applying what you have learned. The information you are given in the formula instructions is intended primarily to encourage you to think and to learn a technique, not just to turn out a product. You should consult your instructor when you have a question about a procedure.

2. **Variations and optional ingredients.** Many formulas are followed by variations. These are actually whole formulas given in abbreviated terms. It is possible to write them out as separate, full-length formulas. (You are encouraged to do this before preparing a variation, as a learning experience.)

   Giving formulas as variations rather than as separate formulas helps you to see the patterns behind each. Again, you are learning techniques, not just formulas. You develop greater understanding of what you are doing when you see, for example, coconut cream pie and chocolate pudding as variations of the same basic techniques rather than as separate, unrelated formulas.

   Your instructors may have their own variations, or they may wish to make changes in the basic formulas in order to teach you certain points. Unlike standardized formulas, instructional formulas are not engraved in stone.

Reading Formulas and Recipes

Before starting production, you must read the entire recipe carefully and completely. The following are some of the tasks you must carry out as you read the recipe and get ready for production. Chefs call these advance preparations their *mise en place* (MEEZE on plahss; French for "put in place"). A good mise en place is essential for efficient operation of a bakeshop or kitchen.

Formula Modifications

- Determine the yield of the printed recipe and decide whether it needs modification. If you need to convert the recipe to a different yield (discussed later in this chapter), do all the math beforehand.

- Determine whether any other changes are needed, such as ingredient substitutions, to get the desired result. Write them down.

Ingredients

- Assemble and measure all ingredients. If all ingredients are scaled in advance, production can go quickly and without interruption. Also, it's better to find out in advance that you don't have enough of an ingredient so you can get more before starting production.

- Prepare all ingredients as necessary, such as sifting flour, separating eggs, and bringing butter to room temperature. Many of these steps are indicated in the recipe, but others may not be. Professional formulas often assume that the experienced baker knows, for example, that butter should be removed from the refrigerator in advance so it is soft enough to be used in creaming-method cake batters.

Procedures

- Read the entire procedure or method of preparation carefully, and make sure you understand it.

- If a mixing method is indicated only by name, such as creaming method, look up and review the procedure if you need to refresh your memory. Make sure you understand each step of the general procedure and how to apply it to your specific formula.

- Look up any terms or key words you don't know.

Tools and Equipment

- Determine what equipment you need. Required equipment is generally listed in standardized recipes but not in those from other sources. Read every step of the procedure and write down which tools and equipment you need in each step.
- Assemble all tools and equipment.
- Prepare equipment as needed. For example, line sheet pans with parchment, grease cake pans, preheat ovens.

KEY POINTS TO REVIEW

▌ Is this statement true: "If you have a good formula, you don't need to know how to bake, because the formula tells you what to do."? Explain.

▌ What are standardized recipes? How are they used?

MEASUREMENT

One of the primary functions of a formula is to indicate the ingredients and their correct quantities or measurements to be used to make a product.

Ingredients are almost always weighed in the bakeshop, rather than measured by volume, because measurement by weight is more accurate. (There are some exceptions, noted below.) Accuracy of measurement, as we have said, is essential in the bakeshop. Unlike home baking recipes, a professional baker's formula will not call for 6 cups flour, for example.

To demonstrate to yourself the importance of weighing rather than measuring by volume, measure 1 cup flour in two ways: (a) Sift some flour and lightly spoon it into a dry measure. Level the top and weigh the flour. (b) Scoop some unsifted flour into the same measure and pack it lightly. Level the top and weigh the flour. Note the difference. No wonder home recipes, which usually indicate volume measures of dry ingredients, can be so inconsistent!

The baker's term for weighing ingredients is *scaling.*

The following ingredients, and *only* these ingredients, may sometimes be measured by volume, at the ratio of 1 pint per pound or 1 liter per kilogram:

- Water
- Milk
- Eggs

Volume measure is often used when scaling water for small or medium-sized batches of bread. Results are generally good. However, whenever accuracy is critical, it is better to weigh. This is because 1 pint water actually weighs slightly more than 1 pound, or approximately 16.7 ounces. (This figure varies with the temperature of the water.)

For convenience, volume measures of liquids are frequently used when products other than baked flour goods—such as sauces, syrups, puddings, and custards—are being made.

Units of Measure

The system of measurement used in the United States is complicated. Even people who have used it all their lives sometimes have trouble remembering factors such as how many fluid ounces are in a quart and how many feet are in a mile.

The Units of Measure: U.S. System table lists equivalents among the units of measure used in the bakeshop and kitchen. You should memorize these now so you don't lose time in the future making simple calculations. The Abbreviations for U.S. Units of Measure Used in This Book table lists those used in this book.

UNITS OF MEASURE: U.S. SYSTEM		
WEIGHT		
1 lb	=	16 oz
VOLUME		
1 gal	=	4 qt
1 qt	=	2 pt
		or
		4 cups
		or
		32 (fl) oz*
1 pt	=	2 cups
		or
		16 (fl) oz
1 cup	=	8 (fl) oz
1 fl oz	=	2 tbsp
1 tbsp	=	3 tsp
LENGTH		
1 ft	=	12 in.

***NOTE:** One fluid ounce (fl oz)—often simply called ounce—of water weighs 1 ounce. One pint of water weighs approximately 1 pound.

The Metric System

The United States is the only major country that uses the complex system of measurement we have just described. Other countries use a much simpler system called the *metric system*, detailed here.

Basic Units

In the metric system, there is one basic unit for each type of measurement:

The *gram* is the basic unit of weight.

The *liter* is the basic unit of volume.

The *meter* is the basic unit of length.

The *degree Celsius* is the basic unit of temperature.

Larger or smaller units are made by simply multiplying or dividing by 10, 100, 1000, and so on. These divisions are expressed by prefixes. The ones you need to know are:

kilo- = 1000

deci- = 1/10, or 0.1

centi- = 1/100, or 0.01

milli- = 1/1000, or 0.001

Once you learn these basic units, you will not need complicated tables such as the one on page 19. The Metric Units table summarizes the metric units you need to know in the bakeshop.

Converting to Metric

Most Americans think the metric system is much harder to learn than it really is. This is because they think about metric units in terms of U.S. units. They read, for example, that there are 28.35 grams in 1 ounce and are immediately convinced they will never be able to learn metrics.

Most of the time, you will not need to worry about converting U.S. units into metric units, and vice versa. This is a very important point to remember, especially if you think the metric system might be hard to learn. The reason is simple: You will usually be working in either one system or the other, and you will rarely have to convert from one to the other. Many people

METRIC UNITS

BASIC UNITS

Quantity	Unit	Abbreviation
Weight	Gram	g
Volume	Liter	L
Length	Meter	m
Temperature	degree Celsius	°C

DIVISIONS AND MULTIPLES

Prefix/Example	Meaning	Abbreviation
kilo-	1000	k
Kilogram	1000 grams	kg
deci-	1/10	d
Deciliter	0.1 liter	dL
centi-	1/100	c
Centimeter	0.01 meter	cm
milli-	1/1000	m
Millimeter	0.001 meter	mm

today own imported cars and repair them with metric tools without worrying about how many millimeters are in 1 inch. Occasionally, you might find a metric formula you want to try in a U.S. kitchen. Even then, much modern equipment, such as digital scales, measures in both metric and U.S. units, so conversion isn't needed. When it is necessary to convert, you can refer to a table such as the one in Appendix 2, Metric Conversion Factors, without having to memorize exact conversion factors. For most purposes, all you have to remember is the information in the table on page 20.

To become accustomed to working in metric units, it is helpful to have a feel for how large the units are. Use the following rough equivalents to help you visualize metric units. These are *not* exact conversion factors; when you need exact conversion factors, see Appendix 2.

A *kilogram* is slightly more than 2 pounds.

A *gram* is about ¹⁄₃₀ ounce. A half-teaspoon of flour weighs a little less than 1 gram.

A *liter* is slightly more than 1 quart.

A *deciliter* is slightly less than ½ cup.

A *centiliter* is about 2 teaspoons.

A *meter* is slightly longer than 3 feet.

A *centimeter* is about ⅜ inch.

0°C is the freezing point of water (32°F).

100°C is the boiling point of water (212°F).

An increase or decrease of 1 degree Celsius is equivalent to about 2 degrees Fahrenheit.

Metric Formulas and Recipes

American industry will probably adopt the metric system someday. Many recipe writers are getting a head start by including metric equivalents. As a result, you will see recipes calling for, for example: 454 g flour, 28.35 g butter, or a baking temperature of 191°C. No wonder some people are afraid of the metric system!

Kitchens in countries that use the metric system do not work with such impractical numbers any more than we normally use figures like 1 lb 1¼ oz flour, 2.19 oz butter, or a baking temperature of 348°F. That would defeat the purpose of the metric system, which is to be simple and practical. If you have a chance to look at a French cookbook, you will see nice, round numbers such as 1 kg, 200 g, and 4 dL.

The metric measures in the formulas in this book are NOT equal to the U.S. measures given alongside them. When working with a formula, do not measure some ingredients in ounces and others in grams. You should think of the metric portion of the formulas as separate formulas with yields that are close to but not the same as the yields of the U.S. formulas. To give exact equivalents would require using awkward, impractical numbers. If you have metric equipment, use the metric units; if you have U.S. equipment, use the U.S. units. As noted earlier, rarely should you have to worry about converting between the two.

For the most part, the total yield of the metric formulas in this book is *close* to the yield of the U.S. formulas, while keeping the ingredient proportions the same. Unfortunately, it is not always possible to keep the proportions exactly the same because the U.S. system is not decimal-based like the metric system. In some cases, the metric quantities produce slightly different results due to the varying proportions, but these differences are usually extremely small.

Measuring by Weight

A good balance scale should be accurate to ¼ oz (0.25 oz) or, if metric, to 5 g. Dry ingredients weighing less than ¼ oz can be scaled by physically dividing larger quantities into equal portions. For example, to scale ¹⁄₁₆ oz (0.06 oz), first weigh out ¼ oz, then divide this into four equal piles using a small knife.

For fine pastry work, a small, battery-operated digital scale is often more useful than a large balance scale. A good digital scale is relatively inexpensive. It can instantly measure quantities to the nearest ⅛ oz or the nearest 2 g. Even more sensitive scales are available at a somewhat higher

Digital professional scale.

Courtesy of Cardinal Detecto.

SCONE FLOUR

British bakers have a convenient method for measuring baking powder when small quantities are needed. They use a mixture called *scone flour*. To make 1 lb scone flour, combine 15 oz flour and 1 oz baking powder; sift together three times. One oz (1⁄16 lb) scone flour thus contains 1⁄16 (0.06 oz) baking powder. For each 1⁄16 oz baking powder you need in a formula, substitute 1 oz scone flour for 1 oz of the flour called for in the formula.

price. Most digital scales have a zero, or *tare*, button that sets the indicated weight to zero. For example, you may set a container on the scale, set the weight to zero, add the desired quantity of the first ingredient, again set the weight to zero, add the second ingredient, and so on. This speeds the weighing of dry ingredients to be sifted together, for example. Be careful, however, when using this method, as opposed to weighing ingredients one at a time. If you add too much of one ingredient, you will likely have to discard the whole mixture and start again.

When very small quantities of items such as spices are required in formulas in this book, an approximate volume equivalent (usually in fractions of a teaspoon) is also included. However, remember that careful weighing on a good scale is more accurate. Approximate volume equivalents of selected ingredients are given in Appendix 4.

To make formula conversions and calculations easier, fractions of ounces that appear in the ingredient tables of the formulas in this book are written as decimals. Thus, 1½ oz is written as 1.5 oz, and ¼ oz is written as 0.25 oz. A list of decimal equivalents is included in Appendix 3.

AP Weight and EP Weight

In the hot kitchen, cooks are regularly concerned with the trimming yield of vegetables, fruits, meats, and other ingredients. For example, 1 lb raw, whole turnips yields much less than 1 lb trimmed, peeled turnips. In the bakeshop, bakers need not be concerned with trimming yield of the ingredients they use most: flour, sugar, fats, and so on. However, it is important to be able to make the proper yield calculations when working with fresh fruits. How many pounds of whole apples must the baker order, for example, if 5 lb peeled, sliced apples are needed?

The percentage yield of a fruit or vegetable indicates, on the average, how much of the *AP weight* (as purchased weight) is left after trimming to produce the ready-to-cook item, or *EP weight* (edible portion weight).

PROCEDURE: Using a Baker's Balance Scale

The principle of using a baker's scale is simple: The scale must balance before setting the weights, and it must balance again after scaling. The following procedure applies to the most commonly used type of baker's scale:

1. Set the scale scoop or other container on the left side of the scale.

2. Balance the scale by placing counterweights on the right side and/or by adjusting the ounce weight on the horizontal bar.

3. Set the scale for the desired weight by placing weights on the right side and/or by moving the ounce weight.

   For example, to set the scale for 1 lb 8 oz, place a 1-lb weight on the right side and move the ounce weight to the right 8 oz. If the ounce weight is already over 8 oz, so you cannot move it another 8, add 2 lb to the right side of the scale and subtract 8 ounces by moving the ounce weight 8 places to the left. The result is still 1 lb 8 oz.

4. Add the ingredient being scaled to the left side until the scale balances.

Courtesy of Cardinal Detecto.

To determine the percentage yield of a fruit, follow these steps:

1. Weigh the item before trimming. This is the AP weight.

2. Trim and peel the item as necessary to get the edible portion.

3. Weigh the trimmed item. This is the EP weight.

4. Divide the EP weight by the AP weight. For example,

$$\textbf{5 lb trimmed (EP)} \div \textbf{10 lb before trimming (AP)} = \textbf{0.5}$$

5. Multiply this number by 100 to get the percentage. For example,

$$\textbf{0.5} \times \textbf{100} = \textbf{50\%}$$

The most accurate yield percentages are the ones you calculate yourself, because they are based on the items you actually use in your bakeshop. For approximate or average yield percentages of most commonly used fruits, refer to the section on fruits in Chapter 21, page 570.

Once you have a yield percentage for an item, save this number to refer to as necessary. You can use this figure to do two basic calculations.

1. **Calculating yield.** Example: You have 10 lb AP apples. Yield after trimming is 75%. What will the EP weight be?

   a. First, change the percentage to a decimal number by moving the decimal point two places to the left.

   $$\textbf{75\%} = \textbf{0.75}$$

   b. Multiply the decimal by the AP weight to get EP yield.

   $$\textbf{10 lb} \times \textbf{0.75} = \textbf{7½ lb or 7 lb 8 oz}$$

1. **Calculating amount needed.** Example: You need 10 lb EP apple slices. What amount of untrimmed fruit do you need?

   a. Change the percentage to a decimal number.

   $$\textbf{75\%} = \textbf{0.75}$$

   b. Divide the EP weight needed by this number to get the AP weight.

   $$\frac{\textbf{10 lb}}{\textbf{0.75}} = \textbf{13.33 lb or 13 lb 5⅓ oz}$$

KEY POINTS TO REVIEW

▍ How are most formula ingredients measured?

▍ In the metric system, what are the units of measure for weight, volume, and length?

▍ What are the steps in the procedure for using a baker's balance scale?

▍ What are AP quantities and EP quantities? Explain how to perform yield calculations.

USING BAKER'S PERCENTAGES

The most important information conveyed by a baker's formula is the *ratios* of the ingredients to each other. For example, if you know a particular bread dough requires exactly two-thirds as much water as flour, you can always determine the exact amount of water to add to the flour, whether you are making a large or a small quantity. *Ratios are the simplest and most basic way of expressing a formula.*

Bakers use a simple but versatile system of percentages for expressing their formulas. *Baker's percentages* indicate the amount of each ingredient used as a percentage of the amount of flour used. Flour is used as the basis of baker's percentages because it is the main ingredient in nearly all baked goods.

PERCENT

A little math review may be in order. What does *percent* mean?

The word percent literally means "per hundred." 100%, then, could also be written $^{100}/_{100}$. Similarly, 10%, for example, is the same as $^{10}/_{100}$. This same fraction, written in decimals, is 0.1.

Whenever you need to work with a percentage in a math problem, you must first change it to a fraction, as we did above. To do this, simply move the decimal point two places to the left. For example

$$15\% = 0.15$$
$$80\% = 0.80 \text{ or, more simply, } 0.8$$
$$100\% = 1.00$$
$$150\% = 1.15$$

To put it differently, the percentage of each ingredient is its total weight divided by the weight of the flour, multiplied by 100%, or:

$$\frac{\text{Total weight of ingredient}}{\text{Total weight of flour}} \times 100\% = \% \text{ of ingredient}$$

Thus, flour is always 100%. If two kinds of flour are used, their total is 100%. Any ingredient that weighs the same as the amount of flour used is also given as 100%. The cake formula ingredients listed on page 26 illustrate how these percentages are used. Check the figures with the above equation to make sure you understand them.

Please remember these numbers do not refer to the percentage of the total yield. They are simply a way of expressing *ingredient proportions.* The total yield of these percentage numbers is always greater than 100%.

Baker's percentages make it easy to see at a glance the ingredient ratios and, therefore, the basic structure and composition of the dough or batter. In addition, they make it easy to adapt the formula for any yield, as you will see in a later section. A third advantage is that single ingredients may be varied, and other ingredients added, without changing the whole formulation. For example, you can add raisins to a muffin mix formula while keeping the percentages of all the other ingredients the same.

Using baker's percentages is the most basic way of expressing a formula, so they are also a useful tool for developing new formulas. When devising a new formula, a baker thinks about the best ratio of ingredients, as indicated by percentages. Once the proper ratios are established, the baker can then translate them into weights, so that the formula can be tested. Most of the formulas in this book were devised this way.

Clearly, a percentage system based on the weight of flour can be used only when flour is a major ingredient, as in breads, cakes, and cookies. However, the principle can be used in other formulas as well, by selecting a major ingredient and establishing it as 100%. Many bakers use the percentage system for flour goods only (doughs and batters), but it is helpful to extend the benefits of this system to other products. In this book, *whenever an ingredient other than flour is used as the base of 100%, this is indicated at the top of the formula above the percentage column.* See, for example, the formulas for Almond Filling on page 196. These recipes indicate "almond paste at 100%," and the weights of the sugar, eggs, and other ingredients are expressed as percentages of the weight of the almond paste. (In some formulas in this book, especially those without a predominant ingredient, percentages are not included.)

Formula Yields

Yields for the formulas in this book are indicated in one of two ways. In most cases, the yields are given as a total of the ingredient quantities. For example, in the sample formula on page 26, the yield tells us how much cake batter the formula makes. This is the figure we need to know for the purpose of scaling the batter into pans. The actual weight of the baked cake will vary, depending on pan size and shape, oven temperature, and so on.

Other formulas of this type, in which the yield is the total weight of the ingredients, include formulas for bread doughs, coffee cake fillings, pastry doughs, and cookie doughs.

In some formulas, however, the yield is not the same as the total weight of ingredients. For example, see the recipe for French Buttercream, page 421. When sugar and water are boiled to make a syrup, about half the water evaporates. Thus, the actual yield is less than the total weight of the ingredients.

In this book, when the yield is not the same as the total weight of the ingredients, the yield is indicated *above* the ingredients list rather than below it.

Also, please note that all yields, including percentage totals, are rounded off to the next lower whole number. This eliminates insignificant fractions and makes reading easier.

Basic Formula and Recipe Conversion

Unless you are working in an operation that uses only its own standardized formulas, you frequently will be required to convert formulas to different quantities. For example, you may have a formula for 20 lb dough but need only 8 lb.

Knowing how to convert formulas and recipes is an important skill. You will no doubt need to use it many times, not only in this book but also during your career.

There is no "best" yield to write recipes for, as every operation, every school, and every individual has different needs. This section explains two methods for converting recipe yields. The first, using a conversion factor, can be applied to nearly all recipes, not just those for baking. The second method uses baker's percentages and is appropriate for most of the formulas in this book.

Conversion Calculations Using Conversion Factors

Nearly everyone can, instinctively, double a formula or cut it in half. It seems more complicated, though, to change a formula from, say, 10 to 18 kg, or from 20 to 12 qt. Actually, the principle is exactly the same: You multiply each ingredient by a number called a *conversion factor*, as in the procedure given here.

The procedure on this page is a general one. It is also used for recipes in the hot kitchen.

Conversion Calculations Using Percentages

Using baker's percentages simplifies formula and ingredient calculations. The two procedures on page 26 are used regularly in the bakeshop.

PROCEDURE: Calculating Conversion Factors

Divide the desired yield by the yield stated on the recipe. This formula may be written like a mathematical calculation, as on a calculator, or as a fraction:

$$\text{Mathematical Calculation: New yield} \div \text{Old yield} = \text{Conversion factor}$$

$$\text{Fraction: } \frac{\text{New yield}}{\text{Old yield}} = \text{Conversion factor}$$

Example 1: You have a recipe with a yield of 8 portions and you want to make 18 portions.

$$18 \div 8 = 2.25$$

Your conversion factor is 2.25. If you multiply each ingredient in your recipe by 2.25, you will prepare 18 portions, not the 8 of the original recipe.

Example 2: You have a recipe that makes 4 liters of sauce, and you want to make 1 liter.

$$1 \div 4 = 0.25$$

Your conversion factor is 0.25. That is, if you multiply each ingredient by 0.25, you will prepare only 1 liter.

Notice in the second example that the conversion factor is a number less than 1. This is because the recipe yield is decreased. You are making the recipe smaller. This is a good way to check your math. Decreasing the recipe yield will involve a conversion factor less than 1. Increasing the yield of a recipe will involve a conversion factor larger than 1.

PROCEDURE: Calculating the Weight of an Ingredient When the Weight of Flour Is Known

1. Change the ingredient percentage to decimal form by moving the decimal point two places to the left.
2. Multiply the weight of the flour by this decimal figure to get the weight of the ingredient.

   Example: A formula calls for 20% sugar and you are using 10 lb flour. How much sugar do you need?

   $$20\% = 0.20$$
   $$10 \text{ lb} \times 0.20 = 2 \text{ lb sugar}$$

   Note: In the U.S. system, weights normally must be expressed all in one unit, either ounces or pounds, in order for the calculations to work. Unless quantities are very large, it is usually easiest to express weights in ounces.

Example (U.S.): Determine 50% of 1 lb 8 oz.

$$1 \text{ lb } 8 \text{ oz} = 24 \text{ oz}$$
$$0.50 \times 24 \text{ oz} = 12 \text{ oz}$$

Example (metric): A formula calls for 20% sugar and you are using 5000 g (5 kg) flour. How much sugar do you need?

$$20\% = 0.20$$
$$5000 \text{ g} \times 0.20 = 1000 \text{ g sugar}$$

PROCEDURE: Converting a Formula to a New Yield

1. Change the total percentage of the formula to a decimal form by moving the decimal point two places to the left.
2. Divide the desired yield by this decimal figure to get the weight of flour needed.
3. If necessary, round off this number to the next highest figure. This will allow for losses in mixing, makeup, and panning, and it will make calculations easier.
4. Use the weight of flour and remaining ingredient percentages to calculate the weights of the other ingredients, as in the previous procedure.

Example: In the sample cake formula in the table below, how much flour is needed if you require 6 lb (or 3000 g) cake batter?

$$377.5\% = 3.775$$
$$6 \text{ lb} = 96 \text{ oz}$$

96 oz / 3.775 = 25.43 oz; or, rounded off, 26 oz (1 lb 10 oz)

3000 g / 3.775 = 794.7 g; or, rounded off, 800 g

INGREDIENTS	U.S. WEIGHT	METRIC WEIGHT	%
Cake flour	5 lb	2500 g	100
Sugar	5 lb	2500 g	100
Baking powder	4 oz	125 g	5
Salt	2 oz	63 g	2.5
Emulsified shortening	2 lb 8 oz	1250 g	50
Skim milk	3 lb	1500 g	60
Egg whites	3 lb	1500 g	60
Total weight:	**18 lb 14 oz**	**9438 g**	**377.5%**

Problems in Converting Formulas

For the most part, converting baking formulas to different yields works well. As long as ingredient ratios stay the same, you are making the same dough or batter. But when you make very large conversions—say, from 2 lb dough to 100 lb—you may encounter problems. In general, the major pitfalls are in one of the following categories.

Surface and Volume

If you have studied geometry, you may remember that a cube with a volume of 1 cubic foot has a top surface area of 1 square foot. But if you double the volume of the cube, the top surface area is not doubled but is in fact only about 1½ times as large.

What in the world, you ask, does this have to do with cooking? Consider the following example.

Suppose you have a good recipe for ½ gallon of dessert sauce, which you normally make in a small saucepan. But now you want to make 16 gallons of sauce, so you multiply all ingredients by a conversion factor of 32 and make the sauce in a steam kettle. To your surprise, not only do you end up with more sauce than you expected, but it turns out rather thin and watery. What happened?

Your converted recipe has 32 times as much volume to start, but the amount of surface area has not increased nearly as much. Because the ratio of surface area to volume is less, evaporation is less. This means less reduction and less thickening occur, and the flavors are not as concentrated. To correct this problem, you would have to either simmer the sauce longer or use less liquid.

The surface/volume problem shows up in the difference between making a single loaf of bread at home and making a large quantity of bread in the bakery. The home bread baker uses warm water to make a bread dough, and must find a way to keep the dough warm enough so it ferments properly. The ratio of surface area to volume in a small amount of dough is so high the dough cools quickly. The commercial baker, in contrast, often uses ice water when making bread dough to ensure the dough doesn't become too warm (see p. 123). The ratio of surface to volume is low, and the dough retains the heat generated by mixing.

When making large adjustments in formula yields, you must also determine whether adjustments in procedure or ingredient percentages are needed.

Equipment

When you change the size of a formula, you must often use different equipment, too. This often means the recipe does not work in the same way. Bakers and cooks must be able to use their judgment to anticipate these problems and modify their procedures to avoid them. The example just given, of cooking a large batch of dessert sauce in a steam kettle, is among the kinds of problems that can arise when you change cooking utensils.

Other problems may arise because of mixers or other processing equipment. For example, if you break down a dough formula to make only a small quantity, you might find there is so little dough in the mixing machine that the beaters don't blend the ingredients properly.

Or you might have a recipe for a muffin batter you usually make in small quantities, mixing the batter by hand. When you increase the recipe greatly, you find you have too much to do by hand. Therefore, you use a mixer but keep the mixing time the same. Because the mixer does the job so efficiently, you overmix the batter and end up with poor-quality muffins.

Many mixing and stirring jobs can be done only by hand. This is easy with small quantities but difficult with large batches. The result is often an inferior product. On the other hand, some handmade products are better when they are produced in large batches. It is hard, for example, to make a small batch of puff pastry because the dough cannot be rolled and folded properly.

Selection of Ingredients

In addition to measuring, there is another basic rule of accuracy in the bakeshop: Use the exact ingredients specified.

As you will learn in Chapter 4, different flours, shortenings, and other ingredients do not function alike. Baker's formulas are balanced for specific ingredients. For example, do not substitute bread flour for pastry flour or regular shortening for emulsified shortening. They won't work the same way.

Occasionally, a substitution may be made, such as instant dry yeast for fresh yeast (see p. 79), but not without adjusting the quantities and rebalancing the formula.

COST CALCULATIONS

Food service operations are businesses. Chefs and bakers must be aware of the basics of food cost calculations, even if they aren't responsible for the management of budgets, invoices, and expenses. This section discusses the most basic calculations.

Ingredient Unit Costs

The first simple calculation you need for all further calculations is for *unit cost.* Often, the purveyor's invoice indicates unit cost; for example, 10 lb apricots at $2.00 per pound, totaling $20.00 ($10 \times \$2.00 = \$20.00$). In other cases, you must make this calculation, using the following formula:

$$\text{Total cost} \div \text{Number of units} = \text{Unit cost}$$

Example 1: A case of mangoes weighing 15 lb costs $25.00. What is the cost per pound?

$$\$25.00 \div 15 \text{ lb} = \$1.67 \text{ per lb}$$

Example 2: A 45-kg sack of patent flour costs $20.00. What is the cost per kilogram?

$$\$20.00 \div 45 \text{ kg} = \$0.45 \text{ per kg (rounded up)}$$

EP Unit Costs

Calculation of AP and EP quantities, as discussed on pages 22–23, is necessary not only for determining quantities needed for preparing formulas and recipes but also for determining costs. After all, when you buy fresh fruit by weight, for example, you are paying for the entire fruit, even if you discard peels, cores, and pits.

In the first example above, you determined that you are paying $1.67 per AP pound of mangoes. But you discard the peel and pit, so the cost per EP pound is greater than $1.67. You use the following formula to calculate the yield cost, or EP unit cost:

$$\text{AP unit cost} \div \text{Yield percentage} = \text{EP unit cost}$$

Using a yield percentage of 75% (see p. 23), you can calculate the cost of our peeled, pitted mangoes using this formula. First you convert the percentage to a decimal by moving the decimal point two places to the left:

$$75\% = 0.75$$
$$\$1.67 \div 0.75 = \$2.23 \text{ per EP lb}$$

Formula Costs

To determine the cost of preparing a formula or recipe, you first determine the cost of each ingredient. Then you add the costs of all the ingredients to get the total cost of the formula.

When you have calculated the total cost, you can then determine the unit cost of the finished product. Units may be any measure you require: per ounce, per kilogram, or per serving portion (portion cost).

For the most accurate costing, you should determine the number of units actually sold, rather than the unit yield of the formula. Keep in mind that ingredients or product lost through spillage or other waste must still be accounted and paid for. Using units sold or served accounts for these costs.

The general procedure on page 29 explains the basic steps in calculating formula cost.

PROCEDURE: Calculating Formula Costs

1. List all ingredients and quantities of the formula as prepared.

2. Determine the EP unit cost of each ingredient (see p. 28).

3. Convert the quantities in the formula to the same units used for the EP costs. (For example, to convert ounces to pounds, divide by 16, as in the following example.)

4. Calculate the total cost of each ingredient by multiplying the EP unit cost by the number of units

needed. Round up fractions of a cent to the next highest cent.

5. Add the ingredient costs to get the total formula cost.

6. To get unit costs, divide the total formula cost by the number of units produced (or, for better accuracy, the number of units actually sold, as explained in the text). Round up fractions of a cent to the next highest cent.

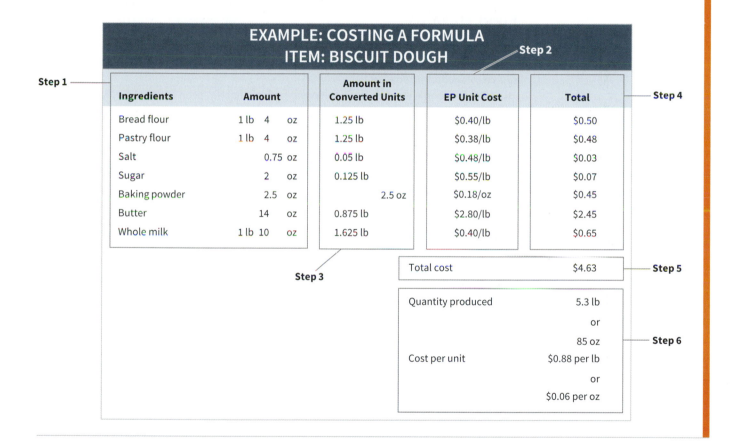

EXAMPLE: COSTING A FORMULA
ITEM: BISCUIT DOUGH

Step 1 · Step 2 · Step 3 · Step 4 · Step 5 · Step 6

Ingredients	Amount			Amount in Converted Units	EP Unit Cost	Total
Bread flour	1 lb	4	oz	1.25 lb	$0.40/lb	$0.50
Pastry flour	1 lb	4	oz	1.25 lb	$0.38/lb	$0.48
Salt		0.75	oz	0.05 lb	$0.48/lb	$0.03
Sugar		2	oz	0.125 lb	$0.55/lb	$0.07
Baking powder		2.5	oz	2.5 oz	$0.18/oz	$0.45
Butter		14	oz	0.875 lb	$2.80/lb	$2.45
Whole milk	1 lb	10	oz	1.625 lb	$0.40/lb	$0.65

Total cost	$4.63

Quantity produced	5.3 lb
	or
	85 oz
Cost per unit	$0.88 per lb
	or
	$0.06 per oz

KEY POINTS TO REVIEW

- What are baker's percentages?
- Using baker's percentages, what is the procedure for calculating the weight of an ingredient when the weight of flour is known?
- Using baker's percentages, what is the procedure for converting a formula to a new yield?
- What is the procedure for calculating formula costs?

FOOD SAFETY AND SANITATION

IN CHAPTER 1 we discussed some of the requirements for success in the food service industry, including professional pride. One of the most important ways of demonstrating professional pride is in the area of sanitation and safety. Pride in quality also is reflected in your personal appearance and work habits. Poor hygiene, grooming, and personal care, and sloppy work habits are nothing to be proud of.

In addition, poor sanitation can cost a lot of money. Poor food-handling procedures and unclean kitchens cause illness and unhappy customers, and may even result in fines, summonses, and lawsuits. Food spoilage raises food costs. Finally, poor sanitation and safety habits show lack of respect for your customers, your fellow workers, and yourself.

This section briefly outlines the guidelines for food safety and sanitation in the bakeshop, presenting enough information to build basic awareness. Be aware, however, that entire books and courses of study are devoted to food safety and sanitation. Consult the bibliography at the end of this book to find sources of more detailed information on these important subjects.

Food Hazards

Preventing foodborne illness is one of the most critical challenges facing every food service worker. To prevent illness, a food worker must begin by recognizing and understanding the sources of foodborne disease.

Most foodborne illness is the result of eating food that has been *contaminated*. To say that a food is contaminated means it contains harmful substances that were not present originally in the food. In other words, contaminated food is food that is not pure.

We begin this section by discussing the substances that can contaminate food and cause illness. Next, we consider how these substances get into food to contaminate it and how food workers can prevent contamination and avoid serving contaminated food.

Any substance in food that can cause illness or injury is called a *hazard*. Food hazards are of three types:

1. Biological
2. Chemical
3. Physical

Biological Hazards

The most important kinds of biological hazard to consider are microorganisms. A *microorganism* is a tiny, usually single-celled organism that can be seen only with a microscope. A microorganism that can cause disease is called a *pathogen*. Although these organisms sometimes occur in clusters large enough to be seen with the naked eye, they are not usually visible. This is one reason why they can be so dangerous. Just because food looks good doesn't mean it is safe.

Four kinds of microorganisms can contaminate food and cause illness: *bacteria*, *viruses*, *fungi*, and *parasites*. Most foodborne diseases are caused by bacteria, and these are the pathogens we focus on here. Many of the measures we take to protect food from bacteria also help prevent the other three kinds of microorganisms.

BACTERIAL GROWTH

Bacteria multiply by splitting in half, repeatedly. Under ideal conditions for growth, they can double in number every 15 to 30 minutes. This means a single bacterium can multiply to 1 million in less than 6 hours! The following conditions are needed for bacterial growth:

1. **Food.** Bacteria require food in order to grow. They like many of the same foods we do. Foods with sufficient amounts of protein are best for bacterial growth. These include meats, poultry, fish, dairy products, and eggs, as well as some grains and vegetables.

2. **Moisture.** Bacteria require water in order to absorb food. Dry foods do not support bacterial growth. Foods with a very high salt or sugar content are also relatively safe, because these ingredients make the bacteria unable to use the moisture present.

3. **Temperature.** Bacteria grow best at warm temperatures. Those between 41°F (5°C) and 135°F (57°C) promote the growth of disease-causing bacteria. This temperature range is called the *Temperature Danger Zone* or the *Food Danger Zone*. (Note that your state or county may have a different definition of the danger zone. See the Local Health Resources and Regulations sidebar on page 35.)

4. **Acidity or alkalinity.** In general, disease-producing bacteria thrive in a neutral environment, neither too acidic nor too alkaline. The acidity or alkalinity of a substance is indicated by a measurement called *pH*. The scale ranges from 0 (strongly acidic) to 14 (strongly alkaline). A pH of 7 is neutral. Pure water has a pH of 7.

5. **Oxygen.** Some bacteria require oxygen to grow. These are called *aerobic*. Other bacteria are *anaerobic*, which means they can grow only if no air is present, such as in metal cans. Botulism, one of the most dangerous forms of food poisoning, is caused by anaerobic bacteria. A third category of bacteria can grow either with oxygen or without it. These bacteria are called *facultative*. Most bacteria in food that cause disease are facultative.

6. **Time.** When bacteria are introduced to a new environment, they need time to adjust to their surroundings before they start growing. This time is called the *lag phase*. If other conditions are good, the lag phase may last about an hour or somewhat longer.

   If it weren't for the lag phase, foodborne disease would be much more common than it is. This time delay makes it possible to maintain foods at room temperature *for very short periods* in order to work on them.

PROTECTION AGAINST BACTERIA

Because we know how and why bacteria grow, we should be able to keep them from multiplying. Likewise, because we know how bacteria get from place to place, we should know how to prevent them from getting into our food.

There are three basic principles of protecting food against bacteria. These principles are the reasons behind nearly all the sanitation techniques we discuss in the rest of this chapter.

1. **Keep bacteria from spreading.** Don't let food touch anything that may contain disease-producing bacteria, and protect food from bacteria in the air.

2. **Stop bacteria from growing.** Take away the conditions that encourage bacteria to grow. In the kitchen, our best weapon is temperature. *The most effective way to prevent bacterial growth is to keep foods below 41°F (5°C) or above 135°F (57°C).* These temperatures won't necessarily kill bacteria; they'll just slow down their growth greatly.

3. **Kill bacteria.** Most disease-causing bacteria die when they are subjected to a temperature of 170°F (77°C) for 30 seconds, or higher temperatures for shorter periods. This enables us to make food safe by cooking and to sanitize dishes and equipment with heat. The term *sanitize* means to kill disease-causing bacteria. Certain chemicals also kill bacteria. These may be used for sanitizing equipment.

OTHER BIOLOGICAL HAZARDS

Viruses are even smaller than bacteria. They consist of genetic material surrounded by a protein layer. Viruses cause disease when they multiply inside the body. They do not grow or multiply in food, as bacteria do. Therefore, foodborne viral diseases are usually caused by direct contact with contaminated people, food contact surfaces, or water.

Parasites are organisms that can survive only by living on, with, or inside another organism. They take their nourishment from the organism they are living in, with, or on. Human parasites are usually very small, but they are larger than bacteria. Most foods that can carry parasites are found in the hot kitchen rather than the bakeshop, although raw fruits and milk may be contaminated.

Molds and yeasts are examples of *fungi* (singular form: fungus). These organisms are usually associated with food spoilage rather than foodborne disease. Certain fungi, like bread yeasts, are valuable to us. Some molds, however, produce toxins that can cause disease. Peanuts, tree nuts, corn, and milk can carry a serious mold-produced toxin that can be fatal to some people.

Some plants are naturally poisonous because they carry *plant toxins*. The best-known plant toxins are those found in certain wild mushrooms. The only way to avoid plant toxins is to avoid the plants in which they occur, as well as products made with those plants. In some cases, the toxins can be transferred in milk from cows that have eaten the plant (such as jimsonweed and snakeroot) or in honey from bees that have gathered nectar from the plants (such as mountain laurel). Other toxic plants to avoid are rhubarb leaves, water hemlock, apricot kernels, and nightshade.

An *allergen* is a substance that causes an allergic reaction. Allergens affect only some people, and these people are said to be *allergic* to that specific substance. Not all allergens are biological hazards, but the most important ones are, so we discuss them together in this section.

Foods to which some people are allergic include wheat products, soy products, peanuts and tree nuts, eggs, milk and dairy products, fish, and shellfish. Nonbiological allergens include food additives such as nitrites, used in cured meats, and monosodium glutamate (MSG), often used in Asian foods. These products are common and perfectly safe for most people, so it is difficult to avoid serving them. Nevertheless, for the sake of people who are sensitive to these foods, food service personnel, especially dining room staff, must be well informed of the ingredients in all menu items so they can inform customers, as needed.

Chapter 26 includes more detailed information on eliminating not only allergens but also other food compounds that some people can't tolerate in their diets.

Chemical and Physical Hazards

Specific kinds of chemical poisoning are caused by the use of defective or improper equipment, or equipment that has been handled improperly. The following toxins (except lead) produce symptoms that appear quickly, usually within 30 minutes of eating poisoned food. By contrast, symptoms of lead poisoning can take years to appear. To prevent these diseases, do not use the materials that cause them.

1. **Antimony.** Caused by storing or cooking acid foods in chipped gray enamelware.
2. **Cadmium.** Caused by cadmium-plated ice-cube trays or containers.
3. **Cyanide.** Caused by silver polish containing cyanide.
4. **Lead.** Caused by lead water pipes, solder containing lead, or utensils containing lead.
5. **Copper.** Caused by unclean or corroded copper utensils, acid foods cooked in unlined copper utensils, or carbonated beverages that come in contact with copper tubing.
6. **Zinc.** Caused by cooking foods in zinc-plated (galvanized) utensils.

Other chemical contamination can result from exposure of foods to chemicals used in commercial food service establishments. Examples include cleaning compounds, polishing compounds, and insecticides. Prevent contamination by keeping these items physically separated from foods. Do not use them around food. Label all containers properly. Rinse cleaned equipment thoroughly.

Physical contamination is contamination of food by objects that may not be toxic but may cause injury or discomfort. Examples include pieces of glass from a broken container, metal shavings from an improperly opened can, stones from poorly sorted dried beans, soil from poorly washed fruits, insects or insect parts, and hair. Proper food handling is necessary to avoid physical contamination.

KEY POINTS TO REVIEW

▮ What are the six conditions necessary for bacterial growth?

▮ What are three ways to protect against bacteria?

▮ Besides bacteria, what other hazards can make foods unsafe?

Personal Hygiene and Safe Food Handling

Earlier in this section, we said that most foodborne disease is caused by bacteria. Now we expand that statement slightly to say that *most foodborne disease is caused by bacteria spread by food workers.*

Cross-Contamination

At the beginning of this section, we defined *contamination* as harmful substances not present originally in the food. Some contamination occurs before we accept delivery of food, which means that proper purchasing and receiving procedures are important parts of a sanitation program. But most food contamination occurs as a result of *cross-contamination*, which may be defined as the transfer of hazardous substances, mainly microorganisms, to a food from other foods or surfaces, such as equipment, worktables, or hands.

Personal Hygiene

For the food worker, the first step in preventing foodborne disease is good personal hygiene. Even when we are healthy, we have bacteria all over our skin, in our nose and mouth, and in our eyebrows and eyelashes. Some of these bacteria, if given the chance to grow in food, will make people ill. To lower the chance of this occurring:

1. Do not work with food if you have any communicable disease or infection.
2. Bathe or shower daily.
3. Wear clean uniforms and aprons.
4. Keep hair neat and clean. Always wear a hat or hairnet.
5. Keep mustaches and beards trimmed and clean. Better yet, be clean-shaven.
6. Remove all jewelry: rings, low-hanging earrings, watches, bracelets. Avoid facial and/or body piercings; if you have them, don't touch them when you are at work.
7. Wash hands and exposed parts of arms before work and as often as necessary during work, including:
   - After eating, drinking, or smoking
   - After using the toilet
   - After touching or handling anything that may be contaminated with bacteria
8. Cover your mouth when you cough or sneeze, then wash your hands.
9. Keep your hands away from your face, eyes, hair, and arms while handling food.
10. Keep your fingernails clean and short. Do not wear nail polish.
11. Do not smoke or chew gum while on duty.
12. Cover cuts or sores with clean bandages.
13. Do not sit on worktables.

USE OF GLOVES

When used correctly, gloves can help protect foods against cross-contamination. When used incorrectly, they can spread contamination just as easily as bare hands. Health departments in most localities require the use of some kind of barrier between hands and foods that are ready to eat—that is, foods that will be served without further cooking. Gloves, tongs, and other serving implements, and bakery or deli tissue all can serve as barriers. To be sure to use gloves correctly, observe the following guidelines.

PROCEDURE: Washing Hands

1. Wet your hands with hot running water. Make the water as hot as you can comfortably stand, but at least 100°F (38°C).
2. Apply enough soap to make a good lather.
3. Rub hands together thoroughly for 20 seconds or longer, washing not only the hands but the wrists and the lower part of the forearms.
4. Using a nail brush, clean beneath the fingernails and between the fingers.
5. Rinse hands well under hot running water. If possible, use a clean paper towel to turn off the water to avoid contaminating the hands by contact with soiled faucets.
6. Dry hands with clean single-use paper towels or a warm-air hand dryer.

GUIDELINES Using Disposable Gloves

1. Wash hands before putting on gloves or when changing to another pair. Gloves are not a substitute for proper handwashing.

2. Remove and discard gloves, wash hands, and change to a clean pair of gloves after handling one food item and before starting work on another. In particular, never to fail to change gloves after handling raw meat, poultry, or seafood. Gloves are for single use only. Remember that the purpose of wearing gloves is to avoid cross-contamination.

3. Change to a clean pair of gloves whenever gloves become torn, soiled, or contaminated by contact with an unsanitary surface.

Food Handling and Preparation

We face two major sanitation problems when handling and preparing food. The first is *cross-contamination*, just discussed. The second is that while we are working on food, it is usually at a temperature between 41°F (5°C) and 135°F (57°C), or in the Temperature Danger Zone. The lag phase of bacteria growth (p. 31) protects us a little, but to be safe, we must keep foods out of the danger zone whenever possible. Here's how:

1. Start with clean, wholesome foods from reputable purveyors. Whenever applicable, buy government-inspected dairy and egg products.

2. Handle foods as little as possible. Use tongs, spatulas, or other utensils instead of hands when practicable.

3. Use clean, sanitized equipment and worktables.

4. Clean and sanitize cutting surfaces and equipment after handling raw foods and before working on another food.

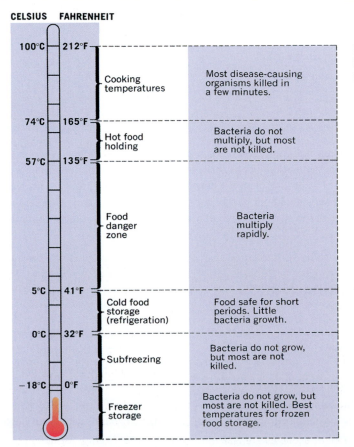

Important temperatures in food sanitation and preparation.

5. Clean as you go. Don't wait until the end of the workday.

6. Wash raw fruits thoroughly.

7. When bringing foods out of refrigeration, do not take out more than you can process in an hour.

8. Keep foods covered unless in immediate use.

9. Limit the time foods spend in the Temperature Danger Zone.

10. Taste foods properly. Using a ladle or other serving implement, transfer a small amount of the food to a small dish. Then taste this sample using a clean spoon. After tasting, do not use the dish and spoon again. Send them to the warewashing station, or, if using disposables, discard them.

11. Don't mix leftovers with freshly prepared foods.

12. Cool and chill foods quickly and correctly, as explained in the following Guidelines for Cooling Foods. Chill custards, cream fillings, and other hazardous foods as quickly as possible by pouring them into shallow, sanitized pans, covering them, and refrigerating. Do not stack the pans.

LOCAL HEALTH RESOURCES AND REGULATIONS

Because local (county or municipal) health departments are responsible for enforcing food safety regulations, they are the best sources for information on food sanitation and food handling guidelines. Even though the federal government has set many standards, local rules often differ, and food service operators are responsible for following the applicable rules in their own locales.

The definition of the Temperature Danger Zone is an important example. In the United States, the FDA has set the standard as indicated in this text (41° to 135°F/5°to 57°C), according to rules published in 2013. However, many state and county governments have more restrictive standards, such as 41°F to 140°F (5° to 60°C) or 40°F to 140°F (4.5° to 60°C). Be sure to observe the regulations in force in your own community.

GUIDELINES: Cooling Foods

1. Never put hot foods directly into the cooler. Not only will they cool too slowly but they will also raise the temperature of other foods in the cooler.

2. If they are available, use quick-chill units or blast chillers to cool foods quickly before transferring them to cold storage.

3. Use ice-water baths to bring down temperatures of hot foods quickly.

4. Stir foods as they are cooling to redistribute the heat in the food and help it cool more quickly.

5. Divide large batches into smaller batches. This increases the amount of surface area for the volume of food and helps it cool more quickly. Pouring foods into flat, shallow pans also increases surface area and cooling speed.

KEY POINTS TO REVIEW

▌ What is cross-contamination?

▌ What are the important rules of personal hygiene? List as many as you can.

▌ What is the Temperature Danger Zone (Food Danger Zone)?

Equipment Sanitation and Safety

Food handling in the bakeshop requires the safe and sanitary use of bakeshop equipment, ranging from small hand tools to large ovens and floor-model mixers. In addition to the guidelines for food safety already discussed in this chapter, the following additional points should be made with respect to equipment usage.

Sanitation

Thorough, regular cleaning of all equipment is essential. Most large equipment can be partially disassembled for cleaning. Read the operating manual, which should describe these procedures in detail, or get the information from someone who knows the equipment.

When purchasing equipment, look for models that have been tested and endorsed for food safety by recognized agencies that certify products and write standards for food, water, air, and consumer goods. Three prominent agencies are NSF International (www.nsf.org; formerly the

NSF International certification mark.

Courtesy NSF International.

The CSA sanitation mark.

Courtesy of the Canadian Standard Association.

The Underwriters Laboratory logo.

Reproduced with permission of Underwriters Laboratory, Inc.

National Sanitation Foundation), CSA International (www.csa-international.org), and Underwriters Laboratory (www.ul.com). These agencies are accredited by the American National Standards Institute (ANSI) as Standards Developing Organizations (SDOs). They are also accredited by ANSI to certify equipment (such as baking and other commercial food equipment) against the American National Standards that have been developed by each of these SDOs. The standards, and the certifications of these three agencies, are recognized internationally.

Products meeting the testing requirements of these agencies are labeled or marked accordingly, as shown in the illustrations. Criteria govern such factors as design and construction (for example, sealed joints and seams, as well as accessible component parts), materials used (for example, nontoxic materials, smooth and easily cleanable surfaces), and performance testing.

Safety

Baking equipment can be dangerous. From large mixers to small hand tools such as knives, much of the equipment found in the bakeshop can inflict serious injuries if not used carefully and properly. Two guidelines are in order here:

- Never use a piece of equipment until you are thoroughly familiar with its operation and its features. You must also learn to recognize when a machine is not operating correctly so you can shut it down immediately and report the malfunction to a supervisor.

- Be aware that not all models are alike. Each manufacturer introduces slight variations on the basic equipment. While all deck ovens or all vertical mixers, for example, operate on the same basic principles, each model is slightly different, if only in the location of the switches. It is important to study the operating manual supplied with each item, or be taught by someone who already knows the item well.

The HACCP System

Once you have learned the principles of food safety, you must apply them in the bakeshop or kitchen. Many food service operations have designed food safety systems that enable food workers to keep a close check on food items whenever there is a risk of contamination or of the growth of pathogens. One effective food safety system is called the *Hazard Analysis and Critical Control Point* system, or *HACCP*. Versions of this system have been widely adopted throughout the food service industry.

The following is a brief introduction to the basic concepts of HACCP. For a more detailed explanation, refer to other published material listed in the Bibliography (p. 748). The discussion here is based on information presented in those books and applies to all food service work, not just the bakeshop. Also, keep in mind that this discussion applies to food service operations in general, not just bakeshops.

The Steps of the HACCP System

The purpose of the HACCP system is to identify, monitor, and control dangers of food contamination. It has seven steps:

1. Assess hazards.
2. Identify critical control points (CCPs).
3. Set up standards or limits for CCPs.
4. Set up procedures for monitoring CCPs.
5. Establish corrective actions.
6. Set up a recordkeeping system.
7. Verify that the system is working.

These steps are the basis of the following discussion.

The Flow of Food

HACCP begins with a concept called the *flow of food*. This term refers to the movement of food through a food service operation, from receiving through the stages of storage, preparation, and service, until it is served to the consumer.

The flow of food is different for each item prepared. Some menu items involve many steps, including receiving of ingredients, storing ingredients, preparing ingredients (such as trimming fruit), cooking, holding, serving, cooling, storing leftovers, reheating leftovers, and so on. Even the simplest items undergo several steps. For example, a cake that is bought already prepared from a commercial baker and served as dessert goes through at least three steps on its way to the customer: (1) receiving, (2) storing, (3) serving.

Assessing Hazards

At each step in the flow of foods through the operation, risks may arise that can lead to dangerous conditions, or *hazards*. Assessing hazards is the process of identifying which of these dangerous conditions may occur at every step of the process. These hazards can be divided into three categories:

1. **Contamination**, such as cross-contamination from a soiled cutting surface, torn packaging that permits insect infestation, a worker handling food without washing hands, or spilling cleaning chemicals on food.

2. **Growth of bacteria and other pathogens** due to such conditions as inadequate refrigeration or storage and holding hot foods below 135°F (57°C).

3. **Survival of pathogens or the continued presence of toxins**, usually because of inadequate cooking or heating or inadequate sanitizing of equipment and surfaces.

Note these hazards correspond to the sanitation techniques discussed on page 31: keep bacteria from spreading, stop bacteria from growing, kill bacteria. The important difference is that the hazards addressed by HACCP include chemical and other hazards, in addition to disease-causing organisms. Naturally, however, most of the hazards we are concerned with are those that affect potentially hazardous foods.

Identifying Critical Control Points

Once the potential hazards are identified, the next step is to decide at which stages a worker can control the hazards, called control points. For any given hazard there may be several control points, or several opportunities to control the hazard. The last control point at which a worker can control a particular hazard is especially important to determine because this is the last chance to prevent a possible danger. These control points are called *critical control points (CCPs)*. Identifying CCPs is the second step in a HACCP program.

In simple language, setting up a HACCP system starts with reviewing the flow of food to figure out where something might go wrong, and then deciding what can be done about it. In the language of HACCP, these steps are called *assessing the hazards* and *identifying critical control points*.

Setting Standards or Limits for CCPs

The next step in designing a HACCP food safety system is setting up procedures for CCPs. At each such point, food workers need to know which standards must be met, which procedures to follow to meet the standards, and what to do if they aren't met. To reduce the chances for making mistakes, these standards and procedures are written out. Whenever possible, they should be included in the operation's recipes.

Some procedures are general and include the sanitation rules discussed earlier in this chapter. For example: Wash hands before handling food and after handling raw foods; hold foods above 135°F (57°C) or below 41°F (5°C). Others apply to specific items. For example: Cook a beef roast to an internal temperature of at least 145°F (63°C) and ensure it stays at that temperature at least three minutes.

Setting Up Monitoring Procedures

Careful observation is needed to verify when standards are met. This often involves measuring. The only way to know, for example, that a roast has reached the required internal temperature is to measure it, using a clean, sanitized thermometer.

Managers must ensure that all employees are trained to follow procedures and have the equipment needed to do the job.

Establishing monitoring procedures includes determining how a CCP is to be monitored or measured, when it is to be monitored, who is responsible for doing the measuring, and what equipment is needed to do the monitoring.

Taking Corrective Action

A *corrective action* is a procedure that must be followed whenever a critical limit is not met. Corrective actions should be identified in written procedures that clearly tell the worker what must be done in each situation.

For example, a monitoring procedure might show the internal temperature of a roast turkey just out of the oven is 155°F (68°C). But the critical limit for roast turkey is 165°F (74°C). The corrective action might be to return the turkey to the oven until the temperature reaches the critical limit.

Other corrective actions might be more complicated, but the written procedure should describe clearly what steps must be taken and who must take them.

Setting Up a Recordkeeping System

Keeping records of all the procedures described above is important for a HACCP system to succeed. Time and temperature logs, records of corrective actions taken, and documentation of when and how measuring devices were calibrated are examples of the kinds of records that enable an establishment to ensure food safety. Each establishment should develop clear, easy-to-use forms for entering all needed information.

Verifying the System Works

Accurate records enable you to make sure a HACCP system is working as intended. Review records regularly to check that all CCPs are being correctly monitored and that corrective actions are taken according to the proper procedures and adequate to control hazards. Revise procedures as necessary.

Accurate records also demonstrate to health inspectors that your operation is following correct safety procedures. In addition, records will help you determine what went wrong if a foodborne illness does occur.

To maintain accuracy of your establishment's records, whenever purchasing specifications are changed, new items are added to the menu, or new equipment is put into use, you must review procedures and revise them if needed. For example, if an operation starts buying larger beef steamship rounds for roasting, the internal temperature of the roasts will not meet critical limits unless the roasting time allowed for the beef is increased.

As this brief introduction to HACCP implies, establishing such a system to control all aspects of food production requires more information than this chapter can cover, so refer to the Bibliography for more detailed information.

Learning More about Food Safety

It is important to understand that food safety and sanitation are large and complex topics, so you should regard the second half of this chapter as only an introduction to them. To advance in a food service career, you will be required to demonstrate a detailed knowledge of the subject, well beyond what can be presented in such a limited space.

You will find entire textbooks devoted to kitchen sanitation and safety. Many organizations, including local and regional health departments and organizations such as the National Restaurant Association (in the United States), sponsor training programs leading to certificates of competency in food safety. Food-service employees in supervisory positions in the United States may be required to hold such a certificate by state or local law. In Canada, many provinces have their own safety regulations, and food-service operators should be familiar with these, as well as with federal regulations. The health and safety of your clientele depend on your diligent study of these important topics.

KEY POINTS TO REVIEW

▪ What does the term *flow of food* mean?
▪ What does the term *critical control point* refer to?
▪ What are the seven steps of the HACCP system?

TERMS FOR REVIEW

recipe	deci-	pathogen	fungus
formula	centi-	Temperature Danger Zone or Food Danger Zone	plant toxin
standardized formula	milli-		allergen
scaling	scone flour	aerobic	cross-contamination
metric system	AP weight	anaerobic	HACCP
gram	EP weight	facultative	flow of food
liter	baker's percentage	lag phase	critical control point (CCP)
meter	contaminated	virus	corrective action
degree Celsius	hazard	parasite	
kilo-	microorganism		

QUESTIONS FOR REVIEW

1. Below are ingredients for a white cake. The weight of the flour is given, and the proportions of other ingredients are indicated by percentages. Calculate the weights required for each.

Cake flour	3 lb (100%)
Baking powder	4%
Shortening	50%
Sugar	100%
Salt	1%
Milk	75%
Egg whites	33%
Vanilla	2%

2. In the formula in question 1, how much of each ingredient is needed if you want a total yield of 4½ lb batter?

3. Why are baking ingredients usually weighed, rather than measured by volume?

4. Make the following conversions in the U.S. system of measurement:

   3½ lb = ___ oz

   6 cups = ___ pt

   8½ qt = ___ fl oz

   ¾ cup = ___ tbsp

   46 oz = ___ lb

   2½ gal = ___ fl oz

   5 lb 5 oz divided by 2 = _____

   10 tsp = ___ fl oz

5. Make the following conversions in the metric system:

   1.4 kg = ___ g

   53 dL = ___ L

   15 cm = ___ mm

   2590 g = ___ kg

   4.6 L = ___ dL

   220 cL = ___ dL

6. Which foods can become contaminated by disease-causing organisms?

   chocolate éclairs

   dinner rolls

   baked custard

   biscotti cookies

   crisp baked meringues

   breadsticks

   chocolate bars

7. How often should you wash your hands when working on food?

8. Why is temperature control an effective weapon against bacterial growth? What are some important temperatures to remember?

3

BAKING AND PASTRY EQUIPMENT

AFTER READING THIS CHAPTER, YOU SHOULD BE ABLE TO:

1. Identify the principal pieces of large equipment used in baking and pastry making and indicate their uses.
2. Identify the principal pans, container, and molds used in baking and pastry making and indicate their uses.
3. Identify the principal hand tools and other equipment used in baking and pastry making and indicate their uses.

MUCH OF A baker's art and craft involves simple tools. Learning to become a successful baker requires developing a great deal of manual skill using these tools. For example, a pastry bag is nothing more than a cone-shaped piece of fabric or plastic, open at both ends. Although its construction is simple, and no operating manual is required to understand how it works, hours of practice are necessary to become skilled at using a pastry bag for decorative work.

At the other extreme are large machines such as floor-model mixers, ovens of many types, and dough-handling equipment such as molders, dividers, and sheeters. Of these, perhaps only ovens are essential to a baker's work. The other items are important labor-saving devices that enable workers to produce goods in large quantities with greater speed. Without this equipment, much of the output of a bakeshop would not be economically feasible.

This chapter is an outline of the most important pieces of equipment used by bakers and pastry chefs, from large equipment to containers and molds to hand tools. In addition to these tools, most bakeshops contain an array of equipment also found in most kitchens, including pots and pans, spoons, ladles, spatulas, knives, and so on. Learning to use these tools is the subject of much of this book.

LARGE EQUIPMENT

Small table-model mixer.

Courtesy of Hobart Corporation.

MIXERS, OVENS, AND dough-handling equipment take up most of this category.

Mixers

Mixers of various types are essential tools in the bakeshop. While small quantities of doughs and batters can be mixed by hand, commercial baking in any quantity would be next to impossible without power mixers.

Two main types of mixer are used in small and medium-size bakeshops: vertical and spiral. Other types of specialized equipment are used in large industrial bakeries.

Vertical Mixer

Also called a *planetary mixer*, the vertical mixer is the most common type used in baking, as well as in cooking. The term *planetary* is descriptive of the motion of the beater attachment. Just as a planet spins on its axis while revolving around the sun, so, too, does the beater attachment spin on its axis while rotating in an orbit to reach all parts of the stationary bowl.

Tabletop mixers range in capacity from 5 to 20 quarts (4.75 to 19 L). Floor models are available as large as 140 quarts (132 L).

Vertical mixers have three main mixing attachments:

1. The *paddle* is a flat blade used for general mixing.
2. The *wire whip* is used for such tasks as beating egg foams and cream.
3. The *dough arm* or *hook* is used for mixing and kneading yeast doughs. Dough hooks may be standard *J*-hooks or spiral hooks.

Large floor-model mixer.

Courtesy of Hobart Corporation.

Be sure to use the right-size attachment for the bowl. Using a 40-quart paddle with a 30-quart bowl could cause serious damage the equipment. Make sure both the bowl and the mixing attachment are firmly in place before turning on the machine. Always turn off the machine before scraping down the bowl or inserting a scraper, spoon, or hand into the bowl.

Additional special attachments are also available. These include the following:

- The *sweet dough arm* combines the actions of the dough arm and the flat paddle and is used for mixing sweet doughs.
- The *wing whip* is used for mixing materials too heavy for the standard wire whip.
- The *pastry blender* is used to blend fat and flour, as in making pie doughs.

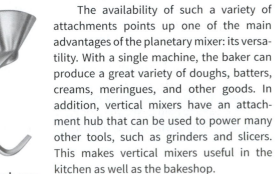

The availability of such a variety of attachments points up one of the main advantages of the planetary mixer: its versatility. With a single machine, the baker can produce a great variety of doughs, batters, creams, meringues, and other goods. In addition, vertical mixers have an attachment hub that can be used to power many other tools, such as grinders and slicers. This makes vertical mixers useful in the kitchen as well as the bakeshop.

Mixer attachments (left to right): whip, paddle, dough arm.

Courtesy of Hobart Corporation.

Spiral Mixer

Spiral mixers are designed for doughs and heavy batters and are used primarily for making large quantities of yeast doughs for breads and bagels. Unlike vertical mixers, spiral mixers do not have interchangeable bowls and agitator arms. The agitator arm is in the shape of a spiral, and both the bowl and the spiral arm rotate to develop the dough quickly and efficiently. In a typical model, the bowl may be set to rotate in either direction.

Dough capacities range from 5 to 30 pounds (2.3 to 14 kg) for small machines to more than 500 pounds (230 kg) in large machines.

Because spiral mixers are used exclusively for mixing doughs, they do not have the versatility of vertical mixers, as just described. However, they do have several important features and advantages that make them the preferred mixers of bread bakers and pizza makers:

- Spiral mixers blend and develop dough more efficiently than planetary mixers. Because of their design, they develop dough more intensively and in less time, resulting in lower machine friction and dough warming (see p. 123).

- The design of the bowl and beater allows for a wide range of dough capacity for each machine. For example, a medium-size mixer may handle as little as 10 pounds (4.5 kg) of dough or as much as 200 pounds (90 kg). By contrast, a vertical mixer bowl handles only a narrow range of dough weights; too large or too small a quantity will not mix properly.

- Spiral mixers are sturdier and more rugged than vertical mixers. They handle more dough, last longer, and require less repair and maintenance.

Three main varieties of spiral mixer are available:

1. **Fixed-bowl mixers.** These have a nonremovable bowl. The dough must be lifted out by hand.
2. **Removable-bowl mixers.** These have a bowl that may be removed from the machine, usually on a wheeled trolley. They are useful for high-volume operations, because a new bowl of ingredients may be wheeled into place as soon as the earlier batch is removed.
3. **Tilt mixers.** On these machines, the entire machine tilts up to deposit the finished dough onto a tray or another container.

Most spiral mixers have two operating speeds, although some specialized machines for stiff doughs have only one speed. In a typical mixing procedure, the baker uses the first speed for the first phase of dough mixing, when the ingredients are blended, and switches to the second speed for the later phase of dough development. Machines with automated controls have timers to regulate each phase of mixing.

Similar to spiral mixers are *fork mixers*. Instead of a single spiral agitator or beater, these machines have a two-pronged fork-shaped beater that enters the bowl at about a 45-degree angle. Like spiral mixers, fork mixers are used specifically for bread doughs.

Horizontal Mixer

Horizontal mixers are large, industrial-size machines capable of handling as much as several thousand pounds of dough at a time. Each model is designed to work best with a specific range of products, such as bread doughs, pastry doughs, or soft doughs and batters. Beater or agitator designs differ for each of these specialized models.

Many horizontal mixers are equipped with water jackets that surround the mixing container. Water of the desired temperature is circulated through the jacket, enabling the operator to control the dough temperature with great precision.

Dough-Handling Equipment

Dough Fermentation Trough

This item is used to hold mixed yeast doughs during fermentation. Small operations might simply use large mixing bowls on stands instead.

Divider

Dividers cut scaled pieces of dough into equal portions by means of a die or cutter attached to a hydraulic or mechanical lever assembly. For example, a divider may

Spiral mixer.

Courtesy of TMB Baking, Inc.

CONTINUOUS MIXER

Another type of mixer used in large bakeries is the *continuous mixer*. Here, small amounts of scaled ingredients enter the machine continuously at one end. The ingredients are blended and developed into a dough as they move through the machine. The finished dough emerges at the other end of the machine. These mixers are efficient because instead of having to blend, say, 200 pounds of flour into a dough all at once, they can take in the flour in 5-pound increments, making the blending much easier.

Horizontal mixer.

Courtesy of Topos Mondial (Model THM-14OT 3 roller bar mixer).

Divider.

Courtesy of American Baking Systems and S.A. Jac NV.

cut a 3-pound piece of dough (called a *press*) into 36 pieces, 1⅓ ounces each, for making dinner rolls. After they are divided, the individual pieces must be rounded by hand (see p. 109).

Divider-Rounder

This machine divides the dough, as does a simple divider, and it then automatically rounds the individual portions, greatly speeding makeup of the dough products.

Dough Sheeter

A sheeter rolls out portions of dough into sheets of uniform thickness. It consists of a canvas conveyor belt that feeds the dough through a pair of rollers. To make thin sheets, the dough usually must be passed through the rollers several times. The operator decreases the space between the rollers after each pass.

Molder

A molder rolls and forms pieces of bread dough for standard loaves, baguettes, and rolls, eliminating the need to perform these tasks by hand.

Sheeter.

Courtesy of American Baking Systems and S.A. Jac NV.

Divider-rounder.

Courtesy of TMB Baking, Inc.

Proofer

A proofer is a special box in which the ideal conditions for fermenting yeast doughs can be created. The box maintains a preset warm temperature and humidity level appropriate to the specific dough.

Retarder

Chilling or refrigerating yeast dough slows or retards the rate of fermentation so the dough can be stored for later baking. A retarder is a refrigerator that maintains a high level of humidity to prevent the dough from drying out or crusting.

Retarder-Proofer

This machine is, as its name suggests, a combination retarder and proofer. A dough can be retarded for a preset time, after which the machine switches to proofing mode and warms up to a second preset temperature and humidity level. For example, breakfast breads can be made up the previous day, held, and be fully proofed and ready to bake when the shop opens the next morning.

Molder.

Courtesy of American Baking Systems and S.A. Jac NV.

Proofer.

Courtesy of Bevles.

Retarder-proofer.

Courtesy of TMB Baking, Inc.

Ovens

Ovens are, of course, the workhorses of the bakery and pastry shop. They are essential for producing breads, cakes, cookies, pastries, and other baked items. Ovens are enclosed spaces in which food is heated, usually by hot air (except in the case of microwave ovens, which are not especially useful in a bakeshop). Several kinds of oven are used in baking.

Steam is important in baking many kinds of breads, as discussed in Chapter 6. Ovens used in bakeshops, including deck ovens, rack ovens, and mechanical ovens, may have steam injected into them during part of the baking cycle.

Deck oven.

Courtesy of Baxter/ITW Food Equipment Group, LLC.

Deck Oven

Deck ovens are so called because the items to be baked—either on sheet pans or, in the case of some breads, freestanding—are placed directly on the bottom, or deck, of the oven. There are no racks for holding pans in deck ovens. Deck ovens are also called *stack ovens* because several may be stacked on top of one another. Breads baked directly on the floor of the oven rather than in pans are often called *hearth breads*, so another name for these ovens is *hearth ovens*. Deck ovens for baking bread are equipped with steam injectors.

Rack oven.

Courtesy of Lang Manufacturing Company.

Rack Oven

A rack oven is a large oven into which entire racks full of sheet pans can be wheeled for baking. Normal baker's racks hold 8 to 24 full-size sheet pans, but racks made specifically to go into rack ovens usually hold 12 to 20 pans. Rack ovens hold 1 to 4 of these racks at once. The ovens are also equipped with steam injectors.

Although this usage is not strictly correct, you may hear the term *rack oven* used for conventional ovens, such as those found in restaurant ranges, because the pans are placed on racks rather than directly on the bottom, as in deck ovens.

Mechanical Oven

In a mechanical oven, the food is in motion while it bakes. The most common type is a revolving oven, in which the mechanism is like that of a Ferris wheel. This mechanical action eliminates the problem of hot spots, or uneven baking, because the mechanism rotates the foods throughout the oven. Because of their size, mechanical ovens are especially useful in high-volume operations. Revolving ovens can be equipped with steam injectors.

A typical revolving oven is shown in the illustration. Each of the multiple trays in such an oven holds one or more sheet pans. The operator loads one tray at a time through the narrow door in the front.

WOOD-FIRED OVENS

Wood-fired brick ovens are similar in function to deck ovens in that items are baked directly on the oven floor. These ovens are used in some operations that produce artisan breads, as well as in some restaurants that serve pizzas and similar items. The heat is generated by a wood fire built inside the oven. The fire heats the thick brick floor and walls, which retain enough heat to bake foods. Gas-fired brick ovens are similar, but the heat in them is easier to control.

Revolving oven.

Courtesy of Baxter/ITW Food Equipment Group, LLC.

Convection oven.

Courtesy of Vulcan-Hart Company.

Convection Oven

Convection ovens contain fans that circulate the air and distribute the heat rapidly throughout the interior. The forced air makes foods cook more quickly at lower temperatures. However, the strong forced air can distort the shape of items made with batters and soft doughs, and the air-flow may be strong enough to blow baking parchment off sheet pans. Therefore, convection ovens are not as versatile for the baker as are the other kinds of ovens discussed here.

Steam-Jacketed Kettle

Steam-jacketed kettles, or steam kettles, have double walls between which steam circulates. Liquids in the kettle itself are heated quickly and efficiently. Although restaurants may use large floor-mounted kettles for making stocks, smaller table models are more useful in the bakeshop for making custards, creams, and fillings.

Tilting kettles with a pouring lip are called *trunnion kettles*. Table models range in capacity from a few quarts or liters to 40 quarts (38 L).

Steam-jacketed kettle.

Courtesy of Vulcan-Hart Company.

Fryer

Fryers are needed in the bakeshop for doughnuts and other fried items. Small operations often use standard deep fryers (or even stovetop kettles), but larger doughnut fryers are best if you make dough-nuts in quantity. They should be used in conjunction with screens, for lowering the doughnuts into the fat and removing them when fried.

In the fryer in the illustration, the proofed doughnuts are arranged on the screen at the right side of the fry kettle. The operator then manually lowers the screen into the hot fat by means of the two raised handles. The illustration also shows, on the left side, a batter depositor for cake doughnuts.

Doughnut fryer.

Courtesy of Belshaw Adamatic Bakery Group

PANS, CONTAINERS, AND MOLDS

MANY OF THE pots and pans found in the hot kitchen are also used in the bakeshop. For example, saucepans are used to boil syrups and to cook creams and fillings. This section, however, concentrates on specialty containers and molds for the bakery. The following list gives a representative sample of the more important of these, in alphabetical order. Molds are of two types: those for baking dough or batter items, and those for giving shape to refrigerated items such as mousses and bombes. Other containers, such as mixing bowls, are included in the list.

Baba mold. A small thimble-shaped mold for making babas (p. 186).

Banneton. A bentwood basket, available in various shapes, for holding and giving shape to certain hearth bread doughs as they proof. Similar canvas-lined baskets are also available.

Baba mold.

Banneton.

Barquette. A small boat-shaped mold for petits fours and small tartlets.

Bombe mold. A dome-shaped mold for frozen desserts (p. 558).

Brioche mold. A flared pan with fluted sides for making brioche (p. 201).

Cake pans. Most cake pans are round, but other shapes, such as hearts, are available for specialty cakes. Cake pans come in many sizes.

Cake ring. See *Charlotte ring*.

Charlotte mold. The classic charlotte mold is round, tapered, and flat-bottomed, with two handles near the top rim. Except for the Apple Charlotte (p. 583), which is baked in this mold, classic charlottes are made with a Bavarian cream filling and refrigerated until set, not baked.

Charlotte ring. Also called *cake rings*, these are stainless-steel rings in various diameters and heights, most often used for making molded desserts and for shaping and holding desserts made of layers of cake, pastry, and fillings. The rings are removed after the fillings have set and before serving or display. (See Chapter 17, where a charlotte ring in use is illustrated on page 445.)

Chocolate molds. Used for all sorts of chocolate work, from large display pieces to bite-size truffles. (See Chapter 23.)

Cornstick pan. Special baking pan with indentations shaped like small ears of corn. Used for baking cornbread items.

Flexipan. This is the brand name for a line of nonstick baking pans made of a flexible silicone material. Flexipans are available in dozens of shapes and sizes to make a wide range of products, from muffins and quick-bread loaves to petits fours.

Hotel pan. A rectangular pan, usually made of stainless steel. Designed to hold foods in service counters. Also used for baking and steaming, and often for baked items such as bread pudding. The standard size is 10 × 20 inches (325 × 530 mm). Fractions of this size (½, ⅓, and so on) are also available. Standard depth is 2½ inches (65 mm), but deeper pans are also available.

Loaf pan. A rectangular pan, usually with slightly flared sides, used for baking loaf breads. Loaf pans can also be used for molding refrigerated and frozen desserts. A special type of loaf pan is the Pullman pan, which has straight, not flared sides, and a removable lid, for baking Pullman loaves of bread (p. 148).

Barquette.

Charlotte mold.

Full-size and
half-size hotel pans.

Loaf pan.   Pullman pan.

Madeleine pan. A special baking pan with shell-shaped indentations, used for baking madeleines (p. 412).

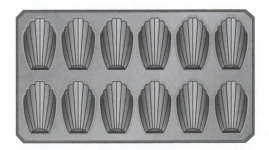

Madeleine pan.

Mixing bowls. The most useful mixing bowls are made of stainless steel and have round bottoms. They are used for general mixing and whipping. The round construction enables the whip to reach all areas, for thorough mixing or whipping.

Muffin pan. Metal baking pan with cup-shaped indentations for baking muffins (see Chapter 10). Pans are available for making muffins in several sizes.

Petit four molds. Tiny metal molds in a variety of shapes, used for baking an assortment of little tartlets, financiers (p. 368), and other petits fours.

Pie pan. Shallow pan with sloping sides, used for baking pies. Disposable aluminum pie pans are usually used in retail bakeshops.

Savarin mold. Small ring-shaped or doughnut-shaped metal mold for baking savarins (p. 186).

Savarin mold.

Sheet pan. A shallow, rectangular pan (1 inch/25 mm deep) for baking sheet cakes, cookies, rolls, and other baked goods. A full sheet pan measures 18 × 26 inches (46 × 66 cm). Half-sheet pans are 13 × 18 inches (33 × 46 cm). Perforated sheet pans are the same size, but the bottom is full of tiny holes. These allow even baking and browning of breads and rolls because the holes let the oven's hot air circulate freely around the items as they bake.

Pan extenders are metal or fiberglass frames that fit inside sheet pans. They give straight sides to sheet cakes and make the pan deeper. Extenders are usually 2 inches (5 cm) high.

Sheet pan.

Springform pan. A cake pan with a removable bottom. Used primarily for baking cheesecakes and other items too delicate to be easily and cleanly removed from standard cake pans.

Tart pan. A shallow (1 inch/2.5 cm deep) metal pan, usually with fluted sides, used for baking tarts. Standard pans are round, but square and rectangular pans are also available. They may be made in one piece or with a removable bottom to make removal of the baked tart from the pan easier.

Tart pans make multiserving pastries, but smaller tartlet pans make single-portion tartlets. Like tart pans, these come in a variety of sizes. The smallest usually are in one piece and lack the removable bottom.

Tube pan. A deep cake pan with a tube in the center. The tube promotes even baking of angel food cakes and similar items.

Springform pan.

Tart pan.

Tube pan.

HAND TOOLS AND MISCELLANEOUS EQUIPMENT

Hand Tools

The category of hand tools is a broad one, encompassing large and small items, some more familiar than others. Those described here are considered indispensable to a bakeshop or commercial baking establishment.

Blowtorch. A tool used for caramelizing and controlled browning of various pastry items, and for caramelizing the sugar topping of crème brûlée. Butane or propane is used as fuel, depending on the model.

Bowl knife. Also called a *straight spatula* or *palette knife*, this tool has a long, flexible blade with a rounded end. Used mostly for spreading icing on cakes and for mixing and bowl scraping. A variant with an angled blade is called an *offset spatula*. The bent blade allows spreading and smoothing batters and fillings inside pans.

Brushes. Pastry brushes are used to brush items with egg wash, glaze, and so on. Larger bench brushes are used to brush flour from tabletops and from the surface of dough. Oven brushes are used to clean excess flour from deck ovens.

Chinois and china cap. A chinois is a conical strainer with a fine mesh, used mostly for straining sauces. A china cap is also a conical strainer, but it is made of perforated steel, so it doesn't strain as finely. A china cap is usually lined with several layers of cheesecloth if the liquid must be well strained.

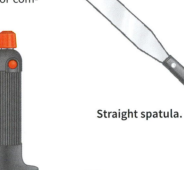

Straight spatula.

Blowtorch.

Bench brush.

Chinois.

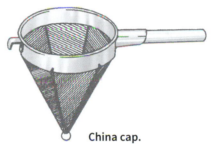

China cap.

Comb, icing. A small plastic tool, usually triangular, with serrated edges in various patterns, for decorating icings and other pastry and decorative items.

Cutters. Many types of cutters are used in the pastry department. Cookie cutters and pastry cutters, available in many shapes, cut decorative shapes by stamping them from rolled-out dough. Roller cutters have a handle on each end, like a rolling pin, and are rolled over rolled-out dough to cut repetitive shapes quickly and efficiently, with minimal loss of dough to trimmings and scraps. Roller cutters are often used for croissants (p. 200).

Pastry bag. A cone-shaped cloth or plastic bag with an open end that can be fitted with metal or plastic tubes or tips of various shapes and sizes. Used for shaping and decorating with items such as icing; for filling certain kinds of pastries and other items, such as éclairs; and for portioning creams, fillings, and doughs. Use of the pastry bag and tubes for decorative work is discussed and illustrated in Chapter 17.

Peel. A thin, flat wooden board or steel sheet with a long handle, used for inserting and removing hearth breads from deck ovens. Because they are thinner than traditional wooden peels, steel peels are easier to slide under baked loaves.

Icing comb.

Cookie cutters and pastry cutters.

Peel.

Roller cutter.

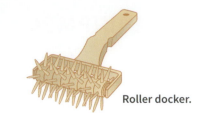

Roller docker.

Bench scraper.

Bowl scraper.

Sieve.

Roller docker. A tool that pierces holes in rolled-out dough to prevent bubbling during baking. It consists of a handle attached to a rotating tube fitted with rows of spikes.

Rolling pins. Many types of rolling pin are used in the bakeshop for rolling out doughs. Perhaps the most versatile pin, used for most general rolling tasks, is simply a solid hardwood rod, about 2 inches (5 cm) thick and 20 inches (50 cm) long. A French rolling pin is about 2 inches (5 cm) thick at the center and tapered toward the ends. It is useful for rolling pie doughs and other doughs that must be rolled to a circular shape. For large quantities or heavy work, a heavy ball-bearing pin may be used. This pin is 3 to 4 inches (8 to 10 cm) thick and has a swiveling rod inserted through the center, with a handle at each end. Textured rolling pins are used to emboss designs, such as a basketweave pattern, in sheets of marzipan, pastillage, and similar pastes and doughs.

Ball-bearing rolling pins, straight wooden rolling pins, and textured rolling pin.

Scrapers. A bench scraper, also called a *dough scraper*, is a small rectangle of stainless steel with a handle along one of the long edges. It is used for cutting and portioning dough and for scraping tabletops. A bowl scraper is a piece of plastic about the same size, but with one curved edge and no handle. It is used for scraping out the contents of mixing bowls.

Sieve. A round metal screen supported in a stainless-steel hoop frame. It is used for sifting flour and other dry ingredients. Also called a *drum sieve* or *tamis* (pronounced tah-mee).

Strainer. A round-bottomed, cup-shaped tool made of screen mesh or perforated metal, with a handle on one side. Used for separating solids from liquids, such as draining the juice from fruit. Screen-mesh strainers can also be used for sifting dry ingredients, like a sieve.

Turntable. A round, flat disk that swivels freely on a pedestal base. Used for holding cakes for decorating.

Wire rack. A wire grate used to hold baked goods as they are cooling, or to hold items such as cakes while liquid icings, such as fondant, are applied.

Whip. Loops of stainless-steel wire fastened to a handle. Whips with a few stiff wires are used for mixing and blending, and whips with many flexible wires are used for whipping foams, such as whipped cream and egg foams. Also called *whisk*.

Turntable.

Whips.

Miscellaneous Tools and Equipment

A number of other tools and equipment, which together may be categorized as miscellaneous, also should be considered essentials to the bakeshop or commercial bakery kitchen.

Acetate. A type of clear plastic. Acetate strips are used for lining charlotte molds (described in Pans, Containers, and Molds) in the production of certain cakes, pastries, and refrigerated desserts. For retail display, the strips can be left on after the charlotte rings are removed to support the dessert while displaying the layers. Acetate sheets are most often used in decorative chocolate work, as illustrated in Chapter 22.

Couche. A sheet of heavy linen or canvas, used for supporting certain breads, such as baguettes, as they are proofed. The cloth is placed on a sheet pan and pleated to form troughs to hold the loaves so they can proof without spreading.

Hydrometer. Also called a *sugar densimeter*, *saccharometer*, and *Baumé hydrometer*. Used to test the density of sugar syrups. (Sometimes called a *thermometer*, but this is inaccurate because it doesn't measure temperature.) It is a glass tube, weighted at one end, that is floated in the solution to be tested. Because it floats higher in denser solutions, the density can be read off the scale marked along the length of the tube at the point where the surface of the liquid meets the tube.

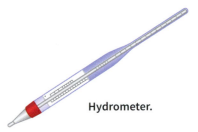

Hydrometer.

Ice cream freezer. Machine for churning and freezing ice creams and sorbets. It consists of a large refrigerated canister or container with a paddle, called a *dasher*, that rotates inside. The ice cream or sorbet mix freezes against the walls of the canister and is continually scraped off and remixed to prevent the formation of ice crystals. Unlike home models, which depend on a salted ice water mixture to create freezing temperatures, commercial ice cream freezers contain a built-in electrically operated freezing unit.

Marble. A stone material used for tabletop or work surfaces in pastry shops. The hard, cool surface of marble is ideal for working with pastry doughs, as well as for tempering chocolate and for some decorative work, such as pastillage. Marble slabs may be installed on top of under-the-counter refrigerated storage boxes. This keeps the marble cool even in warm weather.

Ice cream freezer.

Parchment paper. Also called *baking paper* or *silicone paper*, this is a sheet of treated nonstick paper sized to fit standard sheet pans. When used to line pans, parchment eliminates the need for greasing them. Also used to make piping cones for decorative work. (See Chapter 17.)

Rack, cooling. A wire rack used to hold baked goods while cooling. The rack allows air circulation around the items.

Silicone mat. Flexible fiberglass mat coated with nonstick silicone, used to line baking sheets. Available to fit full and half-size sheet pans. Also used in sugar work (see Chapter 25). The mats withstand temperatures up to about 480°F (250°C) and can be reused indefinitely if well cared for and not folded or creased. There are several manufacturers of silicone mats, but they are often known by one brand name, Silpat.

Thermometers. Thermometers have many uses in the bakery, and there are many types of specialized thermometers. The sugar thermometer, also called a *candy thermometer*, is one of the most important. It is used for measuring the temperature, and hence the concentration, of boiling sugar syrups (p. 252). The chocolate thermometer is used for tempering chocolate (p. 627). Other thermometers measure the temperature of bread doughs, frying fat, and the interiors of ovens, refrigerators, and freezers (to check the accuracy of the equipment's thermostat).

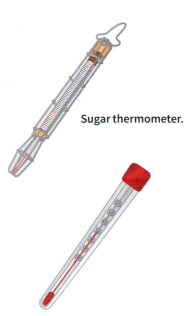

Sugar thermometer.

Chocolate thermometer.

In addition to the above items, other tools for special decorative work are illustrated in the appropriate chapters. See the following pages:

Chocolate, page 627

Pastillage, page 652

Sugar, page 663

Marzipan, page 649

KEY POINTS TO REVIEW

▪ What are the principal types of mixers and attachments?

▪ What are the principal types of dough-handling equipment used in the bakeshop?

▪ What are the four principal types of ovens used in the bakeshop?

4

INGREDIENTS

1. Describe the characteristics and functions of wheat flours.

2. Describe the characteristics and functions of other flours, meals, and starches.

3. Describe the characteristics and functions of sugars.

4. Describe the characteristics and functions of fats.

5. Describe the characteristics and functions of milk and milk products.

6. Describe the characteristics and functions of eggs.

7. Describe the characteristics and functions of leavening agents.

8. Describe the characteristics and functions of gelling agents.

9. Describe the characteristics and functions of fruits and nuts.

10. Describe the characteristics and functions of chocolate and cocoa.

11. Describe the characteristics and functions of salt, spices, and flavorings.

THE INTRODUCTION TO baking ingredients provided in this chapter is necessarily simplified. Hundreds of pages could be—and have been—written on wheat flour alone. Much of this information is, however, of a technical nature and of concern primarily to large industrial bakers. In contrast, this chapter covers the information you will need to produce a full range of baked items in a small bakeshop or a hotel or restaurant kitchen.

WHEAT FLOUR

WHEAT FLOUR IS the most important ingredient in the bakeshop. It provides bulk and structure to most of the baker's products, including breads, cakes, cookies, and pastries. Unlike the home cook who depends almost entirely on a product called *all-purpose flour*, the professional baker has access to a wide variety of flours with different qualities and characteristics. To select the proper flour for each product, and to handle each correctly, you need to understand the characteristics of each type of flour and how it is milled.

Wheat Varieties

The characteristics of a flour depend on the variety of wheat from which it is milled, the location where it is grown, and its growing conditions. The most important fact the baker needs to know is that some wheats are *hard* and some are *soft*. *Hard wheats* contain greater quantities of the proteins called *glutenin* and *gliadin*, which together form gluten when the flour is moistened and mixed. The subject of gluten is discussed in more detail later in this chapter and in Chapter 5.

Gluten development, as you will learn, is one of the baker's major concerns when mixing doughs and batters. *Strong flours*—that is, flours from hard wheats with high protein content—are used primarily to make breads and other yeast products. *Weak flours*—that is, flours from *soft wheats* with low protein content—are important in the production of cakes, cookies, and pastries.

Six principal classes of wheat are grown in North America:

1. **Hard red winter.** This wheat is grown in large quantities. It has a moderately high protein content (see the Protein Content of North American Wheat Varieties table) and is used primarily for *bread flours*. The word "red" in the name refers to the dark color of the bran and husk layers of the wheat berry, not the interior of the grain, which is white.

2. **Hard red spring.** This wheat has the highest protein content of North American wheats and is an important component of strong bread flours. It is often blended with flours from other wheat varieties to make bread flour. Flour made only from hard red spring wheat contains gluten proteins that are often too strong and difficult to stretch for making hand-shaped breads.

3. **Hard white.** This high-protein winter wheat is grown in small quantities for bread flours. One interesting use for this wheat is to make whole wheat flours that are lighter in color and not as strong in flavor as whole wheat flours made from red wheat.

4. **Soft white.** This is a low-protein wheat useful for pastries, cakes, crackers, and other products in which a softer wheat is required.

5. **Soft red winter.** This is another low-protein wheat used for cake and pastry flours.

6. **Durum.** This hard wheat is used primarily for spaghetti and other macaroni products.

Different wheat varieties are grown in Europe. For example, four principal wheat strains grown in France—Recital, Scipion, Soissons, and Textel—are softer—that is, lower in protein—than most North American varieties.

PROTEIN CONTENT OF NORTH AMERICAN WHEAT VARIETIES	
WHEAT VARIETY	**PROTEIN CONTENT**
Soft winter wheat (red and white)	8–11%
Hard winter wheat (red and white)	10–15%
Hard red spring wheat	12–18%
Durum wheat	14–16%

Composition of Wheat

The wheat kernel consists of three main parts:

1. The *bran* is the hard outer covering of the kernel. Darker in color than the interior of the grain, bran is present in whole wheat flour as tiny brown flakes, but is removed in the milling of white flour. (In the case of whole wheat flour made from white wheat, the bran flakes are a much lighter, creamy white color.)

    Bran is high in dietary fiber and contains B vitamins, fat, protein, and minerals.

2. The *germ* is the part of the kernel that becomes the new wheat plant if the kernel is sprouted. It has a high fat content that can quickly become rancid. Therefore, whole wheat flour containing the germ has poor keeping qualities.

   Wheat germ is high in nutrients, containing protein, vitamins, and minerals, as well as fat.

3. The *endosperm* is the white, starchy part of the kernel that remains when the bran and germ are removed. This is the portion of the wheat kernel that is milled into white flour. Depending on its source, the wheat endosperm contains about 68 to 76% starch and 6 to 18% protein. The endosperm also contains small amounts of moisture, fat, sugar, minerals, and other components. These are discussed in more detail when we consider the composition of flour in a later section.

The Milling of Wheat

The purpose of milling wheat is twofold: (1) to separate the endosperm from the bran and germ; and (2) to grind the endosperm to a fine powder.

Stone Grinding

Until modern roller milling (described next) was invented, wheat was made into flour by grinding it between two large stones. Once the grain was ground, it was sifted to remove some of the bran. This sifting is called *bolting*. Bolted flour is lighter in color and finer in texture than whole wheat flour. However, some of the flavor and nutrients are removed along with the bran and germ. In specialty markets, one can still find stone-ground flour, especially unbolted whole wheat flour, and other stone-ground meals, such as cornmeal.

Stone-grinding is laborious and time-consuming, and it does not produce a product that is easy to separate into the precise grades of flour demanded by modern baking. It wasn't until the break system was invented in the nineteenth century that the full range of flour grades in use today became available.

Roller Milling and the Break System

Modern milling of wheat into flour is accomplished by a fairly complex and highly refined system that uses grooved steel rollers. In what is called the *break system*, the rollers are set so the space between them is slightly smaller than the width of the kernels, and the rollers rotate at different speeds. When the wheat is fed between them, the rollers flake off the bran layers and germ and crack the endosperm into coarse pieces. By sifting the broken grains, the parts can be separated. Approximately 72% of the wheat kernel can be separated as endosperm by this process and milled into flour. The remaining 28% consists of bran (about 14%), germ (about 3%), and other outer portions called *shorts* (about 11%).

To further understand how milling works, you must understand that the outer parts of the endosperm—that is, the parts closest to the bran—are higher in protein than the inner parts. When the grain is cracked in the mill, the outer parts break into larger pieces and the inner parts into smaller pieces. In addition, the parts closest to the bran are darker in color than the creamy white interior of the endosperm.

Sifting separates the flour into *streams*. This means the grain is passed through the rollers many times, with the rollers closer together each time. After each pass through the rollers, part of the endosperm is fine enough to be sifted off as flour. The first streams come from the interior of the kernels. Later streams consist of the outer portions of the endosperm. By repeated sifting and breaking, different grades of flour can be obtained from one type of wheat. These grades are described in the following section.

Flour Grades

As just described, different grades of flour come from different portions of the endosperm. Modern milling processes were developed to separate these portions.

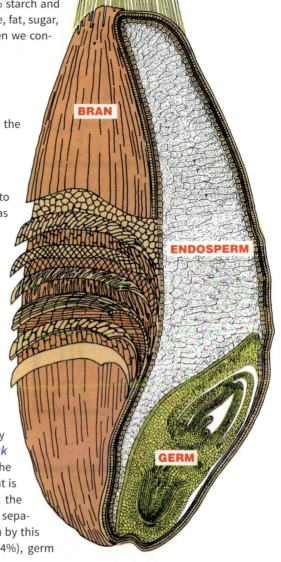

Kernel of wheat.

Provided by the Wheat Foods Council.

PATENT FLOUR

Flour from the interior of the endosperm, extracted during the first streams of milling, is considered the highest grade of flour and is called *patent flour*. It is fine in texture because the granules from the interior of the grain are the smallest. It is also whiter in color than other grades and has high-quality protein. It is nearly completely free of any trace of bran or germ.

Different grades of patent flour are available, depending on the amount of endosperm extracted. Fancy patent, also called *extra short*, is made from only the inner 40 to 60% of the endosperm. Short patent may contain up to 80% of the endosperm, while long patent consists of up to 95% of the endosperm.

Most bakers use the term *patent flour* to mean strong patent flour used for breads. However, any flour made from the interior of the endosperm is patent flour, even if made from soft wheat. Cake flour and pastry flour are also patent flours. You should be aware of these two uses of the term to avoid confusion.

CLEAR FLOUR

The portion of the endosperm left after the patent flour has been removed is called *clear flour*. This flour comes from the outer parts of the endosperm and thus is darker in color and higher in protein. Clear flour is usually separated into more than one grade. *First clear* is a dark flour, tan in color, that is often used in rye breads, where its dark color is not noticed and its high protein content contributes much-needed gluten. Even though it is dark, first clear is lighter in color than *second clear*, which is a low-grade flour not usually used in food production.

It was stated earlier that the outer parts of the endosperm are higher in protein than the interior. Thus, for each type of wheat, clear flour is higher in protein than patent flour. However, the quality of the protein in patent flour is better. This means that the gluten that is formed from these proteins stretches well and makes a strong, elastic film.

STRAIGHT FLOUR

Straight flour is made by combining all the streams of the milling process. In other words, it is made from the entire endosperm. Because it contains the darker parts of the grain as well as the whiter interior, straight flour is darker in color than patent flour. In addition, it contains small amounts of bran and germ that weren't separated during milling.

Straight flour is not often used in North American baking. Some European flours are straight flours.

EXTRACTION

Extraction refers to the amount of flour milled from a given amount of grain. It is expressed as a percentage of the total amount of grain. For example, whole wheat flour is said to be 100% extraction because if you start with 100 pounds of grain, you end up with 100 pounds of whole wheat flour. As a second example, if a grade of flour is described as 60% extraction, this means it would take 100 kilograms whole grain to produce 60 kilograms of this grade of flour. The remaining 40% is bran, germ, shorts, and darker, lower grades of flour. Patent flour is a low-extraction flour, while straight flour is a high-extraction flour.

Composition of Flour

White flour consists mostly of starch. This starch supplies the bulk in baked goods such as breads. Yet the other components of flour, especially protein, are of greatest concern to the baker because of the way they affect the dough-making and baking processes. This section describes each of the major components of white flour.

STARCH

White flour consists of about 68 to 76% starch. Starches are complex carbohydrates whose molecules consist of long chains of simpler sugars bound together. The starches in flour are contained in tiny granules. Most of these remain intact until they come in contact with water during the mixing process, at which time they absorb water and swell in size. Starch can absorb from one-quarter to one-half its weight in water.

A very small amount of the starch is broken down into sugars during milling or storage. This sugar is available as food for yeast.

PROTEIN

About 6 to 18% of white flour is protein, depending on the variety of wheat. Proteins act as binding agents that hold the starch granules together in the endosperm.

About 80% of the proteins in flour are called *glutenin* and *gliadin*. These two proteins, when combined with water and mixed in a dough, form an elastic substance called *gluten*. Controlling the development of gluten, as you will learn in the next chapter, is one of the primary concerns of the baker. Without gluten, it is impossible to make familiar yeast-raised breads, because gluten provides their structure. Gluten proteins can absorb about two times their weight in water.

Other proteins present in white flour are enzymes, most importantly *amylase*, also called *diastase*. This enzyme breaks down starch into simple sugars, which is important for yeast fermentation. Yeast is able to ferment sugars but not starch; amylase makes fermentation possible even in bread doughs with no added sugar.

MOISTURE

The moisture content of flour in good condition ranges from 11 to 14%. If it becomes higher than this, spoilage is likely to occur. For this reason, flour should always be stored covered in a dry place.

GUMS

Like starches, *gums* are forms of carbohydrate. Gums make up 2 to 3% of white flour. The most important gums are called *pentosans*. They are significant because they have a much greater capability to absorb water than either starches or proteins. Pentosans absorb 10 to 15 times their weight in water, so even though they are present in small quantities, they have an important effect on dough formation.

Gums also serve as a source of dietary fiber.

FATS

Fats and fatlike substances (*emulsifiers*) comprise only about 1% of white flour, but it is necessary to be aware of them. First, they are important for gluten development. Second, they spoil easily, giving flour an "off" flavor. For this reason, flour has a limited shelf life and should be used in a timely manner.

ASH

Ash is another term for the mineral content of flour. When bakers are buying flour, they look at two important numbers in the flour's description: the protein content and the ash content. The ash content is determined by burning a sample of flour in a controlled environment. The starch and protein, when burned completely, turn to carbon dioxide gas, water vapor, and other gases, but the minerals do not burn and are left as ash. In general, the higher the ash content, the darker the flour. This is because the bran and the outer parts of the endosperm contain more minerals than the whiter, inner portions of the endosperm. Similarly, whole-grain flour is higher in ash than white flour. In conventional baking, bakers like a relatively low ash content because it makes whiter breads. Today, many artisan bakers of handmade breads look for darker flour with a higher ash content because it makes breads with a more robust wheat flavor.

Ash content for wheat flours ranges from about 0.3% for white cake flour to about 1.5% for whole wheat flour.

PIGMENTS

Orange-yellow pigments called *carotenoids* are present in flour in tiny amounts. Because of these pigments, unbleached flour is creamy in color rather than pure white. As flour ages after it is milled, oxygen in the air bleaches some of these pigments, turning the flour somewhat whiter in color.

Absorption

Absorption refers to the amount of water a flour can take up and hold while being made into a simple dough, based on a predetermined standard dough consistency or stiffness. It is expressed as a percentage of the weight of flour. Thus, if the absorption ratio of a certain grade of flour is

---

KEY POINTS TO REVIEW

▪ What are the three main parts of the wheat kernel?

▪ How is flour milled, using the roller milling system?

▪ What is meant by *extraction*?

▪ What are the three main grades of flour as produced by the roller milling process? Describe them.

described as 60%, this means 60 pounds water combined with 100 pounds flour would yield a dough of standard consistency.

What accounts for differences in absorption ratio of different flours? Remember that the starch, protein, and pentosan gums in flour all absorb water (pp. 56–57). Consider these facts:

- Because starch is the largest component of flour, it absorbs most of the water. However, it absorbs only one-quarter to one-half its weight in water, so a small variation in starch content results in a small variation in absorption.

- Pentosan gums absorb 10 to 15 times their weight in water, but because they are present in such tiny quantities, they don't account for much variation in absorption ratios.

- Proteins are present in significant amounts and absorb up to twice their weight in water. Thus, variations in the absorption ratio of different flours are caused primarily by variations in protein content.

For all practical purposes, the absorption ratio of water by flour is a function of the protein content. *The higher the protein content of the flour, the more water it can absorb.* Obviously, this is an important consideration for bakers. They will have to adjust the water in their bread formulas if they start using flour of a different protein content.

Flour Treatments and Additives

Millers may add small amounts of various compounds to improve the dough-making and baking qualities of flour. All additives must be indicated on the product label. Bakers also may purchase additives and add them to flour as needed.

ENZYMES

As described above, the enzyme amylase, more commonly called *diastase* by bakers, is naturally present in flour, but usually in too small a quantity to be helpful for yeast. Malt flour (described on p. 66) is high in diastase. It may be added by the miller, or the baker may add it in the bakeshop.

AGING AND BLEACHING

Freshly milled flour is not good for bread making. The gluten is somewhat weak and inelastic, and the color may be yellowish. When the flour is aged for several months, the oxygen in the air matures the proteins so they are stronger and more elastic, and it bleaches the color slightly.

Aging flour is costly and haphazard, however, so millers may add small quantities of certain chemicals to accomplish the same results quickly. Bromates, specifically potassium bromate, added to bread flours mature the gluten but do not bleach the flour a great deal. Bromate use is decreasing because of concerns about its safety, and it is not used at all in Canada and Europe. Other additives, such as ascorbic acid (vitamin C), are used instead.

Chlorine is added to cake flour for two reasons: as a maturing agent, and to bleach the flour to pure white.

NUTRIENTS

Enriched flour is flour to which vitamins and minerals (primarily iron and B vitamins) are added to compensate for the nutrients lost when the bran and germ were removed. Most white flour used in North America is enriched.

DOUGH CONDITIONERS

Dough conditioners, also called *dough improvers*, are sometimes added by the baker for the production of yeast products. They contain a variety of ingredients that improve gluten development, aid yeast fermentation, and delay staling. The use of dough conditioners is regulated by law in Canada and the United States, so it is important not to use too much. Also, adding too much to yeast doughs decreases bread quality.

VITAL WHEAT GLUTEN

Vital wheat gluten is wheat gluten in a concentrated form, usually about 75% by weight. It is added to flour to improve the quality of yeast-raised doughs. It can increase the volume of yeast breads and aid in the development of gluten during mixing.

Types of Patent Flour

Bakers generally use the term *patent flour* to mean *patent bread flour*. Technically, all white flour except clear flour and straight flour is patent flour, including cake and pastry flours.

Bread Flour

Patent flour made from hard wheat has enough good-quality gluten to make it ideal for yeast breads. Patent bread flours typically range from 11 to 13.5% protein and 0.35 to 0.55% ash. They are available bleached or unbleached. *Bread flour* with added malt flour to provide extra diastase enzymes is also available.

Bread flour.

In North America, most patent bread flour is formulated for large commercial bakeries. Thus, its gluten proteins are strong enough to tolerate machine handling and molding. Protein content of up to 13.5% is suitable for highly mechanized bakeries. Hand-made artisan breads, on the other hand, generally require a somewhat softer flour, because stronger flours make doughs that are difficult to make up by hand. Look for flour with a protein content of 10.5 to 12%.

High-Gluten Flour

Flour with an especially high protein content is sometimes used in hard-crusted breads and in such specialty products as pizza dough and bagels. It is also used to strengthen doughs made from flours that contain little or no gluten. See, for example, the formula for Chestnut Bread on page 137. (The name of this flour is slightly misleading, as the flour is high not in gluten but in gluten-forming proteins. There is no gluten in flour until certain proteins absorb water and a dough is mixed.)

A typical high-gluten flour has 14% protein and 0.5% ash.

Cake flour.

Cake Flour

Cake flour is a weak or low-gluten flour made from soft wheat. It has a soft, smooth texture and a pure white color. Cake flour is used for cakes and other delicate baked goods that require low gluten content.

Protein content of cake flour is approximately 8%, and ash content is approximately 0.3%.

Pastry Flour

Pastry flour is also a weak or low-gluten flour, but it is slightly stronger than cake flour. It has the creamy white color of patent flour rather than the pure white of cake flour. Pastry flour is used for pie doughs and for some cookies, biscuits, and muffins.

Pastry flour has a protein content of about 9% and an ash content of about 0.4 to 0.45%.

Pastry flour.

European Flour Types

In much of Europe, a flour grading system based on ash content is dominant. For example, the French grades T45 and T55 are white wheat flours with low ash, for breads and pastries. T65 includes high-gluten flours, and T80, T110, and T150 are whole wheat flours of increasing darkness. Other flours are included in this grading system. For example, T170 is dark rye flour.

Bread flours from European wheats are generally lower in protein than North American bread flours. Typically, they have a protein content of around 11 to 11.5%. Some North American mills have begun supplying similar flour to artisan bread bakers seeking to imitate classic European breads.

TYPES OF FLOUR		
FLOUR	**PROTEIN**	**ASH**
Straight flour	13–15%	0.4–0.45%
Patent bread flour	11–13.5%	0.35–0.55%
Clear flour	17%	0.7–0.8%
High-gluten flour	14%	0.5%
Cake flour	8%	0.3%
Pastry flour	9%	0.4–0.45%
All-purpose flour	10–11.5%	0.39–4.4%

HAND TEST FOR FLOUR STRENGTH

A typical small bakery keeps three white wheat flours on hand: cake flour, pastry flour, and a bread flour such as patent. You should be able to identify these three by sight and touch, because sooner or later someone will dump a bag of flour into the wrong bin or label it incorrectly, and you will need to be able to recognize the problem.

▊ Bread flour feels slightly coarse when rubbed between the fingers. If squeezed into a lump in the hand, it falls apart as soon as the hand is opened. Its color is creamy white.

▊ Cake flour feels very smooth and fine. It stays in a lump when squeezed in the hand. Its color is pure white.

▊ Pastry flour feels smooth and fine, like cake flour, and can also be squeezed into a lump. However, it has the creamy color of bread flour, not the pure white color of cake flour.

Hand test for flour strength (from left to right): bread flour, pastry flour, cake flour.

Other Wheat Flours

Other wheat flours you should be familiar with include the following:

All-purpose flour, commonly found in retail markets, is less often found in bakeshops, although it is often used as a general-purpose flour in restaurants, where it is purchased under the name *restaurant and hotel flour*. This flour is formulated to be slightly weaker than bread flour so it can be used for pastries as well. All-purpose flour has a protein content of about 10 to 11.5%.

Durum flour is made from durum wheat, a high-gluten wheat of a different species than those used for most flour. It is used primarily to make spaghetti and other dried pasta. In the bakeshop, it is occasionally used in specialty products, such as Italian semolina bread (*semolina* is another name for durum flour or durum meal). Durum flour has a protein content of 12 to 16%.

Self-rising flour is a white flour to which baking powder and, sometimes, salt has been added. Its advantage is that the baking powder is blended in uniformly. However, its use is limited by two factors. First, different formulas call for different proportions of baking powder. No single blend is right for all purposes. Second, baking powder loses its aerating, or leavening, power with time, so the quality of baked goods made from this flour can fluctuate.

Whole wheat flour is made by grinding the entire wheat kernel, including the bran and germ. The germ, as you have learned, is high in fat, which can become rancid, so whole wheat flour does not keep as well as white flour.

Because it is made from wheat, whole wheat flour contains gluten-forming proteins, so it can be used alone in bread making. (Protein content is typically 12 to 13%.) However, bread made with 100% whole wheat flour is heavier than white bread because the gluten strands are cut by the sharp edges of the bran flakes. Also, the fat from the wheat germ may contribute to the shortening action. This is one reason why most whole wheat breads are strengthened with white flour. Another reason is that the flavor of 100% whole wheat is stronger than many people care for, and the lighter flavor imparted by a blend of flours is often preferred by customers.

Bran flour is flour to which bran flakes have been added. The bran may be coarse or fine, depending on specifications.

Cracked wheat is not a flour but a type of meal, in which the grains are broken into coarse pieces. It is used in small quantities to give texture and flavor to some specialty breads.

Whole wheat flour.

OTHER FLOURS, MEALS, AND STARCHES

WHEAT FLOUR IS the only flour with gluten of sufficient quantity and quality for making regular yeast breads. Some other grains, primarily rye and spelt, also contain gluten proteins, a fact important to people with gluten sensitivity or celiac disease. Unfortunately, the proteins do not form a good, elastic gluten useful for bread making. With the exception of a few specialty baked goods, these other flours and meals are mixed with wheat flour for most baking purposes.

Rye

Next to white and whole wheat, rye is the most popular flour for bread making. Although *rye flour* contains some proteins, these do not form gluten of good quality. This is because although it contains enough gliadin, rye flour does not contain enough glutenin. Therefore, breads made with 100% rye flour are heavy and dense. To make a lighter rye loaf, it is necessary to use a mixture of rye and hard wheat flours. Typical formulas call for 25 to 40% rye flour and 60 to 75% hard wheat flour.

Rye flour is also high in pentosan gums—about four times as much as wheat flour. The gums give some structure to rye breads, but they also interfere with gluten development and make rye doughs stickier than wheat doughs.

Rye flour is milled much like wheat flour. The lightest rye flours, from the inner part of the kernel, have a low extraction rate, corresponding to patent flour. The following grades and types are generally available:

Light rye. The lightest is nearly white. It has a very fine texture and a high percentage of starch, with little protein.

Medium rye. This is a straight flour, milled from the whole rye grain after the bran is removed. Thus, it is darker than light rye and has a higher protein content.

Dark rye. Like clear flour milled from wheat, dark rye comes from the part of the rye grain closest to the bran. Thus, it is darker than other rye flours and has a lower percentage of fine starch particles.

Whole rye flour. This product is made from the whole rye kernel, including the bran and germ.

Rye meal or pumpernickel flour. *Rye meal* is a dark, coarse meal made from the entire rye grain, including the bran and germ. Products labeled *pumpernickel* are sometimes cut into flakes rather than ground into coarse meal. Rye meal is used for pumpernickel bread and similar specialty products.

Rye blend. This is a mixture of rye flour (generally 25 to 40%) and a strong wheat flour, such as clear flour.

Dark rye flour.

Corn

Wheat and rye account for the great majority of the grain flours and meals used in the bakeshop. Other grains are used mainly to add variety to baked goods. Of these other grains, corn is perhaps the most important. (*Note:* In Great Britain, corn is referred to as *maize*, while the word *corn* simply means "grain.")

Corn contains no gluten-forming proteins, although it does contain significant quantities of other proteins, and is therefore important in vegetarian diets.

Corn is most often used by the baker in the form of yellow cornmeal. Blue cornmeal is also available. Most cornmeal is made from only the endosperm, because the oil in the germ becomes rancid quickly. However, whole-grain cornmeal is also available. Cornmeal is available in grinds from fine to coarse. Coarse cornmeal produces a crumbly, somewhat gritty texture in cornbreads, a quality that is desirable in some products.

Yellow cornmeal.

Other important corn products are discussed on page 63 in the section on starches.

Spelt

Spelt is considered an ancestor of modern wheat. Like wheat, it contains gluten proteins, but they form a rather weak gluten structure that can't withstand much mixing. Spelt has a lower absorption ratio than wheat.

Spelt was unheard of by most bakers until not long ago. More recently, it has enjoyed increased popularity, partly because of increased interest in vegetarian diets and the desire for greater variety in dietary sources of protein. It is found increasingly as an ingredient in specialty breads.

Oats

Long familiar as breakfast porridge, oats in various forms also find uses in the bakeshop. Although rich in protein, including enough gluten proteins to make them off-limits for people allergic to gluten, oats do not form a gluten structure when mixed into a dough. Oats are high in gums, which supply dietary fiber. The gum content accounts for the gummy or gluey texture of oatmeal porridge.

Rolled oats, commonly used for porridge, are made by steaming oat grains to soften them and then flattening them between rollers. They are used to give textural interest to multi-grain breads, as toppings for specialty loaves, and as an ingredient in some cookies.

Steel-cut oats are whole grains that have been cut into small pieces. They are occasionally used in small quantities in specialty breads. They have a long cooking time and a chewy texture.

Oat flour is whole-grain oats ground into fine flour, which can be mixed with wheat flour in small quantities for specialty breads.

Oat bran is a good source of dietary fiber that is often used as a muffin ingredient.

Buckwheat

Buckwheat is technically not a grain because it is the seed not of a grass but of a plant with branched stems and broad, arrow-shaped leaves. Whole buckwheat is often ground into a dark, strong-tasting flour, while buckwheat endosperm alone is ground into a lighter-colored flour with a somewhat milder taste. When the grains are crushed into small pieces, they are called *buck-wheat groats* and can be cooked like rice.

Buckwheat flour is most commonly used for pancakes and crêpes, but it can also be used in small quantities in specialty breads and multigrain products.

Soy

Soy is not a grain; it is a bean, or legume. Nevertheless, it may be ground into a flour like a grain. Unlike regular grains, however, it is low in starch. It is also high in fat and protein, although it contains no gluten proteins. The rich protein content makes it valuable in vegetarian diets.

Soy flour used in baking usually has had part of the fat removed. Raw soy flour contains enzymes that make it useful in baking. These enzymes aid yeast action and bleach the pigments in wheat flour. Raw or untoasted soy flour should be used in small quantities in yeast breads, generally about 0.5%. Higher quantities give an unpleasant beany flavor to breads and produce poor texture.

When soy flour is toasted, the enzymes are destroyed and the flour has a pleasanter flavor. Toasted soy flour can be used to add flavor and nutritional value to baked products.

Rice

Rice flour is smooth white flour milled from white rice. It has a small amount of protein but no gluten, so it is often used in gluten-free baked products.

Other Grains and Flours

Many other grains, such as amaranth, millet, teff, and barley, have limited used in the bakeshop, either as flour or as whole grains. Other starchy nongrain foods, such as potatoes and chestnuts, can be dried and ground into flour for special products. See, for example, the formula for Chestnut Bread on page 137. Cooked potato starch is sometimes added to yeast breads, because the starch is easily broken down by diastase enzymes into forms of sugar that yeast can use.

Starches

In addition to flours, other starch products are used in the bakeshop. Unlike flour, they are used primarily to thicken puddings, pie fillings, and similar products. The three most important starches in dessert production are as follows:

1. *Cornstarch* has a special property that makes it valuable for certain purposes. Products thickened with cornstarch set up almost like gelatin when cooled. For this reason, cornstarch is used to thicken cream pies and other products that must hold their shape.

2. *Waxy maize* is made from a different type of corn. It is almost always manufactured into a form called *modified food starch*. Waxy maize and other modified starches have valuable properties. Because they do not break down when frozen, they are used for products that are to be frozen. Also, they are clear when cooked and give a brilliant, clear appearance to fruit pie fillings.

   Waxy maize does not set up firm like cornstarch but rather makes a soft paste that has the same consistency hot and cold. Thus, it is not suitable for cream pie fillings.

3. *Instant starches* are precooked or pregelatinized so they thicken cold liquids without further cooking. They are useful when heat will damage the flavor of the product, as in fresh fruit glazes such as strawberry.

AMYLOSE AND AMYLOPECTIN STARCHES

Starch molecules fall into two principal categories. Amylose molecules are long, straight chains, while amylopectin molecules have many branches. Most grain starches are high in amylose starches; starches from roots and tubers, such as potatoes and arrowroot, are high in amylopectin starches. The differences between the two types can be summarized as follows:

- Amylose starches, after cooking, get thicker and cloudier as they cool. They form a firm gel when cooled. They tend to break down and release liquid after long storage or after freezing.

- Amylopectin starches do not get thicker as they cool, and they remain fairly clear. They also remain stable when frozen and do not release liquid in storage or after freezing.

KEY POINTS TO REVIEW

- What is meant by *absorption*? Why is it important?
- What are the most important characteristics of bread flour, high-gluten flour, pastry flour, and cake flour?
- What are the main types of rye flour?

SUGARS

SUGARS OR SWEETENING agents have the following purposes in baking:

- They add sweetness and flavor.
- They create tenderness and fineness of texture, partly by weakening the gluten structure.
- They give crust color.
- They increase keeping qualities by retaining moisture.
- They act as creaming agents with fats and as foaming agents with eggs.
- They provide food for yeast.

We customarily use the term *sugar* to refer to regular refined sugars derived from sugarcane or beets. The chemical name for these sugars is *sucrose*. However, other sugars of different chemical structure are also used in the bakeshop.

Sugars belong to a group of substances called *carbohydrates*, a group that also includes starches. There are two basic groups of sugars: *simple sugars* (or *monosaccharides*, which means "single sugars") and *complex sugars* (or *disaccharides*, meaning "double sugars"). Starches, or *polysaccharides*, have more complex chemical structures than sugars. Sucrose is a disaccharide, as are maltose (malt sugar) and lactose (the sugar found in milk). Examples of simple sugars are glucose and fructose.

All these sugars have different degrees of sweetness. For example, lactose is much less sweet than regular table sugar (sucrose), while fructose (or fruit sugar, one of the sugars in honey) is much sweeter than sucrose.

All sugars share one characteristic that is important for bakers and pastry chefs to understand: They are *hygroscopic*. This means they attract and hold water. Some sugars are more hygroscopic than others. Fructose, found in honey, is much more hygroscopic than sucrose, or table sugar.

For some purposes, this characteristic is desirable. For example, baked goods containing sugar stay moist longer than those with little or no sugar. For other purposes, this is undesirable. For example, spun sugar (p. 663) can be held for only a limited time, because it attracts moisture from the air and becomes sticky. Sugar used for dusting can attract moisture and dissolve.

Invert Sugar

When a sucrose solution is heated with an acid, some of the sucrose breaks down into equal parts of two simple sugars, dextrose and levulose. A mixture of equal parts of dextrose and levulose is called *invert sugar*. It is about 30% sweeter than regular sucrose.

Invert sugar has two properties that make it interesting to the baker. First, it holds moisture especially well—that is, it is very hygroscopic—and, therefore, helps keep cakes fresh and moist. Second, it resists crystallization. Thus, it promotes smoothness in candies, icings, and syrups. This is why an acid such as cream of tartar is often added to sugar syrups. The acid inverts some of the sugar when it is boiled, preventing graininess in the candy or icing.

Invert sugar is produced commercially and is available as a syrup. It is also present in honey.

Regular Refined Sugars, or Sucrose

Refined sugars are classified by the size of the grains. However, there is no standard system of labeling, so the names of the granulations vary depending on the manufacturer.

Granulated Sugar

Solid sugars (clockwise from top left): 10X sugar, brown sugar, regular granulated sugar, superfine granulated sugar.

Regular granulated sugar, also called *fine granulated sugar* or table sugar, is the most familiar and the most commonly used.

Very fine and **ultrafine sugars** (also called *caster sugar*) are finer than regular granulated sugar. They are prized for making cakes and cookies because they produce a more uniform batter and can support higher quantities of fat.

Sanding sugars are coarse and are used for coating cookies, cakes, and other products.

Pearl sugar is a type of sanding sugar. It consists of opaque, white grains and does not easily dissolve in water. This characteristic, as well as its appearance, makes it useful for decorating sweet dough products. Pearl sugar is also called *sugar nibs*.

In general, finer granulations are better for mixing into doughs and batters because they dissolve relatively quickly. Coarse sugars are likely to leave undissolved grains, even after long mixing. These show up after baking as dark spots on crusts, irregular texture, and syrupy spots. Also, fine sugars are better for creaming with fats because they create a finer, more uniform air cell structure and better volume.

Coarse sugar, on the other hand, can be used in syrups, where its mixing properties are not a factor. Even a very coarse sugar dissolves readily when boiled with water. In fact, coarse crystalline sugar is often purer than fine sugar and makes a clearer syrup.

Confectioners' or Powdered Sugars

Confectioners' sugars are ground to a fine powder and mixed with a small amount of starch (about 3%) to prevent caking. They are classified by coarseness or fineness.

10X is the finest sugar. It gives the smoothest texture in icings.

6X is slightly coarser in texture than 10X. For this reason, it is less likely to form lumps or to dissolve in moisture. It is used mostly for dusting the tops of desserts.

Coarser types (XXXX and XX) are used for dusting and whenever 6X or 10X are too fine.

Confectioners' sugar is also known as *icing sugar* because of its importance in making many kinds of icing.

Dehydrated Fondant

Dehydrated fondant, also known as *fondant sugar*, is a dried form of fondant icing. It is different from confectioners' sugar in that it is much finer than even 10X, and it does not contain any starch to prevent caking.

During the manufacture of fondant, part of the sucrose is changed to invert sugar. This helps keep the sugar crystals tiny, which makes for a very smooth, creamy icing with a good shine.

Fondant is discussed with other icings in Chapter 17.

Brown Sugar

Brown sugar is mostly sucrose (about 85 to 92%), but it also contains varying amounts of caramel, molasses, and other impurities, which give it its characteristic flavor and color. The darker grades contain more of these impurities. Basically, brown sugar is regular cane sugar that has not been completely refined. However, it can also be made by adding measured amounts of these impurities to refined white sugar.

Brown sugar was, at one time, available in 15 grades that ranged from very dark to very light. Today, only two to four grades are generally available.

Because it contains a small amount of acid, brown sugar can be used with baking soda to provide some leavening (see p. 79). It is used in place of regular white sugar when its flavor is desired and its color will not be objectionable. Of course, it should not be used in white cakes.

Keep brown sugar in an airtight container to prevent it from drying out and hardening.

Demerara sugar is a crystalline brown sugar. It is dry rather than moist like regular brown sugar. Demerara sugar is sometimes used in baking, but it is more often served as a sweetener with coffee and tea.

Nonnutritive Sweeteners

Also known as *sugar substitutes*, these products are discussed together with other dietary issues in Chapter 26.

Syrups

Syrups consist of one or more types of sugar dissolved in water, often with small amounts of other compounds or impurities that give the syrup flavor. The most basic syrup in the bakeshop, called **simple syrup**, is made by dissolving sucrose in water. *Dessert syrup* is simple syrup with added flavorings. These sucrose syrups are discussed in more detail in Chapter 12.

Molasses

Molasses is concentrated sugarcane juice. Sulfured molasses is a byproduct of sugar refining. It is the product that remains after most of the sugar is extracted from cane juice. Unsulfured molasses is not a byproduct but a specially manufactured sugar product. It has a less bitter taste than sulfured molasses.

Molasses contains large amounts of sucrose and other sugars, including invert sugar. It also contains acids, moisture, and other constituents that give it its flavor and color. Darker grades are stronger in flavor and contain less sugar than lighter grades.

Molasses retains moisture in baked goods and therefore prolongs freshness. Crisp cookies made with molasses can soften quickly because the invert sugars absorb moisture from the air.

Liquid sugars (clockwise from top left): molasses, honey, low-conversion glucose syrup, corn syrup.

Glucose Corn Syrup

Glucose is the most common of the simple sugars (monosaccharides). In syrup form, it is an important bakeshop ingredient. Glucose is usually manufactured from cornstarch. Starch, as explained on page 63, consists of long chains of simple sugars bound together in large molecules. The manufacturing process breaks these starches into glucose molecules.

Not all the starch is broken into simple sugars during the process. In low-conversion syrups, only one-fourth to one-third of the starch is converted to glucose. As a result, these syrups are only slightly sweet. They are also very thick, because there are many larger molecules in the solution. Low-conversion syrups are less likely to burn or caramelize. They are useful for icings, candies, and sugar pieces, such as pulled sugar.

Regular, all-purpose *corn syrups* are medium-conversion glucose syrups in which nearly half the starch is converted to glucose. Corn syrup is useful for imparting moistness and tenderness to baked goods.

Dark corn syrup is regular corn syrup with added flavorings and colorings. In bakeshop usage, it is considered similar to a very mild molasses.

Invert Sugar Syrup

As explained on page 64, invert sugar is available as a syrup. It is often used in cakes and other products for its moisture-retaining properties. Bakers often refer to invert sugar syrup as *trimoline*, which is the brand name used by one of its manufacturers.

Honey

Honey is a natural sugar syrup consisting largely of the simple sugars glucose and fructose, plus other compounds that give it its flavor and color. Honeys vary considerably in flavor and color, depending on their source. Flavor is the major reason for using honey, especially as it can be expensive.

Because honey contains invert sugar, it helps retain moisture in baked goods. Like molasses, it contains acid, which means it can be used with baking soda as a leavening.

Malt Syrup

Malt syrup, also called *malt extract*, is used primarily in yeast breads. It serves as food for the yeast and adds flavor and crust color to the loaves. Malt is extracted from barley that has been sprouted (malted) and then dried and ground.

There are two basic types of malt syrup: *diastatic* and *nondiastatic*. Diastatic malt contains a group of enzymes called *diastase*, which breaks starch into sugars that can be acted on by yeast. Thus, diastatic malt, when added to bread dough, is a powerful food for yeast. It is used when fermentation times are short. It should not be used when fermentation times are long because too much starch will be broken down by the enzyme. This results in bread with a sticky crumb.

Diastatic malt is produced with high, medium, or low diastase content.

Nondiastatic malt is processed at high temperatures that destroy the enzymes and give the syrup a darker color and stronger flavor. It is used because it contains fermentable sugar and contributes flavor, crust color, and keeping qualities to breads.

Whenever malt syrup is called for in formulas in this book, nondiastatic malt is intended. Only one formula (Bagels, p. 136) requires diastatic malt. If malt syrup is not available, you may substitute regular granulated sugar.

Malt is available in two other forms. *Dried malt extract* is simply malt syrup that has been dried. It must be kept in an airtight container to keep it from absorbing moisture from the air. *Malt flour* is the dried, ground, malted barley that has not had the malt extracted from it. It is obviously a much less concentrated form of malt. When used in bread making, it is blended with the flour.

KEY POINTS TO REVIEW

▮ What are the six functions of sugars in baked goods?

▮ What forms of sucrose are used in the bakeshop?

▮ What are the main syrup products used in the bakeshop?

FATS

THE MAJOR FUNCTIONS of fats in baked items are:

- To add moistness and richness.
- To increase tenderness by shortening gluten strands.
- To increase keeping quality.

- To add flavor.
- To assist in leavening when used as a creaming agent, or to give flakiness to puff pastry, pie dough, and similar products.

Many fats are available to the baker. Each has distinctive properties that make it suitable for different purposes. Among the properties a baker must consider when selecting a fat for a specific use are its melting point, its softness or hardness at different temperatures, its flavor, and its ability to form emulsions (described later in this section).

Saturated and Unsaturated Fats

Some fats are solid at room temperature, while others are liquid. The liquid fats we usually refer to as *oils*. Whether the fats are solid or liquid depends on the fatty acids that make up the fat molecules (see the Lipids sidebar).

Fatty acids consist primarily of long chains of carbon atoms to which hydrogen atoms are attached. If a fatty acid chain contains as many hydrogen atoms as it can possibly hold, it is called a *saturated fat*. If the chain has empty spaces that could hold more hydrogen, it is called an *unsaturated fat*. (One or more places along the carbon chain may lack hydrogen atoms.) Saturated fats are solid at room temperature, while unsaturated fats are liquid.

Natural fats consist of a mixture of many fat compounds. The more saturated fats there are in the mixture, the more solid the fat. The more unsaturated fats there are in the mixture, the softer it is.

To produce solid, pliable fats for the bakeshop, manufacturers submit oils to a treatment called *hydrogenation*. This process bonds hydrogen atoms to the empty spaces in fatty acid chains, changing them from unsaturated to saturated. By controlling the process, the manufacturer can give the fat exactly the desired blend of saturated and unsaturated fats to produce a shortening with the exact characteristics desired, such as softness, moldability, and melting point.

Fat Emulsions

Most bakery ingredients mix easily with water and other liquids and actually undergo a change in form. For example, salt and sugar dissolve in water; flour and starch absorb water, and the water becomes bound up with the starch and protein molecules. Fat, on the other hand, does not change form when it is mixed with liquids or other bakery ingredients. Instead, it is merely broken down into smaller and smaller particles during mixing. These small fat particles eventually become more or less evenly distributed in the mix.

A uniform mixture of two normally unmixable substances, such as a fat and water, is called an *emulsion*. Mayonnaise is a familiar example of an emulsion from outside the bakeshop—in this case, an emulsion of oil and vinegar. There are also emulsions of air and fat, such as that formed when shortening and sugar are creamed together in the production of cakes and other products (see p. 80).

LIPIDS

Fats are members of a larger group of compounds called *lipids*. Lipids are organic compounds that are not soluble in water. Other lipids include cholesterol and emulsifiers, such as lecithin.

Technically, fats are *triglycerides*, which are molecules made up of three fatty acid chains attached to the three carbon atoms of a glycerin molecule. The physical characteristics of each fat are determined by the kind of fatty acid chains that make up the compound.

HYDROGENATION AND FAT STABILITY

As explained in the text, one purpose of hydrogenation is to produce fats with desired physical characteristics. A second reason is to reduce the tendency of the fat to spoil, or become *rancid*, by reacting with the oxygen in the air. The more unsaturated a fat is, the more likely it is to become rancid. Saturated fats are more stable, because all the places along the carbon chain are filled by hydrogen atoms, which gives oxygen less opportunity to react with the fat.

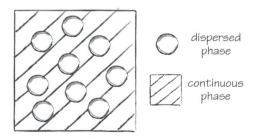

In an emulsion, droplets of one substance (called the *dispersed phase*) are evenly mixed in another substance (called the *continuous phase*).

Reprinted with permission of John Wiley & Sons, Inc.

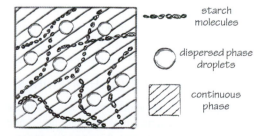

Particles (such as starch) in the continuous phase stabilize an emulsion by helping keep droplets of the dispersed phase from coming together and merging.

Reprinted with permission of John Wiley & Sons, Inc.

Fats have differing abilities to form emulsions. For example, if the wrong shortening is used in certain cakes, the emulsion may fail because the batter contains more water than the fat can hold. We then say that the batter curdles, or breaks.

Shortenings

Any fat acts as a shortening in baking because it shortens gluten strands and tenderizes the product. However, we generally use the word *shortening* to mean any of a group of solid fats, usually white and tasteless, that are especially formulated for baking. Shortenings generally consist of nearly 100% fat.

Shortenings may be made from vegetable oils, animal fats, or both. During manufacturing, the fats are hydrogenated. This process turns liquid oils into solid fats. Shortenings are used for many purposes, so manufacturers have formulated different kinds of fats with various properties. There are three main types: regular or all-purpose (AP) shortenings, high-ratio plastic shortenings, and high-ratio liquid shortenings.

REGULAR SHORTENINGS

Regular shortenings, or all-purpose shortenings, have a fairly tough, waxy texture, and small particles of the fat tend to hold their shape in a dough or batter. They are called *plastic* shortenings, which means they are moldable at room temperature. Regular shortenings can be manufactured to varying degrees of hardness. They have a good creaming ability. This means that a good quantity of air can be mixed into them to give a batter lightness and leavening power (see p. 80). Also, this type of shortening melts only at a high temperature.

Because of their texture, regular shortenings are used for flaky products such as piecrusts and biscuits. They are also used in many other pastries, breads, and products mixed by creaming, such as certain pound cakes, cookies, and quick breads.

Fats (from left): lard, butter, margarine, shortening.

Unless another shortening is specified in a formula, regular shortening is generally used.

HIGH-RATIO PLASTIC SHORTENINGS

These are soft shortenings that spread easily throughout a batter and quickly coat the particles of sugar and flour. They are called *high-ratio* because they were devised for use in cake batters that contain a high ratio of sugar and liquid to flour. They also contain added emulsifying agents, so they can hold a larger quantity of liquid and sugar than regular shortenings. Thus, they give a smoother and finer texture to cakes, and make them moister. Because of the added emulsifiers, this shortening is also commonly referred to as *emulsified shortening*.

On the other hand, high-ratio shortening does not cream well. When recipe instructions call for creaming shortening and sugar, regular shortening rather than high-ratio shortening should be used.

When emulsified shortening is used to make high-ratio cakes—cakes with a high ratio of sugar and liquid to flour—a simpler mixing method can be used because this shortening spreads so well (see Chapter 16). In addition, high-ratio shortening is often used in icings because it can hold more sugar and liquid without curdling.

The term *emulsified shortenings* is not, strictly speaking, an accurate one. Pure fat cannot be emulsified, because an emulsion is a mixture of at least two substances. It would, perhaps, be more accurate to call them *emulsifier* or *emulsifying* shortenings. However, the term *emulsified shortenings* is the more widely recognized and commonly used term.

HIGH-RATIO LIQUID SHORTENINGS

High-ratio liquid shortenings, also called *liquid cake shortenings*, are less hydrogenated than plastic shortenings, making them liquid and pourable, although they are thick and cloudy or opaque in appearance. They contain more emulsifiers than high-ratio plastic shortenings, and are effective shortenings in high-ratio cakes. The emulsifiers make the cakes moist and fine-textured. Also, because air is incorporated so easily during mixing, these shortenings increase the volume and tenderness of cakes.

High-ratio liquid shortenings, because they spread through the batter so well, simplify mixing. Also, the quantity of shortening in a batter can often be reduced because the shortening is so effective. For example, in the formula for Yellow Cake batter on page 400, the shortening quantity can be reduced to 50% with only a small change in quality; the cake will be only slightly drier and firmer.

Butter

Fresh butter in North America consists of about 80% fat, about 15% water, and about 5% milk solids. Most North American butter is made from sweet cream. Many European butters have a higher fat content—about 82%, or even more—and a lower moisture content. In addition, they are more likely to be made from cultured cream (crème fraîche, p. 71, and sour cream are examples of cultured cream used in the kitchen), which gives them a somewhat fuller flavor.

Butter is graded according to U.S. Department of Agriculture (USDA) standards, although grading is not mandatory. Grades are AA, A, B, and C. Most operations use grades AA and A because flavors of the lower grades may be off. In Canada, grades are Canada 1, Canada 2, and Canada 3.

Butter is available salted and unsalted. Unsalted butter is more perishable, but it has a fresher, sweeter taste and is thus preferred in baking. Also, salt masks flavors that might be absorbed during storage, making it is harder to tell if salted butter has foreign flavors that might detract from the finished baked goods. If salted butter is used, the salt in the formula may have to be reduced. It is difficult to know for sure, however, how much to reduce the salt content, because salted butters vary in their composition.

Shortenings are manufactured to have certain textures and levels of hardness to suit them for particular uses. Butter, on the other hand, is a natural product that doesn't have this advantage. It is hard and brittle when cold, very soft at room temperature, and it melts easily. Consequently, doughs made with butter are much harder to handle. Also, butter is more expensive than shortening.

On the other hand, butter has two major advantages:

1. **Flavor.** Shortenings are intentionally flavorless, but butter has a highly desirable flavor.
2. **Melting qualities.** Butter melts in the mouth. Shortenings do not. After eating pastries or icings made with shortening, one can be left with an unpleasant film of shortening coating the mouth.

For these reasons, many bakers and pastry chefs feel the advantages of butter outweigh its disadvantages for many purposes. Shortening is not often used in fine French pastries, for example. Frequently, you may blend 50% butter and 50% shortening to get both the flavor of butter and the handling qualities of shortening.

Margarine

Margarine is manufactured from various hydrogenated animal and vegetable fats, plus flavoring ingredients; emulsifiers; coloring agents; and other ingredients. It contains 80 to 85% fat, 10 to 15% moisture, and about 5% salt, milk solids, and other components. Thus, it may be considered a sort of imitation butter consisting of shortening, water, and flavoring.

Unlike the margarines sold by retail grocers, baker's margarines are formulated in different ways for different purposes. Following are the two major categories.

Cake and Baker's Margarines

These types of margarine are soft and have good creaming ability. They are used not only in cakes but also in a wide variety of other products.

Pastry Margarines

These margarines, also called *roll-in compounds*, are tougher and more elastic than cake margarines and have a waxy texture. They are especially formulated for doughs that form layers, such as Danish dough and puff pastry.

Puff pastry margarine, the toughest of these fats, is sometimes called *puff pastry shortening*. Puff pastry made with this margarine generally rises higher than pastry made with butter.

However, as the fat doesn't melt in the mouth like butter, many people find the pastry unpleasant to eat.

Roll-in margarine is somewhat softer in texture than puff pastry margarine and has a lower melting point. It can be used in Danish pastries, croissants, and puff pastry.

Oils

Oils are liquid fats. They are not often used as shortenings in baking because they spread through a batter or dough too thoroughly and shorten too much. Some breads and a few cakes and quick breads use oil as a shortening. Beyond this, the usefulness of oil in the bakeshop is limited primarily to greasing pans, deep-frying doughnuts, and serving as a wash for some kinds of rolls.

Lard

Lard is the rendered fat of hogs. Because of its plastic quality, it was once highly valued for making classic American flaky piecrusts and biscuits—and it is still sometimes used for these products. Since the development of modern shortenings, however, it is not often used in the bakeshop.

Storage of Fats

All fats become rancid when exposed to the air too long. Also, they tend to absorb odors and flavors from other foods. Highly perishable fats, such as butter, should be stored, well wrapped, in the refrigerator. Other fats and oils should be kept in tightly closed containers in a cool, dry, dark place.

> **KEY POINTS TO REVIEW**
>
> - What are the four functions of fats in baked goods?
> - What is an emulsion?
> - What types of shortenings are used in the bakeshop?
> - What is the composition of butter? What are the advantages and disadvantages of using butter in baked goods?

MILK AND MILK PRODUCTS

NEXT TO WATER, milk is the most important liquid in the bakeshop. As we will discuss in Chapter 5, water is essential for the development of gluten. Fresh milk, being 88 to 91% water, fulfills this function. In addition, milk contributes to the texture, flavor, crust color, keeping quality, and nutritional value of baked products.

In this section, we discuss milk products in two parts: first, an explanation and definition of the available products; and second, guidelines for using milk products in baking.

The Composition of Milk Products table on page 71 lists the water, fat, and milk solids content of the most important milk products. Milk solids include protein, lactose (milk sugar), and minerals.

Categories and Definitions

When we talk about milk and cream used in food service, we are nearly always talking about milk from cows. Milk from other animals, including goats, sheep, and water buffaloes, is used to make some cheeses, but most of the liquid milk we see, except for a small amount of goat milk, is milk from dairy cattle.

Milk is used as a beverage and in cooking. Similarly, other milk products, including cream, butter, and cheese, are eaten as purchased and used in cooking.

Pasteurization

Liquid milk, directly as it comes from the cow and before it has had anything done to it, is called *raw milk*. Because raw milk may contain disease-causing bacteria or other organisms, it is almost always *pasteurized* before being sold or before being processed into other products. Pasteurized milk has been heated to 161°F (72°C), held at this temperature for 15 seconds to kill disease-causing organisms, and then quickly chilled. By law, all Grade A liquid milk and cream must be pasteurized. (Grades B and C are used in food processing and industrial uses and are rarely seen in food service or in the retail market.)

Even after pasteurizing, milk and cream are highly perishable products. Some cream products are **ultrapasteurized** or **UHT pasteurized** (ultra-high temperature or ultra-heat treated) to extend their shelf life. Heating the product to a much higher temperature (275°F/135°C) for one to three seconds kills not only disease-causing bacteria but nearly all organisms that cause spoilage. If packed in sterile conditions, UHT milk keeps at room temperature until opened, but then must be refrigerated.

UHT milk has a somewhat cooked taste and is better suited to cooking than for drinking.

Fresh Milk Products

Whole milk is fresh milk as it comes from the cow, with nothing removed and nothing (except vitamin D) added. It contains about 3½% fat (known as **milk fat** or **butterfat**), 8½% nonfat milk solids, and 88% water.

Skim or **nonfat milk** has had most or all of the fat removed. Its fat content is 0.5% or less.

Low-fat milk has a fat content of 0.5 to 2%. Its fat content is usually indicated, usually 1% and 2%.

Fortified nonfat or low-fat milk contains added substances that increase its nutritional value, usually vitamins A and D and extra nonfat milk solids.

Except, of course, for nonfat milk, natural liquid milk contains fat, which, because it is lighter than water, will gradually separate and float to the top in the form of cream. **Homogenized milk** has been processed so the cream doesn't separate. This is done by forcing the milk through very tiny holes, which breaks the fat into particles so small they stay distributed in the milk. Nearly all liquid milk on the market has been homogenized.

COMPOSITION OF MILK PRODUCTS

	WATER (%)	FAT (%)	MILK SOLIDS (%)
Fresh, whole	88	3.5	8.5
Fresh, skim	91	Trace	9
Evaporated, whole	72	8	20
Evaporated, skim	72	Trace	28
Condensed, whole[1]	31	8	20
Dried, whole	1.5	27.5	71
Dried, skim	2.5	Trace	97.5

[1] Condensed milk also contains 41% sugar (sucrose).

Fresh Cream Products

Whipping cream has a fat content of 30 to 40%. Within this category, you may find light whipping cream (30 to 35%) and heavy whipping cream (36% or more). Extra-heavy cream, also called *manufacturer's cream*, has a fat content of 38 to 40% or more and is generally available only on the wholesale market. Whipping cream labeled *ultrapasteurized* keeps longer than regular pasteurized cream. Pure ultrapasteurized cream does not whip as well as regular pasteurized cream, so additives such as vegetable gums are added to make it more whippable.

Light cream, also called *table cream* or *coffee cream*, contains 18 to 30% fat, usually about 18%.

Half-and-half has a fat content of 10 to 18%, too low to be called *cream*.

Fermented Milk and Cream Products

Sour cream has been cultured or fermented by added lactic acid bacteria, which makes it thick and slightly tangy in flavor. It has about 18% fat.

Crème fraîche (krem fresh) is a slightly aged, cultured heavy cream. It is widely used for sauce making in Europe because of its pleasant, slightly tangy flavor and its ability to blend easily into sauces. Unlike regular heavy cream, it usually doesn't require tempering and can be added directly to hot sauces. It is available commercially but is expensive. A close approximation can be made by warming 1 quart (1 L) heavy cream to about 100°F (38°C), adding 1½ ounces (50 mL) buttermilk, and letting the mixture stand in a warm place until slightly thickened, about 6 to 24 hours.

Buttermilk is fresh, liquid milk, usually skim milk, which has been cultured or soured by bacteria. It is usually called *cultured buttermilk* to distinguish it from the original buttermilk, which was the liquid left after butter making. Buttermilk is used in recipes calling for sour milk.

Yogurt is milk (whole or low-fat) cultured by special bacteria. It has a custardlike consistency. Most yogurt has additional milk solids added, and some of it is flavored and sweetened.

Baker's cheese.

Cream cheese.

Milk Products with Water Removed

Evaporated milk is milk, either whole or skim, with about 60% of the water removed. It is then sterilized and canned. Evaporated milk has a somewhat cooked flavor.

Condensed milk is whole milk that has had about 60% of the water removed and is heavily sweetened with sugar. It is available canned and in bulk.

Dried whole milk is whole milk that has been dried to a powder. *Nonfat dry milk* is skim milk that has been dried in the same way. Both are available in regular form and in instant form, which dissolves in water more easily.

Cheese

Two types of cheese are used in the bakeshop, primarily in the production of cheese fillings and cheesecakes.

Baker's cheese is a soft, unaged cheese with a very low fat content. It is dry and pliable and can be kneaded somewhat like a dough. Generally available in 30-pound (13.6-kg) and 50-pound (22.6-kg) packs, it can be frozen for longer storage.

Cream cheese is also a soft, unaged cheese, but it has a higher fat content, about 35%. It is used mainly in rich cheesecakes and in a few specialty products.

Two other cheeses are occasionally used for specialty products. *Mascarpone* is a type of Italian cream cheese with a tangier flavor than American-style cream cheese. It is used to make the filling for tiramisù (p. 467). Another Italian cheese, *ricotta*, was originally made from the whey left over from making cheese from cow's milk or sheep's milk, although now it is more often made from whole milk than from whey. It has many uses in the kitchen and bakeshop. A smooth, relatively dry ricotta called *ricotta impastata* is used to make a filling for cannoli (p. 239). Regular ricotta has too much moisture for this purpose.

Mascarpone.

Ricotta.

Ricotta impastata.

Artificial Dairy Products

A wide variety of imitation cream and dessert topping products are made from various fats and chemicals, which are listed on the label. They are used in some institutions because they keep longer and are generally less expensive than dairy products. Some people feel they are acceptable, but many find their flavors objectionable.

Guidelines for Using Milk Products in Baking

Fresh Liquid Milk

Whole milk contains fat, which must be calculated as part of the shortening in a dough. For this reason, whole and skim milk are not interchangeable in a formula unless adjustments are made for the fat. (Refer to the Composition of Milk Products table on page 71 for the fat content of milk products.)

Acid ingredients, such as lemon juice, cream of tartar, and baking powder, normally should not be added directly to milk, as they will curdle it.

Fresh liquid milk, even regular pasteurized milk, contains an enzyme that can be harmful to gluten formation. For this reason, bakers often heat milk to just below the boiling point (called *scalding*) and cool it again to room temperature before incorporating it in yeast doughs. If you find you have difficulty properly developing doughs containing fresh milk, you might try scalding the milk to see if this solves the problem. Alternatively, use ultrapasteurized or UHT milk, which has been processed at higher temperatures.

Buttermilk

When buttermilk is produced, the lactose in the milk is converted to lactic acid. When buttermilk is used in place of regular milk in baked goods such as cakes or muffins, this acidity must, in most cases, be neutralized by adding baking soda to the formula. Then, because the soda and acid together release carbon dioxide, this extra leavening power must be compensated for by reducing the baking powder, as follows:

For each quart (2 lb) buttermilk:

1. Add 0.5 oz baking soda.

2. Subtract 1 oz baking powder.

For each liter (1 kg) buttermilk:

1. Add 15 g baking soda.

2. Subtract 30 g baking powder.

Substituting plain milk for buttermilk requires a different calculation. If a formula includes buttermilk and baking soda, you must add another acid to react with the soda when you substitute plain milk. Adding cream of tartar is usually the simplest method of supplying acid. For each teaspoon (5 mL) baking soda, add 2 teaspoons (10 mL) cream of tartar to make up for the lost acid of the buttermilk.

Cream

Cream is not often used as a liquid in doughs and batters, except in a few specialty products. In these instances, because of its fat content, cream functions as a shortening as well as a liquid.

Cream is more important in the production of fillings, toppings, dessert sauces, and cold desserts such as mousses and Bavarian creams. For detailed instructions on whipping heavy cream into a foam, see Chapter 12, page 255.

Dried Milk

Dried milk is often used because of its convenience and low cost. In many formulas, it is not necessary to reconstitute it. The milk powder is included with the dry ingredients and water is used as the liquid. This practice is common in bread making and in no way reduces quality. Unlike fresh liquid milk, which must be heated to destroy enzymes that can be harmful to bread doughs, dried milk contains no active enzymes and can be used without further preparation.

Proportions for reconstituting dry milk can be calculated from the Composition of Milk Products table on page 71. For convenience, the equivalents in the Substituting Dry Milk for Liquid Milk table can be used.

Heat-treated dry milk, not low-heat-processed dry milk, should be purchased by the bakeshop. In the heat-treated product, certain enzymes that can break down gluten have been destroyed.

SUBSTITUTING DRY MILK FOR LIQUID MILK	
TO SUBSTITUTE FOR	**USE**
1 lb skim milk	14.5 oz water + 1.5 oz nonfat dry milk
1 lb whole milk	14 oz water + 2 oz dried whole milk
1 lb whole milk	14 oz water + 1.5 oz nonfat dried milk + 0.5 shortening or 0.7 oz butter
1 kg skim milk	910 g water + 90 g nonfat dry milk
1 kg whole milk	880 g water + 120 g dried whole milk
1 kg whole milk	880 g water + 90 g nonfat dry milk + 30 g shortening or 40 g butter

Storage of Milk Products

Fresh milk and cream, buttermilk and other fermented milk products, and cheese must be kept refrigerated at all times.

Evaporated milk in unopened cans may be kept in a cool storage area. After opening, however, it must be stored in the refrigerator.

Condensed milk in large containers keeps for a week or more after opening if kept covered and in a cool place. The sugar acts as a preservative. Stir before using because the sugar tends to settle to the bottom and sides.

Dried milk does not need refrigeration, but should be kept in a cool, dark place, well away from ovens and other heat sources. Keep the container tightly closed, to prevent the milk from absorbing moisture from the air.

EGGS

EGGS SHOULD BE well understood by the baker because they are used in large quantities in the bakeshop and are more expensive than many of the other high-volume ingredients, such as flour and sugar. For example, half or more of the ingredient cost of the average cake batter is for the eggs.

Composition

A whole egg consists primarily of a yolk, a white, and a shell. In addition, it contains a membrane that lines the shell and forms an air cell at the large end, and two white strands called *chalazae* that hold the yolk centered.

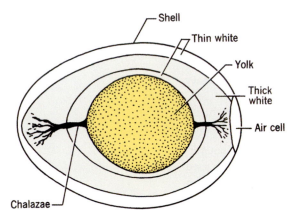

Labels: Shell, Thin white, Yolk, Thick white, Air cell, Chalazae

The parts of an egg. The diagram shows, in simplified form, the location of the parts of an unbroken egg, as described in the text.

Courtesy of USDA.

- The yolk is high in both fat and protein, and contains iron and several vitamins. Its color ranges from light to dark yellow, depending on the diet of the chicken.
- The white is primarily albumin protein, which is clear and soluble when raw but white and firm when coagulated. The white also contains sulfur.
- The shell is *not* the perfect package, in spite of what you may have been told. It is not only fragile but also porous, allowing odors and flavors to be absorbed by the egg and allowing the egg to lose moisture even if unbroken.

The Average Composition of Fresh Liquid Eggs table lists the average water, protein, and fat content of whole eggs, whites, and yolks.

AVERAGE COMPOSITION OF FRESH LIQUID EGGS			
	WHOLE EGGS (%)	WHITES (%)	YOLKS (%)
Water	73	86	49
Protein	13	12	17
Fat	12	—	32
Minerals and other components	2	2	2

Grades and Quality

Grades

In the United States, eggs are graded for quality by the USDA. There are three grades: AA, A, and B. The best grade (AA) has a firm white and yolk that stand up high when broken onto a flat surface and do not spread over a large area.

As eggs age, they become thinner and are graded lower. The figure on page 75 shows the differences among U.S. grades AA, A, and B.

In Canada, there are four egg grades: A, B, C, and Canada Nest Run.

As a baker, you will not be concerned so much with the firmness of yolks and whites. Rather, you will want eggs that are clean and fresh-tasting, free of bad odors and tastes caused by spoilage or absorption of foreign odors. One bad-smelling egg can ruin an entire batch of cakes.

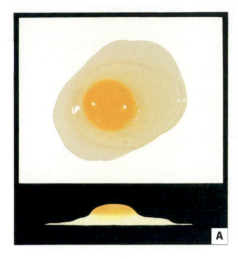 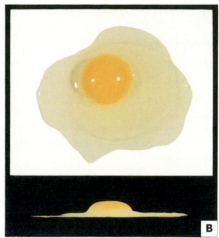 

Egg grades: (a) Grade AA, (b) Grade A, and (c) Grade B, as seen from the top and side. Note how the white and yolk lose thickness and spread more in the lower grades.

Maintaining Quality

Proper storage is essential for maintaining egg quality. Eggs keep for weeks when held at 36°F (2°C) but lose quality quickly when held at room temperature. In fact, they can lose a full grade in one day at warm bakeshop temperatures. There's no point in paying for Grade AA eggs if they are Grade B by the time you use them. Store eggs away from other foods that might pass on undesirable flavors or odors.

Size

Eggs are also graded by size. The Egg Size Classifications table gives the minimum weight per dozen (including shell) of each size category. Note that each size differs from the next by 3 ounces (85 g) per dozen. European eggs are also graded by size, with size 1 being the largest (70 g each, or about 2.5 oz) and 7 being the smallest (45 g each, or about 1.6 oz). This weight includes the shell.

Large eggs are the standard size used in baking and in food service. Shelled large whole eggs, yolks, and whites have the following approximate weights.

Average Large Eggs: Approximate Weights without Shell

One whole egg = 1.67 oz	47 g		
One egg white = 1 oz	28 g		
One yolk = 0.67 oz	19 g		
9½ whole eggs = 1 lb	21 whole eggs = 1 kg		
16 whites = 1 lb	36 whites = 1 kg		
24 yolks = 1 lb	53 yolks = 1 kg		

To measure small quantities or odd quantities of whole egg, such as 0.5 oz or 15 g, beat the whole egg or eggs and then measure by weight.

EGG SIZE CLASSIFICATIONS

	MINIMUM WEIGHT PER DOZEN	
SIZE	**U.S.**	**METRIC**
Jumbo	30 oz	850 g
Extra large	27 oz	765 g
Large	24 oz	680 g
Medium	21 oz	595 g
Small	18 oz	510 g
Peewee	15 oz	425 g

Market Forms

1. **Fresh eggs** or **shell eggs.**

2. **Frozen eggs.** Frozen eggs are usually made from high-quality fresh eggs and are excellent for use in baking. They are pasteurized and usually purchased in 30-pound (13.6-kg) tins.

   To thaw, place them unopened in the refrigerator and hold for two days, or place in a defrosting tank containing running water at 50° to 60°F (10° to 15°C) for about six hours. Do not defrost at room temperature or in warm water. Stir well before using.

   The following egg products are available frozen:

   Whole eggs

   Whole eggs with extra yolks

   Whites

   Yolks

   Frozen yolks usually contain a small amount of sugar (usually about 10%; check the label) to keep the components from separating while frozen. When sugared yolks are used in products such as cakes, you should allow for their sugar content by reducing the sugar in the formula by the same amount. For example, if you are using 20 ounces of yolks with 10% sugar, subtract 2 oz (20 oz × .10) from the sugar in the formula.

3. **Dried eggs.**

   The following egg products are available dried:

   Whole eggs

   Yolks

   Whites

   Dried eggs are sometimes used in the bakeshop, though less often than frozen eggs. The whites are frequently used for making meringue powders. Dried egg products are also used by commercial manufacturers of cake mixes.

   Dried eggs are incorporated in baked goods in two ways: by reconstituting them with water to make liquid eggs, or by mixing them with the dry ingredients and adding the extra water to the liquid portion of the formula.

   It is important to follow manufacturers' instructions for the ratio of egg to water because egg products vary. After mixing, let the eggs stand to allow time for the water to be absorbed. This takes an hour for whole eggs and yolks, and sometimes three hours or more for whites. Mix again before using. The following are typical ratios for reconstituting eggs:

Product	Ratio of Egg to Water by Weight
Whole eggs	1:2.5
Yolks	1:1 to 1:1.5
Whites	1:5.5 to 1:6

Unlike most dried products, dried eggs do not keep well. Keep refrigerated or frozen, tightly sealed.

Pasteurized Eggs and Sanitation

In recent years, cases of salmonella food poisoning have been caused by raw or undercooked eggs. As a result, cooks have been made more aware of sanitation concerns with respect to eggs. Pasteurized egg products are used in more operations. For a more detailed discussion of eggs and food safety, see Appendix 6, page 738.

Functions

Eggs perform the following functions in baking:

1. **Structure.** Like gluten protein, egg protein coagulates to give structure to baked products. This is especially important in high-ratio cakes, in which the high content of sugar and fat weakens the gluten.

   If used in large quantities, eggs make baked products more tough or chewy unless balanced by fat and sugar, which are tenderizers.

2. **Emulsifying of fats and liquids.** Egg yolks contain natural emulsifiers that help produce smooth batters. This action contributes to volume and to texture.

3. **Leavening.** Beaten eggs incorporate air in tiny cells, or bubbles. In a batter, this trapped air expands when heated and aids in leavening.

4. **Shortening action.** The fat in egg yolks acts as a shortening. This is an important function in products that are low in other fats.

5. **Moisture.** Eggs are mostly water (see the Average Composition of Fresh Liquid Eggs table on p. 74). This moisture must be calculated as part of the total liquid in a formula. If yolks are substituted for whole eggs, for example, or if dried eggs are used, adjust the liquid in the formula to allow for the different moisture content of these products.

6. **Flavor.**

7. **Nutritional value.**

8. **Color.** Yolks impart a yellow color to doughs and batters. Also, when baked in doughs, eggs brown easily and contribute to crust color.

KEY POINTS TO REVIEW

▮ What are the main types of milk and cream products used in the bakeshop?

▮ What types of egg products are used in the bakeshop?

▮ Why are pasteurized eggs used for many preparations?

▮ What are the eight functions of eggs in baked goods?

LEAVENING AGENTS

UNLIKE LIQUIDS AND solids, gases expand greatly when they are heated. *Leavening* is the production or incorporation of gases in a baked product to increase volume and produce shape and texture. These gases must be retained in the product until the structure is set enough (by the coagulation of gluten and egg proteins and the gelatinization of starches) to hold its shape.

The three main gases that leaven baked goods are carbon dioxide, steam, and air. Two of these gases, steam and air, are present in all baked goods.

An essential part of the leavening process is the formation of *air cells* during mixing. Even if a properly mixed dough or batter appears dense and compact, it actually contains millions of tiny air cells. Leavening gases are trapped in these air cells, which expand as they fill with gases and as the gases are heated. The walls of the cells are formed largely from gluten proteins and sometimes egg proteins. They hold the gases and form the structure of the baked item. More details of the leavening process are discussed in Chapter 5. In this section, we discuss the most important ingredients or agents that supply gases for leavening.

Exact measurement of leavening agents is important because minor changes can produce major defects in baked products.

Yeast

Yeast is the leavening agent in breads, dinner rolls, Danish pastries, and similar products. This section describes the characteristics of yeast. The handling of yeast and its use in yeast doughs are discussed in Chapter 6.

Yeast Fermentation

Fermentation is the process by which yeast acts on sugars and changes them into carbon dioxide gas and alcohol. This release of gas produces the leavening action in yeast products. The alcohol evaporates completely during and immediately after baking.

Fermentable sugar in bread dough comes from two sources:

1. It is added to the dough by the baker.

2. It is produced from flour by enzymes that break down the wheat starch into sugar. These enzymes are present in the flour and/or are added by the baker in the form of diastatic malt (see p. 66).

Yeast is a microscopic plant that accomplishes this fermentation process by producing enzymes. Some of these enzymes change complex sugars (sucrose and maltose) into simple sugars. Others change the simple sugars into carbon dioxide gas and alcohol. The following formula describes this reaction in chemical terms:

$$C_6H_{12}O_6 \quad \rightarrow \quad 2CO_2 \quad + \quad 2C_2H_5OH$$

simple sugar   carbon dioxide   alcohol

Because yeast is a living organism, it is sensitive to temperature, as shown here.

34°F (1°C)	Inactive (storage temperature)
60° to 70°F (15° to 20°C)	Slow action
70° to 90°F (20° to 32°C)	Best growth (fermentation and proofing temperatures for bread doughs)
Above 100°F (38°C)	Reaction slows
140°F (60°C)	Yeast is killed

In addition to leavening gases, yeast also contributes flavor to bread doughs. Flavor molecules are produced by the yeast during fermentation. For this reason, breads produced by long fermentations usually have more flavor than short-fermentation products.

Types of Yeast

The yeast added to bread dough by the baker may be a commercially produced yeast or a wild yeast culture that is present in *sourdough starter*. The preparation, use, and handling of sourdough starters is discussed in Chapter 8.

Commercial yeast is available in three forms:

Fresh yeast.

1. *Fresh yeast*, also called *compressed yeast*, is moist and perishable. Before the development of instant yeast (see number 3), it was the preferred form of yeast for most baking purposes and is still widely used by professional bakers. It is usually purchased in 1-pound (454-g) cakes. Under refrigeration and carefully wrapped to avoid drying, fresh yeast lasts up to two weeks. For longer storage (up to four months), it may be frozen. Avoid using fresh yeast that has discolored or become moldy.

   Some bakers crumble compressed yeast and add it directly to the dough in a straight-dough procedure. However, the yeast is mixed more evenly into the dough if it is first softened in twice its weight of warm (100°F/38°C) water. See Chapter 6 for information on mixing procedures.

Active dry yeast; instant dry yeast.

2. *Active dry yeast* is a dry, granular form of yeast. It must be rehydrated in four times its weight of warm water (105°F/41°C) before use. When using active dry yeast in a bread formula, use part of the water in the formula to dissolve the yeast. Do not add additional water.

   About 25% of the yeast cells in active dry yeast are dead, due to the harsh conditions of the drying process. The presence of the dead cells can have a negative effect on dough quality. For this reason, active dry yeast has never been popular with professional bakers.

3. *Instant dry yeast*, sometimes called *rapid-rise* or *quick-rise* yeast, is a fairly new product (it was invented in the 1970s). Like active dry yeast, it is also a dry granular form of yeast, but it does not have to be dissolved in water before use. (As the illustration shows, instant yeast is nearly identical in appearance to active dry yeast. You must rely on the packaging for proper identification.) It can be added in its dry form because it absorbs water much more quickly than regular dry yeast. In fact, the preferred way of incorporating it in a bread formula is to mix it with the dry flour.

Unlike active dry yeast, instant yeast contains very little dead yeast, so less of it is needed. In general, you need only 25 to 50% as much instant yeast as fresh compressed yeast, or about 35% on average.

Instant yeast also produces more gas, and produces it more quickly than regular dry yeast. This characteristic makes it appropriate for short fermentations or no-time doughs (explained on p. 120). For long fermentations and pre-ferments (see p. 156), fresh yeast may be a better choice. Fermentation times for instant yeast must be carefully monitored to avoid overfermentation or overproofing.

In doughs with a high sugar content, a special type of instant yeast called **osmotolerant yeast** is often indicated in the formula, as this yeast performs better in sweet doughs (see the Osmotolerant Yeast sidebar). If osmotolerant yeast is called for in the formula and you have only regular instant yeast, increase the quantity of yeast by 30%.

OSMOTOLERANT YEAST

In small quantities, sugar helps yeast to ferment by providing food for the yeast. When the quantity of sugar becomes high, however, as in many sweet dough products, sugar inhibits fermentation. This is because the sugar attracts a lot of water to itself and makes it unavailable to the yeast, thus slowing fermentation. The scientific explanation is that the sugar creates *osmotic pressure*.

Special strains of yeast are available that can tolerate this osmotic pressure and be more active when sugar levels are high. These are called *osmotolerant yeasts*.

Most formulas in this book specify either instant yeast or fresh yeast when yeast is required. To substitute another type of yeast for the one specified, follow these guidelines. And for information on how to add each type of yeast during the mixing process, refer to the previous discussion.

- To convert fresh yeast to regular active dry yeast, multiply the quantity by 0.5. For example, if the formula calls for 1.5 ounces fresh yeast, multiply by 0.5 to get 0.75 ounces active dry yeast.
- To convert fresh yeast to instant dry yeast, multiply the quantity by 0.35. For example, if the formula calls for 40 grams fresh yeast, multiply by 0.35 to get 14 grams instant yeast.
- To convert instant dry yeast to fresh yeast, multiply the quantity by 3. For example, if the formula calls for 0.5 ounces instant yeast, multiply by 3 to get 1.5 ounces fresh yeast.
- To convert instant dry yeast to active dry yeast, multiply the quantity by 1.4. For example, if the formula calls for 30 grams instant yeast, multiply by 1.4 to get 42 grams active dry yeast.

Chemical Leaveners

Chemical leaveners are those that release gases produced by chemical reactions.

Baking Soda

Baking soda is the chemical *sodium bicarbonate*. If *moisture* and an *acid* are present, soda releases carbon dioxide gas, which leavens the product.

Heat is not necessary for the reaction to take place (although the gas is released faster at high temperatures). For this reason, products leavened with soda must be baked at once, or gases will escape and leavening power will be lost.

Acids that react with soda in a batter include honey, molasses, brown sugar, buttermilk, sour cream, yogurt, fruit juices and purées, chocolate, and natural cocoa (not Dutch-processed). Sometimes cream of tartar is used for the acid. The amount of soda used in a formula is generally the amount needed to balance the acid. If more leavening power is needed, baking powder, not more soda, is used.

Baking Powders

Baking powders are mixtures of baking soda plus one or more acids to react with it. They also contain starch, which prevents lumping and brings the leavening power down to a standard level. Because baking powders do not depend for their leavening power on acid ingredients in a formula, they are more versatile.

- *Single-acting baking powders* require only moisture to release gas. Like baking soda, they can be used only if the product is to be baked immediately after mixing. For all practical purposes, no single-acting baking powders are sold today, although you can make one yourself, as explained in the Making Single-Acting Baking Powder sidebar. Practically, single-acting baking powders release gas too quickly to be useful for most products.
- *Double-acting baking powders* release some gas when cold, but they require heat for complete reaction (see the Acid Salts sidebar). Thus, cake batters made with these can incorporate the leavening agent early in the mixing period and then stand for some time before being baked.

Do not include more baking powder than necessary in a formula, because undesirable flavors may be produced. Also, excess

MAKING SINGLE-ACTING BAKING POWDER

A simple, homemade baking powder may be made by mixing the following ingredients in the proportions indicated (using volume measure rather than weight).

Baking soda	1 tbsp	15 mL
Cornstarch	1 tbsp	15 mL
Cream of tartar	2 tbsp	30 mL
Yield:	4 tbsp	60 mL

ACID SALTS

Technically, the ingredients in baking powder are not acids but acid salts. This means they do not release an acid or act like an acid until they are dissolved in water. For simplicity, however, we refer to these compounds as acids.

Different baking powders contain varying combinations of acid salt that react at different speeds. How they react is referred to as their *dough reaction rate*, or DRR. Fast-acting baking powders release about two-thirds of their gases during mixing and one-third during baking. Slow-reacting powders release about one-third of their gases during mixing and two-thirds during baking.

Release of some gases during mixing helps create the air cells needed for leavening, as explained previously. However, it is important that some gases are also released during baking for proper leavening to occur.

Fast-acting acids include cream of tartar (potassium acid tartrate) and monocalcium phosphate (MCP). Slow-acting acids include sodium aluminum sulfate (SAS) and sodium acid pyrophosphate (SAPP).

leavening may create an undesirably light, crumbly texture. Cakes may rise too much and then fall before they become set.

Baking Ammonia

Baking ammonia is a mixture of ammonium carbonate, ammonium bicarbonate, and ammonium carbamate. It decomposes rapidly during baking to form carbon dioxide gas, ammonia gas, and water. Only heat and moisture are necessary for it to work. No acids are needed.

Baking ammonia decomposes completely, leaving no solid residue that could affect flavor when it is properly used. However, it can be used only in small products that are baked until dry, such as cookies. Only in such products can the ammonia gas be completely driven off.

Because ammonia releases gases very quickly, it is sometimes used in products in which rapid leavening is desired, such as cream puffs. Use of ammonia enables the baker to lower the cost of such products by reducing the quantity of eggs. However, the quality of the resulting goods is lowered as well.

Storage of Chemical Leaveners

Baking soda, powder, and ammonia must always be kept tightly closed when not in use. If left open, they can absorb moisture from the air and lose part of their leavening power. They must be stored in a cool place, because heat also causes them to deteriorate.

Air

Air is incorporated into all doughs and batters during mixing. The formation of air cells is important even in products leavened by yeast or baking powder because the air cells collect and hold the leavening gases.

Some products are leavened mostly or entirely by air. In these products, air is incorporated into the batter primarily by two methods: creaming and foaming. This air expands during baking and leavens the products.

1. *Creaming* is the process of beating fat and sugar together to incorporate air. It is an important technique in cake and cookie making. Some pound cakes and cookies are leavened almost entirely by this method.

2. *Foaming* is the process of beating eggs, with or without sugar, to incorporate air. Foams made with whole eggs are used to leaven sponge cakes, while angel food cakes, meringues, and soufflés are leavened with egg-white foams.

Steam

When water turns to steam, it expands to 1,100 times its original volume. Because all baked products contain some moisture, steam is an important leavening agent.

Puff pastry, cream puffs, popovers, and piecrusts use steam as their primary or only leavening agent. If the starting baking temperature for these products is high, steam is produced rapidly and leavening is greatest.

GELLING AGENTS

THE TWO INGREDIENTS discussed in this section are chemically and nutritionally unrelated. Gelatin is a protein, and pectin is a soluble fiber, a type of carbohydrate that is not absorbed by the body. However, they both are used to thicken or to solidify (gel) soft or liquid foods.

Other thickening and gelling agents include starches, discussed on page 63.

Gelatin

Gelatin is a water-soluble protein extracted from animal connective tissue. When a sufficient quantity of gelatin is dissolved in hot water or other liquid, the liquid will solidify when cooled or chilled. When used in smaller quantities, the liquid will thicken but not solidify.

KEY POINTS TO REVIEW

- What three gases are responsible for leavening baked goods?

- What types of yeast are used in the bakeshop?

- What calculations can you do to substitute one type of yeast for another?

- At what temperatures is yeast active? At what temperatures is it inactive or killed?

- What kinds of chemical leaveners are used in the bakeshop?

Gelatin thickens and gels because of the nature of its proteins, which form long strands. When present in small quantities, the strands get tangled with one another, so the liquid does not flow as freely. When present in large enough quantities, the strands bond with one another to form a network that traps the liquid to keep it from flowing at all.

Gelatin Forms

Culinary gelatin is available in powdered form and in sheets. Powdered gelatin is most widely available to North American kitchens, although sheet gelatin, also called *leaf gelatin*, is also available and often preferred by pastry chefs. The sheet form is especially easy to use because it is premeasured (the sheets are of uniform weights). Also, when using sheet gelatin, it is not necessary to measure the liquid for soaking it. This is explained below.

BLOOM

When used in connection with gelatin, the term *bloom* has two meanings:

1. The process of softening gelatin in water is called *blooming*. To bloom gelatin, combine it with water or other liquid according to the procedures explained in the text.

2. The *bloom rating* is a measure of the strength of the gel formed by the gelatin. The higher the number, the stronger the gel. Gelatins with higher bloom ratings set faster and have less taste to detract from the main ingredients.

Powdered gelatin usually has a bloom rating of about 230.

Sheet gelatin varies in bloom rating, but sheets with lower bloom rating weigh more, so the gelling power per sheet is the same no matter the bloom rating. Typically, manufacturers label sheet gelatin "gold," "silver," and "bronze," as follows:

Gold	200 bloom	2 g per sheet	0.07 oz per sheet
Silver	160 bloom	2.5 g per sheet	0.09 oz per sheet
Bronze	130 bloom	3.3 g per sheet	0.12 oz per sheet

As explained in the Bloom sidebar, equal weights of powdered and sheet gelatin do not have the same gelling power. The following equivalents are useful:

- 10 teaspoons powdered gelatin equal 1 ounce.
- 1 ounce (30 g) powdered gelatin has the same gelling power as 20 sheets of sheet gelatin.
- 1 teaspoon powdered gelatin weighs about 2.8 grams or $\frac{1}{10}$ ounce.
- 1 teaspoon powdered gelatin has the same gelling power as 2 sheets of gelatin.

The Weight-Volume Equivalents table lists volume equivalents for a range of weights of gelatin.

Sheet gelatin is available in sizes ranging from 1.7 grams to 3.3 grams (see the Bloom sidebar).

Powdered gelatin and sheet gelatin can be used interchangeably, but they are handled differently. Guidelines for handling the two products and for substituting one for the other are described next.

Sheet and granulated gelatin.

WEIGHT-VOLUME EQUIVALENTS FOR POWDERED GELATIN

U.S.		METRIC	
WEIGHT	**APPROXIMATE VOLUME**	**WEIGHT**	**APPROXIMATE VOLUME**
0.1 oz	1 tsp	1 g	1.75 mL
0.12–0.13 oz	1¼ tsp	2 g	3.5 mL
0.16–0.17 oz	1⅔ tsp	3 g	3 mL
0.2 oz	2 tsp	4 g	7 mL
0.25 oz	2½ tsp	6 g	10 mL
0.33 oz	3⅓ tsp	8 g	14 mL
0.4 oz	4 tsp	10 g	18 mL
0.5 oz	5 tsp	12 g	21 mL
0.75 oz	7½ tsp	14 g	25 mL
1 oz	10 tsp	16 g	28 mL
		20 g	36 mL
		30 g	54 mL

Using Gelatin in Formulas

Using gelatin in a formula requires three main steps:

1. The gelatin is softened in water or other liquid. It absorbs five times its weight in water.

2. The softened gelatin is added to hot ingredients, or is heated with other ingredients, until it dissolves.

3. The mixture is chilled until it sets.

Most of the formulas in this book that require gelatin were developed using powdered gelatin (the remainder were developed using sheet gelatin). The following guidelines will help you use recipes requiring gelatin:

- When a formula was developed using sheet gelatin, no soaking liquid is indicated in the ingredient list. In the procedure, the instructions direct you to soften the gelatin in cold water. To use sheet gelatin, add the indicated weight of gelatin to a generous quantity of cold water and soak until soft. Remove the soaked sheets from the water, drain well, and incorporate into the formula. (See p. 264 for an illustration of using sheet gelatin to make Chiboust Cream.)

- Always use very cold water to soak sheet gelatin. If the water is warm, some gelatin will dissolve and be lost.

- To substitute powdered gelatin when no quantity of soaking liquid is given, measure the gelatin, then add five times its weight of cold water. Let stand until the water is absorbed.

- When a formula was developed using powdered gelatin, the quantity of water for soaking is usually indicated. Either powdered gelatin or sheet gelatin can be used in these formulas. Add the measured gelatin to the measured water and soak. Then add the gelatin and the soaking liquid to the mixture in the formula.

For an example of a formula developed using sheet gelatin but indicating no soaking liquid in the ingredient list, see Fruit Glaçage, page 428. For an example of a formula developed using powdered gelatin and for which the quantity of soaking liquid is indicated, see Vanilla Bavarian Cream, page 528.

Bavarian creams, chiffon pie fillings, and many mousses depend on gelatin for their texture. More information on the use of gelatin in these products is included in Chapter 13.

Pectin

Vegetable gums are carbohydrates that consist of molecules in long chains, somewhat like starches. They can absorb a great deal of water, which makes them useful for thickening or gelling liquids.

Pectin is perhaps the most familiar of these gums. It is present in many fruits. In general, unripe fruits have more pectin than ripe fruits. One of the reasons fruits get softer as they ripen is that the pectin breaks down.

VEGETABLE GUMS

In addition to pectin, several other gums are used in food production. Most of these are used by manufacturers and are not likely to be found in the bakeshop. The following three gums, however, are sometimes used by pastry chefs and retail bakers:

Agar-agar, also known simply as *agar* or *kanten* (its Japanese name) is derived from seaweed and sold in the form of dry strands or powder. It is used much like gelatin, except it does not need to be refrigerated in order to gel. This makes it especially good for use in warm weather and for products that will not be refrigerated. Unlike gelatin, which is an animal product, agar-agar can be used on vegetarian menus.

As a rule of thumb, 1 part agar by weight has as much gelling power as 8 parts gelatin.

Gum tragacanth, often called *gum trag*, is extracted from a bush native to the Middle East. It is used by pastry chefs to make gum paste, a decorative product similar to pastillage (p. 653).

Xanthan gum (ZAN than) is often used to provide structure in gluten-free formulas (see p. 694).

Pectin is extracted from fruits and used to thicken or gel fruit preserves, jams, and jellies. It can also be used to make fruit glazes, because the pectin thickens or sets fruit juices and purées. An important advantage of pectin over an ingredient such as cornstarch is that it makes a clear, not cloudy, gel.

Pectin alone, when added to a liquid, thickens but does not solidify or gel. For pectin to gel, an acid (such as fruit juice) and a high sugar content are necessary. This is one reason jams and jellies contain so much sugar.

Fruits high in pectin will gel naturally, without needing additional pectin. Such fruits include cranberries, apples, and plums. Citrus peels also contain pectin; this characteristic is useful in the production of marmalade.

For making jellies, the amount of pectin you need to add varies with the fruit. As a rule of thumb, 1.75 ounces (50 g) powdered pectin gels 2 quarts (2 L) fruit juice or fruit pulp.

Several fruit preparations in Chapter 21 require the use of pectin.

> **KEY POINTS TO REVIEW**
>
> ▪ What forms of gelatin are used in the bakeshop?
>
> ▪ What are the three basic steps in using gelatin in a formula?
>
> ▪ What are the blooming or soaking procedures for powdered gelatin and sheet or leaf gelatin?

FRUITS AND NUTS

Fruit Products

Nearly any kind of fresh fruit can be used in the production of desserts. In addition, a wide variety of dried, frozen, canned, and processed fruit products are important ingredients in the bakeshop. The lists here specify a number of the most important fruit products, in five categories. You will learn how to use these products in appropriate chapters throughout the book. For more detailed information on fresh fruits, turn to Chapter 21.

Fresh

apples

apricots

bananas

berries

cherries

figs

grapefruit

grapes

kiwi

kumquats

lemons

limes

mangoes

melons

nectarines

oranges

papayas

passion fruit

peaches

pears

pineapples

plums

rhubarb (actually, not a fruit but a stem)

Canned and Frozen

apples, sliced

apricots, halves

blueberries

cherries, sour and sweet

peaches, slices and halves

pineapple, rings, chunks, nibs, crushed, juice

strawberries

Dried

apricots

currants (actually, very small raisins)

dates

figs

raisins, light and dark

prunes

Candied and Glace

cherries

citron

figs

fruitcake mix

lemon peel

orange peel

pineapple

Other Processed Fruits

apricot glaze or coating

jams, jellies, and preserves

prepared pie fillings

fruit purées and fruit compounds, usually frozen (widely used for such products as fruit Bavarians, sauces, soufflés, and other desserts)

Nuts

Most nuts are available whole, halved, or broken or chopped. Because they are high in oil, all nuts can become rancid. Store them, tightly closed, in a cool, dark place. The most common types of nuts found in the bakeshop are these:

Almonds. The most important nut in the bakeshop. Available natural (skin on) and blanched (skin off) in many forms: whole, split, slivered, chopped, and ground (almond flour).

Almonds.

Brazil nuts.

Cashews.

Chestnuts. Must be cooked. Forms used in bakeshops are purée and glacé (in syrup).

Coconut. Sweetened coconut is used primarily for cake decoration. Unsweetened coconut is used as an ingredient in a wide variety of goods, such as cookies, macaroons, cakes, and fillings. Many types are available, based on the size of the individual grains, flakes, or shreds. The smallest types are extra-fine, about the texture of granulated sugar, and macaroon, close to the texture of cornmeal. Large sizes include short and long shred, chip, and flake.

Brazil nuts.

Hazelnuts. Best if toasted before use. Also available ground (hazelnut flour or meal). One of the most important nuts in the bakeshop, along with almonds and walnuts.

Macadamia nuts.

Hazelnuts.

Pecans. More expensive than walnuts. Used in premium goods.

Peanuts.

Macadamia nuts.

Pine nuts, or pignoli. Small kernels that are usually toasted to enhance flavor. Especially important in Italian pastries.

Pistachios. Often used in decorations because of the attractive green color of the kernel.

Walnuts. One of the most important nuts in the bakeshop, along with almonds and hazelnuts.

Pecans.

Nut Products

These seven nut products are standard bakeshop ingredients:

Almond paste. An expensive but highly versatile nut paste, used in a variety of cakes, pastries, cookies, and fillings. It is made from two parts finely ground almonds and one part sugar, plus enough moisture to bring it to the proper consistency.

Pine nuts, or pignoli.

Kernel paste. A product similar to almond paste, but less expensive. It is made from apricot kernels, which have a strong almondlike flavor.

Macaroon paste. This product stands between almond paste and kernel paste in that it is made from a blend of almonds and apricot kernels.

Marzipan. Essentially a sweetened almond paste, used in decorative and confectionery work. This product can be purchased or made in the bakeshop from almond paste.

Pistachios.

Pistachio paste. Similar to almond paste, but made with pistachios.

Praline paste. A confectionery paste made from almonds and/or hazelnuts and caramelized sugar, all ground to a paste. It is used as a flavoring for icings, fillings, pastries, and creams.

Nut flours. Nuts ground to a powder but not so fine as to turn to a paste. Almond flour is the most widely used. Nut flours are often used in fine pastries.

Walnuts.

CHOCOLATE AND COCOA

CHOCOLATE AND COCOA are derived from cocoa or cacao beans. When the beans are fermented, roasted, and ground, the resulting product is called *chocolate liquor*, which contains a white or yellowish fat called *cocoa butter*.

Much more information on the characteristics of chocolate and on handling chocolate can be found in Chapter 23, which is devoted to this specialty. The brief summary of chocolate products in this chapter offers an overview of those used in the bakeshop.

Cocoa

Cocoa is the dry powder that remains after part of the cocoa butter has been removed from chocolate liquor. **Dutch process cocoa**, or *dutched cocoa*, is processed with an alkali. It is slightly darker, smoother in flavor, and more easily dissolved in liquids than natural cocoa.

Natural cocoa.

Dutched cocoa.

Natural cocoa is somewhat acidic. When it is used in such products as cakes, it is possible to use baking soda (which reacts with acid) as part of the leavening power.

Dutched cocoa, on the other hand, is generally neutral or even slightly alkaline. Therefore, it does not react with baking soda (see the Baking Soda Needed to Balance the Acidity of Typical Cocoa Products table). Instead, baking powder is used as the sole leavening agent. If you are substituting dutched for natural cocoa, you must increase the baking powder by 1 ounce (30 g) for each ½ ounce (15 g) soda omitted.

If not enough soda is used in chocolate products, the color of the finished product may range from light tan to dark brown, depending on the quantity used. If too much is used, the color will be reddish brown. This color is desired in devil's food cakes but it may not be wanted in other products. When switching from one kind of cocoa to another, you may have to adjust the soda in your recipes.

BAKING SODA NEEDED TO BALANCE THE ACIDITY OF TYPICAL COCOA PRODUCTS		
	AMOUNT OF BAKING SODA PER LB	**AMOUNT OF BAKING SODA PER KG**
Natural cocoa	1.25 oz	80 g
Dutched cocoa	0	0
Unsweetened chocolate	0.8 oz	50 g
Sweet chocolate	0.4 oz	25 g

Unsweetened or Bitter Chocolate

Unsweetened chocolate is straight chocolate liquor. It contains no sugar and has a strongly bitter taste. Because it is molded in blocks, it is also referred to as *block cocoa* or *cocoa block*. It is used to flavor items that have other sources of sweetness.

Unsweetened chocolate is also known as *bitter chocolate*. Do not confuse this product with *bittersweet chocolate*, which is a category of sweetened chocolate with a low sugar content.

In some less expensive brands of unsweetened chocolate, some of the cocoa butter may be replaced by another fat.

Sweetened Dark Chocolate

Sweetened dark chocolate is bitter chocolate with the addition of sugar and cocoa butter in varying proportions. Based on the amount of sugar added, dark chocolate is divided into the following categories:

- *Sweet chocolate* has the highest percentage of sugar and the lowest percentage of chocolate liquor. A product labeled sweet chocolate may contain as little as 15% chocolate liquor, although it may contain as much as 50%. Because of the low cocoa content, this product is used primarily in inexpensive candies, not in the finest chocolate work.

- *Semisweet chocolate* must contain a minimum of 35% chocolate liquor, but it usually contains about 50 to 65%. It is widely used in confectionery, pastry, and dessert products.

- *Bittersweet chocolate* contains the highest proportion of chocolate liquor, usually from 65 to 85%. Products at the upper end of this range are sometimes labeled *extra bittersweet*. Because of its higher cocoa content, bittersweet chocolate is used in the finest baked goods, pastries, desserts, and confections.

Note: According to government regulations, there is no difference between semisweet and bittersweet chocolate. Both have a minimum chocolate liquor content of 35%. However, most manufacturers use the term *bittersweet* for their products with higher cocoa content.

In this book, when a sweetened dark chocolate is required in a formula, semisweet chocolate is usually specified. Bittersweet chocolate is specified when a good grade of chocolate with a high chocolate liquor content is essential for the best results.

Because sweetened chocolate has, on average, only half the chocolate content of bitter (unsweetened) chocolate, it is usually not economical to add to products that are already highly sweetened, because twice as much will be needed. For example, it is better to use bitter chocolate when making chocolate fondant from plain white fondant.

Good-quality chocolate products—including not only dark chocolate but also milk chocolate and white chocolate (see below)—are often called *couverture*, which means "coating" in French. When couverture is used to coat candies, cookies, and other products, the chocolate must be prepared by a process called *tempering*. This involves carefully melting the chocolate without letting it get too warm, then bringing the temperature back down to a certain level. The process requires a fair amount of skill (see p. 627).

Coating Chocolate

Less expensive chocolates, which have part of the cocoa butter replaced by other fats, are easier to handle and don't require tempering. However, they do not have the flavor and eating qualities of good chocolate. These products are sold under such names as *cookie coating*, *cake coating*, *baking chocolate*, *coating chocolate*, and *compound chocolate*. Do not confuse coating chocolate with couverture. These two products are entirely different, even though *couverture* means "coating." It would be less confusing if this lower-quality chocolate were referred to only as *baking chocolate*, without using the word *coating*.

Milk Chocolate

Milk chocolate is sweet chocolate to which milk solids have been added. It is usually used as a coating chocolate and in various confections. Milk chocolate is seldom melted and then incorporated in batters because it contains a relatively low proportion of chocolate liquor.

FAT CONTENT OF COCOA

When chocolate liquor is pressed to remove cocoa butter from cocoa solids, not all the cocoa butter is pressed out. Therefore, cocoa powder contains some fat in the form of cocoa butter. In Canada and the United States, a product labeled cocoa contains a minimum of 10% cocoa butter. Regular cocoa has a fat content of 10 to 12% and is known as 10/12 cocoa. High-fat cocoa has a fat content of 22 to 24% and is known as 22/24 cocoa. Both types are used in the bakeshop. For hot cocoa beverage, 22/24 cocoa is more often used. European cocoa usually has a fat content of 20 to 22% and is called 20/22 cocoa.

Low-fat cocoa, with a fat content below 10%, must be specially labeled and is more difficult to manufacture. It is expensive and not generally used in the bakeshop.

Cocoa Butter

Cocoa butter is the fat pressed out of chocolate liquor when cocoa is processed. Its main use in the bakeshop is to thin melted couverture to a proper consistency.

White Chocolate

White chocolate consists of cocoa butter, sugar, and milk solids. It is used primarily in confectionery. Technically, it should not be called chocolate, because it contains no cocoa solids. However, the name white chocolate is in common use. Some inexpensive brands, in which another fat is substituted for the cocoa butter, not only contain no cocoa solids, but none of the other components of chocolate either. These products don't deserve the name *chocolate* at all.

Substituting Cocoa and Chocolate

Cocoa, remember, is the same as bitter (unsweetened) chocolate, but with less cocoa butter. Therefore it is often possible to substitute one product for the other in baked goods. Shortening is usually used to take the place of the missing fat. It's important to keep in mind, however, that different fats behave differently in baking. Regular shortening, for example, has about twice the shortening power of cocoa butter, so only half as much is needed in many products, such as cakes. The procedures given here take this difference into account.

Because of these varying factors, as well as the different baking properties of cakes, cookies, and other products, it is recommended that you test-bake a small batch when making a substitution in a formula. You can then make additional adjustments, if necessary. *No single substitution ratio is adequate for all purposes.*

PROCEDURE: Substituting Natural Cocoa for Unsweetened Chocolate

1. Multiply the weight of the chocolate by ⅝. The result is the amount of cocoa to use.

2. Subtract the weight of the cocoa from the original weight of chocolate. Divide this difference by 2. The result is the amount of shortening to add to the formula.

Example: Replace 1 lb chocolate with natural cocoa.

$$⅝ × 16\ oz = 10\ oz\ cocoa$$

$$\frac{16\ oz - 10\ oz}{2} = 3\ oz\ shortening$$

PROCEDURE: Substituting Unsweetened Chocolate for Natural Cocoa

1. Multiply the weight of the cocoa by ⅝. The result is the amount of chocolate to use.

2. Subtract the weight of cocoa from the weight of chocolate. Divide by 2. Reduce the weight of shortening in the mix by this amount.

Example: Substitute bitter chocolate for 1 lb natural cocoa.

$$⅝ × 16\ oz = 26\ oz\ chocolate\ (rounded\ off)$$

$$\frac{26\ oz - 16\ oz}{2} = \frac{10}{2} = 5\ oz\ less\ shortening$$

Starch Content of Cocoa

Cocoa contains starch, which tends to absorb moisture in a batter. Consequently, when cocoa is added to a mix—for example, to change a yellow cake to a chocolate cake—the quantity of flour is reduced to compensate for this added starch. Exact adjustments will vary depending on the product. However, the following may be used as a rule of thumb:

> Reduce the flour by ⅜ (37.5%) of the weight of cocoa added. Thus, if 1 pound cocoa is added, the flour is reduced by 6 ounces. Or, if 400 grams cocoa is added, reduce the flour by 150 grams.

> Chocolate, of course, also contains starch. When melted chocolate is added to fondant, for example, the fondant gets stiffer because of this starch and usually requires thinning. Often, however, the drying effect of the starch is balanced by the tenderizing effect of the cocoa butter. Methods of incorporating both chocolate and cocoa in various products are discussed in appropriate chapters.

SALT, SPICES, AND FLAVORINGS

Salt

Salt plays an important role in baking. More than just a seasoning or flavor enhancer, it has these other functions:

- Salt strengthens gluten structure and makes it more stretchable. Thus, it improves the texture and grain of breads. When salt is present, gluten holds more water and carbon dioxide, allowing the dough to expand more while holding its structure.
- Salt inhibits yeast growth. It is therefore important for controlling fermentation in bread doughs and preventing the growth of undesirable wild yeasts.

For these reasons, the quantity of salt in a formula must be carefully controlled. If too much salt is used, fermentation and proofing are slowed. If not enough salt is used, fermentation proceeds too rapidly. The yeast uses too much of the sugar in the dough and, consequently, the crust doesn't brown well. Other results of overfermentation are described in Chapter 6. Because of the effect of salt on yeast, never add salt directly to the water in which yeast is softened.

Spices

Spices are plant or vegetable substances used to flavor foods. Plant parts used as spices include seeds, flower buds (such as cloves), roots (such as ginger), and bark (such as cinnamon). Spices are generally available whole or ground. Ground spices lose their flavor rapidly, so it is important to have fresh spices always on hand. Keep them tightly sealed in a cool, dark, dry place.

A small amount of spice usually has a great deal of flavoring power, so it is important to weigh spices carefully and accurately. A quarter ounce too much of nutmeg, for example, could make a product inedible. In most cases, it is better to use too little than too much.

The following are the most important spices and seeds in the bakeshop:

Allspice.

Anise.

Caraway.

Cardamom.   Cinnamon.   Cloves.

Ginger.   Mace.   Nutmeg.

Poppy seeds.   Sesame seeds.   Zest of lemon and orange (the outer colored part of the peel).

Vanilla

Vanilla is the most important flavoring in the pastry shop. The source of the flavor is the ripened, partially dried fruit of a tropical orchid. This fruit, called *vanilla bean* or *vanilla pod*, is readily available, but at a high price. In spite of their cost, vanilla beans are valued by pastry chefs for making the finest-quality pastries and dessert sauces and fillings.

Vanilla beans.

There are several ways to flavor products directly with vanilla beans. The simplest is simply to add one to a liquid when the liquid is heated, allowing the flavors to be extracted. Then remove the bean. For a stronger flavor, split the bean lengthwise before adding it. Then, after removing the bean, scrape out the tiny black seeds from inside the pod (see p. 261) and return them to the liquid.

Vanilla beans can also be used to flavor items that are not heated, such as whipped cream. Simply split the bean lengthwise, scrape out the seeds, and add them to the preparation.

A more common and economical way of flavoring with vanilla is to use vanilla extract. Vanilla extract is made by dissolving the flavoring elements of vanilla beans in an alcohol solution. To use, simply add the indicated quantity of the liquid as directed in the recipe.

If a formula calls for vanilla beans, there is no exact equivalent if you must substitute vanilla extract. This is because the strength of the flavor extracted from the bean depends on many factors, such as how long it was left in the liquid, whether or not it was split, and so on. However, a rule of thumb is to substitute ½ to 1 teaspoon (2.5 to 5 mL) extract for each vanilla bean.

Pure natural vanilla powder also is available. Pure white in color, it can be used to give a good vanilla flavor to white products, such as flat icing or whipped cream, without discoloring them.

Extracts and Emulsions

Extracts are flavorful oils and other substances dissolved in alcohol. These include vanilla, lemon, bitter almond, cinnamon, and coffee. Coffee extract can be approximated if it is not available. Dissolve 5 ounces (150 g) instant coffee powder in 12 ounces (360 g) water.

Emulsions are flavorful oils mixed with water with the aid of emulsifiers such as vegetable gums. Lemon and orange are the most frequently used emulsions. Their flavor is strong. For example, it takes less lemon emulsion than lemon extract to give the same flavor.

Flavorings in general may be divided into two categories: natural and artificial. Natural flavorings are usually more expensive but have a superior flavor. Artificial vanilla, for example, is a compound called *vanillin*, widely used in industrially made baked goods but lacking the rich, complex flavor profile of natural vanilla. Because flavorings and spices are used in small quantities, it is not much more expensive to use the best quality. Trying to save a few pennies on a cake by using inferior flavorings is false economy.

Alcohols

Various alcoholic beverages are useful flavoring ingredients in the pastry shop. These include sweet alcohols, often called *liqueurs*, nonsweet alcohols, and wines.

Many liqueurs are fruit-flavored. The most important of these are orange (including Cointreau, Grand Marnier, and Triple Sec) and cassis or blackcurrant. Other important flavors are bitter almond (amaretto), chocolate (crème de cacao), mint (crème de menthe), and coffee (crème de café, Kahlúa, Tía Maria).

Nonsweet alcohols include rum, cognac, Calvados (a brandy made from apples), and kirschwasser (a colorless brandy made from cherries; see p. 576).

The two most important wines are both sweet wines: Marsala (from Sicily) and Madeira (from the Portuguese island of the same name).

KEY POINTS TO REVIEW

▮ What are the components of unsweetened chocolate?

▮ What are the main types of sweetened chocolate used in the bakeshop? Describe them.

▮ What are the functions of salt in baked goods?

TERMS FOR REVIEW

hard wheat	all-purpose flour	emulsion	baker's cheese
strong flour	durum flour	shortening	cream cheese
weak flour	self-rising flour	regular shortening	leavening
soft wheat	whole wheat flour	emulsified shortening	fermentation
bran	bran flour	margarine	fresh yeast
germ	cracked wheat	pasteurized	compressed yeast
endosperm	rye flour	ultrapasteurized	active dry yeast
bolting	rye meal	UHT pasteurized	instant dry yeast
break system	sucrose	whole milk	osmotolerant yeast
stream	carbohydrate	milk fat	chemical leavener
patent flour	simple sugar	butterfat	sodium bicarbonate
clear flour	complex sugar	skim milk	single-acting baking powder
straight flour	invert sugar	nonfat milk	double-acting baking powder
extraction	granulated sugar	low-fat milk	baking ammonia
gluten	confectioners' sugar	fortified nonfat or low-fat milk	creaming
amylase	brown sugar	homogenized milk	foaming
diastase	syrup	whipping cream	gelatin
pentosan	simple syrup	light cream	pectin
ash	dessert syrup	half-and-half	chocolate liquor
carotenoid	molasses	sour cream	cocoa butter
absorption	glucose	crème fraîche	cocoa
enriched flour	corn syrup	buttermilk	dutch process cocoa
dough conditioner	malt syrup	yogurt	couverture
vital wheat gluten	oil	evaporated milk	tempering
bread flour	saturated fat	condensed milk	extract
cake flour	unsaturated fat	dried whole milk	
pastry flour	hydrogenation	nonfat dry milk	

QUESTIONS FOR REVIEW

1. Why is white wheat flour used in rye breads? In whole wheat breads? Some bakeries in Europe produce a kind of pumpernickel bread with 100% rye flour. What would you expect its texture to be like?

2. Describe how to distinguish bread, pastry, and cake flours by touch and sight.

3. Why does white flour have better keeping qualities than whole wheat flour?

4. What is the importance of aging in the production of flour? How is this accomplished in modern flour milling?

5. What is clear flour? What products is it used for?

6. List five functions of sugars in baked foods.

7. What is invert sugar? What properties make it useful in baking?

8. True or false: 10X sugar is one of the purest forms of sucrose. Explain your answer.

9. What is the difference between regular and emulsified shortening? Between cake margarine and pastry margarine?

10. What are some advantages and disadvantages in using butter as the fat in pie dough?

11. List eight functions of eggs in baked goods.

12. What is the difference between single-acting and double-acting baking powders? Which is most frequently used, and why?

13. Explain how to use sheet gelatin in a recipe. Explain how to substitute powdered gelatin for sheet gelatin.

5

BASIC BAKING PRINCIPLES

AFTER READING THIS CHAPTER, YOU SHOULD BE ABLE TO\:

1. Explain the factors that control the development of gluten in baked products.
2. Explain the changes that take place in a dough or batter as it bakes.
3. Explain ways to prevent or retard the staling of baked items.

WHEN YOU CONSIDER that most bakery products are made of the same few ingredients—flour, shortening, sugar, eggs, water or milk, and leavenings—you should have no difficulty understanding the importance of accuracy in the bakeshop, as slight variations in proportions or procedures can mean great differences in the final product. To achieve the desired results, it is not only important to weigh all ingredients accurately, as discussed in Chapter 2. It is also important to understand all the complex reactions that take place during mixing and baking, so you can control these processes.

In this chapter, you are introduced to bakeshop production through a discussion of the basic processes common to nearly all baked goods.

MIXING AND GLUTEN DEVELOPMENT

MIXING DOUGHS AND batters is a complex process. It involves more than just blending the ingredients together. To help you control the mixing processes or methods that apply to the products in this book, from bread doughs to cake batters, you need to understand the many reactions that take place during mixing.

Basic Mixing Processes

In general, there are three phases of mixing in the production of doughs and batters:

1. Blending the ingredients.
2. Forming the dough.
3. Developing the dough.

These phases overlap one another. For example, the dough begins to form and develop even before the ingredients are uniformly blended. Nevertheless, thinking of mixing processes in this way helps understand what is going on.

Different products contain different ingredients in varying proportions. Compare, for example, French bread dough with cake batter. The first has no fat or sugar, while the second has large quantities of both. The first has a smaller percentage of liquid in the mix, so it is a stiff dough, which bakes into a chewy product, rather than a semiliquid like the cake batter, which bakes into a tender product. Because of these and other differences, the two products require different mixing methods.

For much of the rest of this book, we focus a great deal on the correct mixing methods for the many products made in the bakery. For each of the mixing methods, a primary goal is to control the three stages of mixing just listed. In this discussion, we pay particular attention to three special processes that occur during mixing: air cell formation, hydration of the components, and oxidation.

Air Cell Formation

Air cells are visible in the cut surface of bread and other baked items. These air cells form the porous texture of the interior of the item. (The interior of baked goods is referred to by bakers as the *crumb*. In other words, a loaf of bread, for example, consists of two parts, the crust and the crumb.)

Air cell formation is a necessary part of the leavening process. The cells consist of open spaces surrounded by elastic cell walls made primarily of proteins such as gluten or egg albumin. When gases are formed by leavening agents, they collect inside the air cells. As the gases expand during baking, the cell walls stretch and enlarge. Eventually, the heat of baking causes the cell walls to become firm, giving structure and support to the baked item.

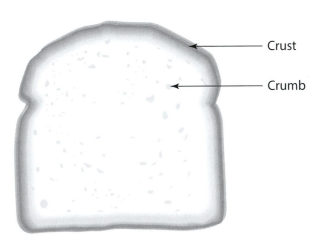
Crust
Crumb

The crumb and crust of bread.

It is important to understand that no new air cells form during baking. All the air cells that enable leavening are formed during mixing. Air cells begin forming as soon as the mixing process starts. Plenty of air is present between the particles of flour and other dry ingredients. In some cases, as with certain cakes, additional air cells are introduced when certain liquid ingredients are added, as when egg foams are folded in.

Air cells are usually rather large at the beginning of mixing, but as mixing continues, these large cells become divided into smaller ones as gluten and other proteins develop and stretch to form more cell walls. This means the length of mixing determines the final texture of the item. In other words, proper mixing is required to get the desired texture.

Hydration

Hydration is the process of absorbing water. The many ingredients in baked goods absorb or react with water in different ways. All these processes are necessary for dough formation.

Starch is, by weight and volume, the largest component of bread doughs and most other doughs and batters. It does not dissolve in water, but it does attract and bind with water molecules and undergoes a change in form. Water molecules are not absorbed by the starch granules but become attached to the surface of them, forming a kind of shell around them. During baking, the heat causes the starch to absorb water and gelatinize. Gelatinization helps form the structure of baked goods; it is discussed later in this chapter (p. 99). Without hydration during mixing, gelatinization could not take place.

Proteins, too, are mostly insoluble in water, but they also attract and bind with water molecules during mixing. Gluten proteins in dry flour form tight coils. Once they come into contact with water, they begin to uncoil. Mixing then causes the straightened proteins to stick together and form long gluten fibers. In other words, water is essential for the formation of gluten.

Yeast requires water to become active and begin fermenting sugars and releasing carbon dioxide gas for leavening. Likewise, salt, sugar, and chemical leaveners such as baking powder have no effect on baked items in their dry form. They must be dissolved in water to carry out their many functions.

Water has many other functions. For example, controlling water temperature enables the baker to control the temperature of the dough or batter. And adjusting the quantity of water or other liquid enables the baker to adjust the consistency or softness of a dough or batter.

Oxidation

Oxidation is the process that occurs when oxygen from the air reacts with proteins and other components of flour during mixing. Oxidation increases when mixing times are long. Therefore, it is an important factor in the mixing of yeast doughs. When mixing times are short, as with products such as cakes, cookies, and pastry doughs, oxidation is less important and is not usually taken into consideration by the baker.

The most important effects of oxidation are on gluten proteins and pigments in the flour. During mixing, oxygen combines with gluten proteins and makes them stronger. This results in better structure for the bread dough. As mixing continues, oxygen combines with pigments in the flour and bleaches them, resulting in whiter bread. The same process, however, destroys some of the flavor and aroma, resulting in bread with less flavor.

Salt slows oxidation. Adding salt early in the mixing process delays the bleaching of pigments and results in a bread that is not as white but that has more flavor. If a whiter bread is desired, salt can be added later in the mixing process, after much of the pigment has already been oxidized.

You can see, then, that some oxidation is desirable, because it creates better gluten structure. But bakers try to avoid too much oxidation in order to preserve flavor. The amount of oxidation in bread dough is controlled by using the proper mixing time.

Controlling Gluten Development

Flour is mostly starch, as you know, but it is the content of gluten-forming proteins, not the starch, that concerns the baker most. Gluten proteins are needed to give structure to baked goods. Bakers must be able to control the gluten, however. For example, we want French bread to be firm and chewy, which requires a lot of gluten. On the other hand, we want cakes to be tender, which means we want very little gluten development in them.

Glutenin and *gliadin* are two proteins found in wheat flour and, in much smaller quantities, in a few other grains, such as rye and spelt. During mixing, these two proteins combine with water (that is, they are hydrated) and form a stretchable substance called *gluten*. As already explained, gluten forms when hydrated glutenin and gliadin proteins uncoil and attach to each other to form long chains. During mixing, these protein chains gradually stretch and become intertwined, forming an elastic network we call the *gluten structure*.

Coagulation is the firming or hardening of gluten proteins, usually caused by heat. When gluten proteins coagulate during baking, they solidify into a firm structure. Soft, pliable bread

Note that loss of moisture goes on even after the product is removed from the oven, as it cools.

Crust Formation and Browning

As just described, crust is formed as water evaporates from the surface and leaves it dry. Browning cannot occur until the surface temperature rises to about 300°F (150°C), and this can't happen until the surface dries. Browning begins before the interior of the item is completely baked and continues throughout the rest of the baking period.

Browning occurs when chemical changes occur to starches, sugars, and proteins. Although this is often referred to as *caramelization*, it is only part of the story. Caramelization involves only the browning of sugars. A similar process, called the *Maillard reaction*, causes most of the crust browning of baked goods. This process occurs when proteins and sugars together are subjected to high heat. Maillard browning also takes place on the surface of meats and other high-protein foods.

The chemical changes caused by caramelization and Maillard browning contribute to the flavor and appearance of the baked item. Milk, sugar, and egg, when included in doughs and batters, increase browning.

AFTER BAKING

MANY OF THE processes that take place during baking continue after the item is removed from the oven, while some of these processes reverse. We can divide this period into two stages, cooling and staling, although there is no exact dividing line between the two. In a sense, staling begins immediately, and cooling is only the first part of this process.

Cooling

Moisture continues to escape after the item is removed from the oven. At the same time, cooling begins, which causes the gases still inside the item to contract. If the protein structure is completely set, the product may shrink slightly but hold its shape. If the product is underbaked, however, the contraction of gases may cause it to collapse.

When baked goods are removed from the oven, the surface is drier than the interior crumb. During cooling, the moisture content tries to equalize throughout the item. As a result, crisp crusts gradually become softer.

Proteins continue to solidify and bond to one another during cooling. Many products are fragile when they are still hot, but cooling makes them firm enough to handle. It is best not to handle or cut most baked goods until they have cooled.

Fats that melted during baking resolidify. This process also helps make the texture firmer.

Starches continue to gelatinize while the interior is still hot. Also, starch molecules bond with each other and become more solid as the product cools. This process, called *starch retrogradation,* is responsible for staling.

Staling

Staling is the change in texture and aroma of baked goods due to a change of structure and a loss of moisture by the starch granules. Stale baked goods have lost their fresh-baked aroma and are firmer, drier, and more crumbly than fresh products. Prevention of staling is a major concern of the baker, because most baked goods lose quality rapidly.

As indicated, starch retrogradation begins as soon as the item begins to cool. As starch molecules bond with each other, the starch forces out moisture and becomes harder and drier. Even though this moisture may then be absorbed by other ingredients such as sugar, the result is that the texture of the item feels drier. Because this is a chemical reaction of the starch, breads become drier in texture even when tightly wrapped.

Starch retrogradation is more rapid at refrigerator temperatures than at room temperature, but it nearly stops at freezer temperatures. Thus, bread should not be stored in the refrigerator. It should be left at room temperature for short-term storage or frozen for long-term storage.

Chemical staling, if it is not too great, can be partially reversed by heating. Breads, muffins, and coffee cakes, for example, are frequently refreshed by placing them briefly in an oven. Remember, however, that this also results in more loss of moisture to the air, so the items should be reheated only just before they are to be served.

Loss of crispness is caused by absorption of moisture, so, in a sense, it is the opposite of staling. The crusts of hard-crusted breads absorb moisture from the crumb and become soft and leathery. Reheating these products to refresh them not only reverses chemical staling of the crumb but also recrisps the crusts.

Loss of crispness is also a problem with low-moisture products such as cookies and piecrusts. The problem is usually solved by proper storage in airtight wraps or containers to protect the products from moisture in the air. Prebaked pie shells should be filled as close to service time as possible.

In addition to refreshing baked goods in the oven, three main techniques are used to slow staling:

1. **Protecting the product from air.** Two examples of protecting baked goods are wrapping bread in plastic and covering cakes with icing, especially icing that is thick and rich in fat.

   Hard-crusted breads, which stale rapidly, should not be wrapped, or the crusts will quickly become soft and leathery. These bread products should always be served very fresh.

2. **Adding moisture retainers to the formula.** Fats and sugars are good moisture retainers, so products high in these ingredients keep best.

   Some of the best French bread has no fat at all, so it must be served within hours of baking or it will begin to stale. For longer keeping, bakers often add a very small amount of fat and/or sugar to the formula.

3. **Freezing.** Baked goods frozen before they become stale maintain quality for longer periods. For best results, freeze soon after baking in a blast freezer at –40°F (–40°C), and maintain at or below 0°F (–18°C) until ready to thaw. Breads should be served quickly after thawing. Frozen breads may be reheated with excellent results if they are to be served immediately.

   Refrigeration, on the other hand, speeds staling. Only baked goods that could become health hazards, such as those with cream fillings, are refrigerated.

KEY POINTS TO REVIEW

- What are the seven changes that take place in baked goods during the baking process?

- Why is protein coagulation important in the baking process?

- What is staling? How can it be controlled?

TERMS FOR REVIEW

crumb	gluten	mature (dough)	Maillard reaction
hydration	coagulation	dough relaxation	starch retrogradation
oxidation	shortening	dough conditioners	staling
glutenin	water hardness	gelatinization	
gliadin	pH	caramelization	

QUESTIONS FOR REVIEW

1. List and describe briefly the three stages of mixing a dough or batter.

2. What are air cell walls made of? Describe how air cells are formed. Name two functions of air cells.

3. Describe what happens when gluten proteins come in contact with water during mixing.

4. What is the result of overmixing on bread dough? Pie dough?

5. Discuss seven factors that affect the development of gluten in batters and doughs.

6. Why do some cakes fall if they are removed from the oven too soon?

7. Which kind of cake would you expect to have better keeping qualities: a sponge cake, which is low in fat, or a high-ratio cake, which is high in both fat and sugar?

6

UNDERSTANDING YEAST DOUGHS

1. Describe the principal types of yeast-raised products.

2. Describe the 12 basic steps in the production of yeast goods.

3. Explain how to judge the quality of yeast goods and correct defects in them.

IN ITS SIMPLEST form, bread is nothing more than a baked dough made of flour and water and leavened by yeast. In fact, some hard-crusted French breads contain only these ingredients, plus salt. Other kinds of bread contain additional ingredients, including sugar, shortening, milk, eggs, and flavorings. But flour, water, and yeast are still the basic building blocks of all breads.

Yet, for something that seems so simple, bread can be one of the most exacting and complex products to make. Success in bread making depends largely on your understanding of two basic principles: gluten development, which was discussed in Chapter 5, and yeast fermentation, which was introduced in Chapter 4 and is described in further detail here.

7

LEAN YEAST DOUGHS: STRAIGHT DOUGHS

AFTER READING THIS CHAPTER, YOU SHOULD BE ABLE TO:

1. Explain the mixing methods for straight doughs, and prepare straight doughs.
2. Mix doughs using appropriate mixing times and speeds, based on the three basic techniques for developing yeast doughs.
3. Describe the factors affecting dough fermentation and how to control them.
4. Make up and bake a variety of yeast dough products.

AFTER READING the general overview of yeast bread production in Chapter 6, you are ready to study mixing and fermentation methods in depth and to begin making yeast breads. Yeast dough production methods and formulas are divided into three chapters. This chapter focuses on lean yeast doughs mixed by straight dough methods, the simplest of the mixing methods. These formulas will give you good experience with all the steps of bread production and a feel for mixing and handling various doughs. Chapter 8 builds on this knowledge by introducing sponge mixing methods and pre-ferments of various types. Chapter 9 completes the study of yeast products with a range of rich doughs and laminated doughs, including Danish, brioche, and sweet roll doughs.

MIXING METHODS

THE TWO MIXING methods discussed in this chapter are the straight dough method and the modified straight dough method.

Straight Dough Method

In its simplest form, the *straight dough method*, also called the *direct dough method*, consists of only one step: Combine all ingredients in the mixing bowl and mix. With fresh yeast, many bakers make good-quality products using this procedure. However, the yeast may not be evenly distributed in the dough. It is therefore safer to mix the yeast separately with a little of the water. If active dry yeast is used, it is, of course, essential to mix the yeast with water before incorporating it in the dough.

Instant dry yeast, on the other hand, need not be blended with water for use because it is moistened and becomes active in the dough so quickly. The usual method for incorporating instant dry yeast is to mix it in dry form with the flour.

PROCEDURE: Straight Dough Mixing Method for Yeast Products

1a. In the bowl that is to be used for mixing the dough, soften fresh yeast or active dry yeast in a little of the water.

Fresh yeast: Mix with about 2 times its weight in water, or more.

- Ideal water temperature: 100°F (38°C)

Active dry yeast: Mix with about 4 times its weight in water.

- Ideal water temperature: 105°F (40°C)

1b. If using instant dry yeast, mix it directly with the flour.

2. Add the flour to the mixing bowl.

3. Add the remaining ingredients to the top of the flour in the mixing bowl.

4. Mix to a smooth, developed dough.

Modified Straight Dough Method

For rich, sweet doughs, the straight dough method is modified to ensure even distribution of the fat and sugar. In this procedure, the fat, sugar, eggs, and flavorings are first blended until uniform before the dough is developed.

PROCEDURE: Modified Straight Dough Method

1. If using fresh or active dry yeast, soften the yeast in part of the liquid, using a separate container. If using instant dry yeast, mix it with the flour.

2. Combine the fat, sugar, salt, milk solids, and flavorings and mix until well combined, but do not whip until light.

3. Add the eggs gradually, but as fast as they are absorbed.

4. Add the liquid; mix briefly.

5. Add the flour and yeast. Mix to a smooth dough.

Mixing Times and Speeds

The first two purposes of mixing—combining the ingredients into a dough and distributing the yeast—are accomplished during the first part of the mixing process. Additional time is necessary to develop the gluten.

To understand mixing times and speeds in detail, it is important to remember that gluten development occurs not only during mixing. It continues during bulk fermentation and folding. Therefore, mixing times, fermentation periods, and number of folds must be balanced. Short mixing time, for example, can be balanced against a long fermentation with numerous folds to yield a properly developed dough. By contrast, if long mixing is followed by long fermentation, the result is an overdeveloped dough.

Three basic mixing techniques are used for most yeast products: the *short mix* technique, the *improved mix* technique, and the *intensive mix* technique (see sidebar). Following the explanation of these techniques, the basic information is summarized in the two tables following this discussion (p. 122).

- First and second sp[...]
  dough hook or othe[...]
  tions for whichever [...]
- Some lightweight m[...]
  long periods. If this [...]
  gluten developmen[...]
- Times also depend [...]
  incorporate the ing[...]

In the end, it is up [...]
oped to the proper deg[...]
called a windowpane te[...]
a thin membrane. For t[...]
the improved mix, the g[...]
developed and regular. [...]
dows as easily because [...]

Dough Strength

The desired goal of glute[...]
can be described as the [...]

Extensibility is the [...]
pulled into differen[...]
made up into loave[...]

Elasticity is the ab[...]
dough has extensib[...]
up high and round[...]

Tenacity refers to [...]
tenacity is difficult[...]
are difficult to roll [...]

The baker must lea[...]
dough is properly devel[...]

In general, it is bet[...]
mixed, this can be large[...]
hand, if it is overmixed, [...]

Matching the Tec[...]

What's the best mixin[...]
can be used for any ye[...]
flavor, you might thinl[...]
of the long fermenta[...]
schedules.

Perhaps the impro[...]
shorter and it still yiel[...]
products—pullman loa[...]
that the intensive mix [...]
schedule for one or mo[...]

In other words, it'[...]
mula. It depends on y[...]
each mix achieves (see[...]

In the formulas in[...]
techniques in each cas[...]
ticular bread. In parti[...]
because the shorter fe[...]
feel free to experiment[...]
that if you change the [...]
to allow for the differe[...]

Short Mix

The short mix technique combines a short mix and long bulk fermentation. In a typical planetary mixer, mixing time is 3 to 4 minutes to incorporate ingredients, plus an additional 5 to 6 minutes to develop the gluten. All mixing time is at low speed. Of the three techniques, this is the closest to handmixing. Because of the short mixing time, the dough is very underdeveloped at the end of the mixing period. Gluten strands have formed but are not well aligned into a smooth dough. As a result, air cells are uneven in size, resulting in an open, irregular crumb structure in the finished bread.

Furthermore, because the dough is underdeveloped after mixing, a long fermentation time is necessary, 3 to 4 hours or even longer. During this long bulk fermentation time, the dough is folded often, generally 4 or 5 times (see p. 107). Because the dough is less developed, it can't hold as much gas and rises less during final proof and baking. Final proof is less than for other mixing techniques.

Shorter mixing also means less oxidation, because less air is mixed into the dough. Less oxidation means less dough strength (a disadvantage). On the other hand, it also means less loss of flavor and color (an advantage). (See the discussion of oxidation on p. 95.)

The short mix technique is especially suitable for lean doughs with an open crumb, such as baguettes and ciabatta. It is also used for laminated doughs, such as croissant dough, in which additional dough development takes place when the butter is rolled in.

Improved Mix

The improved mix technique combines medium mixing and bulk fermentation times. During mixing, the dough is first mixed for 3 to 4 minutes at low speed to incorporate ingredients. Then mixing is continued an additional 5 minutes at medium speed. (Note that the total mixing time is about the same as in the short mix technique, but because second speed is used to develop the gluten, the dough is much more developed than in the short mix.)

Because the dough is more developed after mixing, a shorter fermentation time is needed, usually 1 to 2 hours. Only one or two folds are given during this time.

Improved mix doughs have a slightly whiter color than short mix doughs, due to oxidation, but they still retain good flavor. Also, the crumb structure is tighter than in short mix products.

This technique is used for many yeast products but is especially appropriate for lean doughs with a slightly open, more regular crumb, and for sweet doughs.

Intensive Mix

The intensive mix technique combines long mixing with short fermentation. After an initial 3 to 4 minutes at first speed to incorporate ingredients, the dough is then mixed for 8 to 15 minutes at second speed. When the dough leaves the mixer, it has a well developed gluten structure.

YEAST DOUGH METHODS AND TECHNIQUES

In this discussion, we describe two procedures for combining ingredients and incorporating them into a dough. As we do throughout the book, we refer to these as "mixing methods."

In the production of yeast doughs, however, bakers often use the expression "mixing method" in different ways. Later in this chapter, we describe three techniques for developing doughs, using different mixing times and fermentation periods. In many references, these are also called "mixing methods." However, in order to avoid confusion, in this book, we refer to them as "mixing techniques" rather than as "mixing methods."

BREAD MIXING: A HISTORICAL PERSPECTIVE

For most of human history, bakers mixed bread dough by hand. Because so much manual labor was involved, bakers didn't completely develop the dough by handkneading, but relied on longer fermentation and numerous folds to complete the development of gluten.

Not until the 1800s did machines for mixing dough become available. The first of these machines were slow and inefficient. Although they saved a great deal of hand labor for bakers, they were not able to mix doughs much more quickly than by hand. As with handmixing, early mechanical mixing techniques combined short mixing periods with longer fermentation and several folds. This technique is comparable to the short mix technique described in the text. Breads made this way resemble handmixed breads.

As mixers became faster and more powerful (around the middle of the twentieth century), bakers found that they could mix doughs longer, give them a much shorter bulk fermentation, and, as a result, make larger quantities in a shorter time. This so-called intensive mix technique made bakeries much more efficient. Being able to get a dough ready for dividing and shaping into loaves in only an hour, rather than four to five hours as before, meant that bakers suddenly had shorter workdays. The entire process, from scaling ingredients to removing the baked bread from the oven now took less than 5 hours instead of 10 hours or more as before.

Eventually, however, people began to realize that bread had lost much of its flavor. Longer mixing means that more oxygen is mixed with the dough, destroying pigments, flavor, and aroma. Also, short fermentation gives little opportunity for flavors to develop. In an effort to regain some of the qualities of old-fashioned "short mix" breads without forcing bakers to go back to their 12-hour workdays, experts developed the improved mix technique, in which shorter mixing times can be combined with bulk fermentation periods that are only slightly longer.

BREAD CHARACTERISTICS BASED ON MIXING TECHNIQUE			
MIXING TECHNIQUE	**CRUMB COLOR**	**CRUMB STRUCTURE**	**FLAVOR AND AROMA**
Short mix	Creamy	Open, irregular	Complex
Improved mix	Creamy white	Somewhat open and irregular	Good but mild; not as complex as short mix
Intensive mix	White	Tight and regular	Bland

MIXING TIMES, FERMENTATION, AND FOLDS*				
MIX TECHNIQUE	**FIRST STAGE AT FIRST SPEED**	**SECOND STAGE AT SECOND SPEED**	**FERMENTATION TIME**	**FOLDS**
Short mix	9–10 minutes (3–4 minutes for dough formation; 6 minutes for development)	0	4–5 hours for straight doughs; 3–4 hours for doughs with sponge or pre-ferment	4–5
Improved mix	3–4 minutes	5 minutes	1–2 hours	1–2
Intensive mix	3–4 minutes	8–12 minutes	20–30 minutes	0

*Mixing and fermentation times are for a full batch in a standard planetary mixer, and are approximate. Adjust times as necessary (see p. 120–121). When using a lightweight machine not strong enough to mix a dough at second speed, use first speed and double the mixing time.

> **KEY POINTS TO REVIEW**
>
> - What are the steps in the straight dough mixing method? The modified straight dough mixing method?
> - What are the three basic techniques for mixing and fermenting yeast doughs? Describe each.
> - What do the following terms mean: *extensibility, elasticity,* and *tenacity*?

CONTROLLING FERMENTATION

PROPER FERMENTATION—THAT IS, fermentation that produces a dough that is neither underripe (young) nor overripe (old)—requires a balance of time, temperature, and yeast quantity.

Time

Fermentation times vary, so the time to fold the dough is indicated not by clock but by the appearance and feel of the dough. Thus, the fermentation times given in the formulas in this book and in the table above should be regarded as guidelines only.

To vary the fermentation time, you must control the dough temperature and the amount of yeast.

Temperature

Ideally, dough is fermented at the temperature at which it is taken from the mixer. Large bakeries have special fermentation rooms for controlling temperature and humidity, but small bakeshops and restaurant kitchens seldom have this luxury. If a short-fermentation process is used, however, the fermentation is complete before the dough is greatly affected by changes in shop temperature.

Water Temperature

Dough must be at the proper temperature, usually 78° to 80°F (25.5° to 26.7°C), in order to ferment at the desired rate. The temperature of the dough is affected by several factors:

- Shop temperature
- Flour temperature

- Water temperature
- Friction caused by mixing

Of these, water temperature is the easiest to control in the small bakeshop. Therefore, when the water is scaled, it should be brought to the required temperature. On cold days, it may have to be warmed, and on hot days, using a mixture of crushed ice and water may be necessary. Also, if a long fermentation is used, the dough temperature must be reduced in order to avoid overfermenting.

Friction caused by mixing warms the dough. This machine friction factor varies, depending on the type of mixer, the size of the batch, and the type of dough. This means that, to be accurate in a regular production situation, you need to calculate the machine friction for each dough you produce. Appendix 5 (p. 736) explains the procedure for making this calculation. In a learning situation, you can use an average number as explained in the Procedure for Determining Water Temperature.

PROCEDURE: Determining Water Temperature

1. Multiply the desired dough temperature by 3.

2. Add together the flour temperature and room temperature, plus 20°F (11°C) to allow for the friction caused by mixing (see **Note**).

3. Subtract the result of step 2 from that of step 1. The difference is the required water temperature.

   Example: Dough temperature needed = 80°F
   Flour temperature = 68°F
   Room temperature = 72°F
   Machine friction = 20°F
   Water temperature = ?

1. $80° \times 3 = 240°$
2. $68° + 72° + 20° = 160°$
3. $240° - 160° = 80°$

Therefore, the water temperature should be 80°F.

Note: This procedure is precise enough for most purposes in the small bakeshop. However, there are other complications, such as variations in machine friction, that you may want to consider if you wish to be even more exact. To learn how to make these calculations, see Appendix 5.

Yeast Quantity

If other conditions are constant, the fermentation time may be increased or decreased by decreasing or increasing the quantity of yeast (see Procedure for Modifying Yeast Quantities). In general, use no more yeast than is needed. Excessive yeast results in inferior flavor.

Small Batches

When very small quantities of dough—only a few pounds—are made, the dough is more likely to be affected by shop temperature. Thus, it may be necessary to slightly increase the yeast quantity in cool weather and slightly decrease it in hot weather.

PROCEDURE: Modifying Yeast Quantities

1. Determine a factor by dividing the old fermentation time by the fermentation time desired.

2. Multiply this factor by the original quantity of yeast to determine the new quantity.

   $$\frac{\text{Old fermentation time}}{\text{New fermentation time}} \times \frac{\text{Old yeast}}{\text{quantity}} = \frac{\text{New yeast}}{\text{Quantity}}$$

   Example: A formula requiring 12 oz yeast has a fermentation time of 2 hours at 80°F. How much yeast is needed to reduce the fermentation time to 1½ hours?

   $$\frac{\text{2 hours}}{\text{1½ hours}} \times 12 \text{ oz yeast} = 16 \text{ oz yeast}$$

   Caution: This procedure should be used within narrow limits only. An excessive increase or decrease in yeast quantities introduces many other problems, and results in inferior products.

Other Factors

The salt in the formula, the minerals in the water, and the use of dough conditioners or improvers affect the rate of fermentation. See page 88 for a discussion of salt and its effect on fermentation.

Water that is excessively soft lacks the minerals that ensure proper gluten development and dough fermentation. On the other hand, water that is very hard—that has high mineral content and, as a result, is alkaline—also inhibits the development of the dough. These conditions are more of a problem for lean doughs than for rich doughs. In most localities, small bakeshops can overcome these problems with the proper use of salt or, in areas with alkaline water, by adding a very small amount of a mild acid to the water. Dough conditioners, buffers, and improvers that can correct these conditions are available from bakers' suppliers. Their use should be determined by local water conditions.

The richness of the dough must also be considered. Doughs high in fat or sugar ferment more slowly than lean doughs. This problem can be avoided by using a sponge instead of a straight dough (see Chapters 8 and 9).

Retarding

Retarding means slowing the fermentation or proof of yeast doughs by refrigeration. This may be done in regular refrigerators or in special retarders that maintain a high humidity. If regular refrigerators are used, the product must be covered to prevent drying and the formation of a skin.

Retarded Fermentation

Dough to be retarded in bulk is usually given partial fermentation. It is then flattened on sheet pans, covered with plastic wrap, and placed in the retarder. The layer of dough must not be too thick because the inside will take too long to chill and thus will overferment. When needed, the dough is allowed to warm before molding. Some doughs high in fat are made up while chilled so they do not become too soft.

Retarded Proof

Made-up units to be retarded are made from young dough. After makeup, they are immediately placed in the retarder. When needed, they are allowed to warm and finish their proof, if necessary. They are then baked.

A valuable laborsaving tool for medium to large bakeshops is the *retarder-proofer*. As the name suggests, this equipment is a combination of freezer/retarder and proofer, with thermostats for both functions and with timers to automate the process. For example, the baker can make up a batch of rolls in the afternoon or evening and place them in the retarder-proofer with the controls set for retarding or freezing. The baker sets the timer for the proper hour the following morning. The machine automatically begins to raise the temperature, proofing the rolls so they are ready to bake in time for breakfast.

> **KEY POINTS TO REVIEW**
>
> ▪ What are the three main factors that determine proper fermentation of a yeast dough?
>
> ▪ What procedure is used to control the final temperature of a dough as it comes from the mixer?

PRODUCING HANDCRAFTED BREADS

NOT MANY YEARS ago, bread was something of an afterthought in most restaurants. They offered little in the way of variety and paid scant attention to quality in most cases. In many cities today, however, fine restaurants vie with one another to serve the most interesting selections of fresh artisan breads. Customers are often given a choice from among four, five, or even more types. Likewise, handcrafted specialty breads are appearing in neighborhood bakeries, and everyone seems to have discovered the delights of sourdough.

Traditional formulas such as hard and soft rolls, Italian bread, white and whole wheat loaf breads, and American-style rye bread form the core of this section. It is important to learn well the basics of yeast dough production, and this is easiest to do when you are working on familiar formulas that do not require unusual techniques and exotic ingredients. Not only will you learn how to mix basic yeast doughs, but you will also practice making up a variety of loaf and roll types by hand to develop your manual skills. Then you can proceed with confidence to specialty handcrafted items. Working with sourdoughs (Chapter 8), in particular, is more challenging than working with straight doughs, so your earlier practice and experience will benefit you later.

Making and fermenting dough is a craft distinct from making up rolls and loaves using these doughs. Each dough may be made into many types of loaves and rolls, and each makeup method may be applied to many formulas. Therefore, most makeup techniques—except for a few unique procedures for specialty items—are described in a section at the end of the chapter rather than repeated after every formula.

Using the Formulas

Procedures and techniques for mixing and fermenting bread doughs are explained in detail in the first part of this chapter and in Chapter 6. Be sure to read and understand that material thoroughly before trying the formulas that follow.

In the formulas in the first two sections that follow (pp. 125–134), mixing techniques and procedures are indicated by name, along with page references. Refer to those pages if you need to review the procedures. Mixing and fermentation times are summarized in the Mixing Times, Fermentation, and Folds table on page 122.

Many of the formulas, especially those at the beginning, use the intensive mix technique (p. 119). These enable you to produce doughs that can be mixed and fermented in a short time, so you can move on to practicing makeup techniques for various breads and rolls. After you have developed skill in mixing and handling doughs, you might try making some of these intensive mix doughs using the improved mix technique to gain further experience and to see how the mixing technique affects bread characteristics. When changing the mixing technique, keep in mind that you may need to adjust the yeast quantity to allow for the different fermentation time. See the discussion on page 120.

Note that in a few formulas, more than one mixing technique is indicated. This is done to give you the most opportunities to experience producing a wide variety of products within limited schedules. For example, see the formula for Italian Bread on page 127: Both intensive mix and improved mix are indicated. In such cases, you may use the intensive mix technique to produce an acceptable product if your schedule does not allow time for the improved mix. However, the improved mix is more appropriate for that product. *As a general rule, when given more than one choice of mixing technique, use the one with the longest fermentation time permitted by your schedule.*

In many baking operations, instant yeast has replaced fresh yeast as the preferred leavening. Still, some bakers continue to prefer fresh yeast for at least some preparations, such as yeast pre-ferments. However, to simplify your purchasing and storage needs, with a few exceptions, the formulas in this book specify only instant yeast. To substitute another form of yeast, see page 79 for the necessary calculations.

Crisp-Crusted Bread Formulas

The crisp, thin crusts of French, Italian, and Vienna breads and hard rolls are achieved by using formulas with little or no sugar and fat and by baking with steam. Because the crust is part of the attraction of these items, they are often made in long, thin shapes that increase the proportion of crust.

These breads are usually baked freestanding, either directly on the hearth or on sheet pans. (Perforated sheet pans are especially useful, as they allow better circulation of hot air around the product.) The water content must be low enough that the units hold their shape in the oven.

In practice, French and Italian bread formulas in North America are widely interchangeable. Some of them, in fact, have little resemblance to breads in France and Italy, but nevertheless they may be popular and of good quality. The best practice is to follow regional preferences and to produce good-quality products that appeal to your customers.

FRENCH BREAD (STRAIGHT DOUGH)

For large-quantity measurements, see page 709.

Ingredients	U.S.		Metric	%
Bread flour	1 lb 12	oz	750 g	100
Water	1 lb 2	oz	480 g	64
Yeast, instant	0.25	oz	7 g	0.9
Salt	0.5	oz	15 g	2
Malt syrup	0.13	oz	4 g	0.5
Sugar	0.5	oz	12 g	1.75
Shortening	0.5	oz	12 g	1.75
Total weight:	**2 lb 15**	**oz**	**1280 g**	**170** **%**

PROCEDURE

MIXING AND FERMENTATION

Straight dough method (p. 118)

Improved mix (See Mixing Times, Fermentation, and Folds table on p. 122 for mixing and fermentation times.)

Desired dough temperature: 77°F (25°C)

MAKEUP

See pages 143–144.

PROOFING

80°F (27°C) at 80% humidity

BAKING

425°F (218°C) for loaves; 450°F (230°C) for rolls. Steam for first 10 minutes.

VARIATION

WHOLE WHEAT FRENCH BREAD

For large-quantity measurements, see page 709.

Use the following proportions of flour in the above formula.

Ingredients	U.S.	Metric	%
Whole wheat flour	12 oz	325 g	43
Bread flour	1 lb	425 g	57

Increase the water to 66–67% to allow for the extra absorption by the bran. Mix 8 minutes.

FRENCH BREAD

The long, slender loaf called the baguette (bah GET) is the classic French loaf familiar to most people in North America. However, the terms *French bread* and *baguette* are not interchangeable. Many types of bread are produced in France other than the light, crusty baguette.

Baguettes should be made only with lean doughs that produce a crisp crust. It is not a good practice to make baguette-shaped loaves with ordinary soft-crusted white bread and sell it labeled as French bread.

BAGUETTE

For large-quantity measurements, see page 708.

Ingredients	U.S.			Metric	%
Bread flour	2 lb	2	oz	1000 g	100
Salt		0.67	oz	20 g	2
Yeast, instant		0.25	oz	8 g	0.8
Water	1 lb	6	oz	650 g	65
Total weight:	**3 lb**	**8**	**oz**	**1678 g**	**167** %

PROCEDURE

MIXING AND FERMENTATION

Straight dough method (p. 118)

Improved mix (See Mixing Times, Fermentation, and Folds table on p. 122 for mixing and fermentation times.)

Desired dough temperature: 77°F (25°C)

MAKEUP

See page 143.

PROOFING

80°F (27°C) at 80% humidity

BAKING

425°F (218°C) for loaves; 450°F (230°C) for rolls. Steam for first 10 minutes.

--- VARIATIONS ---

For baguettes with a more open crumb, increase the water to 70% (1 lb 7.8 oz/700 g), decrease the instant yeast to 0.3% (0.1 oz/3 g), and use the short mix technique.

FOUGASSE

Scale dough at 18 oz (540 g). See page 145 for makeup.

CUBAN BREAD

For large-quantity measurements, see page 709.

Ingredients	U.S.			Metric	%
Bread flour	1 lb	8	oz	750 g	100
Water		15	oz	465 g	62
Yeast, instant		0.35	oz	11 g	1.5
Salt		0.5	oz	15 g	2
Sugar		1	oz	30 g	4
Total weight:	**2 lb**	**8**	**oz**	**1271 g**	**169** %

PROCEDURE

MIXING

Straight dough method (p. 118)

Improved mix (see Mixing Times, Fermentation, and Folds table on p. 122), but mix a total of 12 minutes at first speed.

Desired dough temperature: 77°F (25°C)

MAKEUP

Scale at 20 oz (625 g). Shape into round loaves (p. 144).

PROOFING

80°F (27°C) at 80% humidity

BAKING

Score top with a cross.

400°F (200°C)

Soft-Crusted Bread and Rye Bread Formulas

This category includes sandwich-type breads baked in loaf pans, braided breads, soft rolls, and straight-dough rye (sour rye breads are covered in the next section). Many of these formulas incorporate milk, eggs, and higher percentages of sugar and fat.

WHITE PAN BREAD

For large-quantity measurements, see page 709.

Ingredients	U.S.			Metric	%
Bread flour	1 lb	4	oz	500 g	100
Water		12	oz	300 g	60
Yeast, instant		0.4	oz	10 g	2
Salt		0.5	oz	12 g	2.5
Sugar		0.75	oz	18 g	3.75
Nonfat milk solids		1	oz	25 g	5
Shortening		0.75	oz	18 g	3.75
Total weight:	**2 lb**	**3**	**oz**	**883 g**	**177　%**

PROCEDURE

MIXING AND FERMENTATION
Straight dough method (p. 118)

Intensive mix (See Mixing Times, Fermentation, and Folds table on p. 122 for mixing and fermentation times.)

Desired dough temperature: 77°F (25°C)

MAKEUP
See page 148.

PROOFING
80°F (27°C) at 80% humidity

BAKING
400°F (200°C)

——————— **VARIATION** ———————

WHOLE WHEAT BREAD

For large-quantity measurements, see page 709.

Use the following proportions of flour in the above formula.

Ingredients	U.S.	Metric	%
Bread flour	8 oz	200 g	40
Whole wheat flour	12 oz	300 g	60

Whole Wheat Bread.

EGG BREAD AND ROLLS

For large-quantity measurements, see page 710.

Ingredients	U.S.			Metric	%
Bread flour	1 lb	5	oz	625 g	100
Water		10.5	oz	312 g	50
Yeast, instant		0.4	oz	12 g	1.9
Salt		0.4	oz (2 tsp)	12 g	2
Sugar		2	oz	60 g	9.5
Nonfat milk solids		1	oz	30 g	4.75
Shortening		1	oz	30 g	4.75
Butter		1	oz	30 g	4.75
Eggs		2	oz	60 g	9.5
Total weight:	**2 lb**	**7**	**oz**	**1171 g**	**187　%**

PROCEDURE

MIXING AND FERMENTATION

Straight dough method (p. 118)

Intensive mix (see Mixing Times, Fermentation, and Folds table on p. 122 for mixing and fermentation times.)

Desired dough temperature: 77°F (25°C)

MAKEUP

See pages 145–152.

PROOFING

80°F (27°C) at 80% humidity

BAKING

400°F (200°C)

SOFT ROLLS

For large-quantity measurements, see page 710.

Ingredients	U.S.	Metric	%
Bread flour	1 lb 5 oz	625 g	100
Water	12.5 oz	375 g	60
Yeast, instant	0.4 oz	12 g	1.9
Salt	0.4 oz (2 tsp)	12 g	2
Sugar	2 oz	60 g	9.5
Nonfat milk solids	1 oz	30 g	4.75
Shortening	1 oz	30 g	4.75
Butter	1 oz	30 g	4.75
Total weight:	**2 lb 7 oz**	**1174 g**	**187 %**

PROCEDURE

MIXING AND FERMENTATION

Straight dough method (p. 118)

Intensive mix (See Mixing Times, Fermentation, and Folds table on p. 122 for mixing and fermentation times.)

Desired dough temperature: 77°F (25°C)

MAKEUP

See pages 145–152.

PROOFING

80°F (27°C) at 80% humidity

BAKING

400°F (200°C)

VARIATIONS

CINNAMON BREAD

Make up Soft Roll Dough as for loaves (p. 148), but after flattening each unit, brush with melted butter and sprinkle with Cinnamon Sugar (p. 193). After baking and while still hot, brush tops of loaves with melted butter or shortening and sprinkle with cinnamon sugar.

RAISIN BREAD

Scale 75% raisins (1 lb/470 g). Soak in warm water to soften; drain and dry. Add to Soft Roll Dough 1–2 minutes before end of mixing.

100% WHOLE WHEAT BREAD

For large-quantity measurements, see page 710.

Ingredients	U.S.	Metric	%
Whole wheat flour	1 lb 10 oz	750 g	100
Water	1 lb 2 oz	515 g	69
Yeast, instant	0.4 oz	11 g	1.5
Sugar	0.5 oz	15 g	2
Malt syrup	0.5 oz	15 g	2
Nonfat milk solids	0.75 oz	22 g	3
Shortening	1 oz	30 g	4
Salt	0.5 oz	15 g	2
Total weight:	**3 lb**	**1373 g**	**183 %**

PROCEDURE

MIXING AND FERMENTATION

Straight dough method (p. 118)

Intensive mix (See Mixing Times, Fermentation, and Folds table on p. 122 for mixing and fermentation times.)

Desired dough temperature: 77°F (25°C)

MAKEUP

See page 148.

PROOFING

80°F (27°C) at 80% humidity

BAKING

400°F (200°C)

CHALLAH

For large-quantity measurements, see page 710.

Ingredients	U.S.			Metric	%
Bread flour	1 lb	4	oz	500 g	100
Water		8	oz	200 g	40
Yeast, instant		0.4	oz	10 g	2
Egg yolks		4	oz	100 g	20
Sugar		1.5	oz	38 g	7.5
Malt syrup		0.13	oz	2 g	0.6
Salt		0.4	oz (2 tsp)	10 g	1.9
Vegetable oil		2	oz	62 g	10
Total weight:	**2 lb**	**4**	**oz**	**922 g**	**182 %**

PROCEDURE

MIXING AND FERMENTATION

Straight dough method (p. 118)

Intensive mix (See Mixing Times, Fermentation, and Folds table on p. 122 for mixing and fermentation times, but extend fermentation time as necessary, up to 1½ hours.)

Desired dough temperature: 77°F (25°C)

MAKEUP

See pages 149–152.

PROOFING

80°F (27°C) at 80% humidity

BAKING

400°F (200°C)

MILK BREAD (PAIN AU LAIT)

For large-quantity measurements, see page 710.

Ingredients	U.S.			Metric	%
Bread flour	2 lb	4	oz	1000 g	100
Yeast, instant		0.35	oz	10 g	1
Milk, scalded and cooled	1 lb	2	oz	500 g	50
Sugar		3.5	oz	100 g	10
Salt		0.75	oz	20 g	2
Eggs		3.5	oz	100 g	10
Butter or margarine		5	oz	150 g	15
Malt syrup		0.33	oz	10 g	1
Total weight:	**4 lb**	**3**	**oz**	**1890 g**	**189%**

PROCEDURE

MIXING AND FERMENTATION

Straight dough method (p. 118)

Intensive mix (See Mixing Times, Fermentation, and Folds table p. 122 for mixing and fermentation times, but extend fermentation time as necessary up to 1½ hours.)

Desired dough temperature: 77°F (25°C)

MAKEUP

Any method for soft rolls, pages 145–148.

PROOFING

80°F (27°C) at 80% humidity

BAKING

Glaze with egg wash.

425°F (218°C)

Assorted rolls made with milk bread (pain au lait) dough.

LIGHT AMERICAN RYE BREAD AND ROLLS

For large-quantity measurements, see page 711.

Ingredients	U.S.		Metric	%
Light rye flour	8	oz	250 g	40
Bread flour or clear flour	12	oz	375 g	60
Water	12	oz	375 g	60
Yeast, instant	0.25	oz	7 g	1.25
Salt	0.4	oz (2 tsp)	12 g	2
Shortening	0.5	oz	15 g	2.5
Molasses or malt syrup	0.5	oz	15 g	2.5
Caraway seeds (optional)	0.25	oz	8 g	1.25
Rye flavor	0.25	oz	8 g	1.25
Total weight:	**2 lb 2**	**oz**	**1065 g**	**170 %**

PROCEDURE

MIXING AND FERMENTATION

Straight dough method (p. 118)

Improved mix (See Mixing Times, Fermentation, and Folds table on p. 122 for mixing and fermentation times, but reduce second-speed mixing time to 3 minutes.)

Desired dough temperature: 77°F (25°C)

MAKEUP

See pages 141–152.

PROOFING

80°F (27°C) at 80% humidity

BAKING

400°F (200°C). Steam for first 10 minutes.

--- **VARIATION** ---

Add up to 10% Rye Starter (p. 168) to the formula to contribute flavor.

ONION RYE

For large-quantity measurements, see page 711.

Ingredients	U.S.		Metric	%
Light rye flour	7	oz	175 g	35
Clear flour	13	oz	325 g	65
Water	12	oz	300 g	60
Yeast, instant	0.25	oz	6 g	1.25
Dried onions, scaled, soaked in water, and well drained	1	oz	25 g	5
Salt	0.4	oz (2 tsp)	10 g	1.9
Caraway seeds	0.25	oz	6 g	1.25
Rye flavor	0.25	oz	6 g	1.25
Malt syrup	0.5	oz	12 g	2.5
Total weight:	**2 lb 2**	**oz**	**865 g**	**173 %**

PROCEDURE

MIXING AND FERMENTATION

Straight dough method (p. 118)

Improved mix (See Mixing Times, Fermentation, and Folds table on p. 122 for mixing and fermentation times, but reduce second-speed mixing time to 3 minutes.)

Desired dough temperature: 77°F (25°C)

MAKEUP

See pages 141–152.

PROOFING

80°F (27°C) at 80% humidity

BAKING

400°F (200°C). Steam for first 10 minutes.

--- **VARIATION** ---

ONION PUMPERNICKEL (NONSOUR)

For large-quantity measurements, see page 711.

Use the following proportions of flour in the above formula.

Ingredients	U.S.	Metric	%
Rye meal (pumpernickel flour)	4 oz	100 g	20
Medium rye flour	3 oz	75 g	15
Clear flour	13 oz	325 g	65

Dough may be colored with caramel color or cocoa powder.

SEVEN-GRAIN BREAD

Ingredients	U.S.		Metric	%
Bread flour	1 lb 8	oz	750 g	57
Rye flour	6	oz	185 g	14
Barley flour	2	oz	65 g	5
Cornmeal	3	oz	90 g	7
Rolled oats	3	oz	90 g	7
Flax seeds	2	oz	65 g	5
Millet	2	oz	65 g	5
Water	1 lb 10	oz	815 g	62
Yeast, instant	0.33 oz		10 g	0.8
Salt	0.75 oz		24 g	1.8
Total weight:	**4 lb 5**	**oz**	**2159 g**	**164** **%**

NOTE: For the purposes of calculating with percentages, all seven grains are included as part of the total flour, even though three of them are not ground.

VARIATION

MULTIGRAIN BREAD

1. Use 80% bread flour and 20% whole wheat flour in the basic recipe and omit the remaining flours and grains.
2. Separately, prepare a cold soaker (see the Soakers sidebar) using 35% commercial nine-grain mixture and 35% water.
3. Let stand, covered, until the grains are soft and the water is absorbed, 8 hours or more.
4. Drain the soaker.
5. Mix the bread dough 5 minutes, add the soaker, and then continue mixing until the gluten is developed.

> ### KEY POINTS TO REVIEW
> ▌ What factors produce crisp crusts in certain breads?
> ▌ What factors produce soft crusts in certain breads?
> ▌ What are soakers, and how are they used?

PROCEDURE

MIXING AND FERMENTATION

Straight dough method (p. 118)

Sift together the bread flour, rye flour, barley flour, and cornmeal; add the oats, flax seeds, and millet and mix well. This ensures even distribution of the flours.

Improved mix (See Mixing Times, Fermentation, and Folds table on p. 122 for mixing and fermentation times, but reduce second-speed mixing time to 3 minutes.)

Desired dough temperature: 77°F (25°C)

MAKEUP

See pages 144 and 148. Make up as desired for loaf pans or round loaves.

PROOFING

80°F (27°C) at 80% humidity

BAKING

425°F (220°C)

SOAKERS

Adding large quantities of whole or cracked grains to bread doughs can have two undesirable effects. First, the grains absorb water from the dough, resulting in a dry baked loaf. Second, the grains may not hydrate sufficiently, resulting in hard chunks in the bread that are difficult to eat.

The seven-grain bread formula given here contains a relatively small quantity of small, fairly tender grains, and there is sufficient water in the formula to hydrate them. Thus, they can be added directly to the other ingredients.

However, if larger quantities of grains are added, especially if those grains include large, hard grains such as wheat berries, it is better to prepare what is known as a *soaker*. This procedure hydrates the grains before they are included in the bread dough.

Two kinds of soakers, hot and cold, are used. For large, hard grains, a hot soaker is preferred. To prepare a hot soaker, bring the required quantity of water to a boil, as indicated in the formula. Pour the water over the grains and stir. Cover tightly and let stand four hours or more, or until the grains are softened and cooled. Drain and add to the dough as indicated in the formula.

Use a cold soaker for smaller and softer grains. Pour cold or room-temperature water over the grains, stir, cover, and let stand until softened. If a cold soaker is used for hard grains, it may be necessary to prepare it one day ahead of time. In warm weather, store the soaker in the refrigerator to inhibit fermentation or enzyme activity.

Specialty Breads

The final formulas in the chapter include a number of specialty breads and other yeast dough items. Some of these are produced by methods unlike those of other breads. *English muffins* and crumpets, for example, are made on a griddle rather than baked in an oven. Both of these items are toasted before being eaten. But English muffins are split in half before toasting, whereas crumpets are toasted whole. True *bagels*—dense, chewy, and boiled in a malt syrup before baking—are unlike the soft imitation bagels widely sold today (see the Bagels sidebar and formula on p. 136).

Production methods for these items are modified here for use in a small bakeshop. Large producers have special equipment for bagels, English muffins, and crumpets.

Additional formulas in this chapter include two popular ones for focaccia, which is closely related to pizza dough; an unusual and flavorful bread made with chestnut flour; a flatbread called *pita*, which puffs up when baked to form a hollow center; and an Amish-style soft pretzel.

ENGLISH MUFFINS

For large-quantity measurements, see page 712.

Ingredients	U.S.	Metric	%
Bread flour	1 lb	500 g	100
Yeast, instant	0.08 oz	2.5 g	0.5
Water (see Mixing)	12 oz	375 g	75
Salt	0.25 oz	8 g	1.5
Sugar	0.25 oz	8 g	1.5
Nonfat milk solids	0.4 oz (2 tsp)	12 g	2.3
Shortening	0.25 oz	8 g	1.5
Total weight:	**1 lb 13 oz**	**913 g**	**182 %**

PROCEDURE

MIXING

Straight dough method (p. 118)

20–25 minutes at second speed (see p. 121)

This dough is intentionally overmixed in order to develop its characteristic coarse texture. Because of this long mixing time, use twice your normal machine friction factor (see p. 123) when calculating water temperature. For this reason, and because of the low fermentation temperature, it is usually necessary to use very cold water or part crushed ice when making large batches.

FERMENTATION

Dough temperature: 70°F (21°C). Ferment 2½–3 hours.

SCALING AND MAKEUP

Because this dough is very soft and sticky, you must use plenty of dusting flour.

1. Scale at 2 oz (60 g) per unit. Round and relax the units, then flatten with the palms of the hands.
2. Place on cornmeal-covered trays to proof.

BAKING

Bake on both sides on a griddle at low heat.

BAGELS

For large-quantity measurements, see page 712.

Ingredients	U.S.		Metric	%
High-gluten flour	1 lb		500 g	100
Yeast, instant	0.16 oz		5 g	1
Water	9 oz		280 g	56
Diastatic malt powder	0.1 oz (1 tsp)		3 g	0.6
Salt	0.33 oz		10 g	2
Total weight:	**1 lb 9 oz**		**798 g**	**159 %**

PROCEDURE

MIXING

Straight dough method (p. 118)

8–10 minutes at low speed

FERMENTATION

1 hour at 75°F (24°C)

MAKEUP AND BAKING

1. Scale at 4 oz (110 g) per unit.

2. One of two methods may be used for shaping bagels by hand:
   - Roll with the palms of the hands into ropes (as for knotted or tied rolls). Loop around palms into doughnut shape (a). Seal the ends together well by rolling under the palms on the bench (b, c).
   - Round the scaled unit and flatten into a thick disk. Press a hole in the center and tear open with the fingers. Pull the hole open and smooth the edges.

3. Give half proof.

4. Boil in a malt solution (⅓ qt malt syrup per 4 gal water, or 3 dL malt per 15 L water) about 1 minute.

5. Place on sheet pans about 1 in. (2.5 cm) apart. Bake at 450°F (230°C) until golden brown, turning them over when they are half baked. Total baking time is about 20 minutes. If desired, sprinkle bagels with sesame seeds, poppy seeds, diced onion, or coarse salt before baking.

BAGELS

As bagels have become more popular, bagel-like rolls that are really only ordinary bread shaped like bagels have proliferated. True bagels are dense, chewy rolls made with high-gluten flour and a low proportion of water. They are boiled in a malt solution before being baked to give them a glossy, distinctively flavored crust. Also, flavorings for true bagels are generally limited to toppings, such as poppy seeds, sesame seeds, coarse salt, and chopped onion or garlic. Two popular exceptions are pumpernickel bagels and cinnamon-raisin bagels.

The traditional baking method is to arrange bagels on wet canvas-covered boards and partially bake them in a hearth oven. When half done, they are tipped over directly onto the hearth to finish baking. They should be baked until well-browned. Proper bagels are not pale.

OLIVE FOCACCIA

For large-quantity measurements, see page 712.

Ingredients	U.S.		Metric	%
Bread flour	1 lb 8	oz	750 g	100
Water	15	oz	470 g	62.5
Yeast, instant	0.17	oz	5 g	0.7
Salt	0.5	oz	15 g	2
Olive oil	1	oz	25 g	3.5
Chopped, pitted oil-cured black olives	8	oz	250 g	33
Total weight:	**3 lb**		**1515 g**	**201 %**

PROCEDURE

MIXING

Straight dough method (p. 118)

Add the olives after the other ingredients have formed a dough.

12 minutes at first speed.

FERMENTATION

1½ hours at 77°F (25°C)

MAKEUP AND BAKING

See Herb Focaccia (p. 167).

This dough, without the olives, may also be used as a base for pizza (see p. 126).

CHESTNUT BREAD

For large-quantity measurements, see page 713.

Ingredients	U.S.		Metric	%
High-gluten flour	15	oz	450 g	75
Chestnut flour	5	oz	150 g	25
Water	12	oz	360 g	60
Yeast, instant	0.4	oz	12 g	2
Salt	0.5	oz	15 g	2.5
Butter	0.6	oz	18 g	3
Total weight:	**2 lb 1**	**oz**	**1005 g**	**167 %**

PROCEDURE

MIXING

Straight dough method (p. 118)

10 minutes at first speed

FERMENTATION

40 minutes at 80°F (27°C)

MAKEUP

Scale at 10–11 oz (300–330 g). Make up into oval-shaped loaves.

BAKING

450°F (230°C)

--- **VARIATION** ---

For a more developed flavor, add 30% Basic Yeast Starter (p. 168)

PITA

Ingredients	U.S.			Metric	%
Bread flour	1 lb	4	oz	625 g	83
Whole wheat flour		4	oz	125 g	17
Water		14	oz	435 g	58
Yeast, instant		0.4	oz	10 g	1.4
Salt		0.5	oz	15 g	2
Sugar		0.67	oz	22 g	3
Yogurt, plain low-fat		3	oz	90 g	12.5
Oil, preferably olive		1	oz	30 g	4
Total weight:	**2 lb 12**		**oz**	**1352 g**	**18 %**

PROCEDURE

MIXING AND FERMENTATION

Straight dough method (p. 118)

Improved mix (See Mixing Times, Fermentation, and Folds table on p. 122 for mixing and fermentation times.)

Desired dough temperature: 77°F (25°C)

MAKEUP AND BAKING

1. Scale at 3 oz (90 g). Round the units and bench rest.

2. With a rolling pin, roll out into circles about 4–5 in. (10–12 cm) in diameter.

3. Bake on oven hearth or dry sheet pans at 500°F (260°C) until lightly golden around edges, about 5 minutes. Do not overbake, or the pitas will be dry and stiff. They should be soft when cool.

KEY POINTS TO REVIEW

▎ What is mixed fermentation?

▎ What precautions should be taken when mixing, handling, and proofing sourdoughs?

▎ How is a basic sourdough starter produced?

▎ What equipment is used to bake English muffins and crumpets?

MAKEUP TECHNIQUES

THE OBJECT OF yeast dough makeup is to shape the dough into rolls or loaves that bake properly and have an attractive appearance. When you shape a roll or loaf correctly, you stretch the gluten strands on the surface into a smooth skin. This tight gluten surface holds the item in shape. This is especially important for loaves and rolls that are baked freestanding, not in pans. Units that are not made up correctly develop irregular shapes and splits and may flatten out.

Large bakeries have machinery that automatically forms loaves and rolls of many types. In a small bakeshop, however, the baker still makes up most products by hand. Learning how to shape loaves, rolls, and pastries is an important part of the art and craft of fine baking.

Use of Dusting Flour

In most cases, the bench and the dough must be dusted lightly with flour to prevent the dough from sticking to the bench and hands. Some bakers use light rye flour for dusting. Others prefer bread flour.

Whichever dusting flour you use, one rule is very important: Use as little as possible. Excessive flour makes seams difficult to seal and shows up as streaks in the baked product.

PROCEDURE: Scaling and Dividing Dough for Rolls

This procedure involves the use of a dough divider. A dough divider cuts a large unit of dough, called a *press*, into small units of equal weight. If this equipment is not available, you must scale individual roll units.

1. Scale the dough into presses of desired weight. One press makes 36 rolls.

2. Round the presses and allow them to relax.

3. Divide the press using a dough divider. Separate the pieces, using a little dusting flour to prevent sticking.

4. Make up the rolls as desired. In some cases, the pieces are rounded first. In other cases, the rolls are made up without rounding, just as they come from the divider.

Crisp-Crusted Products and Rye Products

Round Rolls

1. Scale the dough as required, such as 3½ lb (1600 g) per press or 1½ oz (45 g) per roll. Divide the presses into rolls.

2. Holding the palm of the hand fairly flat, roll the dough in a tight circle on the workbench (a). Do not use too much flour for dusting, as the dough must stick to the bench a little for the technique to work.

3. As the ball of dough takes on a round shape, gradually cup the hand (b, c).

4. The finished ball of dough should have a smooth surface, except for a slight pucker on the bottom.

5. Place rolls 2 in. (5 cm) apart on sheet pans sprinkled with cornmeal.

6. Proof, wash with water, and bake with steam.

A   B   C

Oval Rolls

1. Scale and round the rolls as indicated for round rolls.

2. Roll the rounded units back and forth under the palms of the hands until they become slightly elongated and tapered.

3. Proof and wash with water. Score with one lengthwise cut or three diagonal cuts.

4. Bake with steam.

Split Rolls

1. Round the rolls as for round rolls. Let them rest a few minutes.

2. Dust the tops lightly with rye flour. Using a lightly oiled ¾-in. (2-cm) thick wooden pin, press a crease in the center of each roll.

3. Proof upside down in boxes or on canvas dusted with flour. Turn right-side up and place on pans or peels dusted with cornmeal. Do not score. Bake as for other hard rolls.

Round Loaves and Oval Loaves

These techniques are used for many types of breads, including pain de campagne and French rye. A round loaf is called a *boule*.

For round loaves, like pain de campagne:

1. Flatten the rounded, relaxed dough into a circle. Fold the sides over the center, then round again. Shape the dough into a seam-free ball (a).

2. Place on pans sprinkled with cornmeal or flour. Proof, wash the tops with water, and score the tops in a crosshatch pattern (b, c). Bake with steam.

A   B   C

Canvas-line banneton.

For oval loaves, like French rye:

1. As for round loaves, flatten the rounded, relaxed dough into a circle. Fold the sides over the center, then round again. Roll the dough under the palms of the hands into a smooth oval loaf (a).

2. Place on pans sprinkled with cornmeal or flour (b). Proof, wash the tops with water, and dredge with flour. Score as shown (c).

As an alternative to proofing on pans, proof upside down in special baskets called *bannetons*. Dust the inside of the banneton with flour and push the dough firmly into the basket (d). When the dough is proofed, turn out onto a sheet pan or a peel, score as desired, and slide into the oven.

A   B

C   D

Fougasse

1. Roll out the dough into a large, thin oval, letting it rest at intervals to allow the gluten to relax.
2. Oil a sheet pan with olive oil. Place the dough on the sheet pan and brush the dough well with olive oil (a).
3. Press the fingertips into the dough at regular intervals, as for focaccia (b) (see p. 167).
4. Cut slits in the dough (c). Stretch the dough to open the slits (d).
5. Proof for 30 minutes at room temperature.

A

B

C

D

Soft Roll Doughs, Pan Loaves, and Braided Breads

Tied or Knotted Rolls

1. Scale the dough into presses of desired size. Divide the presses.
2. With the palms of the hands, roll each unit on the workbench into a strip or rope of dough.
3. Tie the rolls as shown below.
4. Place rolls 2 in. (5 cm) apart on greased or paper-lined baking sheets.
5. Proof, egg-wash, and bake without steam.

Single-knot rolls.

Figure-eight rolls.

Double-knot rolls.

Braided rolls.

Sawtooth Rolls

1. Prepare elongated oval rolls.
2. With scissors, cut a row of snips down the tops of the rolls.

Crescent Rolls

1. Make up as for hard crescent rolls, except brush the triangles with melted butter before rolling up.
2. Proof, egg-wash, and sprinkle with poppy seeds. Bake without steam.

Pan Rolls

1. Scale the dough into presses of desired size. Divide.
2. Make up as for round hard rolls.
3. Place on greased pans ½ in. (1 cm) apart.

Parker House Rolls

1. Scale the dough into presses of desired size. Divide.
2. Round the scaled piece of dough (a).
3. Flatten the center of the dough with a narrow rolling pin (b).
4. Fold the dough over and press down on the folded edge to make a crease (c).
5. Place on a greased baking sheet ½ in. (1 cm) apart. The baked rolls have a seam that splits open easily (d).

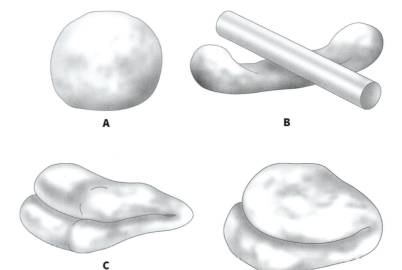

A   **B**

C

D

Butterflake Rolls

1. Roll out the dough into a very thin rectangular shape. Brush it with melted butter. Cut it into strips 1 in. (2.5 cm) wide (a).
2. Stack 6 strips. Cut into 1½-in. (3.5-cm) pieces (b).

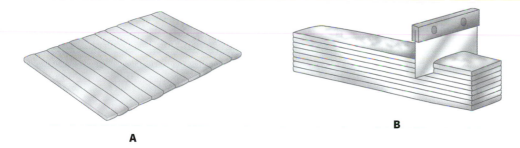

A   **B**

3. Place the pieces on end in greased muffin tins (c). Proof. The baked rolls have a flaky appearance (d).

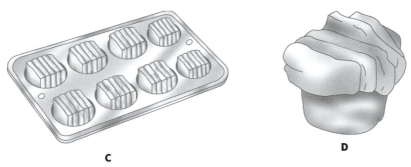

C   **D**

Cloverleaf Rolls

1. Scale the dough into presses of desired size. Divide each piece of dough into 3 equal parts and shape them into balls.

2. Place 3 balls in the bottom of each greased muffin tin (a). The balls merge as they bake to form a cloverleaf shape (b).

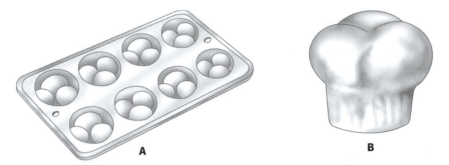

A   B

Pan Loaves

1. Start with the rounded, benched dough (a).

2. Stretch it into a long rectangle (b).

3. Fold into thirds (c, d).

4. Roll the dough into a tight roll that has the same length as the pan it is to be baked in (e). Seal the seam well and place the dough seam-side down in the greased pan.

   For split-top loaves, make one cut from end to end in the top of the loaf after proofing.

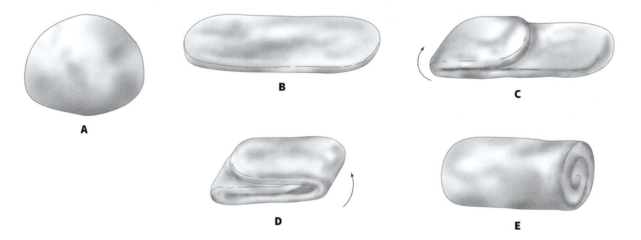

A   B   C   D   E

Pullman Loaf

Pullman loaves are baked in loaf pans with sliding lids so slices from the baked loaf are square, ideal for sandwiches. Pans are usually of standard sizes to make 1-lb (450-g), 1½-lb (675-g), 2-lb (900-g), and 3-lb (1350-g) loaves.

1. Scale the dough to fit the loaf pans. Add an extra 2 oz (50 g) dough per pound (450 g) to allow for baking loss.

2. Make up loaves in one of two ways:
   - Make up as standard pan loaves as in the preceding technique.
   - Divide each scaled unit into 2 pieces. Roll out into strips and twist the 2 strips together. Seal the ends well. This method is preferred by many bakers because it gives extra strength to the loaf structure. The sides of the loaf are less likely to collapse.

3. Place the made-up loaves in lightly greased pans. Put on the lids (greased on the underside), but leave them open about 1 in. (2.5 cm).

4. Proof until the dough has risen almost to the lids.

5. Close the lids. Bake at 400°–425°F (200°–218°C) without steam.

6. Remove the lids after 30 minutes. The bread should be taking on color by this time. If the lid sticks, it may be because the bread requires a few more minutes of baking with the lid. Try again after a few minutes.

7. Complete baking with the lids off to allow moisture to escape.

Braided Loaves

Egg-enriched soft roll dough and challah dough are the most appropriate for braided loaves. The dough should be relatively stiff so the braids hold their shape.

Braids of one to six strands are commonly made. More complicated braids of seven or more strands are not presented here because they are rarely made.

Braided breads are egg-washed after proofing. If desired, they may also be sprinkled with poppy seeds after washing.

ONE-STRAND BRAID

1. Roll the dough into a smooth, straight strip with the palms of the hands. The strip should be of uniform thickness from end to end.

2. Tie or braid the strip as for a braided roll (see p. 146).

TWO-, THREE-, FOUR-, FIVE-, AND SIX-STRAND BRAIDS

1. Divide the dough into equal pieces, depending on how many strips are required.
   For a double three-strand braid, divide the dough into 4 equal pieces, then divide one of these pieces into 3 smaller pieces to yield 3 large and 3 small pieces.

2. Roll the pieces with the palms of the hands into long, smooth strips. The pieces should be thickest in the middle and gradually taper toward the ends.

3. Braid the strips as shown in the illustrations. Please note that the numbers used in these descriptions refer to the positions of the strands (numbered from left to right). At each stage in the braiding, number 1 always indicates the first strand on the left.

Two-Strand Braids

1. Cross the 2 strands in the middle (a).

2. Fold the two ends of the bottom strand over the upper one (b).

3. Now fold the ends of the other strand over in the same way (c).

4. Repeat steps 2 and 3 until the braid is finished (d).

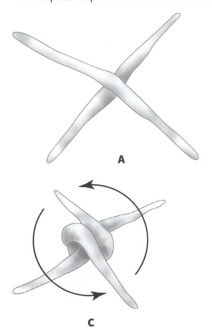

A

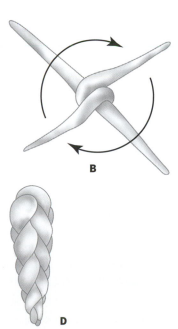

B

C

D

Three-Strand Braids

1. Lay the 3 strands side by side. Starting in the center, fold the left strand over the center one (1 over 2) (a).
2. Now fold the right strand over the center (3 over 2) (b).
3. Repeat the sequence (1 over 2, 3 over 2) (c).
4. When you reach the end of the strands, turn the braid over (d).
5. Braid the other half (e).
6. If desired, a smaller three-strand braid can be placed on top (f).

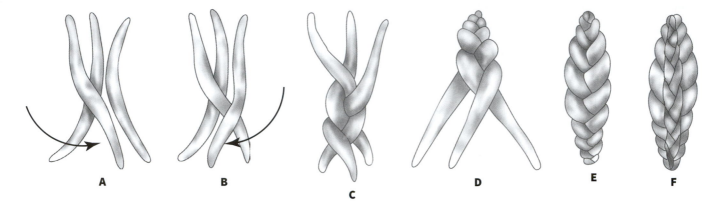

A   B   C   D   E   F

Four-Strand Braids

1. Start with 4 strands, fastened at the end (a).
2. Move 4 over 2 (b).
3. Move 1 over 3 (c).
4. Move 2 over 3 (d).
5. Repeat steps 2, 3, 4 until the braid is finished (e, f).

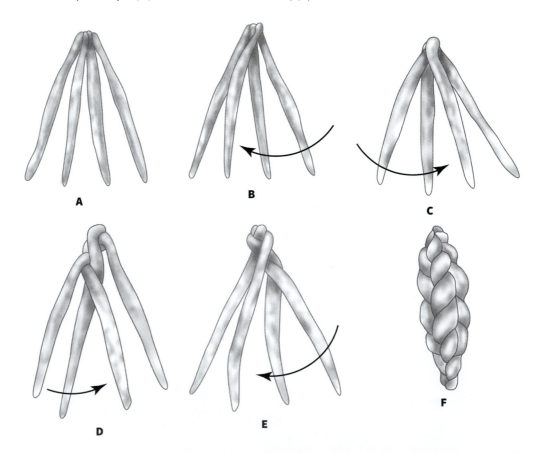

A   B   C   D   E   F

Five-Strand Braids

1. Start with 5 strands, fastened at the end (a).
2. Move 1 over 3 (b).
3. Move 2 over 3 (c).
4. Move 5 over 2 (d).
5. Repeat steps 2, 3, 4 until the braid is finished (e, f).

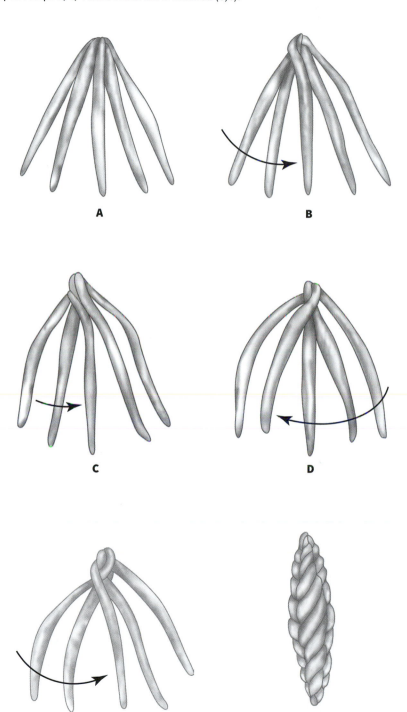

Six-Strand Braids

1. Start with 6 strands, fastened at the end (a).
2. The first step, 6 over 1, is not part of the repeated sequence (b).
3. The repeated sequence begins with 2 over 6 (c).
4. Move 1 over 3 (d).
5. Move 5 over 1 (e).
6. Move 6 over 4 (f).
7. Repeat steps 3 to 6 until the braid is finished (g).

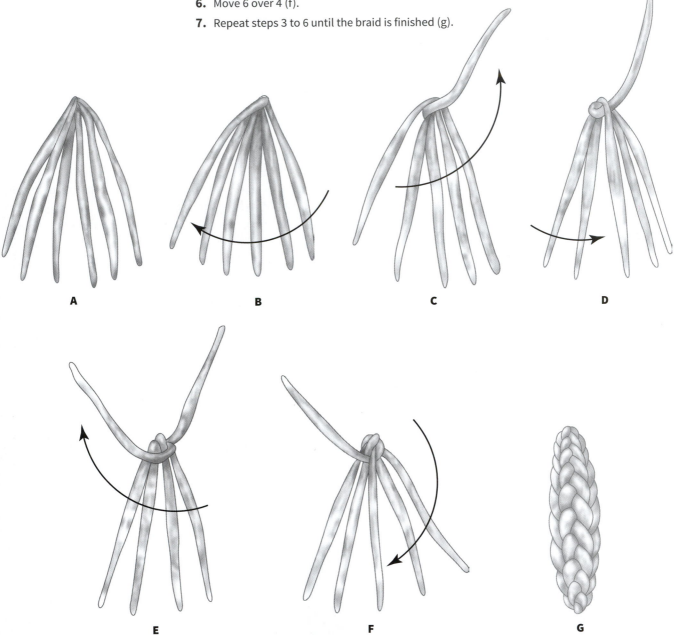

A B C D

E F G

KEY POINTS TO REVIEW

- What are the steps in the procedure to scale and divide dough for rolls using a dough divider?
- What is the procedure for making basic round rolls?
- What is the procedure for making round loaves?
- What is the procedure for making French baguettes?
- What is the procedure for making basic pan loaves?

TERMS FOR REVIEW

straight dough method

short mix

improved mix

intensive mix

short-fermentation
straight dough

no-time dough

gluten window

dough strength

extensibility

elasticity

tenacity

fougasse

French bread

English muffin

bagel

press

pullman loaf

QUESTIONS FOR REVIEW

1. What are the steps in the straight dough mixing method? How is the straight dough method sometimes modified for sweet doughs, and why is this necessary?

2. Explain the differences between the short mix technique, the improved mix technique, and the intensive mix technique.

3. What is the importance of water temperature in mixing yeast doughs?

4. How would the baked loaves be different if you increased the shortening in the French bread formula (p. 128) to 7%?

5. Why is the baking temperature for Italian bread (p. 127) higher than that for challah (p. 132)?

6. How could you modify the formula for Vienna bread (p. 126) if you didn't have any malt?

7. Why is it important not to use too much dusting flour when making up breads and rolls?

8. Describe the procedure for using a dough divider.

9. Describe the procedure for rounding rolls.

10. Describe the procedure for makeup of baguettes.

8

LEAN YEAST DOUGHS: SPONGES, PRE-FERMENTS, AND SOURDOUGHS

AFTER READING THIS CHAPTER, YOU SHOULD BE ABLE TO:

1. Explain the methods for preparing sponge doughs, and prepare sponge doughs and yeast pre-ferments.

2. Prepare and maintain sourdough starters, and use them to mix doughs.

3. Ferment and bake sponge dough and sourdough products.

CONSUMER INTEREST IN flavorful, handmade breads has grown tremendously in recent years. In North America, this has stimulated bakers to research and experiment with traditional European breads in order to offer their customers distinctive, handcrafted products. More and more restaurants are either making their own breads on the premises or purchasing from local bakers who practice baking more as a craft than as an industry. Many fine European bakeries have preserved and practiced these techniques for generations, but to most practitioners in North America, they are new discoveries.

155

In Chapter 7, you learned the basic procedures for producing conventional yeast products of many types, all using the straight-dough method. This chapter introduces the additional complexities of sponge processes and sourdough starters, to enable you to make a greater range of yeast products.

SPONGES AND OTHER YEAST PRE-FERMENTS

SPONGE DOUGHS ARE prepared in two stages. For this reason, the procedure is often called the *sponge-and-dough method*. This procedure gives the yeast action a head start.

The first stage is called a *sponge*, a *yeast starter*, or a *yeast pre-ferment*. All of these terms can mean the same thing (although bakers often reserve the term *sponge* specifically for a yeast pre-ferment with a hydration [water content] of about 60 to 63%).

There are many variations of the *sponge method*, so the steps indicated in the procedure here are general. Variations on the sponge method are discussed in more detail following the basic procedure. The procedure given here, however, will enable you to prepare the conventional sponge doughs in this book.

There are a number of advantages of the sponge mixing method over the straight-dough method:

- Shorter fermentation time for the finished dough.
- Scheduling flexibility. Sponges can usually be held longer than finished dough.
- Increased flavor, developed by the long fermentation of the sponge.
- Stronger fermentation of rich doughs. High sugar and fat content inhibits yeast growth. When the sponge method is used, most of the fermentation is complete before the fat and sugar are incorporated.
- Less yeast is needed, because it multiplies during the sponge fermentation.

A note on the system of baker's percentages (pp. 23–26) is in order here. There are two possible ways to express percentages when using a sponge:

1. Consider the sponge or pre-ferment as a separate formula. Express the flour in the sponge as 100%. Then, in the main formula, express the total weight of the sponge as a percentage of the flour weight in the main formula.

2. Consider the sponge as part of the main formula. Express the flour in the sponge as a percentage of the total flour in the complete formula.

Each method has advantages, and bakers have their own preferences. In this book, both methods are used, depending on the formula, so you can have experience working with each.

Yeast Pre-Ferments

The procedure for the sponge mixing method given on page 157 is useful for a wide variety of bread doughs. To mix the sponge doughs in the first part of the recipe section in this chapter, this method provides all the information you need to mix the dough successfully. To produce a wider variety of artisan breads, however, it is helpful to have more information about the many types of sponges and pre-ferments that have been used.

There are two basic types of pre-ferments: *yeast pre-ferments*, sometimes called *yeast starters*, and *sourdough pre-ferments,* usually called *sourdough starters* or *natural starters*. (Note that some bakers use the term *pre-ferment* only for yeast starters. In this book, we use the term generically for any fermented dough used to provide leavening.) Sourdough starters are similar to yeast pre-ferments except they are made with wild yeasts. As a result, they are handled somewhat differently and are covered in a later section.

PROCEDURE: Sponge Method

1. Combine part or all of the liquid, all of the yeast, and part of the flour (and, sometimes, part of the sugar). Mix into a thick batter or soft dough (a). Let ferment until double in bulk (b).

2. Fold (punch down) and add the rest of the flour and the remaining ingredients. Mix to a uniform, smooth dough.

A

B

Many traditional terms are used for types of pre-ferment. Unfortunately, the terminology is not used consistently. Some of the terms are introduced here, but you may find that various bakers use them in different ways. As artisan breads become more common, these terms will probably become more standardized. Even the word *sponge* is used in different ways. When this text refers to the sponge mixing method, the term *sponge* can indicate any yeast pre-ferment. Other bakers use the word *sponge* only for a specific kind of yeast pre-ferment that has a hydration of around 60%.

Unlike sourdoughs, which can last indefinitely, yeast starters have a limited life and are best made fresh for each new batch of dough. Overfermented yeast pre-ferments should be discarded because a dough made from them will not handle well, and the bread will have undesirable flavors.

When mixing a pre-ferment, keep in mind that developing gluten is not necessary at this stage, so mix only to blend the ingredients into a uniform dough or batter. If the pre-ferment is overmixed, the gluten is likely to become overdeveloped when it is added to the final dough and mixed again.

The most important types of pre-ferments are described in the following sections.

Poolish

This type of starter is said to have originated in Poland, and the word *poolish* comes from "Polish." A poolish (or *poolisch*) is a thin yeast starter made with equal parts flour and water (by weight), plus commercial yeast. In other words, a formula for poolish is 100% flour, 100% water, and varying percentages of yeast, depending on the desired speed of fermentation.

To contribute maximum flavor, a poolish is made with only a small quantity of yeast and given a long fermentation at room temperature. The poolish bubbles up and increases in volume, and when it is at its peak, it starts to fall back slightly and the top surface appears wrinkled. A poolish given a slow fermentation may hold its peak quality for several hours. After this period, the acidity will increase and the quality will deteriorate.

Because of the high level of water in a poolish, the yeast is very active. For this reason, a lower percentage of yeast is used than for drier pre-ferments. A lower quantity of yeast is sufficient to ferment the poolish, creating flavor and developing gluten. However, it is not always enough to leaven the finished dough. Frequently, additional yeast is added to the final dough to boost fermentation. See the discussion of *mixed fermentation* on page 158.

YEAST QUANTITIES AND APPROXIMATE POOLISH FERMENTATION TIMES

QUANTITY OF FRESH YEAST (PERCENT OF FLOUR USED IN POOLISH)	QUANTITY OF INSTANT YEAST (PERCENT OF FLOUR USED IN POOLISH)	APPROXIMATE FERMENTATION TIME AT ROOM TEMPERATURE (65°–68°F OR 18°–20°C)
(3%)	(1%)	(2 hours)*
1.5%	0.5%	4 hours
0.8%	0.28%	8 hours
0.25%	0.08%	12–16 hours

*A 2-hour fermentation is possible, so quantities are given. However, such a short fermentation for a poolish is not recommended if a quality product is desired.

If a shorter fermentation is needed, use more yeast. In this case, however, the starter will be at its peak of quality for a shorter time before it starts to deteriorate. In addition, a short fermentation for the poolish will lose much of the advantage of using a pre-ferment—that is, the flavor improvement given by a long fermentation. See the Yeast Quantities and Approximate Poolish Fermentation Times table for yeast quantities and fermentation times.

Biga

Biga is the Italian term for pre-ferment. Although the word can, in theory, refer to a starter of any consistency, it is usually used for stiff pre-ferments. Stiffer doughs ferment more slowly than wet ones. Therefore, a biga is generally made with more yeast. Use about two times the quantity of yeast as in a poolish to get the same fermentation time.

A typical biga contains 100% flour, 50 to 60% water, and about 0.8 to 1.5% fresh yeast.

Levain-Levure

This is the general French term for yeast pre-ferment. It is usually stiff like a biga, but the term is sometimes used for thin pre-ferments like the poolish as well. The word *levure* means "yeast." Do not confuse *levain-levure* with the word levain alone. *Levain* means "sourdough" or "culture starter," and *pain au levain* means "sourdough bread."

Pre-Fermented Dough or Scrap Dough

Scrap dough is simply a piece of fermented bread dough saved from a previous batch. It is sometimes known as *pâte fermentée* (pot fer mawn TAY), meaning "fermented dough." Saving a piece of fermented dough, preferably in the retarder so it doesn't overferment, is an easy and common way to get the benefits of using a pre-ferment without having to make one separately. Of course, it is also possible to make a batch of bread dough just to use as a pre-ferment.

A lean dough containing only flour, water, yeast, and salt is the best choice for a pre-fermented dough because it can be used in any kind of dough. If the scrap dough contains fat, eggs, or other ingredients, of course it can be used only in bread formulas that contain those ingredients, and so are more limited in their uses.

Because scrap dough is actually bread dough, it differs from other ferments in that it contains salt as well as flour, water, and yeast. The salt slows the fermentation. To balance the salt, a scrap dough contains more yeast than the other types of pre-ferments we have discussed.

Scrap dough can be used in almost any quantity in a dough formula, but the usual amount is around 40 to 50%, based on the total weight of flour in the final dough. For example, if the formula contains 10 pounds flour, 4 to 5 pounds of scrap dough might be added by the baker. Scrap dough should be added to the final dough near the end of mixing time. This is because its gluten is already developed. Other pre-ferments, such as biga and poolish, are added at the beginning of mixing, because their gluten has not been developed.

Mixed Fermentation

When pure pre-ferments like a sponge or biga are used in bread, they may be the only source of leavening. But scrap dough may not be strong enough to ferment the bread on its own in the desired time. Therefore, yeast may be added to the scrap dough when the final bread dough is mixed. In other words, such a bread dough is a straight dough (p. 118) to which scrap dough is added as an ingredient. This method, in which both a pre-ferment and a fresh addition of yeast are used to provide leavening, is sometimes called *mixed fermentation*.

Doughs with other pre-ferments, especially poolish (see above), may also be given added yeast in the finished dough to boost fermentation and shorten the bulk fermentation time. Some sourdoughs are also produced using mixed fermentation—that is, they contain commercial yeast in addition to the sourdough starter.

Autolyse

An extra step during the mixing of the final dough is helpful to create a good gluten structure. This step is called *autolyse* (pronounced auto-lees). To mix a bread dough in this fashion, first combine the flour and water and mix at low speed just until all the flour is moistened and a dough is formed. Turn off the mixer and let stand for 20 to 30 minutes.

During the autolyse, the flour hydrates fully, meaning the water is completely absorbed by the flour's proteins and starches. Also, the enzymes in the dough begin acting on the proteins before they are too stretched by mixing. This improves the gluten structure in the bread, making the finished dough easier to handle and mold. It also improves the texture of the baked bread. Because of the improved gluten structure, mixing time is reduced, meaning less air is mixed into the dough. Therefore, the color and flavor of the bread are improved, because of less oxidation.

Notice that only the flour and water are included in the autolyse. The yeast or starter, the salt, and other ingredients are not added until after this rest period. If the yeast or starter were added to the dough before the autolyse, the yeast action would increase the acidity of the dough, and this acidity would affect dough strength, making the dough less extensible. If the salt were added, it would interfere with water absorption by the gluten proteins and interfere with the action of the enzymes.

After the autolyse period is over, add the remaining ingredients and finish mixing the dough.

YEAST AND AUTOLYSE

According to the text, autolyse should take place without the presence of yeast. Some bakers, however, make exceptions to this rule.

If instant yeast is used, it is sometimes added just before autolyse. This is because the yeast takes time to absorb water. By the time the yeast is fully dissolved, the autolyse period may be mostly over.

Similarly, a poolish that contains a low quantity of yeast is sometimes added before autolyse, because the small amount of yeast is believed to have little effect on the gluten.

KEY POINTS TO REVIEW

▌ What are the steps in the sponge mixing method for yeast doughs?

▌ What are the characteristics of a poolish? A biga? Pre-fermented dough?

▌ What is mixed fermentation?

▌ What is autolyse?

SOURDOUGH STARTERS

FOR PURPOSES OF this discussion, we define a *sourdough* as a dough leavened by a sourdough starter. A *sourdough starter* is a dough or batter that contains wild yeasts and bacteria, has a noticeable acidity as a result of fermentation by these organisms, and is used to leaven other doughs.

Sourdough starter is also called a *natural sour* or *natural starter*. Before commercially prepared yeast was available, bread was started by mixing flour and water and letting this mixture stand until wild yeasts began to ferment it. This starter was then used to leaven bread. A portion of the starter was saved, mixed with more flour and water, and set aside to leaven the next day's bread. This process is still used today.

These starters are "sour" because of the acidity created in the dough during the long fermentation. This acidity affects not only the flavor of the bread but also the texture. The starches and proteins are modified by the acids, resulting in a moister crumb and better keeping qualities. Note that some sourdough cultures produce only a mild acidity, resulting in a bread that does not taste particularly sour (see the following discussion of bacterial fermentation). The term *sourdough*, however, is commonly used for wild cultures of any degree of acidity. Some bakers prefer the terms *levain* (p. 158) or *culture starter* to describe this category, reserving *sourdough* for only those cultures with a strong acidity.

There are two important points to notice in these definitions: the presence of wild yeasts, not commercial yeasts, and the importance of bacteria.

Wild Yeasts

The wild yeasts in sourdough starters are not the same organisms as commercial yeasts. Consequently, they act somewhat differently. Also, different wild yeasts are found in different regions and environments. For example, the wild yeast that gives San Francisco sourdough its distinctive flavor is not the same as wild yeasts found in other parts of the world. If a starter is brought from one region to another, the sour may gradually change character because the yeasts in the new location apparently take over.

Wild yeasts can tolerate more acidity than commercial yeasts. If a dough made with commercial yeast becomes too sour or acidic, the yeast is likely to die, and the resulting bread will have an "off" taste. Wild yeasts used in starters can tolerate and grow in higher levels of acidity.

Although you can approximate sourdough breads using yeast pre-ferments, the complex flavor and moist texture or crumb of a true sourdough can be made only with a true natural starter containing wild yeasts.

Bacterial Fermentation

The second important point is that sourdough starters contain bacteria as well as yeast. The most important of these bacteria belong to a group called **Lactobacilli** (singular form: *Lactobacillus*). Like the yeast, these bacteria ferment some of the sugars in the dough and produce carbon dioxide gas. In addition, they create acids. These acids give sourdough its sourness. As in the case of wild yeasts, the exact strains of bacteria present vary from starter to starter, so each starter has unique characteristics.

Two kinds of acid are created by the bacteria: *lactic acid* and *acetic acid*. Lactic acid is a weak or mild acid. Acetic acid, which is the acid in vinegar, is a strong acid. Getting a good balance of these two acids is an important goal of the baker. The balance of these acids gives the bread its characteristic sourdough flavor. Too much acetic acid in the dough makes the bread taste harsh and vinegary. Lactic acid is necessary to balance the flavor, but if the dough contains only lactic acid and little or no acetic acid, the bread has little sourdough flavor.

The ways in which the baker maintains the starter and controls the fermentation process affect the formation of these two acids.

Starting and Maintaining Natural Starters

As we have said, the microorganisms (yeasts and bacteria) that create sourdough starters differ from place to place. In addition, individual bakers look for different results in their sourdough breads. Thus, the procedures for creating, maintaining, and using natural starters vary considerably. We begin this section with a general explanation of the important factors that should be considered. We then present a general procedure for making a natural starter. Please keep in mind that, until your starter is well established and strong and you have baked breads with consistent quality with this starter, your procedures will be somewhat experimental.

Source of Microorganisms

As you have read, if a flour-and-water dough or batter is left to stand long enough, sooner or later it is likely to start fermenting, either from yeasts and bacteria in the air and environment or from yeasts and bacteria that were already present in the flour. Unfortunately, however, just letting a dough stand, and hoping for the best, is not the ideal way to make a batch of bread. To create a starter, the baker usually looks for a more reliable source of fermentation.

Wild yeasts are naturally present on the surface of fruits and on the surface of whole grains, and these are the most common sources used for creating natural sours. Mixing whole wheat flour or whole-grain rye flour into a batter or dough with water and letting it stand until it ferments is one of the best and most reliable ways of creating a starter. The initial fermentation usually takes at least two or three days. Rye is a good environment for wild yeasts, and starters begun with rye are more likely to be more successful than starters begun with wheat flour only. Whole-grain rye generally contains more of these organisms, but if it is not available, use the darkest rye you can find. Light rye is made from the interior of the grain and contains fewer organisms.

Another popular way to create a sour is to mix a batter or loose dough with regular bread flour (wheat) and bury pieces of fruit (grapes are often used) or vegetable in it until it begins to ferment. Then remove the fruit. Some bakers feel this method is not as good as using rye because grain is the natural environment for the yeasts on rye, whereas the yeasts on fruit are not as well adapted for growing in grain or flour.

Formulas for both types of starter are included in this chapter. Just keep in mind that results will vary, depending on your location.

Refreshing the Starter

After the initial fermentation has begun, the starter must be refreshed, or fed, regularly so the yeasts and bacteria are nourished and will multiply until they are strong enough to ferment a bread dough. Depending on the environment and other factors, this can take several weeks. The yeasts and bacteria must be supplied regularly with fresh food, in the form of wheat flour, so they can grow. The basic procedure is to combine a portion of the fermenting starter with additional flour and water in the correct ratio (see the next section) and again let the mixture ferment.

You can imagine that if you continually add more flour and water to a starter, soon you will have more starter than you can use. For this reason, part of the starter is discarded each time it is refreshed.

Because every starter is different, it is impossible to predict how much time is needed between refreshments. Generally, it may take two days or more at the beginning of the process, but as the yeasts and bacteria multiply, the starter gets stronger and faster-acting. A developed starter is usually refreshed every day, or more often if the temperature is warm.

The starter should always be given a final refreshment before using it in a dough. Starters that have been in storage are not as active and don't work as well for leavening bread.

Flour/Water Ratio in the Starter

Some sourdough starters are stiff doughs, similar to the type of pre-ferment called a *biga* (p. 158). A stiff starter is sometimes referred to by its French name, *levain*. Others are looser batters, with the same consistency as a poolish (p. 157). Thin starters are sometimes called **barms** or **liquid levains**. The two types are handled somewhat differently and yield slightly different results.

A thick, doughlike starter is relatively stable and does not need to be refreshed as often. It can be refrigerated without being refreshed for several days, or even a week. Stiff starters favor the production of both lactic acid and acetic acid. Furthermore, the starter will produce more acetic acid under refrigeration than at room temperature. Often, a baker will retard a stiff starter with the goal of increasing the ratio of acetic to lactic acid.

A thin starter is less stable and must be refreshed more often. It ferments more quickly than a stiff starter and can become strongly acidic in a short time, so it must be monitored carefully. Thin starters favor the production primarily of lactic acid.

The type of starter you choose to make depends on the flavor profile (balance of acids) you would like and on your production schedule. Professional bakeshops can usually manage the demanding feeding schedule of a thin starter. The fact that wet starters ferment more quickly may make them more adaptable to a bakeshop's schedule. Casual or amateur bakers often start with a thin starter because it is easier to mix, but they may find that a stiff starter is easier to maintain in the long run. Production techniques are outlined in the General Procedure for Making a Sourdough Starter (p. 162).

GENERAL PROCEDURE: Making a Sourdough Starter

This is only a general procedure and is, therefore, subject to many variations, as described in the accompanying text.

1. Combine the ingredients for the first stage as directed in the formula. Most starters fall into two groups:

   - Mix together whole rye flour and water (a).

A

   - Or mix together bread flour and water. Add the selected fresh fruit or vegetable.

2. Cover the starter and let stand at room temperature until it begins to ferment. Continue to let ferment until it bubbles up, increases in volume, and then falls back (b). This will probably take two or three days.

B

3. Refresh the starter. Mix together bread flour, water, and all or some of the starter from step 1. Use the quantities or ratios in your formula, or use the following guidelines:

   - A typical stiff starter, or *levain*, may use the following ratio:

Flour	100%
Water	50–60%
Fermented starter	67%

   - A typical thin starter, or *barm*, may use the following ratio:

Flour	100%
Water	100%
Fermented starter	200%

4. Cover and let stand at room temperature until well fermented. It should be sticky and full of bubbles, and it should have increased in volume at least 50% (c). This may take about two days, depending on the room temperature.

C

5. Repeat the refreshment as in step 3.

6. Continue to ferment and refresh as in steps 4 and 5. As the starter becomes stronger and more active, the fermentation will eventually take only one day or less. Once the starter has reached this level of activity, it is ready to use (d). Total time varies greatly, but will average about two weeks.

D

7. After the starter is fully developed, it can be refrigerated to slow its rate of activity and increase the time between refreshments. Do not refrigerate a starter unless it has been refreshed recently, or the yeast may use up its food. Bring a refrigerated starter to room temperature and refresh it again before using it to make bread.

8. The developed starter may be used as is in formulas, or it may be used as a *storage starter*. This means it is a source of leavening that the baker keeps and maintains in storage. To use this storage starter, the baker removes a quantity of it as needed and refreshes this portion of it with the amounts of flour and water specified in an individual bread formula. This starter is then called an *intermediate starter*. For best results, always use either a refreshed starter or an intermediate starter in a bread formula. A storage starter taken from the refrigerator may not be active enough to provide the best fermentation.

FROM FERMENTATION TO BAKING

AFTER YOU HAVE mixed a dough using a pre-ferment, the rest of the 12 basic steps in yeast dough production, beginning with fermentation, continue as they were explained in Chapter 6 and as they are applied to straight doughs in Chapter 7. Review the material in those chapters as necessary before continuing with the bread formulas in this chapter.

Because doughs made with pre-ferments are slightly different from straight doughs, some additional information on the fermentation and baking steps is helpful.

Fermentation

One of the advantages of using pre-ferments is the improvement in flavor and texture resulting from the extended fermentation time. This holds true for the fermentation of the finished bread dough as well. Yeast will ferment at any temperature between 33° and 105°F (1° to 40°C). If the temperature is too low, however, fermentation will be slow and acidity will be produced. On the other hand, a high temperature promotes excessively rapid fermentation and the development of "off" flavors. As you recall from earlier chapters, most production breads are fermented at a temperature of about 77° to 80°F (25° to 27°C).

A lower temperature is preferable for sourdough breads and some breads made with yeast pre-ferments. Before the development of proof boxes, doughs were simply fermented at room temperature. Attempting to duplicate these conditions, artisan bakers may use fermentation temperatures in the range of 72° to 75°F (22° to 24°C). At these slightly cooler temperatures, doughs made with a yeast pre-ferment may take two to three hours to ferment until doubled in bulk.

Sourdoughs ferment more slowly. A sourdough may take eight hours to ferment at these cooler temperatures. Some bakers make sourdoughs at the end of the workday and allow them to ferment overnight. The following morning, they then make up, proof, and bake the loaves.

It is possible to ferment any of these doughs—yeast pre-ferment doughs and sourdoughs—at a still lower temperature of about 68°F (20°C). Keep in mind, however, that the fermentation period will be longer. More acidity will develop because the acid-forming bacteria will be more active than the yeast. This increased acidity may or may not be desirable, depending on the product. You may want to experiment with the results of various fermentation temperatures and times.

Baking

Many of the breads described in this chapter are baked as hearth breads. That is, they are baked directly on the deck or floor of deck or hearth ovens. If you must bake them in rack ovens, it is best to use perforated pans rather than solid pans, because the perforated pans allow for better heat circulation and more even browning of the crust.

Underbaking is a common fault. Most lean hearth breads are best baked in a hot oven preheated to 425° to 450°F (218° to 232°C) until the crust takes on a rich, deep brown color. Use the lower end of this range for large loaves and the hotter temperatures for small products. Small products need a higher temperature so the crust browns sufficiently in the shorter baking time. A well-browned crust has a richer flavor because of the well-caramelized carbohydrates and the browned proteins. Pale golden crusts have a blander flavor. In addition, taking care to bake the bread fully ensures a crisp crust that is less likely to be softened by excessive moisture from the interior of the bread.

Steam should be used for at least the first 15 minutes of baking. Injecting moisture into the oven delays the formation of the crust so the bread can expand fully. Thus, the crust will be thin and crisp rather than thick and hard. The moisture also affects the starches on the surface of the bread, aiding in creating a more attractively browned crust.

The breads in this chapter are formed into loaves and rolls using the makeup techniques described in Chapter 7. They are not repeated in this chapter. Refer to pages 140–152 for makeup methods.

Sponge Doughs and Yeast Pre-Ferments

The formulas in this chapter begin with several basic sponge doughs that are made using the procedure for mixing a yeast dough by the sponge method, described on page 157. Following these are three formulas for general-purpose yeast pre-ferments, one made with wheat flour and two with rye flour. Next are a collection of formulas using yeast pre-ferments. Some of these use

Artisan bread maker at work.

Courtesy of iStockphoto.com.

mixed fermentation (described on p. 158), and some use the pre-ferment as the only source of yeast. When mixed fermentation is used, the formula can be expressed as if it were a straight dough formula, and the separately made starter is one of the ingredients.

KEY POINTS TO REVIEW

▍ Which organisms provide the fermentation of a sourdough starter?

▍ How does a baker start and maintain a sourdough starter?

▍ What precautions should be taken when mixing, handling, and proofing sourdoughs?

▍ What measures should be taken to make sure sourdough breads and other artisan hearth breads are properly baked?

FRENCH BREAD (SPONGE)

For large-quantity measurements, see page 709.

Ingredients	U.S.		Metric	%
Sponge (poolish)				
Bread flour	8	oz	250 g	33
Water	8	oz	250 g	33
Yeast, instant	0.17 oz		5 g	0.7
Malt syrup	0.25 oz		8 g	1
Dough				
Bread flour	1 lb		500 g	67
Water	8	oz	250 g	33
Salt	0.44 oz (2¼ tsp)		13 g	1.75
Total weight:	**2 lb 8**	**oz**	**1276 g**	**169 %**

PROCEDURE

MIXING AND FERMENTATION

Sponge method (p. 157)

Improved mix (See Mixing Times, Fermentation, and Folds table p. 122).

Ferment poolish for 4 hours at 75°F (24°C) or overnight at 65°F (18°C).

See the table on page 122 for final dough fermentation times.

Desired dough temperature: 77°F (25°C)

MAKEUP

See pages 141–145.

PROOFING

80°F (27°C) at 80% humidity

BAKING

425°F (218°C) for loaves; 450°F (230°C) for rolls. Steam for first 10 minutes.

─────────────── **VARIATION** ───────────────

COUNTRY-STYLE FRENCH BREAD

For large-quantity measurements, see page 709.

Use the following proportions of flour and water in the dough stage of the above formula.

Ingredients	U.S.		Metric	%
Clear or bread flour	6	oz	200 g	25
Whole wheat flour	10	oz	300 g	42
Water	8.5 oz		260 g	35

Make up the dough into round loaves.

CIABATTA

For large-quantity measurements, see page 709.

Ingredients	U.S.		Metric	%
Sponge				
Bread flour	1 lb		450 g	67
Water	1 lb	1 oz	480 g	72
Yeast, instant		0.33 oz	9 g	1.33
Virgin olive oil		0.72 oz	20 g	3
Dough				
Salt		0.5 oz	13 g	2
Bread flour	8	oz	220 g	33
Total weight:	**2 lb 10**	**oz**	**1192 g**	**202 %**

PROCEDURE

MIXING

Sponge method

1. Combine the sponge ingredients. Mix to form a soft batter. Beat well for approximately 5 minutes or until the sponge starts to become smooth.

2. Cover and leave at room temperature until doubled in size, approximately 1 hour.

3. Stir down and add the ingredients for the dough. Beat for a few minutes to form a smooth dough, which will be very soft and sticky.

FERMENTATION

Cover and allow to ferment at room temperature until doubled in size, approximately 1 hour. Do not fold.

MAKEUP AND BAKING

1. Flour a work surface well. Handling the fermented dough as little as possible, turn it out onto the work surface and shape into a rectangle (a).

2. Cut the dough into equally sized rectangles the shape and size of the desired loaves (b).

3. Carefully lift the loaves onto parchment-lined sheet pans, handling the dough as little as possible to avoid deflating it (c).

4. Proof at room temperature until the dough doubles in volume.

5. Bake at 425°F (220°C) for about 30 minutes, until golden. Cool on a wire rack.

A

B

C

CIABATTA

The word *ciabatta* (cha BAHT ta) is Italian for "slipper," and indeed the bread resembles a beat-up old house slipper. The bread is made with a very slack dough. Because it is so sticky, it is handled as little as possible and simply deposited on sheet pans without being shaped into loaves. This gives it a very light, open texture.

WHITE PAN BREAD (SPONGE)

For large-quantity measurements, see page 710.

Ingredients	U.S.		Metric	%
Sponge				
Flour	1 lb		500 g	67
Water	11	oz	340 g	45
Yeast, instant	0.2	oz	6 g	0.8
Malt syrup	0.13	oz	4 g	0.5
Dough				
Flour	8	oz	250 g	33
Water	3.5	oz	112 g	15
Salt	0.5	oz	15 g	2
Nonfat milk solids	0.75	oz	22 g	3
Sugar	1.25	oz	38 g	5
Shortening	0.75	oz	22 g	3
Total weight:	**2 lb 10**	**oz**	**1309 g**	**174 %**

PROCEDURE

MIXING AND FERMENTATION

Sponge method (p. 157)

Improved mix (See Mixing Times, Fermentation, and Folds table on p. 122 for mixing and fermentation times.)

Ferment sponge about 4 hours at 75°F (24°C)

Desired dough temperature: 77°F (25°C)

MAKEUP

See page 148. Especially suitable for pullman loaf.

PROOFING

80°F (27°C) at 80% humidity

BAKING

400°F (200°C)

HERB FOCACCIA (SPONGE METHOD)

For large-quantity measurements, see page 713.

Ingredients	U.S.		Metric		%
Sponge					
Flour	8	oz	225	g	29
Water	6	oz	175	g	21
Yeast, instant	0.06	oz	1.6	g	0.2
Flour	1 lb 4	oz	575	g	71
Water	14	oz	400	g	50
Yeast, instant	0.06	oz	1.6	g	0.2
Salt	0.5	oz	15	g	1.75
Olive oil	1	oz	30	g	3.5
Rosemary and salt (see Makeup)					
Total weight:	**3 lb 1**	**oz**	**1423**	**g**	**176** %

PROCEDURE

MIXING AND FERMENTATION

Sponge method (p. 157)

Ferment sponge: 8–16 hours at 70°F (21°C)

Mix dough using short mix technique (see table, p. 122): Reduce fermentation time to 60 minutes. Fold every 15 to 20 minutes.

Desired dough temperature: 77°F (25°C)

MAKEUP AND BAKING

1. Scale at 3 lb (1400 g) for each half-size sheet pan.

2. Oil pans heavily with olive oil.

3. Roll and stretch the dough into a rectangle to fit the pans. Place in the pans (a).

4. Proof until doubled in thickness.

5. Top each unit with 2 oz (60 mL) olive oil (b). With your fingertips, poke holes heavily at regular intervals (c).

6. Top each unit with 2 tbsp (30 mL) fresh rosemary and with coarse salt to taste (d).

7. Bake at 400°F (200°C) for 30 minutes.

A

B

C

D

BASIC YEAST STARTER (BIGA)

For large-quantity measurements, see page 711.

Ingredients	U.S.		Metric		%
Bread flour	15	oz	450	g	100
Water	9	oz	270	g	60
Yeast, instant	0.015	oz	0.5	g	0.1
Total weight:	**1 lb 8**	**oz**	**720**	**g**	**160 %**

PROCEDURE

MIXING

Straight dough method (p. 118). Mix just until a dough forms.

FERMENTATION

12–14 hours at 77°F (25°C) or 18 hours at 70°F (21°C)

RYE STARTER I

For large-quantity measurements, see page 711.

Ingredients	U.S.		Metric		%
Rye flour	1 lb		400	g	100
Yeast, instant	0.08 oz (1 tsp)		2	g	0.5
Water	12	oz	300	g	75
Onion, halved (optional)	1		1		
Total weight:	**1 lb 12**	**oz**	**702**	**g**	**175 %**

PROCEDURE

1. Mix the yeast with the rye flour.
2. Add the water and mix until smooth.
3. Bury the onion in the mix.
4. Let stand 24 hours. Desired temperature: 70°F (21°C)
5. Remove the onion.

RYE STARTER II

For large-quantity measurements, see page 711.

Ingredients	U.S.		Metric		%
Rye flour	1 lb		500	g	100
Water, warm (85–90°F/30–35°C)	1 lb		500	g	100
Yeast, instant	0.08 oz		2.5	g	0.5
Total weight:	**2 lb**		**1002**	**g**	**200 %**

PROCEDURE

1. Mix together all ingredients.
2. Cover and let ferment at room temperature for about 15 hours.

OLD-FASHIONED RYE BREAD

For large-quantity measurements, see page 711.

Ingredients	U.S.		Metric		%
Water	8	oz	200	g	50
Fermented Rye Starter I (p. 168)	9.5	oz	240	g	60
Clear flour	1 lb		400	g	100
Yeast, instant	0.06	oz	1.5	g	0.35
Salt	0.33	oz	8	g	2
Total weight:	**2 lb 1**	**oz**	**849**	**g**	**212 %**
Optional Ingredients					
Caraway seeds	up to 0.25	oz	up to 6 g		up to 1.5
Molasses or malt syrup	up to 0.5	oz	up to 12 g		up to 3
Caramel color	up to 0.25	oz	up to 6 g		up to 1.5

PROCEDURE

MIXING

1. Combine water and starter. Mix to break up the starter.
2. Mix together the flour, yeast, and salt.
3. Add the flour mixture and optional flavoring ingredients to the mixing bowl with the water and starter. Develop the dough 3 minutes at low speed and then 3 minutes at second speed. Do not overmix.

FERMENTATION

30 minutes at 77°F (25°C)

MAKEUP

See pages 141–145. Give only ¾ proof.

BAKING

425°F (218°C) with steam for first 10 minutes.

PUMPERNICKEL BREAD

For large-quantity measurements, see page 712.

Ingredients	U.S.		Metric	%
Water	12	oz	375 g	50
Fermented Rye Starter I (p. 168)	10	oz	315 g	42
Rye meal (pumpernickel)	5	oz	150 g	20
Clear flour	1 lb 3	oz	600 g	80
Yeast, instant	0.12	oz	4 g	0.5
Salt	0.5	oz	15 g	2
Malt syrup	0.25	oz	8 g	1
Molasses	0.5	oz	15 g	2
Caramel color (optional)	0.38	oz	12 g	1.5
Total weight:	**2 lb 15**	**oz**	**1494 g**	**199 %**

PROCEDURE

MIXING

1. Combine the water and starter. Mix to break up the starter.
2. Combine the rye meal, flour, yeast, and salt. Mix to combine.
3. Add the flour mixture, malt, molasses, and color. Develop the dough 3 minutes at low speed and then 2–3 minutes at second speed. Do not overmix.

FERMENTATION

30 minutes at 77°F (25°C)

MAKEUP

See pages 141–145. Give only ¾ proof.

BAKING

425°F (218°C) with steam for first 10 minutes.

FRENCH RYE

For large-quantity measurements, see page 712.

Ingredients	U.S.		Metric	%
Rye Starter II (p. 168)	1 lb 8	oz	750 g	600
Bread flour	4	oz	125 g	100
Salt	0.33	oz	10 g	8
Total weight:	**1 lb 12**	**oz**	**885 g**	**708%**

PROCEDURE

MIXING

1. Place the starter in a mixing bowl. Add the flour and salt.
2. Mix at low speed for 10 minutes. The dough will be soft and somewhat sticky, and therefore a little difficult to handle.

FERMENTATION

30 minutes at warm room temperature

MAKEUP

1. Scale at 14 oz (440 g). Shape into round or slightly oval loaves.
2. Brush or spray with water and dust heavily with flour.
3. Proof 30–60 minutes at 85°F (27°C), or until about double in volume.
4. Score the tops of the loaves.

BAKING

450°F (230°C) with steam, 40–45 minutes

PAIN DE CAMPAGNE (COUNTRY-STYLE BREAD)

For large-quantity measurements, see page 712.

Ingredients	U.S.		Metric	%
Rye Starter II (p. 168)	6	oz	200 g	20
Bread flour	1 lb 8	oz	800 g	80
Rye flour	6	oz	200 g	20
Salt	0.6	oz	20 g	2
Yeast, instant	0.15	oz	5 g	0.5
Water	1 lb 4	oz	650 g	65
Lard or goose fat (optional)	0.6	oz	20 g	2
Total weight:	**3 lb 9**	**oz**	**1895 g**	**189 %**

PROCEDURE

MIXING AND FERMENTATION

Straight dough method (mixed fermentation, pp. 118, 158)

Improved mix (See Mixing Times, Fermentation, and Folds table on p. 122.)

Reduce mixing at second speed to 3 minutes.

Desired dough temperature: 70°F/21°C

MAKEUP

1. Scale at 1 lb 12 oz (950 g). Shape into tight, round loaves.
2. Dust with flour before proofing.
3. Before baking, score in a crosshatch or grid pattern.

BAKING

425°F (218°C) with steam, about 45 minutes

FOUR-GRAIN BREAD

Ingredients	U.S.		Metric	%
Water	1 lb 10	oz	770 g	63
Bread flour	1 lb 4	oz	600 g	49
Rye flour	14	oz	415 g	34
Barley flour	3	oz	85 g	7
Oat flour	4	oz	125 g	10
Yeast, instant	0.16	oz	5 g	0.4
Salt	0.75	oz	24 g	2
Basic Yeast Starter (p. 168) or fermented dough	1 lb		490 g	40
Total weight:	**5 lb 3**	**oz**	**2514 g**	**205 %**

PROCEDURE

MIXING AND FERMENTATION

Straight dough method (p. 118). Sift the flours together before mixing to ensure even distribution.

Improved mix or short mix (For short mix, reduce the yeast quantity to 0.2%. See Mixing Times, Fermentation, and Folds table on p. 122 for mixing and fermentation times.)

Desired dough temperature: 75°F (24°C)

MAKEUP

See pages 144 and 148. Make up as desired for loaf pans or round loaves.

PROOFING

80°F (27°C) at 80% humidity

BAKING

425°F (220°C)

PROSCIUTTO BREAD

For large-quantity measurements, see page 713.

Ingredients	U.S.		Metric		%
Bread flour	1 lb		500	g	100
Water	9	oz	285	g	57
Yeast, instant	0.11	oz	3.5	g	0.7
Salt	0.33	oz	10	g	2
Rendered lard or prosciutto fat	1	oz	30	g	6
Basic Yeast Starter (p. 168) or fermented dough	3.25	oz	100	g	20
Prosciutto, chopped or diced into small pieces	3.25	oz	100	g	20
Total weight:	**2 lb 1**	**oz**	**1028**	**g**	**205 %**

PROCEDURE

MIXING

Straight dough method (mixed fermentation, pp. 118, 158)

1. Mix the water, yeast, flour, salt, and fat 6 minutes at first speed.

2. Add the Basic Yeast Starter and mix another 4 minutes.

3. Add the prosciutto and mix another 1–2 minutes.

FERMENTATION

1 hour at 77°F (25°C)

MAKEUP

Scale at 12–18 oz (360–540 g) or as desired. Shape like long Italian loaves. See page 143.

BAKING

425°F (220°C) with steam

OLIVE BREAD

For large-quantity measurements, see page 713.

Ingredients	U.S.		Metric	%
Bread flour	15	oz	450 g	75
Whole wheat flour	2	oz	60 g	10
Rye flour	3	oz	90 g	15
Yeast, instant	0.1	oz	3 g	0.5
Water	12.5	oz	370 g	62
Salt	0.4	oz	12 g	2
Olive oil	1	oz	30 g	5
Basic Yeast Starter (p. 168) or fermented dough	4	oz	120 g	20
Pitted black olives, whole or halved (see *Note*)	6	oz	180 g	30
Total weight:	**2 lb 12**	**oz**	**1315 g**	**220 %**

NOTE: Use a flavorful brined olive such as Greek kalamata. Do not use canned, water-packed olives, as they have little flavor.

PROCEDURE

MIXING

Straight dough method (mixed fermentation, pp. 118, 158)

1. Mix all the ingredients except the olives 10 minutes at first speed.
2. Add the olives and mix another 4–5 minutes.

FERMENTATION

90 minutes at 75°F (24°C)

MAKEUP

Same as Prosciutto Bread (p. 171)

BAKING

425°F (220°C) with steam

Sourdoughs

This section begins with several formulas for sourdough starters, also called *natural starters*. Following these are formulas for sourdoughs that incorporate these starters. Review the information on sourdoughs (pp. 159–162) as necessary before using these formulas.

True sourdough breads use only a sour starter for leavening. However, it is also possible to use a starter primarily as an ingredient to improve flavor and texture and to rely on additional yeast for leavening. This type of process is a mixed fermentation, which we have already encountered in the previous section. Mixed fermentation can be used with any type of pre-ferment, whether it is a natural starter or yeast starter. When mixed fermentation is used, the formula can be expressed as if it were a straight dough formula, and the separately made starter is one of the ingredients. This section includes an example of a mixed fermentation sourdough, in addition to a number of pure sourdough formulas.

Sourdoughs, especially sour rye doughs, are stickier than regular doughs, so handling the dough and making up loaves requires more skill and practice. Take care not to overmix the dough, and use low speed to avoid damaging the gluten.

Underproof sourdough breads slightly. Proofed units are fragile. Steam should be used in baking to allow the crust to expand without breaking.

BASIC SOURDOUGH STARTER

Yield: 1 lb 10 oz (815 g)

Ingredients	U.S.	Metric	%
Stage 1			
Water, warm	8 oz	250 g	100
Whole rye flour	8 oz	250 g	100
Stage 2			
Bread flour	8 oz	250 g	100
Starter from stage 1	1 lb	500 g	200
Stage 3			
Bread flour	12 oz	375 g	100
Water	6 oz	190 g	50
Starter from stage 2	8 oz	250 g	67
To refresh starter as needed			
Bread flour	12 oz	375 g	100
Water	6 oz	190 g	50
Starter	8 oz	250 g	67

PROCEDURE

1. Combine the water and rye flour and mix together. Place in a nonreactive container (such as stainless steel or plastic) and cover. Let stand at room temperature until the mixture becomes bubbly and fermented and has a noticeable fermented aroma. This should take 2 or 3 days.

2. Mix together the ingredients in stage 2 to make a stiff dough. Cover and let stand until well fermented. This may take 1 or 2 days.

3. Combine the ingredients in stage 3, discarding the leftover starter from the previous step. Mix into a stiff dough. Cover and let stand until the starter has fermented and the volume has increased by about half. This will probably take at least 1 day, possibly longer, depending on conditions and the strength of the wild yeast.

4. Continue to refresh the starter as in step 3 until it is strong enough to double in volume in 8 to 12 hours. The procedure may take about 2 weeks in all. At this point, the starter is ready to use in bread.

5. Refresh the starter at least once a day to keep it healthy and vigorous. If this is not possible, refresh the starter, let it ferment for a few hours, then refrigerate, tightly covered, for up to 1 week. To return the starter to active use, let it come back to room temperature and refresh it at least once before using in bread.

YOGURT SOUR

Ingredients	U.S.	Metric	%
Skim milk	7 oz	225 g	180
Plain yogurt	3 oz	90 g	72
Bread flour	4 oz	125 g	100
Total weight:	**14 oz**	**440 g**	**352%**

PROCEDURE

1. Warm the milk to about 98°F (37°C), or body temperature.

2. Stir in the yogurt.

3. Mix in the flour until smooth.

4. Pour into a sterile container, cover with a damp cloth, then cover tightly with plastic film.

5. Allow to stand in a warm place for 2–5 days, until bubbles form.

APPLE SOUR

Yield: 2 lb (900 g)

Ingredients	U.S.		Metric
Starter			
Whole apple, cored	12	oz	360 g
Sugar	2	oz	60 g
Water	1.33	oz	40 g
First build			
Honey	0.67	oz	20 g
Water, warm	4	oz	120 g
Apple starter (above)	5	oz	160 g
Bread flour (see *Note*)	13	oz	390 g
Second build			
Honey	0.2	oz	6 g
Water, warm	3	oz	85 g
Starter from first build	1 lb 6	oz	650 g
Bread flour	6	oz	195 g

NOTE: For best results, use unbleached organic bread flour.

The total weight is less than the summed weights of the ingredients due to losses from evaporation and from skimming and other mixing losses.

PROCEDURE

1. Leaving the skin on, grate the cored apple.

2. Combine the ingredients for the starter. Cover with a damp cloth and plastic film. Keep in a warm place for 8–10 days.

3. Each day, dampen the cloth, but do not mix the starter. Once the mixture starts to give off gases, it is ready. Remove any crust that may have formed on the surface.

4. For the first build, dissolve the honey in warm water. Mix in the apple starter and mash to a paste. Mix in the flour. Knead by hand 5–10 minutes to form a dough.

5. Place in a clean bowl and cover with a damp cloth and plastic film. Allow to ferment 8–10 hours.

6. Repeat step 3 with the ingredients for the second build.

7. Allow to ferment 5–8 hours. The dough should be well risen.

RUSTIC SOURDOUGH BREAD

Ingredients	U.S.			Metric	%
Bread flour	2 lb	10	oz	1320 g	88
Whole wheat flour		3	oz	90 g	6
Dark rye flour		3	oz	90 g	6
Water	2 lb	0.5	oz	1020 g	68
Basic Sourdough Starter (p. 173), refreshed 8–12 hours earlier		9.5	oz	300 g	20
Salt		1	oz	30 g	2
Total weight:	**5 lb**	**11**	**oz**	**2850 g**	**190%**

PROCEDURE

MIXING

1. Combine all the flours and the water and mix just until combined.

2. Let stand 30 minutes (autolyse).

3. Add the starter and salt. Mix at low speed 5–8 minutes, to develop the dough.

FERMENTATION

Ferment at 75°F (24°C) until almost double in bulk, about 8 hours.

MAKEUP AND PROOFING

1. Scale at 1 lb 12 oz (900 g).

2. Make up into round loaves.

3. Proof until almost double in bulk, about 3–4 hours.

BAKING

425°F (218°C) with steam, 40–45 minutes

VARIATION

Omit the rye flour and whole wheat flour and use instead 100% bread flour. If possible, use a high-extraction, high-ash European-style flour (see sidebar. p. 106). You may need to use slightly less water, depending on the protein content of the flour.

WHITE SOURDOUGH (MIXED FERMENTATION)

Ingredients	U.S.			Metric		%
Starter						
Bread flour		7	oz	210	g	30
Water		3.5	oz	105	g	15
[Basic Sourdough Starter (p. 173)] (see *Note*)		[4.8	oz]	[140	g]	[20]
Dough						
Bread flour	1 lb	1	oz	490	g	70
Instant yeast		0.1	oz	2.8	g	0.4
Water		12.5	oz	364	g	52
Salt		0.5	oz	14	g	2
Total weight:	**2 lb**	**8**	**oz**	**1185**	**g**	**169** %

NOTE: The Basic Sourdough Starter is not included in ingredient weight totals in this formula, since it is subtracted from the starter before the dough is mixed (see Procedure).

PROCEDURE

MIXING AND FERMENTATION

Sponge method (p. 157)

The sponge in this formula is an intermediate pre-ferment (see p. 162). It uses a sourdough starter rather than a commercial yeast. After the starter has fermented, subtract the original weight of starter and set it aside so that it can be refreshed and used again. Add the remaining starter to the dough formula.

Improved mix (See Mixing Times, Fermentation, and Folds table on p. 122 for mixing and fermentation times.)

Desired dough temperature: 75°F (24°C)

MAKEUP

See page 144. Shape into round or oval loaves.

PROOFING

80°F (27°C) at 80% humidity

BAKING

425°F (218°C) with steam for first 10 minutes

FIG HAZELNUT BREAD

Ingredients	U.S.		Metric	%
Bread flour	2 lb	9 oz	1290 g	86
Whole wheat flour		2 oz	60 g	4
Medium or light rye flour		5 oz	150 g	10
Water	1 lb 15	oz	975 g	65
Basic Sourdough Starter (p. 173), refreshed 8–12 hours earlier		12 oz	375 g	25
Salt		1.2 oz	38 g	2.5
Dried figs, diced (see *Note*)	1 lb		500 g	33
Hazelnuts, lightly toasted (see *Note*)		8 oz	250 g	17
Total weight:	**7 lb 4**	**oz**	**3638 g**	**242 %**

NOTE: The quantities of fruit and nuts in this formula makes the dough somewhat difficult to handle. If desired, reduce the quantities of figs and nuts to taste.

--- VARIATION ---

FIG ROLLS

Omit the hazelnuts. Make up into round rolls scaled at 4 oz (125 g) each. Bake at 450°F (232°C).

PROCEDURE

MIXING

1. Combine all the flours and the water and mix just until combined.
2. Let stand 30 minutes (autolyse).
3. Add the starter and salt. Mix at low speed 5–8 minutes to develop the dough.
4. Remove the dough from the mixer to a worktable. Add the figs and nuts and knead in by hand until evenly distributed in the dough.

FERMENTATION

Ferment at 75°F (24°C) until almost double in bulk, about 8 hours.

MAKEUP

1. Scale at 1 lb 8 oz (750 g).
2. Make up into bâtard loaves (thick French-type loaves, p. 143).
3. Proof until almost double in bulk, 3–4 hours.

BAKING

425°F (218°C) with steam, 40–45 minutes

APPLE SOURDOUGH

Yield: 5 lb 10 oz (2400 g)

Ingredients	U.S.		Metric	%
Granny Smith apples	15	oz	450 g	64
Butter	2.5	oz	80 g	11
Cinnamon	0.25	oz	8 g	1
Yeast, active dry	0.25	oz	8 g	1
Water, warm	12	oz	360 g	51
Honey	0.2	oz	6 g	0.85
Salt	0.5	oz	15 g	2
Apple Sour (p. 173)	1 lb 14	oz	900 g	129
Bread flour (see *Note*)	1 lb 2	oz	525 g	75
Rye flour	6	oz	175 g	25
Raisins or dried cranberries	7	oz	200 g	29

NOTE: For best results, use unbleached organic flour for this bread.

The dough yield is less than the summed weights of the ingredients, due mostly to trimming and cooking loss of the apples.

PROCEDURE

MIXING

1. Peel, core, and chop the apples into ¼-in. (5-mm) pieces. Sauté in the butter with the cinnamon until tender. Pour onto a tray and allow to cool.
2. Dissolve the yeast with half of the warm water. Mix to dissolve. Dissolve the honey and salt in the remaining water.
3. Cut the apple sour into pieces and place in the bowl of a mixer fitted with the dough hook.
4. Add the yeast liquid and then the honey, salt, and water, adding slowly to make a smooth paste.
5. Add the flour slowly until a soft dough is formed.
6. Add the sautéed apples and raisins. Mix until combined.
7. Turn out the dough onto a lightly floured work surface and knead gently to form a smooth dough.

FERMENTATION

2½–3 hours at 77°F (25°C)

MAKEUP

1. Scale at 1 lb 6 oz (600 g).
2. Make up into long loaves like Italian or Vienna loaves (p. 143).
3. Allow 2–3 hours for proofing.

BAKING

425°F (220°C) for 20 minutes. Reduce the temperature to 375°F (190°C) for another 20 minutes.

WHOLE WHEAT, RYE, AND NUT SOURDOUGH

Ingredients	U.S.		Metric	%
Sponge				
Yogurt Sour (p. 173)	10	oz	290 g	27
Water, warm	13	oz	375 g	35
Whole wheat flour	12	oz	350 g	32
Dough				
Water	8.5	oz	250 g	23
Yeast, instant	0.35	oz	11 g	1
Salt	0.33	oz	10 g	0.9
Whole wheat flour	11	oz	325 g	30
Rye flour	8	oz	225 g	21
Bread flour	6	oz	180 g	17
Walnuts, chopped and lightly toasted	2.5	oz	70 g	6.5
Pecans, chopped and lightly toasted	2.5	oz	70 g	6.5
Total weight:	**4 lb 10**	**oz**	**2156 g**	**200 %**

VARIATION

The nuts used may be varied—as, for example, all walnuts, all pecans, all hazelnuts, or all almonds. Raisins may be included in addition to the nuts.

PROCEDURE

MIXING

Sponge method (p. 157)

The sponge in this formula is an intermediate pre-ferment (see p. 162). It uses a sourdough starter rather than a commercial yeast.

FERMENTATION

Sponge: 8 hours or overnight at room temperature

Dough: 1 hour at warm room temperature

MAKEUP

1. Scale at 2 lb 4 oz (1050 g) for large loaves, 1 lb 8 oz (700 g) for medium loaves.

2. Shape into round or elongated oval loaves. Spray tops with water and dust heavily with flour. Proof until double in volume.

3. Score tops with desired pattern.

BAKING

425°F (220°C) for 30 minutes. Reduce to 350°F (180°C) until done.

KEY POINTS TO REVIEW

▌ What is autolyse?

▌ What are the preferred temperatures for fermenting typical artisan bread doughs?

▌ What measures are taken to make sure artisan breads are properly baked?

TERMS FOR REVIEW

sponge	biga	mixed fermentation	natural starter
yeast starter	levure	autolyse	*Lactobacilli*
yeast pre-ferment	levain-levure	sourdough	barm
sponge method	levain	sourdough starter	liquid levain
poolish	pâte fermentée	natural sour	

QUESTIONS FOR REVIEW

1. What are the advantages of using a sponge or yeast pre-ferment to make bread doughs?

2. What are the two steps in the basic sponge mixing method?

3. What is the difference between a natural starter and a yeast starter? Describe the source of yeast for each.

4. Describe the kinds of acids that make a sourdough sour. Where do these acids come from?

5. Describe how to mix a bread dough using the technique called *autolyse*.

6. What is the difference between fermenting artisan bread doughs and fermenting conventional bread doughs?

9

RICH YEAST DOUGHS

1. **Produce simple sweet doughs.**
2. **Produce laminated yeast doughs.**
3. **Make up a variety of products using sweet doughs, laminated doughs, and sweet-dough fillings and toppings.**

THIS CHAPTER COMPLETES the study of yeast doughs with a survey of the most important rich yeast doughs. As explained in Chapter 6, rich doughs are those with higher proportions of fat and, sometimes, sugar and eggs as well.

Simple sweet-roll doughs are the easiest of these products to handle. Even these, however, require care, as they are usually softer and stickier than bread doughs. Because their gluten structure is not as strong as that of lean doughs, more care must be taken in proofing and baking sweet dough products.

Laminated doughs, such as those for Danish pastries and croissants, are especially rich in fat because they consist of layers of butter between layers of dough. Like other sweet doughs, these yeast-leavened doughs are often the responsibility of

181

the pastry chef rather than the bread baker. Considerable practice and skill are required for the makeup of fine Danish products.

As in Chapter 7, the dough formulas and makeup techniques covered in this chapter are given in separate sections because each dough can be made up into a great many items. This chapter also includes a selection of fillings and toppings suitable for rich yeast-dough products.

Review Chapters 6, 7, and 8 with respect to the basic mixing methods and other production procedures for yeast doughs.

SWEET DOUGH AND RICH DOUGH FORMULAS

IT IS IMPORTANT to remember that high percentages of fat and sugar in yeast dough inhibit fermentation. For this reason, most of the doughs in this section are mixed by the sponge method so that most of the fermentation can take place before the sugar and fat are added. The major exception is regular sweet dough, or bun dough, which is low enough in fat and sugar to be mixed by the modified straight dough method. The quantity of yeast is also increased. Refer to Chapter 7, pages 188, and Chapter 8, pages 156–157, to review information about these basic mixing methods. For your convenience, the basic steps of the modified straight dough method from Chapter 7 are repeated below.

High levels of fat and eggs make rich doughs very soft. The amount of liquid is reduced to compensate for this. High levels of sugar and fat hinder gluten development, so sweet, nonlaminated doughs are often mixed using the intensive mix technique (pp. 119–120), to produce gluten strength. Be careful not to overmix the dough, however. Likewise, do not let the dough get too warm (due to machine friction). If the dough is warmer than the desired temperature after mixing, refrigerate briefly to cool the dough to the proper temperature.

Rich doughs, because they are so tender, are generally underfermented and underproofed. About three-quarters proof is best for rich doughs. Overproofed units may collapse in baking.

Line bun pans with silicone paper whenever there is danger of sticking. This is especially pertinent for items with fruit fillings or other sugary fillings or toppings.

Note that the recipes in this section exemplify two ways of mixing rich sponge doughs. Rich sweet dough and kugelhopf dough are high in sugar, as is *panettone*, an Italian sweet bread containing dried and candied fruit. To ensure even distribution in the dough, the sugar is creamed with the fat, just as in the modified straight dough method. *Brioche* and *baba* doughs contain relatively little sugar, so this method is not used. The fat is mixed into the dough last.

PROCEDURE: Modified Straight Dough Method

1. If using fresh or active dry yeast, soften the yeast in part of the liquid, using a separate container. If using instant dry yeast, mix it with the flour.
2. Combine the fat, sugar, salt, milk solids, and flavorings and mix until well combined, but do not whip until light.
3. Add the eggs gradually, but as fast as they are absorbed.
4. Add the liquid; mix briefly.
5. Add the flour and yeast. Mix to a smooth dough.

Yeast Selection

When the percentage of sugar is 12% or greater, the preferred yeast to use is *osmotolerant yeast* (see page 78). Regular yeast becomes fairly inactive when sugar quantities are high. Osmotolerant yeast, in contrast, can tolerate high sugar levels.

The formulas in this chapter specify osmotolerant instant yeast whenever the sugar levels are 12% or higher. If osmotolerant yeast is unavailable, multiply the quantity by 1.3 to get the amount of regular instant yeast to substitute. For example, if a formula calls for 0.5 oz osmotolerant yeast, you could substitute 0.65 oz (0.5 × 1.3) regular instant yeast.

Makeup and Baking of Sweet Dough Products

Each of the dough formulas in this chapter can be used for a wide variety of products. Similarly, each makeup method can be applied to more than one dough. As in Chapter 7, makeup methods are grouped together later in the chapter.

From makeup to finished product, take note of a number of techniques especially applicable to rich doughs.

1. **Egg wash.** Unlike lean breads, many sweet, nonlaminated dough products and nearly all laminated dough products are egg-washed before baking to give them a shiny, evenly browned, tender crust.

   For best results, Danish and other laminated dough goods should be egg-washed twice, once immediately after makeup and panning and again just before baking. After makeup, use a pastry brush to coat each item lightly but completely with egg wash. Be careful not to leave a pool of wash around the bottom of the item on the pan. When giving a second wash to the items before baking, remember that they will have been proofed and are more delicate and easily deflated, so brush gently.

2. **Proofing.** For most rich dough goods, keep the proofing temperature at 80°F (27°C) or lower. Too high a proofing temperature can melt the butter in the dough, especially in laminated doughs.

3. **Baking.** As for lean dough goods, some steam is beneficial at the beginning of baking. Because it delays crust formation, steam allows the products to rise more fully while baking and take on a lighter texture. However, too much steam can damage the egg-wash coating on Danish and other sweet dough products, so use less steam than when baking lean breads.

   After baking, allow the items to cool slightly before removing them from pans or handling them. Their structure is still fragile when hot, but becomes stronger as they cool.

KEY POINTS TO REVIEW

▪ What precautions must be taken when fermenting and proofing rich dough products?

▪ What is the preferred yeast for doughs high in sugar?

▪ How are sweet dough products egg-washed?

SWEET ROLL DOUGH

For large-quantity measurements, see page 713.

Ingredients	U.S.		Metric	%
Butter, margarine, or shortening (see *Note*)	4	oz	100 g	20
Sugar	4	oz	100 g	20
Salt	0.4	oz	10 g	2
Nonfat milk solids	1	oz	25 g	5
Eggs	3	oz	75 g	15
Bread flour	1 lb		400 g	80
Cake flour	4	oz	100 g	20
Yeast, instant osmotolerant	0.4	oz	10 g	2
Water	8	oz	200 g	40
Total weight:	**2 lb 8**	**oz**	**1020 g**	**204%**

Note: Any of the fats listed may be used alone or in combination.

PROCEDURE

MIXING AND FERMENTATION

Modified straight dough method (p. 182)

Intensive mix (See the Mixing Times, Fermentation, and Folds table, p. 122, for mixing time. Do not overmix or overheat the dough. Desired dough temperature: 75°F [24°C])

Ferment 45–60 minutes, then retard.

MAKEUP

See Sweet Rolls and Danish Rolls makeup, pages 200–209.

PROOFING

80°F (27°C) at 80% humidity

BAKING

375°F (190°C)

RICH SWEET DOUGH

For large-quantity measurements, see page 714.

Ingredients	U.S.		Metric	%
Milk, scalded and cooled	8	oz	200 g	40
Yeast, instant osmotolerant	0.4	oz	10 g	2
Bread flour	10	oz	250 g	50
Butter	8	oz	200 g	40
Sugar	4	oz	100 g	20
Salt	0.4	oz	10 g	2
Eggs	5	oz	125 g	25
Bread flour	10	oz	250 g	50
Total weight:	**2 lb 13**	**oz**	**1145 g**	**229%**

PROCEDURE

MIXING

Sponge method

Intensive mix (See Mixing Times, Fermentation, and Folds table, p. 122.)

1. Make a sponge with the first 3 ingredients. Ferment until double.

2. Cream butter, sugar, and salt until well blended. Blend in eggs.

3. Add the sponge. Mix to break up the sponge.

4. Add the flour and develop the dough. Mixing time: about 3–4 minutes at first speed and 8 minutes at second speed. Do not overmix or overheat the dough.

Desired dough temperature: 75°F (24°C)

FERMENTATION

40–60 minutes and then retard; or retard immediately. Retarding makes it easier to handle the dough, which is very soft.

VARIATIONS

STOLLEN

For large-quantity measurements, see page 714.

Ingredients	U.S.		Metric	%
Almond extract	0.12 oz (¾ tsp)		2 g	0.5
Lemon rind, grated	0.12 oz (1½ tsp)		2 g	0.5
Vanilla extract	0.12 oz (¾ tsp)		2 g	0.5
Raisins (light, dark, or a mixture)	6	oz	150 g	30
Mixed glacéed fruit	7	oz	175 g	35

Add almond extract, lemon rind, and vanilla extract to the butter and sugar during the blending stage. Knead raisins and mixed glacéed fruit into the dough.

MAKEUP

1. Scale, round, and let rest. Scaling weights may range from 12 oz to 2 lb (350 g to 1 kg), depending on individual needs.

2. With hands or a rolling pin, flatten slightly into an oval shape.

3. Wash the top with butter.

4. Make a crease down the length of the oval about ½ in. (1 cm) off-center. Fold one side (the smaller side) over the other, as though you were making a large, wide Parker House Roll (see p. 147).

5. Give three-quarters proof. Wash the tops with melted butter.

6. Bake at 375°F (190°C).

7. Cool. Dredge heavily with 4X or 6X sugar.

BABKA

For large-quantity measurements, see page 714.

Ingredients	U.S.		Metric	%
Vanilla extract	0.12 oz (¾ tsp)		2 g	0.5
Cardamom	0.06 oz (¾ tsp)		1 g	0.25
Raisins	4	oz	100 g	20

Add vanilla and cardamom to the butter during blending. Knead the raisins into the dough.

MAKEUP

Loaf Coffee Cake (p. 208). May be topped with streusel.

BAKING

350°F (175°C). Be sure to bake thoroughly; underbaked units will have sticky crumbs and may collapse.

KUGELHOPF

Ingredients	U.S.		Metric		%
Milk, scalded and cooled	6	oz	190	g	30
Yeast, instant osmotolerant	0.4	oz	12.5	g	2
Bread flour	6	oz	190	g	30
Butter	8	oz	250	g	40
Sugar	4	oz	125	g	20
Salt	0.4	oz	13	g	2
Eggs	7	oz	220	g	35
Bread flour	14	oz	440	g	70
Raisins	2.5	oz	75	g	12.5
Total weight:	**3**	**lb**	**1515**	**g**	**241** **%**

PROCEDURE

MIXING

Sponge method

Intensive mix (See Mixing Times, Fermentation, and Folds table, p. 122.)

1. Make a sponge with the first 3 ingredients. Ferment until double.

2. Cream the butter, sugar, and salt until well blended. Blend in the eggs.

3. Add the sponge. Mix to break up the sponge.

4. Add the flour and develop the dough. Mixing time: about 3–4 minutes at first speed, 8 minutes at second speed. Do not overmix or overheat the dough. Desired dough temperature: 75°F (24°C). Dough will be very soft and sticky.

5. Carefully blend in the raisins.

FERMENTATION

Needs only 15–20 minutes bench rest before scaling and panning. Or retard immediately.

MAKEUP

1. Heavily butter kugelhopf molds or tube pans.

2. Optional step: Line molds with sliced almonds (which will stick to the buttered sides).

3. Fill molds halfway with dough (each quart of volume requires about 1 lb dough, or each liter requires about 500 g).

4. Give three-quarters proof.

BAKING

375°F (190°C)

Unmold and cool completely. Dust with confectioners' sugar.

HOT CROSS BUNS

For large-quantity measurements, see page 714.

Ingredients	U.S.			Metric	
Sweet Roll Dough (p. 183)	2 lb	8	oz	1250	g
Dried currants		4	oz	125	g
Golden raisins		2	oz	60	g
Mixed candied peel, diced		1	oz	30	g
Ground allspice		0.07 oz (1 tsp)		2.5	g
Total weight:	**2 lb 15**		**oz**	**1467**	**g**

VARIATION

For a more traditional cross on top of the buns, mix together the ingredients for Cross Paste (below) until smooth. Pipe crosses onto the buns after they are proofed but before they are baked.

CROSS PASTE

Ingredients	U.S.		Metric	%
Water	10	oz	300 g	111
Pastry flour or cake flour	9	oz	270 g	100
Shortening	2	oz	60 g	22
Milk powder	1	oz	30 g	11
Baking powder	0.06 oz (⅓ tsp)		2 g	0.7
Salt	0.06 oz (⅓ tsp)		2 g	0.7

PROCEDURE

1. Undermix the Sweet Roll Dough. Mix together the fruits and spice until thoroughly mixed, then work into the dough until well incorporated.
2. See Sweet Roll Dough formula, page 183, for fermentation and baking.

MAKEUP

1. Scale into 2-oz (60-g) units and round.
2. Place on greased or parchment-lined sheet pans, just touching. Egg-wash.
3. After baking, brush with Clear Glaze (p. 194). Pipe Flat Icing (p. 425) into a cross shape on each roll.

BABA/SAVARIN DOUGH

For large-quantity measurements, see page 714.

Ingredients	U.S.		Metric	%
Milk, scalded and cooled	4	oz	120 g	40
Yeast, instant	0.25 oz		8 g	2.5
Bread flour	2.5	oz	75 g	25
Eggs	5	oz	150 g	50
Bread flour	7.5	oz	225 g	75
Sugar	0.25 oz		8 g	2.5
Salt	0.2 oz (1 tsp)		4 g	2
Butter, melted	4	oz	120 g	40
Total weight:	**1 lb 7**	**oz**	**710 g**	**237 %**

VARIATION

Add 25% raisins (10 oz/300 g) to baba dough.

PROCEDURE

MIXING

Sponge method

1. Make a sponge with the first 3 ingredients. Ferment until double.
2. Using the paddle attachment, gradually mix in eggs and then dry ingredients to make a soft dough.
3. Beat in butter a little at a time until it is completely absorbed and the dough is smooth. Dough will be very soft and sticky.

MAKEUP AND BAKING

1. Fill greased molds half full. Average baba molds require about 2 oz (60 g). For savarin molds (ring molds), the following are averages:

5-in. ring: 5–6 oz	13-cm ring: 140–170 g
7-in. ring: 10–12 oz	18-cm ring: 280–340 g
8-in. ring: 14–16 oz	20-cm ring: 400–450 g
10-in. ring: 20–24 oz	25-cm ring: 575–675 g

2. Proof until dough is level with top of mold.
3. Bake at 400°F (200°C).
4. While still warm, soak in Dessert Syrup (p. 254) flavored with rum or kirsch. Drain.
5. Glaze with Apricot Glaze (p. 194). If desired, decorate with candied fruits.

PANETTONE

Ingredients	U.S.		Metric		%
Raisins	1.75 oz		50	g	11
Golden raisins or sultanas	1.75 oz		50	g	11
Mixed candied peel	3.4 oz		100	g	21
Blanched almonds, chopped	1.75 oz		50	g	11
Grated lemon zest	0.1 oz (1¼ tsp)		2.7 g		0.6
Grated orange zest	0.1 oz (1¼ tsp)		2.7 g		0.6
Lemon juice	1.5 oz		40	g	9
Orange juice	1.5 oz		40	g	9
Rum	0.5 oz		13	g	3
Nutmeg	0.04 oz (½ tsp)		1.2 g		0.25
Bread flour	8 oz		235	g	50
Water	6.4 oz		188	g	40
Yeast, instant osmotolerant	0.37 oz		11	g	2.3
Egg yolks	2.7 oz		80	g	17
Salt	0.1 oz (½ tsp)		3.3 g		0.7
Sugar	2.7 oz		80	g	17
Milk solids	0.33 oz		9	g	2
Bread flour	8 oz		235	g	50
Butter, softened	3.2 oz		94	g	20
Total weight:	**2 lb 12**	**oz**	**1285**	**g**	**275** %

PROCEDURE

PREPARE THE MARINATED FRUIT MIXTURE

Combine the raisins, peel, almonds, zest, juice, rum, and nutmeg in a bowl. Cover and allow to marinate several hours; or refrigerate overnight.

MIXING AND FERMENTATION

1. Make a sponge with the first quantity of flour, the milk, and the yeast. Let stand at room temperature for 1 hour.

2. Mix the egg yolks, salt, sugar, and milk powder until well blended.

3. Add the sponge and mix to break it up.

4. Add the last quantity of flour and develop into a dough, about 4–5 minutes at first speed. Do not overdevelop the dough, as it will develop more when the fruit and butter are added.

5. Ferment at room temperature until doubled in size.

6. Drain the marinated fruit. Add the fruit and the butter to the dough, and mix until smooth and well incorporated. Put back into the bowl and let ferment a second time at room temperature until doubled in size.

PAN PREPARATION AND BAKING

1. Have ready a 7-in. (18-cm) paper panettone mold. If such a mold is not available, line the side of a 7-in. (18-cm) buttered cake pan with a double layer of parchment extending about 4½ in. (12 cm) high and tied with a string.

2. Punch down the dough and round it into a smooth ball.

3. Place the dough in the prepared cake tin and press down lightly with the knuckles.

4. Cover and proof at room temperature until doubled in volume.

5. Cut a cross into the top of the dough and brush with melted butter.

6. Bake in a preheated oven at 375°F (190°C). Cover the top of the panettone with foil when golden to prevent excessive browning.

7. Reduce oven temperature to 325°F (160°C). Continue baking until a skewer inserted in the center comes out clean, approximately 1¾–2 hours in all.

8. Remove from the oven and brush with melted butter.

9. Once cold, dust the top with confectioners' sugar, if desired.

BRIOCHE

For large-quantity measurements, see page 714.

Ingredients	U.S.		Metric	%
Milk, scalded and cooled	2	oz	60 g	20
Bread flour	2	oz	60 g	20
Yeast, instant osmotolerant	0.2	oz	6 g	2
Eggs	5	oz	150 g	50
Bread flour	8	oz	240 g	80
Sugar	0.5	oz	15 g	5
Salt	0.2 oz (1 tsp)		6 g	2
Butter, softened (see *Note*)	6	oz	180 g	60
Total weight:	**1 lb 8**	**oz**	**717 g**	**239%**

NOTE: To make the dough less sticky and easier to handle, the butter may be reduced to 50% (5 oz/150 g) or as low as 35% (3.5 oz/105 g). However, the product will not be as rich and delicate.

PROCEDURE

MIXING

Sponge method

1. Make a sponge with the milk, flour, and yeast. Let rise until double.

2. Using the paddle attachment, gradually mix in the eggs and then the dry ingredients to make a soft dough.

3. Beat in the butter a little at a time until it is completely absorbed and the dough is smooth. Dough will be very soft and sticky.

FERMENTATION

1. If the dough will require much handling in makeup, as for small brioche rolls, it is easiest to retard the dough overnight. Making it up while chilled reduces stickiness.

2. If the dough is to be simply deposited in pans, its stickiness and softness will not be problems, so it need not be retarded. Ferment 20 minutes, then scale and pan.

MAKEUP

See Brioches makeup, page 201. Egg-wash after proofing.

BAKING

400°F (200°C) for small rolls; 375°F (190°C) for large units.

LAMINATED DOUGH FORMULAS

LAMINATED OR ROLLED-IN doughs contain many layers of fat sandwiched between layers of dough. These layers create the flakiness you are familiar with in Danish pastry.

In the classic pastry shop, there are two basic rolled-in yeast doughs:

1. *Croissant dough* (also called *Danish pastry dough, croissant-style*) resembles a puff pastry (see Chapter 14) with the addition of yeast. It is based on a dough made of milk, flour, a little sugar, and, of course, yeast. The rolled-in butter gives the dough its flaky texture.

2. *Danish dough, brioche-style*, is a richer dough containing eggs, although it is not as rich in eggs as regular brioche. This dough is also called *brioche feuilletée*, or flaky brioche.

Both these doughs are used in making Danish pastries, although only the first one is generally used for *croissants*. In addition to the classic French recipes for these two pastry doughs, this section includes two formulas similar to those widely used in North American bakeshops.

Unlike nonlaminated sweet doughs, which are often mixed using the intensive method, laminated doughs require much less mixing. This is because the gluten continues to be developed during the rolling-in process. A dough that comes from the mixer fully developed will be overdeveloped by the time the lamination process is completed.

Butter is the preferred fat because of its flavor and melt-in-the-mouth qualities. The highest-quality products use butter for at least part of the rolled-in fat. However, butter is difficult to work because it is hard when cold and soft when a little too warm. Specially formulated shortenings and margarines (called *roll-in compounds*) can be used when lower cost and greater ease of handling are important considerations.

VIENNOISERIE

Viennoiserie (vee en wahz REE), or Viennese pastry, is the general term given to sweet yeast-raised dough goods, both laminated and nonlaminated. Brioche, Danish, and croissants are classic examples of viennoiserie.

ROLLING-IN PROCEDURE: Danish and Croissant Dough

The rolling-in procedure has two major parts: enclosing the fat in the dough, and rolling out and folding the dough to increase the number of layers.

In these doughs, you use a *simple fold*, or three-fold, which means you fold the dough in thirds. Each complete rolling and folding step is called a *turn*. Give Danish dough three turns, resting the dough in the refrigerator for 30 minutes after the first turn to allow the gluten to relax.

After each turn, use the fingertips to press indentations in the dough near the edge—one indentation after the first turn, two after the second, three after the third. This helps you keep track of your production if you have several batches in progress; and it is essential if you have several people working on the same dough.

1. Roll out the dough into a rectangle. Smear softened butter over two-thirds of the dough, leaving a margin around the edges (a, b).

2. Fold the unbuttered third of the dough over the center (c).

3. Fold the remaining third on top (d).

4. Rotate the dough 90 degrees on the countertop. This step is necessary before each rolling-out of the dough so that it is stretched in all directions, not just lengthwise. In addition, always place the more uneven side up before rolling so it will be hidden after folding and the smoother side will be on the outside. Roll out the dough into a long rectangle (e).

5. Fold the dough into thirds by first folding the top third over the center (f).

6. Fold over the remaining third. This is the first turn, or first fold (enclosing the butter doesn't count as a turn). Let the dough rest in the refrigerator 30 minutes to relax the gluten. Repeat this rolling and folding two more times for a total of three turns (g).

CROISSANTS

For large-quantity measurements, see page 715.

Ingredients	U.S.		Metric		%
Milk	8	oz	225	g	57
Sugar	0.5	oz	15	g	4
Salt	0.25	oz	8	g	2
Butter, softened	1.5	oz	40	g	10
Bread flour	14	oz	400	g	100
Yeast, instant	0.2	oz	5.5	g	1.4
Butter	8	oz	225	g	57
Total weight:	**2 lb**		**918**	**g**	**231** %

PROCEDURE

MIXING

Straight dough method

1. Scald the milk and cool to lukewarm.

2. Add the remaining ingredients except the last quantity of butter.

3. Mix into a smooth dough, but do not develop the gluten. Gluten development will take place during rolling-in procedure.

FERMENTATION

1–1½ hours at 75°F (24°C)

Punch down, spread out on a flat pan, and rest in refrigerator or retarder 30 minutes.

ROLLING IN

Incorporate the last amount of butter and give 3 three-folds (see Rolling-in Procedure for Danish and Croissant Dough, p. 189). Rest in retarder overnight.

MAKEUP

See Croissant Dough makeup, page 200.

Proof at 75°F (24°C) and 65% humidity. Egg-wash before baking.

BAKING

400°F (200°C)

THE CROISSANT LEGENDS

Several stories are often told about the origin of the croissant. The most popular of these tales says that the pastry was invented in 1683, in Vienna, to commemorate the defeat of the Turks, who had laid siege to the city. According to the legend, bakers were the first to alert the city to the coming attack because they were working at night while everyone else slept. The crescent shape of the pastry mirrors the crescent on the Turkish flag.

Other stories trace the origin of the croissant to the defeat of a Muslim invasion of France in 732, or to a particular whim of Marie Antoinette in the 1700s. Although all these stories have been disproved long ago, they continue to be told.

What is known is that croissant-shaped pastries and breads have been made in various regions of Europe at least since the thirteenth century. The modern French croissant apparently dates to 1839, with the founding of the Boulangerie Viennoise (Viennese Bakery) in Paris.

DANISH PASTRY

For large-quantity measurements, see page 715.

Ingredients	U.S.		Metric	%
Butter	2.5	oz	62 g	12.5
Sugar	3	oz	75 g	15
Nonfat milk solids	1	oz	25 g	5
Salt	0.4	oz	10 g	2
Cardamom or mace (optional)	0.04 oz (½ tsp)		1 g	0.2
Whole eggs	4	oz	100 g	20
Egg yolks	1	oz	25 g	5
Bread flour	1 lb		400 g	80
Cake flour	4	oz	100 g	20
Yeast, instant osmotolerant	0.4	oz	10 g	2
Water	8	oz	200 g	40
Butter (for rolling in)	10	oz	250 g	50
Total weight:	**3 lb 2**	**oz**	**1258 g**	**251 %**

PROCEDURE

MIXING

Modified straight dough method (p. 182).

1. Develop the dough 3–4 minutes at second speed (see p. 121).
2. Rest in retarder 30 minutes.
3. Roll in last quantity of butter. Give 4 three folds (see Rolling-In Procedure for Danish and Croissant Dough, p. 189).

MAKEUP

See Sweet Rolls and Danish Rolls and Coffee Cakes makeup, pages 201–209.

Proof at 75°F (24°C) with little steam. Egg-wash before baking.

BAKING

375°F (190°C)

MAKEUP OF RICH-DOUGH PRODUCTS

MANY IF NOT most rich-dough products are made with a filling or topping, so preparing fillings is an important part of making sweet rolls, Danish pastry, and croissant-dough products. This section begins with a collection of recipes for fillings and toppings and concludes with makeup for a variety of items.

Fillings and Toppings

The formulas in this section include many of the most popular fillings and toppings for Danish pastry, coffee cakes, and other sweet yeast products. Several of these items, such as cinnamon sugar, streusel topping, almond filling, and clear glaze, are used for many other bakery products, including cakes, cookies, puff pastries, pies, and tarts. However, their primary use is in the production of yeast goods.

Note that many of these and similar fillings are available ready-made from bakery supply houses. For example, good-quality prune, poppy, apricot, and other fruit and nut fillings can be purchased in No. 10 cans.

CINNAMON SUGAR

For large-quantity measurements, see page 715.

Ingredients	U.S.	Metric	Sugar at 100% %
Sugar	8 oz	250 g	100
Cinnamon	0.5 oz (8 tsp)	16 g	6
Total weight:	**8 oz**	**258 g**	**103%**

PROCEDURE

Stir the ingredients together thoroughly.

CLEAR GLAZE

Ingredients	U.S.	Metric	Corn syrup at 100% %
Water	8 oz	250 g	50
Light corn syrup	1 lb	500 g	100
Granulated sugar	8 oz	250 g	50
Total weight:	**2 lb**	**1000 g**	**200%**

PROCEDURE

1. Mix the ingredients together and bring to a boil. Stir until the sugar is completely dissolved.
2. Apply while hot, or reheat before use.

APRICOT GLAZE I

Yield: 1 lb 10 oz (1880 g)

For large-quantity measurements, see page 715.

Ingredients	U.S.		Metric	Fruit at 100% %
Apricots, canned	1 lb		500 g	50
Apples	1 lb		500 g	50
Sugar	1 lb 14	oz	950 g	95
Water	1	oz	25 g	2.5
Sugar	2	oz	50 g	5
Pectin	0.67	oz	20 g	2

PROCEDURE

1. Cut the fruit into small pieces, including the skins and seeds. Place in a heavy saucepan.
2. Add the first quantity of sugar and water. Cook slowly, covered, over medium heat until the fruit is soft.
3. Pass through a food mill into a clean saucepan.
4. Return to pan and bring back to a boil.
5. Mix the second quantity of sugar and pectin together and add to the fruit. Cook another 3–4 minutes.
6. Strain through a chinois, skim, and pour into a plastic container. Cool, then refrigerate.

APRICOT GLAZE II

Yield: 7 oz (220 g)

For large-quantity measurements, see page 715.

Ingredients	U.S.	Metric	Preserves at 100% %
Apricot preserves	8 oz	240 g	100
Water	2 oz	60 g	25

PROCEDURE

1. Combine the preserves and water in a heavy saucepan. Bring to a simmer. Stir and cook until the preserves are melted and well mixed with the water. Simmer until reduced and thickened slightly.
2. Pass the mixture through a fine sieve.
3. Test the mixture by placing a small spoonful on a plate and refrigerating for a few minutes to see if it gels. If necessary, cook down for a few more minutes to make it thicker. Or, if it is too thick, add more water.

STREUSEL OR CRUMB TOPPING

For large-quantity measurements, see page 715.

Ingredients	U.S.		Metric	%
Butter and/or shortening	4	oz	125 g	50
Granulated sugar	2.5	oz	75 g	30
Brown sugar	2	oz	60 g	25
Salt	0.04 oz (¼ tsp)		1 g	0.5
Cinnamon or mace	0.02–0.04 oz (¼–½ tsp)		0.6–1 g	0.25–0.5
Pastry flour	8	oz	250 g	100
Total weight:	**1 lb**		**514 g**	**206 %**

PROCEDURE

Rub all ingredients together until the fat is thoroughly blended in and the mixture appears crumbly.

— VARIATION —

NUT STREUSEL

Add 25% chopped nuts (2 oz/60 g).

LEMON CHEESE FILLING

For large-quantity measurements, see page 715.

Ingredients	U.S.		Metric	Cheese at 100% %
Cream cheese	5	oz	150 g	100
Sugar	1	oz	30 g	20
Grated lemon zest	0.1 oz (1¼ tsp)		3 g	2
Total weight:	**6**	**oz**	**183 g**	**122%**

PROCEDURE

Mix together the cheese, sugar, and zest until well blended.

DATE, PRUNE, OR APRICOT FILLING

Yield: 1 lb 8 oz (750 g)

For large-quantity measurements, see page 716.

Ingredients	U.S.	Metric	Fruit at 100% %
Dates, prunes (pitted), or dried apricots	1 lb	500 g	100
Sugar	3 oz	100 g	20
Water	8 oz	250 g	50

PROCEDURE

1. Pass the fruit through a grinder.

2. Combine all ingredients in a saucepan. Bring to a boil. Simmer and stir until thick and smooth, about 10 minutes.

3. Cool before using.

— VARIATIONS —

1. Flavor date or prune filling with lemon and/or cinnamon.   2. Add 12.5% (8 oz/250 g) chopped walnuts to date or prune filling.

ALMOND FILLING I (FRANGIPANE)

For large-quantity measurements, see page 716.

Ingredients	U.S.	Metric	Almond paste at 100% %
Almond paste	8 oz	250 g	100
Sugar	8 oz	250 g	100
Butter and/or shortening	4 oz	125 g	50
Pastry or cake flour	2 oz	62 g	25
Eggs	2 oz	62 g	25
Total weight:	**1 lb 8 oz**	**750 g**	**300%**

PROCEDURE

1. With the paddle attachment, mix the almond paste and sugar at low speed until evenly mixed.
2. Mix in the fat and flour until smooth.
3. Beat in the eggs, a little at a time, until smooth.

ALMOND FILLING II (FRANGIPANE)

Ingredients	U.S.	Metric	Almond paste at 100% %
Almond paste	8 oz	200 g	100
Sugar	1 oz	25 g	12.5
Butter	4 oz	100 g	50
Cake flour	1 oz	25 g	12.5
Eggs	4 oz	100 g	50
Total weight:	**1 lb 2 oz**	**450 g**	**225%**

PROCEDURE

1. With the paddle attachment, mix the almond paste and sugar at low speed until evenly blended.
2. Blend in the butter.
3. Blend in the flour.
4. Blend in the eggs until smooth.

ALMOND CREAM (CRÈME D'AMANDE)

For large-quantity measurements, see page 716.

Ingredients	U.S.		Metric
Butter	3	oz	90 g
Fine granulated sugar	3	oz	90 g
Grated lemon zest	0.03 oz (⅜ tsp)		1 g
Whole egg	1.67 oz (1 egg)		50 g
Egg yolk	0.67 oz (1 yolk)		20 g
Vanilla extract	2	drops	2 drops
Powdered almonds	3	oz	90 g
Cake flour	1	oz	30 g
Total weight:	**12**	**oz**	**371 g**

PROCEDURE

1. Cream together the butter, sugar, and zest until pale and light.
2. Add the eggs, egg yolks, and vanilla a little at a time, beating well after each addition.
3. Stir in the powdered almonds and flour.

FRANGIPANE

The term *frangipane* is given to a variety of almond-flavored fillings. In classical French pastry, it generally refers to a filling consisting of two parts (by weight) Almond Cream Filling (see recipe) mixed with one part Pastry Cream (p. 263). Today, however, many almond filling formulas, such as the ones on page 196, are referred to as frangipane. Almond paste is widely used in place of powdered almonds.

The name Frangipane can be traced back to a noble Italian family who, in the eleventh century, took it from the phrase *frangere il pane*, or "break the bread." In the early 1600s, one member of this family was appointed perfumer for Louis XIII of France. *Frangipani* also refers to a fragrant tropical tree.

LEMON FILLING

Ingredients	U.S.	Metric	Pie Filling at 100% %
Lemon Pie Filling (p. 300)	1 lb	500 g	100
Cake crumbs (yellow or white)	8 oz	250 g	50
Lemon juice	2 oz	62 g	12.5
Total weight:	**1 lb 10 oz**	**812 g**	**162** %

PROCEDURE

Mix the ingredients together until smooth.

APPLE COMPOTE FILLING

Yield: About 1 lb (500 g), or 9 oz (275 g) drained

For large-quantity measurements, see page 716.

Ingredients	U.S.	Metric	Apple at 100% %
Apples, peeled and cored	9 oz	275 g	100
Butter	2.5 oz	75 g	27
Sugar	4 oz	120 g	44
Water	2 oz	60 g	22

PROCEDURE

1. Cut the apples into ¼-in. (5–6-mm) dice.
2. Combine all ingredients. Simmer, covered, over low heat about 15 minutes, until the apples are tender but still hold their shape.

CINNAMON RAISIN FILLING

For large-quantity measurements, see page 716.

Ingredients	U.S.	Metric	Almonds at 100% %
Powdered almonds	3.5 oz	100 g	100
Sugar	2 oz	60 g	60
Maple syrup	1 oz	30 g	30
Egg whites	2 oz	60 g	60
Cinnamon	0.33 oz	10 g	10
Raisins, golden	1.67 oz	50 g	50
Total weight:	**10.5 oz**	**310 g**	**310%**

PROCEDURE

1. Using a wire whip (if mixing by hand) or the paddle attachment (if mixing by machine), stir together the almonds, sugar, syrup, egg whites, and cinnamon until smooth.
2. The raisins may be mixed in at this point. For more even distribution, however, sprinkle them evenly over the filling after it has been spread.

PECAN MAPLE FILLING

For large-quantity measurements, see page 716.

Ingredients	U.S.	Metric	Hazelnuts at 100% %
Powdered hazelnuts	3.5 oz	100 g	100
Sugar	2 oz	60 g	60
Egg whites	2 oz	60 g	60
Maple syrup	1 oz	30 g	30
Pecans, finely sliced or chopped	2 oz	60 g	60
Total weight:	**10 oz**	**310 g**	**310%**

PROCEDURE

Mix all ingredients together.

CHEESE FILLING

Ingredients	U.S.	Metric	Cheese at 100% %
Baker's cheese	1 lb	500 g	100
Sugar	5 oz	150 g	30
Salt	0.12 oz	4 g	0.7
Eggs	3 oz	100 g	20
Butter and/or shortening, softened	3 oz	100 g	20
Vanilla	0.25 oz	8 g	1.5
Grated lemon zest (optional)	0.12 oz (1½ tsp)	4 g	0.7
Cake flour	1.5 oz	50 g	10
Milk	3–5 oz	100–150 g	20–30
Raisins (optional)	4 oz	125 g	25
Total weight:	**2 lb to 2 lb 6 oz**	**1016 g to 1191 g**	**202% to 237 %**

PROCEDURE

1. Using the paddle attachment, cream the cheese, sugar, and salt until smooth.

2. Add the eggs, fat, vanilla, and zest. Blend in.

3. Add the flour. Blend just until absorbed. Add the milk a little at a time, adding just enough to bring the mixture to a smooth, spreadable consistency.

4. Stir in the raisins, if desired.

HAZELNUT FILLING

For large-quantity measurements, see page 716.

Ingredients	U.S.	Metric	Nuts at 100% %
Hazelnuts, toasted and ground	4 oz	125 g	100
Sugar	8 oz	250 g	200
Cinnamon	0.12 oz (2 tsp)	4 g	3
Eggs	1.5 oz	50 g	37.5
Cake crumbs (yellow or white)	8 oz	250 g	200
Milk	4–8 oz	125–250 g	100–200
Total weight:	**1 lb 9 oz to 1 lb 13 oz**	**804 g to 929 g**	**640% to 740 %**

PROCEDURE

1. Blend together all ingredients except milk.

2. Mix in enough milk to bring the mixture to a spreadable consistency.

POPPY SEED FILLING

Ingredients	U.S.		Metric	Poppy seeds at 100% %
Poppy seeds	8	oz	200 g	100
Water	4	oz	100 g	50
Butter, softened	3	oz	75 g	38
Honey	2	oz	50 g	25
Sugar	3	oz	75 g	38
Cake crumbs (yellow or white)	8	oz	200 g	100
Eggs	1.5	oz	40 g	19
Lemon zest, grated	0.12 (1½ tsp)	oz	3 g	1.5
Cinnamon	0.06	oz	1 g	0.75
Water	as needed		as needed	
Total weight: or more, depending on amount of water added	**1 lb 13**	**oz**	**744 g**	**372 %**

PROCEDURE

1. Soak the seeds in the water overnight. Grind to a paste.
2. Add the remaining ingredients and blend until smooth.
3. Add water as needed to bring to a spreadable consistency.

CHOCOLATE FILLING

For large-quantity measurements, see page 716.

Ingredients	U.S.		Metric	Cake crumbs at 100% %
Sugar	4	oz	100 g	33
Cocoa	1.25	oz	40 g	12
Cake crumbs (preferably chocolate)	12	oz	300 g	100
Eggs	1	oz	25 g	8
Butter, melted	1.25	oz	40 g	12
Vanilla	0.25	oz	6 g	2
Water (as needed)	3	oz	75 g	25
Total weight:	**1 lb 6**	**oz**	**586 g**	**192%**

PROCEDURE

1. Sift together the sugar and cocoa.
2. Mix in the cake crumbs.
3. Add the eggs, butter, vanilla, and a little of the water. Blend in. Add enough additional water to bring to a smooth, spreadable consistency.

— **VARIATION** —

Mix 50% (6 oz/150 g) miniature chocolate chips into the filling.

HONEY PAN GLAZE (FOR CARAMEL ROLLS)

For large-quantity measurements, see page 717.

Ingredients	U.S.		Metric	Brown sugar at 100% %
Brown sugar	10	oz	25 g	100
Butter, margarine, or shortening	4	oz	100 g	40
Honey	2.5	oz	60 g	25
Corn syrup (or malt syrup)	2.5	oz	60 g	25
Water, as needed	1	oz	25 g	10
Total weight:	**1 lb 4**	**oz**	**270 g**	**200%**

PROCEDURE

1. Cream together the sugar, fat, honey, and corn syrup.
2. Add enough water to bring the mixture to a spreadable consistency.

A

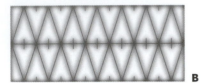

B

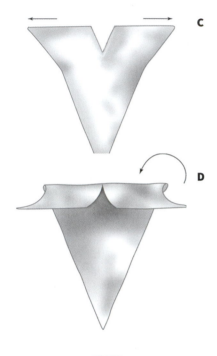

C

D

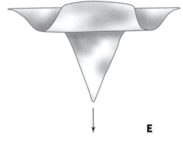

E

F

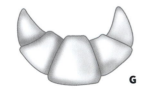

G

Makeup Techniques

Just as for lean doughs, the object of rich dough makeup is to shape the dough into items that bake properly and have an attractive appearance. Most of the guidelines for making up lean yeast breads also hold true for rich doughs. In particular, review the use of dusting flour, discussed on page 140.

While lean doughs usually can be handled vigorously, rich doughs require a lighter touch. Temperature control, too, is important when handling rolled-in doughs, to ensure the butter is neither too hard nor too soft and that the dough does not become overproofed while you are making it up. Study the procedures for these doughs carefully.

Many sweet dough products, including most Danish pastries, are finished with a clear glaze or apricot glaze after baking, preferably while they are still slightly warm. After cooling, they may also be decorated with Flat Icing (p. 425). Note that flat icing is drizzled over the products; it doesn't cover them completely.

Croissant Dough

Plain Croissants

1. Roll out the dough into a rectangle 10 in. (25 cm) wide and about ⅛ in. (3 mm) thick. The length will depend on the amount of dough used (a).
2. Cut the rectangle into triangles (b). (Special roller cutters that do this quickly are available.) Cut a small slit in the base of the rectangle, as in the illustration (b).
3. Place one of the triangles on the bench in front of you. Stretch the back corners outward slightly, as shown by the arrows (c).
4. Begin to roll the dough toward the point (d).
5. Stretch the point of the triangle slightly as you roll it up (e).
6. Finish rolling the dough (f).
7. Bend the roll into a crescent shape. The point of the triangle must face the inside of the crescent and be tucked under the roll so it won't pop up during baking (g).

Filled Croissants

Make up as for plain croissants, except place a small amount of desired filling on the base of each triangle before rolling up.

The technique used for petits pains au chocolat (which follows) can also be used to create filled croissant-dough products with a variety of fillings. These rolls are often called *croissants*, but this use of the term is not accurate because the rolls are not crescent shaped (*croissant* is French for "crescent").

Petits Pains au Chocolat (Chocolate Rolls)

1. Roll out croissant dough into a sheet, as for croissants.
2. Cut into rectangles 6 × 4 in. (15 × 10 cm).
3. Arrange a row of chocolate chips, or, preferably, special pain-au-chocolat bars, about 1½ in. (4 cm) from the narrow end of each rectangle. Use ⅓ oz (10 g) chocolate per roll.
4. Egg-wash the opposite end of each rectangle so the rolls will seal.
5. Roll the dough tightly around the chocolate.
6. Proof, egg-wash, and bake, as for croissants.

Brioche

The traditional brioche shape, called *brioche à tête*, is shown here. Brioches may also be baked as simple round rolls or as pan loaves in many sizes and shapes.

1. For a small brioche, roll the dough into a round piece (a).

2. Using the edge of the hand, pinch off about one-fourth of the dough without detaching it. Roll the dough on the bench so both parts are round (b).

3. Place the dough in the tin, large end first. With the fingertips, press the small ball into the larger one (c).

4. For a large brioche, separate the two parts of the dough. Place the large ball in the tin and make a hole in the center. Form the smaller ball into a pear shape and fit it into the hole (d). The baked loaf has the traditional brioche shape (e).

A

B

C

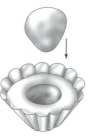

D

E

Sweet Rolls and Danish Rolls

Many sweet dough products, including most Danish products, are finished with Clear Glaze (p. 194) after baking, while still warm. After cooling, they may also be decorated with Flat Icing (p. 425). Note that flat icing is drizzled over the products; it doesn't cover them completely.

Crumb Buns

1. With a rolling pin, roll out sweet dough about ½-in. (12-mm) thick.

2. Cut into 2-in. (5-cm) squares.

3. Arrange the squares in rows on paper-lined sheet pans so they touch each other.

4. Brush with egg wash or milk.

5. Sprinkle the tops heavily with Streusel Topping (p. 195).

6. Proof. Bake at 400°F (200°C).

7. When the buns are cool, they may be dusted lightly with 6X sugar.

Filled Buns

1. Scale the sweet dough into presses of the desired size. (Suggested size: 3 lb (1400 g) for 36 rolls.) Round the presses, relax, and divide.

2. Round the units and place them on paper-lined sheet pans in one of two ways:

   - Place them 2 in. (5 cm) apart so they bake without touching.
   - Place them in rows so they are just touching. Rolls baked in this way will rise higher and must be broken apart before being served.

3. Give the rolls a half proof.

4. Using either the fingers or a small, round object, press a round 1-in. (2.5-cm) indentation in the center of each roll.

5. Egg-wash the tops of the rolls.

6. Fill the centers with desired filling, using about ½ oz (15 g) per roll.

7. Continue proofing to about three-quarters proof. Bake at 400°F (200°C).

8. When cool, drizzle Flat Icing (p. 425) over the rolls.

Cinnamon Raisin Rolls

1. Prepare Cinnamon Raisin Filling (p. 197), leaving the raisins separate for now; you will need 1 small batch, or about 10 oz (300 g), for each unit of dough, as scaled in step 2.

2. Scale Danish Pastry Dough (Brioche-Style) (p. 191) or Danish Pastry (p. 193) into 22-oz (615-g) units. Roll out each unit into a rectangle 20 × 10 in. (50 × 25 cm). For the neatest results, roll slightly larger and trim to size with a knife or pastry wheel.

3. Spread the filling evenly over the dough with a palette knife, sprinkling the raisins over the dough after the filling has been spread. Leave a narrow band of dough uncovered along the top edge (a).

4. Roll up tightly from the bottom edge into a cylinder 20 in. (50 cm) long (b).

5. Cut into 8 slices 2½ in. (6 cm) thick (c).

6. Place on a baking sheet lined with parchment and tuck the loose edge of the roll underneath. With the palm of the hand, flatten each roll to about 1 in. (2.5 cm) thick (d).

7. Proof for 25 minutes at 85°F (30°C).

8. Bake at 350°F (180°C) for 15 minutes.

9. Brush with clear glaze or apricot glaze when cool.

A

B

C

D

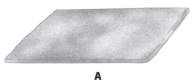
A

B

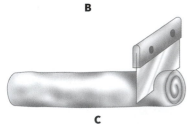
C

Cinnamon Rolls

1. Scale sweet dough into 20-oz (570-g) units or as desired. On a floured bench, roll each piece of dough into a 9 × 12-in. rectangle about ¼-in. thick (23 × 30 × 0.5 cm). Brush off excess flour.

2. Brush with butter and sprinkle with 2 oz (60 g) cinnamon sugar (a).

3. Roll up like a jelly roll 12 in. (30 cm) long (b).

4. Cut into 1-in. (2.5-cm) rolls (c).

5. Place cut side down in greased muffin tins or on greased sheet pans. One full-size 18 × 26-in. (46 × 66-cm) pan holds 48 rolls arranged in 6 rows of 8.

Pecan Maple Rolls

1. Prepare Pecan Maple Filling (p. 198); you will need 1 small batch, or about 10 oz (300 g), for each unit of dough, as scaled in step 2.

2. Scale Danish Pastry Dough (Brioche-Style) (p. 191) or Danish Pastry (p. 193) into 22-oz (615-g) units. Roll out each unit into a rectangle 20 × 10 in. (50 × 25 cm). For the neatest results, roll slightly larger and trim to size with a knife or pastry wheel.

3. Spread the filling evenly over the dough with a palette knife. Leave a narrow band of dough uncovered along the top edge (a).

4. Roll up from the bottom edge into a cylinder 20 in. (50 cm) long (b).

5. Cut into 20 slices 2 in. (5 cm) thick.

6. Butter and sugar 10 small brioche molds.

7. Place 1 slice of the dough roll, cut side up, in each mold, tucking the loose end of the roll underneath. Press lightly into molds (c).

8. Egg-wash the tops.

9. Proof for 25 minutes at 85°F (30°C).

10. Egg-wash a second time.

11. Bake at 350°F (180°C) for 20 minutes.

12. Brush with clear glaze when cool.

Caramel Rolls

1. Prepare like cinnamon rolls.

2. Before panning, spread the bottoms of the pans with Honey Pan Glaze (p. 199). Use about 1 oz (30 g) per roll.

Caramel Nut Rolls or Pecan Rolls

Prepare like caramel rolls, but sprinkle the pan glaze with chopped nuts or pecan halves before placing the rolls in the pans.

Danish Spirals

1. Roll out Danish dough into a rectangle, as for cinnamon rolls. The width of the roll may vary, depending on the desired size of the finished units. A wider rectangle will produce a thicker roll and, therefore, larger finished units.

2. Spread or sprinkle the rectangle with the desired filling. For example:

   Butter, cinnamon sugar, chopped nuts, and cake crumbs

   Butter, cinnamon sugar, and raisins

   Almond filling

   Prune filling

   Chocolate filling

   Note: Loose fillings, such as chopped nuts, should be pressed on gently with a rolling pin.

3. Roll up like a jelly roll.

4. Slice to desired size.

5. Place the rolls on paper-lined pans and tuck the loose ends underneath.

6. Proof, egg-wash, and bake at 400°F (200°C).

Clockwise from top left: pecan maple rolls, cinnamon raisin rolls, lemon cheese pastries.

Variations Made from Filled Dough Roll or Danish Spiral

The filled dough roll is the starting point for a variety of sweet dough and Danish products.

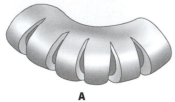

A

1. *Filled Spirals.* Make up like Danish Spirals, above. Give half proof, then press an indentation in the center and fill with desired filling. Complete the proof and bake as above.

2. *Combs and Bear Claws.* Make the Danish Spiral roll thinner, and cut it into longer pieces. Flatten the pieces slightly and cut partway through each in three to five places. Leave straight or bend into a curve to open the cuts (a).

3. *Figure-Eight Rolls.* Cut the Danish spiral rolls almost through. Open them up and lay them flat on the baking sheet (b).

4. *Three-Leaf Rolls.* Cut Danish spiral pieces in two places and spread the three segments apart (c).

5. *Butterfly Rolls.* Cut off slightly larger pieces from the Danish spiral rolls. Crease them by pressing the center firmly with a wooden rod (d).

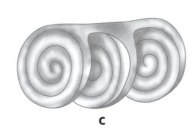

B　　　　**C**　　　　**D**

Filled Danish Crescents

Make up like filled croissants (p. 200).

Danish Twists or Snails

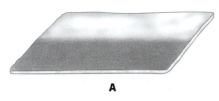

A

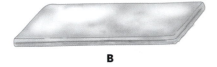

B

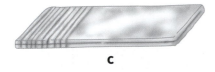

C

1. Roll out the dough into a rectangle 16 in. (40 cm) wide and less than ¼ in. (5 mm) thick. (The length of the rectangle will depend on the quantity of dough.) Brush the dough with melted butter. Sprinkle half of it with cinnamon sugar (a).

2. Fold the unsugared half over the sugared half. You now have a rectangle 8 in. (20 cm) wide. Roll the dough very gently with a rolling pin to press the layers together (b).

3. Cut the dough into strips ½ in. (1 cm) wide (c).

4. Place one strip crosswise in front of you on the bench (d).

5. With the palms of your hands on the ends of the strip, roll one end toward you and the other end away from you, so the strip twists. Stretch the strip slightly as you twist it (e).

6. Curl the strip into a spiral shape on the baking sheet. Tuck the end underneath and pinch it against the roll to seal it in place (f). If desired, press a hollow in the center of the roll and place a spoonful of filling in it.

D　　　　**E**　　　　**F**

Lemon Cheese Pastries

1. Prepare Lemon Cheese Filling (p. 195). You will need 3 oz (90 g) filling for each unit of dough, as scaled in step 2. Fill a pastry bag capped with a small plain tip with the filling.

2. Scale Danish Pastry Dough (Brioche-Style) (p. 191) or Danish Pastry (p. 193) into 22-oz (615-g) units. Roll out each unit into a rectangle 16 × 2 in. (40 × 0 cm). For the neatest results, roll slightly larger and trim to size with a knife or pastry wheel.

3. Cut 4 × 3 into 12 squares, 4 in. (10 cm) on each side.

4. Egg-wash the surface of each square.

5. Pipe the cheese mixture in a line down the center of each square (a).

6. Fold in half to make a rectangle. Press the edges well to seal (b).

7. Turn upside down and arrange on sheet pans lined with parchment. Egg-wash the tops.

8. Proof for 15 minutes at 85°F (30°C).

9. Egg-wash a second time. Sprinkle with sugar.

10. Bake at 350°F (180°C) for 12 minutes.

11. If desired, decorate the tops with slices of poached lemon.

A

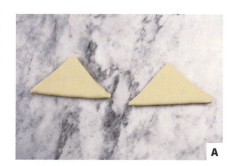

B

Cherry Vol-au-Vents

1. Scale Danish Pastry Dough (Croissant-Style) (p. 190) into 14-oz (400-g) units.

2. Roll out into a rectangle 7 × 11 in. (18 × 27 cm) in size.

3. Cut into 2 strips 3½ × 11 in. (9 × 27 cm), then cut each strip into 3½-in. (9-cm) squares.

4. Fold each square in half diagonally to form a triangle (a).

5. With a chef's knife, cut a strip ½ in. (1 cm) wide along the two short sides of the triangle, starting at the folded edge and stopping about ¾ in. (2 cm) from the opposite corner (b).

6. Unfold the square. Brush with egg wash.

7. Fold each cut strip to the opposite side to make a diamond-shaped pastry with a raised border all around. Press corners to seal (c).

8. Proof for 20 minutes at 85°F (30°C).

9. Egg-wash again.

10. With a pastry bag or spoon, deposit about 2 tsp (10 g) pastry cream in the center of each pastry. Fill with cherries. You will need about 1 oz (25 g) cherries for each pastry (d).

11. Bake at 350°F (180°C) for 15 minutes.

12. Cool and brush with apricot glaze.

A

B

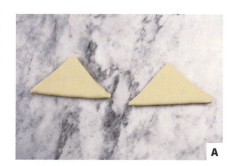

C

D

Danish Pockets

1. Roll out the dough less than ¼ in. (5 mm) thick. Cut it into 5-in. (13-cm) squares. Place the desired filling in the center of each square (a). Brush the four corners lightly with water to help seal them when pressed together.

2. Fold two opposite corners over the center. Press down firmly to seal them together (b). (If desired, rolls may be left in this shape.)

3. Fold the other two corners over the center and again press them firmly together (c).

 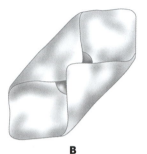 

A   B   C

Apricot Pinwheels

1. Scale Danish Pastry Dough (Croissant-Style) (p. 190) into 14-oz (400-g) units.

2. Roll out into a rectangle about ½ in. (3 mm) thick and approximately 8 × 12 in. (20 × 30 cm). (For the neatest results, roll slightly larger and trim to size with a knife or pastry wheel.)

3. Cut into 6 squares, 4 in. (10 cm) on a side (a).

4. Make a cut about 1½ in. (4 cm) long from the corner of each square toward the center (b).

5. Brush each square with egg wash. Fold alternating corner flaps toward the center to make a pinwheel (c).

6. Proof for 20 minutes at 85°F (30°C).

7. Egg-wash again.

8. With a pastry bag or spoon, deposit about 2 tsp (10 g) pastry cream at the center of each pinwheel. Place an apricot half on top of the pastry cream, cut side down (d).

9. Bake at 350°F (180°C) for 15 minutes.

10. Cool and brush with clear glaze or apricot glaze.

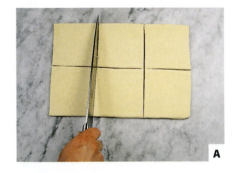

A

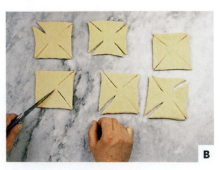

B

C

D

Apple Rosettes

1. Scale Danish Pastry Dough (Croissant-Style) (p. 190) into 14-oz (400-g) units.

2. Roll out into a rectangle about ⅛ in. (3 mm) thick and approximately 8 × 12 in. (20 × 30 cm).

3. With a 4-in. (10-cm) round cutter, cut into 6 circles (a).

4. Make 4 equidistant cuts about 1½ in. (4 cm) long from the outside edge of each circle toward the center (b).

5. Brush each circle with egg wash. Fold alternating corner flaps toward the center to make a pinwheel. Press down corners to seal (c, d).

6. Proof for 20 minutes at 85°F (30°C).

7. Egg-wash again.

8. With a pastry bag or spoon, deposit about 2 tsp (10 g) pastry cream at the center of each pinwheel (e). Top the pastry cream with about 1 oz (25 g) Apple Compote Filling (p. 197) (f). By hand, carefully press each mound of apple into place.

9. Bake at 350°F (180°C) for 15 minutes.

10. Cool and brush with clear glaze or apricot glaze.

Left to right:
apple rosettes,
cherry vol-au-vents,
apricot pinwheels.

Coffee Cakes

Coffee cakes can be made up into many sizes and shapes. The weight of the dough required and the size of the cake can be varied greatly according to the needs of the bakeshop. Except when a specific dough is indicated, the following can be made with either a sweet dough or Danish dough.

Wreath Coffee Cake

1. Using a sweet dough or Danish dough, make a filled dough roll, as for cinnamon rolls, but do not cut into separate pieces. Other fillings, such as prune or date, may be used instead of butter and cinnamon sugar.

2. Shape the roll into a circle (a). Place on a greased baking sheet. Cut partway through the dough at 1-in. (2.5-cm) intervals (b). Twist each segment outward to open the cuts (c).

3. Egg-wash after proofing. Bake at 375°F (190°C).

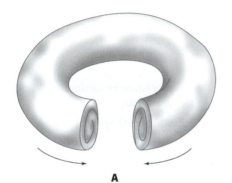

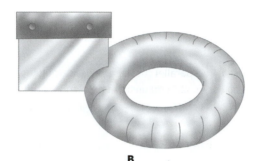

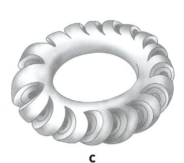

A   B   C

Filled Coffee Cake

1. Scale sweet dough or Danish dough into 12-oz (340-g) units.

2. Roll each unit into a rectangle 9 × 18 in. (23 × 46 cm).

3. Spread half of each rectangle with about 6 oz (170 g) desired filling.

4. Fold the unspread half over the spread half to make a 9-in. (23-cm) square.

5. Place in a greased 9-in. (23-cm) square pan.

6. Sprinkle with streusel topping, about 4 oz (110 g) per pan.

7. Proof. Bake at 375°F (190°C).

Loaf Coffee Cake

1. Using babka dough, make a filled dough roll, as for cinnamon rolls, using desired filling.

2. Fold the roll in half, then twist it up.

3. Place the twisted roll in a greased loaf pan, or coil the twist like a snail and place in a round pan.

4. Proof, wash with melted butter, and bake at 350°F (175°C).

Danish Pretzel

1. Using almond filling, make up Danish dough into a long, thin dough roll, as for cinnamon rolls.

2. Twist the roll into a pretzel shape. Place on a sheet pan.

3. Proof, egg-wash, and bake at 375°F (190°C).

Strip Coffee Cake or Danish Strip

1. Roll out the Danish dough about ¼ in. (6 mm) thick into a rectangle the length of the desired strip and about twice as wide.
2. Spread the desired filling lengthwise down the center of the dough, leaving a ½-in. (1-cm) margin at both ends.
3. Brush both ends and one edge of the rectangle with egg wash, to seal the seams.
4. Fold the side of the rectangle without the egg wash over the center of the filling. Fold the other side over the center, overlapping the first side by ½ in. (1 cm).
5. Turn the strip over and place it seam side down on a paper-lined pan. Make 5 or 6 diagonal slashes in the top of the dough; cut through to the filling but not to the bottom layer of dough.
6. Proof, egg-wash, and bake at 375°F (190°C).

Danish Spiral Coffee Cake

1. Using desired filling, make up Danish dough into a filled dough roll, as for cinnamon rolls, but longer and thinner.
2. Flatten the roll slightly with a rolling pin. Make 2 parallel cuts lengthwise through the dough; cut through the bottom layer leaving about 1 in. (2.5 cm) uncut at both ends.
3. Twist the strip as for Danish Twists (p. 204). Coil the twist into a spiral. Tuck the loose end underneath to secure it.
4. Proof and egg-wash. If desired, sprinkle with chopped or sliced nuts. Bake at 375°F (190°C).

> **KEY POINTS TO REVIEW**
>
> ▪ What is the main difference between croissant and Danish dough formulas?
>
> ▪ What is the rolling-in procedure for laminated yeast doughs?
>
> ▪ What are the principal makeup procedures for laminated and nonlaminated sweet dough products?

TERMS FOR REVIEW

panettone	baba	simple fold
brioche	croissant	

QUESTIONS FOR REVIEW

1. Which mixing method is used for brioche dough and kugelhopf dough? Why?
2. Because butter is hard when cold and melts easily at room temperature, what precautions are necessary when using butter as the rolling-in fat for Danish pastry dough?
3. Explain the difference between croissant-style Danish dough and brioche-style Danish dough.
4. Describe the rolling-in procedure for Danish dough.

10

QUICK BREADS

QUICK BREADS ARE the perfect solution for food service operations that want to offer their patrons fresh, homemade bread products but can't justify the labor cost of making yeast breads. Retail bakeries have discovered a great demand for such items as fresh muffins. Also, quick breads have the advantage of being easy to make in almost unlimited varieties using such ingredients as whole wheat flour, rye flour, cornmeal, bran, oatmeal, and many kinds of fruits, nuts, and spices. Even breads made with vegetables have become popular.

As their name implies, quick breads are quick to make. Because they are leavened by chemical leaveners and steam, not by yeast, no fermentation time is necessary. And because they are usually tender products with little gluten development, mixing them takes just a few minutes.

211

Although prepared biscuit and muffin mixes are available, the only extra work required to make these products from scratch is the time to scale a few ingredients. With a careful and imaginative selection of ingredients, and an understanding of basic mixing methods, you can create superior products.

MUFFIN MIXING AND PRODUCTION METHODS

DOUGH MIXTURES FOR quick breads are generally of two types:

- *Batters* may be either *pour batters*, which are liquid enough to be poured, or *drop batters*, which are thick enough to be dropped from a spoon in lumps.
- *Soft doughs* are used for biscuits, discussed in the next section. These products are, with a few exceptions, rolled out and cut into desired shapes, so a stiffer dough is required than for muffins.

Tunneling.

Only slight gluten development is desirable in most quick breads. Tenderness is a desirable quality, rather than the chewy quality of many yeast breads. In addition, chemical leavening agents do not create the same kind of texture yeast does, and they are not strong enough to produce a light, tender product if the gluten is too strong.

Muffin, loaf bread, and pancake batters are mixed as little as possible—only until the dry ingredients are moistened. This, plus the presence of fat and sugar, keeps gluten development low. Overmixing muffin batter not only causes toughness but also produces irregular shapes and large, elongated holes inside the muffins. This condition is called *tunneling*.

Mixing Methods

The *muffin method* is used for muffins, pancakes, waffles, and many loaf-type or sheet-type quick breads. This method is fast and easy. However, the danger is the dough can quickly become overmixed, resulting in toughness. *Muffin batter should be mixed only until the dry ingredients are just moistened.* Do not attempt to achieve a smooth batter. Some loaf breads and coffee cakes are higher in fat and sugar than muffins, so they can withstand a little more mixing without becoming tough.

This mixing method is not as suitable for formulas high in fat, unlike the creaming method described next. Consequently, quick breads mixed by this method are not as rich and cakelike as muffins and other products mixed by the creaming method. They tend to be a little drier, more like breads than cake. High-fat muffins sell better in today's market (in spite of the public's concern about fat), so the muffin method is not used as often as it once was. Keep this in mind as you try the muffin-method formulas in this chapter.

The *creaming method* is a cake-mixing method that is sometimes applied to muffins and loaf breads. Actually, there is no exact dividing line between muffin products and cakes, and if they are rich enough, muffin products may be considered cakes rather than breads.

The creaming method is a more time-consuming procedure than the muffin method. However, it produces fine-textured goods and carries less danger of overmixing. The creaming method is especially useful for products with high fat and sugar content because it helps mix the ingredients more uniformly.

PROCEDURE: Muffin Method

1. Sift together the dry ingredients (a).

2. Combine all liquid ingredients, including melted fat or oil.

3. Add the liquids to the dry ingredients and mix just until all the flour is moistened. The batter will look lumpy. Be careful not to overmix (b).

4. Pan and bake immediately (c). The dry and liquid mixtures may be prepared in advance, but once the mixtures are combined, the batter should be baked without delay, or loss of volume may result.

Makeup and Panning of Muffin Products

Muffin tins and loaf pans should be greased with shortening or pan spray and dusted with flour or greased with a commercial pan grease preparation. Sheet pans for cornbreads and other sheet products may be lined with silicone paper.

Paper liners may be used for muffin tins. However, because muffins do not stick to greased tins, they rise more freely and take a better shape and crust without paper liners.

When portioning batter into muffin tins, be careful not to stir the mix and toughen it. For best results, scoop the batter from the outside edge of the bowl, using a portion scoop.

Batters for muffins and quick loaf breads are generally interchangeable. In other words, formulas for banana bread or date nut bread, for example, may be baked as muffins instead of as loaves. Similarly, standard muffin batters may also be baked as loaves or sheets.

Please note that some of the muffin and loaf bread formulas included here, especially those mixed by the muffin method, should be thought of as breads rather than as tea cakes. In particular, their fat and sugar contents are intentionally kept lower than those of the rather rich, oily muffins sometimes sold today. Formulas for richer, more cakelike muffins are included later in the chapter. If you wish to experiment with the two basic muffin recipes to make them richer in fat and sugar, first read the section on cake formula balance beginning on page 385.

PROCEDURE: Creaming Method for Muffins, Loaves, and Coffee Cakes

1. Combine the fat, sugar, salt, spices, and milk powder (if used) in the bowl of a mixer fitted with the paddle attachment.

2. Cream the ingredients together until light (a).

3. Add the eggs in two or three stages. Cream well after each addition and before adding more eggs (b).

4. Sift together the flour, baking powder, and other dry ingredients.

5. Stir together the liquid ingredients until well combined.

6. Add the sifted dry ingredients alternately with the liquids. Do this as follows:

   • Add one-fourth of the dry ingredients. Mix just until blended in (c).

   • Add one-third of the liquid. Mix just until blended in (d)

   • Repeat until all ingredients are used. Scrape down the sides of the bowl occasionally for even mixing.

BISCUIT MIXING AND PRODUCTION METHODS

Mixing Methods

The *biscuit method* is used for biscuits, scones, and similar products. It is sometimes called the *pastry method* because it is like that used for mixing pie pastry. In a few instances, biscuit products are mixed with a variation of the *creaming method*.

Biscuit dough is often lightly kneaded, enough to help develop some flakiness but not so much as to toughen the product. Biscuit dough that has been lightly kneaded rises more than dough that has not been kneaded. Unkneaded dough spreads more than kneaded dough and has a more cakelike texture.

Some biscuits are mixed by the creaming method. These have a texture that is more cakelike and less flaky than that produced by the biscuit method. Fat and sugar for creamed biscuit dough should be mixed only until just combined. Continued creaming makes the biscuits excessively cakelike.

PROCEDURE: Biscuit Method

1. Scale all ingredients accurately.
2. Sift the dry ingredients together into a mixing bowl.
3. Cut in the shortening, using the paddle attachment or the pastry knife attachment; if you prefer, cut in the fat by hand, using a pastry blender or your fingers. Continue until the mixture resembles a coarse cornmeal (see variations).
4. Combine the liquid ingredients.
5. Add the liquid to the dry ingredients. Mix just until the ingredients are combined and a soft dough is formed. Do not overmix.
6. Bring the dough to the bench and knead it lightly by pressing it out and folding it in half. Rotate the dough 90 degrees between folds.
7. Repeat this procedure 6 to 10 times, or for about 30 seconds. The dough should be soft and slightly elastic but not sticky. Overkneading toughens the biscuits.

   The dough is now ready for makeup.

VARIATIONS

Changes in the basic procedure produce different characteristics in the finished product:

1. Using slightly more shortening, and cutting it in less—only until the pieces are the size of peas—produces a flakier biscuit.
2. Omitting the kneading step produces very tender, crusty biscuits, but with less height.

PROCEDURE: Creaming Method for Biscuits

1. Combine the fat, sugar, salt, and milk powder (if used) in the bowl of a mixer fitted with the paddle attachment.
2. Blend just to a smooth paste. Do not continue to cream, as this would make the biscuits too cakelike in texture (a).

A

3. Add the eggs gradually and blend in thoroughly (b).

B

4. Sift together the flour, baking powder, and other dry ingredients.
5. Combine the liquid ingredients.
6. Add the sifted dry ingredients alternately with the liquids. Do this as follows:
   - Add one-fourth of the dry ingredients. Mix just until blended in.
   - Add one-third of the liquid. Mix just until blended in (c).

C

   - Repeat until all ingredients are used. Scrape down the sides of the bowl occasionally for even mixing (d).

D

Makeup of Biscuits

Follow these steps to produce biscuits from biscuit dough:

1. Roll out the biscuit dough into a sheet about ½ inch (1 cm) thick, being careful to roll it evenly and to a uniform thickness. Biscuits approximately double in height during baking.

2. Cut into desired shapes. When using a round hand cutter, cut straight down. Do not twist the cutter. Space the cuts as closely as possible, to minimize scraps. Reworked scrap dough produces tougher biscuits. Cutting into squares or triangles with a pastry cutter knife eliminates scraps that would have to be rerolled. Roller cutters also eliminate or reduce scraps. If cutting with a knife, cut straight down without dragging the knife.

3. Place the biscuits ½ inch (1 cm) apart on greased or paper-lined baking sheets. For straighter sides, place the biscuits upside down. For softer biscuits without crusty sides, arrange the units so they touch each other; these must be broken apart after baking.

4. If desired, brush the tops with egg wash or milk to aid browning.

5. Bake as soon as possible.

BISCUITS I

Ingredients	U.S.			Metric	%
Bread flour	1 lb 4	oz		600 g	50
Pastry flour	1 lb 4	oz		600 g	50
Salt		0.75	oz	24 g	2
Sugar		2	oz	60 g	5
Baking powder		2.5	oz	72 g	6
Butter and/or shortening (regular)		14	oz	420 g	35
Milk	1 lb 10	oz		800 g	65
Total weight:	**5 lb 5**	**oz**		**2576 g**	**213%**

PROCEDURE

MIXING

Biscuit method (p. 215)

SCALING

Approximately 1 lb (450 g) per dozen 2-in. (5-cm) biscuits

BAKING

400°F (200°C), about 15–20 minutes

─── **VARIATIONS** ───

BUTTERMILK BISCUITS

Use buttermilk in place of regular milk. Reduce the baking powder to 4% (1.5 oz/50 g) and add 1% baking soda (0.4 oz/12 g).

CHEESE BISCUITS

Ingredients	U.S.	Metric	%
Grated cheddar cheese	12 oz	360 g	30

Add the cheese to the dry ingredients.

CURRANT BISCUITS

Ingredients	U.S.	Metric	%
Sugar	4 oz	120 g	10
Dried currants	6 oz	180 g	15

Increase the sugar to the above amount. Add the currants to the dry ingredients. Sprinkle the tops with Cinnamon Sugar (p. 193) before baking.

HERB BISCUITS

Ingredients	U.S.	Metric	%
Fresh chopped parsley	2 oz	60 g	5

Add the parsley to the dry ingredients.

BISCUITS II

Ingredients	U.S.		Metric		%
Shortening	6	oz	150	g	15
Sugar	4	oz	100	g	10
Salt	0.5	oz	12.5	g	1.25
Nonfat milk solids	2	oz	50	g	5
Eggs	3	oz	75	g	7.5
Bread flour	1 lb 12	oz	700	g	70
Cake flour	12	oz	300	g	30
Baking powder	2	oz	50	g	5
Water	1 lb 8	oz	600	g	60
Total weight:	**5 lb 1**	**oz**	**2037**	**g**	**203** %

VARIATION

Ingredients	U.S.	Metric	%
Butter	7.5 oz	190 g	19

Substitute butter for the shortening.

PROCEDURE

MIXING

Creaming method for biscuits (p. 215)

BAKING

400°F (200°C)

Biscuits II, without and with egg wash.

PLAIN MUFFINS

Ingredients	U.S.		Metric	%
Pastry flour	2 lb 8	oz	1200 g	100
Sugar	1 lb 12	oz	840 g	70
Baking powder	2.5	oz	72 g	6
Salt	0.5	oz	15 g	1.25
Eggs, beaten	12	oz	360 g	30
Milk	1 lb 12	oz	840 g	70
Vanilla extract	1	oz	30 g	2.5
Butter or shortening, melted	1 lb		480 g	40
Total weight:	**8 lb**		**3837 g**	**319 %**

PROCEDURE

MIXING

Muffin method (p. 213)

PANNING

Grease and flour muffin tins. Fill them one-half to two-thirds full. Exact weight depends on pan size. Average sizes are 2 oz (60 g) for small muffins, 4 oz (110 g) for medium muffins, and 5–6 oz (140–170 g) for large muffins.

BAKING

400°F (200°C), about 20–30 minutes

VARIATIONS

RAISIN SPICE MUFFINS

Ingredients	U.S.	Metric	%
Raisins	8 oz	240 g	20
Cinnamon	0.17 oz (2½ tsp)	5 g	0.4
Nutmeg	0.08 oz (1 tsp)	2.5 g	0.2

Add raisins, cinnamon, and nutmeg to dry ingredients.

BLUEBERRY MUFFINS

Ingredients	U.S.	Metric	%
Blueberries (washed and well drained)	1 lb	480 g	40

Fold blueberries into finished batter.

WHOLE WHEAT MUFFINS

Ingredients	U.S.	Metric	%
Pastry flour	1 lb 12 oz	840 g	70
Whole wheat flour	12 oz	360 g	30
Baking powder	1.5 oz	50 g	4
Baking soda	0.3 oz (2 tsp)	10 g	0.75
Molasses	4 oz	120 g	10

Adjust the flour and leavening as listed above. Add the molasses to the liquid ingredients.

CORN MUFFINS

Ingredients	U.S.	Metric	%
Pastry flour	1 lb 10 oz	780 g	65
Cornmeal	14 oz	420 g	35

Adjust the flour as listed above. (See also the Corn Bread formula on p. 219.)

CORN CHEESE MUFFINS

Ingredients	U.S.	Metric	%
Grated cheddar cheese	1 lb 4 oz	600 g	50

Add the cheese to the dry ingredients in the above corn muffin formula. Use half the amount of sugar.

BRAN MUFFINS

Ingredients	U.S.	Metric	%
Pastry flour	12 oz	360 g	30
Bread flour	1 lb	480 g	40
Bran	12 oz	360 g	30
Raisins	6 oz	180 g	15
Butter, melted	1 lb 4 oz	600 g	50
Milk	1 lb 14 oz	900 g	75
Molasses	6 oz	180 g	15

Adjust the flour, butter, and milk as listed above. Add the raisins to the dry ingredients and the molasses to the liquid ingredients.

CRUMB COFFEE CAKE

Ingredients	U.S.	Metric	%
Butter or shortening	1 lb 4 oz	600 g	50
Streusel (p. 195)	2 lb	960 g	80

Increase the fat as listed above. Pour the batter into a greased, paper-lined sheet pan and spread smooth. Top with streusel. Bake at 360°F (182°C) about 30 minutes.

Muffins, clockwise from top: blueberry, corn, bran.

MUFFINS (CREAMING METHOD)

Ingredients	U.S.		Metric	%
Shortening and/or butter	1 lb 4	oz	500 g	50
Sugar	1 lb 10	oz	650 g	65
Salt	0.5	oz	12 g	1.25
Nonfat milk solids	3	oz	70 g	7
Eggs	12	oz	300 g	30
Cake flour	2 lb 8	oz	1000 g	100
Baking powder	2	oz	50 g	5
Vanilla extract	1	oz	25 g	1.25
Water	1 lb 14	oz	750 g	75
Total weight:	**8 lb 6**	**oz**	**3357 g**	**334 %**

PROCEDURE

MIXING

Creaming method (p. 214)

SCALING

Fill tins one-half to two-thirds full.

BAKING

400°F (200°C), about 20–30 minutes

VARIATIONS

CHOCOLATE CHIP MUFFINS

Ingredients	U.S.	Metric	%
White granulated sugar	1 lb 4 oz	500 g	50
Brown sugar	6 oz	150 g	15
Chocolate chips	12 oz	300 g	30

Adjust the sugar as listed above. Add the chocolate chips to the formula. Top with Cinnamon Sugar (p. 193) before baking.

BLUEBERRY MUFFINS

Ingredients	U.S.	Metric	%
Blueberries (washed and well drained)	1 lb 4 oz	500 g	50

Fold the blueberries into the finished batter.

RAISIN SPICE MUFFINS

Ingredients	U.S.	Metric	%
Raisins	10 oz	250 g	25
Cinnamon	0.2 oz (3 tsp)	5 g	0.5
Nutmeg	0.1 oz (1½ tsp)	2.5 g	0.25

Add the raisins, cinnamon, and nutmeg to the dry ingredients.

CORN BREAD, MUFFINS, OR STICKS

Ingredients	U.S.		Metric	%
Pastry flour	1 lb 4	oz	600 g	50
Cornmeal	1 lb 4	oz	600 g	50
Sugar	1 lb		408 g	40
Baking powder	2	oz	60 g	5
Nonfat milk solids	3	oz	90 g	7.5
Salt	0.75 oz		24 g	2
Eggs, beaten	8	oz	240 g	20
Water	1 lb 12	oz	840 g	70
Corn syrup	2	oz	60 g	5
Butter or shortening, melted	12	oz	360 g	30
Total weight:	**6 lb 15**	**oz**	**3354 g**	**279 %**

PROCEDURE

MIXING

Muffin method (p. 213)

SCALING

60 oz (1700 g) per half-sheet pan (13 × 18 in./ 33 × 6 cm)

24 oz (680 g) per 9-in. (23-cm) square pan or per dozen small muffins

10 oz (280 g) per dozen corn sticks

BAKING

400°F (200°C) for corn bread, 25–30 minutes

425°F (218°C) for muffins or sticks, 15–20 minutes

VARIATION

Use buttermilk instead of water and omit nonfat milk solids. Reduce baking powder to 2.5% (1 oz/30 g) and add 1.25% (0.5 oz/15 g) baking soda.

ZUCCHINI CARROT NUT MUFFINS

Ingredients	U.S.		Metric		%
Pastry flour	1 lb		480	g	80
Bran	4	oz	120	g	20
Salt	0.25	oz	7.5	g	1.25
Baking powder	0.3	oz (1¾ tsp)	9	g	1.5
Baking soda	0.2	oz (1 tsp)	6	g	1
Cinnamon	0.08	oz (1¼ tsp)	2.4	g	0.4
Nutmeg	0.04	oz (½ tsp)	1.2	g	0.2
Ginger	0.02	oz (¼ tsp)	0.6	g	0.1
Pecans or walnuts, chopped	5	oz	150	g	25
Shredded, unsweetened coconut	2	oz	60	g	10
Eggs	8	oz	240	g	40
Sugar	15	oz	450	g	75
Zucchini, grated	6	oz	180	g	30
Carrot, grated	6	oz	180	g	30
Vegetable oil	8	oz	240	g	40
Water	9.5	oz	360	g	60
Total weight:	**5 lb**		**2486**	**g**	**414** %

PROCEDURE

MIXING

Modified muffin method

1. Sift the flour, leavenings, and spices. Stir in the bran, nuts, and coconut. (Note that the flour and bran together are calculated as 100% in this formula.)

2. Beat the eggs and sugar until well mixed, but do not whip into a foam. Stir in the grated vegetables, oil, and water.

3. Add the egg mixture to the dry ingredients and mix just until combined. The batter may seem too wet, but the bran will absorb a great deal of water as the muffins bake.

SCALING

Fill the tins two-thirds full.

BAKING

400°F (200°C), about 30 minutes

SCONES

Ingredients	U.S.			Metric	%
Bread flour	1 lb	8	oz	600 g	50
Pastry flour	1 lb	8	oz	600 g	50
Sugar		6	oz	150 g	12.5
Salt		0.5	oz	12 g	1
Baking powder		3	oz	72 g	6
Shortening and/or butter	1 lb	3	oz	480 g	40
Eggs		7	oz	180 g	15
Milk	1 lb	5	oz	540 g	45
Total weight:	**6 lb**	**8**	**oz**	**2634 g**	**219 %**

Left to right: Raisin Scones, Cranberry Drop Scones.

PROCEDURE

MIXING

Biscuit method (p. 215)

Chill dough after mixing if it is too soft to make up.

MAKEUP VARIATIONS

Scale at 1 lb (450 g), round up, and flatten to ½ in. (12 mm) thick. Cut into 8 wedges.

- Roll out into a rectangle ½ in. (12 mm) thick and cut into triangles as for croissants (see p. 200).
- Roll out into a rectangle ½ in. (12 mm) thick and cut out with cutters, like biscuits.

Place on greased or paper-lined sheet pans. Egg-wash tops.

BAKING

400°F (200°C) for 15–20 minutes

VARIATION

Ingredients	U.S.	Metric	%
Raisins or currants	12 oz	300 g	25

Add the raisins or currants to the dry ingredients after cutting in the fat.

CRANBERRY DROP SCONES

For large-quantity measurements, see page 717.

Ingredients	U.S.			Metric	%
Butter		6	oz	185 g	25
Sugar		5	oz	150 g	21
Salt		0.25	oz	8 g	1
Egg yolks		1.33	oz	40 g	5.5
		(2 yolks)		(2 yolks)	
Pastry flour	1 lb	8	oz	750 g	100
Baking powder		1.25	oz	38 g	5
Milk		14	oz	435 g	58
Dried cranberries		4	oz	125 g	17
Total weight:	**3 lb**	**7**	**oz**	**1731 g**	**232 %**

PROCEDURE

MIXING

Creaming method (p. 215)

MAKEUP AND BAKING

Using a 2-oz (60-mL) scoop, drop mounds onto parchment-lined sheets pans. Bake as for regular scones, above.

ENGLISH CREAM SCONES

Ingredients	U.S.		Metric		%
Pastry flour	1 lb		450	g	100
Baking powder		0.7 oz (4 tsp)	20	g	4.4
Salt		0.2 oz (1 tsp)	5.6	g	1.25
Sugar	2	oz	56	g	12.5
Butter	5	oz	140	g	31
Egg	4	oz	112	g	25
Heavy cream	8	oz	225	g	50
Total weight:	**2 lb 3**	**oz**	**1008**	**g**	**224 %**

PROCEDURE

MIXING

Biscuit method (p. 215)

MAKEUP

1. Flatten with palms of hands (or roll out) to 1–1½ in. (3 cm) thick.

2. Cut out 2½-in. (6-cm) rounds. Arrange on sheet pans.

3. Brush tops with heavy cream and sprinkle with granulated sugar.

BAKING

425°F (220°C), about 9–11 minutes

STEAMED BROWN BREAD

Ingredients	U.S.		Metric	%
Bread flour	8	oz	250 g	28.5
Whole wheat flour	4	oz	125 g	14
Light rye flour	8	oz	250 g	28.5
Cornmeal	8	oz	250 g	28.5
Salt	0.25	oz	9 g	1
Baking soda	0.5	oz	15 g	1.8
Baking powder	0.5	oz	15 g	1.8
Raisins	8	oz	250 g	28.5
Buttermilk	2 lb		1000 g	114
Molasses	15	oz	475 g	54
Oil	2	oz	60 g	7
Total weight:	**5 lb 6**	**oz**	**2699 g**	**307 %**

PROCEDURE

MIXING

Muffin method (p. 213)

SCALING AND COOKING

Fill well-greased molds one-half full, about 16 oz for each quart of capacity (500 g per liter). Cover molds and steam for 3 hours.

ORANGE NUT BREAD

Ingredients	U.S.		Metric	%
Sugar	12	oz	350 g	50
Orange zest, grated	1	oz	30 g	4
Pastry flour	1 lb 8	oz	700 g	100
Nonfat milk solids	2	oz	60 g	8
Baking powder	0.75	oz	21 g	3
Baking soda	0.3	oz (2 tsp)	10 g	1.4
Salt	0.3	oz (2 tsp)	10 g	1.4
Walnuts, chopped	12	oz	350 g	50
Eggs	5	oz	140 g	20
Orange juice	6	oz	175 g	25
Water	1 lb		450 g	65
Oil or melted butter or shortening	8	oz	230 g	33
Total weight:	**5 lb 7**	**oz**	**2526 g**	**360 %**

PROCEDURE

MIXING

Muffin method (p. 213)

Blend the sugar and orange zest thoroughly before adding the remaining ingredients, to ensure even distribution.

SCALING

1 lb 4 oz (575 g) per 7⅜ × 3⅝-in. (19 × 9-cm) loaf pan

1 lb 10 oz (750 g) per 8½ × 4½-in. (22 × 11-cm) loaf pan

BAKING

375°F (190°C), about 50 minutes

——— VARIATION ———

LEMON NUT BREAD

Substitute grated lemon zest for the orange zest. Omit the orange juice and add 8% (2 oz/60 g) lemon juice. Increase the water to 83% (1 lb 4 oz/580 g).

BANANA BREAD

Ingredients	U.S.			Metric	%
Pastry flour	1 lb	8	oz	700 g	100
Sugar		14	oz	400 g	58
Baking powder		1.25	oz	35 g	5
Baking soda		0.14	oz (¾ tsp)	4 g	0.6
Salt		0.33	oz (1½ tsp)	9 g	1.25
Walnuts, chopped		6	oz	175 g	25
Eggs		10	oz	280 g	40
Ripe banana pulp, puréed	1 lb	8	oz	700 g	100
Oil or melted butter or shortening		9.5	oz	280 g	40
Total weight:	**5 lb**	**9**	**oz**	**2583 g**	**369** %

PROCEDURE

MIXING

Muffin method (p. 213)

SCALING

1 lb 4 oz (575 g) per 7⅜ × 3⅝-in. (19 × 9-cm) loaf pan

1 lb 10 oz (750 g) per 8½ × 4½-in. (22 × 11-cm) loaf pan

BAKING

375°F (190°C), about 50 minutes

DATE NUT BREAD

Ingredients	U.S.		Metric	%
Shortening and/or butter	8	oz	200 g	40
Brown sugar	10	oz	250 g	50
Salt	0.25	oz	6 g	1.25
Nonfat milk solids	1.5	oz	35 g	7
Eggs	6	oz	150 g	30
Cake flour	1 lb		400 g	80
Whole wheat flour	4	oz	100 g	20
Baking powder	0.75	oz	20 g	3.75
Baking soda	0.25	oz	6 g	1.25
Water	15	oz	375 g	75
Dates (see *Note*)	10	oz	250 g	50
Walnuts, chopped	6	oz	150 g	30
Total weight:	**4 lb 13**	**oz**	**1942 g**	**388** %

NOTE: After scaling the dates, soak them in hot water until very soft. Drain and chop.

PROCEDURE

MIXING

Creaming method (p. 214)

Fold the dates and nuts into the finished batter.

SCALING

1 lb 4 oz (575 g) per 7⅜ × 3⅝-in. (19 × 9-cm) loaf pan

1 lb 10 oz (750 g) per 8½ × 4½-in. (22 × 11-cm) loaf pan

BAKING

375°F (190°C), about 50 minutes

— VARIATION —

Substitute other nuts, or a mixture, for the walnuts. For example: pecans, toasted hazelnuts, or toasted almonds.

Substitute other dried fruits for the dates. For example: prunes, dried apples, raisins, dried figs, or dried apricots.

PLUM CAKE

Ingredients	U.S.			Metric		%
Pastry flour	1 lb	4	oz	600	g	100
Nonfat milk solids		0.5	oz	15	g	3
Salt		0.25	oz	8	g	1.5
Cinnamon		0.06 oz (1 tsp)		2	g	0.3
Brown sugar		10	oz	300	g	50
Butter		10	oz	300	g	50
Eggs		9	oz	270	g	45
Milk	1 lb	2	oz	540	g	90
Topping						
Italian-style prune plums, halved and pitted	3 lb	12	oz	1800	g	300
Cinnamon Sugar (p. 193)		4	oz	120	g	20
Total weight:	**8 lb**	**3**	**oz**	**3955**	**g**	**659** %

PROCEDURE

MIXING

Biscuit method (p. 215)

Because of the moisture in the brown sugar, the dry ingredients must be rubbed through a sieve when sifted.

SCALING AND MAKEUP

One recipe is enough for one half-sheet pan, three 9-in. (23-cm) square pans, or four 8-in. (20-cm) square pans. Spread the dough in greased and floured pans. Arrange plum halves, cut side up, on top of the dough. Sprinkle with cinnamon sugar.

BAKING

400°F (200°C) for 35 minutes

VARIATION

For a more cakelike texture, mix the dough using the creaming method for biscuits.

Top the cake with Streusel (p. 195) instead of cinnamon sugar before baking.

ALMOND POPPY SEED MUFFINS

Ingredients	U.S.			Metric	%
Butter		14	oz	450 g	60
Sugar	1 lb	2	oz	560 g	75
Eggs		12	oz	375 g	50
Pastry flour	1 lb	8	oz	750 g	100
Baking powder		0.25 oz (1½ tsp)		8 g	1
Baking soda		0.16 oz (1 tsp)		5 g	0.7
Salt		0.2 oz (1 tsp)		6 g	0.8
Poppy seeds		1	oz	30 g	4
Almond extract		0.16 oz (1 tsp)		5 g	0.7
Buttermilk	1 lb			500 g	67
Total weight:	**5 lb**	**5**	**oz**	**2689 g**	**359** %

PROCEDURE

MIXING

Creaming method (p. 214)

Mix the poppy seeds with the dry ingredients after sifting.

SCALING

Fill tins two-thirds full.

BAKING

375°F (190°C), about 30 minutes

VARIATION

LEMON POPPY SEED MUFFINS

Flavor the muffins with lemon extract instead of almond extract.

APPLE SPICE MUFFINS

Ingredients	U.S.			Metric		%
Butter		14	oz	435	g	60
Brown sugar	1 lb	2	oz	540	g	75
Salt		0.25 oz (1 tsp)		7	g	1
Cinnamon		0.15 oz (2 tsp)		4	g	0.6
Nutmeg		0.05 oz (¾ tsp)		1.5	g	0.2
Eggs		8	oz	240	g	33
Pastry flour	1 lb	4	oz	600	g	83
Whole wheat flour		4	oz	120	g	17
Baking powder		0.5	oz	15	g	2
Baking soda		0.25 oz (1½ tsp)		7	g	1
Buttermilk		12	oz	360	g	50
Applesauce	1 lb	2	oz	540	g	75
Total weight:	**5 lb 15**		**oz**	**2869**	**g**	**397 %**

PROCEDURE

MIXING

Creaming method (p. 214)

SCALING

Fill tins two-thirds full.

BAKING

400°F (200°C), about 30 minutes

PUMPKIN MUFFINS

Ingredients	U.S.			Metric		%
Butter		12	oz	375	g	50
Brown sugar	1 lb			500	g	67
Ginger		0.05 oz (¾ tsp)		1.5	g	0.2
Cinnamon		0.04 oz (½ tsp)		1.25	g	0.17
Nutmeg		0.03 oz (⅓ tsp)		0.75	g	0.1
Allspice		0.05 oz (¾ tsp)		1.5	g	0.2
Salt		0.14 oz (½ tsp)		4.5	g	0.6
Eggs		6	oz	190	g	25
Pastry flour	1 lb	8	oz	750	g	100
Baking powder		0.33 oz (2 tsp)		10	g	1.4
Baking soda		0.33 oz (1¾ tsp)		10	g	1.4
Buttermilk		12	oz	375	g	50
Pumpkin purée, canned		10	oz	300	g	40
Total weight:	**5 lb**			**2519**	**g**	**336 %**

PROCEDURE

MIXING

Creaming method (p. 214)

SCALING

Fill tins two-thirds full.

BAKING

400°F (200°C), about 30 minutes

DOUBLE CHOCOLATE MUFFINS

Ingredients	U.S.		Metric		%
Butter	10	oz	300	g	40
Sugar	11	oz	340	g	45
Semisweet chocolate	1 lb		500	g	67
Eggs	5	oz	150	g	20
Flour	1 lb 8	oz	750	g	100
Baking soda	0.5	oz	15	g	2
Salt	0.14 oz (½ tsp)		4.5	g	0.6
Buttermilk	1 lb 4	oz	625	g	83
Chocolate chips	12	oz	375	g	50
Total weight:	**6 lb 2**	**oz**	**3059**	**g**	**407 %**

PROCEDURE

MIXING

Creaming method (p. 214)

Melt the chocolate, cool it to room temperature, and cream it into the butter and sugar mixture. Fold the chocolate chips into the finished batter. (Note that there is no baking powder in this formula, only baking soda.)

SCALING

Fill tins two-thirds full.

BAKING

400°F (200°C), about 30 minutes

GINGERBREAD

Ingredients	Old-Fashioned Gingerbread			Pain d'Épices (French Gingerbread)		
	U.S.	Metric	%	U.S.	Metric	%
Pastry flour	2 lb 8 oz	1100 g	100	1 lb 4 oz	550 g	50
Rye flour	—	—	—	1 lb 4 oz	550 g	50
Salt	0.25 oz	7 g	0.6	0.25 oz	7 g	0.6
Baking soda	1.25 oz	33 g	3	1.25 oz	33 g	3
Baking powder	0.6 oz	16 g	1.5	0.6 oz	16 g	1.5
Ginger	0.5 oz	14 g	1.25	0.5 oz	14 g	1.25
Cinnamon	—	—	—	0.25 oz	7 g	0.6
Cloves, ground	—	—	—	0.12 oz	3.5 g	0.3
Anise, ground	—	—	—	0.5 oz	14 g	1.25
Orange rind, grated	—	—	—	0.5 oz	14 g	1.25
Currants	—	—	—	8 oz	220 g	20
Molasses	2 lb 8 oz	1100 g	100	—	—	—
Honey	—	—	—	1 lb 14 oz	825 g	75
Hot water	1 lb 4 oz	550 g	50	1 lb 4 oz	550 g	50
Butter or shortening, melted	10 oz	275 g	25	10 oz	275 g	25
Total weight:	**7 lb 1 oz**	**3095 g**	**281 %**	**6 lb 15 oz**	**3078 g**	**279 %**

PROCEDURE

MIXING

Muffin method (p. 213)

PANNING

Old-Fashioned Gingerbread: greased, paper-lined sheet pans, about 6.5–7 lb (3 kg) per sheet (one recipe per sheet).

Pain d'Épices: greased loaf pans. Fill about one-half full of batter.

BAKING

375°F (190°C)

GINGERBREAD

The name *gingerbread* is given to a wide variety of cakes and shortbreads or cookies. Gingerbread in its various forms dates back to the Middle Ages, when highly spiced foods were common. Different regions of Europe developed their own varieties of gingerbreads, using their own blends of spices.

Originally, gingerbreads were sweetened with honey, just as the French *pain d'épices* (pronounced pan day PEECE, meaning "spice bread") from the city of Dijon still is today. After sugarcane products became more widely available and economical, most regions switched to molasses to sweeten their gingerbreads.

SODA BREAD

Ingredients	U.S.			Metric	%
Pastry flour	2 lb	8	oz	1200 g	100
Baking powder		2	oz	60 g	5
Baking soda		0.5	oz	15 g	1.25
Salt		0.5	oz	15 g	1.25
Sugar		2	oz	60 g	5
Shortening or butter		4	oz	120 g	10
Currants		8	oz	240 g	20
Buttermilk	1 lb	12	oz	840 g	70
Total weight:	**5 lb**	**5**	**oz**	**2550 g**	**212** %

PROCEDURE

MIXING

Biscuit method (p. 215). Stir in currants after cutting in fat. Refrigerate after mixing if too soft to make up.

SCALING

1 lb (450 g) per unit

MAKEUP

Round into a ball-shaped loaf. Place on sheet pan. Cut a deep cross into the top.

BAKING

375°F (140°C), about 30–40 minutes

--- **VARIATION** ---

Add 1.25% (0.5 oz/15 g) caraway seeds. Omit currants or leave them in, as desired.

TERMS FOR REVIEW

pour batter

drop batter

tunneling

muffin method

creaming method

biscuit method

pastry method

QUESTIONS FOR REVIEW

1. If you made a batch of muffins that came out of the oven with strange, knobby shapes, what would you expect to be the reason?

2. What is the most important difference between the biscuit method and the muffin method?

11

DOUGHNUTS, FRITTERS, PANCAKES, AND WAFFLES

AFTER READING THIS CHAPTER, YOU SHOULD BE ABLE TO:

1. **Prepare doughnuts and other deep-fried desserts and pastries.**
2. **Prepare pancakes, waffles, crêpes, and crêpe desserts.**

UNLIKE THE PRODUCTS we have discussed so far, those included in this chapter are cooked not by baking in ovens but by deep-frying, by cooking in greased fry pans or on griddles, or, in the case of waffles, by cooking in specially designed griddles that heat the product from both sides at once.

Several types of doughs or batters are used for these products. To produce the two most popular types of doughnuts, you must understand the principles of yeast dough production (Chapters 6 through 9) and the creaming method used for mixing some quick breads (Chapter 10). French doughnuts are a fried version of the same pastry used to make cream puffs and éclairs (Chapter 14). American pancakes are made from chemically leavened batters mixed by the muffin method, while French pancakes, or crêpes, are made from thin, unleavened batters made of milk, eggs, and flour.

DOUGHNUTS AND OTHER FRIED PASTRIES

Yeast-Raised Doughnuts

The mixing method used to prepare yeast-raised doughnuts is the *modified straight dough method* (p. 182). Review this procedure before beginning doughnut production. In addition, the following points will help you understand and produce high-quality doughnuts. Makeup and finishing procedures follow the formula:

1. The dough used for yeast doughnuts is similar to regular sweet dough or bun dough, except it is often not as rich—that is, doughnuts are made with less fat, sugar, and eggs (compare the formulas on pp. 183 and 232). Doughs that are too rich will brown too fast and absorb too much frying fat. The finished products will be greasy and either too dark on the outside or insufficiently cooked inside. Also, a leaner dough has stronger gluten, which can better withstand the handling involved in proofing and frying.

2. After fermentation, bring the dough to the bench in sufficient time to allow for makeup. Remember that fermentation continues during makeup. If the dough gets too old (proofed too long), the doughnuts will require longer frying to become browned and thus will be greasier. When you are preparing a large quantity of doughnuts, it may be necessary to place some of the dough in the retarder so it doesn't become old.

3. Watch the dough temperature carefully, especially in warm weather. If the dough is much above 80°F (24°C), it will become old more quickly.

4. Proof the doughnuts at a lower temperature and humidity than you do breads. Some bakers proof them at room temperature, if there is a part of the bakeshop that isn't too hot (about 70°F/21°C). Doughnuts proofed this way are less likely to be deformed or dented when handled or brought to the fryer.

5. Handle fully proofed units carefully, as they are soft and easily dented. Many bakers give doughnuts only three-quarters proof. This makes a denser doughnut, but one that is easier to handle.

6. Heat the frying fat to the proper temperature. Fat temperature for raised doughnuts varies from 360° to 385°F (182° to 195°C), depending on the formula. Richer formulas require a lower temperature to avoid excessive browning. The formula in this book requires a frying temperature of 360° (182°C).

7. Arrange the proofed units on screens on which they can be lowered into fat. (For small quantities, you can place them by hand in the fryer, but take care not to burn yourself.) Frying time is about 2½ minutes. The doughnuts must be turned over when they are half done in order to brown evenly on both sides.

8. Lift from the frying fat with the screen, or, if you are frying in smaller quantities, with the frying basket or a spider, holding the doughnuts over the frying fat for a moment to let the fat drain from the doughnuts back into the kettle. Set the doughnuts on brown paper to absorb excess fat.

Cake-Type Doughnuts

Operations that produce cake doughnuts in volume use equipment that drops batter directly into the hot fat. This equipment is usually automatic, although small hand-operated depositors are also available. Automatic depositors use a relatively slack dough that is generally made from prepared mixes. To use these mixes and depositors, follow two important guidelines:

- Follow manufacturers' directions closely when preparing the mix.
- Keep the depositor head 1½ inch (4 cm) above the fat. If the doughnut must drop much farther than this into the fat, poor shape may result.

Operations that make cake doughnuts by hand use a stiffer mix that is rolled out and cut with cutters. Three formulas for this type of mix are included in this chapter. Follow these guidelines when preparing cake doughnuts:

1. Scale ingredients carefully. Even small errors can result in products with unsatisfactory texture or appearance.

2. Mix the dough until smooth, but do not overmix. Undermixed doughs result in a rough appearance and excessive fat absorption. Overmixed doughs result in tough, dense doughnuts.

3. Dough temperature should be about 70° to 75°F (21° to 24°C) when the units are fried. Be especially careful of dough temperature during hot weather.

4. Let the cutout units rest about 15 minutes before frying in order to relax the gluten. Failure to relax the dough results in toughness and poor expansion.

5. Fry at the proper temperature. Normal fat temperature for cake doughnuts is 375° to 385°F (190° to 195°C). Frying time is about 1½ to 2 minutes. Doughnuts must be turned over when half done.

Preparation and Care of Frying Fat

Properly fried doughnuts absorb about 2 ounces (60 g) of fat per dozen. Therefore, frying fat should be of good quality and properly maintained; otherwise, the quality of the doughnuts will suffer. Observe the following guidelines for care of frying fat:

1. Use good-quality, flavorless fat. The best fat for frying has a high smoke point (the temperature at which the fat begins to smoke and to break down rapidly).

   Solid shortenings are popular for frying because they are stable and because they congeal when the doughnuts cool, making them appear less greasy. However, such doughnuts can have an unpleasant eating quality because the fat does not melt in the mouth.

2. Fry at the proper temperature. Using too low a temperature extends frying time, causing excessive greasiness.

   If you do not have automatic equipment with thermostatic temperature controls, keep a fat thermometer clipped to the side of the frying kettle.

3. Maintain the fat at the proper level in the fryer. When additional fat must be added, allow time for it to heat.

4. Do not fry too many doughnuts at a time. Overloading will lower the fat temperature will not allow room for expansion of the doughnuts, and will make it difficult to turn them over.

5. Keep the fat clean. Skim out food particles as necessary. After each day's use, cool the fat until it is warm, strain it, and clean the equipment.

6. Discard spent fat. Old fat loses frying ability, browns excessively, and imparts a bad flavor.

7. Keep the fat covered when not in use. Try to aerate it as little as possible when filtering.

KEY POINTS TO REVIEW

▌ What mixing method is used for yeast-raised doughnuts?

▌ How are yeast doughnuts handled differently from other yeast products, such as breads and rolls?

▌ What are the frying procedures for yeast doughnuts and cake doughnuts?

▌ What are the guidelines for handling frying fat?

YEAST-RAISED DOUGHNUTS

Ingredients	U.S.		Metric	%
Shortening	3	oz	75 g	10
Sugar	4	oz	105 g	14
Salt	0.5	oz	13 g	1.75
Mace	0.09 oz (½ tsp)		2 g	0.3
Nonfat milk solids	1.5	oz	38 g	5
Eggs	4	oz	105 g	14
Bread flour	1 lb 13	oz	750 g	100
Yeast, instant osmotolerant	0.5	oz	13 g	1.7
Water	1 lb		410 g	55
Total weight:	**3 lb 10**	**oz**	**1511 g**	**201** %

PROCEDURE

MIXING

Modified straight dough method (p. 182)

Develop the dough completely, about 6–8 minutes at second speed.

FERMENTATION

About 1½ hours at 80°F (24°C)

SCALING

1.5 oz (45 g) per unit

See below for makeup.

Proof.

FRYING

360°F (182°C)

When the doughnuts are fried, lift them from the fat and let excess fat drip off. Place the doughnuts in one layer on absorbent paper. Cool.

--- **VARIATIONS** ---

Makeup of Yeast-Raised Doughnuts

RING DOUGHNUTS

1. Roll out the dough to ½ in. (12 mm) thick. Make sure the dough is of even thickness. Let the dough relax.
2. Cut out doughnuts with a doughnut cutter. Cut as close together as possible to minimize scrap.
3. Combine the scrap dough and let it relax. Roll it out and let it relax again. Continue cutting doughnuts.

JELLY-FILLED DOUGHNUTS (BISMARCKS)

METHOD 1

1. Scale the dough into 3½ lb (1600 g) presses. Let them relax for 10 minutes.
2. Divide the dough. Round the small units.
3. Let them relax a few minutes, then flatten lightly.

METHOD 2

1. Roll out the dough to ½ in. (12 mm) thick, as for ring doughnuts.
2. Cut out with round cutters (biscuit cutters, or doughnut cutters with the "hole" removed).
3. After frying and cooling, use a doughnut or jelly pump to fill the doughnuts. If a doughnut pump is not available, you can use a special pastry tip for filling small quantities of doughnuts (see illustration). Using a sharp, straight nozzle, pierce the side of the doughnut and inject the jelly into the center. *Note*: Other fillings besides jelly may be used, such as lemon, custard (see Pastry Cream, p. 263), and cream. If using a filling containing egg, milk, or cream, keep the doughnuts refrigerated.

LONG JOHNS

1. Roll out the dough to ½ in. (12 mm) thick, as for ring doughnuts.
2. With a pastry wheel, cut into strips 1½ in. (4 cm) wide and 3½ in. (9 cm) long.

FRIED CINNAMON ROLLS

1. Make up like baked Cinnamon Rolls (p. 202), except omit the butter in the filling.
2. Make sure the edges are well sealed so the rolls don't unwind during frying.

TWISTS

1. Scale into presses, divide the dough, and round the units, as for filled doughnuts.
2. Roll each unit on the bench with the palms of the hands to a strip about 8 in. (20 cm) long.
3. Place one hand over each end of the strip. Roll one end toward you and the other away from you to twist the strip.
4. Holding it by the ends, lift the strip off the bench, and bring the two ends together. The strip will twist around itself.
5. Seal the ends together.

CAKE DOUGHNUTS

Ingredients	U.S.			Metric	%
Shortening		3	oz	90 g	9
Sugar		7	oz	220 g	22
Salt		0.25	oz	8 g	0.8
Nonfat milk solids		1.5	oz	45 g	4.7
Mace		0.12	oz (1¾ tsp)	4 g	0.4
Vanilla extract		0.5	oz	15 g	1.5
Whole eggs		3	oz	90 g	9
Egg yolks		1.5	oz	30 g	3
Cake flour	1 lb	4	oz	750 g	62.5
Bread flour		12	oz	250 g	37.5
Baking powder		1.25	oz	40 g	4
Water	1 lb			500 g	50
Total weight:	**4 lb**	**2**	**oz**	**2042 g**	**204 %**

PROCEDURE

MIXING

Creaming method (p. 214)

Mix the dough until it is smooth, but do not overmix.

MAKEUP

1. Place the dough on the bench and with the hands form into a smooth rectangular shape; rest 15 minutes.
2. Roll out to about ⅜ in. (1 cm) thick. Make sure the dough is of even thickness and does not stick to the bench.
3. Cut out doughnuts with cutters.
4. Collect the scrap dough and let it relax. Roll it out again and continue cutting doughnuts.
5. Place the doughnuts on lightly floured pans and let them relax 15 minutes.

FRYING

375°F (190°C)

Lift the doughnuts from fat, let the excess fat drip off, and place them in one layer on absorbent paper. Cool.

CHOCOLATE CAKE DOUGHNUTS

For large-quantity measurements, see page 717.

Ingredients	U.S.			Metric	%
Shortening		1.5	oz	45 g	9
Sugar		4	oz	125 g	25
Salt		0.13	oz (½ tsp)	4 g	0.8
Nonfat milk solids		0.75	oz	24 g	4.7
Vanilla extract		0.25	oz	8 g	1.5
Whole eggs		1.5	oz	45 g	9
Egg yolks		0.5	oz	15 g	3
Cake flour		10	oz	315 g	62.5
Bread flour		6	oz	185 g	37.5
Cocoa powder		1.25	oz	40 g	7.8
Baking powder		0.25	oz	15 g	3
Baking soda		0.1	oz (½ tsp)	3 g	0.63
Water		8.5	oz	265 g	53
Total weight:	**2 lb**	**2**	**oz**	**1089 g**	**217 %**

PROCEDURE

MIXING

Creaming method (p. 214)

Mix the dough until it is smooth, but do not overmix.

MAKEUP AND FRYING

Same as for Cake Doughnuts. *Caution*: When frying chocolate doughnuts, watch carefully because it is harder to tell doneness by their color.

RICH VANILLA SPICE DOUGHNUTS

For large-quantity measurements, see page 717.

Ingredients	U.S.		Metric	%
Bread flour	12	oz	375 g	50
Cake flour	12	oz	375 g	50
Baking powder	0.75 oz		22 g	3
Nutmeg	0.2	oz (1 tbsp)	6 g	0.8
Cinnamon	0.06 oz (1 tsp)		2 g	0.25
Salt	0.3	oz (1¼ tsp)	9 g	1.25
Whole eggs	5	oz	155 g	21
Egg yolks	1	oz	30 g	4
Sugar	10	oz	315 g	42
Milk	9.5	oz	300 g	40
Vanilla extract	0.75 oz		22 g	3
Butter, melted	3	oz	95 g	12.5
Total weight:	**3 lb 6**	**oz**	**1706 g**	**227 %**

PROCEDURE

MIXING

Muffin method (p. 213), modified as follows:

1. Sift together the flour, baking powder, spices, and salt.
2. Whip together the eggs, egg yolks, and sugar until light. Mix in the milk, vanilla, and melted butter.
3. Fold the liquid ingredients into the dry ingredients to make a soft dough.
4. Refrigerate at least 1 hour before rolling and cutting.

MAKEUP

Same as for Cake Doughnuts (p. 233).

FRYING

375°F (190°C)

Finishing Doughnuts

FRENCH DOUGHNUTS

French doughnuts are made from Éclair Paste (p. 330) that is piped into ring shapes and deep-fried. They are included in the next section on fritters.

Doughnuts should be well drained and cooled before finishing with sugar or other coatings. If they are hot, steam from the doughnuts will soak the coating. The following are some popular coatings and finishes for doughnuts:

- Roll in Cinnamon Sugar (p. 193).
- Roll in 4X sugar. (To keep the sugar from lumping and absorbing moisture, it may be sifted with cornstarch. Use 2 to 3 ounces starch per pound of sugar, or about 150 g per kg.)
- Ice the tops of the doughnuts with a fondant or fudge icing (see Chapter 17).
- To *glaze*, dip in warm Doughnut Glaze (recipe follows) or in a warmed, thinned simple icing or fondant. Place on screens until glaze sets.
- After glazing, and while glaze is still moist, doughnuts may be rolled in coconut or chopped nuts.

DOUGHNUT GLAZE

Ingredients	U.S.		Metric	Sugar at 100% %
Gelatin	0.12 oz		3 g	0.3
Water	8	oz	200 g	20
Corn syrup	2	oz	50 g	5
Vanilla extract	0.25 oz (1½ tsp)		6 g	0.6
Confectioners' sugar	2 lb 8	oz	1000 g	100
Total weight:	**3 lb 2**	**oz**	**1259 g**	**125 %**

PROCEDURE

1. Soften the gelatin in the water.
2. Heat the water until the gelatin dissolves.
3. Add the remaining ingredients and mix until smooth.
4. Dip doughnuts into the warm glaze. Rewarm the glaze as necessary.

--- **VARIATION** ---

HONEY GLAZE

Substitute honey for the corn syrup.

Fritters

The term *fritter* is used for a great variety of fried items, both sweet and savory, including many made with vegetables, meats, or fish. Fried items of all types are often referred to by the French term for fritter, *beignet* (pronounced ben YAY). In the pastry shop, we are concerned with two basic types of fritters:

1. Simple fritters, like doughnuts, are portions of dough that are deep-fried. They are usually dusted with sugar and often served with a sauce or a fruit preserve. This chapter includes recipes for four kinds of simple fritters, including the classic *beignet soufflé*, which is fried éclair paste.

2. Fruit fritters are made by dipping pieces of fresh, cooked, or canned fruit in batter and then deep-frying them, or by mixing chopped fruit into a batter and dropping scoopfuls into frying fat. A basic procedure for making fruit fritters follows. Two recipes for fritter batters also are included.

Also included in this chapter are *cannoli* shells. This type of fried pastry is not generally classified as a fritter. Nevertheless, cannoli shells are made in nearly the same way as two fritters in this chapter, fattigman and beignets de carnival—that is, they are made from a stiff dough that is rolled thin, cut out, and fried. Cannoli, however, are fried in a cylinder shape so they can take various fillings.

PROCEDURE: Preparing Fruit Fritters

1. Prepare batter (see formulas that follow).
2. Prepare the desired fruit. Popular fruits for fritters are:

    Apples Peel, core, and slice into rings ¼ in. (6 mm) thick.

    Bananas Peel, cut in half lengthwise, and then cut crosswise to make four quarters.

    Pineapple Use fresh or canned rings.

    Apricots and plums Split in half and remove the stones.

    For extra flavor, sprinkle fruits heavily with sugar and rum or kirsch and allow to marinate 1 to 2 hours.

3. Drain the fruit pieces well and dip them in batter to coat completely. Dip only as much as can be fried in one batch.
4. Drop into hot fat (375°F/190°C). Fry until golden brown on all sides.
5. Remove from fat and drain well.
6. Serve warm, sprinkled with cinnamon sugar. Crème Anglaise (p. 261) or Fruit Sauce (p. 267) may be served on the side.

FRITTER BATTER I

For large-quantity measurements, see page 717.

Ingredients	U.S.	Metric	%
Pastry flour	9 oz	250 g	100
Sugar	0.5 oz	15 g	6
Salt	0.12 oz (½ tsp)	4 g	1.5
Baking powder	0.12 oz (¾ tsp)	4 g	1.5
Eggs, beaten	4.5 oz	125 g	50
Milk	8 oz	225 g	90
Oil	0.5 oz	15 g	6
Vanilla extract	0.08 oz (½ tsp)	2 g	1
Total weight:	1 lb 6 oz	640 g	256 %

PROCEDURE

MIXING

Muffin method (p. 213)

1. Sift together the dry ingredients.
2. Combine the liquid ingredients.
3. Gradually stir the liquid into the dry ingredients. Mix until nearly smooth, but do not overmix.
4. Let stand at least 30 minutes before using.

FRITTER BATTER II

For large-quantity measurements, see page 717.

Ingredients	U.S.		Metric	%
Bread flour	6	oz	190 g	75
Cake flour	2	oz	60 g	25
Salt	0.12 oz (½ tsp)		4 g	1.5
Sugar	0.25 oz		8 g	3
Milk	9	oz	312 g	113
Egg yolks, beaten	1	oz	30 g	12.5
Oil	1	oz	30 g	12.5
Egg whites	2	oz	60 g	25
Total weight:	**1 lb 5**	**oz**	**694 g**	**267 %**

PROCEDURE

1. Sift together the dry ingredients.
2. Combine the milk, egg yolks, and oil.
3. Stir the liquid into the dry ingredients. Mix until smooth.
4. Let rest until ready to use, at least 30 minutes.
5. Whip the egg whites until stiff but not dry.
6. Fold the egg whites into the batter. Use immediately.

FRENCH DOUGHNUTS (BEIGNETS SOUFFLÉS)

For large-quantity measurements, see page 718.

Ingredients	U.S.		Metric	%
Milk	10	oz	250 g	167
Butter	4	oz	100 g	67
Salt	0.18 oz (¾ tsp)		5 g	3
Sugar	0.18 oz (1 tsp)		5 g	3
Bread flour	6	oz	150 g	100
Eggs	8	oz	200 g	133
Total weight:	**1 lb 12**	**oz**	**710 g**	**473%**

PROCEDURE

MIXING

1. In a saucepan, heat the milk, butter, salt, and sugar until the sugar dissolves and the butter is melted.
2. Bring to a rapid boil. Add the flour all at once and beat in vigorously with a wooden spoon.
3. Over medium heat, beat the mixture for 2–3 minutes, until the mixture pulls away from the sides of the pan.
4. Turn the mixture into a stainless steel bowl and cool slightly.
5. Add the eggs in 3 stages, beating well between additions.
6. Place the dough in a piping bag fitted with a large star tip.

FRYING

The doughnuts may be finished in either of two ways:

Method 1: Pipe the mixture directly into a deep fryer heated to 340°F (170°C), cutting off the dough in 3-in. (7–8-cm) pieces using a knife dipped in the hot fat. Fry until puffed and golden. Drain on kitchen paper.

Method 2: Pipe 2-in. (5-cm) circles onto parchment paper. (To make uniform shapes, mark 2-in./5-cm circles on the paper by tracing around a 2-in./5-cm cutter with a pencil. Turn the paper over and use the outlines as a guide.) Freeze. Fry the frozen units as in method 1.

See page 618 for a presentation suggestion.

BEIGNETS DE CARNIVAL

For large-quantity measurements, see page 718.

Ingredients	U.S.		Metric	%
Bread flour	7	oz	200 g	100
Sugar	0.5	oz	15 g	8
Salt	0.18 oz (¾ tsp)		5 g	2.5
Egg yolks	2	oz	60 g	30
Light cream	2	oz	60 g	30
Kirsch	0.5	oz	15 g	8
Rose water	0.33 oz (2 tsp)		10 g	5
Total weight:	**12**	**oz**	**365 g**	**183 %**

PROCEDURE

MIXING

1. Sift the flour, sugar, and salt into a bowl.
2. In a separate bowl, combine egg yolks, cream, kirsch, and rose water.
3. Make a well in the dry ingredients and pour the liquids into it. Combine to a stiff dough.
4. Turn out onto a lightly floured surface and knead until a smooth ball forms.
5. Place the dough onto a lightly floured plate, cover tightly with plastic film, and chill overnight.

FRYING

1. Bring the dough back to room temperature.
2. Cut the rested dough into pieces ⅓ oz (10 g) each. While you are working, keep dough covered with a damp cloth or plastic film to prevent a crust forming.
3. Taking one piece of dough at a time, roll out very thinly until the dough starts to shrink back. Place under a damp cloth or plastic film and continue rolling the rest of the dough, one piece at a time.
4. Starting again with the first piece, begin rolling the dough a second time, until it is nearly transparent. This process gives the dough time to rest and assists very thin rolling.
5. Once you have rolled the dough for the second time, trim the circles to uniform size using a 4½-in. (11-cm) round cutter. Place the cut pieces on a sheet pan lined with parchment paper. Cover with plastic film.
6. Preheat the fryer to 355°F (180°C). Drop the beignets into the hot fat one at a time. Turn once when golden brown. You can fry the beignets flat, or shape them by holding them under the fat with a long-handled spoon, pressing firmly into the middle of each beignet; this causes them to cup slightly as they fry.
7. When golden, remove, and drain on kitchen paper.
8. Serve with choice of poached fruit or fruit compote.

FATTIGMAN

Ingredients	U.S.	Metric	%
Whole eggs	3.33 oz (2 eggs)	100 g (2 eggs)	24
Egg yolks	1.33 oz (2 yolks)	40 g (2 yolks)	10
Salt	0.13 oz (⅔ tsp)	4 g	1
Sugar	2.5 oz	70 g	18
Cardamom, ground	0.07 oz (1 tsp)	2 g	0.5
Heavy cream	3 oz	85 g	21
Brandy	1.5 oz	45 g	11
Bread flour	14 oz	400 g	100
Confectioners' sugar	as needed	as needed	
Total dough weight:	**1 lb 9 oz**	**746 g**	**185 %**

PROCEDURE

1. Whip the eggs and yolks until foamy.
2. Beat in the salt, sugar, cardamom, and cream.
3. Add the brandy and mix well.
4. Add the flour and blend to make a dough.
5. Wrap or cover the dough and rest, refrigerated, for at least 1 hour.
6. Roll out the dough ⅛ in. (3 mm) thick.
7. Cut into small triangles about 2½ in. (6 cm) on a side.
8. Deep-fry at 375°F (190°C) until lightly browned and crisp.
9. Drain and cool.
10. Dust lightly with 10X sugar.

VIENNOISE

Yield: 10 pastries, 2 oz (60 g) each

For large-quantity measurements, see page 718.

Ingredients	U.S.	Metric
Brioche dough (p. 188)	1 lb 4 oz	600 g
Egg wash	as needed	as needed
Red currant jelly	3.5 oz	100 g

PROCEDURE

1. Scale the brioche dough into 2-oz (60-g) pieces.
2. On a lightly floured work surface, roll each piece into a 4-in. (10-cm) circle.
3. Brush the tops with egg wash.
4. Place ⅓ oz (10 g) jelly in the center of each circle. Enclose the jelly by gathering the edges of the circle together over the jelly to form a "purse." Place upside down (seam on bottom) on a sheet pan lined with parchment. Proof in a warm place until double in size, about 40 minutes.
5. Deep-fry at 340°F (170°C) until golden brown, turning once. Frying time is about 8 minutes.
6. Drain.

CANNOLI SHELLS

For large-quantity measurements, see page 718.

Ingredients	U.S.		Metric	%
Bread flour	6	oz	175 g	50
Pastry flour	6	oz	175 g	50
Sugar	1	oz	30 g	8
Salt	0.04 oz (⅛ tsp)		1 g	0.3
Butter	2	oz	60 g	17
Egg, beaten	1.67 oz (1 egg)		50 g (1 egg)	14
Dry white wine or Marsala	4	oz	125 g	33
Total weight:	**1 lb 4**	**oz**	**616 g**	**172 %**

PROCEDURE

1. Sift the flour, sugar, and salt together into a bowl.
2. Add the butter and work in with your hands until evenly blended.
3. Add the egg and wine and work in to make a dough. Knead it a few times on a floured workbench until it is smooth. Cover and let rest for 30 minutes.
4. Roll out the pastry into a sheet about ⅛ in. (3 mm) thick. Dock it well. For small cannoli, cut into 3½-in. (9-cm) circles; for large cannoli, cut into 5-in. (12-cm) circles. Rework the scraps to cut additional circles. *Note:* 20 oz (600 g) dough is enough for 16–18 large cannoli or 32–36 small ones.
5. Roll the circles around cannoli tubes. Where the edges of the circle overlap, press firmly to seal.
6. Deep-fry at 375°F (190°C) until golden brown. Cool for a few seconds, then carefully slip out the tube. Cool completely before filling. Shells may be filled with a variety of fillings, including vanilla and chocolate pastry creams and other thick creams and puddings.

--- VARIATION ---

SICILIAN CANNOLI

Using a pastry bag, fill cooled cannoli shells from both ends with Ricotta Cannoli Filling (below). Sprinkle lightly with confectioners' sugar. If desired, decorate the filling at the ends of the cannoli with halved candied cherries, colored sugar, or chopped pistachios.

RICOTTA CANNOLI FILLING

For large-quantity measurements, see page 718.

Ingredients	U.S.		Metric	%
Ricotta impastata (see p. 72)	1 lb		500 g	100
Confectioners' sugar	8	oz	250 g	50
Cinnamon extract	0.25 oz (1½ tsp)		7 g	1.5
Candied citron, candied citrus peel, or candied pumpkin, finely diced	1.5	oz	45 g	9
Sweet chocolate, finely chopped, or tiny chocolate bits	1	oz	30 g	6
Total weight:	**1 lb 10**	**oz**	**832 g**	**166 %**

PROCEDURE

1. Process the ricotta in a blender until it is very smooth.
2. Sift the sugar and fold in until well mixed.
3. Mix in the remaining ingredients.

JALEBIS

Yield: approximately 100 pieces

Ingredient	U.S.	Metric	%
Bread flour	8 oz	250 g	50
Pastry flour	8 oz	250 g	50
Plain yogurt	4 oz	125 g	25
Water	12 oz	375 g	75
Powdered saffron	¼ tsp	1 mL	
Water	6 oz	185 g	37.5
Total weight of batter:	**2 lb 6 oz**	**1185 g**	**237 %**
Syrup			
Water	1 lb 12 oz	800 g	
Sugar	1 lb 12 oz	800 g	
Saffron	1 tsp	5 mL	
Ground cardamom	½ tsp	2 mL	
Rose water	1 fl oz	15 mL	

VARIATION

For a less expensive version, omit both quantities of saffron. Instead, color the batter and syrup pale orange using red and yellow food colors, if desired.

PROCEDURE

MIXING

1. Sift together the bread flour and pastry flour into a bowl.
2. Beat the yogurt until smooth.
3. Mix the first quantity of water into the yogurt.
4. Stir the yogurt mixture and the saffron into the flour. Mix until smooth.
5. Stir in the second quantity of water to make a batter.
6. Strain.
7. Let the batter stand several hours or overnight.

PREPARING THE SYRUP

1. Combine the water and sugar in a heavy saucepan. Bring to a boil.
2. Boil until the sugar is completely dissolved and the syrup reaches 230°F (110°C) when tested with a sugar thermometer.
3. Remove from the heat and stir in the saffron and cardamom.
4. When the syrup has cooled but is still warm, stir in the rose water.

FRYING AND FINISHING

1. Before frying, reheat the syrup until it is hot. Set aside.
2. Fill a squeeze bottle with batter. The opening of the squeeze bottle should be about ⅛ in. (3 mm) across, about the same as on a ketchup squeeze bottle.
3. Heat frying fat to 350°F (175°C).
4. With the squeeze bottle, drop the batter into the fat in tight spirals 2½–3 in. (6–7 cm) across.
5. Fry on both sides until very lightly browned.
6. Remove from the fat and drain on absorbent paper for 1 minute.
7. Drop the jalebis into the warm syrup. Leave in the syrup for 2–4 minutes, then remove and drain.

INDIAN DESSERTS

Desserts from India are known for being aromatic and sweet. Many types of pastries are sweetened by soaking them in a flavored syrup. Jalebis are a deep-fried example of a pastry soaked in syrup. Freshly made, hot jalebis are often sold by street vendors in India.

CHINESE SESAME BALLS

Yield: 40 pieces, about 1 oz (25 g) each

Ingredient	U.S.	Metric	%
Water	10 oz	250 g	62.5
Brown sugar	6 oz	200 g	37.5
Glutinous rice powder	1 lb	400 g	100
Red bean paste or lotus paste, canned	8 oz	150 g	50
Sesame seeds	as needed	as needed	
Total weight:	**2 lb 8 oz**	**1000 g**	**250** %

PROCEDURE

MIXING

1. Bring the water to a boil in a saucepan. Add the sugar and stir until dissolved.
2. Place the glutinous rice powder in a mixing bowl.
3. Mix the syrup into the rice powder to make a dough. Knead the dough until it is smooth.

MAKEUP

1. Divide the dough into 4 equal pieces.
2. Using rice powder to dust the workbench and your hands, roll each piece of dough into a cylinder about 10 in. (25 cm) long.
3. Cut each cylinder into 10 equal pieces.
4. Roll each piece between the palms of your hands into a ball.
5. Roll the bean paste or lotus paste into small balls of about 1 tsp (5 g) each. If the paste is too soft to work with, refrigerate or partially freeze it.
6. Make a deep indentation in each rice dough ball with the thumb. Place a ball of bean paste inside and mold the dough to cover the hole completely. Make sure it is well sealed.
7. Place the sesame seeds in a pan or bowl.
8. Dip your hands in water, then roll a filled ball between the palms of the hands to moisten it slightly to help the seeds stick.
9. Roll the ball in the sesame seeds until well coated.

FRYING

1. Heat frying fat to 350°F (175°C).
2. Drop a few sesame balls into the hot fat. Fry about 2 minutes.
3. When the balls are lightly browned, they should be squeezed gently to help them expand in size slightly. For example, use a pair of tongs to squeeze and turn the balls, or use a spatula to press them lightly against the side of the fryer. Release and repeat. (This technique takes a little practice.)
4. Continue frying until the balls are golden brown.
5. Drain. Serve warm.

CHINESE PASTRIES

Chinese pastries are not usually very sweet, at least by European and North American standards, and desserts are not part of a typical Chinese dinner. Pastries are more often eaten as tea snacks or as part of a morning or midday meal of dumplings and other little dishes known as *dim sum*.

Pastes made from seeds, legumes, and nuts are often used as pastry fillings and are available already prepared. The red beans used for the paste in the recipe for sesame balls are small red dried beans known as *azuki beans*. They are also used to make a lightly sweetened soup sometimes served as dessert on banquet menus.

PANCAKES AND WAFFLES

ALTHOUGH PANCAKES AND waffles are rarely produced in the retail bakeshop, they are essential items on the breakfast, brunch, and dessert menus in food service operations. In addition, a French waffle (*gaufre*) formula that is especially well suited for dessert is included here. This batter is actually an éclair paste thinned with cream or milk. French pancakes, or *crêpes*, and desserts made from them are also presented.

American-Style Pancakes and Waffles

American-style pancakes and waffles are made from pourable batters mixed by the muffin method, which is presented in Chapter 10. As with muffins, it is important to avoid overmixing the batters for these products in order to prevent excessive gluten development.

Pancakes and waffles can be made in almost unlimited varieties by substituting other types of flour, such as buckwheat flour, whole wheat flour, and cornmeal, for part of the pastry flour. As some of these absorb more water than others, additional liquid may be needed to thin the batter.

Compare the formulas for pancakes and waffles. In particular, pay attention to these differences:

- Waffle batter contains more fat. This makes the waffles richer and crisper and aids in their release from the waffle iron.
- Waffle batter contains less liquid, so it is slightly thicker. This, too, makes waffles crisp, as crispness depends on low moisture content.
- Whipping the egg whites separately and folding them into the batter gives waffles added lightness.

Advance Preparation for Volume Service

1. Pancake and waffle batters leavened *only by baking powder* may be mixed the night before and stored in the cooler. Some rising power may be lost, so baking powder may have to be increased.

2. Batters leavened by *baking soda* should not be made too far ahead because the soda will lose its power. Mix dry ingredients and liquid ingredients ahead; combine just before service.

3. Batters using beaten *egg whites and baking powder* may be partially made ahead, but *incorporate the egg whites just before service*.

PANCAKES AND WAFFLES

Yield: about 1 qt (1 L)

Ingredients	Pancakes			Waffles		
	U.S.	Metric	%	U.S.	Metric	%
Pastry flour	8 oz	225 g	100	8 oz	225 g	100
Sugar	1 oz	30 g	12.5	—	—	—
Salt	0.08 oz (½ tsp)	2.5 g	1	0.08 oz (½ tsp)	2 g	1
Baking powder	0.5 oz (1 tbsp)	15 g	6	0.5 oz (1 tbsp)	15 g	6
Whole eggs, beaten	3.5 oz (2 large)	100 g	44	—	—	—
Egg yolks, beaten	—	—	—	2 oz	55 g	25
Milk	1 lb	450 g	200	12 oz	340 g	150
Butter, melted, or oil	2 oz	55 g	25	4 oz	112 g	50
Egg whites	—	—	—	3 oz (3 large)	85 g	38
Sugar	—	—	—	1 oz	30 g	12.5

PROCEDURE

MIXING

Muffin method (p. 213)

1. Sift together the dry ingredients.
2. Combine the eggs or egg yolks, milk, and fat.
3. Add the liquid ingredients to the dry ingredients. Mix until just combined. Do not overmix.
4. For waffles: Just before they are to be cooked, whip the egg whites until they form soft peaks, then beat in the sugar until the meringue is stiff. Fold into the batter.

COOKING PANCAKES

1. Using a 2-oz (60-mL) ladle, measure portions of batter onto a greased, preheated griddle (375°F/190°C), allowing space for spreading.
2. Fry the pancakes until the tops are covered with bubbles and begin to look dry, and the bottoms are golden brown.
3. Turn and brown the other side.
4. Serve hot, accompanied by butter, maple syrup, fruit syrup, jams or preserves, applesauce, or fresh berries.

COOKING WAFFLES

1. Pour enough batter onto a lightly greased, preheated waffle iron to almost cover the surface. Close the iron.
2. Cook the waffles until the signal light indicates they are done, or until steam is no longer emitted. The waffles should be brown and crisp.
3. Serve warm with confectioners' sugar, syrup, jam, or fresh fruit.

--- VARIATION ---

BUTTERMILK PANCAKES AND WAFFLES

Use buttermilk instead of milk. Reduce baking powder to 3% (0.25 oz or 1½ tsp/7 g) and add ¾ tsp (3 g) baking soda. If the batter is too thick, thin it with milk or water as necessary (up to 50%).

GAUFRES (FRENCH WAFFLES)

Ingredients	U.S.		Metric	%	PROCEDURE
Milk	1 lb		500 g	200	1. Combine the milk, salt, and butter in a saucepan or kettle. Carefully bring to a boil.
Salt		0.25 oz	8 g	3	
Butter	3	oz	95 g	37.5	2. Add the flour all at once and stir vigorously. Continue to stir until the mixture forms a ball and pulls away from the sides of the kettle.
Bread flour	8	oz	250 g	100	
Eggs	13	oz	400 g	162.5	3. Remove from the heat and transfer to the bowl of a mixer. Let cool 5 minutes.
	(about 8 large eggs)				
Cream	8	oz	250 g	100	4. With the mixer on low speed, add the eggs a little at a time. Wait until each addition is absorbed before adding more.
Milk	4	oz	125 g	50	
Total weight:	**3 lb 4**	**oz**	**1628 g**	**653 %**	5. With the mixer running, slowly pour in the cream, then the milk. Don't worry if the batter is slightly lumpy even after all the milk has been added; this is normal. The batter should be slightly thicker than regular waffle batter. If it is much thicker, add a little more milk.

6. Bake as you would regular waffles.

Crêpes

Crêpes are thin, unleavened pancakes. They are rarely served plain but are instead used to construct a great variety of desserts by being rolled around fillings, layered with fillings, or served with sweet sauces. Unsweetened crêpes are used in similar ways but filled with meat, fish, or vegetable preparations.

Unlike leavened pancakes, crêpes may be made in advance, covered and refrigerated, and used as needed. When the crêpes are filled and rolled or folded, the side that was browned first, which is the more attractive side, should be on the outside.

CRÊPES

Yield: about 50 crêpes

Ingredients	U.S.	Metric	%
Bread flour	8 oz	250 g	50
Cake flour	8 oz	250 g	50
Sugar	2 oz	60 g	12.5
Salt	0.5 oz	15 g	3
Eggs	12 oz (7 large eggs)	375 g (7 large eggs)	75
Milk	2 lb	1000 g	200
Oil or clarified butter	5 oz	150 g	20
Total weight:	**4 lb 3 oz**	**2100 g**	**410 %**

PROCEDURE

MIXING

1. Sift the flour, sugar, and salt into a bowl.
2. Add the eggs and just enough of the milk to make a soft paste with the flour. Mix until smooth and lump-free.
3. Gradually mix in the rest of the milk and the oil. The batter should be about the consistency of heavy cream. If it is too thick, mix in a little water. If it has lumps, pour it through a strainer.
4. Let the batter rest 2 hours before frying.

FRYING

1. Rub a 6- or 7-in. (15–18-cm) crêpe pan or skillet lightly with oil. Heat the pan over moderately high heat until it is very hot. Brush lightly with melted butter and pour off any excess (a).
2. Remove from heat and pour in about 3–4 tablespoons (45–60 mL) of the batter. Very quickly tilt the pan to cover the bottom with a thin layer. Immediately dump out any excess batter, as the crêpe must be very thin (b).
3. Return to the heat for about 1–1½ minutes, until the bottom is lightly browned (c). Flip the crêpe and brown the second side (d). The second side will brown in only a few spots and will not be as attractive as the first side. Therefore the first side should always be the visible side when the crêpe is served (e).
4. Slide the crêpe onto a plate. Continue making crêpes and stacking them as they are finished. Grease the pan lightly when necessary.
5. Cover the finished crêpes and refrigerate until needed.

--- **VARIATION** ---

CHOCOLATE CRÊPES

Ingredients	U.S.	Metric	%
Bread flour	6 oz	190 g	37.5
Cake flour	8 oz	250 g	50
Cocoa powder	2 oz	60 g	12.5

Reduce the quantity of flour in the crêpe formula and add cocoa powder in the proportion listed. Sift the cocoa with the flour in step 1 of the mixing procedure.

Crêpe Desserts

The variety of crêpe desserts you can prepare is limited only by your imagination. The following are only a few of many possible suggestions.

Crêpes Normande. Sauté fresh sliced apples in butter and sprinkle with sugar and a dash of cinnamon. Roll the apples in crêpes and dust with confectioners' sugar.

Banana Crêpes. Sauté sliced bananas quickly in butter and sprinkle with brown sugar and a dash of rum. Roll the filling in the crêpes. Serve with apricot sauce (p. 267).

Crêpes with Jam. Spread apricot jam on crêpes and roll them up. Sprinkle with sugar and run under the broiler quickly to glaze the sugar.

Glazed Crêpes. Fill crêpes with vanilla pastry cream (p. 263) and roll them up. Sprinkle with sugar and run under the broiler to glaze the sugar.

Crêpes Frangipane. Spread the crêpes with Frangipane filling (p. 196) and roll them up or fold them in quarters. Brush with butter and sprinkle with sugar. Place in a buttered baking dish and bake in a hot oven about 10 minutes to heat through. Serve with chocolate sauce or vanilla sauce.

Crêpes Suzette. This most famous of all crêpe desserts is generally prepared at tableside by the waiter according to the procedure in the following recipe. The crêpes, fruit, sugar, and butter are supplied by the kitchen. The dish can also be prepared in the kitchen or pastry department by coating crêpes with hot Sauce Suzette (p. 275).

CRÊPES SUZETTE (DINING ROOM PREPARATION)

Yield: 4 portions

Ingredients	U.S.	Metric
Sugar	3 oz	85 g
Orange	1	1
Lemon	½	½
Butter	2 oz	60 g
Orange-flavored liqueur	1 oz	30 mL
Cognac	2 oz	60 mL
Crêpes	12	12

PROCEDURE

1. In a flambé pan, heat the sugar until it melts and begins to caramelize.

2. Cut several strips of rind from the orange and one from the lemon; add them to the pan.

3. Add the butter and squeeze the juice from the orange and lemon into the pan. Cook and stir until the sugar is dissolved and the mixture is a little syrupy.

4. Add the orange liqueur. One by one, dip the crêpes in the sauce to coat, then fold them into quarters in the pan.

5. Add the cognac and allow it to heat for a few seconds. Flame by carefully tipping the pan toward the burner flame until the cognac ignites.

6. Shake the pan gently and spoon the sauce over the crêpes until the flame dies down.

7. Serve 3 crêpes per portion. Spoon a little of the remaining sauce over each serving.

CRÊPES SOUFFLÉS SUZETTE

Yield: 6 portions

Ingredients	U.S.		Metric
Orange juice	8	oz	250 g
Cornstarch	1	oz	25 g
Water	as needed		as needed
Sugar	1	oz	30 g
Orange liqueur, such as Grand Marnier	1.67 oz		50 g
Vanilla extract	½	tsp	2 g
Egg whites	4	oz	125 g
Sugar	2.5	oz	75 g
Crêpes (p. 245)	18		18
Confectioners' sugar	as needed		as needed
Sauce Suzette (p. 275)	8	fl oz	240 mL
Candied orange zest	as desired		as desired
Berries or other fruit garnish	as desired		as desired

PROCEDURE

1. Heat the orange juice.
2. Mix the cornstarch with enough cold water to make a smooth slurry. Stir into the orange juice and cook, stirring, until thickened.
3. Add the sugar, liqueur, and vanilla. Boil to dissolve the sugar.
4. Cool the mixture.
5. Whip the egg whites to soft peaks. Add the sugar and whip to a firm meringue.
6. Whip one-third of the meringue into the orange base, then fold in the remaining meringue.
7. Fit a pastry bag with a medium plain tip. Fill with the orange meringue mixture.
8. Fold the crêpes into quarters. Using the pastry bag, fill the folded pancakes with the orange meringue mixture. The pancakes may now be frozen for later use if desired.
9. Arrange the filled pancakes on a greased baking sheet. Bake at 375°F (190°C) until well risen and firm to the touch.
10. Dust lightly with confectioners' sugar.
11. Ladle a ring of Sauce Suzette onto each plate. Arrange 3 crêpes on each plate. Garnish as desired with candied zest and berries.

CHOCOLATE SOUFFLÉ CRÊPES

Yield: 6 portions

Ingredients	U.S.		Metric
Milk	8	oz	250 g
Bittersweet chocolate	1.67	oz	50 g
Cornstarch	1	oz	25 g
Rum	1	oz	30 g
Sugar	1.67	oz	50 g
Vanilla extract	½	tsp	2 g
Egg whites	4	oz	125 g
Sugar	2.5	oz	75 g
Chocolate Crêpes (p. 245)	18		18
Chocolate Sauce (p. 269)	8	oz	250 g
Plain yogurt	4	tsp	20 g
Candied orange zest	0.5–1	oz	20 g

PROCEDURE

1. Heat the milk and chocolate together, stirring, until the chocolate is melted and well mixed with the milk. Bring to a simmer.

2. Combine the cornstarch and rum and mix to a smooth paste. Stir into the hot milk and simmer until thickened.

3. Stir in the sugar and vanilla until the sugar is dissolved.

4. Whip the egg whites to soft peaks. Add the sugar and whip to a firm meringue.

5. Whip one-third of the meringue into the chocolate base, then fold in the remaining meringue.

6. Fit a pastry bag with a medium plain tip. Fill with the chocolate meringue mixture.

7. Fold the chocolate crêpes into quarters. Using the pastry bag, fill the folded pancakes with the chocolate meringue mixture. The pancakes may now be frozen for later use if desired.

8. Arrange the filled pancakes on a greased baking sheet. Bake at 375°F (190°C) until well risen and firm to the touch.

9. Dust lightly with confectioners' sugar.

10. Ladle a pool of Chocolate Sauce onto each plate. Arrange 3 crêpes on each plate. Pipe a few dots of yogurt onto the sauce and feather. Garnish with candied orange zest.

CRÊPE GÂTEAU WITH PLUM COMPOTE

Yield: 1 portion

Ingredients	U.S.	Metric
Plum Compote (p. 591)	4 oz	115 g
Crêpes (p. 245)	5	5
Garnish		
Vanilla Ice Cream (p. 550)	as needed	as needed

PROCEDURE

1. Place the plum compote in a fine strainer. Reduce the drained liquid to the consistency of a light sauce.
2. Using a 2½- to 3-inch (6.5- to 7.5-cm) cutter, cut a round out of the center of each crêpe.
3. Place one crêpe round in the center of a plate and set the cutter over it.
4. Spoon one-fourth of the plum compote onto the crêpe and press down with the back of a spoon. Top with another crêpe.
5. Continue with the remaining compote and crêpes, ending with a crêpe. Remove the cutter.
6. Drizzle a little of the reduced liquid around the crêpe stack.
7. Top with a quenelle of ice cream.

KEY POINTS TO REVIEW

- What are the steps in the procedure for preparing fruit fritters?
- What mixing method is used to prepare pancake and waffle batters?
- What are the steps in the procedures for mixing and frying crêpes?

TERMS FOR REVIEW

modified straight dough method	glaze	cannoli	crêpe
	fritter	gaufre	crêpes Suzette
French doughnut	beignet soufflé		

QUESTIONS FOR REVIEW

1. Two yeast doughnut formulas have the same quantities of fat and milk, but one has more sugar than the other. Which one do you expect would require a higher frying temperature? Why?
2. Why is it important to carefully control the mixing time when making cake doughnuts?
3. List seven rules for maintaining frying fat to produce good-quality fried foods.
4. What type of leavening is used in crêpes (French pancakes)? In French doughnuts?
5. Why does waffle batter often contain less liquid (water or milk) than pancake batter?
6. Which mixing method is used to make American-style pancakes? What are the steps in this method?

12

BASIC SYRUPS, CREAMS, AND SAUCES

AFTER READING THIS CHAPTER, YOU SHOULD BE ABLE TO:

1. Cook sugar syrups to various stages of hardness.
2. Prepare whipped cream and meringues.
3. Prepare crème anglaise and pastry cream variations.
4. Prepare dessert sauces, ganache, and other chocolate creams.

MUCH OF THE baker's craft consists of mixing and baking flour goods such as breads, cakes, and pastries. However, the baker also must be able to make a variety of other products, sometimes known as *adjuncts*, such as toppings, fillings, and sauces. These are not baked goods in and of themselves, but they are essential in the preparation of many baked goods and desserts.

Several of the procedures you will learn in this chapter are used in many ways. For example, crème anglaise, or custard sauce, is used not only as a dessert sauce but also as the basis for such items as Bavarian creams and ice creams. Pastry cream, with a variety of flavorings, is also used for pie fillings, puddings, and soufflés.

Pastry Cream

Although it requires more ingredients and steps, pastry cream is easier to make than crème anglaise because it is less likely to curdle. *Pastry cream*, also called *crème pâtissière*, contains a starch-thickening agent that stabilizes the eggs. It can actually be boiled without curdling. In fact, it *must* be brought to a boil or the starch will not cook completely and the cream will have a raw, starchy taste. It may be necessary to boil the cream for up to 2 minutes to eliminate the taste of the starch.

Strict observance of all sanitation rules is essential when preparing pastry cream because of the danger of bacterial contamination. Use clean, sanitized equipment. Do not put your fingers in the cream; do not taste except with a clean spoon. Chill the finished cream rapidly in shallow pans. Keep the cream and all cream-filled products refrigerated at all times.

The procedure for preparing pastry cream is given in the formula that follows. Note the basic steps are similar to those for crème anglaise. In this case, however, a starch is mixed with the eggs and half the sugar to make a smooth paste. (In some formulas with lower egg content, it is necessary to add a little cold milk to provide enough liquid to make a paste.) Meanwhile, the milk is scalded with the other half of the sugar. The egg mixture is then tempered with some of the hot milk and then returned to the kettle and brought to a boil. Some chefs prefer to add the cold paste gradually to the hot milk, but the tempering procedure described here seems to protect better against lumping.

Pastry Cream Variations

Pastry cream has many applications in the bakeshop, so it is important to master the basic technique. Pastry cream and its variations are used as fillings for cakes and pastries, as fillings for cream pies (p. 299), and as puddings (p. 512). With additional liquid, it can also be used as a custard sauce.

Cornstarch should be used as the thickening agent when the cream is to be used as a pie filling so the cut slices hold their shape. For other uses, either cornstarch or flour may be used. Just remember that twice as much flour is needed to provide the same thickening power as cornstarch.

Other variations are possible, as you will see in the recipes. Sometimes whipped cream is folded into pastry cream to lighten it and make a creamier product called *pastry cream mousseline*. Adding a meringue to pastry cream and stabilizing it with gelatin makes a cream called **crème Chiboust** (pronounced shee BOO; p. 264).

PASTRY CREAM (CRÈME PÂTISSIÈRE)

Yield: about 1⅛ qt (1.12 L)

Ingredients	U.S.	Metric	Milk at 100% %
Milk	2 lb (1 qt)	1 L	100
Sugar	4 oz	125 g	12.5
Egg yolks	3 oz	90 g	9
Whole eggs	4 oz	125 g	12.5
Cornstarch	2.5 oz	75 g	8
Sugar	4 oz	125 g	12.5
Butter	2 oz	60 g	6
Vanilla extract	0.5 oz (1 tbsp)	15 mL	1.5

PROCEDURE

1. In a heavy saucepan or kettle, dissolve the sugar in the milk and bring just to a boil.

2. With a whip, beat the egg yolks and whole eggs in a stainless steel bowl.

3. Sift the cornstarch and sugar into the eggs. Beat with the whip until perfectly smooth (a).

4. Temper the egg mixture by slowly beating in the hot milk in a thin stream (b).

5. Return the mixture to the heat and bring to a boil, stirring constantly.

6. When the mixture comes to a boil, continue to stir constantly and boil for up to 2 minutes, until the cream has no raw, starchy taste (c). (As always when tasting, use a clean tasting spoon, and do not reuse the spoon.)

7. Remove from the heat. Stir in the butter and vanilla. Mix until the butter is melted and completely blended in (d).

8. Pour out into a clean, sanitized hotel pan or other shallow pan. Cover with plastic film placed directly in contact with the surface of the cream to prevent a crust from forming (e). Cool and chill as quickly as possible.

9. For filling pastries such as èclairs and napoleons, whip the chilled pastry cream until smooth before using.

A

B

C

D

E

VARIATIONS

DELUXE PASTRY CREAM

Omit the whole eggs in the basic recipe and use 30% egg yolks (10 oz/ 300 g).

PASTRY CREAM MOUSSELINE

For a lighter pastry cream filling, fold whipped heavy cream into the chilled pastry cream. Quantities may be varied to taste. In general, for every 1 qt (1 L) pastry cream, use ½–1 cup (1.25–2.5 dL) heavy cream.

CHOCOLATE PASTRY CREAM

For each 12 oz pastry cream, stir in 4 oz melted semisweet or bittersweet chocolate while the pastry cream is still warm (100 g chocolate for each 300 g pastry cream).

PRALINE PASTRY CREAM

For each 12 oz pastry cream, stir in 4 oz softened praline paste while the pastry cream is still warm (100 g praline paste for each 300 g pastry cream).

COFFEE PASTRY CREAM

Add 2 tbsp (8 g) instant coffee powder or coffee compound (flavoring) to the milk in step 1.

CHIBOUST CREAM

Yield: about 3 lb (1500 g)

Ingredients	U.S.		Metric	Milk at 100% %
Milk	1 pt		500 g	100
Vanilla extract	½	tsp	2 g	0.4
Sugar	1	oz	30 g	6
Egg yolks	5.33 oz		160 g	33
Sugar	1	oz	30 g	6
Cornstarch	1.33 oz		40 g	8
Italian meringue				
Sugar	13	oz	400 g	80
Water	4	oz	120 g	24
Egg whites	8	oz	240 g	48
Gelatin	0.4	oz	12 g	2.5

PROCEDURE

1. Combine the milk, vanilla, and sugar and bring to a boil, stirring to dissolve the sugar.

2. Whip the egg yolks with the second quantity of sugar. Stir in the cornstarch.

3. Temper the egg mixture with half the hot milk. Pour this mixture back into the pan with the remaining milk. Return to a boil and boil for 1 minute, until thickened.

4. Turn out into a bowl and cover the surface with plastic film to prevent a skin from forming. Keep warm while making the Italian meringue.

5. Boil the sugar and water until the temperature of the syrup reaches 258°F (120°C). Whip the egg whites to firm peaks, then slowly pour the syrup into the whites, whipping constantly. Continue whipping until cool.

6. Soak the gelatin in cold water (see pp. 80–82) and add to the hot pastry cream (a).

7. Mix until the gelatin is dissolved (b). (If the pastry cream is not warm enough, rewarm it slightly.)

8. Add one-third of the meringue to the cream and mix quickly to lighten the mixture (c).

9. Gently fold in the remaining meringue until evenly mixed (d, e).

A

B

C

D

E

--- **VARIATIONS** ---

CHOCOLATE CHIBOUST CREAM

Ingredients	U.S.		Metric	%
Rum	1	oz	30 g	6
Bittersweet chocolate	3.5 oz		100 g	20

After step 3 in the basic recipe, stir in the rum and chopped bittersweet chocolate until the chocolate is melted and well blended.

COFFEE CHIBOUST CREAM

Ingredients	U.S.		Metric	%
Coffee liqueur	1	oz	30 g	6
Liquid coffee extract	1.67 oz		50 g	10

After step 3 in the basic recipe, stir in the coffee liqueur and liquid coffee extract.

PRALINE CHIBOUST CREAM

Ingredients	U.S.		Metric	%
Rum	1	oz	30 g	6
Praline paste	2.5 oz		75 g	15

After step 3 in the basic recipe, stir in the rum and praline paste.

CHIBOUST CREAM WITH RASPBERRIES

Yield: about 3 lb (1500 g)

Ingredients	U.S.		Metric	Milk at 100% %
Milk	1 pt		500 g	100
Sugar	1.33 oz		40 g	8
Egg yolks	5.33 oz		160 g	33
Sugar	1.33 oz		40 g	8
Cornstarch	1.67 oz		50 g	10
Italian meringue				
Sugar	13	oz	400 g	80
Water	4	oz	120 g	24
Egg whites	8	oz	240 g	48
Raspberry purée (unsweetened)	6	oz	180 g	36
Gelatin	0.5	oz	16 g	3

NOTE: The quantities of sugar, starch, and gelatin are greater in this recipe than in the basic Chiboust because the addition of raspberry purée requires additional sweetening and thickening.

--- VARIATION ---

CHIBOUST CREAM FLAVORED WITH ALCOHOL

Ingredients	U.S.		Metric	%
Lemon zest, grated	½	tsp	2 g	0.4
Liqueur or other alcohol	1.67 oz		50 g	10

Omit the raspberry purée from the basic recipe. Add grated lemon zest to the egg yolk mixture in step 2, and stir rum, kirsch, brandy, or orange liqueur into the warm pastry cream when adding the gelatin in step 7.

PROCEDURE

1. Combine the milk and sugar and bring to a boil, stirring to dissolve the sugar.

2. Whip the egg yolks with the second quantity of sugar. Stir in the cornstarch.

3. Temper the egg mixture with half the hot milk. Pour this mixture back into the pan with the remaining milk. Return to a boil and boil for 1 minute, until thickened.

4. Turn out into a bowl and cover the surface with plastic film to prevent a skin from forming. Keep warm while making the Italian meringue.

5. Boil the sugar and water until the temperature of the syrup reaches 258°F (120°C). Whip the egg whites to firm peaks, then slowly pour the syrup into the whites, whipping constantly. Continue whipping until cool.

6. Fold the raspberry purée into the meringue.

7. Soak the gelatin in cold water (see pp. 80–82). Stir the gelatin into the warm pastry cream until dissolved and evenly mixed. (If the pastry cream is not warm enough, rewarm it slightly.)

8. Add one-third of the meringue to the cream and mix quickly to lighten the mixture.

9. Gently fold this mixture into the remaining meringue until evenly mixed.

LIME OR LEMON CHIBOUST

Yield: about 1 lb 12 oz (750 g)

Ingredients	U.S.		Metric	Juice at 100% %
Lime or lemon juice	10	oz	250 g	100
Lime or lemon zest, grated	0.16 oz (2 tsp)		4 g	1.5
Sugar	1	oz	25 g	10
Egg yolks	3	oz	80 g	32
Sugar	1	oz	25 g	10
Cornstarch	1	oz	25 g	10
Gelatin	0.25 oz		6 g	2.5
Italian meringue (p. 259)	1 lb		400 g	160

PROCEDURE

1. Heat the juice, zest, and sugar to a simmer.

2. Whip the egg yolks with the second quantity of sugar and the cornstarch. As when making pastry cream, gradually stir the juice into the egg yolk mixture, then return to the saucepan and bring to a boil. Remove from the heat.

3. Soak the gelatin in cold water (see pp. 80–82). Add the gelatin to the egg yolk mixture and stir until dissolved. Cool.

4. Fold in the Italian meringue.

VANILLA CRÈME DIPLOMAT

For large-quantity measurements, see page 719.

Ingredients	U.S.		Metric	Milk at 100% %
Milk	8	oz	250 g	100
Vanilla bean, split (see *Note*)	½		½	
Egg yolks	1.33 oz (2 yolks)		40 g (2 yolks)	16
Fine granulated sugar	1	oz	30 g	12
Cake flour	0.67 oz		20 g	8
Cornstarch	0.55 oz		15 g	6
Orange liqueur, such as Grand Marnier	1	oz	30 g	12
Crème Chantilly (p. 257)	6.55 oz		200 g	80
Total weight:	**1 lb 3**	**oz**	**585 g**	**234%**

PROCEDURE

1. Heat the milk and vanilla bean to just below the boiling point.

2. Whip the egg yolks and sugar until pale. Add the flour and cornstarch and mix well.

3. Temper the egg mixture by gradually stirring in about half the hot milk. Pour this mixture back into the saucepan with the remaining hot milk. Return to a boil, whipping constantly.

4. Remove from the heat and stir in the liqueur.

5. Cover with plastic film and cool the pastry cream thoroughly, then chill.

6. Once the cream is cold, beat well until perfectly smooth.

7. Fold in the crème chantilly.

NOTE: If vanilla beans are not available, flavor the finished cream with vanilla extract to taste.

--- **VARIATIONS** ---

Crème diplomat is often stabilized with gelatin, using the same procedure as for Chiboust Cream (p. 264). For each 8 oz (250 g) milk, use ⅛ oz (4 g, or 2 leaves) gelatin.

CHOCOLATE CRÈME DIPLOMAT

For large-quantity measurements, see page 719.

Ingredients	U.S.	Metric	%
Bittersweet chocolate, finely chopped	2.25 oz	70 g	28

Omit the orange liqueur from the basic recipe. Stir dark chocolate into the hot pastry cream in step 4. Stir until the chocolate is completely melted and well mixed.

Crème diplomat may also be flavored with coffee extract, praline paste, or chestnut purée.

DESSERT SAUCES AND CHOCOLATE CREAMS

IN ADDITION TO the recipes presented in this section, the following types of dessert sauces are discussed elsewhere in this or other chapters or can be made easily without recipes.

Custard Sauces. Vanilla custard sauce, or Crème Anglaise, is presented earlier in this chapter (p. 261). It is one of the most basic preparations in dessert cookery. Chocolate or other flavors may be added to create variations.

Pastry Cream (p. 263) can be thinned with heavy cream or milk and, if necessary, more sugar, to make another type of custard sauce.

Chocolate Sauce. In addition to the three chocolate sauce recipes in this section, chocolate sauce may be made in several other ways. For example:

- Flavor Crème Anglaise with chocolate (see p. 261).
- Prepare Chocolate Ganache I (p. 272) through step 3 in the procedure. Thin to desired consistency with cream, milk, or simple syrup.

Lemon Sauce. Prepare Lemon Filling (p. 300), but use only 1½ ounces (45 g) cornstarch, or use 1 ounce (30 g) waxy maize.

Fruit Sauces. Some of the best fruit sauces are also the simplest. These are of two types:

- Purées of fresh or cooked fruits, sweetened with sugar. Such a purée is often called a *coulis* (pronounced koo LEE).
- Heated, strained fruit jams and preserves, diluted with simple syrup, water, or liquor.

For greater economy, fruit sauces can be stretched by diluting them with water, adding more sugar, and thickening them with starch. Other sauces, such as those made of blueberries or pineapple, may have a more desirable texture when thickened slightly with starch. These may also be flavored with spices and/or lemon juice.

Gelées. A *gelée* is any liquid thickened with gelatin. Although gelatin is usually used to set a product, so that it is firm, it is also possible to use a small amount of gelatin to thicken a liquid just to the consistency of a sauce. In the pastry department, almost any kind of sweetened juice or purée can be used, as well as wines and other alcoholic beverages. Before preparing gelées, review the guidelines for using gelatin on pages 80–82.

Sabayon. A *sabayon* is a foamy sauce made by whipping egg yolks with a liquid, often wine or liqueur. Two recipes are included in this section, one made without wine and a more traditional one made with wine. The Italian version of this sauce, *zabaglione*, is made with Marsala wine.

COULIS

The word *coulis* has had many meanings in the past century or two. Originally, the term referred to juices from cooked meats. By Escoffier's time, at the beginning of the twentieth century, a coulis was a type of thick soup made from puréed meat, game, or fish. More recently, as puréed meat soups were prepared more rarely, the term was used primarily for thick puréed shellfish soups.

The concept of a thick liquid made of puréed ingredients is preserved in the most common usage of the word *coulis* today. In modern cooking, a coulis is a thick sauce made of puréed fruits or vegetables, such as a raspberry coulis or a tomato coulis.

Caramel Sauces

The first section of this chapter explains the stages of sugar cooking, the last stage of which is caramel. In other words, caramel is simply sugar cooked until it is golden. The simplest caramel sauce is merely caramelized sugar diluted with water to sauce consistency. The addition of heavy cream makes a creamy caramel sauce, as shown by the recipe in this section.

Two methods are possible for caramelizing sugar. In the *wet method*, the sugar is first combined with water and boiled to dissolve it, making a syrup. Glucose or an acid such as cream of tartar or lemon juice may be added to help prevent crystallization. The sugar caramelizes after the water has boiled off. The recipe for caramel sauce in this section is prepared using the wet method. Follow the guidelines for preparing syrups given at the beginning of this chapter.

The second method is called the *dry method*. In the dry method, the sugar is melted in a dry pan without first making it into a syrup. Often, an acid in the form of a small amount of lemon juice is added to the sugar and rubbed in so the crystals are slightly moist. Place the sugar in a heavy saucepan or sauté pan. Set it over moderately high heat. When the sugar begins to melt, stir constantly so it caramelizes evenly. Many chefs prefer to add the sugar to the pan a little at a time. More sugar is added only when the previous addition is fully melted. Butter caramel, included in this section, is prepared using the dry method.

Remember that sugar, when turning to caramel, is very hot, well over 300°F (150°C). Water or other liquids added to hot caramel can spatter dangerously. To minimize spattering, allow the caramel to cool slightly. To stop the cooking quickly and prevent the sugar from becoming too brown, dip the bottom of the pan in cold water for just an instant. Alternatively, heat the liquid first, then add it carefully to the caramelized sugar.

A more complex type of caramel is butter caramel. The recipe included in this section is rarely used by itself (except to make hard toffee candies). Rather, it is a component of other preparations, such as caramelized fruits. See, for example, the recipes for Caramelized Apricots (p. 590), Figs in Port Wine (p. 587), and Spiced Pineapple (p. 589) in Chapter 21. Because butter caramel is somewhat difficult to make, it is included here to give you an opportunity to study it by itself and master it before trying one of the recipes mentioned. It is necessary to follow the instructions in the recipe procedure carefully in order to make the butter and caramelized sugar form a uniform, emulsified mixture.

Chocolate Creams

Two basic chocolate preparations are included in this section, chocolate ganache and chocolate mousse. Each has many variations, depending on its intended use, and so you will find additional formulas in other chapters in this book, in connection with specific cakes, pastries, and confections.

Ganache

Ganache (pronounced gah NAHSH) is a rich chocolate cream with many uses, including as a glaze, icing, or filling for cakes and pastries, and as a base for confections. It is one of the fundamental pastry preparations.

In its most basic form, ganache is a smooth mixture of heavy cream and chocolate couverture. The exact proportions of cream and chocolate depend on its intended use. Equal parts chocolate and cream make a soft ganache suitable for using as a glaze, while two parts chocolate to one part cream make a firm ganache that can be used for truffles and other confections.

The hardness of the ganache also depends on the amount of cocoa solids and cocoa butter in the chocolate. Extra bittersweet chocolate makes a firmer ganache than dark chocolates containing more sugar and less cocoa, while milk chocolate and white couverture make even softer ganaches. You may have to adjust the ratio of chocolate and cream in your formulas to take into account these differences.

In addition to chocolate and cream, other ingredients may be added to ganache to adjust the flavor and texture. Corn syrup or glucose syrup are often added to increase the smoothness of the ganache. Flavorings such as fruit juices and alcohols create variety. Butter can also be added, especially when fruit juices are used, in order to improve the texture and body of the ganache.

The formula for Passion Fruit Ganache (p. 273) in this section contains passion fruit juice as a flavoring. You might like to experiment with this recipe, substituting other fruit purées and flavorings for the passion fruit. In Chapters 17 and 19 you'll find formulas for ganache intended specifically for icing cakes, and Chapter 23 explains how ganache is used to make truffles.

Ganache can also be whipped to create a mousselike texture for filling. Whipped ganache, however, is somewhat limited in its usefulness. It must be used at once, because it quickly becomes firm and difficult to spread once it has stood for a short time.

Mousse

Chocolate mousses are chocolate creams that are given a light texture by the addition of egg foams or whipped cream or both. The two chocolate mousse recipes included here are well suited for fillings and pastries. They can also be served by themselves as desserts. Other mousses are included in Chapter 19.

The first of the two formulas is typical of recipes found in many classic cookbooks. But because of food safety concerns, many these classic recipes must be modified to specify the use of pasteurized eggs. If pasteurized eggs are not available, use a different formula, such as the second chocolate mousse in this section, in which the egg products are heated to a safe temperature in the production process.

KEY POINTS TO REVIEW

- What is a fruit coulis?
- What are the two methods for caramelizing sugar?
- How is a basic caramel sauce made?
- What is ganache, and how is it made?

CHOCOLATE SAUCE I

Yield: 1 qt (1 L)

Ingredients	U.S.	Metric
Semisweet chocolate	1 lb	500 g
Water	1 pt	500 mL
Butter	6 oz	190 g

PROCEDURE

1. Chop the chocolate into small pieces.
2. Place the chocolate and water in a saucepan. Heat over low heat or over hot water until the chocolate is melted. Bring to a simmer and simmer 2 minutes. Stir while cooking to make a smooth mixture. The mixture should thicken slightly as it simmers.
3. Remove from the heat and add the butter. Stir until the butter is melted and mixed in.
4. Set the pan in a bowl of ice water and stir the sauce until it is cool.

CHOCOLATE SAUCE II

Yield: 1 lb 8 oz (600 g)

Ingredients	U.S.	Metric
Water	12 oz	300 g
Sugar	7 oz	175 g
Bittersweet chocolate couverture	3 oz	75 g
Cornstarch	1 oz	25 g
Cocoa powder	2 oz	50 g
Water, cold	as needed	as needed

PROCEDURE

1. Combine the water, sugar, and chocolate. Bring to a boil, stirring to mix the chocolate with the syrup.
2. Mix the cornstarch and cocoa powder to a thin paste with a little water.
3. Add this paste to the chocolate syrup mixture and return to a boil. Strain and cool.

CHOCOLATE FUDGE SAUCE

Yield: 1 qt (1 L)

Ingredients	U.S.	Metric
Water	1 pt	0.5 mL
Sugar	2 lb	1 kg
Corn syrup	6 oz	375 g
Unsweetened chocolate	8 oz	250 g
Butter	2 oz	62 g

PROCEDURE

1. Combine the water, sugar, and syrup and bring to a boil, stirring to dissolve the sugar.
2. Boil 1 minute and remove from the heat. Let cool a few minutes.
3. Melt the chocolate and butter together over low heat. Stir until smooth.
4. Very slowly stir the hot syrup into the chocolate.
5. Place over moderate heat and bring to a boil. Boil for 2 minutes.
6. Remove from the heat and cool.

FRUIT COULIS

Yield: 10–11 oz (300 g)

Ingredients	U.S.		Metric
Berries or other soft fruit	7	oz	200 g
Fine granulated sugar	3.5	oz	100 g
Water	1.33 oz (8 tsp)		40 g
Lemon juice	0.5	oz (3 tsp)	15 g
Kirsch or other fruit brandy or liqueur (optional)	0.67 oz (4 tsp)		20 g

PROCEDURE

1. Purée the fruit in a blender or food processor and pass through a fine sieve or chinois.
2. Warm the fruit purée in a saucepan.
3. Separately, make a syrup of the sugar and water and boil to 220°F (105°C). Mix into the fruit purée.
4. Return to a boil, strain, and mix in the juice and alcohol. Cool.

MELBA SAUCE

Yield: about 1 pt (400 mL)

Ingredients	U.S.		Metric
Frozen, sweetened raspberries	1 lb	8 oz	600 g
Red currant jelly		8 oz	200 g

PROCEDURE

1. Thaw the raspberries and force them through a sieve to purée them and remove the seeds.
2. Combine with the jelly in a saucepan. Bring to a boil, stirring until the jelly is melted and completely blended with the fruit purée.

--- **VARIATION** ---

RASPBERRY SAUCE

Purée and sieve frozen sweetened raspberries, or use fresh raspberries and sweeten to taste. Omit the red currant jelly. Use as is or simmer until thickened, as desired.

Other fruits can be puréed and sweetened to taste to make dessert sauces, using the same procedure. If purées from pulpy fruits (such as mangoes) are too thick, thin with water, simple syrup, or an appropriate fruit juice.

CARAMEL SAUCE

Yield: 12 oz (375 mL)

For large-quantity measurements, see page 719.

Ingredients	U.S.	Metric
Sugar	8 oz	250 g
Water	2 fl oz	60 mL
Lemon juice	¾ tsp	4 mL
Heavy cream	6 fl oz	190 mL
Milk or additional cream	4 fl oz	125 mL

Clear caramel sauce and caramel sauce with cream.

PROCEDURE

1. Combine the sugar, water, and juice in a heavy saucepan. Bring to a boil, stirring to dissolve the sugar. Cook the syrup to the caramel stage (see p. 253). Toward the end of the cooking time, turn the heat to very low to avoid burning the sugar or letting it get too dark. It should be a golden color.

2. Remove from the heat and cool 5 minutes. Alternatively, to stop the cooking completely and prevent the sugar from becoming any darker because of residual heat, dip the bottom of the pan in cold water for an instant.

3. Bring the heavy cream to a boil. Add a few ounces of it to the caramel.

4. Stir and continue to add the cream slowly. Return to the heat and stir until all the caramel is dissolved.

5. Let cool completely.

6. Stir the milk or additional cream into the cooled caramel to thin it.

--- VARIATIONS ---

HOT CARAMEL SAUCE

Proceed as directed through step 4. Omit the milk or additional cream.

CLEAR CARAMEL SAUCE

Substitute 2½–3 oz (75–90 mL) boiling water for the heavy cream and omit the milk. If the sauce is too thick when cool, add more water.

BUTTERSCOTCH SAUCE

Use brown sugar instead of white granulated sugar in the basic recipe. Omit the lemon juice. In step 1, cook the syrup only to 240°F (115°C). Add 2 oz (60 g) butter before adding the heavy cream.

CARAMEL CREAM

Prepare 2 oz Clear Caramel Sauce. Soften 0.06 oz (½ tsp/2 g) gelatin in 0.5 oz (1 tbsp/15 mL) water. Add to the warm caramel sauce and stir until dissolved (rewarm if necessary). Cool to room temperature but do not cool until set. Whip 4 oz (125 g) heavy cream to soft peaks. Mix about one-fourth of the cream into the caramel sauce, then fold in the remaining cream.

BUTTER CARAMEL

Yield: 11 oz (330 g)

Ingredients	U.S.	Metric
Sugar	8 oz	250 g
Butter	4 oz	125 g

PROCEDURE

1. Heat the sugar over moderate heat until it melts and then turns to a golden brown caramel.

2. Keep the pan over moderate heat. Add the butter. Stir constantly over heat until the butter has melted and blended into the caramel. It is essential to stir vigorously in order to emulsify the butter and caramel. If you do not stir well enough, the butterfat will tend to separate.

3. The caramel will hold reasonably well for a short time over heat. Stir it from time to time. If the caramel is allowed to cool, it will become a hard, brittle toffee. If it is reheated, the butter will separate, though it can be reincorporated by adding a few drops of water and stirring vigorously.

CHOCOLATE GANACHE I

Ingredients	U.S.	Metric	Chocolate at 100% %
Bittersweet or semisweet chocolate	1 lb	500 g	100
Heavy cream	12 oz	375 g	75
Total weight:	**1 lb 12 oz**	**875 g**	**175%**

A

B

C

PROCEDURE

1. Chop the chocolate into small pieces. Place in a bowl.

2. Bring the cream just to a boil, stirring to prevent scorching. (Use very fresh cream; old cream is more likely to curdle when it is boiled.)

3. Pour the cream over the chocolate (a). Let stand for a few minutes. Stir until the chocolate is completely melted and the mixture is smooth (b). If necessary, warm gently over low heat to completely melt the chocolate. At this point, the ganache is ready to be used as an icing or glaze. Apply it by pouring it over the item to be iced (c), like poured fondant (see p. 416).

4. If the ganache is not to be used warm, let it cool at room temperature. Stir from time to time so it cools evenly. Cooled ganache may be stored in the refrigerator and rewarmed over a water bath when needed.

5. For whipped ganache, the mixture should first be cooled thoroughly, or it will not whip properly. Do not let it become too cold, however, or it will be too hard. With a wire whip or the whip attachment of a mixer, whip the ganache until it is light, thick, and creamy. Use at once. If stored, whipped ganache will become firm and hard to spread.

VARIATION

The proportion of chocolate and cream may be varied. For a firmer product, or if the weather is warm, decrease the cream to as little as 50%. For a very soft ganache, increase the cream to 100%. This proportion makes a ganache that is too soft for truffles but may be whipped into a mousse.

The composition of the chocolate also affects the consistency of the ganache, and the formula may require slight adjustments depending on the chocolate used.

CHOCOLATE GANACHE II

Ingredients	U.S.	Metric	Chocolate at 100% %
Heavy cream	1 lb 2 oz	600 g	100
Vanilla powder	pinch	pinch	
Bittersweet chocolate	1 lb 2 oz	600 g	100
Butter, softened	3 oz	100 g	17
Total weight:	**2 lb 7 oz**	**1300 g**	**217%**

PROCEDURE

1. Bring the cream and vanilla powder to a boil.

2. Chop the chocolate.

3. Pour the hot cream over the chocolate. Stir until the chocolate is melted.

4. When the mixture has cooled to 95°F (35°C), stir in the butter. Use the ganache at once.

PASSION FRUIT GANACHE

For large-quantity measurements, see page 719.

Ingredients	U.S.		Metric	Chocolate at 100% %
Heavy cream	4	oz	120 g	56
Passion fruit juice	4	oz	120 g	56
Butter	2	oz	60 g	28
Egg yolks	1.67	oz	50 g	23
Sugar	2	oz	60 g	28
Bittersweet or semisweet chocolate, chopped	7	oz	215 g	100
Total weight	**1 lb 4**	**oz**	**625 g**	**291%**

PROCEDURE

1. Combine the cream, juice, and butter in a saucepan and bring to a boil.
2. Whip the egg yolks with the sugar until light.
3. Gradually beat the hot liquid into the egg mixture.
4. Return this mixture to the heat and bring it quickly to a boil, then remove from heat.
5. Strain the liquid over the chopped chocolate in a bowl. Stir until all the chocolate is melted and the mixture is evenly blended.

CHOCOLATE MOUSSE I

Ingredients	U.S.		Metric	Chocolate at 100% %
Bittersweet or semisweet chocolate	1 lb		500 g	100
Butter	9	oz	280 g	56
Pasteurized egg yolks	5	oz	155 g	31
Pasteurized egg whites	12	oz	375 g	75
Sugar	2.5	oz	80 g	16
Total weight	**2 lb 12**	**oz**	**1390 g**	**278%**

PROCEDURE

1. Melt the chocolate over hot water.
2. Remove from the heat and add the butter. Stir until the butter is melted and completely mixed in.
3. Add the egg yolks one at a time. Mix in each egg yolk completely before adding the next.
4. Beat the egg whites until they form soft peaks. Add the sugar and beat until the egg whites form stiff but moist peaks. Do not overbeat.
5. Fold the egg whites into the chocolate mixture.

CHOCOLATE MOUSSE II

Ingredients	U.S.		Metric	Chocolate at 100% %
Egg yolks	4.5	oz	120 g	25
Fine granulated sugar	4	oz	105 g	22
Water	3	oz	90 g	19
Bittersweet chocolate, melted	1 lb 2	oz	480 g	100
Heavy cream	2 lb		900 g	190
Total weight:	**3 lb 13**	**oz**	**1695 g**	**356%**

PROCEDURE

1. In a round-bottomed stainless steel bowl, whip the egg yolks until pale.
2. Make a syrup with the sugar and water and boil to 244°F (118°C). Whip the hot syrup into the yolks and continue whipping until cool.
3. Melt the chocolate and fold into the egg mixture.
4. Whip the cream until it forms soft peaks. Whip one-third of the cream into the chocolate mixture. Then fold in the remaining cream until well incorporated.

SABAYON I

Yield: about 1½ pt (750 mL)

Ingredients	U.S.	Metric
Egg yolks	2.67 oz (4 yolks)	80 g (4 yolks)
Simple syrup (p. 254)	3.5 oz	100 g
Whipped cream	2 oz	60 g

PROCEDURE

1. Mix the egg yolks and syrup in a stainless steel bowl. Place the bowl over a hot-water bath and whip until light, frothy, and pale in color.

2. Remove the bowl from the hot-water bath and continue to whip until cool and doubled in volume.

3. Gently fold in the whipped cream.

4. Use as a dessert sauce or topping that can be browned (gratinéed) under a salamander or broiler.

SABAYON II

Yield: about 1 qt (900 mL)

Ingredients	U.S.	Metric
Egg yolks	4 oz (6 yolks)	115 g (6 yolks)
Sugar	8 oz	225 g
Dry white wine	8 oz	225 g

PROCEDURE

1. In a stainless steel bowl, beat the yolks until foamy.

2. Beat in the sugar and wine. Place over a hot-water bath and continue beating until thick and hot.

3. Serve hot as a dessert or as a sauce for fruit or fritters. Serve without delay. If allowed to stand, it will lose some foaminess and begin to separate.

VARIATIONS

COLD SABAYON

Dissolve 0.04 oz (½ tsp/1 g) gelatin in the wine. Proceed as in the basic recipe. When the sauce is done, place the bowl over ice and whip the sauce until it is cool.

ZABAGLIONE

This is the Italian sauce and dessert that is the origin of sabayon. Use sweet Marsala wine instead of the dry white wine, and use only half the sugar. Other wines or spirits may be used, such as port or sherry. Adjust the sugar according to the sweetness of the wine.

SAUCE SUZETTE

Yield: about 1 pt (450 mL)

Ingredients	U.S.		Metric
Orange juice	7	oz	200 g
Lemon juice	2	oz	60 g
Orange zest, grated	0.5	oz	15 g
Sugar	7	oz	200 g
Butter	2.5	oz	80 g
Orange liqueur such as Cointreau	7	oz	100 g
Brandy	2	oz	60 g

PROCEDURE

1. Warm the juice and zest in a saucepan.
2. In a separate pan, cook the sugar to a golden caramel.
3. Remove from the heat and add the butter. Stir to begin to dissolve the caramelized sugar.
4. Add the warmed juices. Reduce by one-third, stirring continuously.
5. Add the liqueur and brandy. Ignite to burn off the alcohol.
6. Serve warm.

BLUEBERRY SAUCE

Yield: about 10 oz (300 mL)

Ingredients	U.S.		Metric
Sugar	1.5	oz	45 g
Water	2	oz	60 mL
Lemon juice	1	fl oz	30 mL
Blueberries, fresh, washed and drained well	12	oz	360 g

PROCEDURE

1. Put the sugar in a heavy saucepan. Heat until the sugar melts and then caramelizes to a rich golden brown.
2. Remove the pan from heat and add the water. Because the pan is very hot, the water will boil immediately, so be careful to avoid being scalded by steam.
3. Simmer until the caramelized sugar is dissolved.
4. Add the lemon juice and simmer 1 minute, until it is well blended.
5. Add the blueberries and cook slowly for 5 to 10 minutes, until the berries pop and the sauce is slightly reduced and thickened.
6. Taste for sweetness. If the berries are tart, add a little more sugar to taste. Cool.

BASIL HONEYDEW GELÉE

Yield: 20 fl oz (600 mL)

Ingredients	U.S.		Metric
Basil leaves	1	oz	30 g
Honeydew melon, diced	1 lb		480 g
Gelatin (see *Note*)	0.33 oz (1 tbsp)		10 g
Water	1.5	fl oz	45 mL
Water	8	fl oz	240 mL
Sugar	2½	oz	75 g
Lime juice	1	fl oz	30 mL

NOTE: To adjust the texture and thickness of the gelée, decrease or increase the gelatin quantity slightly.

PROCEDURE

1. Blanch the basil leaves in boiling water for 5 seconds. Drain. Chill quickly in ice water. Drain again and squeeze dry.

2. In a food processor, purée the basil with the melon until smooth. Let stand 5 minutes or longer so that the green color of the basil is extracted into the juice.

3. Strain through a sieve lined with cheesecloth. Discard the solids.

4. Bloom the gelatin in the first quantity of water.

5. Combine the second quantity of water with the sugar and bring to a boil to dissolve the sugar.

6. Remove from the heat. Add the lime juice and the bloomed gelatin. Stir until the gelatin is dissolved.

7. Combine the gelatin mixture and the honeydew juice and mix until well combined. Chill until set.

8. To use as a sauce, stir the gelée gently with a wire whip to break it up.

DULCE DE LECHE

Yield: about 1 pt (500 mL)

Ingredients	U.S.	Metric
Milk	2 pt	1 L
Sugar	12 oz	375 mL
Baking soda	¼ tsp	1 mL
Vanilla extract	½ tsp	2 mL

PROCEDURE

1. Combine the milk, sugar, and baking soda in a heavy saucepan. Set over medium heat. Bring to a slow boil without stirring.

2. As the mixture approaches the boil, it will foam up. Quickly remove it from the heat before it boils over; stir.

3. Turn the heat to low, set the pan back on the heat, and cook slowly, stirring frequently with a wooden spoon, for about 45–60 minutes. The mixture will gradually caramelize.

4. When the mixture is a rich caramel brown and thickened but still pourable, remove from the heat and stir in the vanilla.

5. Cool thoroughly.

HARD SAUCE

Yield: about 1 pt (500 mL)

Ingredients	U.S.	Metric
Butter	8 oz	250 g
Confectioners' sugar	1 lb	500 g
Brandy or rum	1 oz	30 mL

PROCEDURE

1. Cream the butter and sugar until light and fluffy, as for simple buttercream (see p. 419).
2. Beat in the brandy or rum.
3. Serve with steamed puddings, such as English Christmas pudding.

CREAM SAUCE FOR PIPING

Yield: variable

Ingredients	U.S.	Metric
Sour cream	as needed	as needed
Heavy cream	as needed	as needed

PROCEDURE

1. Stir the sour cream until it is smooth.
2. As this sauce is used for marbling or decorating other sauces, the quantity of cream needed depends on the texture of the other sauces. Gradually stir in heavy cream to thin the sour cream until it is the same consistency as the sauce to be decorated.

TERMS FOR REVIEW

caramelize	common meringue	crème anglaise	sabayon
crystallize	Swiss meringue	pastry cream	zabaglione
simple syrup	Italian meringue	crème Chiboust	ganache
dessert syrup	soft meringue	coulis	
crème chantilly	hard meringue	gelée	

QUESTIONS FOR REVIEW

1. How can you avoid unwanted crystallization when cooking sugar syrups?
2. Why is cream of tartar or lemon juice sometimes added to a sugar syrup before or during cooking?
3. Vanilla custard sauce and pastry cream both contain eggs. Why is it possible to boil pastry cream but not custard sauce?
4. Explain the importance of sanitation in the production of pastry cream. What specific steps should you take to ensure a safe product?
5. Explain the effects of fat, sugar, and temperature on the whipping of egg whites into foams.
6. Describe two simple ways of preparing fruit sauces.

13

PIES

AFTER READING THIS CHAPTER, YOU SHOULD BE ABLE TO:

1. **Prepare pie doughs.**
2. **Roll pie doughs, and assemble and bake single-crust pies, double-crust pies, lattice-topped pies, and unbaked pies.**
3. **Prepare a variety of pie fillings, including fruit, soft or custard-type, cream, and chiffon fillings.**
4. **Judge the quality of pies.**

ON THE EARLY American frontier, it was not uncommon for the pioneer housewife to bake 21 pies each week—one for every meal. Pies were so important to settlers that in winter, when fruits were unavailable, cooks would bake dessert pies out of whatever materials were available, such as potatoes, vinegar, and soda crackers.

Few of us today eat pie at every meal. Nevertheless, pies are still a favorite American dessert. Most customers will order and pay a higher price for a piece of chocolate cream pie than for chocolate pudding, even if the pie filling is the same as the pudding, and even if they leave the crust uneaten.

In this chapter, we study the preparation of pie doughs and fillings and the procedures for assembling and baking pies.

PIE DOUGHS

BEFORE YOU BEGIN studying this section, review the Mixing and Gluten Development section in Chapter 5.

Pie pastry is a simple product in terms of its ingredients: flour, shortening, water, and salt. Yet success or failure depends on how the shortening and flour are mixed and how the gluten is developed. The key to making pie dough is proper technique, and you will remember the techniques better if you understand why they work.

Ingredients

Flour

Pastry flour is the best choice for pie doughs. It has enough gluten to produce the desired structure and flakiness, yet is low enough in gluten to yield a tender product, if handled properly. If stronger flours are used, the percentage of shortening should be increased slightly to provide more tenderness.

Fat

Regular hydrogenated shortening is the most popular fat for piecrusts because it has the right plastic consistency to produce a flaky crust. It is firm and moldable enough to make an easily workable dough. Emulsified shortening should not be used, as it blends too quickly with the flour and makes it difficult to achieve a flaky pastry.

Butter contributes excellent flavor to pie pastry, but it is frequently avoided in volume production for two reasons: It is expensive, and it melts easily, making the dough difficult to work.

It is desirable, if costs permit, to blend a quantity of butter into the shortening used for piecrusts to improve flavor. The large quantity of piecrust dumped into the garbage after customers have eaten the filling is evidence that many people are not satisfied with the taste of shortening piecrusts.

If butter is used to replace all the shortening for pie doughs, the percentage of fat in the formula should be increased by about one-fourth. (If 1 pound shortening is called for, use 1 pound 4 ounces butter.) The liquid can be reduced slightly, as butter contains moisture.

In the case of richer pastries and short doughs, butter is specified as the primary fat in the formulas here. These doughs are used primarily for European-style tarts and pastries, in which the flavor of the butter is an important part of the dessert.

Lard is an excellent shortening for pies because it is firm and plastic, properties that produce good flakiness. However, it is not widely used in food service.

Liquid

Water is necessary to develop some gluten in the flour and to give structure and flakiness to the dough. If too much water is used, the crust will become tough because of too much gluten development. If not enough water is used, the crust will fall apart because of inadequate gluten structure.

Milk makes a richer dough that browns more quickly. However, the crust is less crisp and the production cost is higher. If dry milk is used, it should be dissolved in the water to ensure even distribution in the dough.

PIES IN HISTORY

If we take the word *pie* to mean any of a variety of foods enclosed in pastry and baked, then there have been pies for nearly all of recorded history. In ancient Greece and Rome, doughs made with olive oil were used to cover or enclose various ingredients.

In English, the word *pie* used in this way dates back to at least 1300. It is probably a short form of *magpie*, a bird that collects a variety of things, just as bakers do when they are assembling ingredients to bake in a pie. In the Middle Ages, the word *pie* almost always referred to savory pies containing meats, poultry, or game. Today, in England, the word is still used largely for meat pies, both hot and cold (cold pies being similar to what we might call pâtés), while in North America, savory pies, such as chicken "pot pie," are still enjoyed.

North Americans, however, are responsible for turning the development of pies firmly away from savory and toward sweet. Fruit pies, especially apple, are perhaps still the most popular, but pastry cooks have devised dessert pie fillings from many other ingredients as well.

Pies are so popular that across the continent they are the feature of annual summer festivals. The little town of Braham, for example, which bills itself as the Pie Capital of Minnesota, hosts a popular festival called Pie Day, featuring pie sales, baking contests, art and craft shows, and daylong entertainment, all in celebration of pies.

Whether water or milk is used, it must be added cold (40°F/4°C or colder) to maintain proper dough temperature.

Salt

Salt has some conditioning effect on the gluten (see p. 88). However, it contributes mainly to flavor. Salt must be dissolved in the liquid before being added to the mix to ensure even distribution.

Temperature

Pie dough should be kept cool, about 60°F (15°C), during mixing and makeup, for two reasons:

- Shortening has the best consistency when cool. If it is warm, it blends too quickly with the flour. If it is very cold, it is too firm to be easily worked.
- Gluten develops more slowly at cool temperatures than at warm temperatures.

Pie Dough Types

There are two basic types of pie dough:

- Flaky pie dough.
- Mealy pie dough.

The difference between the two is in how the fat is blended with the flour. Complete mixing procedures are given in the formulas that follow. First, it is important to understand the basic distinction between the two types.

Flaky Pie Dough

For *flaky pie dough*, the fat is cut or rubbed into the flour until the particles of shortening are about the size of peas or hazelnuts—that is, the flour is not completely blended with the fat, and the fat is left in pieces. (Many bakers distinguish between this crust, which they call *short-flake*, and *long-flake crusts*, in which the fat is left in pieces the size of walnuts and the flour is coated even less with shortening. Blitz puff paste, introduced in the next chapter, is actually a long-flake pie dough that is rolled and folded like puff paste.)

When water is added, the flour absorbs it and develops some gluten. When the dough is rolled out, the lumps of fat and moistened flour are flattened and become flakes of dough separated by layers of fat.

Mealy Pie Dough

For *mealy pie dough*, the fat is blended into the flour more thoroughly, until the mixture looks like coarse cornmeal. The more complete coating of the flour with fat has three results:

Fat-and-flour mixtures for flaky pie dough and mealy pie dough.

- The crust is very short and tender because less gluten can develop.
- Less water is needed in the mix because the flour won't absorb as much as in flaky dough.
- The baked dough is less likely to absorb moisture from the filling and become soggy.

Mealy dough is used for bottom crusts, especially in baked fruit pies and soft or custard-type pies, because it resists sogginess. Flaky doughs are used for top crusts and sometimes for prebaked shells.

To produce mealy doughs with even greater resistance to soaking, the flour and fat can be blended together completely to make a smooth paste. Such a dough is very short when baked. It is especially appropriate for custard pies.

The formula called Enriched Pie Pastry included in this section is essentially a mealy dough, except it contains more sugar, is enriched with egg yolks, and works especially well with butter as the only fat. Its delicate, rich flavor makes it suited for European-style tarts and single-crust pies.

3-2-1 Dough

A popular pie dough formula is called 3-2-1 dough. The numbers refer to the ratio of ingredients by weight: 3 parts flour, 2 parts shortening, and 1 part ice water. The ratios of ingredients in this chapter's basic pie dough formulas have been modified slightly from the 3-2-1 standard. In particular, they contain slightly less water to yield a somewhat more tender dough. However, the 3-2-1 ratio is easy to remember and is always reliable. It can be used for both mealy and flaky doughs. To mix the ingredients, use the same procedure as that given in the basic formulas below.

Trimmings

Reworked scraps or trimmings are tougher than freshly made dough. They may be combined with mealy dough and used for bottom crusts only.

Mixing

Hand mixing is best for small quantities of dough, especially flaky dough, because you have more control over the mixing. Quantities up to 10 pounds (4.5 kg) can be mixed almost as quickly by hand as by machine.

For machine mixing, use a pastry knife or paddle attachment. Blend at low speed.

The mixing method for pie doughs is sometimes called the *rubbed dough method*. It is nearly identical to the *sanding method* discussed in the next chapter (p. 312), except that for flaky doughs the fat is rubbed in less thoroughly. Although the procedure has several steps, the two main steps are characteristic of the method:

1. Rub the fat into the sifted dry ingredients.
2. Carefully mix the combined liquid ingredients into the dry ingredients.

The six steps in the pie dough recipe that follows explain the rubbed dough method in more detail. Most pie doughs and several other basic pastries are mixed with this procedure or a variation. Also, compare this procedure with the biscuit method outlined on page 215. Although biscuit dough is softer and contains leavening, it is mixed with a similar procedure.

Crumb Crusts

Graham cracker crusts are popular because they have an appealing flavor and are easier to make than pastry crusts. For variation, vanilla or chocolate wafer crumbs, gingersnap crumbs, or zwieback crumbs may be used instead of graham cracker crumbs. Ground nuts may be added for special desserts.

Crumb crusts are used primarily for unbaked pies, such as cream pies and chiffon pies. They can also be used for such desserts as cheesecake. Be sure the flavor of the crust is compatible with the filling. Lime chiffon pie with a chocolate crumb crust, for instance, is not an appealing combination. And some cream fillings are so delicate in flavor they would be overwhelmed by a crust that is too flavorful.

Baking a crumb crust before filling it makes it firmer and less crumbly, and gives it a toasted flavor.

PIE DOUGH

For large-quantity measurements, see page 720.

Ingredients	Flaky Pie Dough				Mealy Pie Dough			
	U.S.		Metric	%	U.S.		Metric	%
Pastry flour	1 lb	4 oz	500 g	100	1 lb	4 oz	500 g	100
Shortening, regular		14 oz	350 g	70		13 oz	325 g	65
Water, cold		6 oz	150 g	30		5 oz	125 g	25
Salt		0.4 oz (2 tsp)	10 g	2		0.4 oz (2 tsp)	10 g	2
Sugar (optional)		1 oz	25 g	5		1 oz	25 g	5
Total weight:	**2 lb**	**9 oz**	**1035 g**	**207%**	**2 lb**	**7 oz**	**985 g**	**197%**

PROCEDURE

1. Sift the flour into a mixing bowl. Add the shortening.
2. Rub or cut the shortening into the flour to the proper degree:

    For flaky dough, until fat particles are the size of peas or hazelnuts.

    For mealy dough, until mixture resembles cornmeal.
3. Dissolve salt and sugar (if used) in water.
4. Add the water to the flour mixture. Mix very gently, just until the water is absorbed. Do not overwork the dough.
5. Place the dough in pans, cover with plastic film, and place in the refrigerator or retarder for at least 4 hours.
6. Scale portions of dough as needed.

ENRICHED PIE PASTRY

For large-quantity measurements, see page 720.

Ingredients	U.S.		Metric	%
Pastry flour	12	oz	375 g	100
Sugar	2	oz	62 g	17
Butter	6	oz	188 g	50
Egg yolks	1	oz	30 g	8
Water, cold	3	oz	94 g	25
Salt	0.13 oz (⅞ tsp)		4 g	1
Total weight:	**1 lb**	**8 oz**	**753 g**	**201%**

— VARIATION —

For quiches and other savory pies and tarts, omit the sugar.

PROCEDURE

This pastry is mixed somewhat like mealy pie dough, except the quantity of sugar is too large to dissolve easily in the water.

1. Sift the flour and sugar into a mixing bowl.
2. Add the butter and rub it in until it is well combined and no lumps remain.
3. Beat the egg yolks with the water and salt until the salt is dissolved.
4. Add the liquid to the flour mixture. Mix gently until it is completely absorbed.
5. Place the dough in pans, cover with plastic film, and place in refrigerator at least 4 hours. (Alternatively, if the sizes you need are known in advance, scale the dough, form into discs, wrap separately, and refrigerate.)
6. Scale portions as needed.

GRAHAM CRACKER CRUST

Yield: enough for four 9-in. (23-cm) pies or five 8-in. (20-cm) pies

Ingredients	U.S.	Metric	Crumbs at 100% %
Graham cracker crumbs	1 lb	450 g	100
Sugar	8 oz	225 g	50
Butter, melted	8 oz	225 g	50
Total weight:	**2 lb**	**900 g**	**200%**

VARIATION

Substitute chocolate or vanilla wafer crumbs, gingersnap crumbs, or zwieback crumbs for the graham cracker crumbs.

PROCEDURE

1. Mix the crumbs and sugar in a mixing bowl.
2. Add the melted butter and mix until evenly blended; crumbs should be completely moistened by the butter.
3. Scale the mixture into pie pans:
   8 oz (225 g) for 9-in. (23-cm) pans
   6 oz (180 g) for 8-in. (20-cm) pans
4. Spread the mixture evenly on the bottom and sides of the pan. Press another pan on top to pack the crumbs evenly.
5. Bake at 350°F (175°C) for 10 minutes.
6. Cool thoroughly before filling.

KEY POINTS TO REVIEW

- What are the steps in the mixing method for pie doughs?
- What is 3-2-1 dough?
- Flaky dough is best for what kind of piecrusts? Mealy dough is best for what kind of piecrusts?
- What are the ingredients and procedure for making a crumb crust?

ASSEMBLY AND BAKING

PIES MAY BE classified into two groups based on method of assembling and baking.

Baked Pies. Raw pie shells are filled and then baked. *Fruit pies* contain fruit fillings and usually have a top crust. *Soft pies* are those with custard-type fillings—that is, liquid fillings that become firm when their egg content coagulates. They are usually baked as single-crust pies.

Unbaked Pies. Prebaked pie shells are filled with a prepared filling, chilled, and served when the filling is firm enough to slice. *Cream pies* are made with pudding or boiled custard-type fillings. *Chiffon pies* are made with fillings that are lightened by the addition of beaten egg whites and/or whipped cream. Gelatin or starch gives them a firm consistency.

The two main components of pies are the dough or pastry and the filling. These two components are produced in quite separate and distinct operations. Once the pastry and fillings are made, rolling the dough and assembling and baking the pies can proceed rapidly.

Because these operations are separate and involve different kinds of problems and techniques, it is helpful to concentrate on them one at a time. The preparation of pie dough is described above. This section begins with procedures for making pie pastry into pie shells and for filling and baking pies, followed by a discussion of pie fillings in the next section.

Instead of being given a top crust, fruit pies are sometimes topped with Streusel (p. 195) or a *lattice crust* (see the Procedure for Making a Lattice Top Crust). Streusel is especially good on apple pies. Lattice crusts are best for pies with attractive, colorful fruit, such as cherry or blueberry.

PROCEDURE: Rolling Pie Dough and Lining Pans

1. **Select the best doughs for each purpose.** Mealy pie doughs are used whenever soaking is a problem, so they are mainly used for bottom crusts, especially bottom crusts for soft pie fillings such as custard and pumpkin. This is because mealy doughs resist soaking better than flaky doughs.

   Flaky pie doughs are best for top crusts. They can also be used for prebaked pie shells if the shells are filled with cooled filling just before serving. However, if the prebaked shells are filled with hot filling, it is safer to use mealy dough.

2. **Scale the dough.** The following weights are only guidelines. The depth of pie tins, and hence their capacity, varies. For example, disposable tins are often shallower than standard tins.

   > 8 oz (225 g) for 9-in. (23-cm) bottom crusts
   >
   > 6 oz (170 g) for 9-in. (23-cm) top crusts
   >
   > 6 oz (170 g) for 8-in. (20-cm) bottom crusts
   >
   > 5 oz (140 g) for 8-in. (20-cm) top crusts

   Experienced bakers use less dough when rolling out crusts because they know how to roll the dough to a perfect circle of the right size and, therefore, need to trim away little excess dough.

   Be aware that pie pans are often mislabeled to suggest they are larger than they actually are. It is possible to find pans labeled as 9-in. that are actually smaller than 8-in. pans. "Pan size" as used in this book refers to the inside top diameter of the pie pan.

3. **Dust the bench and rolling pin lightly with flour.** Too much dusting flour toughens the dough, so use no more than needed to prevent sticking.

   Instead of rolling the dough directly on the bench, you may roll it out on flour-dusted canvas. Rolling on canvas does not require as much dusting flour.

4. **Roll out the dough.** Flatten the dough lightly and roll it out to a uniform ⅛-in. (3-mm) thickness. Use even strokes and roll from the center outward in all directions. Lift the dough frequently to make sure it is not sticking. The finished dough should be a nearly perfect circle.

5. **Place the dough in the pan.** To lift the dough without breaking it, roll it lightly around the rolling pin. A second method is to fold the dough in half, place the folded dough into the pan with the fold in the center, and unfold the dough.

   Allow the dough to drop into the pan; press it into the corners without stretching it. Stretched dough will shrink during baking. There should be no air bubbles between the dough and the pan.

6. **For single-crust pies, flute or crimp the edges, if desired, and trim off excess dough.** For double-crust pies, fill with cold filling, brush the edge of the crust with water, and top with the second crust, as explained in the Procedure for Preparing Baked Pies (p. 287). Seal the edges; crimp or flute, if desired. Trim off the excess dough.

   The simplest way to trim excess dough is to rotate the pie tin between the palms of the hands while pressing with the palms against the edge of the rim. This pinches off the excess dough flush with the rim.

   Some bakers feel that fluted edges add to the appearance of the product. Others feel that fluting takes too much time and produces nothing more than a rim of heavy dough that most customers leave on their plates. Follow your instructor's directions on this procedure. Whether you flute the edges or not, be sure that double-crust pies are well sealed. Many bakers like to make a raised, fluted rim of dough on pie shells for soft-filled pies such as custard or pumpkin. This raised edge, as shown in the illustration, enables them to fill the shell quite full while reducing the chance of spillover.

7. **Rest the made-up pies for 20–30 minutes, preferably refrigerated.** This helps prevent crust shrinkage.

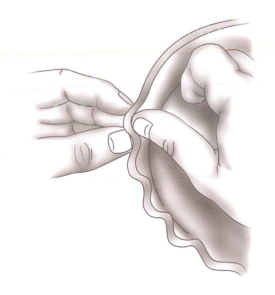

The Soggy Bottom

Underbaked bottom crusts or crusts that have soaked up moisture from the filling are a common fault in pies. Soggy bottoms can be avoided in several ways:

1. Use mealy dough for bottom crusts. Mealy dough absorbs less liquid than flaky dough.

2. Use high bottom heat, at least at the beginning of baking, to set the crust quickly. Bake the pies at the bottom of the oven.

3. Do not add hot fillings to unbaked crusts.

4. For fruit pies, line the bottom of the pie shell with a thin layer of cake crumbs before pouring in the filling. This helps absorb some juice that might otherwise soak into the crust.

5. Use dark metal pie tins, which absorb heat. (Because so many bakers use disposable aluminum pans, other methods must be relied on. Disposable pans with black bottoms are sometimes available.)

6. If finished pies still have underbaked bottoms, they can be set on a flattop range for a few minutes. However, exercise extreme care to avoid scorching.

PROCEDURE: Making a Lattice Top Crust

1. Roll out fresh pie dough (not scraps) ⅛ in. (3 mm) thick.

2. Cut long strips about ⅜ in. (1 cm) wide and long enough to cross the center of the pie.

3. Egg-wash the strips and the rim of the filled pie.

4. Place the strips across the pie about 1 in. (2.5 cm) apart. Be sure they are parallel and evenly spaced. Seal them well onto the rim of the pie shell and trim off excess.

5. Place additional strips across the pie at an angle to the first. They may be at a 45-degree angle to make a diamond pattern or at a 90-degree angle to make a checkerboard pattern. Seal and trim excess.

Note: Instead of laying the strips across each other, you may interweave them (a, b, c), but this is usually too time-consuming for a bakeshop and generally done only in home kitchens. When you interweave the strips, some juices from the filling are likely to cling to the bottoms of the strips, as in the illustration. It is best to remove most of these juices as you go, so that they do not mar the appearance of the crust when baked.

A

B

C

PROCEDURE: Preparing Baked Pies

Note: For pies without a top crust, omit steps 3 to 7.

1. Line pie pans with pie dough as in the basic procedure (a).

2. Fill with cooled fillings (b). (See the table below for scaling instructions.) Do not drop filling on the rims of the pie shells; this will make it harder to seal the rims to the top crusts, and leaking may result during baking.

To avoid spilling custard fillings in single-crust pies, place the empty shells on the racks in the ovens before pouring in the filling.

3. Roll out dough for the top crusts.
4. Cut perforations in the top crusts to allow steam to escape during baking.
5. Moisten the rim of the bottom crusts with water or egg wash to help seal them to the top crusts.
6. Fit the top crusts in place (c). Seal the edges together firmly and trim excess dough. The rims may be fluted or crimped if desired. Pressing with the tines of a fork is a quick way to seal and crimp the edge. An efficient way to trim excess pastry is to rotate the pie tin while pressing on the edges with the palms of the hands (d).

7. Brush tops with desired wash: milk, cream, egg wash, or melted butter. Sprinkle lightly with granulated sugar, if desired. Egg-washed tops have a shiny appearance when baked. Tops brushed with fat, milk, or cream are not shiny but have a home-baked look.

8. Place pies on the lower level of an oven preheated to 425°–450°F (210°–220°C). The high initial heat helps set the bottom crust to avoid soaking. Fruit pies are baked at this high heat until done. For custard pies, reduce heat after 10 minutes to 325°–350°F (165°–175°C) to avoid overcooking and curdling the custard. Custard pies include all those containing large quantities of egg, such as pumpkin pie and pecan pie.

SCALING INSTRUCTIONS FOR BAKED PIES

U.S.		METRIC	
PIE SIZE	WEIGHT OF FILLING	PIE SIZE	WEIGHT OF FILLING
8 in.	26–30 oz	20 cm	750–850 g
9 in.	32–40 oz	23 cm	900–1150 g
10 in.	40–50 oz	25 cm	1150–1400 g

Note: Weights are guidelines only. Exact weights may vary, depending on the filling and the depth of the pans. Disposable tins are usually shallower than standard tins.

PROCEDURE: Preparing Unbaked Pies

1. Line the pie pans with pie dough as in the basic procedure.

2. Dock the crust well with a fork to prevent blistering. (To *dock* means to pierce or perforate the pastry, using a fork or other suitable tool.)

3. Place another pan inside the first one so the dough is between two pans.

4. Place the pans upside down in a preheated oven at 450°F (230°C). Baking upside down helps keep the dough from shrinking down into the pan.

   Some bakers like to chill the crusts at least 20–30 minutes before baking to relax the gluten and help reduce shrinkage.

5. Bake at 450°F (230°C) for 10–15 minutes. One pan may be removed during the last part of baking so the crust can brown.

6. Cool the baked crust completely.

7. Fill with cream filling or chiffon filling. Fill as close as possible to service time to prevent soaking the crust.

8. Chill the pie until it is set enough to slice.

9. Most cream pies and chiffon pies are especially good topped with whipped cream. Some cream pies, especially lemon, are popular when topped with meringue and browned (Procedure for Making Meringue Pie Topping follows).

PROCEDURE: Making Meringue Pie Topping

1. Make common meringue or Swiss meringue, using 1 pound of sugar per pound of egg whites. Whip until just stiff. See pages 258–259 for procedure.

2. Spread a generous amount of meringue on each pie. Mound it slightly, and be sure to attach it to the edge of the crust all around. If this is not done, the meringue may slide around on the finished pie. Leave the meringue in ripples or peaks.

3. Bake at 400°F (200°C) until the surface is attractively browned. Do not use higher temperatures, which will cause the surface of the meringue to shrink and toughen.

4. Remove from the oven and cool.

KEY POINTS TO REVIEW

▪ What are the steps in the procedure for rolling pie dough and lining pans?

▪ What are the steps in the procedure for preparing baked pies?

▪ What are the steps in the procedure for preparing unbaked pies?

FILLINGS

MOST PIE FILLINGS require thickeners of some sort. The two most important thickeners for pies are starches and eggs.

Starches for Fillings

Many kinds of pie filling, especially fruit fillings and cream fillings, depend on starch for their thickness. Some egg-thickened fillings, such as pumpkin, also sometimes contain starch. The starch acts as a stabilizer and may also reduce the cost by allowing for a lower egg content. Starches for fillings include:

> **Cornstarch** is used for cream pies because it sets up into a firm gel that holds its shape when sliced. It may also be used for fruit pies.

Waxy maize or **modified starches** are best for fruit pies because they are clear when set and make a soft paste rather than a firm gel. Waxy maize should be used for pies that are to be frozen, as this starch is not broken down by freezing.

Flour, tapioca, potato starch, rice starch, and other starches are used less frequently for fillings. Flour has less thickening power than other starches and makes fruit fillings cloudy.

Instant or pregelatinized starch needs no cooking because it has already been cooked. When used with certain fruit fillings, it eliminates the need to cook the filling before making up the pie. It loses this advantage, however, when the filling is made of raw fruit that must be cooked anyway. In the case of soft fillings such as pumpkin, *instant starch* can be used to eliminate a problem that often occurs with cornstarch: Cornstarch tends to settle out before gelatinizing. This creates a dense, starchy layer on the bottom and improperly thickened filling on top. Instant starches differ in thickening power, so follow the manufacturer's recommendations.

Cooking Starches

To avoid lumping, starches must be mixed with a cold liquid or sugar before being added to a hot liquid.

Sugar and strong acids, such as lemon juice, reduce the thickening power of starch. When possible, all or part of the sugar and strong acids should be added *after the starch has thickened*.

Fruit Fillings

Fruit fillings consist of solid fruit pieces bound together by a gel. The gel consists of fruit juice, water, sugar, spices, and a starch thickener. As explained, a modified starch such as waxy maize is the preferred thickener for fruit fillings because it makes a clear, not cloudy, gel.

Other starches, such as cornstarch, tapioca, or potato starch, may also be used. Cornstarch is frequently used in food service operations in which baking is only one aspect of the food preparation, making it inconvenient to have on hand all the specialty ingredients found in a bakery.

The functions of the gel are to bind the solid fruit pieces together, to help carry the flavors of the spices and the sweetness of the sugar, and to improve appearance by giving a shine or gloss to the fruit. Of course, the solid fruit is the most important part of the filling. To have a good-quality pie filling, you should have 2 to 3 pounds of drained fruit for each pound of liquid (juice plus water).

The two basic methods in food service for making pie fillings are the *cooked juice method* and the *cooked fruit method*. We also describe a third, the old-fashioned method, at the end of the section. In the cooked juice method, the gel is made separately by cooking fruit juice, water, and sugar with a starch. The gel is then mixed with the fruit. In the cooked fruit method, the fruit, water, and juices (if any) are all cooked together and then thickened with a starch.

Fruits for Pie Fillings

Fresh fruits are excellent in pies if they are at their seasonal peak. Fresh apples are used extensively for high-quality pies. The quality of fresh fruits can vary considerably, however, and many fruits require a lot of labor.

Frozen fruits are widely used for pies because they are consistent in quality and readily available. Frozen fruits for quantity use are commonly packed with sugar in 30-pound (13.6-kg) tins. They may be thawed in the refrigerator for 2 to 3 days, or in a water bath. A third method is to thaw the fruit just enough to free it from its container, add the water to be used in making it into a pie filling, and heat it to 185° to 195°F (85° to 90°C). Then drain the juice well and make the filling. Whichever method you use, be sure the fruit is completely thawed before preparing the filling. If it is partially frozen, you will not be able to drain the juice properly to make the gel, and the frozen, undrained juice will water down the filling later.

Some frozen fruits, especially berries, are packed without sugar. Naturally, the sugar content of any fruit must be taken into account when adding sugar to pie fillings.

Canned fruits are packed in four basic styles: solid pack, heavy pack, water pack, and syrup pack. *Solid pack* means no water is added, although you will be able to drain off a small quantity of juice. *Heavy pack* means only a small quantity of water or juice is added. *Water pack* fruits are canned with the water that was used to process them. Sour cherries are usually packed this way. *Syrup pack* fruits are packed in a sugar syrup, which may be light, medium, heavy, or extra-heavy. Heavy syrup means there is more sugar in the syrup. In general, fruits packed in heavy syrup are firmer and less broken than fruits in light syrup.

With water-pack and syrup-pack fruits, it is important to know the *drained weight* (the weight of the solid fruit without the juice). This information may be indicated on the label or available from the processor. The *net weight* is the weight of the total contents, including juice or syrup.

If the drained weight of a fruit is very low, you may need to add extra drained fruit to a batch of filling in order to get a good ratio of fruit to gel.

Dried fruits must be rehydrated by soaking and, usually, simmering before they are made into pie fillings.

Fruits must have sufficient acid (tartness) to make flavorful fillings. If they lack natural acid, you may need to add some lemon, orange, or pineapple juice to supply the acid.

Cooked Juice Method

The advantage of this method is that only the juice is cooked. Thus, the fruit retains better shape and flavor because it is subjected to less heat and handling. This method is used when the fruit requires little or no cooking before filling the pie. Most canned and frozen fruits are prepared this way. Fresh berries can also be prepared with this method: Part of the berries are cooked or puréed to provide juice, and the remaining berries are then mixed with the finished gel.

PROCEDURE: Cooked Juice Method

1. Drain the juice from the fruit.
2. Measure the juice and, if necessary, add water or other fruit juice to bring to the desired volume.
3. Bring the juice to a boil.
4. Dissolve the starch in cold water and stir it into the boiling juice. Return to a boil and cook until clear and thickened.
5. Add sugar, salt, and flavorings. Stir until dissolved.
6. Pour the thickened juice over the drained fruit and mix gently. Be careful not to break or mash the fruit.
7. Cool.

Cooked Fruit Method

This method is used when the fruit requires cooking or there is not enough liquid for the cooked juice method. Most fresh fruits (except berries) are prepared this way, as are dried fruits such as raisins and dried apricots. Canned fruits should not be prepared by this method because they have already been cooked and are likely to break up or turn to mush.

PROCEDURE: Cooked Fruit Method

1. Bring the fruit and juice or water to a boil. Some sugar may be added to the fruit to draw out juices.
2. Dissolve the starch in cold water and stir into the fruit. Return to a boil and cook until clear and thickened. Stir while cooking.
3. Add sugar, salt, flavorings, and other ingredients. Stir until dissolved.
4. Cool as quickly as possible.

VARIATION

Some fruits, such as fresh apples, may be cooked in butter, rather than boiled in water, for better flavor.

Old-Fashioned Method

This method is commonly used for homemade apple pies and peach pies. However, it is not often used in food service operations because of its disadvantages. First, the thickening of the juices is difficult to control. Second, because raw fruit shrinks as it cooks, it is necessary to pile the fruit high in the shell. The fruit then shrinks, often leaving a large airspace between the crust and fruit, so the top crust becomes misshapen. Also, the juices given off are more likely to boil over than when the filling is cooked and the juice thickened before filling the pie.

For these reasons, the cooked fruit method usually gives better results than the old-fashioned method. See the Apple Pie formula and variations on page 294.

PROCEDURE: Old-Fashioned Method

1. Mix the starch and spices with the sugar until uniformly blended.
2. Mix the fruit with the sugar mixture.
3. Fill the unbaked pie shells with the fruit.
4. Place lumps of butter on top of the filling.
5. Cover with a top crust or Streusel (p. 195) and bake.

KEY POINTS TO REVIEW

▮ What are the steps in the cooked juice procedure for making pie fillings?

▮ What are the steps in the cooked fruit procedure for making pie fillings?

▮ What are the steps in the old-fashioned procedure for making fruit pie fillings?

APPLE PIE FILLING (CANNED FRUIT)

Yield: about 9½ lb (4500 g)—five 8-in. (20-cm) pies; four 9-in. (23-cm) pies; three 10-in. (25-cm) pies

Ingredients	U.S.			Metric
Canned apples, solid pack or heavy pack (one No. 10 can)	6 lb	8	oz	3000 g
Drained juice plus water	1 pt	8	fl oz	750 mL
Water, cold		8	fl oz	250 mL
Cornstarch		3	oz	90 g
or				
Modified starch (waxy maize)		2.5	oz	75 g
Sugar	1 lb	4	oz	570 g
Salt		0.25	oz	7 g
Cinnamon		0.25	oz (3½ tsp)	7 g
Nutmeg		0.08	oz (1 tsp)	2 g
Butter		3	oz	90 g

PROCEDURE

Use the cooked juice method (p. 290).

1. Drain the apples and save the juice. Add enough water to the juice to measure 1½ pt (750 mL).
2. Mix the cold water and starch.
3. Bring the juice mixture to a boil. Stir in the starch mixture and return to a boil.
4. Add the remaining ingredients, except the drained apples. Simmer until the sugar is dissolved.
5. Pour the syrup over the apples and mix gently. Cool completely.
6. Fill the pie shells. Bake at 425°F (220°C) about 30–40 minutes.

VARIATIONS

DUTCH APPLE PIE FILLING

Simmer 8 oz (250 g) raisins in water. Drain and add to apple pie filling.

CHERRY PIE FILLING

Use one No. 10 can sour cherries instead of apples and make the following ingredient adjustments:

Increase starch to 4 oz (125 g) cornstarch or 3 oz (90 g) waxy maize.

Increase sugar to 1 lb 12 oz (825 g).

Add 1½ oz (45 mL) lemon juice in step 4.

Omit cinnamon and nutmeg. Add almond extract to taste (optional).

If desired, color with 2 to 3 drops red coloring.

PEACH PIE FILLING

Use one No. 10 can sliced peaches, preferably solid or heavy pack, instead of apples. Increase liquid in step 1 to 1 qt (1 L). Omit cinnamon and nutmeg.

PINEAPPLE PIE FILLING

Use one No. 10 can crushed pineapple instead of apples. Gently press the fruit in a sieve to squeeze out the juice. Make the following ingredient adjustments:

Increase the liquid in step 1 to 1 qt (1 L).

Increase the starch to 4 oz (125 g) cornstarch or 3 oz (90 g) waxy maize.

Use 1 lb 8 oz (750 g) sugar and 8 oz (250 g) corn syrup.

Omit the cinnamon and nutmeg. If desired, color with 2 to 3 drops yellow coloring.

BLUEBERRY PIE FILLING (FROZEN FRUIT)

Yield: about 7 lb 8 oz (3375 g)—four 8-in. (20-cm) pies; three 9-in. (23-cm) pies

Ingredients	U.S.		Metric
Blueberries, frozen, unsweetened	5 lb		2250 g
Drained juice plus water	12	fl oz	375 mL
Sugar	6	oz	175 g
Water, cold	6	fl oz	190 mL
Cornstarch	3	oz	90 g
or			
Modified starch (waxy maize)	2.25	oz	68 g
Sugar	14	oz	412 g
Salt	0.25	oz	8 g
Cinnamon	0.12	oz (1¾ tsp)	4 g
Lemon juice	1.5	fl oz	45 mL

PROCEDURE

Use the cooked juice method (p. 290).

1. Thaw the berries in their unopened original container.

2. Drain the berries. Add enough water to the juice to measure 12 oz (375 mL). Add the first quantity of sugar.

3. Mix the cold water and the starch.

4. Bring the juice mixture to a boil. Stir in the starch mixture. Return to a boil to thicken.

5. Add the remaining ingredients, except the drained berries. Stir over heat until the sugar is dissolved.

6. Pour the syrup over the drained berries. Mix gently. Cool completely.

7. Fill pie shells. Bake at 425°F (220°C) about 30 minutes.

VARIATIONS

APPLE PIE FILLING

Use 5 lb (2.25 kg) frozen apples instead of blueberries. Make the following ingredient adjustments:

Reduce the starch to 1.5 oz (45 g) cornstarch or 1.25 oz (38 g) waxy maize.

Reduce the second quantity of sugar to 8 oz (225 g).

Add ½ tsp (1 g) nutmeg and 3 oz (87 g) butter in step 5.

CHERRY PIE FILLING

Use 5 lb (2.25 kg) frozen cherries instead of blueberries. Make the following ingredient adjustments:

Increase the liquid in step 2 to 1 pt (500 mL).

Reduce the starch to 2.5 oz (75 g) cornstarch or 2 oz (60 g) waxy maize.

Reduce the second quantity of sugar to 10 oz (285 g).

Omit the cinnamon.

Reduce the lemon juice to 0.75 fl oz (22 mL).

RAISIN PIE FILLING

Yield: about 2 lb (1 kg)—one 9-in. (23-cm) pie

For large-quantity measurements, see page 720.

Ingredients	U.S.		Metric	
Raisins	13	oz	360	g
Water	13	fl oz	400	mL
Water, cold	2	fl oz	50	mL
Cornstarch	0.5	oz	15	g
or				
Modified starch (waxy maize)	0.4	oz	12	g
Sugar	4	oz	114	g
Salt	0.06	oz (¼ tsp)	2	g
Lemon juice	0.6	fl oz	18	mL
Grated lemon zest	0.02	oz (⅛ tsp)	0.6	g
Cinnamon	0.012	oz (⅛ tsp)	0.4	g
Butter	0.6	oz	18	g

PROCEDURE

Use the cooked fruit method (p. 290).

1. Combine the raisins and water in a saucepan. Simmer 5 minutes.

2. Mix the water and starch. Stir into the raisins and simmer until thickened.

3. Add the remaining ingredients. Stir until the sugar is dissolved and the mixture is uniform.

4. Cool thoroughly.

5. Fill the pie shells. Bake at 425°F (220°C) about 30–40 minutes.

FRESH APPLE PIE FILLING I

Yield: about 2 lb 6 oz (1070 g)—one 9-in. (23-cm) pie

For large-quantity measurements, see page 721.

Ingredients	U.S.		Metric	
Apples, peeled and sliced	2 lb		900	g
Butter	1	oz	30	g
Sugar	3	oz	90	g
Water, cold	2	oz	60	g
Cornstarch	0.75 oz		24	g
or				
Modified starch (waxy maize)	0.5	oz	15	g
Sugar	3.5	oz	100	g
Salt	0.06 oz (¼ tsp)		1	g
Cinnamon	0.06 oz (1 tsp)		1	g
Nutmeg	0.02 oz (¼ tsp)		0.5 g	
Lemon juice	0.33 oz (2 tsp)		10	g
Butter	0.25 oz		7	g

PROCEDURE

Use this variation of the cooked fruit method (p. 290).

1. Sauté the apples lightly in the first quantity of butter until they are slightly softened. Add the first quantity of sugar as the apples cook. This will draw juices out of the apples, which will then simmer in these juices.

2. Mix the water and starch until smooth. Add the starch mixture to the apples and boil until the liquid is thick and clear.

3. Remove from the heat. Add the remaining ingredients. Stir gently until the sugar is dissolved and the butter is melted.

4. Cool completely.

5. Fill the pie shells. Bake at 425°F (220°C) about 30–40 minutes.

—— **VARIATIONS** ——

FRESH APPLE PIE FILLING II

For large-quantity measurements, see page 721.

Ingredients	U.S.	Metric
Water	3.5 oz	100 g

Omit the first quantity of butter. Instead, simmer the apples in water and the first quantity of sugar as in the basic cooked fruit method, using the quantity of water listed above.

APPLE GINGER PIE FILLING

For large-quantity measurements, see page 721.

Ingredients	U.S.	Metric
Ground ginger	0.03 oz (¼ tsp)	0.5 g
Candied ginger, finely chopped	0.67 oz	20 g

Prepare as for Fresh Apple Pie Filling I or II, but omit the cinnamon and instead add ground and candied ginger.

APPLE PEAR PIE FILLING

Prepare as for Fresh Apple Pie Filling I or II, but substitute slightly firm pears for half the apples.

APPLE WALNUT PIE FILLING

For large-quantity measurements, see page 721.

Ingredients	U.S.	Metric
Chopped walnuts	2.5 oz	75 g

Mix walnuts into Fresh Apple Pie Filling I or II.

RHUBARB PIE FILLING

For large-quantity measurements, see page 721.

Ingredients	U.S.	Metric
Fresh rhubarb	1 lb 6 oz	650 g

Substitute rhubarb, cut into 1-in. (2.5-cm) pieces, for the apples. Omit the cinnamon, nutmeg, and lemon juice.

APPLES FOR PIES

Which varieties of apples are best for making pies? Two criteria are important: taste and texture. First, the apples should have good flavor and a noticeable level of acidity. Apples that are very mild make pies with little flavor. The sugar content, or sweetness, of the apple, is less important, as the sugar in the recipe can be adjusted.

Second, the apples should hold their shape when cooked. Apples that turn to mush, such as McIntosh, are better for applesauce than for pies.

Popular apple varieties that have good taste and texture for use in pie fillings include Granny Smith, Jonathan, Jonagold, Newton Pippin, Rome, Macoun, Pink Lady, Stayman-Winesap, Haralson, and Golden Delicious.

PEACH SOUR CREAM PIE FILLING

Yield: 2 lb 4 oz (1125 g)—one 9-in. (23-cm) pie

For large-quantity measurements, see page 720.

Ingredients	U.S.		Metric	
Sour cream	8	oz	250	g
Sugar	4	oz	125	g
Cornstarch	0.5	oz	15	g
Eggs, beaten	3.33 oz (2 eggs)		100	g (2 eggs)
Vanilla extract	½ tsp		2	mL
Nutmeg	⅛ tsp		0.5	mL
Fresh peaches, sliced (see *Note*)	1 lb		625	g
Streusel (p. 195)	6	oz	180	g

NOTE: If fresh peaches are not available, substitute canned peaches packed in light syrup. Drain them well before weighing.

PROCEDURE

1. Mix the sour cream, sugar, and cornstarch until smooth.
2. Add the eggs, vanilla, and nutmeg and mix in.
3. Carefully fold the peaches into the sour cream mixture.
4. Fill unbaked pie shells.
5. Top with Streusel (p. 195).
6. Bake at 425°F (220°C) for about 30 minutes, until the filling is set.

--- **VARIATION** ---

PEAR SOUR CREAM PIE

Substitute sliced pears for the sliced peaches.

OLD-FASHIONED APPLE PIE FILLING

Yield: about 11 lb (5 kg)—six 8-in. (20-cm) pies; five 9-in. (23-cm) pies; four 10-in. (25-cm) pies

Ingredients	U.S.		Metric
Apples, peeled and sliced	9 lb		4100 g
Lemon juice	2	fl oz	60 mL
Sugar	2 lb		900 g
Cornstarch	3	oz	90 g
Salt	0.25	oz	7 g
Cinnamon	0.25	oz	7 g
Nutmeg	0.08 oz (1 tsp)		2 g
Butter	3	oz	90 g

PROCEDURE

Use the old-fashioned method (p. 291).

1. Select firm, tart apples. Scale after peeling and coring.
2. Combine the apple slices and lemon juice in a large mixing bowl. Toss to coat apples with the juice.
3. Mix together the sugar, cornstarch, salt, and spices. Add to the apples and toss gently until well mixed.
4. Fill the pie shells, packing down the apples well. Dot the tops with pieces of butter before covering with top crusts. Bake at 400°F (200°C) about 45 minutes.

FRESH STRAWBERRY PIE FILLING

Yield: about 12 lb (5.5 kg)—six 8-in. (20-cm) pies; five 9-in. (23-cm) pies; four 10-in. (25-cm) pies

Ingredients	U.S.		Metric
Fresh whole strawberries	9 lb		4100 g
Water, cold	1 pt		500 mL
Sugar	1 lb 12	oz	800 g
Cornstarch	4	oz	120 g
or			
Modified starch (waxy maize)	3	oz	90 g
Salt	0.17 oz (1 tsp)		5 g
Lemon juice	2	fl oz	60 mL

PROCEDURE

Use the cooked juice method (p. 290).

1. Hull, wash, and drain the berries. Set aside 7 lb (3.2 kg) berries. If small, these may be left whole; if large, cut in halves or quarters.
2. Mash or purée the remaining 2 lb (900 g) berries. Mix with the water. (If a clear filling is desired, strain this mixture.)
3. Mix together the sugar, starch, and salt. Stir into the berry-and-water mixture until no lumps remain.
4. Bring to a boil, stirring constantly. Cook until thickened.
5. Remove from the heat and stir in the lemon juice.
6. Cool to room temperature but do not chill.
7. Stir to eliminate lumps. Fold in the reserved berries.
8. Fill baked pie shells and chill (do not bake).

--- VARIATION ---

FRESH BLUEBERRY TART FILLING

Substitute blueberries for the strawberries. This recipe works best with small berries and with cornstarch rather than modified starch. Adjust the sugar as desired, depending on the sweetness of the fruit. Force the cooked, thickened juices through a sieve (cooking the juices before straining gives more color to the gel). Fold the glaze into the berries while it is still hot.

This mixture is more suitable for tarts than for pies. Because pie shells are deeper, the filling may not hold its shape when sliced. One recipe makes enough filling for eight or nine 8-in. (20-cm) tarts, seven or eight 9-in. (23-cm) tarts, or six 10-in. (25-cm) tarts.

Custard or Soft Fillings

Custard, pumpkin, pecan, and similar pies are made with an uncooked liquid filling containing eggs. The eggs coagulate during baking, which sets the filling. For more information on custards, see page 515.

The method for one pie in this section is unusual. Key Lime Pie is similar to other soft pies, except it is not baked. Instead, the acidity of the lime juice is sufficient to coagulate the proteins and thicken the pie filling.

Many soft fillings contain starch in addition to eggs. Flour, cornstarch, and instant starch are frequently used. Although starch is unnecessary if enough eggs are used, many bakers prefer to add a little starch because it allows them to reduce the egg content. Also, the use of starch helps bind the liquids and reduce the chance of separating, or "weeping," in the baked pie. If starch is used, be sure the mix is well stirred before filling the pies in order to reduce the danger of the starch settling out.

The greatest difficulty in preparing soft pies is cooking the crust completely without over-cooking the filling. Start the pie at the bottom of a hot oven (425° to 450°F/220° to 230°C) for the first 10 to 15 minutes to set the crust. Then reduce the heat to 325° to 350°F (165° to 175°C) to cook the filling slowly. An alternative approach is to *partially* bake the empty shells before filling. See page 288 for baking empty shells (called *baking blind*), but bake until about half cooked. Cool, fill, and bake the pie.

Use one of these methods to test for doneness:

- Shake the pie very gently. If it is no longer liquid, it is done. The center will still be slightly soft, but its own heat will continue to cook the pie after it is removed from the oven.
- Insert a thin knife blade an inch from the center. If it comes out clean, the pie is done.

CUSTARD PIE FILLING

Yield: 2 lb (0.9 kg)—one 9-in. (23-cm) pie

For large-quantity measurements, see page 720.

Ingredients	U.S.		Metric	
Eggs	8	oz	225	g
Sugar	4	oz	112	g
Salt	0.06	oz (¼ tsp)	1	g
Vanilla extract	0.25	fl oz (1½ tsp)	7.5	mL
Milk (see *Note*)	1.25 pt		600	mL
Nutmeg	0.018–0.035 oz (¼–½ tsp)		0.5–0.75 g	

NOTE: For a richer custard, use part milk and part cream.

PROCEDURE

1. Combine the eggs, sugar, salt, and vanilla and blend until smooth. Do not whip air into the mixture.
2. Stir in the milk. Skim off any foam.
3. Place the unbaked pie shells in preheated oven (450°F/230°C) and carefully ladle in the filling. Sprinkle tops with nutmeg.
4. Bake at 450°F (230°C) for 15 minutes. Reduce heat to 325°F (165°C) and bake until set, about 20–30 minutes more.

VARIATION

COCONUT CUSTARD PIE FILLING

Use 2.5 oz (70 g) unsweetened, flaked coconut. Sprinkle the coconut into the pie shells before adding the custard mixture. The coconut may be lightly toasted in the oven before it is added to the pies. Omit the nutmeg.

PECAN PIE FILLING

Yield: 1 lb 12 oz (820 g) filling plus 5 oz (142 g) pecans—one 9-in. (23-cm) pie

For large-quantity measurements, see page 721.

Ingredients	U.S.		Metric	
Granulated sugar (see *Note*)	7	oz	200	g
Butter	2	oz	60	g
Salt	0.06	oz (¼ tsp)	1.5	g
Eggs	7	oz	200	g
Dark corn syrup	12	oz (about 8½ fl oz)	350	g
Vanilla extract	0.25	oz (1½ tsp)	8	g
Pecans	5	oz	142	g

NOTE: Brown sugar may be used if a darker color and stronger flavor are desired.

PROCEDURE

1. Using the paddle attachment, at low speed, blend the sugar, butter, and salt until evenly blended.
2. With the machine running, add the eggs a little at a time until they are all absorbed.
3. Add the syrup and vanilla. Mix until well blended.
4. To assemble pies, distribute the pecans evenly in the pie shells and then fill with the syrup mixture.
5. Bake at 425°F (220°C) for 10 minutes. Reduce heat to 350°F (175°C). Bake 30–40 minutes more, until set.

VARIATION

MAPLE WALNUT PIE FILLING

Substitute pure maple syrup for the corn syrup. Substitute coarsely chopped walnuts for the pecans.

PUMPKIN PIE FILLING

Yield: about 4.25 lb (2 kg)—two 9-in. (23-cm) pies

For large-quantity measurements, see page 721.

Ingredients	U.S.		Metric	
Pumpkin purée (one No. 2½ can)	1 lb 10.5	oz	750	g
Pastry flour	1	oz	30	g
Cinnamon	0.12	oz	4	g
Nutmeg	0.018 oz (¼ tsp)		0.5 g (1 mL)	
Ginger	0.018 oz (¼ tsp)		0.5 g (1 mL)	
Cloves	0.01	oz (⅛ tsp)	0.3 g (0.5 mL)	
Salt	0.12	oz (⅝ tsp)	4	g
Brown sugar	10	oz	290	g
Eggs (see *Note*)	10	oz	300	g
Corn syrup or half corn syrup and half molasses	2	oz	60	g
Milk	1 pt 4	fl oz	600	mL

NOTE: Pumpkin pie filling should be allowed to stand at least 30 minutes before being poured into the pie shells. This gives the pumpkin time to absorb the liquid and makes a smoother filling that is less likely to separate after baking. If the filling is to stand for much more than 1 hour, do not add the eggs until the pies are to be filled. If the eggs are added earlier, the acidity of the pumpkin and brown sugar may partially coagulate the eggs.

PROCEDURE

1. Place the pumpkin in the bowl of a mixer fitted with the whip attachment.
2. Sift together the flour, spices, and salt.
3. Add the flour mixture and sugar to the pumpkin. Mix at first speed until smooth and well blended. Avoid whipping air into the mix.
4. Add the eggs and mix in. Scrape down the sides of the bowl.
5. With the machine still at low speed, gradually pour in the syrup, then the milk. Mix until evenly blended.
6. Let the filling stand for 30–60 minutes.
7. Stir the filling to remix. Fill the pie shells. Bake at 450°F (230°C) for 15 minutes. Lower the heat to 350°F (175°C) and bake until set, about 30–40 minutes more.

VARIATIONS

SWEET POTATO PIE FILLING

Substitute canned sweet potatoes, drained and puréed, for the pumpkin.

SQUASH PIE FILLING

Substitute puréed squash for the pumpkin.

KEY LIME PIE FILLING

Yield: 1 lb 5 oz (630 g)—one 9-in. (23-cm) pie

For large-quantity measurements, see page 721.

Ingredients	U.S.		Metric
Egg yolks, pasteurized	2.67 oz (4 yolks)		80 g (4 yolks)
Sweetened condensed milk	14	oz	400 g
Freshly squeezed key lime juice (see *Note*)	5	oz	150 g

NOTE: If key limes are not available, substitute regular lime juice. Bottled or frozen key lime juice is also available.

Classic key lime pie filling is pale yellow in color, not green. However, if desired, tint the filling pale green with a few drops of food color.

PROCEDURE

1. Beat the egg yolks lightly, then stir in the sweetened condensed milk.

2. Add the lime juice and beat until smooth.

3. Pour the filling into a baked pie shell or a graham cracker crumb pie shell. Refrigerate overnight. The acidity of the limes will partially coagulate the egg and milk proteins so the filling becomes firm. Key lime pie must be kept refrigerated at all times.

4. Top with a meringue or whipped cream border.

Cream Pie Fillings

Cream pie fillings are the same as puddings, which, in turn, are the same as basic pastry cream with added flavorings such as vanilla, chocolate, or coconut. Lemon filling is made by the same method, using water and lemon juice instead of milk.

There is one difference between pastry cream and pie filling you should note: *Cream pie fillings are made with cornstarch, so slices hold their shape when cut.* Pastry cream may be made with flour, cornstarch, or other starches.

The basic principles and procedures for making pastry cream are included in Chapter 12, pages 262–263. For your convenience, the formula for vanilla pastry cream is repeated here under the name Vanilla Cream Pie Filling. Popular flavor variations for cream pie fillings follow this basic recipe.

Opinion is divided as to whether pie shells should be filled with warm cream fillings, which are then cooled in the shell, or the filling should be cooled first and then added to the shell. For the best-looking slices, warm filling is best. The filling cools to a smooth, uniform mass and the slices hold sharp, clean cuts. However, you must use a well-prepared mealy pie dough that resists soaking, or you risk having soggy bottom crusts. Enriched Pie Pastry (p. 283) is good for this purpose.

Many food service operations prefer to fill each pie shell with cold filling shortly before the pie is to be cut and served. The slice will not cut as cleanly when you do this, but the crusts will be crisp and you can use flaky dough for them.

We use the warm filling method in this book, but you can, of course, modify the procedure to suit your needs.

KEY POINTS TO REVIEW

- What methods can be used to ensure that the crusts of soft pies are fully baked without overcooking the fillings?

- How are custard pies tested for doneness?

- What is the difference between pastry cream and cream pie filling?

VANILLA CREAM PIE FILLING

Yield: about 1⅛ pt (0.5 L) or 13 oz (0.8 kg)—one 9-in. (23-cm) pie

For large-quantity measurements, see page 722.

Ingredients	U.S.		Metric
Milk	1 pt		500 g
Sugar	2	oz	60 g
Egg yolks	1.5	oz	45 g
Whole eggs	2	oz	60 g
Cornstarch	1.25	oz	38 g
Sugar	2	oz	60 g
Butter	1	oz	30 g
Vanilla extract	0.25 oz (1½ tsp)		8 g

PROCEDURE

Before beginning production, review the discussion of pastry cream on pages 262–263.

1. In a heavy saucepan or kettle, dissolve the sugar in the milk and bring just to a boil.
2. With a whip, beat the egg yolks and whole eggs in a stainless steel bowl.
3. Sift the starch and sugar into the eggs. Beat with the whip until perfectly smooth.
4. Temper the egg mixture by slowly beating in the hot milk in a thin stream.
5. Return the mixture to the heat and bring it to a boil, stirring constantly.
6. When the mixture comes to a boil and thickens, remove it from the heat.
7. Stir in the butter and vanilla. Mix until the butter is melted and completely blended in.
8. Pour into baked, cooled pie shells. Cool, then keep chilled. If desired, decorate chilled pies with whipped cream, using a pastry bag with a star tube.

VARIATIONS

BANANA CREAM PIE FILLING

Using vanilla cream filling, pour half the filling into pie shells, cover with sliced bananas, and fill with remaining filling. (Bananas may be dipped in lemon juice to prevent browning.)

CHOCOLATE CREAM PIE FILLING I

For large-quantity measurements, see page 722.

Ingredients	U.S.	Metric
Unsweetened chocolate	1 oz	30 g
Semisweet chocolate	1 oz	30 g

Melt together the unsweetened and semisweet chocolate and mix into the hot vanilla cream filling.

CHOCOLATE CREAM PIE FILLING II

For large-quantity measurements, see page 722.

Ingredients	U.S.		Metric
Milk	14	fl oz	438 mL
Sugar	2	oz	60 g
Egg yolks	1.5	oz	45 g
Whole eggs	2	oz	60 g
Cold milk	2	oz	60 g
Cornstarch	1.25	oz	38 g
Cocoa	0.75	oz	22 g
Sugar	2	oz	60 g
Butter	1	oz	30 g
Vanilla extract	0.25 fl oz		8 mL

This variation uses cocoa instead of chocolate. The cocoa is sifted with the starch. Some of the milk must be included with the eggs in order to provide enough liquid to make a paste with the starch and cocoa. Follow the procedure in the basic recipe, but use the above ingredients.

BUTTERSCOTCH CREAM PIE FILLING

For large-quantity measurements, see page 722.

Ingredients	U.S.	Metric
Brown sugar	8 oz	250 g
Butter	2.5 oz	75 g

Combine brown sugar and butter in a saucepan. Heat over low heat, stirring, until the butter is melted and the ingredients are blended. Prepare the basic vanilla cream filling recipe, but omit all the sugar and increase the starch to 1½ oz (45 g). As the mixture comes to a boil, in step 5, gradually stir in the brown sugar mixture. Finish as in the basic recipe.

LEMON PIE FILLING

For large-quantity measurements, see page 722.

Ingredients	U.S.		Metric	
Water	14	fl oz	400	mL
Sugar	7	oz	200	g
Egg yolks	2.5	oz	75	g
Cornstarch	1.5	oz	45	g
Sugar	2	oz	60	g
Salt	0.025 oz (⅛ tsp)		0.5	g
Lemon zest, grated	0.16	oz (2 tsp)	5	g
Butter	1	oz	30	g
Lemon juice	3	fl oz	90	mL

Follow the procedure for vanilla cream filling, but use the above ingredients. Note that the lemon juice is added after the filling is thickened.

COCONUT CREAM PIE FILLING

Add 2 oz (60 g) toasted, unsweetened coconut to the basic filling.

STRAWBERRY RHUBARB PIE FILLING

Yield: 3 lb 8 oz (1680 g)—two 9-in. (20-cm) pies

For large-quantity measurements, see page 723.

Ingredients	U.S.		Metric
Rhubarb, fresh or frozen, in 1-in. (2.5-cm) pieces	1 lb 4	oz	600 g
Sugar	12	oz	360 g
Water	4	oz	120 g
Egg yolks	2.67 oz (4 yolks)		80 g (4 yolks)
Heavy cream	4	oz	120 g
Cornstarch	1.5	oz	45 g
Fresh strawberries, hulled and quartered	1 lb		480 g

PROCEDURE

1. Place the rhubarb, sugar, and water in a heavy saucepan. Cover and set over low heat. Bring to a simmer. The sugar will help draw juices out of the rhubarb. Simmer until the rhubarb is soft and the sugar is dissolved.

2. Beat the egg yolks with the cream until well mixed. Add the cornstarch and stir until evenly blended.

3. Remove the rhubarb from the heat. Stir in the cream mixture.

4. Return the rhubarb to the heat and bring to a simmer. Simmer about 1 minute, until thickened.

5. Pour out the rhubarb into a bowl and mix in the strawberries. Let stand until slightly warm. Mix again to blend the strawberry juices with the filling, then fill the baked pie shells. Chill until firm.

Chiffon Pie Fillings

Chiffon fillings have a light, fluffy texture created by the addition of beaten egg whites and, sometimes, whipped cream. The egg whites and cream are folded into a cream or fruit base, which is stabilized with gelatin. The folding-in of the egg whites and the filling of the baked pie shells must be done before the gelatin sets. After the pie is chilled to set the gelatin, the filling should be firm enough to hold a clean slice.

When chiffon filling contains both egg whites and whipped cream, most chefs and bakers prefer to fold in the egg whites first, even though they may lose some volume. The reason is that if the cream is added first, there is more danger it will be overbeaten and turn to butter during the folding and mixing procedure.

For a review of the guidelines for beating egg whites, see page 258. For the guidelines for whipping cream, see page 255.

For safety, always use pasteurized egg whites.

Bases for chiffons include the following three main types:

Thickened with starch. The procedure is the same as for fruit pie fillings made by the cooked juice method or cooked fruit method, except the fruit is finely chopped or puréed. Most fruit chiffons are made this way.

Thickened with egg. The procedure is the same as for Crème Anglaise (p. 261). Chocolate chiffons and pumpkin chiffons are sometimes made this way.

Thickened with egg and starch. The procedure is the same as for pastry cream or cream pie fillings. Lemon chiffon is usually made this way.

Guidelines for Using Gelatin

Although some chiffons contain starch as their only stabilizer, most contain gelatin. Gelatin must be handled properly to ensure it is completely dissolved and mixed evenly throughout the filling. (*Note:* All references to gelatin in this book mean unflavored gelatin, not flavored, sweetened gelatin mixes.)

In addition to the guidelines here, please refer to Chapter 4 for additional information on gelatin. There you will find guidelines for using leaf gelatin as well as powdered gelatin.

1. Measure gelatin accurately. Too much gelatin makes a stiff, rubbery product. Too little makes a soft product that does not hold its shape.

2. Do not mix raw pineapple or papaya with gelatin. These fruits contain enzymes that dissolve gelatin. You may use these fruits only if they are cooked or canned.

3. To dissolve unflavored gelatin, stir it into *cold* liquid to avoid lumping. Let it stand for 5 minutes to absorb water. Then heat it until it is dissolved, or combine it with a hot liquid and stir until dissolved.

4. After the gelatin is dissolved in the base, cool or chill it until it is slightly thickened but not set. If the base starts to set, it will be difficult or impossible to fold in the egg whites uniformly.

5. Stir the base occasionally while it is cooling so it cools evenly. Otherwise, the outside edges may start to set before the inside is sufficiently cooled, which creates lumps.

6. If the gelatin sets before you can add the egg whites, warm the base slightly by stirring it over hot water just until the gelatin is melted and there are no lumps. Cool again.

7. When folding in egg whites and whipped cream, work rapidly and without pause, or the gelatin might set before you are finished. Fill the pie shells immediately, before the filling sets.

8. Keep the pies refrigerated, especially in hot weather.

In addition to the following chiffons, you may also use Bavarian creams (p. 525) as pie fillings. Although Bavarian creams contain gelatin and whipped cream, they are not, strictly speaking, chiffons, because they do not contain whipped egg whites. Nevertheless, their texture is similar to that of chiffons because of the lightening effect of the whipped cream.

Finally, this section includes a recipe for a popular pie, French Silk Pie, that doesn't fit any of the standard categories in this chapter. The filling is a rich mixture of creamed butter, sugar, chocolate, and eggs. The procedure is similar to the creaming method for cakes, except that no flour is mixed in. Because the filling contains raw eggs, be careful always to use pasteurized eggs for French Silk Pie filling.

PROCEDURE: Making Chiffon Fillings

1. Prepare the base. Figure (a) shows thickening juice with cornstarch.

2. Soften gelatin in cold liquid. Stir it into the hot base until dissolved (b). Chill until thickened, but not set.

3. Fold in beaten egg whites (c).

4. Fold in whipped cream, if used (d).

5. Immediately pour into pie shells and chill.

STRAWBERRY CHIFFON PIE FILLING

Yield: 1 lb 5 oz (600 g)—one 9-in. (23-cm) pie

For large-quantity measurements, see page 723.

Ingredients	U.S.		Metric
Frozen sweetened strawberries (see *Note*)	13	oz	370 g
Salt	0.04 oz (⅛ tsp)		1 g
Cornstarch	0.2	oz	6 g
Water, cold	1	fl oz	30 mL
Gelatin	0.2	oz	6 g
Cold water	1.5	fl oz	45 mL
Lemon juice	0.2	fl oz	6 mL
Egg whites, pasteurized	3	oz	85 g
Sugar	2.5	oz	70 g

NOTE: To use fresh strawberries, slice or chop 10 oz (285 g) fresh, hulled strawberries and mix with 3 oz (85 g) sugar. Let stand in refrigerator for 2 hours. Drain and reserve juice and proceed as in basic recipe.

PROCEDURE

1. Thaw and drain the strawberries. Chop them coarsely.
2. Place the drained juice and salt in a saucepan. Bring to a boil.
3. Dissolve the cornstarch in the water and stir into the juice. Cook until thick. Remove from the heat.
4. Soften the gelatin in the second quantity of water. Add it to the hot, thickened juice and stir until completely dissolved.
5. Stir in the lemon juice and the drained strawberries.
6. Chill the mixture until thickened, but not set.
7. Beat the egg whites until they form soft peaks. Gradually add the sugar and continue to beat until a thick, glossy meringue is formed.
8. Fold the meringue into the fruit mixture.
9. Pour the mixture into baked pie shells. Chill until set.

VARIATIONS

STRAWBERRY CREAM CHIFFON PIE FILLING

For a creamier filling, reduce the egg whites to 2.5 oz (70 g). Whip 3.25 fl oz (100 mL) heavy cream and fold it in after the meringue.

RASPBERRY CHIFFON PIE FILLING

Substitute raspberries for strawberries in the basic recipe.

PINEAPPLE CHIFFON PIE FILLING

Use 10 oz (285 g) crushed pineapple. Mix the drained juice with an additional 3.25 fl oz (100 mL) pineapple juice and add 1.6 oz (48 g) sugar.

CHOCOLATE CHIFFON PIE FILLING

Yield: 1 lb 6 oz (640 g)—one 9-in. (23-cm) pie

For large-quantity measurements, see page 723.

Ingredients	U.S.		Metric
Unsweetened chocolate	2	oz	60 g
Water	5	fl oz	150 mL
Egg yolks	3	oz	90 g
Sugar	3	oz	90 g
Gelatin	0.2	oz	6 g
Water, cold	1.5	fl oz	45 mL
Egg whites, pasteurized	4	oz	120 g
Sugar	5	oz	150 g

PROCEDURE

1. Combine the chocolate and water in a heavy saucepan. Bring to a boil over moderate heat, stirring constantly until smooth.
2. With the whip attachment, beat the egg yolks and sugar together until thick and light.
3. With the mixer running, gradually pour in the chocolate mixture.
4. Return the mixture to the saucepan and stir over very low heat until thickened. Remove from heat.
5. Soften the gelatin in the second quantity of water. Add it to the hot chocolate mixture and stir until the gelatin is completely dissolved.
6. Chill until thick, but not set.
7. Beat the egg whites until they form soft peaks. Gradually beat in the last quantity of sugar. Continue beating until a firm, glossy meringue is formed.
8. Fold the meringue into the chocolate mixture.
9. Pour the mixture into baked pie shells. Chill until set. Keep refrigerated.

VARIATION

CHOCOLATE CREAM CHIFFON PIE FILLING

For a creamier filling, reduce the egg whites to 3 oz (90 g). Whip 3 fl oz (90 mL) heavy cream and fold it in after the meringue.

PUMPKIN CHIFFON PIE FILLING

Yield: 1 lb 8 oz (680 g)—one 9-in. (23-cm) pie

For large-quantity measurements, see page 722.

Ingredients	U.S.		Metric	
Pumpkin purée	8	oz	240	g
Brown sugar	4	oz	120	g
Milk	2.5	oz	70	g
Egg yolks	2.5	oz	70	g
Salt	0.04	oz (⅛ tsp)	1	g
Cinnamon	0.055	oz (¾ tsp)	1.4	g
Nutmeg	0.028	oz (⅜ tsp)	0.8	g
Ginger	0.014	oz (⅛ tsp)	0.4	g
Gelatin	0.2	oz	6	g
Water, cold	1.5	fl oz	45	mL
Egg whites, pasteurized	3	oz	90	g
Sugar	3	oz	90	g

PROCEDURE

1. Combine the pumpkin, brown sugar, milk, egg yolks, salt, and spices. Mix until smooth and uniform.
2. Place mixture in a double boiler. Cook, stirring frequently, until thickened, or until the temperature of the mix is 185°F (85°C). Remove from heat.
3. Soften the gelatin in the water. Add it to the hot pumpkin mixture and stir until dissolved.
4. Chill until very thick, but not set.
5. Beat the egg whites until they form soft peaks. Gradually add the sugar and continue to beat until a thick, glossy meringue is formed.
6. Fold the meringue into the pumpkin mixture.
7. Fill baked pie shells with mixture. Chill until set.

VARIATION

PUMPKIN CREAM CHIFFON PIE FILLING

For a creamier filling, reduce the egg whites to 2.5 oz (70 g). Whip 3.25 fl oz (100 mL) heavy cream and fold it in after the meringue.

LEMON CHIFFON PIE FILLING

Yield: 1 lb 6 oz (640 g)—one 9-in. (23-cm) pie

For large-quantity measurements, see page 723.

Ingredients	U.S.		Metric
Water	5	fl oz	150 mL
Sugar	1.67	oz	48 g
Egg yolks	2.4	oz	70 g
Water, cold	1	fl oz	25 mL
Cornstarch	0.6	oz	18 g
Sugar	1.6	oz	48 g
Lemon zest, grated	0.1	oz	3 g
Gelatin	0.2	oz	6 g
Water, cold	1.5	fl oz	45 mL
Lemon juice	2.4	fl oz	70 mL
Egg whites, pasteurized	3	oz	90 g
Sugar	3	oz	90 g

PROCEDURE

1. Dissolve the sugar in the water and bring to a boil.
2. Beat together the egg yolks, second quantity of water, cornstarch, sugar, and zest until smooth.
3. Gradually beat the boiling syrup into the egg yolk mixture in a thin stream.
4. Return the mixture to the heat and bring it to a boil, beating constantly with a whip.
5. As soon as the mixture thickens and boils, remove it from the heat.
6. Soften the gelatin in the third quantity of water.
7. Add in the gelatin to the hot lemon mixture. Stir until it is dissolved.
8. Stir in the lemon juice.
9. Chill until thick, but not set.
10. Beat the egg whites until they form soft peaks. Gradually add the sugar and continue to beat until a thick, glossy meringue is formed.
11. Fold the meringue into the lemon mixture.
12. Fill baked pie shells. Chill until set.

VARIATIONS

LIME CHIFFON PIE FILLING

Substitute lime juice and zest for the lemon juice and zest.

ORANGE CHIFFON PIE FILLING

Make the following ingredient adjustments:

Use orange juice instead of water in step 1.

Omit the first 1.67 oz (48 g) sugar.

Substitute orange zest for the lemon zest.

Reduce the lemon juice to 0.8 oz (25 mL).

FRENCH SILK PIE FILLING

Yield: 1 lb 8 oz (720 g)—one 9-in. (23-cm) pie

Ingredients	U.S.		Metric	
Unsweetened chocolate	4	oz	120	g
Butter	6	oz	180	g
Sugar	9	oz	270	g
Vanilla	0.25 fl oz (1½ tsp)		7.5 mL	
Eggs, pasteurized	5	oz	150	g

Garnish				
Sweetened whipped cream	as desired		as desired	
Chocolate shavings or curls	as desired		as desired	

PROCEDURE

1. Melt the chocolate, then cool until just barely warm.

2. Using the paddle attachment, cream together the butter and sugar until light.

3. Beat the melted chocolate into the butter mixture until well blended.

4. Mix in the vanilla.

5. Add about one-third of the eggs. Using the whip attachment, whip at medium speed for 5 minutes.

6. Add another third of the eggs. Whip at medium speed for 5 minutes.

7. Add the remaining eggs. Again whip for 5 minutes. The mixture should be smooth and light.

8. Fill baked pie shells. Chill until firm enough to slice.

9. Before displaying or serving, pipe a generous border of whipped cream around the top edge of the filling. Alternatively, cover the entire top with piped whipped cream. Decorate the top with chocolate shavings or curls.

STANDARDS OF QUALITY FOR PIES

ERRORS IN PIE PRODUCTION may include improper mixing of doughs, improper assembly of pies, faulty production of fillings, and problems in baking. The following chart lists common pie faults and their causes. To judge the quality of a pie, examine it for each of the defects listed in the table, to see if it avoids those defects. In other words, a well-made pie should have the following characteristics:

- Tender crust, but one that holds together and is not crumbly.
- Flaky top crust.
- Tender bottom crust that is fully baked and not soggy.
- Crust that hasn't shrunk or pulled away from the pan.
- Top crust well sealed to bottom crust.
- Filling of good flavor for its type and properly seasoned.
- Filling that is properly cooked and hasn't boiled out of the crust.
- Custard-type fillings properly set and not curdled or weeping.

To correct any faults you find, check the troubleshooting guide here for possible causes and then correct your procedures.

Fault	Causes
CRUST	
Dough too stiff	Not enough shortening Not enough liquid Flour too strong
Tough	Overmixing Not enough shortening Flour too strong Too much rolling or too much scrap dough used Too much water
Crumbly	Not enough water Too much shortening Improper mixing Flour too weak
Not flaky	Not enough shortening Shortening blended in too much Overmixing or too much rolling Dough or ingredients too warm
Soggy or raw bottom crust	Oven temperature too low; not enough bottom heat Filling hot when put in shell Not baked long enough Use of wrong dough (use mealy dough for bottom crusts) Not enough starch in fruit fillings
Shrinkage	Dough overworked Not enough shortening Flour too strong Too much water Dough stretched when put in pans Dough not rested
FILLING	
Filling boils out	No steam vents in top crust Top crust not sealed to bottom crust at edges Oven temperature too low Fruit too acidic Filling hot when put in shell Not enough starch in filling Too much sugar in filling Too much filling
Curdling of custard or soft fillings	Overbaked

KEY POINTS TO REVIEW

- What are the three types of bases for chiffon pie fillings?
- What are the guidelines for using gelatin?
- What is the procedure for making chiffon pie fillings?
- What are the most common faults found in pies, and how can these faults be corrected?

TERMS FOR REVIEW

flaky pie dough	fruit pie	instant starch	water pack
mealy pie dough	soft pie	cooked juice method	syrup pack
rubbed dough method	cream pie	cooked fruit method	drained weight
crumb crust	chiffon pie	solid pack	
	lattice crust	heavy pack	

QUESTIONS FOR REVIEW

1. Discuss the factors that affect tenderness, toughness, and flakiness in pie dough. Why shouldn't emulsifier shortening be used for pie dough?

2. What are some advantages and disadvantages of using butter in pie dough?

3. What would happen to a flaky pie dough if you mixed it too long before adding the water? After adding the water?

4. Describe the difference between mealy pie dough and flaky pie dough.

5. What kind of crust would you use for a pumpkin pie? An apple pie? A banana cream pie?

6. How can you prevent shrinkage when baking empty pie shells?

7. How can you prevent soggy or undercooked bottom piecrusts?

8. Which starch would you use to thicken apple pie filling? Chocolate cream pie filling? Lemon pie filling? Peach pie filling?

9. Why is lemon juice added to lemon pie filling after the starch has thickened the water? Wouldn't this thin the filling?

10. Why is the cooked juice method usually used when making pie fillings from canned fruits?

11. What problem might you have if you make blueberry pie filling out of blueberries that are still partially frozen?

12. How can you test a custard pie for doneness?

14

PASTRY BASICS

AFTER READING THIS CHAPTER, YOU SHOULD BE ABLE TO:

1. Prepare pâte brisée and short pastries.
2. Prepare puff pastry dough, blitz puff pastry dough, and reversed puff pastry dough, and make simple pastries from these doughs.
3. Prepare pâte à choux (éclair paste), and make simple pastries from it.
4. Prepare strudel dough, handle commercial phyllo (strudel) dough, and make pastries using either homemade or commercial dough.
5. Bake meringue and meringue-type sponges, and assemble simple desserts with these meringues.

THE TERM *PASTRY* comes from the word paste, meaning, in this case, a mixture of flour, liquid, and fat. In the bakeshop, pastry refers both to various pastes and doughs and to the many products made from them.

We have already discussed two fundamental types of pastry: yeast-raised pastry, such as Danish dough, in Chapters 6 and 9, and pie doughs in Chapter 13. Besides these two, the most important types of pastry are short doughs of various types, puff pastry, also known as *pâte feuilletée*, and éclair paste, also known as *pâte à choux*. These three pastries are introduced in this chapter. We also take a look at strudel and phyllo doughs, which are important for some specialty items. Finally, we look at crisp meringues and other meringue-type sponges. These are not pastries in the original sense of the word, because they are not made from a flour paste. Nevertheless, they are used like flour pastries in combination with creams, fillings, fruits, and icings to create a wide range of desserts.

This chapter concentrates on production of the doughs themselves. It is important to master the production techniques for these preparations before applying them to more complicated pastry desserts. Some simple applications of puff paste and éclair paste are included to give you practice handling these doughs. In addition, the section on strudel and phyllo includes examples of pastries made with these doughs. Once you understand the fundamentals, continue on to the next chapter, where you'll learn how these doughs are used in specialty pastry work.

PÂTE BRISÉE AND SHORT PASTRIES

THE QUALITY OF the pastry used to make tarts and tartlets is perhaps even more important than the quality of pie dough. Because tarts are generally thinner than pies, and have less filling, the dough is a prominent part of the finished pastry, not just a holder for the filling, as often seems to be the case with American-style pies. The best of these doughs are made with pure butter, not shortening, and they generally are enriched with eggs and sugar.

The three main doughs in this section—pate brisée, pate sucrée, and pate sablée—are basic preparations in classical pastry.

- *Pâte brisée* (pronounced pot bree ZAY), which literally means "broken dough," is mixed using the same method as mealy pie dough—the fat is first combined with the flour. In classical pastry, this is known as *sablage* (sah BLAHZH) or the *sanding method*. The fat and flour are mixed until the mixture resembles coarse meal or sand. Coating the flour with fat protects it from absorbing water, and therefore limits gluten development. This results in tender pastry. (Review pie dough production [pp. 280–282] if necessary. Follow the method for mealy pie dough, combining the eggs with other liquids.) If you compare the formula for pâte brisée in this chapter with the formula for Enriched Pie Pastry on page 283, you will see they are very similar. Pâte brisée is usually used for large tarts.

- *Pâte sucrée* (soo CRAY) means "sugared dough." It is similar to pate brisée but has a much higher sugar content. The high content of sugar acts as a tenderizer, so the dough is fragile and more difficult to handle than pate brisée. It is used primarily for small items such as tartlets and petits fours. Pâte sucrée can be mixed either by the sablage method or the creaming method (as it is in this chapter). The creaming method, in which the fat and sugar are mixed first, is also used for cookies, cakes, and muffins. In fact, both pâte sucrée and, especially, pâte sablée can be used to make plain cookies.

- *Pâte sablée* (sah BLAY) contains even more fat than pâte sucrée and less egg and other moisturizers. Some formulas also contain more sugar as well. It is an extremely tender and crumbly dough that is generally used for cookies but can also be used for small tarts and other pastries. The crumbly, "sandy" texture of the baked dough gives the pastry its name (sable means "sand" in French). Pâte sablée can be mixed using the sablage method, but today it is perhaps more common to use the creaming method, as in a typical cookie dough.

The sablée dough in this chapter is often called a *1-2-3 dough*, because it contains 1 part sugar, 2 parts fat, and 3 parts flour by weight. (Compare with the 3-2-1 dough discussed on page 282.)

The three remaining doughs in this section are variations on the basic pâte sablée formula. All these doughs are known as *short doughs*, because their tender structure is due to short gluten strands.

All these doughs are intended to be tender, so gluten development is kept low. Some gluten is necessary, however, to hold the doughs together. Otherwise they would be impossible to handle and roll out. For many formulas, including the ones in this chapter, pastry flour has enough protein to provide structure, but not so much as to make the dough tough. In other sources, you will find formulas that call for higher-protein flour, such as all-purpose flour or a mixture of pastry flour and bread flour. These flours are especially useful when the fat and sugar content is very high. The extra protein balances the tenderizing effect of the fat and sugar to give adequate structure to the dough.

PÂTE BRISÉE

For large-quantity measurements, see page 724.

Ingredients	U.S.		Metric	%
Pastry flour	12	oz	400 g	100
Salt	0.3	oz (1¼ tsp)	10 g	2.5
Sugar	0.3	oz (1½ tsp)	10 g	2.5
Butter, chilled	6	oz	200 g	50
Eggs	4	oz	130 g	33
Water	0.6	oz (4 tsp)	20 g	10
Vanilla extract	4	drops	4 drops	
Lemon zest, grated	0.12	oz (1½ tsp)	4 g	1
Total weight:	**1 lb 7**	**oz**	**774 g**	**199 %**

PROCEDURE

1. Sift the flour, salt, and sugar into a round-bottomed bowl.

2. Cut the butter into small cubes. Rub it into the flour, using the fingertips, until the mixture looks like fine bread crumbs. Make a well in the center.

3. Mix the eggs, water, vanilla, and lemon zest. Pour the mixture into the well in the flour. Mix to form a soft dough.

4. Turn out the dough onto a lightly floured work surface. Knead gently just until smooth and well mixed.

5. Wrap in plastic film and chill for at least 30 minutes before use.

PÂTE SABLÉE

For large-quantity measurements, see page 724.

Ingredients	U.S.		Metric		%
Butter, softened	6	oz	150	g	67
Confectioners' sugar	3	oz	75	g	33
Salt	0.03	oz (⅛ tsp)	0.7	g	0.3
Lemon zest, grated	0.04	oz (½ tsp)	1	g	0.5
Vanilla extract	2	drops	2	drops	
Eggs, beaten	1	oz	25	g	11
Pastry flour	9	oz	225	g	100
Total weight:	**1 lb 3**	**oz**	**475**	**g**	**211 %**

PROCEDURE

1. Cream together the butter, confectioners' sugar, lemon zest, and vanilla until the mixture is smooth and pale.

2. Add the eggs a little at a time and beat well between each addition.

3. Add the flour. With a plastic scraper, carefully blend into a soft dough.

4. Wrap in plastic film and flatten out. Chill until firm before use.

--- **VARIATION** ---

CHOCOLATE PÂTE SABLÉE

For large-quantity measurements, see page 724.

Ingredients	U.S.		Metric	%
Butter	6	oz	150 g	86
Confectioners' sugar	3	oz	75 g	43
Grated orange zest	0.08	oz (1 tsp)	2 g	0.2
Eggs, beaten	2	oz	50 g	28
Pastry flour	7	oz	175 g	100
Cocoa powder	1	oz	30 g	17

Substitute the above ingredients and follow the basic procedure.

Sift the flour with the cocoa.

PÂTE SUCRÉE

For large-quantity measurements, see page 724.

Ingredients	U.S.		Metric	%
Butter, softened	6.5	oz	216 g	54
Confectioners' sugar	4	oz	132 g	33
Salt	0.06 oz (⅓ tsp)		2 g	0.5
Lemon zest, grated	0.06 oz (¾ tsp)		2 g	0.5
Vanilla extract	4	drops	4 drops	
Eggs, beaten	3	oz	100 g	25
Pastry flour	12	oz	400 g	100
Total weight:	**1 lb 9**	**oz**	**852 g**	**213 %**

PROCEDURE

1. Cream together the butter, confectioners' sugar, salt, lemon zest, and vanilla until the mixture is smooth and pale.
2. Add the eggs a little at a time and beat well between each addition.
3. Add the flour. With a plastic scraper, carefully blend into a soft dough.
4. Wrap in plastic film and flatten out. Chill until firm before use.

SHORT DOUGH I

For large-quantity measurements, see page 724.

Ingredients	U.S.		Metric	%
Butter or butter and shortening	8	oz	250 g	67
Sugar	3	oz	90 g	25
Salt	0.06 oz (¼ tsp)		2 g	0.5
Eggs	2.25 oz		70 g	19
Pastry flour	12	oz	375 g	100
Total weight:	**1 lb 9**	**oz**	**787 g**	**211 %**

PROCEDURE

1. Using the paddle attachment, mix the butter, sugar, and salt at low speed until smooth and evenly blended.
2. Add the eggs and mix just until absorbed.
3. Sift the flour and add it to the mixture. Mix just until evenly blended.
4. Chill several hours before using.

SHORT DOUGH II

For large-quantity measurements, see page 725.

Ingredients	U.S.		Metric	%
Butter	5	oz	150 g	60
Sugar	3.5	oz	100 g	40
Salt	0.07 oz (⅓ tsp)		2 g	0.8
Vanilla powder	0.07 oz		2 g	0.8
Powdered almonds	1	oz	30 g	12
Eggs	1.75 oz		50 g	22
Pastry flour	8	oz	250 g	100
Total weight:	**1 lb 3**	**oz**	**584 g**	**235 %**

PROCEDURE

1. Using the paddle attachment, mix the butter, sugar, salt, vanilla powder, and almonds.
2. Add the eggs and flour. Mix until just combined.
3. Chill several hours before using.

ALMOND SHORT DOUGH

For large-quantity measurements, see page 724.

Ingredients	U.S.		Metric		%
Butter	8	oz	200	g	80
Sugar	6	oz	150	g	60
Salt	0.1 oz (½ tsp)		2.5	g	1
Powdered almonds	5	oz	125	g	50
Eggs	1.6	oz	42	g	16.5
Vanilla extract	¼	tsp	1.25	g	0.5
Pastry flour	10	oz	250	g	100
Total weight:	**1 lb 14**	**oz**	**770**	**g**	**308 %**

PROCEDURE

1. Using the paddle attachment, blend the butter, sugar, and salt at low speed just until smooth and well mixed. Do not continue to cream until light.

2. Add the almonds and blend in.

3. Add the eggs and vanilla. Mix just until absorbed.

4. Sift the flour and add it to the mixture. Mix just until evenly blended.

5. Chill several hours before using.

VARIATIONS

LINZER DOUGH I

For large-quantity measurements, see page 724.

Ingredients	U.S.	Metric	%
Cinnamon	0.06 oz (1⅛ tsp)	1.5 g	0.6
Nutmeg	0.01 oz (⅛ tsp)	0.25 g	0.1

Use ground hazelnuts, ground almonds, or a mixture of the two.

Mix in the cinnamon and nutmeg with the salt in the first step.

LINZER DOUGH II

Prepare as for Linzer Dough I but instead of the raw egg yolks, use finely sieved hard-cooked egg yolks.

PUFF PASTRY

PUFF PASTRY IS one of the most remarkable products of the bakeshop. Although it includes no added leavening agent, it can rise to eight times its original thickness when baked.

Puff pastry is a laminated or rolled-in dough, like Danish and croissant doughs. This means it is made up of many layers of fat sandwiched between layers of dough. Unlike Danish dough, however, puff pastry contains no yeast. Steam, created when the moisture in the dough is heated, is responsible for the spectacular rising power of puff pastry. (See p. 104 for a general discussion of laminated doughs.)

Because puff pastry or puff dough consists of over 1,000 layers, many more than in Danish dough, the rolling-in procedure requires a great deal of time and care.

As with so many other products, there are nearly as many versions of puff pastry as there are bakers. Both formulas and rolling-in techniques vary. The formula provided here contains no eggs, for example, although some bakers add them. Two methods for enclosing the butter and two rolling-in methods are illustrated.

Butter is the preferred fat for rolling in because of its flavor and melt-in-the-mouth quality. Special puff pastry shortening is also available. This shortening is easier to work because it is not as hard when refrigerated and doesn't soften and melt at warm temperatures as easily as butter does. It is also less expensive than butter. However, it can be unpleasant to eat because it tends to congeal and coat the inside of the mouth.

The quantity of rolled-in fat may vary from 50 to 100% of the weight of the flour, or 8 ounces to 1 pound of fat per pound of flour. If the lower quantity of fat is used, the dough should be left slightly thicker when rolled out. Puff pastry that is low in fat will not rise as high and may rise unevenly. This is because there is less fat between the dough layers, so the layers are more likely to stick together.

The illustrations in this section show in detail the procedures for mixing the dough, enclosing the butter, and rolling. The Procedure for Making Puff Pastry Dough shows one complete method for making puff pastry using the *four-fold* method for rolling in. An alternative method for enclosing the butter in the dough is illustrated next. Finally, the *three-fold* method is shown as an alternative rolling-in procedure.

Formulas for *blitz puff pastry* and *reversed puff pastry* are also included. Blitz puff pastry is actually a very flaky pie dough that is rolled and folded like puff pastry. It is easier and quicker to make than classic puff dough (*blitz* is the German word for "lightning"). It does not rise as high as true puff pastry and its texture is not as fine, so it is not suitable for products in which

PROCEDURE: Making Puff Pastry Dough

1. Make a well in the mound of flour and add the liquids.

2. Work the ingredients into a dough.

3. Knead the dough until it is smooth. Refrigerate for 30 minutes. Then roll it out into a large rectangle.

4. To prepare the butter, first soften it by beating it with a rolling pin.

5. Square off the butter. Roll it into a smooth rectangle two-thirds the size of the dough rectangle.

6. Place the butter on the dough so it covers the bottom two-thirds of the rectangle.

7. Fold down the top unbuttered third of the dough so it covers half the butter.

8. Fold the bottom third over the center. The butter is now enclosed.

9. To give the dough its first four-fold, roll the dough into a long rectangle. Before rolling, beat the dough lightly, as shown, so that the butter is evenly distributed.

10. Before folding, always brush off excess dusting flour.

a high, light pastry is desirable. However, it bakes up crisp and flaky and is perfectly suitable for *napoleons* and similar desserts that are layered with cream fillings.

Reversed puff pastry is somewhat unusual and difficult to work with. As the name suggests, the butter and dough are reversed—that is, the butter (which has flour mixed into it) encloses the dough rather than the dough enclosing the butter. Although it is more difficult to prepare, it can be made up and baked without a final rest, as it shrinks less than classic puff pastry.

11. Fold down the top edge of the dough to the center.

12. Fold up the bottom edge to the center.

13. Fold in half to achieve the finished four-fold.

ALTERNATIVE METHOD: ROLLING-IN PROCEDURE

1. Fold the dough rectangle in thirds, as for making Danish Pastry (p. 189).

2. Square off the finished three-fold with the rolling pin.

ALTERNATIVE METHOD: ENCLOSING THE BUTTER IN PUFF PASTRY

1. Roll the dough into a blunt cross shape, as shown, leaving the center thicker than the arms of the cross.

3. Fold the remaining three arms of dough over the center.

2. Place the square of butter in the center. Fold one of the arms of dough over the butter to cover it.

KEY POINTS TO REVIEW

■ What method is used to mix pâte brisée? What mixing methods are used to mix short doughs, including pâte sucrée and pâte sablée?

■ What are the steps in the rolling-in procedure for making puff pastry dough (pâte feuilleté)?

■ What guidelines should be followed when making up and baking puff pastry products?

CLASSIC PUFF PASTRY (PÂTE FEUILLETÉE CLASSIQUE)

For large-quantity measurements, see page 725.

Ingredients	U.S.		Metric	%
Bread flour	1 lb		500 g	100
Salt		0.33 oz	10 g	2
Butter, melted	2.5	oz	75 g	15
Water	8	oz	250 g	50
Butter, for rolling in	9.5	oz	300 g	60
Total weight:	**2 lb 4**	**oz**	**1135 g**	**227%**

PROCEDURE

MIXING

1. Mix the flour and the salt. Place the flour in a mound on a work surface and make a well in the center. (*Note:* For illustrations of the steps in the mixing and laminating procedures, refer to the Procedure for Making Puff Pastry Dough, pages 316–317.)

2. Pour the melted butter and water into the center of the well. Gradually stir from the inside outward to incorporate the flour into the liquids, making a dough.

3. Once the dough has formed, knead briefly, just until smooth. Do not overwork, or the dough will become too elastic and difficult to work. Gather the dough into a smooth ball.

4. Decide which method for enclosing the butter (below) you will use. If method 1, wrap in plastic and refrigerate for 30 minutes. If method 2, cut a cross in the top of the dough and wrap in plastic film. Allow to rest for 30 minutes in the refrigerator.

ENCLOSING THE BUTTER: METHOD 1

1. Roll out the dough into a large rectangle.

2. Place the butter between 2 sheets of plastic film. Soften and flatten it by beating with a rolling pin. Set aside while the dough is rolled out.

3. Keeping the butter between the plastic sheets, roll it out and square the edges using the rolling pin to make a rectangle about two-thirds the size of the dough rectangle.

4. Remove the plastic from the rectangle of butter and place it on the bottom two-thirds of the dough rectangle. Fold the top third of the dough down over the center to cover half the butter. Fold the bottom one-third over the center. The butter is now enclosed in the dough, making 2 layers of butter between 3 layers of dough.

5. Give the dough *4 four-folds*. This will give the dough 1,028 layers of dough and butter. Rest the dough in a cool place between folds to allow the gluten to relax.

    Alternatively, give the dough *5 three-folds*, making a total of 883 layers. (If you wish, you can double this number of layers simply by rolling and folding the dough in half after the last three-fold. This is preferable to giving the dough a sixth three-fold—for over 2,400 layers—because the dough may not rise properly when the layers become this thin.)

ENCLOSING THE BUTTER: METHOD 2

1. With the rolling pin, spread open the four quarters of the dough made by cutting the cross and roll out the dough in the shape of a large, broad cross. Keep the dough thicker in the center than in the four arms of the cross.

2. Place the butter between 2 sheets of parchment or plastic film. Flatten and soften it slightly by beating lightly with a rolling pin. Then roll it out into a square about ¾ in. (2 cm) thick. The size of the square of butter should be smaller than the center section of dough so the butter will not overlap the edges of the dough in step 3.

3. Place the square of butter in the center of the dough cross. Fold the four arms of the dough over the butter to enclose it completely, as in an envelope.

4. Give the dough *6 three-folds*. Rest the dough in a cool place between folds to allow the gluten to relax. This will give the dough 1,459 layers of dough and butter.

ORDINARY PUFF PASTRY

For large-quantity measurements, see page 725.

Ingredients	U.S.		Metric	%
Bread flour	12	oz	375 g	75
Cake flour	4	oz	125 g	25
Butter, softened	2	oz	60 g	12.5
Salt	0.25 oz		8 g	1.5
Water, cold	9	oz	282 g	56
Butter	1 lb		500 g	100
Bread flour (see *Note*)	2	oz	60 g	12.5
Total weight:	**2 lb 13**	**oz**	**1410 g**	**282 %**

NOTE: The purpose of the second quantity of bread flour is to absorb some of the moisture of the butter and help make the dough more manageable. Omit this flour if shop temperature is cool or if puff paste shortening is used instead of butter.

VARIATION

The butter for rolling in may be reduced to 75% or even to as little as 50%. If the butter is reduced, you should also reduce the last quantity of flour (for mixing with the butter) in the same proportion, so it is one-eighth the weight of the butter.

PROCEDURE

MIXING

1. Place the first quantities of flour and butter in a mixing bowl. With the paddle attachment, mix at low speed until well blended.
2. Dissolve the salt in the cold water.
3. Add the salted water to the flour mixture and mix at low speed until a soft dough is formed. Do not overmix.
4. Remove the dough from the mixer and let it rest in the refrigerator or retarder for 20 minutes.
5. Blend the last quantities of butter and flour at low speed in the mixer until the mixture is the same consistency as the dough, neither too soft nor too hard.
6. Roll the butter into the dough following the procedure shown on pages 316–317. Give the dough *4 four-folds* or *5 three-folds*.

BLITZ PUFF PASTRY

Ingredients	U.S.		Metric	%
Bread flour	8	oz	250 g	50
Pastry flour	8	oz	250 g	50
Butter, slightly softened	1 lb		500 g	100
Salt	0.25 oz		8 g	1.5
Water, cold	8	oz	250 g	50
Total weight:	**2 lb 8**	**oz**	**1258 g**	**251 %**

VARIATION

Reduce the butter to 75% (12 oz/375 g).

PROCEDURE

1. Sift the two flours together into a mixing bowl.
2. Cut the butter into the flour as for pie dough, but leave the fat in very large lumps, 1 in. (2.5 cm) across.
3. Dissolve the salt in the water.
4. Add the salted water to the flour/butter mixture. Mix until the water is absorbed.
5. Let the dough rest 15 minutes. Refrigerate it if the bakeshop is warm.
6. Dust the bench with flour and roll out the dough into a rectangle. Give the dough *3 four-folds*.

REVERSED PUFF PASTRY (PÂTE FEUILLETÉE INVERSÉE)

Ingredients	U.S.	Metric	%
Butter	1 lb 4 oz	500 g	100
Bread flour	10 oz	250 g	50
Bread flour	1 lb 4 oz	500 g	100
Salt	1 oz	25 g	5
Water	11 oz	270 g	54
Butter, melted	7 oz	175 g	35
Total weight:	**4 lb 5 oz**	**1720 g**	**344%**

PROCEDURE

1. Combine the first quantities of butter and flour in a mixing bowl and mix together, either by hand or with the paddle attachment of a mixer, until completely blended.

2. Roll the butter mixture between 2 sheets of parchment paper to make a large rectangle ¾ in. (2 cm) thick. Refrigerate for 30 minutes.

3. Mix the remaining ingredients into a dough using the procedure described in steps 1 and 2 of the formula for Classic Puff Pastry (p. 318). Wrap and refrigerate for 30 minutes.

4. Roll out the dough to make a rectangle half the size of the butter rectangle.

5. Place the dough on the top half of the butter rectangle. Fold the butter over it to enclose completely, using the parchment to lift the butter.

6. Chill for 30 minutes.

7. Give the dough *5 three-folds*. Be sure to dust the work surface well with flour so the butter does not stick.

Guidelines for Makeup and Baking of Puff Dough Products

1. The dough should be cool and firm when it is rolled and cut. If it is too soft, layers may stick together at the cuts, preventing proper rising.

2. Using a sharp cutting tool, cut straight down with firm, even cuts.

3. Avoid touching the cut edges with your fingers, or the layers may stick together.

4. For best rising, place units upside down on baking sheets. The reason is, even sharp cutting tools may press the top layers of dough together. Baking upside down puts the stuck-together layers at the bottom.

5. Avoid letting egg wash run down the edges. Egg wash can cause the layers to stick together at the edges.

6. Rest made-up products for 30 minutes or more in a cool place or in the refrigerator before baking. This relaxes the gluten and reduces shrinkage.

7. Trimmings may be used again, although they will not rise as high. Press them together, keeping the layers in the same direction. After rolling them out, give them a three-fold before using.

8. Baking temperatures of 400° to 425°F (200° to 220°C) are best for most puff dough products. Cooler temperatures will not create enough steam in the products to leaven them well. Higher temperatures will set the crust too quickly.

9. Larger products such as Pithiviers (p. 362) are harder to bake through than the small ones. To avoid underbaked, soggy interiors, start large items at a high temperature and bake until they are well risen. Then turn the temperature down to about 350°F (175°C) and finish baking until crisp.

Puff Pastry Desserts

The following recipes include instructions for simple puff pastry products, including petits fours. If any of your products do not turn out well, consult the troubleshooting guide in the Puff Pastry Faults and Their Causes table.

PUFF PASTRY FAULTS AND THEIR CAUSES	
FAULTS	**POSSIBLE CAUSES**
Shrinkage during baking	Dough not relaxed before baking
Poor lift or rising	Too little or too much fat used
	Dough rolled out too thin or given too many turns
	Oven too hot or too cold
Uneven lift or irregular shapes	Improper rolling-in procedure
	Uneven distribution of fat before rolling
	Dough not relaxed before baking
	Uneven heat in oven
Fat running out during baking (*Note*: Some fat running out is normal, but it should not be excessive.)	Too much fat used
	Not enough turns given
	Oven too cool

PINWHEELS

Components
Puff pastry dough
Egg wash
Fruit filling

PROCEDURE

1. Roll out the puff pastry dough ⅛ in. (3 mm) thick.
2. Cut into squares 5 in. (12 cm) per side, or to other size as desired.
3. Cut diagonally from the corners to about 2 in. (5 cm) from the center. Brush the pastry with egg wash.
4. Fold every other corner to the center and press into place, as for making Danish pinwheels (pp. 206–207).
5. Brush with egg wash a second time.
6. Select a thick filling that will not run when baked (see step 9). Place a spoonful of the filling in the center of each pinwheel.
7. Bake at 400°F (200°C) until puffed and golden.
8. Cool. Dust with confectioners' sugar.
9. Pinwheels may also be filled after, instead of before, baking. This method is used for fillings that might run or burn when baked.

  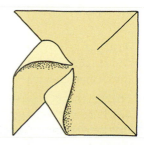 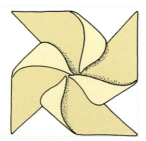

PATTY SHELLS

Components

Puff pastry dough

Egg wash

PROCEDURE

1. Roll out puff pastry dough ⅛ in. (3 mm) thick.
2. Roll out a second piece of dough ¼ in. (6 mm) thick.
3. Cut the same number of circles from each piece of dough with a round 3-in. (7.5-cm) cutter.
4. With a 2-in. (5-cm) cutter, cut out the centers of the *thick* circles (a).

5. Wash the thin circles with water or egg wash and place one of the rings on top of each (b). Wash the top carefully with egg wash (do not allow wash to drip down the edges). Let them rest 30 minutes.
6. Place a sheet of greased parchment over the tops of the shells to prevent their toppling over while baking.
7. Bake at 400°F (200°C) until brown and crisp.

TURNOVERS

Components

Puff pastry dough

Fruit filling

Egg wash

or

Milk or water; granulated sugar

PROCEDURE

1. Roll puff pastry dough ⅛ in. (3 mm) thick.
2. Cut into 4-in. (10-cm) squares. Wash the edges of each with water.
3. Place a portion of the desired filling into the center of each square (a).
4. Fold the squares diagonally and press the edges together. With a knife, puncture the tops in 2 or 3 places to allow steam to escape (b). Let them rest 30 minutes.
5. Brush the tops with egg wash, if desired, or brush with milk or water and sprinkle with sugar.
6. Bake at 400°F (200°C) until crisp and brown.

A

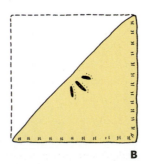

B

BAKED APPLE DUMPLINGS

Components	PROCEDURE
Small, tart baking apples Puff pastry dough Cake crumbs (optional) Cinnamon Sugar (p. 193) Raisins Egg wash	1. Peel and core as many apples as desired. 2. Roll out puff pastry dough to ⅛ in. (3 mm) thick. Cut out squares large enough to cover an apple completely when the points of the square are overlapped at the top of the apple. *Caution:* Do not stretch the dough over the apple or it will pull away during baking. To prevent this, cut out one square and test it to be sure it is large enough to cover the apple. Then cut out the remaining squares. 3. If the dough becomes soft , refrigerate it for 15 to 30 minutes before continuing. 4. Place a teaspoonful of cake crumbs in the center of each pastry square. Then place an apple on top of the crumbs. (*Note:* The crumbs are optional, but they help absorb the juice of the apple.) 5. Fill the center of the apples (where the cores used to be) with cinnamon sugar and raisins. Taste a small piece of apple for tartness to help you judge how much sugar to use. 6. Brush the edges of the dough with water or egg wash. Draw up the four corners of the dough and overlap them at the top of the apple. Press the corners together to seal. Pinch the edges of the dough together to seal the seams. 7. Cut out 1-in. (2.5-cm) circles of dough. Moisten the top of each apple with egg wash and cap with a circle of dough. This covers the overlapping corners and makes the product more attractive. 8. Arrange the apples on parchment-lined pans. Brush with egg wash. 9. Bake at 400°F (200°C) until the pastry is browned and the apples are cooked through but not too soft (or they will sag and flatten out). This will take 45 to 60 minutes, depending on the apples. Test for doneness by piercing one of the apples with a thin skewer. If the pastry browns too fast, cover lightly with a sheet of parchment or foil.

CREAM HORNS

Components	PROCEDURE
Puff pastry dough Granulated sugar Whipped cream or Pastry Cream (p. 263) Confectioners' sugar	1. Roll out puff pastry dough ⅛ in. (3 mm) thick and about 15 in. (38 cm) wide. 2. Cut out strips 1¼ in. (3 cm) wide by 15 in. (38 cm) long. 3. Wash the strips with water. 4. Press one end of a strip, with the washed side facing outward, onto one end of a cream horn tube (a). If you are using conical tubes, start at the small end. 5. Roll the strip diagonally in a spiral by turning the tube (b). Overlap the edges by ⅜ in. (1 cm). Do not stretch the dough. 6. Roll up completely and press the end in place to seal (c). 7. Roll the horns in granulated sugar and lay them on baking sheets. The end of the dough strip should be on the bottom so it will not pop up during baking. 8. Bake at 400°F (200°C) until brown and crisp. 9. Slip out the tubes while still warm. 10. Just before service, fill the horns from both ends (if using cylindrical tubes) or from the large end (if using conical tubes) with whipped cream or pastry cream, using a pastry bag with a star tip. Dust with confectioners' sugar.

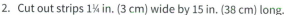

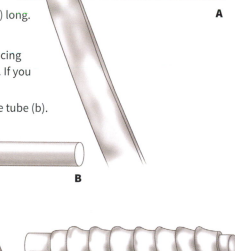

A

B

C

NAPOLEONS

Components

Puff pastry dough

Pastry Cream (p. 263) or mixture of pastry cream and whipped cream

Fondant (p. 417)

Chocolate Fondant (p. 417)

PROCEDURE

1. Roll puff pastry dough into a very thin sheet about the size of a sheet pan. Blitz puff paste or rerolled trimmings may be used.

2. Place on a sheet pan and let rest 30 minutes, preferably in the refrigerator.

3. Dock with a fork to prevent blistering.

4. Bake at 400°F (200°C) until brown and crisp.

5. Trim the edges of the pastry sheet and cut with a serrated knife into equal strips 3–4 in. (7.5–10 cm) wide. Set the best strip aside for the top layer. If one of the strips breaks, it can be used as the middle layer.

6. Spread one rectangle with pastry cream or with a mixture of pastry cream and whipped cream.

7. Top with a second sheet of pastry.

8. Spread with another layer of pastry cream.

9. Place third pastry rectangle on top, with the flattest side up.

10. Ice the top with the fondant (see p. 417).

11. To decorate, pipe 4 strips of chocolate fondant lengthwise on the white fondant (a). Draw a spatula or the back of a knife across the top in opposite directions to feather the design (b, c).

12. Cut into strips 1½–2 in. (4–5 cm) wide (d).

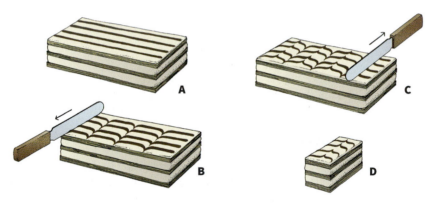

NAPOLEONS

What does the layered puff pastry dessert have to do with the French emperor Napoleon? Actually, nothing. The name comes from the French adjective *napolitain*, meaning "pertaining to the Italian city of Napoli," or, as it is known in English, Naples. The pastry was thought to have originated there, and it has no connection with the emperor Napoleon. A better English name for it would be neapolitan.

In fact, the dessert may have been the invention of Carême (pp. 6–8) rather than of pastry cooks in Naples. Perhaps he was making a dessert in what he considered to be the style of Naples.

In French, the dessert is not called napoleon but *mille-feuille*, meaning "thousand leaves." Italians don't call it *napoleon*, either, but *mille foglie*, also meaning "thousand leaves."

Fruit Tarts

Puff pastry may be used instead of short dough to make fruit tarts. Fruit strips are fruit tarts made in the shape of long strips about 4 to 5 inches (10 to 12 cm) wide.

The procedure for assembling these desserts is the same as that for unbaked fruit tarts described in Chapter 15 (p. 352), except baked puff pastry should be assembled only at the last minute because the pastry quickly becomes soggy.

The shells can be made in any shape, but squares and rectangles are easiest, as in the following procedure.

FRUIT TARTS

Components
Puff pastry dough
Egg wash
Pastry Cream (p. 263)
Fruit, as desired
Apricot Glaze (p. 194) or other glaze

PROCEDURE

1. Roll out the puff pastry dough ⅛ in. (3 mm) thick.
2. Cut out squares or rectangles of desired size.
3. With the remaining dough, cut strips about ¾ in. (2 cm) wide and long enough to make borders for the tarts.
4. Brush the rims of the dough squares with water or egg wash. Lay the strips in place on the moistened edges to make borders. Egg-wash the tops of the borders.
5. With a fork, knife tip, or roller docker, dock the inside of the shell (not the borders) to prevent blistering.
6. Rest in the refrigerator 30 minutes before baking.
7. Bake at 400°F (200°C) until browned and crisp. Cool.
8. Fill with a thin layer of pastry cream, arrange fruit on top, and brush with apricot glaze.

See page 352 for the detailed procedure for filling fruit tarts.

— **VARIATION** —

FRUIT STRIPS

Follow the above procedure, but make the rectangles 4–5 in. (10–12 cm) wide and as long as your sheet pans. Put borders on the two long sides, but leave the ends open.

PETITS FOURS

The term *petit four*, French for "small oven," can be used for any small cake, pastry, or cookie that can be eaten in one or two bites. Petits fours are discussed in more detail on pages 472 and 483. The name may derive from the fact that, in the days of wood-fired brick ovens, petits fours were baked when the oven was cooling down, after the main baking of the day was finished.

For a long time, people in North America thought of petits fours only as small pieces of delicate layer cake individually iced in fondant. (Many of these cakes found in American bakeshops are, in fact, not very "petit.") However, as many more restaurants have adopted the practice of serving a small tray or plate of tiny chocolates and petits fours of many types after dessert, Americans have become more familiar with the broader meaning of the term.

Puff Pastry Petits Fours

CHAUSSONS

Components
Puff pastry dough
Egg wash
Apple Compote (p. 197)

PROCEDURE

1. Roll out puff pastry dough to less than ⅛ in. (2 mm) thick. Place on a sheet pan lined with parchment paper. Chill for 30 minutes.
2. With a 2½-in. (6-cm) round cutter, cut out circles of dough.
3. Brush the edges with egg wash.
4. Spoon about ½ tsp (2–3 mL) apple compote onto the center of each circle.
5. Fold over to make a half-moon shape. Seal the edges by pressing with the reverse edge (the dull edge) of the round cutter.
6. Brush with egg wash. Score the tops lightly with the back of a fork to make a simple decoration.
7. Bake at 375°F (190°C) until puffed and golden brown.

— **VARIATION** —

Use other fruit compotes (see Chapter 21) or Frangipane (p. 196) instead of the apple filling.

PALMIERS

Components

Puff pastry dough

Granulated sugar or sanding sugar

PROCEDURE

1. Line a sheet pan with parchment. Alternatively, thickly butter a sheet pan and chill.
2. Dust the work surface heavily with granulated sugar.
3. Place puff pastry dough on top of the sugar and roll it out into a long strip about 12 in. (30 cm) wide and ⅛ in. (3 mm) thick. Turn it over once or twice as you roll it out to coat both sides with sugar.
4. Trim the sides of the strip so they are straight.
5. Determine the center of the strip. Then fold each side halfway to the center (a). Then fold each side again so the two folds meet in the center (b). Each half of the strip should be 3 layers thick.
6. Fold one half over the other lengthwise to make a strip 6 layers thick and about 2 in. (5 cm) wide (c).
7. Refrigerate until firm.
8. Cut into slices ½ in. (6 mm) thick with a sharp knife (d) and lay on the prepared sheet pan in staggered rows, leaving plenty of space between them to give them room to expand.
9. Press down on the slices with the palm of the hand to flatten lightly.
10. Bake at 375°F (190°C) until golden brown. Turn the palmiers over and bake the second side until well colored. Transfer to a wire rack to cool.

A

B

C

D

VARIATIONS

Serve plain, as a dry petit four.

Sandwich with buttercream and serve as a tea pastry.

Dip halfway into melted chocolate.

ALLUMETTES

Components	PROCEDURE
Puff pastry dough Royal Icing (p. 426)	1. Roll out puff pastry dough to a rectangle ⅛ in. (3 mm) thick. Place on a sheet pan. 2. Spread a thin layer of royal icing thinly over the puff pastry. Freeze until icing sets. 3. Cut the pastry with a wet knife into batons or strips approximately ⅝ × 1½ in. (1.5 × 4 cm). Place on a sheet pan lined with parchment paper. 4. Bake at 375°F (190°C) until risen, then cover with a silicone mat and cook until golden and fully cooked, approximately 20 minutes. 5. Cool on a wire rack.

PAPILLONS (BUTTERFLIES, OR BOW TIES)

Components	PROCEDURE
Puff pastry dough Granulated sugar	1. Line a sheet pan with parchment. Alternatively, thickly butter a baking tray and chill. 2. Scale 1 lb (500 g) puff pastry dough. On a work surface dusted with sugar, roll out to a rectangle 13 × 5 in. (33 × 13 cm). Trim the edges neatly. 3. Cut into 5 equal pieces, measuring about 2½ × 5 in. (6.5 × 13 cm). Brush 4 of them with a little water and stack them, placing the unbrushed one on top. 4. Using the back of a knife, mark a center line down the length of the pastry. Turn over and repeat in the same place on the underside. Chill. 5. Trim the edges of the stack to neaten if necessary. Using a sharp knife, cut crosswise into slices ¼ in. (5 mm) thick with an indention in the middle (a). 6. Twist the slices in the middle to splay the layers. Place on the tray and press down the edges lightly (b). Bake at 375°F (190°C) until golden brown.

A

B

— VARIATION —

Add ground cinnamon or ginger to the sugar.

CONVERSATIONS

Components

Puff pastry dough

Fruit jam, such as raspberry

Frangipane Filling (p. 196)

Royal Icing (p. 426)

PROCEDURE

1. Roll out puff pastry dough as thin as possible. It should be nearly transparent. Chill for 30 minutes on a tray lined with parchment paper.

2. With a round cutter, cut out circles of dough large enough to line 2-in. (5-cm) tartlet cases. Cut out additional circles for the tops of each pastry and set aside. Keep the trimmings flat to use for the decoration.

3. Put about ½ tsp (3 g) jam in the bottom of each tartlet and top with 1 tsp (5 g) frangipane filling.

4. Brush the edges of the pastry with egg wash. Top with a circle of very thin puff pastry and chill.

5. Using a small palette knife, coat the top of the puff pastry with a thin layer of royal icing.

6. Cut strips of puff pastry very thinly and lay on top of the royal icing to form a lattice pattern. The illustration shows one pastry without its top (right) and three ready to bake.

7. Bake at 375°F (190°C) until golden brown and cooked through.

Puff pastry petits fours, left to right: Palmiers, Conversations, Papillons.

SACRISTAINS

Components
Puff pastry dough
Egg wash
Granulated sugar
Almonds, chopped (optional)

PROCEDURE

1. Roll out strips of puff pastry dough ⅛ in. (3 mm) thick. Cut into long strips 4 in. (10 cm) wide.
2. Brush the dough with egg wash and sprinkle with coarse granulated sugar or a mixture of sugar and chopped almonds. With a rolling pin, lightly press the sugar and nuts into the dough.
3. Turn the strips over and coat the other side with egg wash, sugar, and almonds in the same way.
4. Cut the strips crosswise into small strips ¾ in. (2 cm) wide and 4 in. (10 cm) long.
5. Twist each strip to make a shape like a corkscrew. Place on paper-lined baking sheets and press down the ends lightly so the twists do not unwind during baking.
6. Bake at 425°F (220°C) until brown and crisp.

ÉCLAIR PASTE

ÉCLAIRS AND CREAM puffs are made from a dough called *éclair paste*, or *choux paste*. The French name *pâte à choux* (pronounced pot a SHOO) means "cabbage paste," referring to the resemblance of cream puffs to little cabbages.

Unlike puff pastry, éclair paste is extremely easy to make. The dough itself can be prepared in just a few minutes. This is fortunate, because for best baking results the dough should not be prepared more than 1 hour ahead of time.

The exact procedure for making éclair paste is detailed in the formula that follows. In general, the method consists of these steps:

1. Bring the liquid, fat, salt, and sugar (if used) to a boil. The liquid must be boiling rapidly so the fat is dispersed in the liquid, not just floating on top. If this is not done, the fat will not be as well incorporated into the paste, and some of it may run out during baking.

2. Add the flour all at once and stir until the paste forms a ball and pulls away from the sides of the pan. It should leave a thin film on the bottom of the pan (a).

3. Remove the paste from the heat and let it cool to 140°F (60°C) (b). Beat or mix the paste so it cools evenly. If the paste is not cooled slightly, it will cook the eggs when they are added.

4. Beat in the eggs a little at a time (c). Completely mix in each addition of eggs before adding more. If the eggs are added too quickly, it will be difficult to get a smooth batter. When the paste is smooth and moist but stiff enough to hold its shape (d), it is ready to use.

In principle, éclair paste is similar to popover batter, even though the former is a thick dough and the latter a thin batter. Both products are leavened by steam, which expands the product rapidly and causes large holes to form in the center of the item. The heat of the oven then coagulates the gluten and egg proteins to set the structure and make a firm product. A strong flour is necessary in both for sufficient structure. (For comparison with pâte à choux, a formula for popovers is included at the end of this section, p. 330.)

Éclair paste must be firm enough to hold its shape when piped from a pastry bag. You may occasionally find a formula that produces too slack a dough. Correct such a formula by reducing the water or milk slightly. Alternatively, stop adding eggs when the paste arrives at the proper texture. Take care, though, as éclair paste should not be too dry. It should look smooth and moist, not dry and rough. Paste that is too dry does not puff up well and is thick and heavy.

Éclair paste for cream puffs and *éclairs* is normally piped onto parchment-lined pans. It can also be piped onto greased pans, although this method is not used as often.

Proper baking temperatures are important. Start at a high temperature (425°F/220°C) for the first 15 minutes to develop steam. Then reduce the heat to 375°F (190°C) to finish baking and set the structure. The products must be firm and dry before being removed from the oven. If they are removed too soon or cooled too quickly, they may collapse. Some bakers like to leave them in a turned-off oven with the door ajar. However, if the oven must be heated again for other products, this may not be the best idea. It may be better to bake the products thoroughly, remove them carefully from the oven, and let them cool slowly in a warm place.

Note: French doughnuts or crullers, also made with éclair paste, are discussed in Chapter 11 (p. 236).

ÉCLAIR PASTE OR PÂTE À CHOUX

Ingredients	U.S.		Metric	%
Water, milk, or half water, half milk	1 lb 2	oz	560 g	150
Butter or regular shortening	9	oz	280 g	75
Salt	0.18 oz (1 tsp)		5 g	1.5
Bread flour	12	oz	375 g	100
Eggs (approximate quantity; see step 6)	1 lb 4	oz	625 g	167
Total weight:	**3 lb 11**	**oz**	**1845 g**	**493** %

NOTE: If a sweeter product is desired, add ½ oz (15 g) sugar in step 1.

PROCEDURE

1. Combine the liquid, butter, and salt in a heavy saucepan or kettle. Bring the mixture to a full, rolling boil.

2. Add the flour all at once. Stir quickly.

3. Over moderate heat, stir vigorously until the dough forms a ball and pulls away from the sides of the pan.

4. Transfer the dough to the bowl of a mixer. Or, if you wish to mix it by hand, you can leave it in the saucepan.

5. With the paddle attachment, mix at low speed until the dough has cooled slightly. It should be 110°–140°F (43°–60°C), which is still very warm but not too hot to touch.

6. At medium speed, beat in the eggs a little at a time. Add no more than one-quarter of the eggs at once, and wait until they are completely absorbed before adding more. Do not add all the eggs before checking the texture. The paste should be smooth and moist but firm enough to hold its shape. If the paste reaches this texture before all the eggs are added, stop adding eggs. The paste is now ready for use.

Éclair Paste Products

CREAM PUFFS

Components
Éclair paste
Filling of choice
Confectioners' sugar

PROCEDURE

1. Line sheet pans with parchment paper.
2. Fit a large pastry bag with a plain tube. Fill the bag with the éclair paste.
3. Pipe out round mounds of dough about 1½ in. (4 cm) in diameter onto the lined baking sheets. If you prefer, drop the dough from a spoon.
4. Bake at 425°F (215°C) for 10 minutes. Lower the heat to 375°F (190°C) and continue baking until the mounds are well browned and very crisp.
5. Remove them from the oven and let cool slowly in a warm place.
6. When cool, cut a slice from the top of each puff. Fill with whipped cream, Pastry Cream (p. 263), or other desired filling, using a pastry bag with a star tube.
7. Replace the tops and dust with confectioners' sugar.
8. Fill as close to service time as possible. If cream-filled puffs must be held, keep refrigerated.
9. Unfilled and uncut puffs, if thoroughly dry, may be held in plastic bags in the refrigerator for 1 week. Recrisp in the oven for a few minutes before use.

ÉCLAIRS

Components
Éclair paste
Pastry Cream (p. 263)
Chocolate Fondant (p. 417)

PROCEDURE

1. Proceed as for cream puffs, except pipe the dough out into strips about ¾ in. (2 cm) wide and 3–4 in. (8–10 cm) long. Bake as for cream puffs.
2. Fill baked, cooled éclair shells with pastry cream. Two methods may be used:
   - Make a small hole in one end and fill with a pastry bag or a doughnut filling pump.
   - Cut a slice lengthwise from the top and fill with a pastry bag.
3. Dip the tops of the éclairs in chocolate fondant.
4. For service and holding, see Cream Puffs, above.

--- **VARIATION** ---

FROZEN ÉCLAIRS AND PROFITEROLES

1. Fill éclairs or small cream puffs (profiteroles) with softened ice cream. Keep frozen until service.
2. At service time, top with chocolate syrup.

PARIS-BREST

Components
Éclair paste
Sliced or chopped almonds
Filling of choice

PROCEDURE

1. Line a sheet pan with parchment paper. Using a round cake pan of the desired size as a guide, draw a circle on the parchment. An 8-in. (20-cm) circle is a popular size.

2. Fit a large pastry bag with a plain tube. Pipe a ring of éclair paste 1 in. (2.5 cm) thick just inside the drawn circle. Pipe a second ring inside the first one, just touching it. Then pipe a third ring on top of the other two.

3. Egg-wash the paste circles and sprinkle with sliced or chopped almonds.

4. Bake as for cream puffs and éclairs.

5. When cool, cut a slice off the top of the pastry. Fill with whipped cream, vanilla pastry cream (p. 263), Pastry Cream Mousseline (p. 263), or Chiboust Cream (p. 264). Replace the top.

PARIS-BREST-PARIS

The bicycle race from Paris to Brest (in Britanny) and back to Paris again is the oldest regularly run bicycle race; it was begun in 1891. The race is a grueling 1200 kilometers (750 miles). The race is commemorated in the pastry known as Paris-Brest, made in the shape of a bicycle wheel.

CHOUX PASTRY LATTICE

Components
Éclair paste
Poppy seeds

PROCEDURE

1. Draw lattice designs on a sheet of parchment paper. Turn the paper over and place on a sheet pan. The drawings should show through.

2. Fill a paper cone with éclair paste and cut a small opening in the tip. Pipe the pastry over the outlines. If necessary, neaten the joints with the point of a small knife.

3. Sprinkle with poppy seeds.

4. Bake at 375°F (190°C) until evenly golden, 4–7 minutes.

5. Use as a garnish for various cakes and plated desserts.

Choux Petits Fours

PARIS-BREST MINIATURES

Components

Choux pastry

Flaked almonds

Praline Pastry Cream
  (p. 263)

Melted chocolate

Confectioners' sugar

PROCEDURE

1. On a lightly buttered sheet pan, mark circles by dipping a 1-in. (2.5-cm) pastry cutter into flour and then tapping onto the tray.

2. Following this line, pipe a continuous ring of choux pastry using a small star tip.

3. Brush lightly with egg wash. Sprinkle with flaked almonds.

4. Bake at 375°F (190°C) until golden brown and hollow-sounding when tapped. Cool on a wire rack.

5. Slice the rings in half horizontally and pipe ⅓ oz (10 g) praline crème pâtissière in the lower half of each.

6. Flick the tops with melted chocolate, dust with confectioners' sugar, and replace the tops.

Choux Petits Fours, left to right: Paris-Brest, Mini Éclairs, Pralines, Mini Cream Puffs, Choux Florentines.

PRALINES

Components

Choux pastry

Praline Pastry Cream
(p. 263)

Nuts, lightly toasted

Caramelized sugar
(pp. 267–268)

PROCEDURE

1. Line a sheet pan with parchment paper, or butter it lightly. Pipe onto it ¾-in. (2-cm) bulbs of choux pastry. Brush lightly with egg wash.

2. Bake at 375°F (190°C) until golden and well risen. Cool on a wire rack.

3. Once cold, make a small hole in the bottom of each. Pipe praline crème pâtissière into the holes.

4. On a lightly oiled sheet pan, place lightly toasted nuts, one for each pastry, slightly apart.

5. Dip the top of each pastry in caramelized sugar and then place downward directly on top of each nut, allowing the caramel to cool around the nut and onto the flat tray.

6. Serve in paper petit four cases with the nut upward.

CHOUX FLORENTINES

Components

Choux pastry

Flaked almonds

Caramelized sugar
(pages 267–268)

Crème Chantilly (p. 257)

PROCEDURE

1. On a lightly buttered sheet pan, mark circles by dipping a 1-in. (2.5 cm) pastry cutter in flour and then tapping onto the tray. Alternatively, using a round cutter as a guide, draw circles on a sheet of parchment. Turn the parchment over and place on a sheet pan. The circles should show through.

2. Following this line, pipe a ring of choux pastry using a small star tip.

3. Brush lightly with egg wash.

4. Bake at 375°F (190°C) until golden brown and hollow-sounding when tapped. Cool on a wire rack.

5. Dip the tops in caramelized sugar. Fill the center hole by piping a rosette of crème chantilly.

MINI ÉCLAIRS

Components

Choux pastry

Chocolate Pastry Cream
(p. 263)

Chocolate Fondant
(p. 417) or caramelized
sugar (pp. 267–268)

PROCEDURE

1. Line a sheet pan with parchment paper, or butter it lightly. Pipe onto it 2-in. (5-cm) fingers of choux pastry using a medium plain tip.

2. Brush with egg wash. Gently press down with the back of a fork.

3. Bake at 375°F (190°C) until puffed and golden. Cool on wire racks.

4. Make a hole at either end of the éclair. Pipe chocolate crème pâtissière inside, then dip the top in chocolate fondant icing or caramelized sugar.

5. Pipe designs in melted chocolate on the top of each and serve in paper petit four cases.

MINI CREAM PUFFS

Components
Choux pastry
Flaked almonds
Crème Chantilly (p. 257)
Melted chocolate
Confectioners' sugar

PROCEDURE

1. Line a sheet pan with parchment paper, or butter it lightly. Pipe onto it ¾-in. (2-cm) bulbs of choux pastry. Brush lightly with egg wash and sprinkle with flaked almonds.
2. Bake at 375°F (190°C) until golden and hollow-sounding when tapped. Cool on a wire rack.
3. Slice in half horizontally. Pipe crème chantilly onto the bases.
4. Flick the tops with melted chocolate, dust with confectioners' sugar, and replace the tops.
5. Serve in paper petit four cases.

POPOVERS

Ingredients	U.S.		Metric	%
Eggs	1 lb	4 oz	625 g	125
Milk	2 lb		1000 g	200
Salt		0.25 oz	8 g	1.5
Butter or shortening, melted		2 oz	60 g	12.5
Bread flour	1 lb		500 g	100
Total weight:	**4 lb**	**6 oz**	**2193 g**	**439 %**

PROCEDURE

MIXING

1. Beat eggs, milk, and salt together with whip attachment until well blended. Add melted fat.
2. Replace whip with paddle. Mix in flour until completely smooth.
3. Strain the batter (optional but gives the popovers a better appearance).

SCALING AND PANNING

Grease every other cup of muffin tins (to allow room for expansion). Fill cups about one-half full, about 1½ oz (45 g) batter per unit.

BAKING

425°F (218°C) for 30–40 minutes. Before removing them from the oven, be sure popovers are dry and firm enough to avoid collapsing. Remove from pans immediately.

STRUDEL AND PHYLLO

PUFF PASTRY DOUGH, you will remember, consists of over 1,000 layers of dough and fat. Starting with a single thick piece of dough, you fold in butter and then continue to roll out and fold until you have a very flaky pastry of extremely thin layers.

Pastries made from *strudel dough* or phyllo doughs are even flakier than puff pastries. Unlike puff pastries, these desserts start out with paper-thin layers of dough that are brushed with fat and then stacked or rolled up to make many-layered creations.

Strudel is an Eastern European pastry that begins as a soft dough made of strong flour, eggs, and water. After the dough is mixed well to develop the gluten, it is stretched by hand into a very thin, transparent sheet. This is a skilled operation that takes practice to do well.

Phyllo dough (pronounced FEE-lo and sometimes spelled "filo" or "fillo") is a Greek version of this type of paper-thin dough. Although not exactly the same as strudel dough, it is interchangeable with strudel dough for most of our purposes. Because it is available commercially, phyllo dough is widely used today for strudel-making. In fact, commercial phyllo is often labeled "phyllo/strudel dough."

Commercially made phyllo is almost always available frozen; and in some locations it can also be purchased fresh (refrigerated). The sheets usually measure about 11 × 17 in. or 12 × 17 in. (28 × 43 cm or 30 × 43 cm). A 1-pound (454-g) package contains about 25 sheets.

The following recipes are for homemade strudel dough and for two popular strudel fillings, apple and cheese. Included with these are procedures for assembling and baking a strudel using both homemade dough and commercial phyllo leaves. Finally, we include a procedure for assembling and baking baklava, the popular Greek phyllo pastry filled with nuts and soaked with a honey syrup.

STRUDEL DOUGH

Yield: enough for 4 sheets, each about 3 × 4 ft (1 × 1.2 m)

Ingredients	U.S.		Metric	%
Bread flour	2 lb		900 g	100
Water	1 lb	2 oz	500 g	56
Salt		0.5 oz	15 g	1.5
Eggs		5 oz (3 eggs)	140 g (3 eggs)	15
Vegetable oil		2 oz	55 g	6
Total weight:	**3 lb**	**9 oz**	**1610 g**	**178 %**

PROCEDURE

MIXING

1. Mix all ingredients into a smooth dough. To develop the gluten well, mix at moderate speed for about 10 minutes. The dough will be very soft.

2. Divide the dough into 4 equal parts. Flatten each piece into a rectangle. Place the 4 pieces of dough on an oiled sheet pan. Oil the top of the dough lightly and cover it with plastic film.

3. Let the dough rest at least 1 hour at room temperature, or longer in the retarder.

PROCEDURE: Stretching Strudel Dough

1. Strudel dough stretches best if it is slightly warm, so place the dough in a warm place. Allow at least 1 to 2 hours if the dough has been refrigerated.

2. Cover a large table (at least 3 × 4 ft/1 × 1.2 m) with a cloth. Dust the cloth well with flour and rub it in lightly.

3. Using plenty of dusting flour, place one piece of dough in the center of the table and, with a rolling pin, roll it out roughly into an oval or rectangle. This step is meant only to start the stretching, so don't try to roll the dough too thin.

4. With the back of the hands up, slide your hands under the dough. Carefully begin stretching the dough from the center outward, using the backs of your hands, not your fingers, to avoid poking holes in the dough. Work your way around the table, gently stretching the dough little by little in all directions. Concentrate on the thickest parts of the dough, to make it of even thickness all around.

5. Keep stretching the dough until it is paper-thin and nearly transparent. If small holes appear, you can ignore them; if large holes appear, patch them with pieces of dough from the edges after stretching is complete. Each piece of dough should make a sheet about 3 × 4 ft (1 × 1.2 m).

6. With scissors, cut off the heavy rim of dough around the edge and discard it.

7. Let the dough dry about 10 minutes, then fill it and roll it according to the Procedure for Filling, Rolling, and Baking Strudel.

PROCEDURE: Filling, Rolling, and Baking Strudel

METHOD 1, USING HOMEMADE DOUGH

1. Assemble the following ingredients:

1 sheet freshly made strudel dough	3 × 4 ft	1 × 1.2 m
Melted butter	8 oz	250 g
Cake crumbs, bread crumbs, finely chopped nuts, or a mixture of these	8 oz	250 g
Cinnamon	0.25 oz (1 tbsp)	7 g
Cheese filling	5–5½ lb	2300–2600 g
or		
Apple filling	4–4½ lb	2000–2200 g

2. Sprinkle or brush the dough all over with the melted butter. If you brush the fat on, draw the brush very lightly over the dough to avoid tearing it.

3. Mix the crumbs, nuts, and cinnamon and sprinkle them evenly over the dough (a).

4. Arrange the filling in a band 1½-in. (4-cm) thick along one long side of the dough. Leave a margin of about 2 in. (5 cm) between the row of filling and the edge of the dough.

5. Standing on the side of the filling, grasp the edge of the cloth and lift it upward and forward to start the strudel rolling (b). Using the cloth as an aid, roll up the strudel like a jelly roll (c, d).

6. Cut the strudel in lengths to fit on a greased or paper-lined sheet, or bend the strudel to fit it on in one piece. Pinch the ends closed.

7. Brush the top with butter or egg wash. Bake at 375°F (190°C) until browned, about 45 minutes.

8. When cool, dust butter-washed strudel with confectioners' sugar, or brush egg-washed strudel with a clear syrup glaze (p. 194).

A

B

C

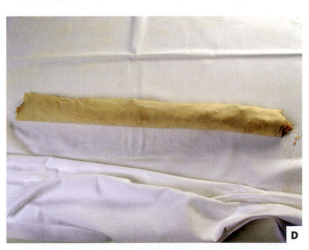
D

METHOD 2, USING PHYLLO LEAVES

Each unit requires 4 phyllo leaves plus one-fourth of the filling ingredients needed in Method 1.

1. Assemble the following ingredients:

Phyllo leaves	4 sheets	4 sheets
Melted butter	2 oz	60 g
Cake crumbs, bread crumbs, finely chopped nuts, or a mixture of these	2 oz	60 g
Cinnamon	1 tsp	2 g
Cheese filling	20–22 oz	575–625 g
or		
Apple filling	16–18 oz	500–550 g

2. Mix together the crumbs, nuts, and cinnamon.

3. Lay a cloth or a sheet of parchment on the bench. Lay a sheet of phyllo on the cloth or paper. Brush it with butter and sprinkle it with one-fourth of the crumb mixture.

4. Lay a second sheet on top of the first one. Brush with butter and sprinkle with crumbs.

5. Repeat with the remaining two sheets.

6. Arrange the filling in a band along the wide side of the sheet, leaving a margin of about 2 in. (5 cm) between the filling and the edge.

7. Roll up and bake as in Method 1 (steps 5 to 7). Each unit will fit crosswise on a standard baking sheet, 4 to 6 units per sheet.

8. In the retail shop, it is customary to cut each of these baked units in half and display the halves with the cut edges toward the customer.

Handling Phyllo Dough

Commercially made phyllo is so thin and delicate it must be handled very carefully. Two guidelines are important:

- First, thaw frozen phyllo completely *before opening the plastic package*. Do not try to handle frozen dough; it will break.

- Second, after opening the package and unfolding or unrolling the sheets of dough, keep the stack of leaves covered to prevent drying. Remove and work with one sheet at a time, keeping the rest covered. (*Note:* Package instructions often say to cover the dough with a damp cloth, but this is risky because the sheets stick together if the dough becomes too damp.)

The modern trend to lighter pastries has inspired chefs to use baked layers of phyllo in place of puff pastry to make desserts such as napoleons.

PROCEDURE: Making Crisp Phyllo Layers for Napoleons

1. On a cutting board, lay out one sheet of phyllo dough. Brush very lightly with butter. It is not necessary to cover the surface thoroughly with butter; use a light hand. Top with a second and third layer, buttering each layer lightly.

2. Cut the pastry into squares or rectangles of desired size for individual pastries—for example, squares 3 in. (8 cm) on a side. Cut 2, 3, or 4 squares for each pastry, depending on the number of layers desired. A typical napoleon requires 3 layers.

3. Arrange the squares on baking sheets. Bake at 400°F (200°C) until brown, about 5 minutes.

4. The pastry squares to be used for top layers may be caramelized to enhance their appearance and flavor.

To caramelize, coat with confectioners' sugar by sifting the sugar over them. Place under a hot broiler until the sugar is caramelized. Watch closely so neither the sugar nor the pastry burns or scorches. Alternatively, caramelize the sugar with a blow torch.

PHYLLO TARTLET SHELLS

Prepare squares of pastry as in steps 1 and 2, making 4 layers. Press each square into a tartlet shell and bake. Use as shells for unbaked fruit tartlets, following the procedure on page 352.

APPLE FILLING FOR STRUDEL

Yield: 4 lb (2000 g)

Ingredients	U.S.		Metric	Apples at 100% %
Apples, peeled and cored (see *Note*)	3 lb		1500 g	100
Lemon juice	1	oz	30 g	2
Sugar	8	oz	250 g	17
Sugar	8	oz	250 g	17
Raisins	4	oz	125 g	8
Walnuts, chopped	4	oz	125 g	8
Cake crumbs, preferably yellow or white	2	oz	60 g	4
Lemon zest, grated	0.25 oz		8 g	0.5
Cinnamon	0.25 oz		8 g	0.5

NOTE: Canned sliced apples may be used. Weigh after draining. Omit the lemon juice and the first quantity of sugar. Omit steps 1 and 2 in the procedure.

PROCEDURE

1. Cut the apples into thin slices or small dice. Mix with the lemon juice and the first quantity of sugar. Let stand for 30 minutes while preparing the pastry.
2. Drain the apples well. The sugar will have drawn out juice that would otherwise run out of the strudel and make the bottom soggy.
3. Mix the apples with the remaining ingredients.

CHEESE FILLING FOR STRUDEL

Yield: enough for 4 strudels (each 16 in./41 cm long) or one 5-ft (1.6-m) strudel, using homemade dough

Ingredients	U.S.		Metric	Cheese at 100% %
Baker's cheese	2 lb 8	oz	1200 g	100
Butter	10	oz	300 g	25
Sugar	12	oz	360 g	30
Cake flour	3	oz	90 g	7.5
Salt	0.5	oz	15 g	1.25
Vanilla extract	0.5	oz	15 g	1.25
Lemon zest, grated	0.25 oz (1 tbsp)		8 g	0.6
Eggs	6	oz	180 g	15
Sour cream	8	oz	240 g	20
Raisins	8	oz	240 g	20
Total weight:	**5 lb 8**	**oz**	**2648 g**	**220 %**

PROCEDURE

1. Combine the cheese and butter (at room temperature) and blend at low speed with the paddle attachment until smooth.
2. Add the sugar, flour, salt, vanilla, and zest. Blend at low speed until just smooth and completely mixed. Do not cream too much air into the mixture or it will expand when baked and may burst the pastry.
3. Add the eggs a little at a time, mixing in at low speed. Mix in the sour cream.
4. Fold in the raisins.

— **VARIATION** —

CREAM CHEESE FILLING FOR STRUDEL

Ingredients	U.S.		Metric	%
Cream cheese	3 lb		1440 g	100
Sugar	12	oz	360 g	25
Cake flour	3	oz	90 g	6
Salt	0.5	oz	15 g	1
Vanilla extract	0.5	oz	15 g	1
Lemon zest	0.25 oz		8 g	0.5
Eggs	6	oz	180 g	12.5
Sour cream	8	oz	240 g	17
Raisins	8	oz	240 g	17

Substitute the above ingredients for those in the main recipe, using cream cheese instead of baker's cheese and omitting the butter. Mix as in basic recipe.

BAKLAVA

Yield: one 15 × 10-in. (38 × 25 cm) pan, about 48 pieces

Ingredients	U.S.		Metric	
Pastry				
Phyllo leaves	1 lb		500	g
Walnuts, chopped	1 lb		500	g
Sugar	2	oz	60	g
Cinnamon	0.06 oz (1 tsp)		2	g
Cloves, ground	0.04 oz (½ tsp)		0.5	g
Butter, melted, or mixture of butter and oil	8	oz	250	g
Syrup				
Sugar	12	oz	375	g
Water	9	oz	280	g
Honey	4.5	oz	140	g
Lemon peel	2 strips		2 strips	
Lemon juice	1	oz	30	g
Cinnamon stick	1		1	

PROCEDURE

1. Unfold the phyllo leaves and keep them covered.
2. Mix together the nuts, sugar, cinnamon, and cloves.
3. Butter the bottom and sides of a 15 × 0-in. (38 × 25-cm) baking pan.
4. Lay 1 phyllo sheet in the bottom of the pan, letting the ends of the dough fold upward at the sides of the pan. Brush the dough with butter (a).
5. Repeat until there are 10 buttered sheets in the pan.
6. Place one-third of the nut mixture in the pan in an even layer (b).
7. Put in 2 more phyllo leaves, buttering each as it is placed in the pan.
8. Put in another third of the nuts, another 2 buttered phyllo leaves, and the rest of the nuts.
9. Finally, lay each of the remaining leaves in the pan, buttering each, including the top one.
10. There will be excess dough sticking up around the edges of the pan. With a sharp knife, trim it level with the top of the pastry.
11. Chill the pastry to congeal the butter. This will make cutting easier.
12. Cut the pastry into 4 rows of 6 squares, each about 2½ in. (6 cm) on a side. Then cut the squares diagonally to make triangles (c). (A traditional method is to cut baklava into diamond shapes, but this always leaves small, odd-shaped pieces at the ends.)
13. Bake at 350°F (175°C) for 50–60 minutes, until golden brown.
14. While the baklava is baking, combine the syrup ingredients and bring to a boil. Simmer for 10 minutes, then cool to lukewarm. Remove the cinnamon stick and lemon peel. Skim off foam, if any.
15. When the pastry is baked, pour the warm syrup carefully over the hot baklava (d).
16. Let the baklava stand overnight to absorb the syrup.

A

B

C

D

BAKLAVA

There are countless varieties of baklava throughout the Mediterranean region, including Greece and southeastern Europe, Turkey, Lebanon, and other countries in the Middle East, and parts of North Africa. The pastry seems to have originated centuries ago with Turkish layered breads. Today, connoisseurs of baklava can tell its origin by its filling (usually chopped nuts, including walnuts, pistachios, and almonds), its shape, and its flavorings (for example, honey and cinnamon in Greece, lemon and rose water in Lebanon).

BAKED MERINGUES

TO REFER TO *baked meringues* as pastries may seem odd, as the term *pastry* usually refers to desserts made from flour goods such as puff pastry, short dough, or éclair paste. However, meringue that is bagged out into shapes and baked until crisp is used in many of the same ways as flour pastry. It can be filled or iced with many kinds of creams, icings, and fruits to make an interesting variety of attractive desserts.

Basic meringue mixtures are discussed in Chapter 12, along with other creams and toppings. Common meringue and Swiss meringue are the types generally used to make crisp, baked shells. The basic procedure for baking meringue is presented in this section, followed by instructions for individual desserts. Also, a special meringue mixture containing nuts, called *japonaise*, is introduced. This flavorful mixture is usually made into round, crisp layers that are used somewhat like cake layers. They may be filled and iced with buttercream, chocolate mousse, whipped cream, or similar light icings and creams.

The most common use for the preparations in this section is to pipe them out into disks and use the baked meringues as bases or layers for a variety of pastries. (To make meringue or sponge layers, mark a circle on a sheet of parchment and pipe the meringue or batter in a spiral to fill the circle.) Chopped or powdered nuts, especially almonds and hazelnuts, may be folded into a meringue before baking, making flavorful, crisp layers for a variety of pastries, as well as specialty cakes. Two formulas of this type are included.

Four of the recipes in this section contain some cake flour and are mixed like sponge cakes. In fact, they are sometimes called *sponges*. The flour contributes structure. The quantity of flour is low, however, and the main ingredients are egg whites and sugar, as in regular meringues. Therefore, these recipes are grouped with meringues rather than with cakes.

You will find pastry recipes using these meringues in Chapter 15. Chapter 17 includes cakes that incorporate one or more layers of meringue.

CRISP BAKED MERINGUES

Components

Common Meringue (p. 258), Chocolate Meringue (p. 258) or Swiss Meringue (p. 259)

PROCEDURE

1. On baking sheets lined with parchment paper, and using a pastry bag, form the meringue into the desired shapes. (Specific shapes are indicated in the procedures for specific desserts.)

2. Bake at 200° to 225°F (100°C) until crisp but not browned. This will take 1 to 3 hours, depending on size.

3. Cool the meringues, then remove them from the parchment. Be careful, because they may be fragile.

ALMOND MERINGUES

For large-quantity measurements, see page 725.

Ingredients	U.S.	Metric	Egg whites at 100% %
Egg whites	4 oz	120 g	100
Fine granulated sugar	4 oz	120 g	100
Powdered almonds	4 oz	120 g	100
Total weight	**12 oz**	**360 g**	**300%**

PROCEDURE

1. Prepare baking sheets by lining them with parchment paper. Draw circles of the desired size on the paper, using cake pans or other round objects as guides. Turn the sheets over so the circles are on the bottom but visible through the paper.
2. Whip the egg whites to soft peaks.
3. Add the sugar and continue whipping until firm and glossy.
4. Fold in the powdered almonds.
5. Using a pastry bag with a ½-in. (12-mm) plain tube, fill in the circles on the baking sheets by making spirals starting in the center of each circle, as on page 341. Fill each circle with a layer of meringue about ½ in. (12 mm) thick.
6. Bake at 325°F (160°C) until firm and dry, about 25 minutes.

JAPONAISE MERINGUES

Ingredients	U.S.	Metric	Egg whites at 100% %
Egg whites	1 lb	500 g	100
Fine granulated sugar	1 lb	500 g	100
Confectioners' sugar, sifted	1 lb	500 g	100
Blanched hazelnuts or almonds, chopped very fine	1 lb	500 g	100
Total weight:	**4 lb**	**2000 g**	**400%**

PROCEDURE

1. Line baking sheets with parchment paper. Draw circles of the desired size on the paper, using cake pans or other round objects as guides. Turn the sheets over so the marks are on the bottom but visible through the paper.
2. With the whip attachment, beat the egg whites at medium speed until they form soft peaks.
3. Add the granulated sugar, a little at a time, with the machine running. Whip until the meringue forms stiff peaks.
4. Stop the machine. Mix together the confectioners' sugar and nuts. Fold this mixture into the meringue.
5. Using a pastry bag with a ½-in. (12-mm) plain tube, fill in the circles on the baking sheets by making spirals starting in the center of each circle, as on page 341. Fill each circle with a layer of meringue about ½ in. (12 mm) thick.
6. Bake at 250°F (120°C) until meringue is crisp and very lightly browned, about 1½–2 hours.
7. Use in place of or in addition to cake layers in assembling cakes and gâteaux (Chapter 17).

MARLY SPONGE

Ingredients	U.S.		Metric	Egg whites at 100% %
Powdered almonds	5	oz	150 g	60
Cake flour	2.25	oz	70 g	28
Sugar	8	oz	250 g	100
Egg whites	8	oz	250 g	100
Sugar	5	oz	150 g	60
Total weight:	**1 lb 12**	**oz**	**870 g**	**248%**

PROCEDURE

1. Line sheet pans with parchment paper. Draw circles of the desired size on the paper, using cake pans or other round objects as guides. Turn the sheets over so the marks are on the bottom but visible through the paper.

2. Sift the almonds, flour, and first quantity of sugar.

3. Whip the egg whites to soft peaks. Add the second quantity of sugar and whip to firm peaks.

4. Fold in the almond powder mixture.

5. Using a pastry bag with a plain tip, pipe disks inside the circles marked on the paper, using the technique on page 341.

6. Bake at 350°F (180°C) for 12–15 minutes.

COCONUT DACQUOISE

Ingredients	U.S.		Metric	Egg whites at 100% %
Powdered almonds	3	oz	90 g	60
Sugar	4	oz	120 g	80
Cake flour	1.5	oz	42 g	28
Coconut, grated	0.5	oz	15 g	10
Egg whites	5	oz	150 g	100
Sugar	4	oz	120 g	80
Total weight:	**1 lb 2**	**oz**	**537 g**	**358%**

PROCEDURE

1. Line baking sheets with parchment paper. Draw circles of the desired size on the paper, using cake pans or other round objects as guides. Turn the sheets over so the marks are on the bottom but visible through the paper.

2. Sift together the almond powder, first quantity of sugar, and flour. Stir in the coconut.

3. Whip the egg whites to soft peaks, add the second quantity of sugar, and continue whipping to firm peaks.

4. Add the sifted dry ingredients and fold in.

5. Using a pastry bag with a medium plain tip, pipe disks inside the circles marked on the paper, using the technique shown on page 341.

6. Bake at 350°F (180°C) for 10 minutes or until golden.

HAZELNUT COCONUT SPONGE

Ingredients	U.S.		Metric	Egg whites at 100% %
Powdered hazelnuts	5	oz	150 g	83
Confectioners' sugar	4	oz	120 g	67
Cake flour	1	oz	30 g	17
Coconut, grated	1.16 oz		35 g	19
Egg whites	6	oz	180 g	100
Granulated sugar	3	oz	90 g	50
Total weight:	**1 lb 4**	**oz**	**605 g**	**336%**

PROCEDURE

1. Sift together the hazelnuts, confectioners' sugar, and cake flour. Stir in the coconut.

2. Whip the egg whites and sugar to firm peaks.

3. Fold in the dry ingredients.

4. Using a pastry bag with a medium plain tip, pipe the mixture onto parchment-lined pans into disks of desired size, as shown on page 341.

5. Bake at 350°F (180°C) for 10–12 minutes.

SUCCÈS

For large-quantity measurements, see page 725.

Ingredients	U.S.	Metric	Egg whites at 100% %
Egg whites	6 oz	180 g	100
Granulated sugar	4 oz	120 g	67
Powdered almonds	4 oz	120 g	67
Confectioners' sugar	4 oz	120 g	67
Cake flour	1 oz	30 g	17
Total weight	**1 lb 3 oz**	**570 g**	**318%**

PROCEDURE

1. Line baking sheets with parchment paper. Draw circles of the desired size on the paper, using cake pans or other round objects as guides. Turn the sheets over so the marks are on the bottom but visible through the paper.

2. Make a French meringue: Whip the egg whites until they form soft peaks. Add the granulated sugar and whip until the meringue is stiff and glossy.

3. Sift together the remaining ingredients. Fold into the meringue.

4. Using a pastry bag with a plain tip, pipe disks inside the circles marked on the paper using the technique shown on page 341.

5. Bake at 350°F (180°C) until dry to the touch but not completely hardened, 20–30 minutes.

--- VARIATION ---

PROGRÈS

This mixture can also be prepared with powdered hazelnuts, in which case it is more properly called progrès. (The final "s" is not pronounced in either succès or progrès.)

Note that this preparation is similar to Marly Sponge (p. 343).

PISTACHIO MACAROON SPONGE

Ingredients	U.S.		Metric	Egg whites at 100% %
Almond paste	9	oz	270 g	90
Heavy cream	2.5	oz	75 g	25
Green pistachio paste	2	oz	60 g	20
Egg whites	10	oz	300 g	100
Sugar	4	oz	120 g	40
Total weight:	**1 lb 11**	**oz**	**825 g**	**275%**

PROCEDURE

1. Line baking sheets with parchment paper. Draw circles of the desired size on the paper, using cake pans or other round objects as guides. Turn the sheets over so the marks are on the bottom but visible through the paper.
2. Soften the almond paste with the heavy cream. Heat the mixture to 105°F (40°C).
3. Mix in the pistachio paste.
4. Whip the egg whites to soft peaks. Add the sugar and whip to firm peaks.
5. Fold into the almond paste mixture.
6. Using a pastry bag with a medium plain tip, pipe disks inside the circles marked on the paper, using the technique shown on page 341.
7. Bake at 350°F (180°C) for 8 minutes.

CHOCOLATE HEADS

Components

Common Meringue (p. 258) *or* Chocolate Meringue (p. 258)

Chocolate Buttercream (p. 418)

Grated chocolate or chocolate sprinkles

PROCEDURE

1. Prepare shells as for Meringue Chantilly (below).
2. Sandwich two shells together with chocolate buttercream.
3. Refrigerate shells until firm.
4. Spread each meringue sandwich with more chocolate buttercream so it is completely covered.
5. Roll in grated chocolate or chocolate sprinkles.

MERINGUE CHANTILLY

Components

Common Meringue (p. 258), Chocolate Meringue (p. 258), *or* Swiss Meringue (p. 259)

Crème Chantilly (p. 257)

PROCEDURE

1. On a baking sheet lined with parchment paper, shape the meringue into round mounds about 2 in. (5 cm) in diameter, using a ¾-in. (2-cm) plain tube in the pastry bag. Bake at 200° to 225°F (100°C) until crisp but not browned.
2. Optional step to allow more room for cream filling: When the shells are firm enough to handle but not completely crisp, remove them from the baking sheet. With your thumb, press a hollow in the base (the flat side). Return them to the oven to finish baking.
3. Cool the shells and store them in a dry place until needed.
4. Just before serving, sandwich two shells together with crème chantilly. Place the filled shells on their sides in paper cases.
5. Using a pastry bag with a star tube, decorate with additional whipped cream in the space between the shells.
6. If desired, the cream may be decorated with nuts or candied fruit.

MERINGUE GLACÉE

Components	PROCEDURE
Common Meringue (p. 258), Chocolate Meringue (p. 258), *or* Swiss Meringue (p. 259) Ice cream Whipped cream	1. Prepare meringue shells as for Meringue Chantilly (p. 345). 2. Sandwich two shells together with ice cream instead of crème chantilly. 3. Decorate with whipped cream.

MERINGUE MUSHROOMS

Components	PROCEDURE
Common Meringue (p. 258)	These are used primarily for decorating Bûche de Noël (Chocolate Christmas Roll), page 470. 1. On baking sheets lined with parchment paper, and using a pastry bag with a small, plain tube, make small mounds of meringue in the shapes of mushroom caps. Make smaller, pointed mounds to use as stems. 2. If desired, sprinkle very lightly with cocoa. 3. Bake as for Crisp Baked Meringues (p. 341). 4. When baked, make a small hole in the bottoms of the caps. Attach the stems with meringue or royal icing.

MERINGUE CREAM CAKES

Components	PROCEDURE
Japonaise Meringues (p. 342) Buttercream (p. 418)	1. For each cake, you will need two 2½-in. (6–7-cm) japonaise meringues and about 2 oz (60 g) buttercream in any flavor. 2. Spread one japonaise circle with a thin layer of buttercream. Top with a second circle. 3. Ice the top and sides smoothly. 4. If desired, coat the iced cakes with chopped nuts, grated chocolate, toasted coconut, etc.

VACHERIN

Components	PROCEDURE
Common Meringue (p. 258), Chocolate Meringue (p. 258), *or* Swiss Meringue (p. 259)	1. For a large vacherin, draw 8-in. (20-cm) or 9-in. (23-cm) circles on sheets of parchment, using a cake pan as a guide. For individual vacherins, draw 2½-in. (6–7-cm) circles.

Components:

- Common Meringue (p. 258), Chocolate Meringue (p. 258), *or* Swiss Meringue (p. 259)
- Sweetened whipped cream
- Fruit of choice
- Sponge cake, cubed, moistened with flavored syrup (optional)
- Fresh or candied fruit

PROCEDURE

1. For a large vacherin, draw 8-in. (20-cm) or 9-in. (23-cm) circles on sheets of parchment, using a cake pan as a guide. For individual vacherins, draw 2½-in. (6–7-cm) circles.
2. Using a pastry bag with a plain tube, make one meringue base for each vacherin. Do this by making a spiral starting in the center of a circle and continuing until the circle is filled in with a layer of meringue about ½ in. (12 mm) thick.
3. For the sides of the vacherin, make rings of meringue the same size as the bases. For each large vacherin, you will need 4 or 5 rings. For each individual vacherin, make 2 rings.
4. Bake as for Crisp Baked Meringues (p. 341).
5. Carefully remove the baked meringues from the parchment. Be especially careful with the rings, as they are fragile.
6. Stack the rings on the bases, using additional unbaked meringue to stick the pieces together.
7. If the rings are neatly and uniformly made, you may leave the shell as is. If the sides are not attractive, you may spread the sides of the shell smoothly with fresh meringue, or later ice the sides of the finished shell with buttercream.
8. Bake the shells again to dry out the fresh meringue. Cool.
9. Fill the shells with sweetened whipped cream and fruit (such as strawberries or sliced peaches). Cubes of sponge cake moistened with a flavored syrup may be used in addition to fruit.
10. Using a pastry bag, decorate the top with more whipped cream. Finally, arrange pieces of fresh or candied fruit in an attractive pattern on the top.

KEY POINTS TO REVIEW

- What are the steps in mixing pâte à choux (éclair paste)?
- What guidelines should be followed when handling phyllo dough? Describe how to make strudel using phyllo dough.
- What is the procedure for making crisp baked meringues?

TERMS FOR REVIEW

pâte brisée	short dough	reversed puff pastry	strudel dough
sablage	puff pastry	napoleon	strudel
pâte sucrée	four-fold	éclair paste	phyllo dough
pâte sablée	three-fold	pâte à choux	baked meringue
1-2-3 dough	blitz puff pastry	éclair	japonaise

QUESTIONS FOR REVIEW

1. Compare the mixing method for pâte brisée with the mixing method for short dough.
2. Describe two methods for enclosing the butter when making puff pastry.
3. Compare the mixing methods for puff pastry dough and blitz puff dough. Compare blitz puff dough and flaky pie dough.
4. What might happen to patty shells during baking if the puff dough is not relaxed before cutting and baking? What might happen to them if they are cut out of soft dough with a dull cutter?
5. Why is it important to bake cream puffs and éclairs thoroughly, and to cool them slowly?
6. What precautions must you take when handling frozen commercial phyllo/strudel dough?
7. In order to bake meringue shells until crisp, should you use a hot, moderate, or cool oven? Why?

15

TARTS AND SPECIAL PASTRIES

AFTER READING THIS CHAPTER, YOU SHOULD BE ABLE TO:

1. Prepare baked and unbaked tarts and tartlets.
2. Prepare a variety of special pastries based on puff pastry, choux pastry, and meringue-type sponges.

TO MANY BAKERS, pastry work is the most exciting and challenging part of their careers. It offers unlimited scope for developing artistic creativity, and it gives them opportunities to display their decorative skills. The basic doughs you learned in the preceding chapter, together with the creams and icings in other chapters, are the components of a nearly infinite variety of delicious and eye-appealing desserts and sweets.

Chapter 14 presented the principal pastry doughs in detail. Procedures for preparing simple items were included for all these preparations (except short doughs) to help you become familiar with handling them. This chapter continues the study of pastries, introducing more elaborate and advanced pastries.

349

Quantity Notice

Ingredient quantities in the following recipes may need to be adjusted. For example, especially sour fruit may need more sugar. Also, fruit may yield more or less than average quantities after trimming (peeling, pitting, etc.).

Most of the recipes on pages 352–358 are for 10-inch (25-cm) tarts. For smaller tarts, *multiply or divide each ingredient quantity by the factors indicated below* to get the approximate quantities needed.

TART SIZE	FACTOR
9-in. (23-cm)	multiply by 0.8 (or ⅘)
8-in. (20-cm)	multiply by 0.66 (or ⅔)
7-in. (18-cm)	divide by 2
6-in. (15-cm)	divide by 3
5-in. (13-cm)	divide by 4
4-in. (10-cm)	divide by 6
3-in. (7.5-cm)	divide by 10

FRESH FRUIT TART

Yield: one 10-in. (25-cm) tart

Ingredients	U.S.	Metric
Fresh fruit (see Procedure)	1.5–2 lb	750–1000 g
Pastry Cream (p. 263)	14 oz	400 g
10-in. (25-cm) baked tart shell	1	1
Apricot Glaze (p. 194)	4 oz or as needed	125 g or as needed

PROCEDURE

1. Select the fruit for the tart. Fresh fruit tarts may be made from all one fruit or a colorful combination of two or more fruits. Prepare fruit as necessary. Trim and wash. Cut large fruits such as peaches or pineapples into even slices or uniform bite-size pieces. Poach hard fruits such as apples or pears (see p. 578 for poaching methods). Drain all fruits well.

2. Spread a layer of pastry cream in the baked shell. Use enough pastry cream to fill it about half full.

3. Carefully arrange the fruit on top of the pastry cream.

4. Warm the apricot glaze; if it is too thick, dilute it with a little water or simple syrup. Brush the glaze on the fruit to coat it completely.

APPLE TART

Yield: one 10-in. (25-cm) tart

Ingredients	U.S.	Metric
Firm, flavorful cooking apples	1 lb 12 oz	750 g
10-in. (25-cm) unbaked tart shell	1	1
Sugar	3 oz	90 g
Apricot Glaze (p. 194)	as needed	as needed

PROCEDURE

1. Peel, core, and cut the apples into thin slices. You should have about 1 lb 6 oz (600 g) apple slices.
2. Arrange the apple slices in the tart shell. Save the best, most uniform slices for the top; arrange them shingle-fashion in concentric rings.
3. Sprinkle the sugar evenly over the apples.
4. Bake at 400°F (200°C), about 45 minutes, or until the pastry is browned and the apples are tender.
5. Cool. Brush with apricot glaze.

VARIATIONS

Saving enough of the best slices for a top layer, chop the rest of the apples and cook them with 2 oz (60 g) of the sugar and 0.5 oz (15 g) butter until they make a thick applesauce. Cool and spread in the bottom of the tart shell. Arrange apple slices on top. Sprinkle with remaining sugar and bake.

If the apple slices are very hard, sauté them lightly in 1–2 oz (30–60 g) butter and 1 oz (30 g) sugar until they begin to get soft and lightly browned. Turn them carefully to avoid breaking them. Proceed as in the basic recipe.

PLUM, APRICOT, CHERRY, OR PEACH TART

Follow the basic recipe, but sprinkle a thin layer of cake crumbs, cookie crumbs, or bread crumbs in the unbaked shell before adding the fruit. Adjust the sugar according to the sweetness of the fruit.

Appropriate spices, such as cinnamon for plums or apples, may be added in small quantities.

APPLE CUSTARD TART

Reduce the apples to 1 lb 4 oz/560 g (or 1 lb/450 g after peeling and coring). Reduce the sugar to 1.5 oz (45 g). Assemble and bake as in the basic recipe. When about half done, carefully pour in a custard mixture made by mixing the following ingredients.

Ingredients	U.S.	Metric
Milk	4 oz	120 mL
Heavy cream	4 oz	120 mL
Sugar	2 oz	60 g
Whole egg	1	1
Egg yolk	1	1
Vanilla extract	1 tsp	5 mL

Continue baking until set. Cool and dust with confectioners' sugar.

LEMON TART

Yield: one 10-in. (25-cm) tart

Ingredients	U.S.		Metric
10-in. (25-cm) tart shell	1		1
Sugar	4	oz	120 g
Lemon zest, grated	1	tbsp	15 mL
Eggs	6.67 oz (4 eggs)		190 g (4 eggs)
Lemon juice	6	oz	175 mL
Heavy cream	2	oz	60 mL

PROCEDURE

1. Bake the tart shell until it is golden but not too brown. Cool.
2. In a mixer fitted with the paddle attachment, blend the sugar and zest together thoroughly.
3. Add the eggs. Mix until well combined, but do not whip.
4. Mix in first the lemon juice and then the cream. Pass the mixture through a strainer.
5. Pour the strained filling into the tart shell. Bake at 325°F (165°C) just until the filling is set, no longer, about 20 minutes.

VARIATION

Arrange a few fresh raspberries on top of the tart. Dust lightly with confectioners' sugar.

PEAR ALMOND TART

Yield: one 10-in. (25-cm) tart

Ingredients	U.S.	Metric
10-in. (25-cm) tart shell	1	1
Frangipane (p. 196) or Almond Cream (p. 196)	12 oz	350 g
Pear halves, canned or poached	8	8
Apricot Glaze (p. 194)	as needed	as needed
Garnish (optional):		
Pear Crisps (p. 593; see variations)	2	2

PROCEDURE

1. Spread the frangipane filling evenly in the tart shell.
2. Drain the pears well. Cut them crosswise into thin slices, but keep the slices together in the shape of pear halves.
3. Arrange the sliced pear halves on top of the frangipane like spokes of a wheel. Do not cover all the filling with the pears. Push them gently into the cream.
4. Bake at 375°F (190°C), about 40 minutes.
5. Cool. Brush the top with apricot glaze.
6. If desired, place two pear crisps in the center of the tart.

VARIATIONS

Cooked or canned peaches, apples, apricots, plums, or cherries may be used instead of pears. For small fruits such as apricots, plums, and cherries, reduce the quantity of frangipane and use enough fruit to cover the top completely.

FRUIT TART WITH PASTRY CREAM

Omit the frangipane and instead cover the bottom of the tart shell with a ½-in. (1-cm) layer of pastry cream. Alternatively, use a mixture of 2 or 3 parts pastry cream blended smooth with 1 part almond paste. Cover the cream with a layer of fruit, arranged attractively.

FRANGIPANE TART

Omit the fruit. Spread the bottom of the tart shell with a thin layer of apricot jam. Fill with frangipane filling. Bake and cool. Instead of glazing, dust lightly with confectioners' sugar. This recipe is especially appropriate for small, individual tartlets.

FRUIT TARTLETS

The ingredients in the main recipe are the basis for all regular baked fruit tartlets. The following fresh or cooked fruits are the most commonly used: apples, pears, cherries, blueberries, pears, apricots, peaches, nectarines. Use only one type of fruit per tartlet. Approximately the following quantities will be needed for ten 3-in. (8-cm) tartlets.

Ingredients	U.S.	Metric
Short Dough (p. 314) or Pâte Sucrée (p. 314)	12 oz	350 g
Frangipane (p. 196) or Almond Cream (p. 196)	14 oz	400 g
Fruit	8–14 oz	250–400 g
Apricot Glaze (p. 194)	3–4 oz	90–120 g

CHOCOLATE TART

Yield: one 10-in. (25-cm) tart

Ingredients	U.S.		Metric
10-in. (25-cm) tart shell made with Short Dough (p. 314) or Chocolate Pâte Sablée (p. 313)	1		1
Heavy cream	6	oz	175 mL
Milk	6	oz	175 mL
Bittersweet chocolate	8	oz	240 g
Egg	1.67 oz (1 egg)		50 g (1 egg)

PROCEDURE

1. Roll the short dough as thin as possible when making the tart shell. Bake until golden but not too brown. Cool.

2. Combine the cream and milk. Bring to a simmer and remove from the heat.

3. Add the chocolate. Stir in until completely melted and blended uniformly with the cream.

4. Beat the egg lightly in a bowl. Gradually stir in the warm chocolate mixture.

5. Pour the chocolate into the tart shell. Bake at 375°F (190°C) until set, about 15 minutes.

VARIATION

CHOCOLATE BANANA TART

In addition to the ingredients above, assemble the following:

Ingredients	U.S.	Metric
Ripe banana	1	1
Lemon juice	0.5 oz	15 g
Butter	0.5 oz	15 g
Sugar	1.5 oz	45 g

Slice the banana and toss the pieces gently with the lemon juice. Heat the butter in a nonstick sauté pan over high heat. Add the banana pieces and then the sugar. Sauté over high heat so the bananas brown and become coated in the caramelized sugar. Do not cook so long that they become soft and mushy. Transfer to a sheet pan lined with parchment and let cool. Arrange the caramelized bananas in the bottom of the tart shell before pouring in the chocolate mixture. Proceed as in the basic recipe.

WALNUT TART

Yield: one 10-in. (25-cm) tart

Ingredients	U.S.	Metric
Brown sugar	8 oz	225 g
Butter	2 oz	55 g
Eggs	5 oz (3 eggs)	150 g (3 eggs)
Flour	1 oz	30 g
Cinnamon	½ tsp	2 mL
Walnuts, broken or coarsely chopped	12 oz	340 g
Unbaked 10-in. (25-cm) tart shell	1	1
Chocolate Glaçage (p. 427) or tempered chocolate	as needed	as needed

PROCEDURE

1. Cream the butter and sugar until well blended.
2. Beat in the eggs one at a time, waiting until one is absorbed before adding the next.
3. Add the flour and cinnamon. Blend in well.
4. Mix in the nuts.
5. Transfer the mixture to the tart shell. Bake at 350°F (175°C) for about 40 minutes, or until the pastry is golden and the filling is set.
6. Cool completely.
7. Using a paper cone (see pp. 436–438), drizzle the chocolate glaçage very lightly over the tart in a crosshatch pattern. Let stand until the chocolate is set.

LINZERTORTE

Yield: one 10-in. (25-cm) tart

Ingredients	U.S.	Metric
Linzer Dough (p. 315)	1 lb 8 oz	700 g
Raspberry jam	14 oz (1¼ cups)	400 g

NOTE: This famous Austrian pastry is called a torte but it is actually a tart filled with raspberry jam.

PROCEDURE

1. Roll out about two-thirds of the linzer dough to ¼–⅓ in. (6–8 mm) thick.
2. Line a greased 10-in. (25-cm) tart pan with the dough. Trim off excess dough.
3. Spread the jam evenly in the shell.
4. Roll out the remaining dough and cut it into strips about ⅜ in. (1 cm) wide. Arrange the strips in a lattice pattern on top of the tarts. Set the strips at an angle so they form diamond shapes rather than squares.
5. Roll small, evenly sized balls of dough and place them tightly against each other around the edge of the tart to cover the ends of the lattice strips and to serve as a border (see illustration).
6. Bake at 375°F (190°C) for 35–40 minutes.

SPECIAL PASTRIES

THIS SECTION PRESENTS a collection of pastries of many types. The first three recipes are for famous classics based on puff pastry, pâte à choux, and short dough. These are items that all pastry chefs should know how to make well. The *gâteau St-Honoré* is a spectacular assembly of choux pastry, short dough, caramel, and cream fillings. It is often decorated with a nest of spun sugar (p. 664) on top. The rich *Pithiviers* and the special napoleon or *millefeuille* test your ability to work with puff pastry.

The remaining recipes are mostly of the type sometimes known in North America as *French pastries*. They are individual portions made up of any of a number of creams, icings, Bavarian creams (from Chapter 19), and layers of meringue, pastry, and even sponge cake. One of the first of these recipes, Passionata, is illustrated in detail to introduce you to the basic techniques for making this type of pastry. You can then apply the same techniques to other pastries in this section.

This chapter focuses primarily on pastries based on the doughs and meringue-type mixtures in Chapter 14, although cake layers (Chapter 16) are often used as well. Many of the cakes in Chapter 17 could also be presented as French pastries, as discussed on page 471. Additional pastries based on cake batters are explained in that chapter. The most common way to make French pastries from cakes is to bake the cake layers as sheets rather than as rounds, cut the sheet cakes into long strips, about 4 inches (10 cm) wide, and then slice the strips crosswise into portions, as explained on page 471. Note that several of the desserts in Chapters 19 and 21 are made in large ring molds. These, too, can be made as individual pastries by assembling them in small ring molds instead.

Finally, the chapter includes a recipe for a popular pastry called *sfogliatelle* (pronounced SFO lee ah TELL eh), a type of filled turnover from southern Italy. It is somewhat difficult to prepare, so follow the instructions carefully.

ST-HONORÉ

Two stories are told to explain the origin of the name of this elegant, classic pastry. One is that the confection was created in honor of the patron saint of pastry cooks, Saint Honoré (san toh no RAY). The other story is that it was developed in a pastry shop on the Paris street Rue Saint-Honoré. As a footnote to this second story, the pastry chef who developed the pastry was M. Chiboust, who supposedly invented a cream (see Chiboust Cream, p. 264) that is often used to fill a gâteau St-Honoré.

GÂTEAU ST-HONORÉ

Yield: two 8-in. (20-cm) gâteaux

Ingredients	U.S.		Metric
Pâte Brisée (p. 313)	10	oz	300 g
Pâte à Choux (p. 330)	1 lb 4	oz	600 g
Egg wash			
Egg yolks	4	oz (6 yolks)	120 g (6 yolks)
Whole egg	1.67	oz (1 egg)	50 g (1 egg)
Sugar	¼	tsp	1 g
Salt	¼	tsp	1 g
Water	2	tsp	10 g
Vanilla Crème Diplomat (p. 266)	12–13	oz	385 g
Chocolate Crème Diplomat (p. 266)	14	oz	425 g
Caramel			
Fine granulated sugar	7	oz	200 g
Water	2	oz	60 g
Glucose or corn syrup	0.67	oz	20 g

PROCEDURE

PREPARING THE PASTRIES

1. Chill the pâte brisée for at least 30 minutes before use.

2. Fit a pastry bag with a medium plain tip and fill with the pâte à choux.

3. Beat together the ingredients for the egg wash. (*Note:* You will not need the total quantity of egg wash. Reserve the remainder for another use.)

4. Roll out the pâte brisée about ⅛ in. (3 mm) thick into a long oval shape (large enough to cut the circles in the next step). Place on a buttered sheet pan and dock well. Chill.

5. Cut two 8-in. (20-cm) circles from the pastry. Leave the circles on the pan and remove the excess dough.

6. Brush around the edges of the circles with egg wash.

7. Pipe a thick band of pâte à choux around the edge of the pastry circles about 1 in. (2.5 cm) from the outer edge. Brush lightly with egg wash. Press down the choux pastry lightly by running the back of a fork along the top. Pipe an additional small spiral of choux pastry in the center of each circle.

8. Onto a parchment-lined or buttered sheet pan, pipe the remaining choux pastry into ¾-in. (2-cm) bulbs and brush with egg wash. (This will make more bulbs than necessary for the finished pastry, allowing you to select those of the best appearance.)

9. Bake all the pastries at 375°F (190°F) until risen and golden and the bulbs sound hollow when tapped. Cool on wire racks.

ASSEMBLING THE GÂTEAUX

1. Select the best choux bulbs for the finished pastries. You will need 12–14 for each. Make a small hole in the bottom of each bulb and use a pastry bag to fill it with vanilla crème diplomat.

2. Spread a layer of chocolate crème diplomat in the bottom of each pastry circle.

3. Fit two pastry bags with St-Honoré tips (see p. 435 for illustration). Fill with the remaining creams.

4. Holding the bag so the V-shaped point of the St-Honoré tip is up, pipe alternating lines of vanilla and chocolate creams to fill the pastry circles. See the photograph of the finished gâteau, as well as page 439, for piping with the St-Honoré tip. Chill the pastries.

5. Make a caramel by heating the sugar and water gently to dissolve the sugar. Bring to a boil, add the glucose, and cook until golden. Plunge the base of the pan into ice water briefly to stop the cooking.

6. Dip the filled choux bulbs into the caramel and then place caramel side down onto an oiled marble slab until cold.

7. Reheat the remaining caramel and use to glue the bulbs around the edges of the pastry circles, keeping the flat caramel tops of the bulbs as level as possible.

PRALINE MILLEFEUILLE

Yield: one pastry, about 6 × 10 in. (15 × 25 cm) and weighing about 2½ lb (1200 g)

Ingredients	U.S.	Metric
Classic Puff Pastry (p. 318)	1 lb 4 oz	630 g
Confectioners' sugar	as needed	as needed
Praline Cream (p. 535)	1 lb	500 g
Praline Pailletine (recipe below)	5 oz	150 g
Garnish		
Caramelized nuts	as desired	as desired

PROCEDURE

1. Roll out the puff pastry to a rectangle about 13 × 20 in. (33 × 52 cm). Place on a sheet pan lined with parchment paper. Dock the dough and refrigerate for 20 minutes.

2. Bake at 400°F (200°C). When the pastry is about four-fifths baked, remove from the oven and dredge generously with confectioners' sugar.

3. Raise the oven heat to 475°F (240°C). Return the pastry to the oven and bake until the sugar caramelizes, 2–3 minutes.

4. Remove from the oven and let cool.

5. With a serrated knife, trim the edges of the pastry so they are straight and square. Then cut crosswise into 3 equal rectangles. (Exact size depends on how much the pastry shrank; approximate size is indicated above in the yield.) Select the best of the rectangles and reserve it for the top layer.

6. Spread one of the pastry rectangles with a layer of praline cream ⅝ in. (1.5 cm) thick. Cover with a second layer of pastry.

7. Top with the praline pailletine and then another layer of the praline cream.

8. Cover with the third layer of pastry.

9. Decorate the top as desired with caramelized nuts.

PRALINE PAILLETINE

Ingredients	U.S.		Metric
Milk chocolate couverture	1	oz	25 g
Cocoa butter	0.25	oz	6 g
Almond-hazelnut praline paste	4	oz	100 g
Ice cream wafers (pailletine), crushed	1	oz	25 g
Total weight:	**6**	**oz**	**156 g**

PROCEDURE

1. Melt the chocolate and cocoa butter in a bowl over a hot-water bath.

2. Mix in the praline paste.

3. Add the crushed wafers and mix in.

4. To use in Praline Millefeuille (above), spread on a sheet pan to a thickness of about ¼ in. (5 mm), making a rectangle about 6 × 10 in. (15 × 25 cm), or the same size as the pastry rectangles.

5. Place in the refrigerator to harden.

APRICOT PITHIVIERS

Yield: two 8-in. (20-cm) pastries, about 11 oz (325 g) each

Ingredients	U.S.		Metric
Classic Puff Pastry (p. 318) (See *Note*)	1 lb		500 g
Almond Cream (p. 196)	12	oz	370 g
Canned apricot halves, drained, syrup reserved (see variations)	5	oz	150 g
Egg wash			
Egg yolks	4	oz (6 yolks)	120 g (6 yolks)
Whole egg	1.67	oz (1 egg)	50 g (1 egg)
Sugar	¼	tsp	1 g
Salt	¼	tsp	1 g
Water	2	tsp	10 g

NOTE: This quantity of pastry allows for about 7 oz (200 g) trimmings. Each Pithiviers uses about 5 oz (150 g) pastry. Chefs who can roll pastry to accurate dimensions can get by with less pastry to start.

VARIATIONS

Other canned fruits, such as pears or plums, may be used.

For a classic plain Gâteau Pithiviers, omit the fruit and increase the quantity of almond cream.

A

B

C

PITHIVIERS

Gâteau Pithiviers (pee tee VYAY) is a specialty of the town of Pithiviers in the Loire region of north central France. The dessert pastry is traditionally made with a filling of almond cream. The swirled design on top is also traditional. Some cooks also make savory pastries in the same shape, filled with meat or vegetable mixtures.

PROCEDURE

1. Roll out the puff pastry to ⅛ in. (3 mm) thick. Place on a sheet pan lined with parchment. Cover with plastic film and chill.

2. Cut out two 8-in. (20-cm) and two 9-in. (23-cm) circles from the pastry. Chill again.

3. Beat together the ingredients for the egg wash.

4. For each pastry, brush egg wash around the outer edge of an 8-in. (20-cm) pastry disk. Dock the center.

5. Spread with a layer of almond cream, staying about 1–1½ in. (3–4 cm) from the edge.

6. Arrange the fruit on the top of the almond cream.

7. With a pastry bag, pipe the remaining almond cream over the apricots to form a dome. Smooth with a palette knife.

8. Cover with the 9-in. (23-cm) pastry circle, pressing lightly to remove any trapped air. Select a bowl slightly larger than the dome of almond cream and invert it over the pastry. Press down to seal.

9. Using a bottle cap cut in half, cut a scalloped edge around the edge. (This can also be done with a knife, but an even finish is harder to achieve.) Remove the pastry trimmings (a).

10. Brush the top of the pastry with egg wash. Allow to dry in the refrigerator. Repeat with another layer of egg wash, and again allow to dry.

11. With a paring knife, cut a pinwheel pattern in the top, stopping short of the scalloped edge (b). Make very shallow cuts; do not cut through the pastry.

12. If desired, score the scalloped edge lightly to decorate (c).

13. Bake at 375°F (190°C) until golden brown and well risen. Reduce the oven temperature to 325°F (160°C) and bake until a knife inserted in the center comes out clean. Total baking time is about 45 minutes.

14. Use the syrup from the canned fruit to brush the hot pastry and return to the oven at 425°F (220°C) until the syrup bubbles and the top is glazed.

15. Cool on a wire rack.

CAPUCINE CHOCOLATE

Yield: 12 pastries, about 3½ oz (100 g) each

Ingredients	U.S.	Metric
Marly Sponge disks (p. 343), 2¾ in. (7 cm) in diameter	24	24
Chocolate Ganache II (p. 272)	1 lb 12 oz	775 g
Chocolate shavings	as needed	as needed
Confectioners' sugar	as needed	as needed
Chocolate Ganache II (p. 272) (optional)	2 oz	60 g

PROCEDURE

1. For each pastry, place a disk of sponge inside a ring mold 2¾ in. (7 cm) in diameter and 1½ in. (4 cm) high. Trim the sponge disks as necessary to fit.

2. Cover the sponge disks with a layer of ganache about ¾ in. (2 cm) thick.

3. Top with a second sponge disk.

4. Place in the freezer until set.

5. Remove the ring molds, using a blowtorch to lightly warm the molds to release them.

6. Press chocolate shavings onto the sides of the pastries.

7. Sprinkle the tops with confectioners' sugar.

8. If desired, for additional decoration, pipe about 1 tsp (5 g) ganache onto the centers of the tops of the pastries.

PASSIONATA

Yield: 12 pastries, about 5 oz (140 g) each

Ingredients	U.S.		Metric
Canned pineapple, drained	10	oz	300 g
Vanilla Syrup (p. 254)	6	oz	175 g
Rum	0.67 oz (4 tsp)		20 g
Coconut Dacquoise disks (p. 343), 2¾ in. (7 cm) in diameter	24		24
Passion Fruit Bavarian (p. 532)	2 lbs		1000 g
Gelatin	0.1	oz	3 g
Poured Fondant (p. 417)	5	oz	150 g
Passion fruit juice	3.5	oz	100 g
Passion fruit, fresh	1		1
Coconut, grated and toasted	as needed		as needed

PROCEDURE

1. Cut the pineapple into ¼ × ¾ in. pieces (5 mm × 2 cm). Add to the vanilla syrup. Simmer 10 minutes. Add the rum and flambé. Cool, then chill the mixture.

2. Select 12 ring molds 2¾ in. (7 cm) in diameter and 1½ in. (4 cm) high. Place a disk of dacquoise on a cake card and set a ring mold over it so the disk is inside the mold. Trim the disks if necessary to fit snugly (a).

3. Drain the pineapple well and arrange half of it on top of the dacquoise (b).

4. Fill the molds halfway with passion fruit Bavarian (c).

5. Cover with a second dacquoise disk and add the remaining pineapple. Fill to the top with the remaining Bavarian and smooth with a palette knife.

A

B

C

D

E

F

G

H

PASSIONATA PROCEDURE CONTINUED

6. Place in the freezer until set.

7. Prepare the passion fruit glaze for the top. Soften the gelatin in water (see pp. 80–82). Combine the fondant and passion fruit juice and bring to a boil. Add the gelatin. Stir to dissolve. Add the seeds and juice from a fresh passion fruit.

8. Spoon a thin layer of this mixture over the tops of the cold pastries to glaze (d); spread it to the edges with a palette knife (e). Allow to set.

9. Remove the ring molds by heating the sides gently with a blowtorch to release them (f). Lift off the mold (g).

10. Coat the sides of the pastries with coconut (h).

─── **VARIATIONS** ───

The procedure and components for making Passionata can be used to create a variety of pastries by substituting other fruits and flavorings. For example, substitute fresh raspberries for the pineapple, and use raspberry Bavarian and raspberry juice in place of the passion fruit.

GÂTEAU SUCCÈS

Yield: 1 gâteau, 7 in. (18 cm) in diameter

Ingredients	U.S.	Metric
Succès layers (p. 344), 7 in. (18 cm) in diameter	2	2
Praline Buttercream (p. 421)	8 oz	225 g
Nougatine (p. 658), crushed	2 oz	60 g
Sliced almonds, toasted	2.5 oz	75 g
Confectioners' sugar	as needed	as needed

PROCEDURE

1. Place one succès layer on a cake card, anchoring it in place with a dab of buttercream.
2. Spread a layer of buttercream on the succès.
3. Sprinkle the crushed nougatine evenly over the buttercream.
4. Top with the second layer of succès.
5. Spread the top and sides of the cake with buttercream.
6. Coat the top and sides with the almonds. Sprinkle the top very lightly with confectioners' sugar.

--- **VARIATION** ---

Individual succès pastries can be made using the same procedure. Use small succès disks 2¾ in. (7 cm) in diameter.

CHOCOLATINES

Yield: 10 pastries, about 2½ oz (75 g) each

Ingredients	U.S.	Metric
Succès disks (p. 344), 2¾ in. (7 cm) in diameter	20	20
Chocolate Mousse I (p. 273)	14 oz	400 g
Confectioners' sugar	2 oz	60 g
Cocoa powder	1 oz	30 g

PROCEDURE

1. For each pastry, place a succès disk in the bottom of a ring mold 2¾ in. (7 cm) in diameter.
2. Fill about two-thirds full with chocolate mousse.
3. Top with a second succès disk and push down gently.
4. Fill the mold with additional chocolate mousse and smooth the top.
5. Chill several hours or overnight.
6. Remove the ring mold by warming it carefully with a blowtorch and lifting off.
7. Sift together the confectioners' sugar and cocoa. Return the mixture to the sieve and sift it over the tops of the pastries.

NOUGATINE PARISIENNE

Yield: 8 pastries, about 5 oz (150 g) each

Ingredients	U.S.		Metric
Pistachio Macaroon Sponge disks (p. 345), 2¾ in. (7 cm) in diameter	16		16
Caramelized Apricots (p. 590)	10	oz	300 g
Nougatine Cream (p. 534)	1 lb 8	oz	750 g
Dark chocolate	7	oz	200 g
Apricot Glaze (p. 194)	3.5	oz	100 g
Garnish			
Caramelized Apricots	as needed		as needed
Pistachios, whole, broken, or chopped	as needed		as needed

PROCEDURE

1. For each pastry, place a sponge disk in the bottom of a ring mold 2¾ in. (7 cm) in diameter.

2. Arrange half the caramelized apricots over the sponge disks.

3. Cover with half of the nougatine cream.

4. Place another sponge disk on top of the cream.

5. Arrange the remaining apricots over the disks.

6. Fill the molds with nougatine cream, smoothing the top with a palette knife.

7. Refrigerate or freeze until set.

8. Carefully remove the ring molds by warming them briefly with a blowtorch.

9. Select strips of acetate of the same width as the height of the molds. Temper the chocolate (see p. 629) and spread it over the strips, as shown on page 634.

10. While the chocolate is still soft, wrap the acetate around the pastries, chocolate side in, and allow to set.

11. Glaze the tops with apricot glaze and decorate as desired with pieces of apricot and pistachios.

12. Peel the acetate off the chocolate just before serving.

CREOLE DÉLICES

Yield: 10 pastries, about 4 oz (120 g) each

Ingredients	U.S.	Metric
Raisins	5 oz	150 g
Dessert Syrup (p. 254) flavored with rum	6 oz	180 g
Almond Meringue disks (p. 342), 2¾ in. (7 cm) in diameter	20	20
Liqueur Bavarian Cream (p. 528) flavored with dark rum	1 lb 10 oz	800 g
Chocolate Glaçage (p. 427)	5 oz	150 g

PROCEDURE

1. Combine the raisins and syrup in a small saucepan. Warm slightly, then remove from heat and let stand 1 hour to allow the raisins to soften. Drain well.

2. Place half the meringue disks in the bottoms of 10 ring molds 2¾ in. (7 cm) in diameter.

3. Mix the raisins with the Bavarian cream. Fill the molds half full with the cream.

4. Place a second meringue disk on top of the cream and press down gently.

5. Cover with the remaining cream and smooth the tops. Chill or freeze until set.

6. Coat the tops with a thin layer of chocolate glaçage. Chill again until set.

7. Warm the ring molds very gently with a blowtorch and lift off.

--- VARIATION ---

CHOCOLATE RUM DÉLICES

Prepare as in the main recipe but with the following changes: Use only half the quantity of Bavarian cream and omit the raisins and syrup. Use the cream in the bottom layer as in the main recipe. After placing the second meringue disk in the mold, fill the mold with Chocolate Mousse I (p. 273). Chill or freeze until set. Glaze the top as in the main recipe.

FINANCIERS AU CAFÉ

Yield: about 150 pastries, ⅐ oz (4 g) each

Ingredients	U.S.	Metric
Raisins	1.67 oz	40 g
Rum	2 oz	60 g
Cake flour	2.25 oz	65 g
Confectioners' sugar	6.5 oz	185 g
Powdered almonds	2.25 oz	65 g
Egg whites	4.5 oz	125 g
Butter, melted	4.5 oz	125 g
Coffee extract	1 drop	1 drop
Dark rum	3.5 oz	100 g
Honey	3.5 oz	100 g
Apricot Glaze (p. 194) or Clear Glaze (p. 194)	as needed	as needed

PROCEDURE

1. Marinate the raisins and rum as long as possible (minimum 45 minutes).

2. Butter 1-in. (2.5-cm) round, rectangular, or boat-shaped molds.

3. Sift flour, sugar, and almonds into a bowl and make a well.

4. Lightly froth the egg whites with a fork. Pour into the well.

5. Cook the butter until it browns and takes on a nutty aroma. Pour it into the well with the coffee extract.

6. Draw all the ingredients together to form a smooth paste.

7. Place the drained, marinated raisins into the prepared molds.

8. Pipe or spoon the mixture to fill the buttered molds three-quarters full.

9. Bake at 340°F (170°C) until firm. Remove from the molds and cool on a wire rack. Turn all the pastries bottom side up.

10. Heat the rum and honey to scalding point. Spoon the mixture over the baked financiers and brush with apricot glaze or clear glaze.

11. Place into paper petit four cases.

PRALINE CAKE (PRALINETTE)

Yield: 12 individual-serving cakes, about 4 oz (110 g) each

Ingredients	U.S.	Metric
Marjolaine Sponge Cake disks (p. 407), 2¾ in. (7 cm) in diameter	24	24
Light Praline Cream (p. 422)	1 lb 8 oz	680 g
Milk chocolate couverture	1 lb 4 oz–1 lb 12 oz	600–800 g
Cocoa powder	as needed	as needed

PROCEDURE

1. For each cake, place one sponge disk in the bottom of a ring mold 2¾ in. (7 cm) in diameter and 1½ in. (4 cm) in height.

2. Using a pastry bag with a large plain tip, fill the mold with praline cream to within ½ in. (1 cm) of the top.

3. Place another sponge disk on top. Refrigerate to set.

4. Remove the ring mold.

5. Following the procedure described for Feuille d'Automne (p. 459), coat the bottoms of sheet pans with melted milk chocolate (see p. 636), and with a scraper, cut long strips of the chocolate to cover the cakes (a). (*Note:* For more information and further illustration of this procedure, refer to the recipe for Feuille d'Automne.)

6. Handling the chocolate as little and as lightly as possible, wrap it around the pastry (b).

7. Fold the top edge of the chocolate over the top of the pastry (c). Decorate the top with additional narrow strips of chocolate.

8. Sprinkle very lightly with cocoa powder.

A

B

C

SFOGLIATELLE

Yield: 10 large pastries, about 3½ oz (100 g) each, or 20 small pastries, about 1¾ oz (50 g) each

Ingredients	U.S.	Metric	
Dough			
Bread flour	12 oz	375	g
Pastry flour	4 oz	125	g
Salt	1 tsp	5	g
Water	7 oz	215	g
Butter	4 oz	125	g
Lard or shortening	4 oz	125	g
Filling			
Water, cold	8 oz	250	g
Sugar	3 oz	90	g
Semolina	3 oz	90	g
Ricotta cheese	12 oz	375	g
Egg yolks	1⅓ oz (2 yolks)	40	g (2 yolks)
Cinnamon extract	⅛ tsp	0.5 mL	
Candied orange peel, finely diced	3 oz	90	g

PROCEDURE

1. To make the dough, sift the flour and salt into a bowl. Add the water and mix to make a dry dough. Turn out the mixture onto a work surface and knead until the dough holds together.

2. Set the rollers of a pasta machine at their widest opening. Pass the dough through the rollers and fold in half. Repeat until the dough is smooth and elastic. Wrap the dough in plastic and rest for 1–2 hours in the refrigerator.

3. Cut the dough into 4 equal pieces. Pass each piece through the rollers. Then set the rollers closer together, and repeat until you reach the narrowest setting of the rollers. You should have 4 long, paper-thin strips of dough.

4. Melt together the butter and shortening or lard. Cool slightly.

5. Lay one strip of dough out on the workbench and brush heavily with the melted fat. Roll up tightly from one end until only about 1 in. (2.5 cm) of the strip remains. Move the roll back to the other end of the bench and lay the second strip out so the beginning of the first strip butts up against the end of the first strip to make a continuous roll. Again, brush heavily with the fat and continue to roll up. If you are making large pastries, repeat with the third and fourth strips. You should now have a roll of dough about 6 in. (15 cm) long and 2½ in. (6 cm) thick. If you are making small pastries, make a new roll with the third and fourth strips of dough, so you have two rolls about 6 in. (15 cm) long and 1¾ in. (4.5 cm) thick. Refrigerate for several hours. Save the remaining melted fat for step 10.

6. Prepare the filling. Combine the water, sugar, and semolina in a saucepan and mix until smooth. Bring to a boil over moderate heat, stirring constantly, and cook until the mixture is thick. Pass the ricotta through a fine sieve and add it to the pan. Cook for 2 or 3 minutes more. Remove from the heat and add the remaining filling ingredients, beating in well. Place in a bowl, cover tightly with plastic film, and chill. When the mixture is cold, beat until smooth and transfer to a pastry bag with a medium plain tip.

7. Remove the dough rolls from refrigeration and square off the ends with a sharp knife. Carefully slice each dough roll into 10 slices ½ in. (1.25 cm) thick. (*Note:* The pastry can be prepared in advance up to this point and frozen for later use.)

8. For each pastry, place a slice of the dough on the workbench. With a small, light rolling pin, very gently roll the circle of dough from the center outward in all directions just until the layers of dough fan outward toward the edges of the circle. At this point, if it is warm in the bakeshop, chill the rolled-out slices briefly. Remove only a few at a time from refrigeration, because they are easier to work with if the fat between the layers is firm.

9. Pick up a circle of pastry with both hands, with the thumbs underneath and the fingers above the center of the circle. The side that was up when the circle was rolled out should be on top. Carefully shape the circle into a cone by working the thumbs into the center of the circle and moving outward so the layers of dough slide away from each other. The side that was on top during rolling should be the outside of the cone. Hold the cone in one hand and, using the pastry bag, fill it with about 1 oz (30 g) filling for small pastries, 2 oz (60 g) for large pastries.

10. Lay the pastries on their sides on a sheet pan lined with parchment. Brush with the remaining fat.

11. Bake at 400°F (200°C) until golden, 25–30 minutes.

SFOGLIATELLE

This distinctive pastry, which somewhat resembles an oyster shell, is an ancient tradition from Naples. The pastry for sfogliatelle (SFO lee ah TELL eh) is sort of an antique form of puff pastry. In Italian, *sfoglia* is a sheet of pasta dough, and *pasta sfoglia* is puff pastry.

KEY POINTS TO REVIEW

- ▌ Which doughs are used to make tarts and tartlets?
- ▌ What is the procedure for making baked tart shells?
- ▌ What is the procedure for making a fresh fruit tart (unbaked)?
- ▌ What are the following pastries: Gâteau St-Honoré? Millefeuille? Pithiviers? Describe each of them.

TERMS FOR REVIEW

tart	gâteau St-Honoré	millefeuille	sfogliatelle
tarte Tatin	Pithiviers	French pastry	

QUESTIONS FOR REVIEW

1. What is the purpose of docking tart shells before they are baked?

2. List four or five ingredients besides fruit and sugar that are sometimes used for filling *baked* fruit tarts.

3. Describe the procedure for making baked tartlet shells.

4. Describe the procedure for making an unbaked fruit tart.

5. Describe, in as much detail as possible, the procedure for making a gâteau St-Honoré.

6. Read the procedures for special cakes in Chapter 18. Which do you think might be appropriate for making up as French pastries? Select one and describe how you would modify the procedure to make French pastries.

16

CAKE MIXING AND BAKING

AFTER READING THIS CHAPTER, YOU SHOULD BE ABLE TO:

1. Explain the three main goals of mixing cake batters.

2. Mix high-fat or shortened cakes.

3. Mix egg-foam cakes.

4. Explain ingredient functions and the concepts behind formula balance.

5. Scale, pan, and bake cakes correctly.

6. Explain how to judge the quality of baked cakes and correct cake defects in them.

7. Adjust formulas for baking at high altitudes.

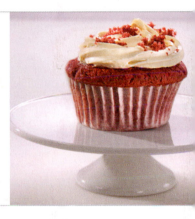

CAKES ARE THE richest and sweetest of all the baked products we have studied so far. From the baker's point of view, producing cakes requires as much precision as producing breads, but for the completely opposite reason. Breads are lean products that require strong gluten development and careful control of yeast action during the long fermentation and proofing periods. Cakes, on the other hand, are high in both fat and sugar. The baker's job is to create a structure that supports these ingredients and yet keeps it as light and delicate as possible.

Cakes owe their popularity not only to their richness and sweetness but also to their versatility. They can be presented in many forms, from simple sheet cakes in cafeterias to elaborately decorated works of art for weddings and other important occasions. With only a few basic formulas and a variety of icings and fillings, the chef or baker can construct the perfect dessert for any occasion or purpose.

The formulas at the end of the chapter will give you practice with all major cake-mixing methods. Many popular North American cake types are included, sometimes in the form of variations on the basic cake types. These variations show that by making small changes in flavoring ingredients, you can make many different cakes from the same basic recipe. Adding new flavorings sometimes requires other ingredient changes. For example, in the case of the Strawberry Cake (p. 398), the flavoring ingredient is high in sugar, so the amount of sugar in the formula is reduced.

In this chapter, we focus on the procedures for mixing and baking the basic types of cakes. In Chapter 17, we discuss how to assemble and decorate many kinds of cake desserts.

PRINCIPLES OF CAKE MIXING

THE SELECTION OF high-quality ingredients is, of course, necessary to produce a high-quality cake. However, good ingredients alone do not guarantee a fine cake. A thorough understanding of mixing procedures is essential. Slight errors in mixing can result in cakes with poor texture and volume.

The mixing methods presented in this chapter are the basic ones used for most types of cakes prepared in the modern bakeshop. Each of these methods is used for particular types of formulas, as listed here:

- High-fat or shortened cakes
    - Creaming method
    - Two-stage method
    - One-stage (liquid shortening) method
    - Flour-batter method
- Egg-foam cakes
    - Sponge method
    - Angel food method
    - Chiffon method
    - Combination creaming/sponge method

We discuss these methods and their variations in detail beginning on page 380. You should learn these methods well. They are not repeated for each of the formulas later in this chapter, but page references in the formulas enable you to review the appropriate method as necessary before beginning production.

The three main goals of mixing cake batters are:

- To combine all ingredients into a smooth, uniform batter.
- To form and incorporate air cells in the batter.
- To develop the proper texture in the finished product.

These three goals are closely related. They may seem fairly obvious, especially the first one. But understanding each of the goals in detail will help you avoid many errors in mixing. For example, inexperienced bakers often grow impatient and turn the mixer to high speed when creaming fat and sugar, thinking high speed will do the same job faster. But air cells do not form as well at high speed, so the texture of the cake suffers.

Let's examine these three goals one at a time.

Combining Ingredients into a Homogeneous Mixture

Two of the major ingredients in cakes—fat and water (including the water in milk and eggs)—are, by nature, unmixable. Therefore, careful attention to mixing procedures is important to reach this goal.

As you recall from Chapter 4 (p. 67), a uniform mixture of two unmixable substances is called an *emulsion*. Part of the purpose of mixing is to form such an emulsion. Properly mixed cake batters contain a water-in-fat emulsion; that is, the water is held in tiny droplets surrounded by fat and other ingredients. Curdling occurs when the fat can no longer hold the water in emulsion. The mixture then changes to a fat-in-water mixture, with small particles of fat surrounded by water and other ingredients.

The following factors can cause curdling:

1. **Using the wrong type of fat.** Different fats have different emulsifying abilities. High-ratio shortening contains emulsifiers that enable it to hold a large amount of water without curdling. You should not substitute regular shortening or butter in a formula that calls specifically for high-ratio, or emulsified, shortening.

    Butter has a desirable flavor but relatively poor emulsifying ability. Butter is, of course, used in many cake batters, but the formula should be specifically balanced so it contains no more liquid than the batter can hold. Also, remember that butter contains some water.

    Egg yolks, as you will recall, contain a natural emulsifier. When whole eggs or yolks are properly mixed into a batter, they help the batter hold the other liquids.

2. **Having the ingredients too cold.** Emulsions are best formed when the temperature of the ingredients is about 70°F (21°C).

3. **Mixing the first stage of the procedure too quickly.** If you do not cream the fat and sugar properly, for example, you will not form a good cell structure to hold the water (see "Forming Air Cells," below).

4. **Adding the liquids too quickly.** In most cases the liquids, including the eggs, must be added in stages—that is, a little at a time. If they are added too quickly, they cannot be absorbed properly.

    In batters made by the creaming method (p. 377), the liquid is often added alternately with the flour. The flour helps the batter absorb the liquid.

5. **Adding too much liquid.** This is not a problem if the formula is a good one. However, if you are using a formula that is not properly balanced, it might call for more liquid than the fat can hold in emulsion.

Forming Air Cells

Air cells in cake batters are important for texture and leavening. A fine, smooth texture is the result of small, uniform air cells. Large or irregular air cells result in a coarse texture. And recall that air trapped in a mix helps leaven a cake when the heat of the oven causes the air to expand (p. 94). When no chemical leavener is used, this trapped air, in addition to steam, provides nearly all the leavening. Even when baking powder or soda is used, the air cells provide places to hold the gases released by the chemical leavener.

Correct ingredient temperature and mixing speed are necessary for good air cell formation. Cold fat (below 60°F/16°C) is too hard to form good air cells, and fat that is too warm (above 75°F/24°C) is too soft. Mixing speed should be moderate (medium speed). If mixing is done on high speed, friction warms the ingredients too much. Not as many air cells are formed, and those that do form tend to be coarse and irregular.

Granulated sugar is the proper sugar for creaming-method cakes. Confectioners' sugar is too fine to produce good air cells.

In the case of egg-foam cakes (sponge, angel food, chiffon), the air cells are formed by whipping eggs and sugar. For the best foaming, the egg and sugar mixture should be slightly warm (about 100°F/38°C). Whipping may be done at high speed at first, but the final stages of whipping should be at medium speed in order to retain air cells.

Developing Texture

Both the uniform mixing of ingredients and the formation of air cells are important to a cake's texture, as we discussed in the preceding sections. Another factor of mixing that affects texture is gluten development. For the most part, we want very little gluten development in cakes, so we use cake flour, which is low in gluten. Some sponge cake formulas call for cornstarch to replace part of the flour, so there is even less gluten (the high percentage of eggs in sponge cakes provides much of the structure). In contrast, some pound cake and fruit cake formulas need more gluten than other cakes for extra structure and to support the weight of the fruit. Thus, you will sometimes see such cake formulas calling for part cake flour and part bread flour.

Recall from Chapter 5 that the amount of mixing affects gluten development. In the creaming method, the sponge method, and the angel food method, the flour is added at or near the end of the mixing procedure so there is very little gluten development in properly mixed batters. If the batter is mixed too long after the flour is added, or if it becomes too warm during mixing, the cakes are likely to be tough.

In the two-stage method, the flour is added in the first step. However, it is mixed with high-ratio shortening, which spreads well and coats the particles of flour with fat. This coating action limits gluten development. It is important to mix the flour and fat thoroughly for the best results. Observe all mixing times closely. Also, keep in mind that high-ratio cakes contain a high percentage of sugar, which is also a tenderizer.

MIXING HIGH-FAT OR SHORTENED CAKES

Creaming Method

The *creaming method*, also called the *conventional method*, was for a long time the standard method for mixing **high-fat cakes**. The development of emulsified, or high-ratio, shortenings led to the development of simpler mixing methods for shortened cakes containing greater amounts of sugar and liquid. The creaming method is still used for many types of butter cakes, however.

The fat specified in creaming-method formulas in this book is butter. Butter cakes are highly prized for their flavor; shortening adds no flavor to cakes. Butter also influences texture because it melts in the mouth, whereas shortening does not.

Nevertheless, many bakers may prefer to substitute shortening for all or part of the butter in these formulas. Shortening has the advantages of being less expensive and easier to mix. In creaming recipes, use regular shortening, not emulsified shortening. Regular shortening has better creaming abilities.

It is usually a good idea *not* to substitute an equal weight of shortening for butter. Remember that butter is only 80% fat, so you will need less shortening. Also, butter contains about 15% water, so you should adjust the quantity of milk or water. The Procedure for Substituting Butter and Shortening in Creaming-Method Batters (p. 378) explains how to adjust formulas for these substitutions.

Two-Stage Method

The *two-stage method* was developed for use with high-ratio plastic shortenings. High-ratio cakes contain a large percentage of sugar, more than 100% based on the weight of the flour. Also, they are made with more liquid than creaming-method cakes, and the batter pours more freely. The two-stage mixing method is a little simpler than the creaming method, and it produces a smooth batter that bakes up into a fine-grained, moist cake. It gets its name because the liquids are added in two stages.

The first step in making high-ratio cakes is to blend the flour and other dry ingredients with shortening. When this mixture is smooth, the liquids (including eggs) are added in stages. Throughout this procedure, it is important to follow two rules:

- Mix at low speed and observe correct mixing times. This is important to develop proper texture.
- Stop the machine and scrape down the sides of the bowl frequently during mixing. This is important to develop a smooth, well-mixed batter.

Note the variation following the basic procedure. Many bakers prefer this variation. It is somewhat simpler because it combines steps 2 and 3.

The two-stage method can sometimes be adapted to butter cakes, especially those high in fat. As an experiment, try making a butter cake formula with the creaming method and the two-stage method and comparing the texture of the finished cakes.

PROCEDURE: Creaming Method

1. Scale ingredients accurately. Have all ingredients at room temperature (70°F/21°C).

2. Place the butter or shortening in the mixing bowl. With the paddle attachment, beat the fat slowly, until it is smooth and creamy.

3. Add the sugar; cream the mixture at moderate speed until the mixture is light and fluffy (a). This will take about 8 to 10 minutes.

   Some bakers prefer to add the salt and flavorings with the sugar to ensure uniform distribution.

   If melted chocolate is used, it may be added during creaming.

4. Add the eggs a little at a time (b). After each addition, beat until the eggs are absorbed before adding more. After the eggs are beaten in, mix until light and fluffy. This step will take about 5 minutes.

5. Scrape down the sides of the bowl to ensure even mixing.

6. Add the sifted dry ingredients (including the spices, if they were not added in step 3), alternating with the liquids. This is done as follows:

   Add one-fourth of the dry ingredients (c). Mix just until blended in.

   Add one-third of the liquid (d). Mix just until blended in.

   Repeat until all ingredients are used. Scrape down the sides of the bowl occasionally for even mixing.

   The reason for adding dry and liquid ingredients alternately is that the batter may not absorb all the liquid unless some of the flour is present.

Variation

A few creaming-method cakes require an extra step: egg whites whipped to a foam with sugar are folded into the batter to provide additional leavening.

PROCEDURE: Substituting Butter and Shortening in Creaming-Method Batters

To substitute regular shortening for all or part of the butter:

1. Multiply the weight of the butter to be eliminated by 0.8. This gives the weight of regular shortening to use.

2. Multiply the weight of the eliminated butter by 0.15. This gives the weight of additional water or milk needed.

   Example: A formula calls for 3 lb butter and 3 lb milk. Adjust it so you use 1 lb (16 oz) butter. How much shortening and milk will you need?

   Weight of butter
   to be eliminated = 2 lb
                    = 32 oz
   0.8×32 oz = 26 oz shortening
                    (rounded off)
   0.15×32 oz = 5 oz extra milk
                    (rounded off)
   Total milk = 3 lb 5 oz

To substitute butter for all or part of the regular shortening:

1. Multiply the weight of the shortening to be eliminated by 1.25. This gives the weight of the butter to use.

2. Multiply the weight of the butter by 0.15. This gives the weight of water or milk to be subtracted from the formula.

   Example: A formula calls for 3 lb regular shortening and 3 lb milk. Adjust it so you use 1 lb (16 oz) shortening. How much butter and milk will you need?

   Weight of shortening
   to be eliminated = 2 lb
                    = 32 oz
   1.25×32 oz = 40 oz butter
   0.15×40 oz = 6 oz milk to be subtracted
                       from the formula
   Total milk = 2 lb 10 oz

PROCEDURE: Two-Stage Method

1. Scale the ingredients accurately. Have all ingredients at room temperature.

2. Sift the flour, baking powder, soda, and salt into the mixing bowl and add the shortening. With the paddle attachment, mix at low speed for 2 minutes. Stop the machine, scrape down the bowl and beater, and mix again for 2 minutes.

   If melted chocolate is used, blend it in during this step.

   If cocoa is used, sift it with the flour in this step or with the sugar in step 3.

3. Sift the remaining dry ingredients into the bowl and add part of the water or milk. Blend at low speed for 3 to 5 minutes. Stop the machine and scrape down the sides of the bowl and the beater several times to ensure even mixing.

4. Combine the remaining liquids and lightly beaten eggs. With the mixer running, add this mixture to the batter in 3 parts. After each part, turn off the machine and scrape down the bowl. Continue mixing for a total of 5 minutes in this stage.

   The finished batter is normally pourable.

Variation

This variation combines steps 2 and 3 above into one step.

1. Scale the ingredients as in the basic method.

2. Sift all dry ingredients into the mixing bowl. Add the shortening and part of the liquid. Mix on low speed for 7 to 8 minutes. Scrape down the sides of the bowl and the beater several times.

3. Continue with step 4 in the basic procedure.

One-Stage (Liquid Shortening) Method

High-ratio liquid shortening, described on page 68, is so effective at emulsifying and at spreading through the batter to tenderize gluten that cake batters made from it can generally be mixed all in one step—thus called the *one-stage method*. Adding the liquid ingredients to the bowl first simplifies the procedure because there is less chance for moistened flour to coat the bottom and sides of the bowl, making scraping down difficult. Mix at low speed until the dry ingredients are moistened, to prevent dry flour from being thrown from the bowl. Then mix for a period at high speed, followed by a period at medium speed, to properly develop air cells and create a smooth, fine-textured batter.

PROCEDURE: One-Stage (Liquid Shortening) Method

1. Scale all ingredients accurately. Have all ingredients at room temperature.

2. Combine all liquid ingredients, including high-ratio liquid shortening, in the mixing bowl (a).

3. Sift the dry ingredients together on top of the liquid ingredients in the bowl (b).

4. With the paddle attachment, mix at low speed for 30 seconds (c), until the dry ingredients are moistened. (The purpose of mixing slowly until the dry ingredients are moistened is to keep them from being thrown out of the bowl.)

5. Mix at high speed for 4 minutes. Stop the machine and scrape down the bowl and beater.

6. Mix at medium speed for 3 minutes (d).

Flour-Batter Method

The *flour-batter method* is used for only a few specialty items. It produces a fine-textured cake, but there may be some toughening due to the development of gluten.

Flour-batter cakes include those made with either emulsified shortening or butter or both. There are no formulas in this book requiring this mixing method, although the batter for Old-Fashioned Pound Cake (p. 394) can be mixed this way instead of by the creaming method.

PROCEDURE: Flour-Batter Method

1. Scale all ingredients accurately. Have all ingredients at room temperature.

2. Sift the flour and other dry ingredients except the sugar into the mixing bowl. Add the fat. Blend together until smooth and light.

3. Whip the sugar and eggs together until thick and light. Add liquid flavoring ingredients, such as vanilla.

4. Combine the flour-fat mixture and the sugar-egg mixture and mix until smooth.

5. Gradually add water or milk (if any) and mix smooth.

KEY POINTS TO REVIEW

▌ What are the steps in the creaming method?

▌ What are the steps in the two-stage method?

▌ What are the steps in the one-stage method?

MIXING EGG-FOAM CAKES

Most *egg-foam cakes* contain little or no shortening and depend on the air trapped in beaten eggs for most or all of their leavening. Growing interest in fine pastries and cakes has led to new appreciation of the versatility of sponge cakes. Therefore, this chapter includes formulas for a great variety of egg-foam batters. These cakes are used in many of the special desserts assembled in Chapter 17.

Egg-foam cakes have a springy texture and are tougher than shortened cakes. This makes them valuable for many kinds of desserts that require much handling to assemble. Most European cakes and tortes are made with sponge or egg-foam cakes. These cakes are baked either in thin sheets or disks or in thick layers that are then sliced horizontally into thinner layers. The thin sponge layers are then stacked with a variety of fillings, creams, mousses, fruits, and icings. In addition, sponge layers in this kind of cake are usually moistened with a flavored sugar syrup, to compensate for their lack of moisture.

Sponge sheets for jelly rolls and other rolled cakes are often made without any shortening so they do not crack when rolled. Because fat weakens gluten, sponge cakes containing fat may split more easily.

Flour for egg-foam cakes must be weak in order to avoid making the cake tougher than necessary. Cornstarch is sometimes added to cake flour for these cakes to weaken the flour further.

Note that at the beginning of this section we said that *most* egg-foam cakes contain little or even no fat. This is true of the most typical cakes in this section: genoise and other sponge cakes, which have little fat, and angel food cakes, which have none. As a result, egg-foam cakes are often called *low-fat cakes*, to distinguish them from the high-fat cakes discussed in the previous section. However, a few formulas are an exception. For example, the Joconde Sponge Cake on p. 405 contains 120% butter, while the Chocolate Fudge Cake on p. 405 contains 400% butter in addition to the fat content of the chocolate. Nevertheless, their mixing method is based on incorporating an egg-and-sugar foam into the other batter ingredients, just as for the other cakes in this section.

Sponge Methods

The many types of *sponge method* cakes have one characteristic in common: they are made with an egg foam that contains yolks. These are usually whole-egg foams but, in some cases, the base foam is a yolk foam, and an egg white foam is folded in at the end of the procedure.

In its simplest form, sponge cake batter is made in two basic steps: (1) eggs and sugar are whipped to a thick foam, and (2) sifted flour is folded in. Additional ingredients, such as butter or liquid, complicate the procedure slightly. It would be too confusing to try to include all the variations in one procedure, so instead we describe four separate procedures.

Please note the difference between the main procedure and the first variation. There may be some confusion because in North American bakeshops, *genoise* nearly always contains butter. Nevertheless, in classical pâtisserie, genoise is often made without butter, and it is still commonly made in European bakeshops with only eggs, sugar, and flour. Furthermore, the main procedure as

PROCEDURE: Plain Sponge or Genoise Method

1. Scale all ingredients accurately.

2. Combine the eggs, sugar, and salt in a stainless steel bowl. Immediately set the bowl over a hot-water bath and stir or beat with a whip until the mixture warms to a temperature of about 110°F (43°C) (a). The reason for this step is that the foam attains greater volume if warm.

3. With a wire whip or the whip attachment of a mixer, beat the eggs at high speed until they are very light and thick and about three times their original volume (b). Toward the end of the mixing period, it is helpful to turn the mixer speed to medium, in order to preserve a more uniform cell structure. Total mixing time may be as long as 10 to 15 minutes if the quantity is large.

4. If any liquid (water, milk, liquid flavoring) is included, add it now. Either whip it in, in a steady stream, or stir it in, as indicated in the recipe.

5. Fold in the sifted flour in 3 or 4 stages, being careful not to deflate the foam. Many bakers do this by hand, even for large batches. Fold gently until all the flour is blended in (c). If any other dry ingredients are used, such as cornstarch or baking powder, sift them first with the flour.

6. Immediately pan and bake the batter. Delays will cause loss of volume.

Variation: Butter Sponge or Butter Genoise

1. Follow the plain sponge procedure through step 5.

2. Carefully fold in the melted butter after the flour has been added. Fold in the butter completely, but be careful not to overmix, or the cake will be tough (d).

3. Immediately pan and bake.

Variation: Hot Milk and Butter Sponge

1. Scale all ingredients accurately. Heat the milk and butter together until the butter is melted.

2. Whip the eggs into a foam, as in the plain sponge method, steps 2 and 3.

3. Fold in the sifted dry ingredients (flour, leavening, cocoa, etc.), as in the basic procedure.

4. Carefully fold in the hot butter and milk in 3 stages. Fold in completely, but do not overmix.

5. Immediately pan and bake.

Variation: Separated-Egg Sponge

1. Follow the basic plain sponge method, steps 1–4, but use yolks for the basic foam (steps 2 and 3). Reserve the egg whites and part of the sugar for a separate step.

2. Whip the egg whites and sugar to firm, moist peaks. Fold into the batter alternately with the sifted dry ingredients. Fold in completely, but do not overmix.

3. Immediately pan and bake.

given here explains sponge cakes in their simplest and most basic form, and this procedure is the foundation for the variations that follow. If you work in a bakeshop in Canada or the United States, however, you can expect to use the first variation instead of the main procedure to mix basic genoise.

Angel Food Method

Angel food cakes are based on egg-white foams and contain no fat. (For success in beating egg whites, review the principles of egg white foams in Chapter 12, p. 258.) Egg whites for the *angel food method* should be whipped until they form soft, not stiff, peaks. Overwhipped whites lose their capability to expand and to leaven the cake. This is because the protein network in stiffly beaten whites has already stretched as far as it can. If the whites are whipped to soft peaks instead, they can stretch more during baking, allowing the cake to rise.

PROCEDURE: Angel Food Method

1. Scale ingredients accurately. Have all ingredients at room temperature. The egg whites may be slightly warmed in order to achieve better volume.

2. Sift the flour with half the sugar. This step helps the flour mix more evenly with the foam.

3. Using the whip attachment, beat the egg whites until they form soft peaks. Add salt and cream of tartar near the beginning of the beating process (a).

4. Gradually beat in the portion of the sugar that was not mixed with the flour (b). Continue to whip until the egg whites form soft, moist peaks (c). Do not beat until stiff. Beat in the flavorings.

5. Fold in the flour-sugar mixture just until it is thoroughly absorbed, but no longer (d).

6. Deposit the mix in ungreased pans (e) and bake immediately.

Chiffon Method

Chiffon cakes and angel food cakes are both based on egg-white foams, but here the similarities in the mixing methods end. In angel food cakes, a dry flour-sugar mixture is folded into the egg whites. In the *chiffon method*, a batter containing flour, egg yolks, vegetable oil, and water is folded into the whites. The oil content of some chiffon cakes makes their fat content as high as that of some two-stage cakes. However, their mixing method is based on egg foams, just as for sponge cakes.

Egg whites for chiffon cakes should be whipped until they are a little firmer than those for angel food cakes, but not so much that they become dry. Chiffon cakes contain baking powder, so they do not depend on the egg foam for all their leavening.

PROCEDURE: Chiffon Method

1. Scale all ingredients accurately. Have all ingredients at room temperature. Use a good-quality, flavorless vegetable oil.

2. Sift the dry ingredients, including part of the sugar, into the mixing bowl.

3. Mixing with the paddle attachment at second speed, gradually add the oil (a), then the egg yolks (b), water (c), and liquid flavorings, all in a slow, steady stream. While adding the liquids, stop the machine several times to scrape down the bowl and the beater. Mix until smooth, but do not overmix.

4. Whip the egg whites until they form soft peaks. Add the cream of tartar and sugar in a stream and whip to firm, moist peaks.

5. Fold the whipped egg whites into the flour-liquid mixture (d).

6. Immediately deposit the batter in ungreased center-tube pans (like angel food cake pans) or in layer pans with only the bottoms greased and dusted, not the sides (like sponge layers).

Combination Creaming/Sponge Method

Some European-style cakes are begun by using the creaming method. In other words, butter is creamed with sugar until the mixture is light. These cakes usually contain no chemical leavening, however. Instead, whipped egg whites are folded into the batter, as for some sponge cakes. Examples of this kind of cake are Hazelnut Sponge Cake (p. 408) and Baumkuchen (p. 409). Mixing hazelnut sponge is illustrated in the Combination Creaming/Sponge Method procedure below.

PROCEDURE: Combination Creaming/Sponge Method

1. Cream the butter and sugar.

2. Add the egg yolks a little at a time.

3. Mix well after each addition.

4. Whip the egg whites and sugar until they form soft peaks, as for angel food cake.

5. Fold the meringue into the butter mixture.

6. Sift the dry ingredients together.

7. Fold in the sifted dry ingredients.

8. Deposit the batter in prepared pans.

9. Level the top of the batter with a plastic scraper.

Prepared Mixes

Many mixes are available that contain all ingredients except water and, sometimes, eggs. These products also contain emulsifiers to ensure an even blending of ingredients. To use them, follow the package instructions exactly.

Most mixes produce cakes with excellent volume, texture, and tenderness. Whether or not they also taste good is a matter of opinion. On the other hand, cakes made from scratch are not necessarily better. They are better only if they are carefully mixed and baked, are prepared from good, tested formulas, and incorporate high-quality ingredients.

> **KEY POINTS TO REVIEW**
>
> ■ What are the steps in the plain sponge method?
>
> ■ What are the steps in the angel food method?
>
> ■ What are the steps in the chiffon method?
>
> ■ What are the steps in the combination creaming/sponge method?

CAKE FORMULA BALANCE

IT IS POSSIBLE to change cake formulas, either to improve them or to reduce costs. However, ingredients and quantities can be changed only within certain limits. A cake formula whose ingredients fall within these limits is said to be "in balance." Knowing the limits helps you not only modify recipes but also judge untested recipes and correct faults.

Keep in mind that new ingredients and procedures are frequently developed. Cake-balancing rules that have worked well until now may be adapted as new developments come along that allow you to break the rules. A baker should be open to new ideas and willing to try them. For example, it was once a rule that the weight of sugar in a mix should not exceed the weight of flour. But the introduction of shortenings with emulsifiers and the development of the two-stage method led to formulas allowing higher proportions of sugar.

Ingredient Functions

For the purpose of balancing cake formulas, we can classify cake ingredients according to four functions: tougheners (or stabilizers), tenderizers, dryers, and moisteners (or moisturizers). The idea of formula balancing is that tougheners should balance tenderizers and dryers should balance moisteners. If, for example, we increase the amount of tougheners in a formula, we must compensate by also increasing the amount of tenderizers.

Many ingredients fill more than one function, sometimes even opposite functions. Egg yolks contain protein, which is a toughener, but they also contain fat, which is a tenderizer. The major cake ingredients act as follows:

Tougheners provide structure: flour, eggs (whites and yolks).

Tenderizers provide softness or shortening of protein fibers: sugar, fats (including butter, shortening, and cocoa butter), chemical leaveners.

Moisteners provide moisture or water: water, liquid milk, syrups and liquid sugars, eggs.

Dryers absorb moisture: flours and starches, cocoa, milk solids.

You can also use this list of ingredients as a troubleshooting guide for cake failures. A cake that fails even if mixed and baked correctly may require formula balancing. For example, if a cake is too dry, you might increase one or more of the moisteners or decrease the dryers. Doing so, however, takes a certain amount of experience. Remember that most ingredients have more than one function. If you decide to increase the eggs in a dry cake, you may wind up with an even harder, tougher cake. Although whole eggs do provide some moisture, they add even more toughening power because of their strong protein content.

As a further complication, many successful cake formulas apparently break the rules. For example, one rule for creaming-method cakes made with butter or regular shortening says the weight of the sugar should not exceed the weight of the flour. In practice, however, there are successful creaming method recipes calling for more than 100% sugar. Many baking manuals insist on these balancing rules rather strongly. But it may be better to think of them not as ironclad laws but as guidelines that give you a starting point for judging or correcting recipes.

In summary, it takes an experienced baker to be consistently successful at adjusting cake formulas. However, even as a novice baker you should have some knowledge of formula balancing. It helps you understand the formulas you are using and practicing, and it helps you understand why you assemble and mix cakes in certain ways and what makes the mixtures work.

In the following discussion of balancing rules, it is helpful to think of ingredients in terms of baker's percentages (see p. 23) rather than as specific weights. This eliminates one variable: Flour is a constant 100%, so other ingredients are increased or decreased with respect to flour.

Balancing Fat-Type or Shortened Cakes

A normal starting point in discussing cake balancing is old-fashioned *pound cake*. This cake is made of flour, sugar, butter, and eggs in equal parts. As bakers experimented with this basic recipe over the years, they reduced the quantities of sugar, fat, and eggs, and compensated by adding milk. This is the origin of the modern butter cake.

The general rules for balancing creaming-method cakes made with butter or regular shortening are as follows (all ingredient quantities are, of course, by weight):

- The sugar (a tenderizer) is balanced against the flour (a toughener). In most creaming-method cakes, the weight of sugar is less than or equal to the weight of flour.
- The fat (a tenderizer) is balanced against the eggs (tougheners).
- The eggs and liquids (moisteners) are balanced against the flour (a dryer).

Balancing one ingredient against another, as indicated in the preceding guidelines, means that if one ingredient is increased or decreased, then the balancing ingredients must also be adjusted. For example, if the fat is increased, then the eggs must be increased to keep the formula in balance.

With the development of emulsified shortening, it became possible to increase the quantities of sugar, eggs, and liquids. For example, the weight of sugar in high-ratio cakes is greater than the weight of flour, yet the formula is still in balance. Similarly, the quantity of liquid may be greater because the emulsifiers in the shortening keep the batter stable. Nevertheless, the general principles of balancing, as outlined above, still hold. If one ingredient is increased, other ingredients must be adjusted to compensate.

A common practice in balancing a formula is to decide on the sugar/flour ratio and then balance the rest of the ingredients against these. The following guidelines are helpful in this regard:

- If eggs are increased, increase the shortening.
- If extra milk solids are added as an enrichment, add an equal weight of water.
- If cocoa is added, add water equal in weight to 75 to 100% of the cocoa.
- If cocoa or bitter chocolate is added, increase the amount of sugar to as much as 180% of the weight of the flour in high-ratio cakes, and to over 100% of the weight of the flour in creaming-method cakes. This is to account for the starch content of the cocoa and chocolate.
- In cakes to be baked in very large units, use less liquid because less water will evaporate during baking.
- If a liquid sugar is added (honey, corn syrup, etc.), reduce other liquids slightly.
- If large quantities of moist ingredients, such as applesauce or mashed bananas, are added, reduce the liquid. Extra-large additions of moist ingredients may also require increasing the flour and eggs.
- Use less baking powder with creamed batters than two-stage batters because the creamed batters get more aeration in the creaming stage.

SCALING, PANNING, AND BAKING

Pan Preparation

Prepare pans before mixing cake batters so cakes can be baked without delay as soon as they are mixed.

- For high-fat cakes, layer pans must be greased, preferably with a commercial pan-greasing preparation. If this is not available, dust the greased pans with flour and tap out the excess.
- For sheet cakes, line the pans with greased parchment. For thin layers, such as for Swiss rolls, it is necessary to use level pans without dents or warps. Silicone mats are especially good to use for lining pans for thin layers.

- For angel food cakes and chiffon cakes, do not grease the pan. The batter must be able to cling to the sides so it doesn't sink back into the pan after rising.
- For sponge cake layers with little or no fat, grease the bottoms but not the sides of the pans.

Scaling

For consistency, cake batters should be scaled into prepared pans by weight, as explained in the Procedure for Scaling Cake Batters. This is the most accurate method for all types of cake batters. However, some chefs prefer alternative methods for certain batters because they believe those methods are faster.

Because two-stage and one-stage batters are pourable, some bakers prefer to scale them by volume, as described in the Alternative Procedure for Scaling Two-Stage and One-Stage Batters. This method is quick and also fairly accurate.

Foam batters should be handled as little as possible and baked immediately to avoid deflating the beaten eggs. While these cake batters may be scaled by weight as in the basic procedure, some bakers prefer to eyeball them in order to minimize handling, as described in the Alternative Procedure for Scaling Egg-Foam Cakes.

Creaming method batters are thick, and so do not pour easily. Thus, they should always be weighed, as in the first procedure.

KEY POINTS TO REVIEW

- Which cake ingredients are tenderizers? Tougheners? Moisteners? Dryers?
- In the concept of cake formula balance, what does it mean to balance one ingredient against another?
- How should cake pans be prepared before batter is deposited in them?
- What is the basic procedure for scaling cake batters?

PROCEDURE: Scaling Cake Batters

Method 1: Using a Balance Scale

1. Place a prepared cake pan on the left side of the balance scale. Balance the scale by placing another pan on the right side.
2. Set the scale to the desired weight.
3. Add batter to the left pan until the scale balances.
4. Remove the pan from the scale and spread the batter smooth with a spatula.
5. Repeat with remaining pans.
6. Give the pans several sharp raps on the bench to free large trapped air bubbles. Bake immediately.

Method 2: Using a Digital Scale

1. Place a prepared cake pan on the scale.
2. Press the tare button to reset the scale to zero or, if the scale is off, turn it on. Verify that the weight reads zero.
3. Add batter to the pan until the digital readout indicates the desired weight of batter.
4. Repeat steps 1–3 with the remaining pans.
5. Give the pans several sharp raps on the bench to free large trapped air bubbles. Bake immediately.

ALTERNATIVE PROCEDURE FOR SCALING TWO-STAGE AND ONE-STAGE BATTERS

1. Place an empty volume measure on the left side of the balance scale. Balance the scale to zero.
2. Set the scale to the desired weight.
3. Pour batter into the measure until the scale balances.
4. Note the volume of batter in the measure.
5. Pour the batter into the prepared pan, quickly scraping out the measure to get all the batter.
6. Scale the remaining cakes with the volume measure, using the volume noted in step 4.
7. Give the pans several sharp raps on the bench to free large trapped air bubbles. Bake immediately.

ALTERNATIVE PROCEDURE FOR SCALING EGG-FOAM CAKES

1. Have all prepared pans lined up on the bench.
2. Scale the first pan as for creamed batters.
3. Quickly fill the remaining pans to the same level as the first pan, judging the level by eye.
4. Spread the batter smooth. Bake immediately.

See the Average Cake Scaling Weights, Baking Temperatures, and Times table (p. 388).

AVERAGE CAKE SCALING WEIGHTS, BAKING TEMPERATURES, AND TIMES

Pan Type and Size	Scaling Weight*		Baking Temperature		Approximate Baking Time in Minutes
	U.S.	Metric	U.S.	Metric	
HIGH-FAT CAKES AND CHIFFON CAKES					
Round layers					
6 in. (15 cm)	8–10 oz	230–285 g	375°F	190°C	18
8 in. (20 cm)	14–18 oz	400–510 g	375°F	190°C	25
10 in. (25 cm)	24–28 oz	680–800 g	360°F	180°C	35
12 in. (30 cm)	32–40 oz	900–1100 g	360°F	180°C	35
Sheets and square pans					
18 × 26 in. (46 × 66 cm)	7–8 lb	3.2–3.6 kg	360°F	180°C	35
18 × 13 in. (46 × 33 cm)	3.5–4 lb	1.6–1.8 kg	360°F	180°C	35
9 × 9 in. (23 × 23 cm)	24 oz	680 g	360°F	180°C	30–35
Loaf (pound cake)					
2¼ × 3½ × 8 in. (6 × 9 × 20 cm)	16–18 oz	450–500 g	350°F	175°C	50–60
2¾ × 4½ × 8½ in. (7 × 11 × 22 cm)	24–27 oz	680–765 g	350°F	175°C	55–65
Cupcakes					
per dozen	18 oz	510 g	385°F	195°C	18–20
FOAM-TYPE CAKES					
Round layers					
6 in. (15 cm)	5–6 oz	140–170 g	375°F	190°C	20
8 in. (20 cm)	10 oz	280 g	375°F	190°C	20
10 in. (25 cm)	16 oz	450 g	360°F	180°C	25–30
12 in. (30 cm)	24 oz	700 g	360°F	180°C	25–30
Sheets (for jelly roll or sponge roll)					
18 × 26 in., ½ in. thick (46 × 66 cm, 12 mm thick)	2.5 lb	1.2 kg	375°F	190°C	15–20
18 × 26 in., ¼ in. thick (46 × 66 cm, 6 mm thick)	28 oz	800 g	400°F	200°C	7–10
Tube (angel food and chiffon)					
8 in. (20 cm)	14–18 oz	400–460 g	360°F	180°C	30
10 in. (25 cm)	24–32 oz	700–900 g	350°F	175°C	50
Cupcakes					
per dozen	10 oz	280 g	375°F	190°C	18–20

*The weights given are averages. Weights may be increased by 25% if thicker layers are desired. Baking times may need to be increased slightly.

Baking and Cooling

Cake structure is fragile, so proper baking conditions are essential to produce high-quality products. Follow these guidelines to help you avoid cake failures.

- Preheat the ovens. To conserve expensive energy, don't preheat longer than necessary.

- Make sure ovens and shelves are level.

- Do not let pans touch each other. If pans touch, air circulation is inhibited and the cakes rise unevenly.

- Bake at the correct temperature:

  Too hot an oven causes the cake to set unevenly with a humped center, or to set before it has fully risen. Crusts will be too dark.

  Too slow an oven causes poor volume and texture because the cake doesn't set fast enough and may fall.

- If steam is available in the oven, use it for creamed, two-stage, and one-stage batters. These cakes bake with a flatter top if baked with steam because the steam delays the formation of the top crust. Do not use steam with sponge and angel food cakes.

- Do not open the oven or disturb cakes until they have finished rising and are partially browned. Disturbing the cakes before they are set may cause them to fall.

Tests for Doneness

- Shortened cakes shrink away slightly from sides of pan.

- Cake is springy. The center of the top of the cake springs back when pressed lightly.

- A cake tester or wooden pick inserted in center of cake comes out clean.

Cooling and Removing from Pans

- Cool layer cakes and sheet cakes 15 minutes in pans and turn out while slightly warm. Because they are fragile, they may break if turned out when hot.

- Turn out layer cakes onto racks to finish cooling.

- To turn out sheet cakes:

  1. Sprinkle the top lightly with granulated sugar.

  2. Set a cake board on top of the cake, and then set an empty sheet pan on top, bottom side down. (If a cake board is not available, just set the upside-down sheet pan on top.)

  3. Invert both pans.

  4. Remove the top pan.

  5. Peel the parchment off the cake.

- Cool angel food cakes and chiffon cakes upside down in pans so they do not fall back into the pans and lose volume. Because they are baked in ungreased pans, they won't fall out of their pans. Support the edges of the pan so the top of the cake is off the bench. When cool, loosen the cake from sides of the pan with a knife or spatula and carefully pull out the cake.

STANDARDS OF QUALITY FOR CAKES

ERRORS IN MIXING, scaling, baking, and cooling cakes result in many kinds of defects and failures. Many of these, along with their possible causes, are summarized, for easy reference, in the Common Cake Faults and Their Causes table on page 390. To judge the quality of a cake, examine it for each of the defects listed in the table to see whether it avoids those defects. In other words, a good-quality cake should have the following characteristics:

- Good volume. Well risen and not fallen.

- Even shape, with a fairly flat top or only slightly domed.

- Slight browning, not too pale or too dark.

COMMON CAKE FAULTS AND THEIR CAUSES

Fault	Causes
VOLUME AND SHAPE	
Poor volume	Too little flour
	Too much liquid
	Too little leavening
	Oven too hot
Uneven shape	Improper mixing
	Batter spread unevenly
	Uneven oven heat
	Oven racks not level
	Cake pans warped
CRUST	
Too dark	Too much sugar
	Oven too hot
Too light	Too little sugar
	Oven not hot enough
Burst or cracked	Too much flour or flour too strong
	Too little liquid
	Improper mixing
	Oven too hot
Soggy	Underbaked
	Cooling in pans or with not enough ventilation
	Wrapping before cool
TEXTURE	
Dense or heavy	Too little leavening
	Too much liquid
	Too much sugar
	Too much shortening
	Oven not hot enough
Coarse or irregular	Too much leavening
	Too little egg
	Improper mixing
Crumbly	Too much leavening
	Too much shortening
	Too much sugar
	Wrong kind of flour
	Improper mixing
Tough	Flour too strong
	Too much flour
	Too little sugar or shortening
	Overmixing
POOR FLAVOR	
	Poor-quality ingredients
	Poor storage or sanitation
	Unbalanced formula

- Intact crust, not burst or cracked.
- Crust that is slightly dry to the touch, not soggy or wet.
- Texture appropriate to the type of cake, not too dense or heavy. Egg-foam cakes have a lighter texture than high-fat cakes, and pound cakes are fairly dense.
- Even, regular crumb, with no large holes in the interior.
- Neither too tender and crumbly nor too tough.
- Good flavor, with no off-tastes.

To correct defects, refer to the table and adjust the formula, the mixing method, or the baking procedure as necessary.

ALTITUDE ADJUSTMENTS

AT HIGH ALTITUDES, atmospheric pressure is much lower than at sea level. This factor must be taken into account in cake baking. Formulas must be adjusted to suit baking conditions more than 2000 or 3000 feet above sea level.

Although general guidelines may be given, the exact adjustments required will vary for different kinds of cakes. Many manufacturers of flour, shortening, and other bakery ingredients supply detailed information and adjusted formulas for any given locality.

In general, these are the adjustments you must make:

Leavening. Leavening gases expand more when air pressure is lower, so you must decrease the amounts of baking powder and baking soda. Also, reduce creaming and foaming procedures so less air is incorporated.

Tougheners: Flour and Eggs. Cakes require firmer structure at high altitudes, so increase both eggs and flour to supply adequate proteins for structure.

Tenderizers: Shortening and Sugar. For the same reason, you must decrease shortening and sugar so that the structure will be firmer.

Liquids. At higher altitudes, water boils at a lower temperature and evaporates more easily. Therefore, increase liquids to prevent excess drying, both during and after baking. This also helps compensate for the decrease in moisturizers (sugar and fat) and the increase in flour, which absorbs moisture.

Baking Temperatures. Increase baking temperatures by about 25°F (14°C) above 3500 feet.

Pan Greasing. High-fat cakes tend to stick at high altitudes. Grease pans more heavily. Remove baked cakes from pans as soon as possible.

Storing. To prevent drying, wrap or ice cakes as soon as they are cool.

> **KEY POINTS TO REVIEW**
>
> - How are cakes tested for doneness?
> - How are cakes removed from their baking pans?
> - What adjustments must be made to cake formulas that are to be baked at high altitudes?

APPROXIMATE FORMULA ADJUSTMENT IN SHORTENED CAKES AT HIGH ALTITUDE

INGREDIENT	INCREASE OR DECREASE	2500 FT (750 M)	5000 FT (1500 M)	7500 FT (2280 M)
Baking powder	decrease	20%	40%	60%
Flour	increase	—	4%	9%
Eggs	increase	2.5%	9%	15%
Sugar	decrease	3%	6%	9%
Fat	decrease	—	—	9%
Liquid	increase	9%	15%	22%

To make adjustments, multiply the percentage indicated by the amount of the ingredient and then add or subtract the result, as indicated.

Example: Adjust 1 lb (16 oz) eggs for 7500 ft:

$$0.15 \times 16 \text{ oz} = 2.4 \text{ oz}$$
$$16 \text{ oz} + 2.4 \text{ oz} = 18.4 \text{ oz}$$

YELLOW BUTTER CAKE

For large-quantity measurements, see page 725.

Ingredients	U.S.		Metric	%
Butter	12	oz	360 g	80
Sugar	13	oz	390 g	87
Salt	0.12	oz (⅔ tsp)	4 g	0.75
Eggs	7.5	oz	225 g	50
Cake flour	15	oz	450 g	100
Baking powder	0.62	oz (3¾ tsp)	18 g	4
Milk	15	oz	450 g	100
Vanilla extract	0.2	oz	8 g	1.5
Total weight:	**3 lb 15**	**oz**	**1905 g**	**423 %**

PROCEDURE

MIXING

Creaming method (p. 377)

SCALING AND BAKING

See table on page 388.

--- **VARIATIONS** ---

UPSIDE-DOWN CAKE

Increase the eggs to 55% (8.25 oz/245 g). Decrease milk to 60% (9 oz/275 g). Add 0.75% (0.12 oz/4 g) lemon or orange flavor. Butter a sheet pan, spread with pan spread (at right), and arrange the desired fruit (pineapple rings, sliced peaches, etc.) on top of the pan spread. Scale the batter as indicated in the table on page 388. Bake at 360°F (180°C). Immediately after baking, turn out of the pan (see p. 389). Glaze with Clear Glaze (p. 194) or Apricot Glaze (p. 194).

WALNUT CAKE

Add 50% (7.5 oz/225 g) finely chopped walnuts to the batter. Bake in small loaf pans. If desired, ice with chocolate buttercream.

PAN SPREAD

For large-quantity measurements, see page 725.
(for 9-in./23 cm square pan)

Ingredients	U.S.		Metric
Brown sugar	4	oz	112 g
Granulated sugar	1.5	oz	42 g
Corn syrup or honey	1	oz	30 g
Water (as needed)			

Cream together the first three ingredients. Add enough water to thin to spreading consistency.

CHOCOLATE BUTTER CAKE

For large-quantity measurements, see page 726.

Ingredients	U.S.		Metric	%
Butter	9	oz	280 g	75
Sugar	15	oz	470 g	125
Salt	0.2	oz (1 tsp)	6 g	1.5
Unsweetened chocolate, melted	6	oz	188 g	50
Eggs	8	oz	250 g	67
Cake flour	12	oz	375 g	100
Baking powder	0.5	oz	15 g	4
Milk	14	oz	430 g	115
Vanilla extract	0.25	oz	8 g	2
Total weight:	**4 lb**		**2022 g**	**539 %**

PROCEDURE

MIXING

Creaming method (p. 377)

Blend in the melted chocolate after the fat and sugar are well creamed.

SCALING AND BAKING

See table on page 388.

BROWN SUGAR SPICE CAKE

Ingredients	U.S.		Metric		%
Butter	12	oz	400	g	80
Brown sugar	15	oz	500	g	100
Salt	0.25	oz	8	g	1.5
Eggs	9	oz	300	g	60
Cake flour	15	oz	500	g	100
Baking powder	0.5	oz	15	g	3
Baking soda	0.05 oz (¼ tsp)		1.5	g	0.3
Cinnamon	0.08 oz (1¼ tsp)		2.5	g	0.5
Cloves, ground	0.05 oz (¾ tsp)		1.5	g	0.3
Nutmeg	0.03 oz (⅜ tsp)		1	g	0.2
Milk	15	oz	500	g	100
Total weight:	**4 lb**	**2 oz**	**2229**	**g**	**445 %**

PROCEDURE

MIXING

Creaming method (p. 377)

SCALING AND BAKING

See table on page 388.

VARIATIONS

CARROT NUT CAKE

Reduce the milk to 90% (13.5 oz/450 g). Add 40% (6 oz/200 g) grated fresh carrots, 20% (3 oz/100 g) finely chopped walnuts, and 1 tsp (3 g) grated orange zest. Omit the cloves.

BANANA CAKE

Omit the cinnamon and cloves. Reduce the milk to 30% (4.5 oz/150 g). Add 125% (1 lb 3 oz/625 g) ripe, puréed bananas. If desired, add 40% (6 oz/200 g) finely chopped pecans.

APPLESAUCE CAKE

Reduce the milk to 50% (7.5 oz/250 g) and add 90% (13.5 oz/450 g) applesauce. Reduce the baking powder to 2% (0.3 oz or 2 tsp/10 g). Increase the baking soda to 1% (0.15 oz or 1 tsp/5 g).

OLD-FASHIONED POUND CAKE

Ingredients	U.S.	Metric	%
Butter *or* part butter and part shortening	1 lb	500 g	100
Sugar	1 lb	500 g	100
Vanilla extract	0.33 oz (2 tsp)	10 g	2
Eggs	1 lb	500 g	100
Cake flour	1 lb	500 g	100
Total weight:	**4 lb**	**2010 g**	**402%**

PROCEDURE

MIXING

Creaming method (p. 377)

After about half the eggs have been creamed in, add a little of the flour to avoid curdling.

SCALING AND BAKING

See table on page 388. Paper-lined loaf pans are often used for pound cakes.

--- **VARIATIONS** ---

Mace or grated lemon or orange zest may be used to flavor pound cake.

RAISIN POUND CAKE

Add 25% (4 oz/125 g) raisins or currants that have been soaked in boiling water and drained well.

CHOCOLATE POUND CAKE

Sift 25% (4 oz/125 g) cocoa and 0.8% (0.12 oz or ¾ tsp/4 g) baking soda with the flour. Add 25% (4 oz/125 g) water to the batter.

MARBLE POUND CAKE

Fill loaf pans with alternating layers of regular and chocolate pound cake batters. Swirl a knife through the batter to marble the mixture.

SHEET CAKE FOR PETITS FOURS AND FANCY PASTRIES

Increase eggs to 112% (1 lb 2 oz/560 g). Bake on sheet pans lined with greased paper. Scale 4 lb (1800 g) for ¼-in. (6-mm) layers to make three-layer petits fours.

Increase the recipe and scale 6 lb (2700 g) for ⅜-in. (9-mm) layers to make two-layer petits fours.

FRUIT CAKE

Use 50% cake flour and 50% bread flour in the basic recipe. Add 250–750% (2.5–7.5 lb/1.25–3.75 kg) mixed fruits and nuts to the batter. Procedure and suggested fruit mixtures follow.

PROCEDURE

1. Prepare fruits and nuts:

   Rinse and drain glazed fruits to remove excess syrup.

   Cut large fruits (such as whole dates) into smaller pieces.

   Mix all fruits and soak overnight in brandy, rum, or sherry.

   Drain well. (Reserve drained liquor for later batches or other purposes.)

2. Mix batter as in basic procedure, using 80% of the flour. If spices are used, cream them with the butter and sugar.

3. Toss the fruits and nuts with the remaining flour. Fold them into the batter.

4. Baking: Use loaf, ring, or tube pans, preferably with paper liners. Bake at 350°F (175°C) for small cakes (1–1½ lb/450–700 g), and 300°F (150°C) for large cakes (4–5 lb/1.8–2.3 kg). Baking time ranges from about 1½ hours for small cakes to 3–4 hours or more for large cakes.

5. Cool. Glaze with Clear Glaze (p. 194), decorate with fruits and nuts, if desired, and glaze again.

──────────── **VARIATIONS** ────────────

Percentages in the following fruit mixes are based on the flour in the basic pound cake recipe.

FRUIT MIX I (DARK)

Ingredients	U.S.		Metric		%
Dark raisins	1 lb		500	g	100
Light raisins	1 lb		500	g	100
Currants	8	oz	250	g	50
Dates	1 lb		500	g	100
Figs	8	oz	250	g	50
Glacé cherries	6.5	oz	200	g	40
Nuts (pecans, walnuts, filberts, Brazil nuts)	9.5	oz	300	g	60
Spices					
Cinnamon	0.08 oz (1¼ tsp)		2	g	0.5
Cloves, ground	0.04 oz (½ tsp)		1.25	g	0.25
Nutmeg	0.04 oz (½ tsp)		1.25	g	0.25
Total weight:	**5 lb**		**2500**	**g**	**700 %**

FRUIT MIX II (LIGHT)

Ingredients	U.S.		Metric	%
Golden raisins	12	oz	375 g	75
Currants	8	oz	250 g	50
Mixed glacé fruit	8	oz	250 g	50
Glacé pineapple	3	oz	100 g	20
Glacé orange peel	2.5	oz	75 g	15
Glacé lemon peel	2.5	oz	75 g	15
Glacé cherries	5	oz	150 g	30
Blanched almonds	4	oz	125 g	25
Spices				
Lemon zest, grated	0.06 oz (¾ tsp)		2 g	0.4
Total weight:	**2 lb 13**	**oz**	**1400 g**	**280 %**

ALMOND CAKE FOR PETITS FOURS

Ingredients	U.S.	Metric	%
Almond paste	3 lb 6 oz	1500 g	300
Sugar	2 lb 8 oz	1150 g	225
Butter	2 lb 8 oz	1150 g	225
Eggs	3 lb 2 oz	1400 g	275
Cake flour	12 oz	340 g	67
Bread flour	6 oz	170 g	33
Total weight:	**12 lb 10 oz**	**5710 g**	**1125%**

PROCEDURE

MIXING

Creaming method (p. 377)

To soften the almond paste, blend it with a little of the egg until smooth before adding the sugar. Proceed as for mixing pound cake.

SCALING AND BAKING

4 lb 3 oz (1900 g) per sheet pan. One recipe is enough for 3 pans. Make sure pans are level and without dents. Spread batter very smooth.

BAKING

400°F (200°C)

See page 472 for makeup of petits fours.

SACHER MIX I

Ingredients	U.S.		Metric	%
Butter	10	oz	250 g	100
Sugar	10	oz	250 g	100
Sweet chocolate, melted	12.5	oz	312 g	125
Egg yolks	10	oz	250 g	100
Vanilla extract	0.33 oz (2 tsp)		8 g	3.3
Egg whites	15	oz	375 g	150
Salt	0.08 oz (½ tsp)		2 g	0.8
Sugar	7.5	oz	188 g	75
Cake flour, sifted	10	oz	250 g	100
Total weight:	**4 lb 11**	**oz**	**1885 g**	**750 %**

NOTE: See page 454 for icing and decorating a Sachertorte. Layers may be iced and decorated like any other chocolate cake, but then the cake should not be called Sachertorte (see the Sachertorte sidebar).

PROCEDURE

MIXING

Modified creaming method:

1. Cream the butter and sugar; add the chocolate; add the egg yolks and vanilla, as in the basic creaming method.
2. Whip the egg whites with the salt. Add the sugar and whip to soft peaks.
3. Fold the egg whites into the batter alternately with the flour.

SCALING

6-in. (15-cm) cake: 14 oz (400 g)
7-in. (18-cm) cake: 19 oz (540 g)
8-in. (20-cm) cake: 24 oz (680 g)
9-in. (23-cm) cake: 30 oz (850 g)
10-in. (25-cm) cake: 36 oz (1020 g)

BAKING

325°F (165°C) for 45–60 minutes

SACHER MIX II

For large-quantity measurements, see page 726.

Ingredients	U.S.		Metric	%
Butter, softened	4.5	oz	135 g	337
Fine granulated sugar	3.67	oz	110 g	275
Egg yolks	4	oz	120 g	300
Egg whites	6	oz	180 g	450
Fine granulated sugar	2	oz	60 g	150
Cake flour	1.33	oz	40 g	100
Cocoa powder	1.33	oz	40 g	100
Powdered almonds, toasted	1.75	oz	55 g	137
Total weight:	**1 lb 8**	**oz**	**740 g**	**1849%**

NOTE: See page 454 for icing and decorating Sachertorte. Layers may be iced and decorated like other kinds of chocolate cake, but then the cake should not be called Sachertorte (see the Sachertorte sidebar).

PROCEDURE

MIXING

Modified creaming method:

1. Cream the butter and sugar. Add the egg yolks as in the basic creaming method.
2. Whip the egg whites and sugar to a stiff meringue.
3. Sift together the flour and cocoa powder. Mix in the almonds.
4. Fold the meringue and dry ingredients alternately into the butter mixture, starting and ending with the meringue.

SCALING

6-in. (15-cm) cake: 7 oz (200 g)
7-in. (18-cm) cake: 10 oz (280 g)
8-in. (20-cm) cake: 12 oz (370 g)
9-in. (23-cm) cake: 16 oz (470 g)

Butter the pans, line the bottoms with parchment, and dust with flour.

BAKING

325°F (160°C), 35–45 minutes, depending on size

SACHERTORTE

The classic chocolate cake Sachertorte originated at the Hotel Sacher, an elegant hotel built in 1876, directly across the street from the Vienna Opera House. The cake became so popular that many bakers tried to imitate it, even though the hotel kept the original formula a secret. As a result, there are many recipes claiming to be authentic. Of course, the original is still available on the menu at the Hotel Sacher.

Austrians serve the cake with a generous portion of unsweetened whipped cream ("mit Schlag," in the Austrian dialect) because the texture of the cake is somewhat dry.

RED VELVET CAKE

Ingredients	U.S.		Metric	%
Butter	10	oz	300 g	50
Sugar	1 lb 4	oz	600 g	100
Salt	0.22	oz	6 g	1
Red food color (liquid) (see **Note**)	0.66	oz	20 g	3.2
Eggs	6.67	oz	200 g	33
Cake flour	1 lb 4	oz	600 g	100
Cocoa	1.2	oz	36 g	6
Baking powder	0.4	oz	12 g	2
Baking soda	0.4	oz	12 g	2
Buttermilk	1 lb 4	oz	600 g	100
Distilled vinegar	1	oz	30 g	5
Total weight:	**5 lb**		**2416 g**	**402 %**

NOTE: Beet juice can be used in place of food coloring, although quantity may have to be adjusted to get the desired effect.

PROCEDURE

MIXING

Creaming method (p. 377)

Add the food coloring after the butter and sugar have been creamed together.

SCALING AND BAKING

See table on page 388.

WHITE CAKE

For large-quantity measurements, see page 726.

Ingredients	U.S.		Metric	%
Cake flour	12	oz	375 g	100
Baking powder	0.75	oz	22 g	6.25
Salt	0.25	oz	8 g	2
Emulsified shortening	6	oz	188 g	50
Sugar	15	oz	470 g	125
Skim milk	6	oz	188 g	50
Vanilla extract	0.18 oz (1⅛ tsp)		5 g	1.5
Almond extract	0.09 oz (½ tsp)		2 g	0.75
Skim milk	6	oz	188 g	50
Egg whites	8	oz	250 g	67
Total weight:	**3 lb 6**	**oz**	**1696 g**	**452 %**

PROCEDURE

MIXING

Two-stage method (p. 378)

SCALING AND BAKING

See table on page 388.

VARIATIONS

Use water instead of milk and add 10% (0.62 oz/18 g) nonfat dry milk to the dry ingredients.

Flavor with lemon extract or emulsion instead of vanilla and almond.

YELLOW CAKE

Make the following ingredient adjustments:

Reduce shortening to 45% (5.5 oz/168 g).

Substitute whole eggs for egg whites, using the same total weight (67%).

Use 2% (0.25 oz/8 g) vanilla and omit the almond extract.

STRAWBERRY CAKE

Make the following ingredient adjustments:

Reduce the sugar to 100% (12 oz/375 g).

Reduce the milk in each stage to 33% (4 oz/125 g).

Thaw and purée 67% (8 oz/250 g) frozen, sweetened strawberries. Mix into the batter.

CHERRY CAKE

Make the following ingredient adjustments:

Reduce the milk in each stage to 40% (4.75 oz/150 g).

Add 30% (3.5 oz/112 g) ground maraschino cherries, with juice, to the batter.

DEVIL'S FOOD CAKE

For large-quantity measurements, see page 726.

Ingredients	U.S.		Metric	%
Cake flour	12	oz	375 g	100
Cocoa	2	oz	60 g	17
Salt	0.25	oz	8 g	2
Baking powder	0.375	oz	12 g	3
Baking soda	0.25	oz	8 g	2
Emulsified shortening	7	oz	220 g	58
Sugar	1 lb		500 g	133
Skim milk	8	oz	250 g	67
Vanilla extract	0.18	oz (1 tsp)	5 g	1.5
Skim milk	6	oz	188 g	50
Eggs	8	oz	250 g	67
Total weight:	**3 lb 12**	**oz**	**1876 g**	**500 %**

PROCEDURE

MIXING

Two-stage method (p. 378)

SCALING AND BAKING

See table on page 388.

DEVIL'S FOOD CAKE

The difference between chocolate cake and devil's food cake is in the amount of baking soda used. As we explained in Chapter 4, an excess of soda produces a reddish color in chocolate. By reducing the amount of soda (and increasing the baking powder to make up the lost leavening power), a devil's food cake can be turned into a regular chocolate cake. Of course, both types of cake can be made with either cocoa powder or chocolate. See page 85 for instructions on substituting one type of cocoa product for another.

HIGH-RATIO POUND CAKE

Ingredients	U.S.			Metric	%
Flour	1 lb	2	oz	500 g	100
Salt		0.25	oz	8 g	2
Baking powder		0.25	oz	8 g	2
Emulsified shortening		12	oz	335 g	67
Sugar	1 lb	5	oz	585 g	117
Nonfat milk solids		1	oz	30 g	6
Water		8	oz	225 g	45
Eggs		12	oz	335 g	67
Total weight:	**4 lb**	**8**	**oz**	**2026 g**	**406%**

PROCEDURE

MIXING

Two-stage method (p. 378)

SCALING AND BAKING

See table on page 388.

--- **VARIATIONS** ---

See variations following Old-Fashioned Pound Cake, page 394.

YELLOW CAKE (LIQUID SHORTENING)

Ingredient	U.S.			Metric	%
Whole eggs	1 lb	8	oz	675 g	150
Milk		8	oz	225 g	50
High-ratio liquid shortening		10	oz	280 g	62.5
Vanilla extract		1	oz	30 g	6.25
Sugar	1 lb	4	oz	560 g	125
Cake flour	1 lb			450 g	100
Baking powder		1	oz	30 g	6.25
Salt		0.5	oz	15 g	3
Total weight:	**5 lb**			**2265 g**	**493** %

PROCEDURE

MIXING

One-stage method (p. 379)

SCALING AND BAKING

See table on page 388.

VARIATIONS

WHITE CAKE (LIQUID SHORTENING)

Reduce the whole eggs to 12.5% (2 oz/60 g) and add 137.5% (1 lb 6 oz/615 g) egg whites. If desired, add 3% (½ oz /15 g) almond extract.

CHOCOLATE CAKE (LIQUID SHORTENING)

In baker's percentages, substitute natural (not Dutched) cocoa powder for part of the flour, so the flour and cocoa together total 100%, as indicated in the following ingredient list. In addition, increase milk and sugar, decrease baking powder, and add baking soda, as indicated. Mix and bake as in the basic formula.

Ingredients	U.S.			Metric	%
Whole eggs	1 lb	8	oz	675 g	150
Milk		10	oz	280 g	62.5
High-ratio liquid shortening		10	oz	280 g	62.5
Vanilla extract		1	oz	30 g	6.25
Sugar	1 lb	6	oz	515 g	137.5
Cake flour		13	oz	365 g	81.25
Natural cocoa powder		3	oz	85 g	18.75
Baking powder		0.5	oz	15 g	3
Baking soda		0.25	oz	7 g	1.5
Salt		0.5		15 g	3

GENOISE

Ingredients	U.S.			Metric	%
Eggs	1 lb	2	oz	562 g	150
Sugar		12	oz	375 g	100
Cake flour		12	oz	375 g	100
Butter (optional; see p. 381)		4	oz	125 g	33
Vanilla extract or lemon flavor		0.25	oz	8 g	2
Total weight:	**2 lb 14**		**oz**	**1445 g**	**385%**

PROCEDURE

MIXING

Genoise or butter genoise method (p. 381)

SCALING AND BAKING

See table on page 388.

VARIATIONS

CHOCOLATE GENOISE

Substitute 2 oz (60 g) cocoa powder for 2 oz (60 g) of the flour.

SPONGE FOR SEVEN-LAYER CAKE

Add 50% (6 oz/188 g) egg yolks and 10% (1.25 oz/38 g) glucose to the first stage of mixing. Scale at 1 lb 12 oz (800 g) per sheet pan or 14 oz (400 g) per half-pan.

ALMOND SPONGE I

Make the following ingredient adjustments:

Add 50% (6 oz/188 g) yolks to the first mixing stage.

Increase the sugar to 150% (1 lb 2 oz/560 g).

Add 117% (14 oz/440 g) almond powder, mixed with the sifted flour.

(For more variations, substitute other nuts for the almonds.)

ALMOND SPONGE II

Blend 125% (15 oz/470 g) almond paste with 50% (6 oz/188 g) egg yolks until smooth. Blend in the sugar (from the basic recipe) until smooth. Add the eggs, and proceed as in the basic recipe. (**Note:** This mix does not develop as much volume as regular genoise, and it makes a layer ⅞-in. (22-mm) thick if scaled like genoise. If desired, scale 25% heavier to make a thicker layer.)

SPONGE ROLL I

Omit the butter from the basic recipe.

CHOCOLATE SPONGE ROLL I

Omit the butter from the chocolate genoise mix.

GENOISE MOUSSELINE

For large-quantity measurements, see page 726.

Ingredients	U.S.			Metric	%
Whole eggs		10	oz	300 g	167
Egg yolks		1.33 oz (2 yolks)		40 g (2 yolks)	22
Sugar		6	oz	180 g	100
Cake flour, sifted		6	oz	180 g	100
Total weight:	**1 lb 7**		**oz**	**700 g**	**389%**

PROCEDURE

MIXING

Plain sponge method (p. 381)

SCALING AND BAKING

See table on page 388.

SPONGE ROLL II (SWISS ROLL)

Ingredients	U.S.		Metric	%
Egg yolks	12	oz	350 g	100
Sugar	8	oz	235 g	67
Cake flour	12	oz	350 g	100
Egg whites	1 lb 2	oz	525 g	150
Salt	0.25	oz	7 g	2
Sugar	6	oz	175 g	50
Total weight:	**3 lb 8**	**oz**	**1642 g**	**469%**

PROCEDURE

MIXING

Separated-egg sponge method (p. 381)

SCALING

1 lb 12 oz (820 g) per sheet pan. Line the pans with greased paper.

BAKING

425°F (220°C), about 7 minutes

VARIATIONS

DOBOS MIX

Blend 100% (12 oz/350 g) almond paste with the sugar. Add a little of the yolks and blend until smooth. Add the rest of the yolks and proceed as in the basic formula.

SCALING AND PANNING

Seven layers are needed to make Dobos torte (see p. 453 for assembly instructions). For a round Dobos torte, spread a thin layer of mix onto the greased, floured bottoms of upside-down cake pans or onto circles traced on parchment. One recipe makes about seven 12-in. (30-cm) circles or fourteen 8- or 9-in. (20–22-cm) circles. For rectangular torten, spread a thin layer of mix on greased, paper-lined pans. Four times the basic recipe makes seven full-size sheets. To make only one strip, scale 20 oz (550 g) onto one sheet pan. When baked, cut into seven 3½-in. (9-cm) wide strips.

BAKING

400°F (200°C)

CHOCOLATE SPONGE ROLL II (CHOCOLATE SWISS ROLL)

Sift 17% (2 oz/60 g) cocoa with the flour. Add 25% (3 oz/90 g) water to the whipped egg yolks.

JELLY ROLL SPONGE

Ingredients	U.S.		Metric	%
Sugar	11	oz	325 g	100
Whole eggs	10	oz	292 g	90
Egg yolks	2	oz	65 g	20
Salt	0.25	oz	8 g	2
Honey *or* corn syrup	1.5	oz	45 g	14
Water	1	oz	30 g	10
Vanilla extract	0.12 oz (⅜ tsp)		4 g	1
Water, hot	4	oz	118 g	36
Cake flour	11	oz	325 g	100
Baking powder	0.16 oz (1 tsp)		5 g	1.5
Total weight:	**2 lb 9**	**oz**	**1217 g**	**374 %**

PROCEDURE

MIXING

Plain sponge method (p. 381)

Add the honey or syrup, the first quantity of water, and the vanilla to the sugar and eggs for the first mixing stage.

SCALING AND BAKING

See the table on page 388. One recipe makes 2 sheet pans. Line the pans with greased paper. Immediately after baking, turn the cakes out of the pans onto a sheet of parchment and remove the paper from their bottoms. Spread with jelly and roll up tightly. When cool, dust with confectioners' sugar.

MILK AND BUTTER SPONGE

For large-quantity measurements, see page 726.

Ingredients	U.S.		Metric	%
Sugar	10	oz	312 g	125
Whole eggs	6	oz	188 g	75
Egg yolks	2	oz	60 g	25
Salt	0.12 oz (⅝ tsp)		4 g	1.5
Cake flour	8	oz	250 g	100
Baking powder	0.25 oz		8 g	3
Skim milk	4	oz	125 g	50
Butter	2	oz	60 g	25
Vanilla extract	0.25 oz		8 g	3
Total weight:	**2 lb**		**1015 g**	**407** %

PROCEDURE

MIXING

Hot milk and butter sponge method (p. 381)

SCALING AND BAKING

Cake layers; see table on page 388.

--- VARIATION ---

Instead of vanilla, add 1.5% (0.5 oz/15 g) lemon flavor.

ANGEL FOOD CAKE

Ingredients	U.S.		Metric	%
Egg whites	2 lb		1000 g	267
Cream of tartar	0.25 oz		8 g	2
Salt	0.17 oz (1 tsp)		5 g	1.5
Sugar	1 lb		500 g	133
Vanilla extract	0.33 oz (2 tsp)		10 g	2.5
Almond extract	0.17 oz (1 tsp)		5 g	1.25
Sugar	1 lb		500 g	133
Cake flour	12	oz	375 g	100
Total weight:	**4 lb 12**	**oz**	**2403 g**	**640** %

PROCEDURE

MIXING

Angel food method (p. 382)

SCALING AND BAKING

See table on page 388.

--- VARIATIONS ---

CHOCOLATE ANGEL FOOD CAKE

Substitute 3 oz (90 g) cocoa for 3 oz (90 g) of the flour.

COCONUT MACAROON CUPCAKES

Increase the first quantity of sugar to 167% (1 lb 4 oz/625 g). Mix 350% (2 lb 10 oz/1300 g) macaroon coconut with the flour/sugar mixture. Scale at 20 oz (575 g) per dozen cupcakes. Bake at 375°F (190°C), about 25 minutes.

YELLOW CHIFFON CAKE

Ingredients	U.S.		Metric	%
Cake flour	10	oz	250 g	100
Sugar	8	oz	200 g	80
Salt	0.25	oz	6 g	2.5
Baking powder	0.5	oz	12 g	5
Vegetable oil	5	oz	125 g	50
Egg yolks	5	oz	125 g	50
Water	7.5	oz	188 g	75
Vanilla extract	0.25	oz	6 g	2.5
Egg whites	10	oz	250 g	100
Sugar	5	oz	125 g	50
Cream of tartar	0.05	oz (⅝ tsp)	1 g	0.5
Total weight:	**3 lb 3**	**oz**	**1288 g**	**515 %**

PROCEDURE

MIXING

Chiffon method (p. 383)

SCALING AND BAKING

See table on page 388. For layers, use the weights for high-fat cakes.

VARIATIONS

CHOCOLATE CHIFFON CAKE

Make the following ingredient adjustments:

Add 20% (2 oz/50 g) cocoa. Sift it with the flour.

Increase egg yolks to 60% (6 oz/150 g).

Increase the water to 90% (9 oz/225 g).

ORANGE CHIFFON CAKE

Make the following ingredient adjustments:

Increase the egg yolks to 60% (6 oz/150 g).

Use 50% (5 oz/125 g) orange juice and 25% (2.5 oz/62 g) water.

Add 0.5 oz (1 tbsp/6 g) grated orange zest when adding the oil.

CHOCOLATE FUDGE CAKE

Ingredients	U.S.		Metric	%
Unsweetened chocolate	1 lb		500 g	400
Butter	1 lb		500 g	400
Eggs	1 lb	4 oz	625 g	500
Sugar	1 lb	4 oz	625 g	500
Bread flour		4 oz	125 g	100
Total weight:	**4 lb**	**12 oz**	**2375 g**	**1900%**

PROCEDURE

MIXING

Plain sponge method (p. 381)

Melt the chocolate and butter together over a hot-water bath. Fold the chocolate mixture into the egg-sugar foam before folding in the flour.

SCALING

7-in. (18-cm) round pan: 19 oz (550 g)

8-in. (20-cm) round pan: 25 oz (750 g)

9-in. (23-cm) round pan: 31 oz (950 g)

10-in. (25-cm) round pan: 38 oz (1100 g)

Butter the pans heavily before panning.

BAKING

350°F (175°C) until slightly underbaked, 20–30 minutes. Set the cake pans on sheet pans to avoid scorching the bottoms.

Cool and glaze with warm Ganache (p. 272).

--- VARIATION ---

CHOCOLATE SURPRISE CAKE

Fill large muffin tins or similar pans three-quarters full of batter. Insert a 1-oz (30-g) ball of cold Ganache (p. 272) into the center of each. Bake at 350°F (175°C), about 15 minutes. Turn out and serve warm with whipped cream or ice cream. The melted ganache will run out when the cake is cut open.

JOCONDE SPONGE CAKE (BISCUIT JOCONDE)

For large-quantity measurements, see page 727.

Ingredients	U.S.		Metric	%
Powdered almonds	3.5	oz	85 g	340
Confectioners' sugar	3	oz	75 g	300
Cake flour	1	oz	25 g	100
Whole eggs	4.75	oz	120 g	480
Egg whites	3.25	oz	80 g	320
Sugar	0.4	oz (2½ tsp)	10 g	40
Butter, melted	1.25	oz	30 g	120
Total weight:	**1 lb 1**	**oz**	**425 g**	**1700%**

PROCEDURE

MIXING

1. Mix together the almonds, confectioners' sugar, and flour in a bowl.

2. Add the eggs a little at a time. Mix well after each addition. Mix until smooth and light.

3. Whip the egg whites with the sugar until they form firm, glossy peaks.

4. Gently fold the egg mixture into the whipped egg whites.

5. Fold in the melted butter.

SCALING AND BAKING

Spread ¼ in. (5 mm) thick in half-sheet pans lined with parchment. Allow 1 lb (425 g) per half-sheet pan. Bake at 400°F (200°C) for 15 minutes, or until golden and firm to the touch. Remove from the pans and cool on a rack.

--- VARIATION ---

HAZELNUT JOCONDE SPONGE CAKE

Substitute powdered hazelnuts for the powdered almonds. Omit the melted butter.

RIBBON SPONGE

Yield: 2 half-sheet pans

Ingredients	U.S.		Metric
Stencil paste			
Butter	7	oz	200 g
Confectioners' sugar	7	oz	200 g
Egg whites	7	oz	200 g
Cake flour	7.75	oz	220 g
Powdered food coloring (see variation)	as needed		as needed
Joconde Sponge batter (p. 405)	2 lb		850 g

NOTE: This cake is used for decorative linings for cake molds and charlotte molds. Chapter 17 includes instructions for using the baked ribbon sponge. The stencil paste used to make the designs is another version of the batter used for Tuile cookies (p. 502).

It is advisable to bake this sponge on a silicone mat so the bottom of the cake doesn't brown. If a mat is not available, double-pan (set one sheet pan on top of another) and bake on the top shelf of the oven.

A

B

C

D

E

F

PROCEDURE

1. Beat the butter until soft. Add the sugar and mix well.

2. Add the egg whites, beating continuously.

3. Sift the flour into the mixture. Mix until smooth.

4. Color the paste with food coloring if desired.

5. Line the bottom of a sheet pan with a silicone mat.

6. Use one of the two following procedures to make the stencil design:

   Cover the bottom of a sheet pan with a silicone mat. Place a stencil on top of the mat, spread with a thin layer of the paste, and remove the stencil.

   or

   Spread a thin layer of the paste onto a silicone mat with a palette knife (a). Comb with a plastic pastry comb to make stripes, as shown here, or zigzags, wavy lines, or other patterns (b). Alternatively, apply an abstract finger-painted design by depositing dabs of colored stencil paste (c) and spreading them thin with a palette knife (d). If desired, make abstract finger-painted designs with your fingers (e).

7. Place the mat in the freezer until the paste is firm.

8. Cover the stencil paste with joconde sponge cake batter, spreading it to an even layer ¼ in. (5 mm) thick (f).

9. Bake in a 475°F (250°C) oven for about 15 minutes.

10. Transfer to a baking rack to cool.

11. Cut the strip to the desired length and use to line ring molds.

--- **VARIATIONS** ---

To make chocolate stencil paste for brown and white ribbon sponge, substitute cocoa powder for *one-fifth* of the cake flour.

Plain genoise may be used instead of joconde sponge.

LADYFINGER SPONGE

Ingredients	U.S.	Metric	%
Egg yolks	6 oz	180 g	60
Sugar	3 oz	90 g	30
Egg whites	9 oz	270 g	90
Sugar	5 oz	150 g	50
Lemon juice	¼ tsp	1 mL	0.4
Pastry flour	10 oz	300 g	100
Total weight:	**2 lb 1 oz**	**990 g**	**340 %**

PROCEDURE

MIXING

Separated-egg sponge method (p. 381)

PANNING AND BAKING

One recipe is enough for one full-size sheet pan. Use one of two methods for sponge sheets:

1. Using a pastry bag fitted with a medium plain tip, pipe the sponge mix in diagonal lines on a sheet pan lined with parchment. Pipe the strips of batter so they touch each other and the entire pan is filled with the sponge batter.

2. Alternatively, simply spread with a palette knife.

3. Bake at 375°F (190°F) for about 10 minutes.

--- VARIATION ---

LADYFINGER COOKIES

Pipe batter as in first method above, but in strips 3½ in. (9 cm) long; and keep them separate, not touching. Dredge the pan generously with confectioners' sugar. Grasp the parchment by two adjacent corners and lift, to let excess sugar fall off. Bake as directed above. One recipe makes about 100 ladyfingers.

MARJOLAINE SPONGE CAKE

For large-quantity measurements, see page 727.

Ingredients	U.S.		Metric	%
Confectioners' sugar	4	oz	120 g	133
Powdered almonds	4	oz	120 g	133
Egg yolks	3.33	oz	100 g	111
Egg whites	2	oz	60 g	67
Egg whites	5	oz	150 g	167
Sugar	3	oz	90 g	100
Pastry flour, sifted	3	oz	90 g	100
Total weight:	**1 lb 8**	**oz**	**730 g**	**811%**

PROCEDURE

MIXING

Sponge method variation:

1. Combine the confectioners' sugar, almonds, and egg yolks. Beat well.

2. Add the first quantity of egg whites. Whip until thick and light.

3. Whip the second quantity of egg whites with the sugar to make a common meringue. Fold into the egg yolk mixture.

4. Fold in the flour.

MAKEUP AND BAKING

Line sheet pans with parchment paper. Fit a pastry bag with a medium plain tip. Pipe disks of the desired size using the technique shown on page 341. Bake for 10 minutes at 350°F (180°C).

HAZELNUT SPONGE CAKE

For large-quantity measurements, see page 727.

Ingredients	U.S.		Metric	%
Butter, softened	4.5	oz	135 g	337
Sugar	3.67	oz	110 g	275
Egg yolks	4	oz	120 g	300
Egg whites	6	oz	180 g	450
Sugar	2	oz	60 g	160
Cake flour	1.33	oz	40 g	100
Cocoa powder	1.33	oz	40 g	100
Ground hazelnuts, toasted	1.75	oz	55 g	138
Total weight:	**1 lb 8**	**oz**	**740 g**	**1860%**

PROCEDURE

MIXING

Combination creaming/sponge method:

1. Cream the butter and first quantity of sugar.
2. Add the egg yolks in several stages, beating well after each addition.
3. Whip the egg whites and second quantity of sugar to a stiff meringue.
4. Sift together the flour and cocoa. Mix in the hazelnuts.
5. Fold the meringue and the dry ingredients alternately into the butter mixture, starting and finishing with the meringue.

SCALING

12 oz (370 g) per 8-in. (20-cm) round pan. Grease the pans and line the bottoms with parchment. Flour the sides of the pans.

BAKING

325°F (160°C), about 40 minutes

ALMOND POUND CAKE (PAIN DE GÊNES)

Ingredients	U.S.		Metric	%
Almond paste	7.5	oz	225 g	167
Confectioners' sugar	5	oz	150 g	111
Egg yolks	4	oz	120 g	89
Whole eggs	1.67	oz	50 g	37
Vanilla extract	0.07 oz (½ tsp)		2 g	1.5
Egg whites	6	oz	180 g	133
Sugar	2.5	oz	75 g	56
Cake flour	4.5	oz	135 g	100
Butter, melted	2.33	oz	70 g	52
Sliced almonds	2	oz	50 g	37
Total weight:	**2 lb 3**	**oz**	**1057 g**	**783 %**

PROCEDURE

MIXING

Modified separated-egg sponge method:

1. Mix the almond paste and confectioners' sugar to a sandlike consistency.
2. Mix in the egg yolks, a little at a time. Then add the whole egg and vanilla. Beat well until smooth and light.
3. Whip the egg whites to soft peaks. Add the sugar and whip to stiff peaks.
4. Fold the meringue into the almond paste mixture.
5. Fold in the flour and melted butter.

PAN PREPARATION, SCALING, AND BAKING

1. Butter the bottom and sides of round or square cake pans. Line the insides of the pans with the sliced almonds.
2. For scaling, use the figures for high-fat cakes in the table on page 388 at the high end of the weight range.
3. Bake at 340°F (170°C) for 20–25 minutes.

BAUMKUCHEN

Ingredients	U.S.		Metric	%
Butter	7	oz	200 g	114
Sugar	5	oz	150 g	85
Vanilla extract	0.07 oz (½ tsp)		2 g	1
Lemon zest, grated	0.03 oz (½ tsp)		1 g	0.5
Egg yolks	2.5	oz	80 g	43
Egg whites	7	oz	210 g	120
Sugar	5	oz	150 g	85
Cornstarch	6	oz	175 g	100
Powdered almonds	2.25 oz		65 g	37
Salt	0.07 oz (⅓ tsp)		2 g	1
Total weight:	**2 lb 2**	**oz**	**1035 g**	**586** %

PROCEDURE

MIXING

Combination creaming/sponge method:

1. Cream the butter, sugar, vanilla, and zest until light.
2. Beat in the egg yolks a little at a time.
3. Whip the egg whites until they form soft peaks. Add the sugar and whip until they form stiff, glossy peaks.
4. Fold the cornstarch into the egg whites.
5. Mix together the almonds and salt.
6. Fold the meringue and the almonds alternately into the butter mixture, starting and finishing with meringue.

BAKING

1. Line the bottom of an 8-in. (20-cm) square cake pan with parchment.
2. Put about 1 oz (30 g) batter in the pan and spread it smooth with a small offset palette knife (a).
3. Place under a salamander or broiler until well and evenly browned (b).
4. Repeat steps 2 and 3 until the cake is about 1½ in. (4 cm) thick (c).
5. Chill.
6. The cut cake reveals a pattern of layers (d). It is used to line charlotte molds (p. 446). It can also be cut into small pieces and served plain or iced with fondant (p. 472) as petits fours.

A

B

C

D

BAUMKUCHEN

Baumkuchen is an unusual cake that deserves explanation. The name means "tree cake" in German. Traditionally, it was made on a revolving wooden spit. The batter was ladled on in thin layers as the spit rotated in front of a heat source. As each layer cooked and browned on the surface, another layer was added. Thus, cutting into the cake revealed a series of concentric rings, resembling tree rings.

Today, baumkuchen is generally made in cake pans, as illustrated. Its unusual striped interior makes it valuable for the decorative lining of cake and charlotte molds.

ALMOND CHOCOLATE SPONGE

For large-quantity measurements, see page 727.

Ingredients	U.S.	Metric	%
Marzipan	4.33 oz	130 g	325
Egg yolks	2.67 oz (4 yolks)	80 g (4 yolks)	200
Egg whites	4 oz (4 whites)	120 g (4 whites)	300
Sugar	1.67 oz (4 tbsp)	50 g	125
Cake flour	1.33 oz	40 g	100
Cocoa powder	1.33 oz	40 g	100
Butter, melted	1.33 oz	40 g	100
Total weight:	**1 lb**	**500 g**	**1250%**

PROCEDURE

MIXING

Modified separated-egg sponge method:

1. Beat the marzipan and egg yolks together until smooth and light.
2. Whip the egg whites and sugar to a stiff meringue.
3. Sift the flour and cocoa together. Fold the meringue and dry ingredients alternately into the egg yolk mixture, starting and ending with the meringue.
4. Fold in the butter.

SCALING AND BAKING

See table on page 388. For sponge circles, (as for Monte Carlo, p. 465), draw circles of the desired size on parchment. Turn the paper over and spread batter to fill the circles. Alternatively, pipe the batter using the technique shown on page 341. One 7-in. (18-cm) circle requires about 8 oz (250 g) batter. Bake at 425°F (220°C) for 10–12 minutes.

CHOCOLATE SPONGE LAYERS

For large-quantity measurements, see page 727.

Ingredients	U.S.	Metric	%
Egg whites	5 oz	150 g	150
Sugar	4 oz	120 g	120
Egg yolks	3.5 oz	100 g	100
Cake flour	3.5 oz	100 g	100
Cocoa powder	1 oz	30 g	30
Total weight:	**1 lb 1 oz**	**500 g**	**500%**

PROCEDURE

MIXING

1. Whip the egg whites until foamy, then add the sugar and whip to soft peaks.
2. Whip the egg yolks until they are light and pale.
3. Fold the yolks into the whites.
4. Sift the flour with the cocoa powder. Fold into the egg mixture.

MAKEUP AND BAKING

Using a pastry bag fitted with a plain tip, pipe circles of batter on parchment, as shown on page 341. Bake at 350°F (175°C) for 15 minutes.

CHOCOLATE VELVET CAKE (MOELLEUX)

For large-quantity measurements, see page 727.

Ingredients	U.S.		Metric	%
Almond paste	2.5	oz	75 g	188
Confectioners' sugar	1.67	oz	50 g	125
Egg yolks	2	oz	60 g	150
Egg whites	2	oz	60 g	150
Sugar	0.83	oz (5 tsp)	25 g	63
Cake flour	1.33	oz	40 g	100
Cocoa powder	0.33	oz	10 g	25
Butter, melted	0.67	oz	20 g	50
For baking (optional)				
Almonds, chopped	1	oz	30 g	75
Total batter weight:	**11**	**oz**	**340 g**	**851%**

PROCEDURE

MIXING

Modified separated-egg sponge method:

1. Mix the almond paste and confectioners' sugar until the mixture has a sandy consistency.
2. Mix in the egg yolks a little at a time. Beat until the mixture is smooth and light.
3. Whip the egg whites and sugar to a stiff meringue. Fold into the almond paste mixture.
4. Sift together the flour and cocoa. Fold into the batter.
5. Fold in the melted butter.

SCALING AND BAKING

7-in. (18-cm) square pan: 11 oz (340 g)

8-in. (20-cm) square pan: 14 oz (425 g)

9-in. (23-cm) square pan: 19 oz (600 g)

Butter the pans. If desired, line pans with the almonds before filling with batter.

Bake at 340°F (170°C), 20–25 minutes

LEMON MADELEINES

For large-quantity measurements, see page 728.

Ingredients	U.S.		Metric		%
Butter	5	oz	150	g	100
Sugar	4.7	oz	140	g	94
Honey	0.8	oz	24	g	16
Salt	0.01 oz (¹⁄₂₀ tsp)		0.4	g	0.25
Grated lemon zest	0.23	oz	10	g	4.5
Eggs	5.5	oz	165	g	67
Pastry flour	5	oz	150	g	100
Baking powder	0.13 oz (¾ tsp)		3.8	g	2.5
Total weight:	**1 lb 5**	**oz**	**643**	**g**	**427 %**

VARIATION

CHOCOLATE AND ORANGE MADELEINES

For large-quantity measurements, see page 728.

Ingredients	U.S.		Metric		%
Butter	5	oz	150	g	143
Sugar	4.7	oz	140	g	134
Honey	0.8	oz	24	g	2
Salt	0.01	oz	0.4	g	0.3
Grated orange zest	0.35	oz	10	g	10
Eggs	5.5	oz	165	g	157
Pastry flour	3.5	oz	105	g	100
Cocoa powder	1.2	oz	35	g	34
Baking powder	0.18 oz (1 tsp)		5	g	5

Follow the basic procedure, but make changes to the ingredients as listed above.

PROCEDURE

MIXING

Creaming method. Chill the batter for at least 20 minutes.

PANNING AND BAKING

1. Double-butter madeleine pans and dust with flour. Pipe batter into the pans using a pastry bag fitted with a medium plain tip. Each small or petit four-size madeleine (1½ × 1 in. or 4 × 2.5 cm) requires about ⅛ oz (5 g) batter; a large madeleine (2½ × 1½ in. or 6.5 × 4 cm) requires about ⅔ oz (20 g) batter.

2. Bake at 400°F (200°C) until golden but still soft to the touch, about 6–7 minutes for small madeleines, at least twice as long for large.

3. Unmold onto wire racks to cool.

MARRONIER (CHESTNUT CAKE PETITS FOURS)

Ingredients	U.S.	Metric	%
Sweetened chestnut purée	3.5 oz	100 g	133
Rum	0.33 oz (2 tsp)	10 g	13
Egg whites	8 oz	240 g	320
Granulated sugar	1.67 oz	50 g	67
Confectioners' sugar, sifted	5 oz	150 g	200
Powdered almonds	2 oz	60 g	80
Cake flour	2.5 oz	75 g	100
Butter, melted	3.5 oz	100 g	133
Garnish			
Confectioners' sugar	as needed	as needed	
Sugar-glazed chestnut halves	48	48	
Total batter weight:	**1 lb 10 oz**	**785 g**	**1046%**

PROCEDURE

MIXING

1. Soften the chestnut purée by mixing in the rum.

2. Whip the egg whites and granulated sugar to a stiff meringue. Fold into the chestnut purée.

3. Fold in the confectioners' sugar, almonds, and flour.

4. Fold in the melted butter.

SCALING AND BAKING

1. Butter and flour 2-in. (5-cm) tartlet molds.

2. Fill each mold with ½ oz (15 g) batter.

3. Bake at 375°F (190°C) for 8 minutes.

4. Remove from the molds immediately after baking. Cool on racks.

5. When completely cool, dust the tops with confectioners' sugar. Top each cake with a half chestnut.

TERMS FOR REVIEW

emulsion	two-stage method	sponge method	pound cake
air cells	one-stage method	genoise	baumkuchen
creaming method	flour-batter method	angel food method	
high-fat cakes	egg-foam cakes	chiffon method	

QUESTIONS FOR REVIEW

1. What are the three main goals of mixing cake batter?

2. How are the following concepts related to the goals in question 1: (a) emulsion; (b) creaming of fat and sugar; (c) gluten development?

3. What are four precautions you should take to prevent a cake batter from curdling or separating?

4. List the steps in the creaming method of cake mixing.

5. List the steps in the two-stage, or high-ratio, mixing method.

6. List the steps in the sponge method. What extra steps are needed in the butter sponge method? In the hot milk and butter sponge method? In the separated-egg sponge method?

7. What are the advantages and disadvantages of using butter in high-fat cakes?

8. Why is there a lot of emphasis on scraping down the sides of the bowl and the beater in both the creaming and the two-stage methods?

9. How is mixing a creaming-method cake different from mixing a combination creaming/sponge method cake?

10. Which of the following cake ingredients are considered tougheners? Which are tenderizers? Dryers? Moisteners?

flour	egg whites	milk (liquid)
butter	egg yolks	cocoa
sugar	whole eggs	water

11. Why should angel food cake pans not be greased?

17

ASSEMBLING AND DECORATING CAKES

AFTER READING THIS CHAPTER, YOU SHOULD BE ABLE TO:

1. Prepare icings.
2. Assemble and ice simple layer cakes, sheet cakes, and cupcakes.
3. Perform basic cake-decorating techniques using a pastry bag, paper cone, and other basic decorating tools.
4. Assemble cakes using a variety of specialized techniques, including the use of cake rings and the application of glazes and rolled coatings.
5. Prepare a variety of European-style gateaux, Swiss rolls, and small cakes.

MUCH OF THE appeal of cakes is due to their appearance. Cakes are an ideal medium in which a baker can express artistry and imagination. A cake need not be elaborate or complex to be pleasing. Certainly, a simple but neatly finished cake is more appealing than a gaudy, overdecorated cake that is done carelessly or without any plan for a harmonious overall design.

There are, of course, many styles of cake decorating, and within each style hundreds or thousands of designs are possible.

This chapter is, in part, an introduction to basic techniques for finishing cakes. The most important requirement for making effective desserts is practice—hours and hours of practice with the pastry bag and paper cone, the decorator's chief tools.

415

Even the simplest designs (such as straight lines) require a lot of repetition. Only when you have mastered the basic skills should you proceed to the more advanced techniques presented in style manuals and cake decorating books.

A cake must be assembled and iced before it can be decorated. Therefore, we begin with a study of icings, and include recipes for many variations. Then we discuss the procedures for assembling basic layer cakes, sheet cakes, and other simple products. Guidelines for more advanced techniques conclude the chapter.

PREPARING ICINGS

ICINGS, ALSO CALLED *frostings*, are sweet coatings for cakes and other baked goods. Icings have three main functions:

- They contribute flavor and richness.
- They improve appearance.
- They improve keeping qualities by forming protective coatings around cakes.

There are eight basic types of icings and other cake coatings:

- Poured fondant
- Buttercreams
- Foam-type icings
- Fudge-type icings
- Flat-type icings
- Royal or decorator's icing
- Glazes
- Rolled coatings

Use top-quality flavorings for icings so they enhance the cake rather than detract from it. Use moderation when adding flavors and colors. Flavors should be light and delicate.

Poured Fondant

Poured fondant is a sugar syrup that is crystallized to a smooth, creamy white mass. It is familiar as the icing for napoleons, éclairs, petits fours, and some cakes. When applied, it sets up into a shiny, nonsticky coating. (Until the recent popularity of so-called "rolled fondant" (p. 448), poured fondant was known simply as fondant. We now use the longer term in order to avoid confusion.)

A note is in order regarding the word "crystallized" in the previous paragraph. In Chapter 12, in the discussion of cooking sugar syrups, we stressed the importance of avoiding crystallization because it causes graininess. So how can crystallization occur in a smooth icing? When you read Procedure and Guidelines for Using Fondant, you will see this white icing starts as a sugar solution that is as clear as water. It is crystallization that turns it white and opaque. The key is to control the temperature so when the crystals form, they are microscopically tiny. This is what keeps the fondant smooth and shiny. If the fondant is not made correctly, or is heated too much when used, the crystals become larger and the icing loses its shine and smoothness.

Because it is difficult to make in the bakeshop, poured fondant is almost always purchased already prepared, either in the ready-to-use moist form or the dry form, which requires only the addition of water. In an emergency (for instance, if you run out of fondant and there is no time to get more from your supplier), flat icing can be substituted, although it will not perform as well.

For those who wish to try making fondant, a formula is included here. The purpose of the glucose or cream of tartar is to invert some of the sugar in order to get the right amount of crystallization. If none is used, the syrup will set up to be too unworkable, and it will not be smooth and white. When an excess of glucose or cream of tartar is added, not enough crystallization will take place and the fondant will be too soft and syrupy. Also, if the hot syrup is disturbed before it cools sufficiently (step 6 in the procedure), large crystals will form and the fondant will not be smooth and shiny.

ICINGS AND FROSTINGS

Most people use the terms *icing* and *frosting* interchangeably, and for the most part they do mean the same thing. More specifically, however, products applied by pouring over an item, such as fondant and flat icing, are rarely referred to as *frostings*. Royal icing, as well, is always called icing, not frosting. When the term frosting is used, it is likely to mean a thicker product that is applied with a palette knife or spatula, such as buttercream. But these are not absolute definitions. Many pastry chefs are in the habit of calling all these products icings.

PROCEDURE AND GUIDELINES: Using Poured Fondant

1. Heat the fondant over a warm-water bath, stirring constantly, to thin it and make it pourable. Do not heat it over 100°F (38°C), or it will lose its shine.

2. If it is still too thick, thin it with a little simple sugar syrup or water.

3. Add flavorings and colorings as desired.

4. To make *chocolate fondant*, stir melted unsweetened chocolate into the warm fondant until the desired color and flavor are reached (up to about 3 oz bitter chocolate per lb of fondant, or 190 g per kg). Chocolate will thicken the fondant, so the icing may require more thinning with sugar syrup.

5. Apply the warm fondant by pouring it over the item or by dipping items into it.

POURED FONDANT

Yield: 6–7 lb (3–3.5 kg)

Ingredients	U.S.		Metric	Sugar at 100% %
Sugar	6 lb		3000 g	100
Water	1 lb 8	oz	750 g	25
Glucose	1 lb 2	oz	570 g	19
or				
Cream of tartar	0.5 oz		15 g	0.5

PROCEDURE

1. Clean a marble slab well and moisten it with water. Set 4 steel bars on the slab in the shape of a square to hold the hot syrup when it is poured onto the marble.

2. Combine the sugar and water in a heavy kettle and heat to dissolve the sugar. Boil until the temperature reaches 225°F (105°C).

3. If glucose is used, warm it. If cream of tartar is used, disperse it in a little warm water. Add the glucose or the cream of tartar to the boiling syrup.

4. Continue to boil the syrup until it reaches 240°F (115°C).

5. Pour the boiling syrup onto the marble slab and sprinkle it with a little cold water to prevent crystallization.

6. Let the syrup cool undisturbed to about 110°F (43°C).

7. Remove the steel bars and work the sugar with a steel scraper, turning it from the outside to the center. It will turn white and begin to solidify.

8. Continue to work the fondant, either by hand or by putting it in a mixing bowl and working it slowly with the paddle attachment, until it is smooth and creamy.

9. Keep the fondant in a tightly covered container.

Buttercreams

Buttercream icings are light, smooth mixtures of fat and sugar. They may also contain eggs to increase their smoothness or lightness. These popular icings for many kinds of cakes are easily flavored and colored to suit a variety of purposes.

There are many variations of buttercream formulas. We cover five basic kinds in this chapter:

1. **Simple buttercreams** are made by creaming together fat and confectioners' sugar to the desired consistency and lightness. A small quantity of egg whites, yolks, or whole eggs may be whipped in. (For safety, use only pasteurized eggs.) Some formulas also include nonfat milk solids.

   Decorator's buttercream (sometimes called *rose paste*) is a special type of simple buttercream used for making flowers and other cake decorations. It is creamed only a little, at low speed, as too much air beaten into it would make it unable to hold delicate shapes. Because shortening has a higher melting point than butter, it is often used as the only fat in decorator's buttercream, to give maximum stability to the finished décor. However, when possible, a little butter may be included to improve the flavor.

2. **Meringue-type buttercreams** are a mixture of butter and meringue. These are very light icings. The most frequently made of these kinds of buttercreams is Italian buttercream, made with Italian Meringue (p. 259). Swiss Meringue (p. 259) can also be used as the base for buttercream.

3. **French buttercreams** are prepared by beating a boiling syrup into beaten egg yolks, and whipping to a light foam. Soft butter is then whipped in. These are very rich, but light, icings.

4. **Pastry cream-type buttercream**, in its simplest form, is made by mixing together equal parts thick pastry cream and softened butter, and whipping until light. If more sweetness is desired, sifted confectioners' sugar may be mixed in. The recipe included in this chapter (Vanilla Cream, p. 422, contains a lower proportion of butter than usual. To give it the necessary body, a little gelatin is added. This type of preparation is better suited for use as a cake filling rather than an exterior icing.)

5. **Fondant-type buttercream** is simple to make with only a few ingredients on hand. Simply cream together equal parts fondant and butter. Flavor as desired.

Butter, especially unsalted butter, is the preferred fat for buttercreams because of its flavor and melt-in-the-mouth quality. Icings made with shortening only can be unpleasant because the fat congeals and coats the inside of the mouth, where it does not melt. However, butter makes a less stable icing because it melts so easily. There are two ways around this problem:

- Use buttercreams only in cool weather.
- Blend a small quantity of emulsifier shortening with the butter to stabilize it.

Buttercreams may be stored, covered, in the refrigerator for several days. However, they should always be used at room temperature in order to have the right consistency. Before using, remove buttercream from the refrigerator at least 1 hour ahead of time and let it come to room temperature. If it must be warmed quickly, or if it curdles, warm it gently over warm water and beat it well until smooth.

Flavoring Buttercreams

Buttercreams may be combined with many flavorings, making them versatile and adaptable to many kinds of cakes and desserts.

The quantities given in the following variations are suggested amounts for each 1 pound (500 g) buttercream. In practice, flavorings may be increased or decreased to taste, but avoid flavoring icings too strongly. Unless the instructions say otherwise, simply blend the flavoring into the buttercream.

1. **Chocolate.** Use 3 ounces (90 g) semisweet dark chocolate. Melt chocolate and cool slightly. (Chocolate must not be too cool or it will solidify before completely blending with the buttercream.) Blend with about one-quarter of the buttercream, then blend this mixture into the rest.

   If your buttercream base is very sweet, use 1½ ounces (45 g) unsweetened chocolate instead of the sweet chocolate.

2. **Coffee.** Use ⅔ fluid ounces (20 mL) coffee compound (coffee flavoring), or 1½ tablespoon (5 g) instant coffee dissolved in ½ ounce (15 mL) water.

3. **Marron (chestnut).** Use 8 ounces (250 g) chestnut purée. Blend with a little of the buttercream until soft and smooth, then blend this mixture into the remaining buttercream. Flavor with a little rum or brandy, if desired.

4. **Praline.** Use 2 to 3 ounces (60 to 90 g) praline paste. Blend with a little of the buttercream until soft and smooth, then blend this mixture into the remaining buttercream.

5. **Almond.** Use 6 ounces (180 g) almond paste. Soften almond paste with a few drops of water. Blend in a little of the buttercream until soft and smooth, then blend this mixture into the remaining buttercream.

6. **Extracts and emulsions** (orange, lemon, etc.). Add according to taste.

7. **Spirits and liqueurs.** Add according to taste. For example: kirsch, orange liqueur, rum, brandy.

SIMPLE BUTTERCREAM

For large-quantity measurements, see page 728.

Ingredients	U.S.		Metric	Sugar at 100% %
Butter	8	oz	250 g	40
Shortening	4	oz	125 g	20
Confectioners' sugar	1 lb 4	oz	625 g	100
Egg whites, pasteurized	1.25	oz	40 g	7.5
Lemon juice	0.08 oz (½ tsp)		2 g	0.4
Vanilla extract	0.12 oz (¾ tsp)		4 g	0.6
Water (optional)	1	oz	30 g	5
Total weight:	**2 lb 2**	**oz**	**1076 g**	**172 %**

PROCEDURE

1. Using the paddle attachment, cream together the butter, shortening, and sugar until well blended.

2. Add the egg whites, lemon juice, and vanilla. Blend in at medium speed. Then mix at high speed until light and fluffy.

3. For a softer buttercream, blend in the water.

VARIATIONS

For flavored buttercreams, see above.

SIMPLE BUTTERCREAM WITH EGG YOLKS OR WHOLE EGGS

Instead of the egg whites in the above recipe, substitute an equal weight of pasteurized egg yolks or whole eggs. These substitutions make slightly richer icings. Also, the egg yolks help make a better emulsion.

DECORATOR'S BUTTERCREAM OR ROSE PASTE

Use 7 oz (200 g) regular shortening and 3 oz (90 g) butter. Omit the lemon juice and vanilla. Add 0.75 oz (22 g) of either water or egg whites. Blend at low speed until smooth; do not whip.

CREAM CHEESE ICING

Substitute cream cheese for the butter and shortening. Omit the egg whites. If necessary, thin the icing with cream or milk. If desired, flavor with grated lemon or orange zest instead of vanilla, and use orange juice and/or lemon juice instead of milk for thinning the icing.

ITALIAN BUTTERCREAM

Yield: 1 lb 11 oz (850 g)

For large-quantity measurements, see page 728.

Ingredients	U.S.		Metric	Sugar at 100% %
Italian meringue				
Sugar	8	oz	250 g	100
Water	2	oz	60 mL	25
Egg whites	4	oz	125 g	50
Butter, soft	12	oz	375 g	150
Emulsified shortening (or additional butter)	2	oz	60 mL	25
Lemon juice	0.08 oz (½ tsp)		2 mL	1
Vanilla extract	0.12 oz (¾ tsp)		4 mL	1.5

PROCEDURE

1. Make the meringue (Italian Meringue procedure on p. 259). Whip until completely cool.

2. Little by little, add the soft butter and continue to whip (a). Add each piece after the previous one has been incorporated. In the same way, whip in the shortening, if using, or the additional butter.

3. When all the fat has been incorporated, whip in the lemon juice and vanilla.

4. Continue to whip until the buttercream is smooth. The mixture will appear curdled at first (b), but it will become smooth and light with continued whipping (c).

--- **VARIATION** ---

For flavored buttercreams, see pages 418–419.

SWISS BUTTERCREAM

Instead of making Italian buttercream, use the sugar and (pasteurized) egg whites (omitting the water) in the formula to make a Swiss meringue, as described on page 259. When the meringue has cooled to room temperature, continue with step 2 in the basic recipe.

A

B

C

FRENCH BUTTERCREAM

Yield: 1 lb 6 oz (688 g)

For large-quantity measurements, see page 728.

Ingredients	U.S.		Metric	Sugar at 100% %
Sugar	8	oz	250 g	100
Water	2	oz	60 mL	25
Egg yolks	3	oz	90 g	37.5
Butter, softened	10	oz	300 g	125
Vanilla extract	0.12 oz (¾ tsp)		4 mL	1.5

VARIATION

For flavored buttercreams, see pages 418–419.

PROCEDURE

1. Combine the sugar and water in a saucepan. Bring to a boil while stirring, to dissolve the sugar.

2. Continue to boil until the syrup reaches a temperature of 240°F (115°C).

3. While the syrup is boiling, beat the yolks with a wire whip or the whip attachment of a mixer until they are thick and light.

4. As soon as the syrup reaches 240°F (115°C), pour it very slowly into the beaten yolks while whipping constantly.

5. Continue to beat until the mixture is completely cool and the yolks are very thick and light.

6. Whip in the butter a little at a time. Add it just as fast as it can be absorbed by the mixture.

7. Beat in the vanilla. If the icing is too soft, refrigerate it until it is firm enough to spread.

PRALINE BUTTERCREAM

Yield: 1 lb 2 oz (550 g)

For large-quantity measurements, see page 728.

Ingredients	U.S.		Metric	Sugar at 100% %
Water	1.5	oz	40 g	33
Sugar	4	oz	120 g	100
Egg yolks	3.33 oz (5 yolks)		100 g (5 yolks)	83
Butter, softened	6	oz	180 g	150
Praline paste	5	oz	150 mL	125

PROCEDURE

1. Combine the water and sugar in a saucepan, bring to a boil to dissolve the sugar, and cook the syrup to 248°F (120°C).

2. Whip the egg yolks until light. Gradually add the hot syrup to the yolks, whipping constantly. Whip until cool.

3. Whip in the butter and the praline paste.

CARAMEL BUTTERCREAM

Yield: 1 lb (500 g)

For large-quantity measurements, see page 729.

Ingredients	U.S.		Metric	Sugar at 100% %
Water	1	oz	25 g	14
Sugar	6.5	oz	185 g	100
Water	1.75	oz	50 g	27
Heavy cream	1.25	oz	35 g	19
Coffee extract	0.2	oz (1 tsp)	5 g	2.7
Egg yolks	2	oz	60 g	32
Butter, softened	6.75	oz	190 g	103

PROCEDURE

1. Cook the first quantity of water and the sugar to the caramel stage.
2. Let the caramel cool to 250°F (120°C) and then add the second quantity of water and the heavy cream. Cook until dissolved.
3. Add the coffee extract.
4. Whip the egg yolks until light, then whip in the hot caramel. Whip until light; Continue whipping until the mixture has cooled to about 85°F (30°C).
5. Whip in one-third of the butter. When this has been uniformly incorporated, whip in the remaining butter.

VANILLA CREAM

For large-quantity measurements, see page 729.

Ingredients	U.S.		Metric
Pastry Cream (p. 263)	1 lb		450 g
Gelatin		0.25 oz	6 g
Rum	4	tsp	20 g
Butter, softened	7	oz	200 g
Total weight:	**1 lb 7**	**oz**	**676 g**

PROCEDURE

1. Whip the pastry cream until smooth.
2. Soften the gelatin in cold water (see pp. 80–82). Heat the rum. Add the gelatin and stir until dissolved, warming as necessary.
3. Beat the gelatin mixture into the pastry cream.
4. Beat in the butter a little at a time. Whip until smooth and light.

LIGHT PRALINE CREAM

For large-quantity measurements, see page 729.

Ingredients	U.S.		Metric	Sugar at 100% %
Butter, softened	8	oz	200 g	100
Praline paste	4	oz	100 g	50
Cognac	1.5	oz	40 g	20
Italian Meringue (p. 259)	14	oz	340 g	170
Total weight:	**1 lb 11**	**oz**	**680 g**	**340%**

PROCEDURE

1. Whip together the butter and praline paste until smooth and light.
2. Whip in the cognac.
3. Mix in the Italian meringue. Whip until smooth.

Foam-Type Icings

Foam icings, sometimes called *boiled icings*, are simply meringues made with a boiling syrup. Some also contain stabilizing ingredients like gelatin. Foam icings should be applied thickly to cakes and left in peaks and swirls.

These icings are not stable. Therefore, regular boiled icing should be used the day it is prepared. *Marshmallow icing* should be made just before using and applied while still warm, before it sets.

Plain Boiled Icing

Follow the recipe for Italian Meringue (p. 259), but include 2 ounces (60 g) corn syrup with the sugar and water for the boiled syrup. Flavor the icing to taste with vanilla.

Marshmallow Icing

Soak ¼ ounce (8 g) gelatin in 1½ ounces (45 mL) cold water. Warm the water to dissolve the gelatin. Prepare plain boiled icing. Add the dissolved gelatin to the icing after adding the hot syrup. Scrape down the sides of the bowl to make sure that the gelatin is evenly mixed in. Use while still warm.

Chocolate Foam Icing and Filling

Prepare boiled icing. After the syrup has been added, blend in 5 ounces (150 g) melted, unsweetened chocolate.

Fudge-Type Icings

Fudge-type icings are rich and heavy. Many of them are made somewhat like candy. Their predominant ingredient is sugar, and they contain less fat than buttercreams. Fudge icings may be flavored with a variety of ingredients, and are used on cupcakes, layer cakes, loaf cakes, and sheet cakes.

Fudge icings are stable and hold up well on cakes and in storage. Stored icings must, however, be covered tightly to prevent drying and crusting.

To use stored fudge icing, warm it in a double boiler until it is soft enough to spread.

COCOA FUDGE ICING

Yield: 2 lb 6 oz (594 g)

Ingredients	U.S.		Metric	Granulated Sugar at 100% %
Granulated sugar	1 lb		500 g	100
Corn syrup	5	oz	150 g	30
Water	4	oz	125 mL	25
Salt	0.1	oz (½ tsp)	2 g	0.5
Butter or part butter and part emulsified shortening	4	oz	125 g	25
Confectioners' sugar	8	oz	250 g	50
Cocoa	3	oz	90 g	18
Vanilla extract	0.25	oz	8 mL	1.5
Water, hot	as needed		as needed	

PROCEDURE

1. Combine the granulated sugar, syrup, water, and salt in a saucepan. Bring to a boil, stirring to dissolve the sugar. Boil the mixture until it reaches 240°F (115°C).

2. While the sugar is cooking, mix the fat, confectioners' sugar, and cocoa until evenly combined, using the paddle attachment of the mixer.

3. With the machine running at low speed, slowly pour in the hot syrup.

4. Mix in the vanilla. Continue to beat until the icing is smooth, creamy, and spreadable. If necessary, thin with a little hot water.

5. Use while still warm, or rewarm in a double boiler.

--- **VARIATION** ---

VANILLA FUDGE ICING

Use evaporated milk or light cream instead of water for the syrup. Omit the cocoa. Adjust consistency with additional confectioners' sugar (to thicken) or water (to thin). Other flavorings, such as almond, maple, peppermint, or coffee, may be used in place of vanilla.

CARAMEL FUDGE ICING

Yield: 2 lb (1 kg)

Ingredients	U.S.			Metric	Sugar at 100% %
Brown sugar	1 lb	8	oz	750 g	100
Milk		12	oz	375 g	50
Butter or part butter and part shortening		6	oz	188 g	25
Salt		0.1	oz (½ tsp)	2 g	0.4
Vanilla extract		0.25	oz	8 mL	1

PROCEDURE

1. Combine the sugar and milk in a saucepan. Bring to a boil, stirring to dissolve the sugar. Boil the mixture until it reaches 240°F (115°C).
2. Pour the mixture into the bowl of a mixer. Let it cool to 110°F (43°C).
3. Turn on the machine and mix at low speed with the paddle attachment.
4. Add the butter, salt, and vanilla, and continue to mix at low speed until cool. Beat the icing until it is smooth and creamy in texture. If it is too thick, thin it with a little water.

QUICK WHITE FUDGE ICING I

Ingredients	U.S.			Metric	Sugar at 100% %
Water		4	oz	125 mL	12.5
Butter		2	oz	60 g	6
Emulsified shortening		2	oz	60 g	6
Corn syrup		1.5	oz	45 g	4.5
Salt		0.1	oz (½ tsp)	2 g	0.25
Confectioners' sugar	2 lb			1000 g	100
Vanilla extract		0.25	oz	8 mL	0.75
Total weight:	**2 lb**	**9**	**oz**	**1300 g**	**130** %

PROCEDURE

1. Place the water, butter, shortening, syrup, and salt in a saucepan. Bring to a boil.
2. Sift the sugar into the bowl of a mixer.
3. Using the paddle attachment, and with the machine running on low speed, add the boiling water mixture. Blend until smooth. The more the icing is mixed, the lighter it will become.
4. Blend in the vanilla.
5. Use while still warm, or rewarm in a double boiler. If necessary, thin with hot water.

—————————— VARIATION ——————————

QUICK CHOCOLATE FUDGE ICING

Omit the butter in the basic recipe. After step 3, blend in 6 oz (188 g) melted unsweetened chocolate. Thin the icing with hot water, as needed.

QUICK WHITE FUDGE ICING II

Ingredients	U.S.		Metric	Fondant at 100% %
Fondant	1 lb 4	oz	500 g	100
Corn syrup	2	oz	50 mL	10
Butter, softened	2	oz	50 g	10
Emulsified shortening	3	oz	75 g	15
Salt	0.12 oz		3 g	0.6
Flavoring (see procedure)				
Liquid, to thin (see procedure)				
Total weight:	**1 lb 11 oz or more**		**678 g or more**	**135 % or more**

PROCEDURE

1. Warm the fondant to 95°F (35°C).

2. Combine the fondant, corn syrup, butter, shortening, and salt in the bowl of a mixer. Blend with the paddle attachment until smooth.

3. Blend in the desired flavoring (see below).

4. Thin to spreading consistency with appropriate liquid (see below).

FLAVORING VARIATIONS

Add desired flavoring to taste, such as vanilla, almond, maple, lemon, or orange (extract, emulsion, or grated zest), or instant coffee dissolved in water. Crushed fruit, such as pineapple, strawberries, or ground maraschino cherries, may be used.

For *chocolate icing*, add 6 oz (180 g) melted unsweetened chocolate.

LIQUIDS FOR ADJUSTING CONSISTENCY

With fruit flavorings such as orange or lemon, use lemon juice and/or orange juice. With other flavors, use simple syrup or evaporated milk.

Flat Icings

Flat icings, also called *water icings*, are simply mixtures of confectioners' sugar and water, sometimes with corn syrup and flavoring added. They are used mostly for coffee cakes, Danish pastry, and sweet rolls.

Flat icings are warmed to 100°F (38°C) for application and are handled like poured fondant.

FLAT ICING

For large-quantity measurements, see page 729.

Ingredients	U.S.		Metric	Sugar at 100% %
Confectioners' sugar	1 lb		500 g	100
Water, hot	3	oz	90 mL	19
Corn syrup	1	oz	30 g	6
Vanilla extract	0.12 oz (¾ tsp)		4 g	0.8
Total weight:	**1 lb 4 oz**		**624 g**	**125 %**

PROCEDURE

1. Mix all ingredients together until smooth.

2. To use, place the desired amount in a double boiler. Warm to 100°F (38°C) and then apply to the product to be iced.

Royal Icing

Royal icing, also called *decorating* or *decorator's icing*, is similar to flat icings except it is much thicker and made with egg whites, which make it hard and brittle when dry. It is used almost exclusively for decorative work. Pure white royal icing is most often used, but it may also be colored as desired. Because it consists mostly of confectioners' sugar, it is sweet but has little taste.

Royal icing dries easily and quickly, which makes it useful for fine decorations; but it also requires special handling and storage. Cover it tightly whenever it is not in use. For even greater protection from drying, place a clean, damp towel on the surface of the icing, and then cover the container tightly with plastic film. If any icing dries or crusts on the sides of the container during storage, remove the dried sections carefully, so that it does not fall back into the moist icing. Dried particles can clog the tips of paper cones and writing tubes.

Using a paper cone or, even better, a pastry bag fitted with a writing tip (a pastry tip with a small, round opening), royal icing can be piped into designs onto parchment or plastic and allowed to dry. They can then be lifted off carefully and stored in airtight containers for later use. See pages 436–437 for a discussion of using the paper cone.

A second use for royal icing is called *string work*, in which delicate strands or filaments of icing are suspended between two attachment points, as illustrated in the decoration of the pastillage showpiece on page 655. This technique is also used on some styles of wedding cakes. To produce string work, touch the tip of the paper cone to the first attachment point, then pull the bag away while squeezing the cone with constant pressure. Allow the loop to drop to the desired length, then touch the tip to the second attachment point.

A third use of royal icing is *flooding* outlined areas of a design with colored icing. This technique requires much thinner icing than that used for string work. Thin the icing with water until a teaspoonful dropped into the bowl of icing flattens to a smooth surface in about 10 seconds. The first step in flooding is to draw an outline using medium-stiff royal icing, either white or colored, as desired. Pipe the outline on the desired surface, such as a sheet of acetate. Allow the outline to dry at least until the surface of the icing is firm. Using a pastry bag with a small (No. 2) plain tip, pipe thinned icing, colored as desired, in a line next to but not touching the inside of the dried outline. The icing should be thin enough to flow up to the outline. Continue to pipe along the inside edge of the icing until the area is filled with a smooth layer of icing. When dry, the design can be lifted off and placed on the surface of a cake.

As you can see, the correct consistency or thickness of royal icing depends on its use. Piped designs and string work require fairly thick icing, while flood work requires a thinner product. For this reason, many pastry chefs do not use a recipe for royal icing but prepare small batches as needed, using the Procedure for Preparing Royal Icing, below. For those who prefer working with a recipe, one is provided.

PROCEDURE: Preparing Royal Icing

1. Place desired amount of confectioners' sugar in a mixing bowl. Add a small quantity of cream of tartar (for whiteness), about ⅛ tsp per pound of sugar (0.6 g per kilogram).

2. Beat in egg whites (pasteurized), a little at a time, until the sugar forms a smooth paste. You will need 2 to 3 oz egg whites per pound of sugar (125 g per kilogram).

3. Keep unused icing covered with a damp cloth or plastic film at all times to prevent hardening.

ROYAL ICING

Ingredients	U.S.	Metric
Confectioners' sugar	1 lb	500 g
Cream of tartar	⅛ tsp	0.3 g (0.5 mL)
Egg whites, pasteurized (see *Note*)	3 oz	95 g
Total weight:	**1 lb 3 oz**	**595 g**

NOTE: Vary the quantity of egg whites depending on the consistency desired.

PROCEDURE

1. Sift the sugar and cream of tartar into the bowl of a mixer fitted with the paddle attachment.

2. In a small bowl, beat the egg whites briefly, to break them up.

3. With the mixer running on low speed, gradually add the egg whites.

4. Continue to mix until the ingredients are well blended and the icing stands in soft peaks.

Glazes

Glazes are thin, glossy, transparent coatings that give a shine to baked products and help prevent drying.

The simplest glaze is a sugar syrup or diluted corn syrup brushed while hot onto coffee cakes or Danish pastries (see p. 190 for recipe). Syrup glazes may also contain gelatin or waxy maize starch.

Fruit glazes for pastries, the most popular of which are apricot and red currant, are available commercially prepared. They are melted, thinned with a little water, syrup, or liquor, and brushed on while hot. Fruit glazes may also be made by melting apricot or other preserves and forcing them through a strainer. It helps to add melted, strained preserves to commercial glazes because these products usually have little flavor.

The glaze recipes included in this chapter are of two types: chocolate and gelatin-based. Chocolate glazes are usually melted chocolate containing additional fats or liquids, or both. They are applied warm and set up to form a thin, shiny coating. Gelatin-based glazes, which include many fruit glazes, are usually applied only to the tops of cakes and charlottes made in ring molds. There are several recipes in this chapter, and Chapter 19 contains examples of products finished with gelatin-based glazes.

CHOCOLATE GLAÇAGE OR SACHER GLAZE

Ingredients	U.S.	Metric	Chocolate at 100% %
Heavy cream	6 oz	150 g	100
Semisweet or bittersweet chocolate, chopped	6 oz	150 g	100
Butter	2 oz	50 g	33
Total weight:	**14 oz**	**350 g**	**233%**

PROCEDURE

1. Prepare a ganache (p. 272) with the cream and chocolate: Heat the cream to boiling and pour over the finely chopped chocolate. Stir until the chocolate is melted and the mixture is uniformly blended.

2. Add the butter and stir to mix in. Use as soon as possible.

GANACHE ICING (GANACHE À GLACER)

Ingredients	U.S.	Metric	Chocolate at 100% %
Heavy cream	10 oz	250 g	100
Sugar	2 oz	50 g	20
Glucose	2 oz	50 g	20
Semisweet or bittersweet chocolate couverture	10 oz	250 g	100
Total weight:	**1 lb 8 oz**	**600 g**	**240%**

PROCEDURE

1. Heat the cream, sugar, and glucose to the boiling point. Remove from the heat.

2. Finely chop the chocolate and place in a bowl.

3. Pour the hot cream over the chocolate. Stir until the chocolate is melted and well blended with the cream.

4. Allow to cool slightly before use. This makes a thin, shiny coating when poured over cakes and charlottes.

OPERA GLAZE

For large-quantity measurements, see page 729.

Ingredients	U.S.		Metric
Coating chocolate (see p. 86)	8	oz	250 g
Semisweet or bittersweet chocolate couverture	3.5	oz	100 g
Peanut oil	1.33	oz	40 g
Total weight:	**12**	**oz**	**390 g**

VARIATION

If couverture is used alone instead of part coating chocolate and part couverture, increase the quantity of oil so the icing has the proper texture and can be cut easily with a cake knife.

For large-quantity measurements, see page 729.

Ingredients	U.S.	Metric
Dark chocolate couverture	11.5 oz	350 g
Peanut oil	2 oz	60 g

PROCEDURE

1. Melt both chocolates in a hot-water bath.
2. Stir in the oil.
3. Allow to cool slightly before use. Makes a thin coating that sets solid but can be cut with a hot knife.

FRUIT GLAÇAGE

Ingredients	U.S.		Metric
Gelatin	0.5	oz	12 g
Sugar	3	oz	90 g
Water	2	oz	60 g
Glucose	1	oz	30 g
Fruit purée	5	oz	150 g
Total weight:	**11**	**oz**	**342 g**

VARIATION

Two charlottes in this book, Passion Fruit Charlotte (p. 533) and Charlotte au Cassis (p. 533), use fruit glaçage. Passion fruit purée or juice and blackcurrant or cassis purée, respectively, are used to make the glaçage. For other uses, most fruit purées can be used.

PROCEDURE

1. Soften the gelatin in cold water (see pp. 80–82).
2. Heat the sugar, water, and glucose until dissolved. Remove from the heat and stir in the gelatin until dissolved.
3. Add the fruit purée.
4. Strain through a chinois or fine strainer.
5. To use, rewarm if necessary. Pour over the top of a cake or charlotte and, with a palette knife, quickly spread to the edges of the cake. One small batch makes enough glaze for a 7- or 8-in. (18–20-cm) cake.

COCOA JELLY

For large-quantity measurements, see page 729.

Ingredients	U.S.		Metric	Fondant at 100% %
Water	4	oz	100 g	67
Fondant	6	oz	150 g	100
Glucose	1	oz	25 g	17
Gelatin	0.25	oz	7 g	4.7
Cocoa powder	1.2	oz (6 tbsp)	30 g	20.8
Total weight:	**12**	**oz**	**312 g**	**209 %**

PROCEDURE

1. Combine the water, fondant, and glucose. Bring to a boil and skim if necessary.

2. Soften the gelatin in cold water (see pp. 80–82).

3. Add the gelatin and cocoa powder to the hot fondant mixture. Mix quickly and strain through a chinois or fine strainer.

4. This mixture is ready to use once the temperature has dropped to 95°F (35°C).

COFFEE MARBLE GLAZE

Yield: about 11 oz (350 g)

For large-quantity measurements, see page 729.

Ingredients	U.S.		Metric
Gelatin	0.33	oz	8 g
Water	8	oz	250 g
Sugar	1.33	oz	40 g
Glucose	1.33	oz	40 g
Vanilla bean, split (see *Note*)	1		1
Coffee liqueur	4	tsp	20 g
Coffee extract	2	tsp	10 g

NOTE: If vanilla beans are not available, add ½ tsp vanilla extract.

PROCEDURE

1. Soften the gelatin in cold water (see pp. 80–82).

2. Simmer the water, sugar, glucose, and vanilla bean until the sugar and glucose are completely dissolved.

3. Remove from the heat, cool slightly, and add the gelatin. Stir until dissolved. Scrape the seeds from the vanilla bean and add to the syrup.

4. When ready to use, rewarm the glaze if necessary. Add the coffee liqueur and extract and swirl them in slightly; do not mix them in. Swirl the glaze over the surface of the cake so the coffee extract gives a marbled effect (see the photo of Julianna on p. 466).

Rolled Coatings

The three commonly used rolled cake coatings are rolled fondant, marzipan, and modeling chocolate. Rather than being applied by spreading or pouring like the other products discussed in this chapter, these are rolled into thin sheets, using a rolling pin, and draped over the cake to cover it. To ensure the coating adheres to the cake, the cake is first brushed with apricot glaze (p. 194) or a similar product, or iced with a thin layer of buttercream before the rolled coating is applied.

Marzipan is a paste made of ground almonds and sugar. Preparation and use of marzipan is discussed in Chapter 24.

Rolled fondant is a doughlike product consisting primarily of confectioner's sugar combined with small quantities of glucose, water, gelatin, and other ingredients to give it the proper consistency. It is firm and stiff enough to be kneaded, and pliable enough to be rolled out in thin sheets. Like poured fondant, it is almost always purchased ready-prepared.

Modeling chocolate is a stiff paste made of melted chocolate and corn syrup. It is discussed in Chapter 23.

Guidelines for applying rolled coatings are discussed on pages 447–448.

KEY POINTS TO REVIEW

- What are the eight basic types of icings and cake coatings?

- What is the procedure for using fondant?

- What are the basic types of buttercream? Describe how they are made.

- What are foam icings?

- How is royal icing made? What is it used for?

ASSEMBLING AND ICING SIMPLE CAKES

THIS SECTION DEALS with simple North American-style cakes. Typical examples of this type are cupcakes, sheet cakes, and layer cakes made of two or three high-ratio or butter-cake layers. These are popular items in bakeshops and are standard desserts in many food service operations. They may be iced but otherwise undecorated, or they may be given some decorative touches.

In contrast, the typical European-style cake is a sponge cake, split into thin layers, moistened with flavored syrup, filled and iced, and frequently set on a base of baked meringue, japonaise, or short dough. It is sometimes filled with fruit between the layers, and is almost always decorated on top. It is usually less than 3 inches (7.5 cm) tall, and has a broad flat top that serves as an excellent canvas for pastry chefs to display their decorating skills.

This section focuses on the basic skills needed to assemble and ice simple North American-style cakes, with basic decorating techniques discussed in the next section. After mastering these techniques, you are then introduced to more complex cakes in the last sections of the chapter.

Planning the Cake

Most cakes have up to four components:

- Cake
- Icing
- Filling
- Décor

The simplest cakes have only the first two of these components: cake and icing. For example, the simplest sheet cake consists of only a single layer of cake topped by a single layer of icing. Simple layer cakes have two or three layers of cake, with icing between the layers and the same icing on the top and sides.

In a slightly more complex cake, the filling between the layers may be different from the icing on the outside of the cake.

Finally, a cake may be decorated with additional elements as décor, such as fruit and nuts.

When planning a cake, a pastry chef must consider the characteristics of each of these four components in order to produce an appealing and attractive cake. In particular, the chef should take into account the following characteristics:

- Flavor
- Color
- Texture
- Shape

Cake layers, icings, and fillings come in an endless variety of flavors, colors, and textures. The fourth characteristic, shape, applies primarily to the cake layers (round, rectangular, novelty cutout) and to the décor elements.

When matching flavors and textures of cake, icing, and filling, select combinations that complement each other (such as chocolate icing and chocolate cake) or that make a pleasing contrast (such as raspberry filling in chocolate cake).

Selection of Icing

The flavor, texture, and color of the icing must be compatible with the cake. In general, use heavy frostings with heavy cakes and light frostings with light cakes. For example, ice angel food cakes with a simple flat icing, fondant, or a light, fluffy, boiled icing. High-ratio cakes go well with buttercreams and fudge-type icings. Sponge layer cakes are often combined with fruits or fruit fillings, light French or Italian buttercreams, whipped cream, or flavored fondants.

Because heavier icings are usually richer in texture and more intense in flavor, they are applied in thinner layers than lighter icings. The icing should not overpower or overwhelm the cake.

Use the best-quality flavorings, and use them sparingly. The flavor of the frosting should not be stronger than that of the cake. Fudge-type icings may be flavored most strongly, as long as the flavor is of good quality.

Use colors carefully. For traditional cakes, use colors sparingly. Light pastel shades are more appetizing than strong colors. Modern taste in cakes, however, runs more to strong colors. Consider your audience when planning use of colors. Paste colors give the best results. To use either paste or liquid colors, mix a little color with a small portion of the icing, then use this icing to color the rest.

Selection of Décor

Elements of cake decoration fall into two general categories: piped icing decoration and additional décor items. Both these categories serve several functions, adding eye appeal as well as flavor and textural interest. All of these should be taken into consideration when planning cakes. Flavor, color, texture, and shape of décor should be appropriate to the cake.

The list of cake décor items is nearly limitless. Popular categories of décor include fruits, nuts, crisp meringue, chocolate décor (see Chapter 23); pastillage, pulled sugar flowers and other items (Chapters 24 and 25); and candies and confections, either made in-house or commercially made.

Sheet Cakes

Sheet cakes are ideal for volume service because they require little labor to bake, ice, and decorate, and they keep well as long as they remain uncut.

For special occasions, sheet cakes are sometimes decorated as a single unit with a design or picture in colored icing, and a "Happy Special Occasion" message. It is more common, however, to ice them for individual service, as in the Procedure for Icing Sheet Cakes on page 433.

Cupcakes

There are three main methods for icing cupcakes. The first of these, dipping, is used for soft icings. The other methods are used when the icing is too stiff for dipping.

Before icing the top of the cupcake, you might want to inject a filling into the cake to make a specialty product. To fill a cupcake with a light buttercream or other cream filling, use a pastry bag fitted with a small, plain tip. Pierce the top center of the cupcake so that the tip is about an inch deep in the cake. Squeeze gently to force about ½ to ¾ fl oz (15–22 mL) filling into the center.

To ice the top of the cupcake, use one of these three methods:

1. Dip the tops of the cupcakes in the icing. Do not dip them too deeply; only the tops should touch the icing.
   - If the icing is reasonably stiff, not flowing, twist the cakes slightly and pull them out quickly in one smooth motion.
   - If the icing is flowing (such as flat icing or fondant), pull the cakes straight out of the icing. Hold them sideways for a moment so the icing runs to one edge. Then turn them upright and wipe the icing from the edge of the cakes with your finger. Do not let icing run down the sides.

2. Spread the icing with a spatula. Take enough icing for one cake on the tip of a bowl knife and cover the top of the cake in a single smooth, neat motion, twisting the cake in one hand. Practice is necessary to develop speed and efficiency.

3. With a pastry bag fitted with a star or plain tube, apply a swirl of icing to each cake. This is perhaps the most popular method for modern cupcakes. It makes it possible to apply a generous quantity of icing to the cupcake—a style favored by consumers.

Before the icing dries, cupcakes may be decorated with glazed fruit, coconut, nuts, colored sugar, chocolate sprinkles, and so on.

Layer Cakes

A basic method for assembling and icing simple layer cakes is explained in detail in the Procedure for Assembling Simple Layer Cakes, which follows. This is the simplest and most direct way of icing a layer cake. In addition, two other icing techniques should be mentioned here: applying a thin masking layer of icing and applying glaze.

PROCEDURE: Assembling Simple Layer Cakes

This is the basic procedure for assembling popular American-style layer cakes made with high-fat (that is, creaming method, two-stage, and one-stage method) batters. Layered sponge cakes are assembled slightly differently, as shown on page 443.

1. Assemble all tools and equipment and have them ready.

2. Have all ingredients prepared and at the proper temperature. Cool cake layers completely before assembling and icing. Icings and fillings should be spreadable and at the correct temperature.

3. Trim cake layers, if necessary. Remove any ragged edges. Slightly rounded tops are easily covered by icing, but excessively large bumps may have to be cut off.

   If desired, split layers in half horizontally. This makes the cake higher and increases the proportion of filling to cake (see p. 443).

4. Brush all crumbs from cakes. Loose crumbs make icing difficult.

5. Place the bottom layer upside down (to give a flat surface for the filling) on a cardboard cake circle of the same diameter. Place the cake in the center of a cake turntable. If a cake circle or turntable is not available, place the cake on a serving plate; slip sheets of wax paper or parchment under the edges of the cake to keep the plate clean.

6. Spread filling on the bottom layer, out to the edges. If the filling is different from the outside frosting, be careful not to spread the filling over the edges. One way to avoid spilling the filling over the edge is to pipe a row of the icing used for the cake sides around the edge of the cake layer to form a barrier to hold the filling inside.

   Use the proper amount of filling. If applied too heavily, filling will ooze out when top layer is put in place.

7. Place the top layer on the bottom layer, right side up.

8. Optional step: Apply a masking layer of icing, as described in the next section.

9. Ice the cake:

   a. If a thin or light icing is used, pour or spread the icing onto the center of the cake. Then spread it to the edges and down the sides with a spatula.

   b. If a heavy icing is used, it may be necessary to spread the sides first, then place a good quantity of icing in the center of the top and push it to the edges with the spatula.

   Steps 6–9 on page 443 illustrate how to ice the cake.
   Pushing the icing, rather than pulling or dragging it with the spatula, prevents pulling up crumbs and getting them mixed with the icing.

   Use enough icing to cover the entire cake generously, but not excessively, with an even layer.

   Smooth the icing with the spatula, or leave it textured or swirled, as desired.

   An alternative way to apply icing is to pipe it on using an oversize basketweave tip, sometimes called a *speed icer*, in a pastry bag.

   The finished, iced cake should have a perfectly level top and perfectly straight, even sides.

Applying a Masking Layer

As an alternative to applying the finishing directly to the cake, it is often useful to add an intermediate step. Apply a thin coating of icing to the cake, using the technique given in the basic procedure but making only a thin layer. This optional step has three advantages:

1. The masking layer locks in any loose crumbs that might otherwise get mixed with the final icing and mar its appearance. The finish coat of icing is then easier to apply. For this reason, a masking layer is sometimes called a *crumb coat*.

2. The masking layer protects from drying when longer storage is needed. A pastry chef might want to mask a number of cakes and then store them for later icing and decoration. This enables a more flexible production schedule.

3. The masking layer can be used to even out any irregularities in the cake. For example, if the top layer is domed in the center, the masking layer can be used to level the top so that it is flat. The masked cake should have perfectly smooth, even sides and a smooth, level top.

After applying the masking layer, refrigerate the cake long enough for the surface to become firm before applying the final coat of icing.

Applying Glaze

Unlike regular spreadable icings such as buttercream, glazes (p. 427) are applied by pouring them over the cake. A masking coat of icing is always applied if the cake is to be finished with a glaze rather than a spread icing. A detailed Procedure for Applying Glaze can be found on page 447.

PROCEDURE: Icing Sheet Cakes

1. Turn out the cake onto a cake board or the bottom of another sheet pan or tray, as described on page 389. Cool the cake thoroughly.

2. Trim the edges evenly with a serrated knife.

3. Brush all crumbs from the cake.

4. Place a quantity of icing in the center of the cake and, with a spatula, push the icing to the edges. Smooth the top with the spatula, giving the entire cake an even layer of icing.

5. With a long knife or spatula, mark the entire cake into portions by pressing the back of the knife lightly into the icing. Do not cut the cake.

6. Using a paper cone or pastry bag fitted with a star tube, pipe a rosette or swirl onto the center of each marked-off portion. (If you prefer, select another kind of decoration.) Whatever decorations you use, keep them simple, and make them the same for every portion.

7. Cut portions as close as possible to service time to keep the cake from drying.

Cake-cutting guides for sheet cakes and round layer cakes. For half-size sheets (13 × 18 in./33 × 46 cm), simply halve the diagrams for full-size sheet cakes below.

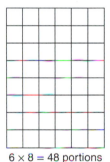

6 × 8 = 48 portions

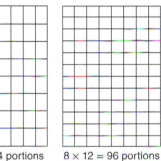

8 × 8 = 64 portions

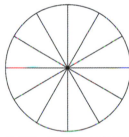

8 × 12 = 96 portions

8–10 in. (20–25 cm) layers
12 portions

10–12 in. (25–30 cm) layers
16 portions

Specialty Items

A number of popular cake items don't fit in the categories just described—layer cake, sheet cake, or cupcake. We discuss those here.

Boston Cream Pie

Boston cream pie is not a pie at all but a simple layer cake. Bake sponge cake in standard layer pans or pie tins. When cool, split each cake into two layers. Fill with Pastry Cream (p. 263) and ice the tops with chocolate fondant, or sprinkle with confectioners' sugar.

Cake Rolls

Besides jelly rolls (p. 402), sponge rolls can be made with a variety of fillings, such as whipped cream, vanilla or chocolate boiled icing, marshmallow icing, or buttercream. Cake rolls are discussed in more detail in the section on European-style cakes (p. 469).

Ice Cream Cakes

Ice cream may be used in place of icing to fill layer cakes or cake rolls. If the bakeshop is cool, or if you have a walk-in refrigerator to work in, you can spread slightly softened ice cream on the layers or inside the rolls. Round cakes are best assembled inside cake rings lined with acetate (pp. 50–51). If the temperature is warm, however, it is better to cut slices of hard-frozen ice cream to fill the cakes. Work quickly; do not allow the ice cream to melt and drip out of the cake.

As soon as the layers are stacked or the rolls are tightly rolled, return them to the freezer until they are firm. Then quickly frost the tops and sides with whipped cream. Store in the freezer until needed.

French Pastry

In parts of North America, the term *French pastry* is used to refer to a wide range of decorated pastry and cake products usually made in single-portion pieces. The simplest of the cake-based varieties are tiny decorated layer cakes made in a variety of shapes. They are assembled as follows:

1. Using thin (½–¾-in./1–2-cm) sheet cakes, stack two or three sheets with filling or icing between them. The filled cake layers together should be about 1½–2 in. (4–5 cm) thick.

    Buttercream is the most popular filling. Fruit jams and fudge icings may also be used.

2. Press the layers together firmly and chill or freeze.

3. Using a sharp knife dipped in hot water before each cut, cut the sheet into desired shapes, such as squares, rectangles, or triangles. Circles may be cut out using large cutters. Pieces should be the size of a single portion.

4. Ice the sides and top of each piece with buttercream or fondant. After icing, sides may be coated with chopped nuts, coconut, chocolate sprinkles, and so on.

5. Decorate the tops neatly.

    French pastries are discussed further in the section on European-style cakes (pp. 471–472).

KEY POINTS TO REVIEW

■ What are the four possible components of a simple cake?

■ What are the steps in the procedure for assembling and icing simple layer cakes?

■ How are sheet cakes and cupcakes iced?

BASIC DECORATING TECHNIQUES

A NUMBER OF essential decorating techniques are discussed in this section. Of these, perhaps the most difficult to learn are the ones using the pastry bag and paper cone. Others take less practice to master, but do require a steady hand, neatness, and a strong sense of symmetry.

Tools

You will need the following tools for assembling and decorating cakes:

Palette knife.

Palette knife or steel spatula. A spatula with a long, flexible blade for spreading and smoothing icings and fillings.

Offset palette knife. A palette knife with an angled blade for spreading batters and creams inside pans.

Offset palette knife.

Serrated knife.

Serrated knife. A scalloped-edge knife for cutting cakes and splitting cake layers horizontally into thinner layers.

Icing screens, **or grates.** Open-mesh screens for holding cakes being iced with a flow-type icing such as fondant. Excess icing drips off the cake and is collected on a tray under the rack.

Turntable. A pedestal with a flat, rotating top, to simplify the process of icing cakes.

Icing screen.

Icing comb. A plastic triangle with toothed or serrated edges used for applying a grooved or ridged pattern to the sides of iced cakes. The edge of the comb is held stationary in a vertical position against one side of the cake while the turntable is rotated.

Plastic or steel scraper. A tool with a flat edge for making the icing on the sides of cake perfectly smooth. The technique is the same as that for working with the icing comb (see preceding page).

Pastry brushes. Used to remove crumbs from a cake, apply dessert syrups to sponge cake layers, and glaze the surfaces of cakes with apricot glaze and other coatings.

Sugar dredger. Resembling a large metal saltshaker, a dredger is used to dust cakes with confectioners' sugar.

Cake rings or charlotte rings. Stainless steel rings of varying diameters and heights. Cakes are assembled inside these rings when they include soft fillings, such as Bavarian creams and other gelatin-based fillings, that must be held in place while the filling sets. Also used for charlottes (Chapter 19).

Cake cards and doilies. Layer cakes are placed on cardboard circles (same diameter as the cake) when being assembled. Sheet cakes are placed on half- or full-size cardboard cake boards. This makes them easy to ice and to move after icing. For easy, attractive display, place a paper doily 4 inches (10 cm) larger than the cake on a cake card 2 inches (5 cm) larger than the cake. For example, to assemble, ice, and display a 10-inch cake, use a 10-inch circle, a 12-inch circle, and a 14-inch doily.

Parchment paper. For making paper cones.

Pastry bag and tips. For making borders, inscriptions, flowers, and other designs out of icing. The basic tips are described below.

Pastry brushes.

Sugar dredger.

Plain (round) tips: For writing words and drawing lines, beads, dots, and so forth. Also used to pipe sponge batters, creams, and choux paste, and to fill choux pastries and other items.

Star tips: For making rosettes, shells, stars, and borders.

Rose tip: For making flower petals. These tips have a slit-shaped opening that is wider at one end than the other.

Leaf tips: For making leaves.

Ribbon or basketweave tips: For making smooth or ridged stripes or ribbons. These have a slit opening that is ridged on one side.

St-Honoré tip: For filling gâteaux St-Honoré (p. 360). This tip has a round opening with a V-shaped slit on one side.

Many other specialized tips are used for unusual shapes. However, the plain and star tips are by far the most important. The beginner is advised to concentrate on these at first. They make a wide variety of decorations. With the exception of roses and other flowers, the majority of cake decorations are made using the plain and star tips.

The usual way of using a pastry tip is simply to fit it inside the pastry bag. When you need to use more than one tip with the same icing, you must use a separate bag for each one or empty the bag to change the tip. However, special *couplers* are available that allow you to attach the tip to the outside of the bag. It is then a simple matter to change tips even when the pastry bag is full of icing.

Using the Paper Cone

The *paper cone* is widely used in decorative work. It is inexpensive, easy to make, and can simply be discarded after use. It is especially valuable if you are working with different colors; simply make a separate cone for each color icing.

Although it is possible to fit metal decorating tubes inside paper cones, the cones are usually used without metal tubes for writing inscriptions and for making line drawings and patterns. In other words, they are used the same way you would use a pastry bag fitted with a small plain tube. Because paper cones can be made rather small and are easy to control, pastry chefs generally prefer them to pastry bags when they are doing delicate work. For the most delicate work, a special type of plastic or cellophane is available that makes finer lines than paper because a smaller, cleaner opening can be cut on the tip.

Two factors are important to be successful using both the paper cone and the pastry bag:

1. **Consistency of the icing.** Icing must be neither too thick nor too thin. With the paper cone or the writing tube, the icing must be thin enough to flow freely from the opening, but not too thin to form a solid thread. Stiff icing is difficult to force through the opening and tends to break off. For flowers and large decorations, however, the icing must be stiffer so the items hold their shapes.

2. **Pressure on the cone or bag.** Pressure control is necessary to make neat, precise decorations. As described below, sometimes you must keep the pressure steady and even. For other types of decorations, such as shell borders, you must vary the pressure from heavy to light, and then stop the pressure at the right moment. Learning to control the pressure with which you squeeze the decorator's cone or pastry bag takes a lot of practice.

Two methods are used to make decorations: the *drop-string method* and the *contact method*.

The drop-string method, also known as the *falling method*, is so called because the cone is held above the surface and the icing is allowed to fall or drop from the tip of the cone onto the surface being decorated. This method is used to make lines of even thickness on horizontal surfaces. Much, if not most, paper cone work is done this way, generally with royal icing, fondant, chocolate fondant, melted chocolate, or piping chocolate (p. 637).

To use the drop-string method, begin by holding the cone vertically. Touch the tip of the cone to the surface to attach the icing to the point where you want the line to start. Then, as you begin to squeeze the cone, lift the tip of the cone from the surface and start your line. Hold the cone about 1 inch (2.5 cm) from the surface as you trace your pattern. The thread of icing will be suspended in air between the tip of the cone and the surface being decorated. Keep the pressure light and constant. To finish a line, lower the tip of the cone and touch the surface at the point where you want the line to end. At the same time, stop squeezing the cone.

The drop-string method allows you to make fine, delicate lines and patterns while keeping the thickness of the line perfectly even. Make sure the opening in the tip of the cone is cut quite small. At first, it may seem difficult to control the line while holding the cone an inch above the surface, but with practice, you will be able to make precise patterns.

The contact method is used in two situations: (1) when you want to vary the thickness of the line, and (2) when you want to decorate a vertical surface, such as the side of a cake.

For the contact method, begin by holding the cone as you would a pen, with the tip in contact with the surface and at an angle of about 30 to 45 degrees. Draw lines as though you were drawing on paper with a pen. Control the thickness of the line by adjusting the pressure of your thumb. Squeezing harder makes a thicker line.

Normally, it is best to work with the drop-string method first, until you are able to make simple lines and patterns easily. Then, when you move to the contact method, you can concentrate on controlling pressure. In addition to royal icing, fondant, and chocolate, buttercream is also used for decorating with the contact method.

Note: The instructions that follow for using the cone and pastry bag are written for right-handed people. If you are left-handed, simply reverse the hands in the instructions.

PROCEDURE: Decorating with a Paper Cone

1. Make the paper cone, as shown.

2. Fill the cone about half full with icing. If the cone is too full, it is harder to squeeze, and icing is likely to come out the top.

3. Fold down the top of the cone to close the open end.

4. With scissors, cut off a very small piece of the tip of the cone. (Be sure to discard the tiny paper tip immediately, or it may get mixed in with the icing.) It is better to make the opening too small than too large. Squeeze out a little of the icing to test the cone. If necessary, cut off a little more of the tip to enlarge the opening.

5. Hold the top end of the cone between your thumb and the first two fingers of your right hand. Position your fingers so they can hold the folded end closed and at the same time apply pressure to squeeze the icing from the cone.

6. Do not squeeze the cone with your left hand. Instead, lightly hold the index finger of your left hand against the thumb of your right hand or against the cone, in order to steady your right hand and help guide it.

7. Use either the contact method or the drop-string method (discussed on p. 436) to create different types of decorations and inscriptions.

Make a single cone out of a small triangle of parchment paper. Hold the cone with the fingertip in the center of the long side and curl one side.

For a sturdier double cone, cut a longer triangle. Start as for a single cone.

Curl the other side around to complete the cone.

Twist the long end around twice to complete the cone.

Fold over the peak at the open end of the cone to secure it.

Complete single and double cones.

(continues)

(continued)

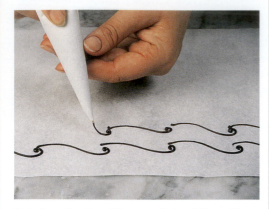

Note how the tip of the cone is held above the surface, allowing the icing to drop into place.

An assortment of borders made with the paper cone.

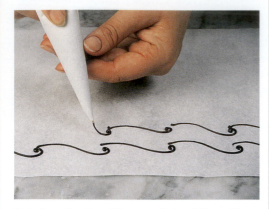

Paper-cone designs made by the contact method.

Using the Pastry Bag

An advantage of the pastry bag is that it makes it easy to use many different metal tips to create a wide variety of designs. Also, a pastry bag holds more icing than a paper cone. This is important when you are decorating with whipped cream or meringue. Buttercream flowers, shell borders, and many other decorations are made with the pastry bag.

Most pastry bags are made of one of the following four materials:

- *Disposable plastic bags* are designed to be thrown away after use. As a result, they are hygienic.

- *Reusable plastic bags* are made of a soft, reinforced plastic, making them durable and easy to use. Also, they do not easily absorb odors and flavors. However, they must be thoroughly cleaned after use.

- *Nylon bags* are soft and flexible. They, too, must be cleaned thoroughly after use, but because they are made of a synthetic fabric, they are easier to clean than cotton.

- *Cotton* is the traditional material for pastry bags, but because it is highly absorbent, bags made with cotton are harder to clean. It is important to wash them well and sterilize them after each use.

PROCEDURE: Filling and Using a Pastry Bag

1. Fit the desired metal tip into the pastry bag.

2. If the filling or icing is thin, twist the bag just above the tip and force it into the tip. This prevents the filling from running out of the bag while the bag is being filled.

3. Turn down the top of the bag into a sort of collar. Slip your hand under this collar and hold the top open with your thumb and forefinger.

4. Fill the bag half to three-quarters full. Remember that stiff icings are relatively hard to force from the bag, so fill the bag less when you are working with these. With meringue and whipped cream, the bag can be fuller.

5. Turn up the top of the bag again. Gather the loose top together and hold it shut with the thumb and forefinger of your right hand.

6. To force out the icing or cream, squeeze the top of the bag in the palm of your right hand.

7. Use the fingers of your left hand to lightly guide the tip of the bag, *not to squeeze the bottom of the bag*. The left hand is sometimes used to hold the item being filled or decorated.

Piping basic shells and shell borders.

Simple bulbs, bead borders, and rosettes.

Scrolls and borders made with a star tip.

Additional scrolls and borders made with a star tip; plus, at the bottom, an example of piping using a St-Honoré tip.

Other Decorating Techniques

There are many dozens of techniques for decorating cakes. In this section, we describe some of the simpler, more commonly used ones. Later in this chapter and in the accompanying illustrations, you will see examples of these and other techniques.

A popular way of organizing the decoration of a round cake is to divide the cake into portions by marking the icing on top with the back of a long knife: First mark the cake in quarters. Then divide each quarter in half, thirds, or fourths, depending on the size of the cake and the number of pieces desired. Decorate the cake in a repetitive pattern so each slice has the same decorations. For example, you might decorate a Black Forest Torte (p. 451) with a rosette of cream at the wide end of each wedge, then place a cherry on each rosette.

The advantages of marking the cake into wedges are that it enables portion control and ensures that each piece is decorated equally. Thus, this approach is often used in restaurants and in retail shops that sell cakes by the slice. Each slice, when cut and served, retains an attractive decoration.

Examples of marbled icing patterns.

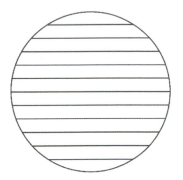

Masking the Sides

This technique (not to be confused with applying a masking layer of icing, as explained on p. 432) is used to apply a coating of chopped or sliced nuts, coconut, chocolate sprinkles, chocolate shavings, cake crumbs, or another material to the sides of the cake.

Hold the freshly iced cake (on a cardboard circle) in your left hand over the tray of nuts or other material. With your right hand, lightly press a handful of the material against the side of the cake, and let the excess fall back onto the tray. Turn the cake slightly and repeat until the coating is complete. You can coat the sides completely or just the bottom edge.

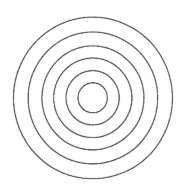

Stenciling

You can add designs to a cake by masking part of the top with paper cutouts or paper doilies and then sprinkling the top of the cake with confectioners' sugar, cocoa, ground nuts, shaved chocolate, cake crumbs, praline powder, or another fine material. Alternatively, spray the top of the cake with a chocolate sprayer, as shown on page 637. Carefully remove the paper pattern to reveal the design. A simple type of stenciling that is effective on chocolate icings is to lay parallel strips of paper on the cake and dust with confectioners' sugar.

Marbling

The *marbling* technique is most frequently used with fondant.

Ice the top of the cake with fondant, then pipe lines or spirals in fondant of a contrasting color. Quickly, before the icing sets, draw the back of the knife through the icing to marble it. This is the same technique used to ice napoleons (p. 324). You can make more elaborate marbled icing patterns by piping lines, circles, or spirals of a contrasting color fondant onto an iced cake top, then drawing the back of a knife or spatula across the lines before the icing sets.

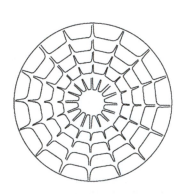

Palette Knife Patterns

You can texture icing quickly and easily with a palette knife as soon as the cake is iced. To make a spiral pattern, leave the cake on the turntable and press the rounded end of the blade lightly into the icing at the center of the cake. Slowly turn the turntable and, at the same time, gradually draw the tip of the palette knife to the outer edge of the cake.

If you wish, you can marble this spiral with the edge of the knife the same way you would marble fondant stripes. Other patterns, such as straight, parallel ridges, can be made with the palette knife and then marbled.

Piping Jelly

Piping jelly is a transparent, sweet jelly used for decorating cakes. It is available in various colors and in a clear, colorless form you can color yourself. Piping jelly can be applied directly to a cake with a paper cone. For example, you can add a touch of color to borders by first decorating them with one of the designs on page 438 and then filling in some of the small loops with colored piping jelly.

Another way to use piping jelly is to make jelly transfers. These are colored pictures that are made ahead of time and applied to cakes as needed. Their advantage is that they can be made during slack hours and stored until called for.

PROCEDURE: Making Piping Jelly Transfers

1. Trace the desired drawing onto a sheet of tracing paper; or, if you wish, draw a picture freehand.

2. Turn the drawing over so the tracing is underneath but can be seen through the paper. (You turn the paper over so the pen or pencil marks don't come off with the jelly.)

3. Outline the drawing with brown piping jelly.

4. Fill in the outlines with piping jelly of appropriate colors.

5. Let the jelly dry. This takes 1 day.

6. Turn the transfer over and place it, jelly side down, on the iced cake.

7. Moisten the back of the paper lightly with a brush dipped in water.

8. Let the cake and paper stand a few minutes. Then carefully peel off the paper, leaving the jelly picture on the cake.

Adding Fruits, Nuts, and Other Items

Arranging fruits, nuts, and other items in an attractive pattern is an easy and effective way to decorate a cake while adding to its flavor and appeal to the customer. This technique is especially appropriate for cakes marked off into portions, as described at the beginning of this section. Each portion can be topped with an appropriate item, such as cherries on the Black Forest Torte (p. 451).

Many fresh or juicy fruits should be added as close to service or display time as possible, as they deteriorate quickly. Fruits in juice or syrup should be drained and dried well before applying.

Naturally, you should use items appropriate to the flavor of the cake. For example, you might place candy coffee beans on a mocha cake or mandarin orange segments on an orange-flavored cake.

Here are several examples of items that can be arranged decoratively on cakes:

- Whole strawberries
- Sweet cherries
- Mandarin orange segments
- Pineapple wedges
- Glacéed fruits
- Candied chestnuts
- Pecan halves
- Walnut halves

- Small, crisp meringues
- Chocolates, such as chocolate truffles
- Chocolate curls or other chocolate decorations.
- Small candies (no hard candies, because a customer might break a tooth)
- Marzipan cutouts—cut from colored marzipan (p. 649) rolled out in sheets—and marzipan figures.

Decorating Sequence

Although the order in which decorations are placed on the cake depends on the cake and the baker's preferences, many pastry chefs prefer the following sequence:

1. Mask the sides of the cake with nuts, crumbs, or other coatings, either before or after decorating. If the top decorations are delicate and might be damaged if the cake is handled, mask the sides first. However, if you are marbling the top of the cake or using some other technique that disturbs the icing on the sides of the cake, then mask the sides afterward.

2. If the cake is to have an inscription or message, such as a person's name or a holiday or birthday greeting, put this on first. (This guideline does not apply to retail bakeshops that display an array of cakes for their customers to choose from. In such operations, decorate the cake completely, leaving space for the inscription. The customer chooses the cake and indicates the inscription, which is then applied by the baker at the time of sale.)

3. Add borders and paper cone designs.

4. Add flowers, leaves, and similar decorations made with a pastry bag.

5. Add additional items such as fruits, nuts, or candies.

KEY POINTS TO REVIEW

- What basic tools are needed for decorating cakes?

- What is the procedure for decorating with a paper cone?

- What is the procedure for filling and using a pastry bag?

PLANNING AND ASSEMBLING SPECIALTY CAKES

GÂTEAUX AND TORTEN

Two words you will see often in connection with European-style cakes are *gâteau* and *torte*. Gâteau is French for "cake" (the plural is *gâteaux*; both singular and plural are pronounced gah-toe). The term is nearly as general as the English word *cake*, as it is used to refer to a wide range of products. For example, Chapter 15 included recipes for Gâteau Pithiviers (p. 362), made of puff pastry and almond filling, and Gâteau St-Honoré (p. 360), made of short dough and éclair paste and filled with a type of pastry cream. Gâteaux may also refer to more conventional layer cakes.

The German word *torte* (plural *torten*) is generally used to describe layer cakes, but it has many definitions, which often contradict each other. According to a British definition, a torte is a sponge layer cake marked off into individual wedges that are individually decorated. An entirely different definition says a torte is a cake baked from a batter that contains nuts and/or crumbs but little or no flour. Yet there are classic torten that fit neither definition.

Rather than try to decide the issue or add to the confusion, we will use the words torte and gâteau when they are parts of a generally accepted name of a classic dessert, such as sachertorte and gâteau St-Honoré.

AS WE HAVE pointed out several times in this book, much of a pastry cook's job is assembly work. Starting with basic elements such as creams, fillings, and baked doughs and batters, the pastry cook builds desserts by putting these elements together in different and attractive ways. This is especially true of the construction of European-style cakes.

Although the number of ingredients that may go into a cake is nearly limitless, the most commonly used are those listed in the Basic Cake Components section, next. This list is followed, first, by a general procedure for assembling a basic European-style cake, and then with more specific procedures for making a number of desserts, most of which are popular classics.

Once you are familiar with the general procedure, you should be able to go beyond the examples included here and put together your own cakes. As you do, keep in mind that a cake that has too many flavors is less pleasing than one with fewer flavors that blend well or have a pleasing contrast. Make sure the flavors you choose for the cake layers, fillings, icings, and syrups go well together. Texture, too, is an important consideration. A mixture of creamy, crisp, and cake-like textures is more interesting to the palate than a cake that consists mostly of mousse. Ingredients such as fruits, nuts, nougatine, caramel, chocolate, crisp meringue, and puff pastry add textural interest.

Note that sponge cakes or other egg-foam cakes are almost always the basis of these desserts. Sponge cakes are sturdy enough to be split into thin layers and to undergo the handling necessary for these constructions. The butter cakes and high-ratio cakes discussed earlier in this chapter are too tender to be handled this way. In addition, they are not able to stand up to the amount of liquid in some of the fillings used.

Basic Cake Components

Following are some of the more important types of components pastry chefs use to construct specialty cakes.

Optional bottom layer	Baked short dough circle (p. 314)
	Baked meringue or japonaise (pp. 341–342)
Optional cake ring linings	(p. 445)
Cake layers	Genoise or other plain sponge (p. 401)
	Almond sponge or other nut sponge (pp. 401, 407, 408, 410)
	Chocolate sponge (pp. 401, 408, 410)
Additional specialty layers	Puff paste disks (pp. 318–321)
	Japonaise or meringue disks (pp. 341–342)
For moistening and flavoring cake layers	Dessert syrup (p. 254)
Fillings	Jam or jelly (especially apricot and raspberry)
	Buttercream (pp. 418–422)
	Crème chantilly (p. 257)
	Ganache (pp. 272–273)
	Chocolate mousse (p. 273)
	Pastry cream and variations (pp. 262–263)
	Bavarian cream (p. 525)
	Fruits (fresh, poached, or canned)
Icings and coatings	Buttercream (pp. 418–422)
	Poured Fondant (pp. 416–417)
	Whipped cream (pp. 255–256)
	Marzipan (p. 649)
	Glazes (pp. 427–429)
	Rolled coatings (p. 429)

Basic Assembly Techniques

This chapter builds on the skills described in the first part of this chapter. If necessary, review the basic cake assembly and decoration techniques laid out on pages 436–441 before continuing with the more specialized techniques in this section.

Because there are so many types of specialty cakes, some of which can be quite complex, we introduce the methods for making them in two stages. The first procedure, below, is for assembling a basic layered sponge cake from baked cake layers and icing. Note that this procedure is somewhat different from the one used for high-fat cakes, explained on page 432. The most important difference is the use of flavored syrups.

PROCEDURE: Assembling a Basic Layered Sponge Cake

1. Trim the edges of the cake as necessary.

2. Cut a notch in the edge of the cake so the layers can be lined up again after cutting.

3. Split the cake in half horizontally.

4. Place one half on a cake card and moisten it with a flavored syrup.

5. Applying the filling with a pastry bag is an easy way to get a layer of uniform thickness.

6. Top with the second layer, and mask the top . . .

7. . . . and sides with the desired icing.

8. Smooth the sides with a plastic scraper.

9. With a palette knife, smooth the top. The cake is now ready for glazing, if desired (p. 447), and decorating.

The second procedure introduces many of the techniques used for some of the more elaborate cakes later in this chapter. Be aware that this is only a general procedure. Some of the same steps appear in both procedures.

GENERAL PROCEDURE: Assembling European-Style Specialty Cakes

1. Assemble all ingredients and equipment.

2. Place a cake card on a turntable or the work surface. The cake will be assembled on top of the card.

3. Split the sponge cake horizontally into two or three layers, depending on the thickness of the cake. Alternatively, use a sponge baked in a thin layer and cut it to the desired shape and size if necessary.

4. If using a charlotte ring (cake ring), line it as desired (see below).

5. If using a japonaise, meringue, or short-dough base, place it on the cake card. Stick it down with a dab of icing or jam so it doesn't slide off the card. (If you are using a cake ring, place the base inside the ring.) Spread with a thin layer of filling or jam. Raspberry or apricot jam is often used on short-dough bases.

6. Place one sponge layer on top of the base; or, if you are not using a base layer, place the sponge layer directly on the card.

7. Brush the cake layer with dessert syrup. Use enough to moisten the cake well, but not so much that it becomes soggy.

8. If you are using fruit pieces, arrange them either on top of the base or on top of the filling after the next step.

9. Apply a layer of the desired filling. Either spread it on with a palette knife or, to quickly apply an even layer, pipe it on as shown in step 5 the Procedure for Assembling a Basic Layered Sponge Cake.

10. Top with another sponge layer and brush it with syrup.

11. If you are using a third sponge layer, repeat steps 9 and 10.

    Note: It is sometimes recommended that the top sponge layer be placed cut side up, as opposed to crust side up. This is especially helpful if a light, translucent icing such as fondant is being used. A dark crust will show through a thin fondant layer and detract from the appearance of the cake.

12. Ice the cake with the desired icing or glaze. If using buttercream or other spreadable icing, you may ice the cake directly or first give it a thin masking coat, as explained on page 432. Note that cakes to be covered with glaze (see the Procedure for Applying Glaze, p. 447) must first be given a masking coat of icing.

13. Decorate.

Rectangular Cakes or Strips

Most popular cakes can also be made in a rectangular shape or strip about 2½ to 3½ inches (6 to 9 cm) wide and 16 to 18 inches (40 to 46 cm) long (the width of a sheet pan) or any fraction of that length. A cake baked in a standard sheet pan can be cut crosswise into seven pieces of this size.

To produce one cake, cut strips of the desired size from sheet cakes and then layer with fillings as in the basic procedure. Ice the top and sides. Ends may be iced or be left un-iced to show an attractive pattern of cake layers and fillings. Using a sharp serrated knife, trim a thin slice off each end for a more attractive appearance. Wipe the knife clean and dip it in hot water before cutting each slice.

To produce rectangular or strip cakes in quantity, use full cake sheets and layer as in the basic procedure. Cut into strips of the desired width, then ice the top and sides of each strip.

Strip cakes are divided into portions by cutting off rectangular slices about 1½ inches (4 cm) wide. The tops may be marked into portions and decorated in a regular pattern, in the same way that round cakes are often marked into wedges.

Lining Charlotte Rings or Cake Rings

Sometimes a soft filling or mousse, such as Bavarian cream or other gelatin-based filling, is used in a layer cake. In these cases, it is necessary to use a ring mold to hold the filling in place until the cake is chilled enough to set the filling. These ring molds are often called *charlotte rings* because they are used to make charlottes, molded desserts made of Bavarian cream (see Chapter 19). They may also be called *cake rings*.

Using a charlotte ring allows the pastry chef to create a decorative edge for the cake. The cake is finished by applying an icing or glaze only to the top. The decorated sides of the cake are revealed when the ring is removed.

For the neatest results, line the cake ring with a strip of acetate before assembling the cake. This makes it easier to remove the metal ring from the finished cake without marring the sides. Sponge cake, for example, sometimes sticks to the ring if acetate is not used.

Four popular linings for charlotte rings are sponge strips, sliced sponge, chocolate, and fruit.

Sponge Strips

Sponge used to line a ring must be thin (about ¼ inch/0.5 cm) and flexible enough to bend without breaking (see the Procedure for Lining a Ring Mold with a Sponge Strip). Sponges made with almond powder are good for this purpose because they stay moist and flexible. Joconde Sponge Cake (p. 405) is especially suitable. Ladyfinger Sponge (p. 407) is another good choice, even though it does not contain nut powder, because it is strong and flexible.

For a decorative edge, Ribbon Sponge (p. 406) is popular. Using colored stencil paste allows the chef to make many different designs for different cakes. In Chapter 19, Passion Fruit Charlotte (p. 533) and L'Exotique (p. 536) are made with ribbon sponge. Caramelized sponge also makes an attractive lining and is suitable for cakes made with caramelized fruit or other caramel flavor, such as Bananier (p. 468). The Procedure for Caramelizing Sponge (below) details how to do this.

PROCEDURE: Lining a Ring Mold with a Sponge Strip

1. Use the ring as a guide to measure the width and length of the strip of sponge to be cut (a). The strip may be cut slightly narrower than the ring so some of the filling will show above it. It should be slightly longer than the circumference of the ring so it will fit snugly.

2. Brush the sponge with dessert syrup before placing it in the mold, to prevent discoloration by juices seeping through from the filling.

3. Place the ring on a cake card and fit the strip of sponge into the ring (b).

4. Trim the end of the strip with a small knife (c).

PROCEDURE: Caramelizing Sponge

1. Cut a strip of joconde sponge to the desired size for lining the mold.

2. Spread the sponge with a thin coating of Sabayon I (p. 274) and then sprinkle evenly with confectioners' sugar, using a fine sieve.

3. Brown the top of the sponge. For best results, use a handheld electric salamander iron. If this is not available, brown under a salamander or broiler, but watch it closely to prevent it from scorching.

4. Repeat steps 2 and 3 for a second coat.

5. Turn the strip over and caramelize the other side in the same way.

Sliced Sponge

Baumkuchen (p. 409) makes an attractive lining for molds because of the striped pattern of its cut surfaces (see the Procedure for Lining a Mold with Slices of Baumkuchen, below). For a recipe using baumkuchen, see Caramelized Pear Charlotte (p. 588).

Another way to make a sliced sponge lining with attractive vertical stripes is to sandwich together thin layers of sponge with jam, ganache, or other filling. The procedure for cutting the slices and lining the mold is the same as for baumkuchen. Chocolate Indulgence (p. 540) and Charlotte au Cassis (p. 533) are made this way.

PROCEDURE: Lining a Mold with Slices of Baumkuchen

1. Cut a piece of baumkuchen into a strip just as wide as the desired height of the cake border (a).

A

2. Cut this strip crosswise into slices ¼ in. (0.5 cm) thick (b).

B

3. Fit these slices against the inside of the mold so the stripes are vertical (c).

C

Chocolate

Chocolate is an especially popular lining for cake molds. Tempered chocolate is spread on a strip of acetate and placed inside the ring mold. The acetate can remain around the cake for display, but is removed before the cake or charlotte is sliced and served. Plain chocolate may be used, but chocolate with a pattern—such as wood grain or marble—is even more attractive. These techniques are illustrated in Chapter 23 (see pages 633–634). See the procedure for Julianna (p. 466) for an example of a cake made in a ring lined with chocolate.

Fruit

Fruits, too, can be used to line a mold, as in the procedure for Strawberry Cake (p. 456). When using fresh fruits such as strawberries, remember the finished dessert cannot be frozen because the texture of the fruit will be ruined and the fruit will lose juices when thawed, marring the appearance of the cake.

Lining the mold with a strip of acetate gives the best results. (Use parchment if acetate is not available.) Take precautions so the filling does not run between the fruit and the mold, which would detract from the cake's appearance. In the case of halved strawberries or similar fruit, press the cut surface firmly against the side of the mold, but not so tightly as to crush the fruit. Thick fillings and gelatin-based fillings that are about to set are less likely to run between the fruit and mold.

KEY POINTS TO REVIEW

▪ What are the steps in the procedure for assembling a basic layered sponge cake?

▪ What are the steps in the general procedure for assembling European-style specialty cakes?

▪ What are the procedures for lining a cake ring with a sponge strip and with cake slices?

Applying Other Icings or Coatings

The assembly procedures discussed so far focus on coating cakes with spreadable icings such as buttercreams. Other coatings for cakes, particularly glazes and rolled coatings, require other techniques.

Glazes and Poured Fondant

Poured fondant provides a thin, smooth, shiny coating for cakes and serves as an excellent base for paper-cone decorations. Also, in hot weather, it is a good substitute for buttercream, especially for cakes that, for one reason or another, may not be kept in a refrigerated case at all times.

When fondant is used to ice a cake, especially a sponge cake, it is a good idea to first brush the top and sides of the cake with hot apricot glaze. Let the glaze set before applying the fondant. This provides a moisture barrier between the fondant and the cake, and it reduces the chance that the fondant will dry out and lose its shine. Also, it minimizes the problem of loose crumbs, which might spoil the smoothness of the icing layer.

Guidelines for using poured fondant are on page 417. To ice a cake with fondant, set it on an icing screen then pour the warm fondant over the cake, using a bowl knife to guide the fondant evenly over the sides.

To apply other poured glazes, you should also first apply a moisture and crumb barrier, as you do for fondant. However, spreading a masking coat of buttercream icing is generally a more appropriate choice than brushing on apricot glaze.

PROCEDURE: Applying Glaze

1. Assemble all ingredients and equipment.
2. Apply a masking coat of icing to the top and sides of the cake, as explained on page 432. Be sure that the icing is perfectly smooth and level, as any irregularities will show through the glaze.
3. Refrigerate until the icing is set and firm.
4. Have the glaze at a slightly warm temperature, about 80°F (27°C). If it is too warm, it will melt the icing. If it is too cold, it will not flow and spread freely. Spoon off any bubbles on the surface of the glaze.
5. Set the cake on an icing screen or rack above a sheet pan to catch excess glaze.
6. Pour the glaze over the cake, covering it completely and evenly. Pastry chefs have two different preferred methods to ensure even coating:
   a. Start by pouring the glaze around the edge of the cake first and letting it run down the sides; then pour glaze onto the center of the cake to finish. If necessary, tilt the cake slightly from side to side to get the glaze to flow evenly.
   b. Alternatively, start by pouring a generous quantity of glaze over the center of the cake, letting it flow in all directions. With an offset palette knife, quickly draw the glaze toward all sides of the cake so that it covers the sides completely. Sweep the knife off the edges of the cake; do not lift it off the top, as this will leave ridges in the glaze. You must do this quickly before the glaze begins to set.
7. If there are any bubbles in the glaze, remove them by very carefully warming them with a blowtorch. Or, if the glaze is still quite liquid, pop them with a fine skewer.
8. Refrigerate until the glaze is set.

Rolled Coatings

Marzipan and rolled fondant are frequently used to cover cakes. Rolled fondant is most often used for wedding cakes, as it provides a fine, smooth surface as the base for more elaborate decorations. Recall from page 84 that marzipan is a confection or paste made of almonds and sugar. While rolled fondant is always used as the outer layer, marzipan either can be used as an outer layer or covered with a layer of poured fondant or other icing. When used under poured fondant, marzipan, like apricot coating, serves as a moisture barrier to protect the fondant. (Production of marzipan is explained in Chapter 24, p. 649.) Rolled fondant and marzipan can be used as is or colored by kneading in the desired coloring.

Modeling chocolate is used much less often as a cake coating but is found on a few specialty products. It is handled like rolled fondant, except that it is not colored.

ROLLED FONDANT

Not many years ago, the term *fondant*, used by itself, nearly always referred to the icing we are calling *poured fondant*, or to candies that are made the same way. Today, however, the word most often refers to the putty-like substance called *rolled fondant*. However, poured fondant and rolled fondant have almost nothing in common except that they are both mostly sugar. Rolled fondant, strictly speaking, isn't fondant at all. Note that the word itself comes from the French word meaning "melting," a most inappropriate term when applied to the rolled coating.

The following are guidelines for using rolled coatings:

1. Prepare the surface of the cake. Make sure it is perfectly smooth and free of crumbs. Seal the surface of the cake by applying a masking coat of icing (as explained on p. 432) or by brushing with melted jam. Buttercream icing is used most often under rolled fondant, while either icing or melted jam or apricot glaze may be used under marzipan. The seal coat helps the rolled coating stick to the cake and also serves as a moisture barrier between the cake and the coating.

2. Work the coating product in your hands or knead it on the workbench to make it pliable, if necessary. Using confectioners' sugar to dust the bench and rolling pin, roll out the coating into a thin sheet, as though you were rolling out pastry.

3. If marzipan is to be on the outside of the cake—that is, not covered with icing—the sheet can be textured with a ridged rolling pin. Roll the ridged pin over the sheet of marzipan once to make ridges. To make a checked or dimpled texture, roll the pin across the sheet a second time at a right angle to the first.

4. Roll the coating into a thin sheet large enough to cover the top and sides of the cake. Lift it with the rolling pin and drape it over the cake. With a fondant smoother or the palms of the hands, carefully smooth the coating and mold it against the sides of the cake. Mold the sides carefully to avoid making ripples or folds.

5. An easier alternative method for covering a round layer cake with marzipan is to coat only the top layer. Place the layer upside down on a sheet of marzipan and press it on lightly. Trim off the excess marzipan. Set the layer right side up on the cake. You can then ice the sides of the cake in a conventional manner.

6. To coat the sides of a round layer cake after coating the top, first ice the sides so the marzipan will stick. Roll out a strip of marzipan as wide as the cake is high and as long as three times the width of the cake. Roll up the strip loosely, then unroll it against the sides of the cake. The cake can now be coated with fondant or another light icing.

7. To cover a strip cake or a sponge roll (Swiss roll) with marzipan or rolled fondant, roll out a sheet of coating large enough to cover the strip or roll. Coat the cake with apricot glaze or melted jam. Set the cake on the coating at one edge and roll it up in the sheet.

    As an alternative, you can brush the apricot glaze onto the rolled-out coating rather than onto the cake.

8. In humid weather, it is best not to store cakes coated with rolled fondant in the refrigerator. When the cake is removed from refrigeration, moisture that condenses on the surface can mar the appearance of the fondant.

Assembling Tiered Cakes

Amateur bakers sometimes make the mistake of thinking that a tiered cake such as a wedding cake can be made by simply stacking up increasingly smaller layers atop one another. Unfortunately, the result is almost always a collapsed cake, because the bottom layers are not strong enough to support the weight of the layers on top.

Tiered cakes require adequate support to maintain their structure. The procedure given here outlines the steps in building this structure.

Butter cakes or high-ratio cakes are the best choices for tiered cakes, because of their density.

PROCEDURE: Assembling a Tiered Cake

1. Ice each tier separately. Each tier should be on its own cake circle. Use cake circles of the same diameters as the cake layers. They should not be visible when the tier has been completed.

2. Refrigerate the cakes so that they are firm and easy to handle before beginning to assemble. Remove the tiers from refrigeration one at a time, when needed, to keep them firm. (However, see the caution about refrigeration at the end of the guidelines for applying rolled coatings, above.)

3. Place the bottom tier on a cake stand, a heavy cake board, or whatever surface the cake will be displayed on.

(continues)

(continued)

4. Mark the top of the cake tier with an inverted cake pan the same size as the next tier. Center the pan and press it gently into the icing and remove it. This procedure will make a circle in the top of the cake to serve as a guide for placing the next tier. Alternatively, instead of a cake pan, place a cake circle the size of the second tier on top of the lower tier and lightly mark the icing around the edge of the circle with a pick (a).

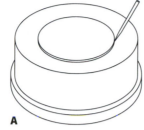

A

5. Insert a thin wooden dowel into the center of the cake, keeping it perfectly vertical. Press it down firmly so that it rests solidly on the bottom cake board. It may be necessary to sharpen the dowel slightly.

6. Using a knife or a pencil, make a mark in the dowel just at the level of the surface of the icing (b).

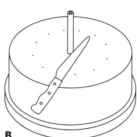

B

7. Remove the dowel. Using the mark as a guide, cut additional dowels of the same length. The number of dowels needed depends on the size of the cake tier. Usually 4 to 7 will be enough. A heavy wire cutter is a convenient tool for cutting the dowels.

8. Insert one cut dowel in the center of the cake and the remaining dowels in a circle around it, remaining about 1 inch (2.5 cm) inside the circle that was marked in the top of the icing (c).

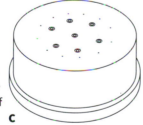

C

9. Repeat steps 5–8 to measure, cut, and insert dowels in each of the remaining layers. As the tiers become smaller, you will need fewer dowels to support them, but always at least three. You will not need dowels in the top tier unless you need to support a heavy top ornament. To support a top ornament, mark the icing of the top tier with the bottom of the ornament, and then cut and insert dowels as in steps 5–8. In most cases, use three dowels placed in a triangle. Even for smaller ornaments, using only one or two dowels makes the ornament unstable.

10. Steps 1–9 may be done well in advance of final assembly and the cakes may be returned to the refrigerator at this point. Even if you proceed immediately to final assembly, it is a good idea to refrigerate the cake tiers briefly to make sure they are firm.

11. To assemble, first pipe a little royal icing onto the tops of the dowels to stick the bottom of the next tier's cake circle in place and keep it from sliding. Some bakers omit this step, but it is recommended, especially if the finished cake must be moved more than a short distance.

12. Place the second tier on top of the bottom tier, aligning it with the circle that you made in step 4 (d). Repeat steps 11 and 12 for the remaining tiers.

D

13. Decorate the cake as desired.

Procedure Summary

1. Ice each tier and refrigerate.
2. Mark guide circles in the top icing of each tier.
3. Insert, mark, and cut dowels.
4. Insert dowels.
5. Pipe royal icing on the tops of the dowels.
6. Stack the tiers.

KEY POINTS TO REVIEW

▪ What are the steps in the procedure for applying glaze?

▪ How are rolled coatings applied to cakes?

▪ What are the steps in the procedure for assembling tiered cakes?

PROCEDURES FOR SPECIALTY CAKES

THE PREVIOUS SECTION of this chapter concentrated on explaining general procedures and techniques for assembling specialty cakes. The remainder of the chapter is devoted to specific procedures for assembling a variety of cakes and cake-based desserts, including Swiss rolls and small cakes.

The instructions for specialty cakes in this chapter are assembly procedures rather than recipes, even though they may resemble recipes with their lists of ingredients or components. These procedures may be used for cakes of any size. In many cases, they can be used not only for round cakes but also for square cakes and rectangular strips. Consequently, the quantities of fillings and icings needed to complete them vary considerably. Presenting the procedures in this way reflects the normal working practices of a bakeshop. In a typical operation, cakes are baked ahead of time, and fillings, icings, and other components are prepared separately and in advance. Depending on demand or sales, individual desserts can be assembled quickly, as needed, using the materials on hand.

For a few of the more complex cakes, approximate quantities for the major components are given as guidelines. These quantities apply only to the size of cake indicated in the procedure. This does not prevent you, however, from using the procedures to make any size cake, changing the quantities as necessary.

Large Cakes

Most of the procedures in this section are for round cakes. Many of these, except those made in ring molds, could also be made as rectangles or strips, as explained on page 444. In addition, most of these cakes can be made in any size. Therefore, specific quantities of the individual components are not given in many cases; you have the freedom to make the cake in any size you wish. Bakeshops generally make cakes from the components they have on hand in larger quantities, so chefs simply use the quantities they feel they need without measuring specific amounts.

A number of more complex cakes are introduced later in the section, and the quantities required for them are included as guidelines, to help you visualize the cakes. Feel free to modify these quantities as necessary.

Finally, many molded desserts and pastries are made in the shape of cakes and decorated like cakes. For example, molded and decorated Bavarian creams, called *charlottes*, are often made in ring molds, as some cakes are. These are included with basic Bavarians in Chapter 19 if they are made without cake layers. Other desserts made in the shape of cakes are found in Chapters 15 and 21. Some of these are mentioned in the section above called Lining Charlotte Rings or Cake Rings.

Each of the procedures in this section is accompanied by a diagram to help you visualize how the components are layered and built to make the completed cake. These drawings are intended to show the structure of the cake and the relationships of its components. They are not necessarily drawn to scale. For example, you may make layers of icings thicker or thinner than those shown. Decorations for the tops of the cakes usually are not shown.

BLACK FOREST TORTE

Components

Chocolate Genoise (pp. 401), split into 3 layers, or 3 Chocolate Sponge Layers (p. 410)

Dessert syrup flavored with kirsch

Whipped cream flavored with kirsch

Sweet, dark, pitted cherries, drained

Chocolate shavings

PROCEDURE

1. Moisten one chocolate sponge layer with syrup.

2. Spread with a thin layer of whipped cream.

3. With a pastry bag fitted with a large, plain tube, pipe a circle of cream in the center of the layer. Pipe a ring of cream around the edge. Then pipe another ring in the space between these two.

4. Fill the two spaces between these rings with well-drained cherries.

5. Top with a second sponge layer. Moisten with syrup.

6. Spread with a layer of whipped cream.

7. Top with a third sponge layer, moistened with syrup.

8. Ice the top and sides with whipped cream.

9. With the back of a knife, mark off the top of the cake into the desired number of wedges.

10. Mask the sides of the cake with chocolate shavings. Sprinkle chocolate shavings in the center of the cake.

11. With a star tube, pipe rosettes of whipped cream around the top edge of the cake so that there is one on each wedge. Place a cherry on each rosette.

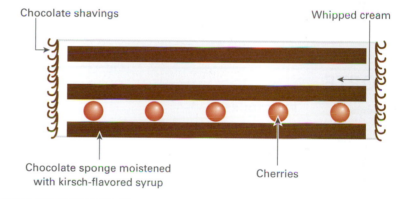

Chocolate shavings

Whipped cream

Chocolate sponge moistened with kirsch-flavored syrup

Cherries

SCHWARZWALDER KIRSCHTORTE

The Black Forest, or Schwarzwald (SHVARTS valt) in German, lies in southwestern Germany, just east of the Rhine River. One of the prominent agricultural products of this scenic region is the cherry, or *kirsche* (keer sheh), which is used to make the clear white brandy (eau-de-vie) called *kirschwasser*. The *Black Forest torte* (Schwarzwalder Kirschtorte), made of chocolate sponge flavored with kirschwasser (or *kirsch*, for short) and layered with cherries and whipped cream, is a popular dessert in this region and is sold in most pastry shops.

MOCHA TORTE

Components

Genoise (p. 401), split into 3 or 4 layers

Buttercream flavored with coffee (p. 419)

Dessert syrup flavored with coffee or coffee liqueur

PROCEDURE

1. Moisten the cake layers with syrup. Sandwich them together with buttercream.
2. Ice the top and sides smoothly with buttercream.
3. Decorate as desired with a pastry bag filled with additional buttercream. Chocolate decorations are also appropriate. Sides may be masked with toasted, sliced almonds, if desired.

VARIATION

Alternate 2 thin layers of vanilla genoise with 2 thin layers of chocolate genoise.

MOCHA

Mocha, also spelled Mukha, is the name of a seaport in Yemen, on the Arabian peninsula. This city was an important exporter of a richly flavored coffee that has been prized since at least the fifteenth century. We know this coffee primarily as one of the two components of the coffee blend *mocha java*. In other words, the term *mocha* originally had nothing to do with chocolate. Today, however, we most often use the word to refer to a blend of coffee and chocolate flavors. The Mocha Torte here honors the original meaning of the word, as it is flavored with coffee only (although the variation offers a chocolate option).

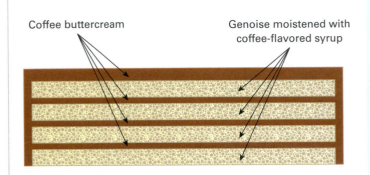

Coffee buttercream   Genoise moistened with coffee-flavored syrup

FRUIT TORTE

Components

Short Dough (p. 314) or Almond Short Dough (p. 315) circle

Genoise (p. 401) or Almond Sponge (p. 401), split into 2 layers

Raspberry or apricot jam

Dessert syrup flavored with vanilla or kirsch

Buttercream flavored with vanilla or kirsch (p. 419)

Small fruits, preferably 3 or 4 kinds, in contrasting colors (such as mandarin orange slices, cherries, grapes, banana slices, strawberries, apricot halves, and pineapple wedges)

Apricot Glaze (p. 194)

Almonds, sliced or chopped

PROCEDURE

1. Spread the short dough base with jam.
2. Top with a sponge layer. Moisten with syrup.
3. Spread with a thin layer of buttercream.
4. Top with second sponge layer.
5. Moisten with syrup.
6. Ice the top and sides with buttercream.
7. Arrange the fruits on the top of the cake in neat, concentric circles, as though you were making an unbaked fruit tart (p. 352).
8. Glaze the fruits with apricot glaze.
9. Mask the sides of the cake with almonds.

VARIATION

Instead of buttercream, use whipped cream or pastry cream for the filling.

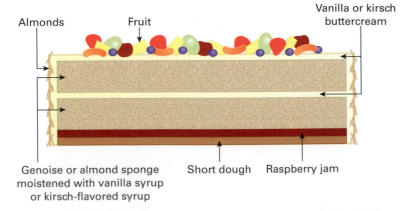

Almonds   Fruit   Vanilla or kirsch buttercream

Genoise or almond sponge moistened with vanilla syrup or kirsch-flavored syrup   Short dough   Raspberry jam

DOBOS TORTE

Components

7 Dobos layers (p. 402)

Chocolate buttercream
(pp. 418–419)

Chopped almonds

Sugar, cooked to the light
caramel stage (p. 253)

PROCEDURE

1. Set aside the best Dobos layer for the top.

2. Sandwich the other 6 layers together with chocolate buttercream.

3. Ice the top and sides completely. Mask the sides with chopped almonds.

4. Cook the sugar to the light caramel stage. Pour the hot caramel over the reserved Dobos layer to coat the top completely with a thin layer.

5. With a heavy, buttered knife, immediately cut the caramel layer into portion-size wedges. This must be done before the caramel hardens.

6. Top the cake with the layer of caramel-covered wedges.

VARIATION

SEVEN-LAYER CAKE

Seven-layer cake is a variation of the Dobos Torte, except it is generally made as a strip or rectangle (see p. 444 for an explanation) rather than as a round cake. Use Dobos Mix (p. 402), seven-layer mix (p. 401), or any thin sponge layers. Sandwich together 7 layers of cake with chocolate buttercream. Coat the top and sides with chocolate buttercream, chocolate fondant, or melted chocolate.

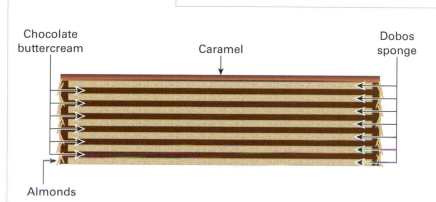

Chocolate buttercream · Caramel · Dobos sponge · Almonds

NAPOLEON GÂTEAU

Components

Blitz Puff Pastry (p. 319) or
scrap puff paste

Pastry Cream (p. 263)

White fondant

Chocolate fondant

Chopped almonds or puff
paste crumbs

NOTE: This is the same as a regular Napoleon but made in the shape of a cake.

PROCEDURE

1. Roll out puff paste ⅛ in. (3 mm) thick. Cut out 3 circles 1 in. (2.5 cm) larger in diameter than the desired cake (to allow for shrinkage during baking). Dock the pastry well. Let rest 30 minutes.

2. Bake the puff paste at 400°F (200°C) until browned and crisp. Cool. With a serrated knife, carefully trim the circles, if necessary, so they are perfectly round and uniform.

3. Sandwich the 3 layers together with generous layers of pastry cream. Use the best pastry layer for the top and place it upside down so the top is flat and smooth.

4. Ice the top with white poured fondant and marble it with chocolate fondant (see p. 440).

5. Carefully smooth the sides, using additional pastry cream if necessary. Mask with almonds or pastry crumbs.

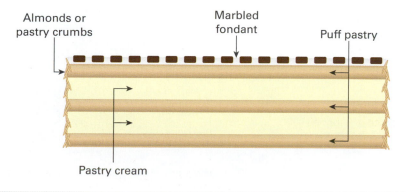

Almonds or pastry crumbs · Marbled fondant · Puff pastry · Pastry cream

SACHERTORTE

Components

1 baked Sacher cake
  (p. 396)

Dessert syrup flavored with
  kirsch

Apricot jam

Ganache (p. 272)

Chocolate Glaçage (p. 427)

Grated dark chocolate

PROCEDURE

1. Trim the cake, if necessary, and cut it into 2 layers. Moisten both layers with kirsch syrup.

2. Sandwich the layers together with a layer of apricot jam.

3. Mask the top and sides of the cake with ganache, spreading it perfectly smooth.

4. Chill the cake until the ganache is firm.

5. Place the cake on a wire rack on a tray. Ice the cake by pouring warm chocolate glaçage over it. Run a palette knife over the top and tap the tray to smooth the icing. Chill until set.

6. Remove from the wire rack, neaten the bottom edge with a knife, and place on a cake board.

7. Using additional ganache, pipe the word "Sacher" across the middle of the cake. Coat the bottom of the sides with grated chocolate. (For background information on this classic Austrian cake, see page 397.)

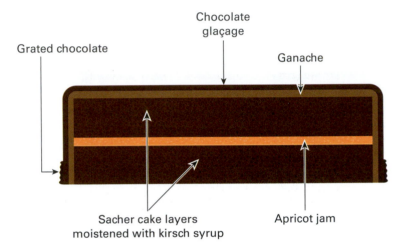

Grated chocolate • Chocolate glaçage • Ganache • Sacher cake layers moistened with kirsch syrup • Apricot jam

KIRSCH TORTE

Components

2 baked meringue or
   japonaise disks (pp. 341
   and 342)

1 baked genoise layer
   (p. 401), about 1 in.
   (2.5 cm) thick

Dessert syrup flavored with
   kirsch

Buttercream flavored with
   kirsch (p. 419)

Confectioners' sugar

Chopped almonds or
   meringue crumbs

PROCEDURE

1. Moisten the genoise with enough kirsch syrup to saturate it well.
2. Place a meringue or japonaise layer upside down (smooth side up) on a cake circle.
3. Spread it with a layer of buttercream.
4. Place the genoise on top and spread it with buttercream.
5. Top with the second meringue layer, smooth side up.
6. Spread the sides smoothly with buttercream and coat them with nuts or meringue crumbs.
7. Dust the top heavily with confectioners' sugar. With the back of a knife, mark the sugar in a diamond pattern.

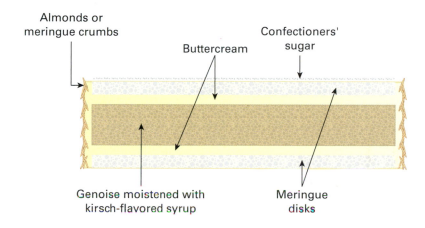

Almonds or meringue crumbs

Buttercream

Confectioners' sugar

Genoise moistened with kirsch-flavored syrup

Meringue disks

ORANGE CREAM CAKE

Components

1 meringue disk (p. 341)

Genoise (p. 401), split into
   2 layers

Orange-flavored dessert
   syrup

Whipped cream lightly
   flavored with orange
   liqueur

Mandarin orange segments

NOTE: This procedure can be
used with any appropriate fruit,
such as strawberries, pineapple,
apricots, and cherries. The
flavor of the syrup and the
cream should be appropriate to
the fruit.

PROCEDURE

1. Spread the meringue layer with whipped cream.
2. Top with a genoise layer and brush it with syrup.
3. Spread with whipped cream.
4. Arrange a layer of orange segments, well drained, on the cream.
5. Top with a second genoise layer. Moisten with syrup.
6. Ice the top and sides of the cake with whipped cream.
7. Mark the top of the cake into the desired number of wedges.
8. Decorate with rosettes of whipped cream around the top edge of the cake. Top each rosette with an orange segment.

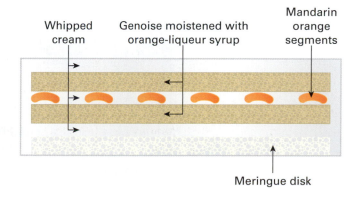

Whipped cream

Genoise moistened with orange-liqueur syrup

Mandarin orange segments

Meringue disk

STRAWBERRY CAKE

Components

2 genoise layers (p. 401), each ½ in. (1 cm) thick

Dessert syrup flavored with kirsch

Fresh strawberries, trimmed

Vanilla Bavarian Cream (p. 528)

Buttercream flavored with vanilla (p. 419)

Piping chocolate (p. 637)

PROCEDURE

1. Line a charlotte ring with a strip of acetate. Set the ring on a cake card.
2. Place a genoise layer in the ring and brush it with syrup.
3. Select the best-looking, most uniformly sized strawberries to line the ring and cut them in half vertically. Place them on the sponge evenly spaced around the edge, with the stem end down and the cut surface against the acetate. Distribute the remaining strawberries evenly on the sponge.
4. Cover the strawberries with the Bavarian cream, which has been cooled until it is thick and just about to set, filling the ring to within ½ in. (1 cm) of the top, making sure there are no airspaces around the berries.
5. Place the second genoise layer on top, pressing down gently. Brush the top with syrup.
6. Spread the top with a thin layer of buttercream.
7. Using a paper cone, decorate the top of the cake with piping chocolate, making desired patterns (see pp. 436–438).
8. Chill until set. Remove the ring, but leave the acetate around the cake until ready to serve.

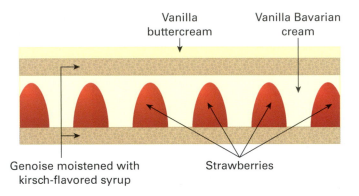

Vanilla buttercream

Vanilla Bavarian cream

Genoise moistened with kirsch-flavored syrup

Strawberries

CHOCOLATE MOUSSE CAKE

Components

3 chocolate meringue disks (p. 341)

Chocolate Mousse (p. 273)

Shaved chocolate

PROCEDURE

1. Sandwich together the chocolate meringue disks with chocolate mousse.
2. Ice the top and sides completely with chocolate mousse.
3. Coat the top and sides of the cake with shaved chocolate.

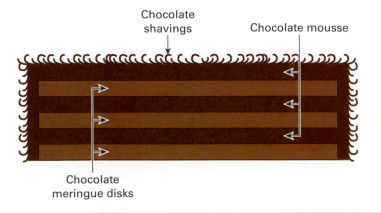

Chocolate shavings

Chocolate mousse

Chocolate meringue disks

CHOCOLATE GANACHE TORTE

Components

1 plain or chocolate
  meringue disk (p. 341)
  (optional)

Whipped ganache (p. 272)

Chocolate Genoise (p. 401),
  split into 3 layers

Dessert syrup flavored
  with rum or vanilla

Chocolate buttercream
  (pp. 418–419)

PROCEDURE

1. Spread the meringue disk with ganache.

2. Top with a genoise layer. Moisten with syrup and spread with a layer of ganache.

3. Repeat with a second genoise layer and more syrup and ganache.

4. Top with the remaining cake layer, moistened with syrup.

5. Ice the top and sides with buttercream.

6. Decorate as desired.

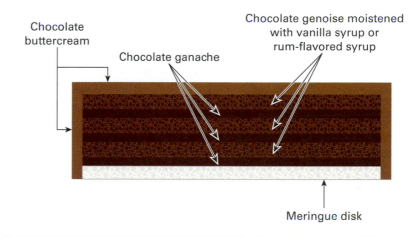

Chocolate
buttercream

Chocolate ganache

Chocolate genoise moistened
with vanilla syrup or
rum-flavored syrup

Meringue disk

ABRICOTINE

Components

Genoise (p. 401), split into
  2 layers

Dessert syrup flavored
  with kirsch

Apricot preserves

Italian Meringue (p. 259)

Sliced almonds

Confectioners' sugar

PROCEDURE

1. Place a layer of genoise on a cake card and brush it with syrup.

2. Spread with a layer of apricot preserves.

3. Top with the second genoise layer and brush with syrup.

4. Coat the top and sides of the cake with Italian meringue.

5. Using a pastry bag with a star tip, pipe a decorative border of Italian meringue on top of the cake.

6. Fill the center of the top of the cake with a layer of sliced almonds and dust with confectioners' sugar.

7. Place in a hot oven (500°F/250°C) until lightly browned.

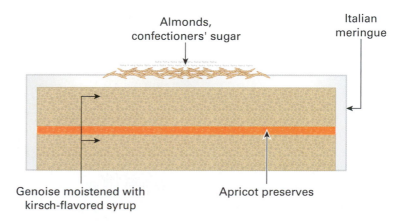

Almonds,
confectioners' sugar

Italian
meringue

Genoise moistened with
kirsch-flavored syrup

Apricot preserves

ALMOND GÂTEAU

Components

Almond Sponge (p. 401), split into 2 layers

Dessert syrup flavored with rum

Apricot jam

Almond macaroon mixture (p. 498)

Apricot Glaze (p. 194)

PROCEDURE

1. Moisten the sponge layers with syrup and sandwich them together with apricot jam.
2. Coat the sides of the cake with the macaroon mixture. Using a star tube or basketweave tube, cover the top of the cake with macaroon mix in a basketweave pattern.
3. Let stand for at least 1 hour.
4. Brown quickly in a hot oven (450°F/230°C), about 10 minutes.
5. While still warm, glaze with apricot glaze.

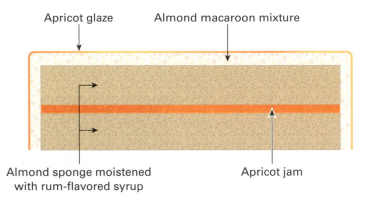

Apricot glaze   Almond macaroon mixture

Almond sponge moistened with rum-flavored syrup   Apricot jam

BAVARIAN CREAM TORTE

Components

Genoise (p. 401) or other sponge cut into 3 very thin layers, about ¼ in. (6 mm) thick

Bavarian Cream in any flavor (pp. 528–529)

Whipped cream flavored to be compatible with that of the Bavarian cream (use chocolate whipped cream with chocolate Bavarian torte)

Dessert syrup, flavored appropriately

PROCEDURE

1. Line the bottom of a charlotte ring, cake pan, or springform pan with a thin sponge layer. Moisten with syrup.
2. Prepare the Bavarian cream. Pour enough of the mixture into the cake pan to make a layer about ¾ in. (2 cm) thick.
3. Place a second layer of sponge cake on top of the cream. Moisten with syrup.
4. Fill with another layer of Bavarian cream.
5. Top with the remaining sponge layer.
6. Chill until set.
7. Unmold.
8. Ice the top and sides with whipped cream.
9. Decorate as desired.

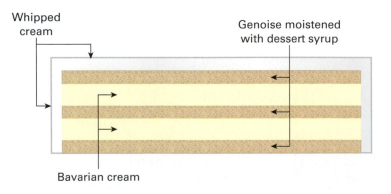

Whipped cream   Genoise moistened with dessert syrup

Bavarian cream

FEUILLE D'AUTOMNE

Components

Almond Meringues (p. 342),
  three 6½-in. (16-cm) disks

Chocolate Mousse IV (p. 538),
  16–20 oz (450–550 g)

Dark chocolate couverture,
  about 14 oz (400 g)

Cocoa powder

PROCEDURE

1. Place a 7-in. (18-cm) charlotte ring on a cake board. Lay one of the meringue disks in the bottom.

2. Fill the ring slightly less than half full of mousse.

3. Place a second meringue on top and press down lightly. Fill nearly to the top with mousse, then place the third meringue on top. Press down lightly.

4. Spread the top with a thin layer of mousse.

5. Chill until firm.

6. Remove the charlotte ring, using a blowtorch to help release the sides. Chill again to firm the sides.

7. Melt the chocolate couverture.

8. Heat 3 clean half-sheet pans at 325°F (160°C) for 4 minutes. Spread the melted chocolate over the bottoms of the trays. Let cool at room temperature until the chocolate begins to get cloudy. (Warming the pans enables you to spread a thinner coat of chocolate; be careful, however, not to get the pans too hot. Some chefs prefer to use cold pans.)

   Note: The procedure used here is illustrated and explained in more detail in Chapter 23 (see p. 636). An experienced chef may need as little as 1 or 1½ pans of chocolate to coat the cake, but it is a good idea to prepare extra, to allow for mistakes.

9. Refrigerate to set completely.

10. Bring back to room temperature. The chocolate must be pliable but not soft. Use a metal scraper to lift strips of chocolate off the trays, as shown on page 636. Wrap these around the sides of the cake. Use the same technique to make ruffles for the top of the cake. Chill until firm.

11. Dust the top with a little cocoa powder. (The cake in the illustration is further decorated with chocolate leaves, made by brushing a leaf mold (real leaves could also be used) with tempered chocolate and letting the chocolate set before peeling off.)

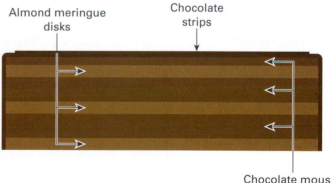

Almond meringue disks

Chocolate strips

Chocolate mousse

ALHAMBRA

Components

One 8-in. (20-cm) round
   Hazelnut Sponge Cake
   (p. 408)

Coffee Rum Syrup (p. 255)

Ganache I (p. 272), made with
   equal parts cream and
   chocolate, about 8 oz (250 g)

Chocolate Glaçage (p. 427),
   5–6 oz (150–175 g)

Decoration

   Chopped pistachios

   Marzipan rose

NOTE: Assembly of this cake is
illustrated on page 443.

PROCEDURE

1. Trim the top of the cake, if necessary, to make it level. Turn it upside down. Cut it in half horizontally to split into 2 layers.

2. Brush both halves with syrup to moisten.

3. Using a pastry bag with a medium plain tip, pipe the ganache onto the bottom layer, making a spiral that starts in the center and covers the layer completely.

4. Place the second layer on top and press down lightly.

5. Mask the top and sides of the cake with the remaining ganache. Chill until firm.

6. Place the cake on a wire rack over a tray. Pour the glaçage over it. Carefully run a palette knife over the top and then tap the tray to ensure the icing is perfectly smooth. Chill until set.

7. When the icing is chilled and set, remove the cake from the wire rack. Neaten the bottom edge with a knife.

8. Press chopped pistachios around the bottom ½ in. (1 cm) of the sides. Place on a cake card.

9. Using the remaining ganache, pipe the word "Alhambra" across the middle of the cake.

10. Make 2 marzipan roses and 2 leaves (see p. 651) and brush them with cocoa powder to highlight them. Arrange them attractively above the writing on top of the cake.

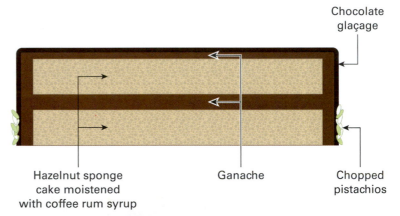

Chocolate glaçage

Hazelnut sponge
cake moistened
with coffee rum syrup

Ganache

Chopped
pistachios

GENOISE À LA CONFITURE FRAMBOISE (GENOISE WITH RASPBERRY FILLING)

Components

Genoise (p. 401), split into 2 layers

Dessert syrup flavored with framboise (raspberry alcohol)

Raspberry preserves or jam (p. 589)

Italian Meringue (p. 259)

Sliced almonds

Fresh raspberries

Confectioners' sugar

PROCEDURE

1. Moisten one genoise layer with the syrup. Spread the top evenly with raspberry preserves.

2. Moisten the bottom of the second cake layer with syrup and place on top of the first layer. Brush the top with additional syrup.

3. Coat the top and sides with the Italian meringue and spread smooth with a palette knife. Using a pastry bag, decorate the top with additional meringue.

4. Press the almonds around the bottom edge of the sides of the cake.

5. Brown the meringue with a blowtorch.

6. Garnish the top of the cake with fresh raspberries and sprinkle with a little confectioners' sugar.

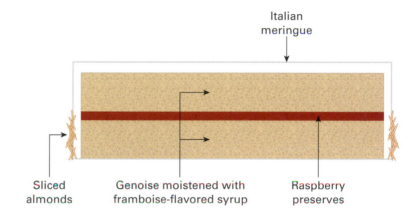

Italian meringue

Sliced almonds

Genoise moistened with framboise-flavored syrup

Raspberry preserves

BRASILIA

Components

1 half-sheet pan Hazelnut Joconde Sponge Cake (p. 405)

Nougatine (p. 658), freshly prepared, 10 oz (300 g)

Dark chocolate, melted, about 2 oz (50 g)

Dessert syrup flavored with rum

Caramel Buttercream (p. 422), 1 lb (500 g)

Tempered white couverture for decoration

PROCEDURE

1. Cut the sponge into 3 equal rectangles, about 6 × 12 in. (15 × 30 cm).

2. Prepare the nougatine. Roll out into a thin rectangle slightly larger than the sponge rectangles. While it is still warm, trim the edges with a sharp knife so they are straight and the rectangle is about ½ in. (1 cm) smaller on a side than the sponge (to allow for later trimming of the sponge). (If you rolled the nougatine on a silicone mat, remove it from the mat before cutting.) Cut portions of the desired size, but leave them together. Let cool.

3. Spread one sponge layer with a thin coat of melted chocolate. Refrigerate to set.

4. Remove from the refrigerator, turn chocolate side down, and brush with the rum syrup.

5. Spread with a layer of buttercream, about ¼ in. (5 mm) thick.

6. Place a second sponge layer on top, brush with syrup, and again spread with buttercream.

7. Repeat with the third layer and spread with buttercream.

8. Trim the edges and top with the nougatine.

9. Put the tempered white chocolate in a paper cone and decorate the top of the cake with a fancy border.

10. If desired, this large cake can be cut in half to make two 6-in. (15-cm) square cakes.

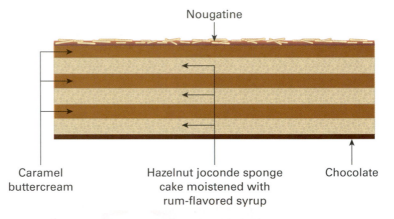

Nougatine

Caramel buttercream

Hazelnut joconde sponge cake moistened with rum-flavored syrup

Chocolate

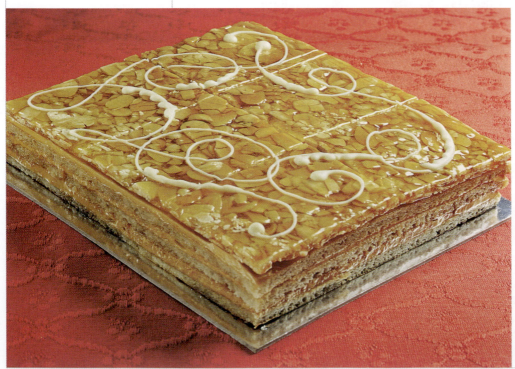

RUSSIAN CAKE

Components

1 half-sheet pan Joconde
  Sponge Cake (p. 405)

Dark chocolate, melted,
  about 2 oz (50 g)

Dessert syrup flavored
  with cognac

Praline Buttercream
  (p. 421), 1 lb (500 g)

Apricot Glaze (p. 194)

Toasted sliced almonds

Confectioners' sugar

PROCEDURE

1. Cut the sponge into 3 equal rectangles, about 6 × 12 in. (15 × 30 cm).

2. Spread one sponge layer with a thin layer of melted chocolate. Refrigerate to set.

3. Remove from the refrigerator, turn chocolate side down, and brush with the cognac syrup.

4. Spread with a layer of buttercream, about ½ in. (1 cm) thick.

5. Place a second sponge layer on top, brush with syrup, and again spread with buttercream.

6. Top with the third layer of sponge and brush with syrup. Trim the sides of the cake neatly.

7. Heat the apricot glaze and thin with water to a consistency that can be poured and spread. Glaze the top of the cake.

8. With the remaining buttercream, decorate the top of the cake with a scroll border, using a pastry bag with a star tip.

9. Garnish the top of the cake with the almonds and dust them very lightly with confectioners' sugar.

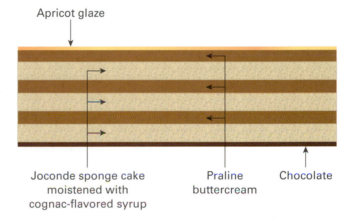

Apricot glaze

Joconde sponge cake
moistened with
cognac-flavored syrup

Praline
buttercream

Chocolate

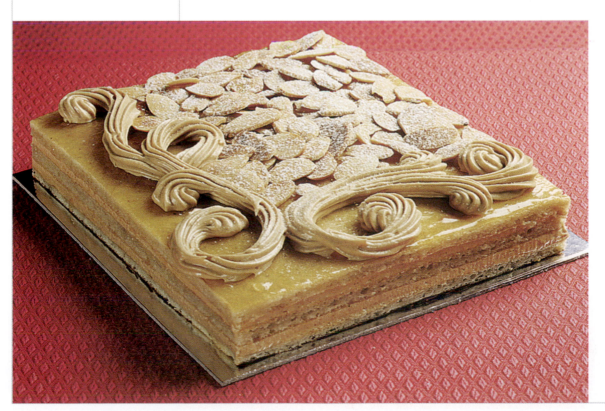

OPERA CAKE

Components

1 half-sheet pan Joconde
  Sponge Cake (p. 405)

Dark chocolate, melted,
  about 2 oz (50 g)

Dessert syrup flavored with
  coffee extract

French Buttercream flavored
  with coffee (p. 421),
  12 oz (350 g)

Ganache, 5–6 oz (150 g)

Opera Glaze (p. 428)

PROCEDURE

1. Cut the sponge into 3 equal rectangles, about 6 × 12 in. (15 × 30 cm).

2. Spread one sponge layer with a thin coat of melted chocolate. Refrigerate to set.

3. Remove from the refrigerator, turn chocolate side down, and brush with the coffee syrup.

4. Spread with a layer of buttercream, about ¼ in. (5 mm) thick.

5. Place a second sponge layer on top, brush with syrup, and spread with a thin layer of ganache.

6. Top with the third layer of sponge and brush with syrup. Spread with a layer of the
    buttercream. Smooth the top carefully with a palette knife. Refrigerate or freeze until firm. The
    cake must be quite cold so the warm glaze does not melt the buttercream.

7. Set the cake on a rack over a tray. Pour warm opera glaze over the cake. Pass a palette knife
    over the top of the cake and then tap the tray to smooth the glaze.

8. Chill until set. Remove from the rack and trim the sides of the cake neatly and squarely with a
    hot knife.

9. With additional ganache in a paper cone, pipe the word Opera on top of the cake.

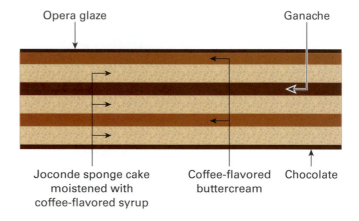

Opera glaze · Ganache · Joconde sponge cake moistened with coffee-flavored syrup · Coffee-flavored buttercream · Chocolate

MONTE CARLO

Components

Common Meringue
  (p. 258), 8 oz (225 g)

Almond Chocolate Sponge
  (p. 410), one circle 5, 6,
  or 7 in. (13–18 cm) in
  diameter

Jelled Spiced Apricot
  Compote (p. 466)

Almond Cream (p. 196),
  14 oz (400 g)

Decoration

Crème Chantilly (p. 257)

Apricot halves

Cocoa powder

Red currants

PROCEDURE

1. Pipe 7-in. (18-cm) circles of common meringue onto parchment paper (see p. 341 for the technique). Use all the meringue—you will need two circles for the cake, plus crumbled meringue for decoration. Bake at 325°F (160°C) until firm. Using a 7-in. (18-cm) charlotte ring like a cookie cutter, trim two of the circles to fit inside the ring.

2. Trim the almond chocolate sponge, if necessary, to fit inside a 5-in. (13-cm) cake pan. Brush generously with the reserved syrup from the apricot compote. Pour warm apricot compote on top of the sponge in the tin. Chill until set.

3. Place one of the meringue layers on a cake card. Turn out the sponge and apricot compote from the tin upside down on top of the meringue so the almond sponge layer is on top. Be sure to center this 5-in. (13-cm) circle on the meringue.

4. Place a 7-in. (18-cm) charlotte ring on the cake card enclosing the meringue layer.

5. Fill to just below the top of the ring with the almond cream. Top with the second meringue layer, pressing down gently. Chill until set.

6. Remove the charlotte ring, carefully using a blowtorch to release the ring from the sides.

7. Mask the top and sides of the cake by spreading on a thin layer of almond cream.

8. Crumble the remaining baked meringue and press the crumbs onto the sides and top of the cake.

9. Using a pastry bag with a star tip, pipe 8 rosettes of crème Chantilly around the top edge of the cake. Top each with a fanned apricot half. Dust the center lightly with cocoa powder. If desired, add a few red currants for further decoration.

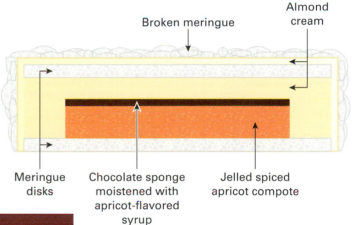

Broken meringue

Almond cream

Meringue disks

Chocolate sponge moistened with apricot-flavored syrup

Jelled spiced apricot compote

JELLED SPICED APRICOT COMPOTE

Ingredients

Canned apricots with
 syrup, 12 oz (350 g)

Cinnamon stick, 1

Lemon peel, strips from
 1 lemon

Gelatin, ⅛ oz (4 g, or
 2 leaves)

Amaretto liqueur, 2 oz
 (60 mL)

PROCEDURE

1. Drain and reserve the syrup from the apricots. Add the cinnamon stick and lemon peel to the syrup and bring to a boil. Add the apricots and simmer until the fruit is beginning to fall apart (if necessary, remove the apricots and chop them). Remove the cinnamon stick and lemon peel. Drain and reserve the syrup to moisten the cake layer as directed in step 2 of the recipe for Monte Carlo.

2. Soften the gelatin in cold water (see pp. 80–82).

3. Add the gelatin to the hot apricots and stir until it is dissolved. Stir in the amaretto.

4. Rewarm, if necessary, to use in the Monte Carlo on the previous page.

JULIANNA

Components

Wood-grain chocolate strip

Plain genoise (p. 401),
 two 7-in. (18-cm) disks,
 ¼–⅜ in. (1 cm) thick

Coffee Syrup (p. 255)

Praline Cream II (p. 535),
 10 oz (300 g)

Vanilla Cream (p. 422),
 10 oz (300 g)

Coffee Marble Glaze
 (p. 429), 3–4 oz
 (100–110 g)

Decoration

Chocolate fan

Chocolate cigarettes

Caramelized hazelnuts

PROCEDURE

1. Line a 7-in. (18-cm) charlotte ring with a strip of acetate coated with wood-grain chocolate (see pp. 633–634). Set the ring on a cake card.

2. Place a disk of genoise sponge in the base of the ring. (*Note:* The sponge circles may be cut from a thin sheet of sponge, or cut horizontally from a thicker sponge layer.)

3. Brush the sponge with coffee syrup.

4. Fill the ring halfway with praline cream.

5. Top with a second sponge layer and press down gently and evenly. Brush the sponge with coffee syrup.

6. Fill the ring to the top with vanilla cream. Smooth with a palette knife. Chill until firm.

7. Add the coffee extract to the marble glaze (see p. 429) and swirl in lightly. Spread over the surface of the cake, swirling to give a marbled pattern. Chill well.

8. Remove the ring and peel away the acetate. Neaten the edge of the glaze with a small knife.

9. Decorate the top of the cake with a chocolate fan dusted with confectioners' sugar, a few chocolate cigarettes (p. 635), and caramelized hazelnuts.

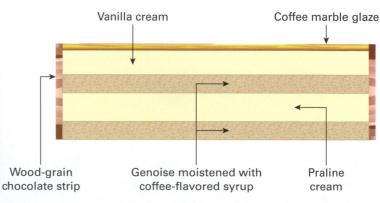

Vanilla cream

Coffee marble glaze

Wood-grain chocolate strip

Genoise moistened with coffee-flavored syrup

Praline cream

TIRAMISÙ

Components

1 sheet Ladyfinger Sponge (p. 407)

Strong espresso coffee, 1 pt (500 mL)

Dessert syrup, 8 oz (250 mL)

Mascarpone Filling (recipe follows)

Cocoa powder

NOTE: This recipe is easily cut in half. Start with a half-size sponge sheet and use half the filling and coffee syrup. Alternatively, use ready-prepared ladyfinger cookies in place of the sponge sheet.

PROCEDURE

1. Cut the sponge sheet in half crosswise.
2. Combine the espresso and syrup. Brush the sponge sheets generously with this syrup—use it all.
3. Place one sponge sheet on a tray. Spread half the filling evenly over the sponge.
4. Top with the second layer of sponge, followed by the remaining filling. Smooth the top. Chill until firm.
5. Dust the top generously with cocoa powder.
6. Cut 6 × 4 into 24 portions.

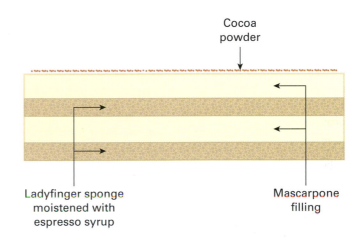

Cocoa powder

Ladyfinger sponge moistened with espresso syrup

Mascarpone filling

MASCARPONE FILLING

Ingredients	U.S.	Metric
Egg yolks	2 yolks	2 yolks
Sugar	6 oz	180 g
Water	4 oz	120 g
Glucose or corn syrup	2 oz	60 g
Mascarpone	1 lb	500 g
Heavy cream	1 lb 8 oz	740 g
Approximate weight:	**3 lb**	**1600 g**

PROCEDURE

1. Whip the egg yolks until light.
2. Make a syrup of the sugar, water, and glucose and cook to 248°F (120°C). Gradually pour into the egg yolks while whipping constantly. Continue whipping until cool.
3. In a mixer fitted with the paddle attachment, mix the mascarpone until soft.
4. With the mixer running at low speed, add the egg yolk mixture a little at a time, waiting until each addition is blended in before adding more.
5. Whip the cream to soft peaks. Fold into the mascarpone mixture.

TIRAMISÙ

Tiramisù has become so popular that many people think it must be an old, classic Italian dessert. Some have even argued that it dates back hundreds of years, to the Renaissance period. In fact, no printed recipes for tiramisù appear until the latter part of the twentieth century, so probably the cake as we know it today is a recent invention.

The cake has been widely copied and modified. There are hundreds of different recipes for it, and almost the only thing they have in common is mascarpone cheese.

The word *tiramisù* means "pick-me-up," in reference to the two ingredients in it that contain caffeine, coffee, and cocoa.

BANANIER

Components

Joconde Sponge (p. 405)

Rum Syrup (p. 255)

Lime Chiboust (p. 266),
7 oz (200 g)

Caramelized Banana Slices
(below)

Banana Mousse (p. 535),
7 oz (200 g)

Chocolate spray (p. 637)

Apricot Glaze (p. 194)

Decoration

Chocolate fans

Slices of lime and banana

PROCEDURE

1. Line a 6½-in. (16-cm) ring mold with a strip of acetate.

2. Cut two 6-in. (15-cm) circles from a sheet of joconde sponge. Cut one strip of joconde to line the side of the ring mold, making it slightly narrower than the height of the ring so the filling will show above it. Caramelize the sponge strip and circles according to the Procedure for Caramelizing Sponge on page 445.

3. Brush the caramelized sponge strip and circles with rum syrup. Line the mold with the strip of sponge and place it on a cake card. Place one sponge circle in the bottom.

4. Prepare the lime chiboust. Before it sets, use it to fill the ring nearly half full, then place the second sponge circle on top and press down gently.

5. Arrange the banana slices on top of the sponge.

6. Prepare the banana mousse. Before it sets, fill the mold to the top and then level it with a palette knife.

7. Place in the freezer for 45 minutes, to set.

8. Lay a decorative stencil on top of the cake and spray with a chocolate sprayer.

9. Coat the top with apricot glaze.

10. Garnish as desired. The cake in the illustration is garnished with 2 chocolate fans and slices of lime and banana coated with apricot glaze.

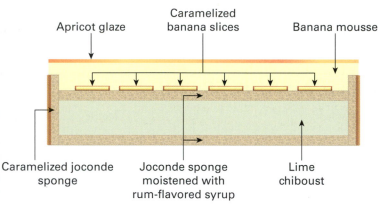

CARAMELIZED BANANA SLICES FOR BANANIER

Ingredients

1 banana

Brown sugar, 1 oz (30 g)

Butter, 2 tsp (10 g)

PROCEDURE

1. Cut the banana into slices ½ in. (1 cm) thick.

2. Heat the sugar in a small sauté pan and add the banana slices. Heat them quickly until caramelized on both sides but not soft.

3. Swirl in the butter.

4. Place the banana slices on a sheet of parchment paper to cool.

Swiss Rolls

Swiss rolls are made up in much the same way as American jelly rolls, except Swiss rolls are usually more delicate. They can be made with a great variety of fillings and are often iced and decorated.

GENERAL PROCEDURE: Making Swiss Rolls

1. Bake Swiss roll sponge as directed in the formula (p. 401 or 402). Turn out onto a sheet of parchment and carefully peel the paper off the back of the sponge. Cool it partially covered so the cake does not dry out. (You may also moisten the cake with dessert syrup.)

2. Trim the edges with a sharp knife (crusty edges do not roll well).

3. Spread with the desired filling, such as:

   Jam or jelly

   Buttercream (pp. 418–422)

   Ganache (pp. 272–273)

   Chocolate Mousse (p. 273, and pp. 537–538)

   Pastry cream variations (pp. 262–263)

   Whipped cream

   Lemon Filling (p. 300)

   Chopped fruits or nuts may be mixed with buttercream or pastry cream.

4. If any items—such as fruit pieces or a thin rope of marzipan—are to be rolled into the center of the roll, place these along one edge of the sheet on top of the filling. Begin rolling from this edge.

5. With the aid of the sheet of parchment under the sponge, roll up the cake tightly.

6. Ice or cover the outside of the roll as desired. For example:

   - Brush with apricot glaze, then ice with fondant.
   - Coat with melted chocolate.
   - Coat with a sheet of marzipan or rolled fondant (see pp. 447–448), using apricot jam or glaze to make the coating stick.
   - Spread with a thin layer of buttercream, then coat with marzipan.
   - Spread with buttercream, then roll in coconut or chopped nuts.

7. Swiss rolls may be sold as whole cakes or cut into individual slices.

VARIATION: HALF ROLLS

1. Before icing the outside of the roll, chill the roll to make it firmer.

2. Cut a sheet of baked short pastry or sponge cake into 2 strips, each as long and as wide as the sponge roll. Spread the strips with a thin layer of icing or jam.

3. With a sharp knife, carefully cut the chilled sponge roll in half lengthwise.

4. Mount each half cut side down on one of the prepared sponge or short dough bases.

5. Ice and decorate as in the basic procedure.

ALMOND SWISS ROLLS

Components
Swiss Roll sponge (p. 402)
Apricot jam
Almond pastry cream
Apricot Glaze (p. 194)
White poured fondant
Toasted almonds

PROCEDURE

1. Spread plain Swiss roll sponge with apricot jam, then with almond pastry cream.
2. Roll up.
3. Brush with apricot glaze and ice with white fondant.
4. While the fondant is soft, lay a row of toasted almonds along the top of the roll.

BLACK FOREST ROLL

Components

Whipped cream fortified with gelatin (p. 256) and flavored with kirsch

Chocolate Swiss Roll sponge (p. 402)

Dark sweet cherries, well drained

Chocolate shavings

PROCEDURE

1. Fit a pastry bag with a plain tube and fill it with the whipped cream.
2. Pipe strips of cream about ⅜ in. (1 cm) apart on a sheet of chocolate Swiss roll so the strips run the length of the roll.
3. Fill in the spaces between the strips with cherries.
4. Roll up.
5. Coat with additional cream and then with chocolate shavings.

BÛCHE DE NOËL (CHOCOLATE CHRISTMAS ROLL)

Components

Plain or Chocolate Swiss Roll sponge (p. 402)

Chocolate Buttercream (p. 418)

Vanilla Buttercream (p. 419)

Meringue Mushrooms (p. 346)

PROCEDURE

1. Spread plain or chocolate Swiss roll sponge with chocolate buttercream.
2. Roll up.
3. The finished roll is intended to look like a log. To create this effect, first spread the ends with white buttercream. Then, using a paper cone, pipe on a spiral of chocolate buttercream or other chocolate icing to look like the end grain of wood.
4. Ice the rest of the roll with chocolate buttercream to resemble bark, either by using a pastry bag with a flattened star tube or by spreading on the cream and then texturing it with an icing comb.
5. Decorate with meringue mushrooms.

HARLEQUIN ROLL

Components

Plain Swiss Roll sponge (p. 402)

Vanilla Buttercream (p. 419)

Chocolate Buttercream (p. 418)

Apricot Glaze (p. 194)

Chocolate rolled fondant, or marzipan colored with cocoa

PROCEDURE

1. On a sheet of plain Swiss roll sponge, pipe alternating rows of vanilla and chocolate buttercream until the roll is completely covered with stripes of buttercream running the length of the roll.
2. Roll up.
3. Coat with apricot glaze.
4. Cover with chocolate rolled fondant or marzipan colored with cocoa.

MOCHA ROLL

Components	PROCEDURE
Plain Swiss Roll sponge (p. 402) Coffee buttercream (p. 419) Chocolate shavings Chocolate for drizzling	1. Spread plain Swiss roll sponge with buttercream and sprinkle with chocolate shavings. 2. Roll up. 3. Ice with more buttercream. Decorate by drizzling chocolate over the icing.

PRALINE GANACHE ROLL

Components	PROCEDURE
Plain Swiss Roll sponge (p. 402) Praline Buttercream (p. 419) Ganache (p. 272) Chopped or sliced hazelnuts	1. Spread plain Swiss roll sponge with praline buttercream. 2. Using a large plain tube, pipe a strip of ganache along one edge. 3. Roll up so the ganache is in the center. 4. Cover with more buttercream. Coat with chopped or sliced hazelnuts.

STRAWBERRY CREAM ROLL

Components	PROCEDURE
Plain Swiss Roll sponge (p. 402) Pastry cream (p. 263) flavored with orange flavor or orange liqueur Fresh strawberries Confectioners' sugar	1. Spread plain Swiss roll sponge with flavored pastry cream. 2. Place a row of fresh strawberries along one edge. 3. Roll up so the strawberries are in the center. Dust with confectioners' sugar.

Small Cakes

Small fancy cakes in individual portion sizes can be made in many shapes and flavors. In some American bakeshops, these are known as *French pastries*. Using a variety of cakes, icings, fillings, and decorations, a baker can make an unlimited variety of small, attractive cakes. This section briefly describes some of the more popular varieties.

Slices

These are simply portion-size slices of rectangular strip cakes (p. 444), Swiss rolls (p. 469), and half rolls (p. 469). An important part of the appearance of slices is the pattern made by the icing and filling layers. Therefore, it is important to cut the slices carefully and neatly.

For best results, chill or freeze the rolls or strips before slicing so the fillings and icings are firm. Use a sharp knife. Wipe the knife clean and dip it into hot water before each cut.

Slices may be lined up on trays or placed in individual paper cases for display.

Triangles

To make triangles, sandwich together four or five layers of ¼-inch (6-mm) thick sponge (such as Swiss roll sponge or seven-layer sponge) with buttercream in a contrasting color. Press the layers together firmly. Chill to solidify the cream. Cut the cake into strips 2 to 2½ inches (5 to 6 cm) wide.

Place a strip at the edge of the bench and, using a sharp knife, cut diagonally into triangles (a). Turn the triangles so the layers are vertical (b). Attach them back to back with a layer of buttercream to form a larger triangle (c).

Coat with marzipan, chocolate glaçage, or icing. Cut into slices.

Squares

Layer two or three sheets of cake and icing or filling so that the assembled layers are 1½ to 1¾ inches (4 cm) high. Press the layers together firmly. Chill until the filling is firm.

Cut the cake into small squares, 2 inches (5 cm) across or less. Ice the sides, then the top, with buttercream. Decorate as desired.

Petits Fours

The term *petit four* can be used to refer to almost any small cake or pastry item small enough to be eaten in one or two bites. *Petit* in French means "little" and *four* means "oven." Most petits fours are small baked items, although a few are not baked.

Petits fours are divided into two categories: *Petits fours secs* (*sec* means "dry") include a variety of small, dainty cookies, baked meringues, macaroons, and puff pastry products. These will be discussed further in the next chapter.

Petits fours glacés are iced petits fours (*glacé* means, in this case, "iced"). This category includes such items as tiny éclairs, tartlets, filled meringues, and cakes. In fact, nearly any iced or creamed pastry or cake item may be called a petit four as long as it is small enough to be eaten in one or two bites.

In North America, the usual type of petit four is a cake cutout iced with fondant. In fact, most people are probably not aware of any other kind. Because of its popularity, the fondant-glazed petit four should be in the repertoire of every pastry cook. See the general Procedure for Making Fondant-Iced Petits Fours below.

PROCEDURE: Making Fondant-Iced Petits Fours

1. Select a firm, close-grained cake. Cake that is too coarse, soft, or crumbly is difficult to cut evenly into small shapes. Of the formulas in this book, Almond Cake for Petits Fours (p. 395) is recommended. Other suitable choices are Almond Sponge II (p. 401) and Pound Cake (see the variation for petits fours on p. 394). For one sheet of petits fours you will need 3 sheets of cake, ¼ in. (6 mm) thick each. The finished, iced petits fours should be no more than 1 in. (2.5 cm) high.

2. Lay one sheet of cake on a sheet pan and spread with a thin layer of hot apricot jam or of buttercream. Top with the second sheet.

3. Repeat with the third sheet. Spread the top with a thin layer of jam or the same filling used between the layers.

4. Roll out a thin sheet of marzipan the same size as the cake sheet. Roll it up loosely on the rolling pin, then unroll it to cover the cake. Run the rolling pin over the top to make sure the layers are stuck together firmly.

5. Place a sheet of parchment on top of the marzipan, then place a sheet pan on the parchment. Invert the entire assembly so the marzipan layer is on the bottom. Remove the top sheet pan.

6. Wrap the cake in plastic film and freeze. This firms the cake so the neatest possible pieces can be cut from it.

7. Using appropriate cutters, cut out small squares, rectangles, diamonds, ovals, circles, or other shapes. Remember to keep them small—no more than 1 in. (2.5 cm) across.

8. Prepare fondant for icing. Thin the fondant with simple syrup so it will coat the cakes with a very thin layer. You may also color it very lightly.

9. Place the petits fours 1 in. (2.5 cm) apart on an icing grate over a tray. Pour the fondant over each one, making sure to cover the top and sides completely.

   Alternatively, you may dip each cake in warm fondant. Push the cake upside down into the fondant until the bottom is level with the icing. With two chocolate forks (see p. 627), one on the bottom and one on the top, lift the cake out of the fondant, invert it, and set it on an icing grate to drain.

10. When the icing is set, use chocolate, piping gel, or colored fondant to decorate the tops of the petits fours.

11. As an interesting variation, before icing the petits fours, pipe a small bulb of buttercream on top of each cake. Refrigerate to harden the buttercream. Then coat the petits fours with fondant.

TERMS FOR REVIEW

poured fondant	glaze	icing comb	charlotte ring
buttercream	marzipan	paper cone	charlotte
boiled icing	rolled fondant	drop-string method	Black Forest torte
marshmallow icing	modeling chocolate	contact method	Swiss roll
flat icing	Boston cream pie	marbling (icing)	petit four
royal icing	French pastry	piping jelly	petit four glacé
string work	icing screen	gâteau	
flooding	turntable	torte	

QUESTIONS FOR REVIEW

1. What is the most important rule to follow when using fondant? Why?

2. What are the advantages and disadvantages of using butter and using shortening in buttercream icings?

3. What are the steps for assembling and icing a two-layer cake?

4. What method would you use to ice cupcakes with fondant? With buttercream?

5. Why is the consistency of the icing important when you are decorating with a paper cone or pastry bag?

6. True or false: If you are right-handed, you should hold the top of the pastry bag shut with your right hand and squeeze the bag with your left hand. Explain your answer.

7. Name four techniques you can use for partially or completely decorating a cake without using a pastry bag or paper cone.

8. Briefly list the steps in assembling a typical basic European-style cake or gâteau.

9. Describe how to cut cake slices to achieve the neatest results.

10. Describe four ways to line a ring mold for a cake.

11. What precautions must be taken when using fruit to line a ring mold?

12. Describe the procedure for caramelizing a strip of sponge.

13. Describe the procedure for covering a cake with a rolled coating.

18

COOKIES

AFTER READING THIS CHAPTER, YOU SHOULD BE ABLE TO:

1. Describe the causes of crispness, softness, chewiness, and spread in cookies.
2. Prepare cookie doughs by using the four basic mixing methods.
3. Prepare eight basic types of cookies: dropped, bagged, rolled, molded, icebox, bar, sheet, and stencil.
4. Bake and cool cookies properly.
5. Explain how to judge the quality of cookies and correct defects in them.

THE WORD *COOKIE* means "small cake," and that's more or less what a cookie is. In fact, some cookies are made from cake batter. For some products, such as certain kinds of brownies, it's difficult to know whether to classify them as cakes or cookies.

Most cookie formulas, however, call for less liquid than cake formulas do. Cookie doughs range from soft to very stiff, unlike the thinner batters for cakes. This difference in moisture content means some differences in mixing methods, although the basic procedures are much like those for cakes.

The most obvious differences between cakes and cookies are in makeup. Because most cookies are individually formed or shaped, a great deal of hand labor is involved. Learning the correct methods and then practicing diligently are essential for efficiency.

COOKIE CHARACTERISTICS AND THEIR CAUSES

COOKIES COME IN an infinite variety of shapes, sizes, flavors, and textures. Characteristics that are desirable in some types are not desirable in others. For example, we want some *cookies* to be crisp, others to be soft. We want some to hold their shape, others to spread during baking. In order to produce the characteristics we want, and to correct faults, it is useful to know what causes these basic traits.

Keep in mind that many of these factors work together to create the specific characteristic. For example, note that three factors that result in crispness are low liquid content, high sugar content, and high fat content. Having a high fat and sugar content doesn't by itself create crispness. Rather, having a high sugar and fat content enables you to lower the liquid content and still have a workable dough. So if you want to make a cookie crisper, it's not enough just to increase the sugar, as you may end up with a badly balanced formula. You should instead lower the liquid content and then balance the formula by increasing the sugar and fat.

Crispness

Cookies are crisp when they are low in moisture. The following factors contribute to crispness:

- Low proportion of liquid in the mix. Most crisp cookies are made from a stiff dough.
- High sugar and fat content. A large proportion of these ingredients makes it possible to mix a workable dough with low moisture content.
- Baking long enough to evaporate most of the moisture. Baking in a convection oven also dries cookies more quickly, contributing to crispness.
- Small size or thin shape. This causes the cookie to dry faster during baking.
- Proper storage. Crisp cookies can become soft when they absorb moisture.

LITTLE CAKES

The word *cookie*—which comes from the Dutch word *koekje*, meaning "little cake"—is used only in North America. In Britain, these little cakes are known as biscuits, although English biscuits are usually smaller than North American cookies and almost always crisp rather than soft and chewy.

Immigrants from many countries brought their favorite recipes for little sweets with them to North America, and as a result we enjoy cookies that originated in Scandinavia, Britain, Germany, France, Eastern Europe, and elsewhere.

Until recently, North American cookies were more likely to be small and crisp—that is, truer to their European origins. Then, in the latter part of the twentieth century, the public began to prefer soft or chewy cookies, and bakers started underbaking them to prevent them from crisping. As a result, it was not unusual to find doughy cookies with partly raw centers. Quickly, however, bakers modified cookie formulas so they could produce soft cookies that were fully baked. At the same time, the North American fondness for large portions led to cookies of increasing size. Today, it is common to find cookies 4 or 5 inches (10–12 cm) in diameter, or even larger.

Softness

Softness is the opposite of crispness, so it has the opposite causes, as follows:

- High proportion of liquid in the mix.
- Low sugar and fat.
- Honey, molasses, or corn syrup included in the formulas. These sugars are *hygroscopic*, which means they readily absorb moisture from the air or from their surroundings.
- Underbaking.
- Large size or thick shape. This enables them to retain more moisture.
- Proper storage. Soft cookies can dry out and become stale if not tightly covered or wrapped.

Chewiness

Moisture is necessary for chewiness, but other factors are also important. In other words, all chewy cookies are soft, but not all soft cookies are chewy. The following factors contribute to chewiness:

- High sugar and liquid content, but low fat content.
- High proportion of eggs.
- Strong flour or gluten developed during mixing.

Spread

Spread is desirable in some cookies, whereas others must hold their shape. Several factors contribute to *spread*, or the lack of it.

- High sugar content increases spread (see photo at right). Coarse granulated sugar increases spread, while fine sugar or confectioners' sugar reduces spread.

- High baking soda or baking ammonia content encourages spread.

- The creaming together of fat and sugar contributes to leavening by incorporating air. Creaming a mixture until light increases spread. Blending fat and sugar just to a paste (without creaming in a lot of air) reduces spread.

- Low oven temperature increases spread. High temperature decreases spread because the cookie sets up before it has a chance to spread too much.

- A slack batter—that is, one with a high liquid content—spreads more than a stiff dough.

- Strong flour or activation of gluten decreases spread.

- Cookies spread more when baked on heavily greased pans.

Sugar increases spread: These cookies were made with the same formula, except that the four at the top contain 50% sugar, while those at the bottom contain 67% sugar.

> **KEY POINTS TO REVIEW**
>
> ▪ What factors cause a cookie to be crisp?
>
> ▪ What factors cause a cookie to be soft?
>
> ▪ What factors cause a cookie to be chewy?
>
> ▪ What factors cause a cookie to spread while baking?

MIXING METHODS

COOKIE MIXING METHODS are much like those for mixing cakes. The major difference is that less liquid is usually incorporated, so mixing is somewhat easier. Less liquid means gluten is less developed by the mixing. Also, it is a little easier to get a smooth, uniform mix.

There are four basic cookie mixing methods:

- One-stage
- Creaming
- Sanding (sablage)
- Sponge

These methods are subject to many variations due to differences in formulas. The general procedures are as follows, but always be sure to follow the exact instructions with each formula.

One-Stage Method

The *one-stage method* is the counterpart of the one-stage cake-mixing method. As just noted, cookie doughs contain less liquid than cake batters do, so blending the ingredients into a uniform dough is easier.

Because all the ingredients are mixed at once, the baker has less control over mixing with this method than with other methods. Therefore, the one-stage method is not frequently used. When overmixing is not a great problem, as with some chewy cookies, it can be used.

PROCEDURE: One-Stage Method

1. Scale ingredients accurately. Have all ingredients at room temperature.

2. Place all ingredients in the mixer. With the paddle attachment, mix the ingredients at low speed until uniformly blended. Scrape down the sides of the bowl as necessary.

Creaming Method

The *creaming method* for cookies is nearly identical to the creaming method for cakes. Because cookies require less liquid than cakes, it is not usually necessary to add the liquid alternately with the flour. It can be added all at once.

Note the importance of step 2 of the procedure, the creaming stage. The amount of creaming affects the texture of the cookie, the leavening, and the spread. Only a small amount of creaming is desired when the cookie must retain its shape and not spread too much. Also, if the cookie is very short (high in fat and low in gluten development), or if it is thin and delicate, too much creaming will make the cookie too crumbly.

PROCEDURE: Creaming Method

1. Scale ingredients accurately. Have all ingredients at room temperature.
2. Place the fat, sugar, salt, and spices in the mixing bowl. With the paddle attachment, cream these ingredients at low speed. Partway through mixing, stop the machine and scrape down the bowl to ensure even mixing.
3. For light cookies, cream until the mix is light and fluffy, in order to incorporate more air for leavening. For denser

cookies, blend to a smooth paste, but do not cream until light.

4. Add the eggs and liquid, if any, and blend in at low speed.
5. Sift in the flour and leavening. Mix until just combined. Do not overmix, or gluten will develop.

Sanding Method

The *sanding*, or sablage, *method* was introduced in Chapter 14 as a mixing methods for rich tart pastries and pâte brisée. There are two basic steps in this method: (1) mixing the dry ingredients with fat until the mixture resembles sand or cornmeal, and (2) mixing in the moist ingredients. In the case of cookies, the sanding method is used primarily with formulas that contain only egg and no other moist ingredient.

PROCEDURE: Sanding Method

1. Scale all ingredients accurately. Have all ingredients at room temperature.
2. Combine the dry ingredients and the fat in the bowl of a mixer. With the paddle attachment, mix until the mixture resembles coarse cornmeal or sand (a).

3. Add the eggs (b). Mix until a uniform dough is formed (c).

Sponge Method

The *sponge method* for cookies is similar to the egg-foam methods for cakes. The procedure varies considerably, however, depending on the ingredients. Batches should be kept small because the batter is delicate.

PROCEDURE: Sponge Method

1. Scale all ingredients accurately. Have all ingredients at room temperature—except the eggs, which you may want to warm slightly for greater volume, as for sponge cakes.

2. Following the procedure given in the formula being used, whip the eggs (whole, yolks, or whites) and the sugar to the proper stage: soft peaks for whites, thick and light for whole eggs or yolks.

3. Fold in the remaining ingredients as specified in the recipe. Be careful not to overmix or to deflate the eggs.

KEY POINTS TO REVIEW

▮ What are the steps in the one-stage mixing method?

▮ What are the steps in the creaming method?

▮ What are the steps in the sanding method?

▮ What are the steps in the sponge method?

TYPES AND MAKEUP METHODS

WE CAN CLASSIFY cookies by their makeup methods as well as by their mixing methods. Grouping them by makeup method is perhaps more useful, from the point of view of production, because cookie mixing methods are relatively simple, while their makeup procedures vary considerably. In this section, you will learn the basic procedures for producing eight cookie types:

- Bagged
- Dropped
- Rolled
- Molded
- Icebox
- Bar
- Sheet
- Stencil

No matter which makeup method you use, you must follow one important rule: *Make all cookies of uniform size and thickness*. This is essential for even baking. Because baking times are so short, small cookies may burn before large ones are done.

If the tops of the cookies are to be garnished with fruits, nuts, or other décor, place the garnishes on the cookies as soon as they are panned; press them on gently. If you wait until the surface of the dough begins to dry, the garnish may not stick and will fall off after baking.

Bagged

Bagged, or pressed, cookies are made from soft doughs. The dough must be soft enough to be forced through a pastry bag but stiff enough to hold its shape. For stiffer doughs, you may want to double-bag the dough (for example, put a disposable bag inside a cloth bag) for extra strength:

1. Fit a pastry bag with a tip of the desired size and shape. Fill the bag with the cookie dough. Review page 439 for tips on the use of the pastry bag.

2. Press out cookies of the desired shape and size directly onto prepared cookie sheets.

Dropped

Like bagged cookies, *dropped* cookies are made from a soft dough. Actually, this method may be considered the same as the bagged method, and many bakers use the term *drop* for both bagging out cookies and for depositing dough with a spoon or scoop. Usually, using a pastry bag is faster, and gives better control over the shape and size of the cookies. However, in the following situations, using a portion scoop to drop cookies may be preferred:

- When the dough contains pieces of fruit, nuts, or chocolate that would clog the pastry tube.
- When you want the cookies to have a rough, homemade look.

1. Select the proper size scoop for accurate portioning.
   - A No. 8 scoop makes a jumbo cookie, about 4 oz (110 g).
   - A No. 16 scoop makes a large cookie, about 2–2½ oz (60–70 g).
   - A No. 30 scoop makes a medium-large cookie, about 1 oz (30 g).
   - A No. 40 scoop makes a medium cookie.
   - A No. 50, 60, or smaller scoop makes a small cookie.

2. Drop the cookies onto the prepared baking sheets. Allow enough space between cookies for spreading.

3. Rich cookies spread by themselves, but if the formula requires it, flatten the mounds of dough slightly with a weight dipped in sugar.

Rolled

Cookies *rolled* and cut from a stiff dough are not made as often in bakeshops and food service operations as they are made in homes because they require excessive labor. Also, there are always scraps left over after cutting, and each time the scraps are rerolled, the dough toughens.

The advantage of this method is that it allows you to make cookies in a great variety of shapes for different occasions.

1. Chill dough thoroughly.

2. Roll out dough ⅛ in. (3 mm) thick on a floured work surface. Use as little flour as possible for dusting because this flour can toughen the cookies. If the dough is especially delicate, roll out between sheets of parchment paper.

3. Cut out cookies with cookie cutters. Cut as close together as possible to reduce the quantity of scraps. Place cookies on prepared baking sheets. Roll scraps into fresh dough to minimize toughness.

4. Some décor may be applied before baking. For example, brush the tops with egg wash and sprinkle with colored sugars.

5. After baking, cutout cookies are often decorated with colored icing (royal icing, flat icing, or fondant) for holidays or special occasions. Cool cookies completely before applying icing.

Molded

Steps 1–3 of the *molded* method are simply a fast and fairly accurate way of dividing cookie dough into equal portions. Each piece is then molded into the desired shape. For some traditional cookies, special molds are used to flatten the dough and, at the same time, stamp a design onto the cookie. The use of such molds gives this procedure its name. However, today a more common method is to flatten the pieces of dough with a weight rather than a special mold. The pieces may also be shaped by hand into crescents, fingers, or other shapes.

1. Refrigerate the dough if it is too soft to handle. Roll it out into long, uniform cylinders of the required size: about ¾ inch (2 cm) thick, for very small cookies, up to 1½ inches (4 cm) or larger for large cookies. The key to uniform portioning is to make the cylinders the same thickness.

2. If necessary, refrigerate the dough cylinders to make them firmer.

3. With a knife or bench scraper, cut the roll into uniform pieces of the desired size (a).

4. Place the pieces on prepared baking sheets, leaving 2 in. (5 cm) space between each.

   Depending on the formula, the pieces may be placed directly on the baking sheets without further shaping, or they may be first rolled into balls in the palms of the hands.

   Additionally, for some cookies, the dough pieces may be rolled in sugar before panning (b).

5. Flatten the cookies with a weight, such as a can, dipped in granulated sugar before pressing each cookie (c). A fork is sometimes used for flattening the dough, as for peanut butter cookies.

6. *Alternative method:* After step 3, shape the dough by hand into desired shapes.

Icebox

The *icebox,* or refrigerator, method is ideal for operations that wish to have freshly baked cookies on hand at all times. The rolls of dough may be made up in advance and stored. Cookies can easily be sliced and baked as needed.

This method is also used to make multicolored cookies in various designs, such as checkerboard and pinwheel cookies. The procedures for making these designs are included with the recipes in this chapter (pp. 486–487).

1. Scale the dough into pieces of uniform size, from 1½ lb (700 g), if you are making small cookies, to 3 lb (1400 g) for large cookies.

2. Form the dough into cylinders 1–2 in. (2.5–5 cm) in diameter, depending on the cookie size desired. For accurate portioning, it is important to make all the cylinders of dough the same thickness and length.

3. Wrap the cylinders in parchment or wax paper, place them on sheet pans, and refrigerate overnight.

4. Unwrap the dough and cut into slices of *uniform thickness*. The exact thickness required depends on the size of the cookie and how much the dough spreads during baking. The usual range is ⅛–¼ in. (3–6 mm).

   A slicing machine is recommended for ensuring even thickness. Doughs containing nuts or fruits, however, should be sliced by hand with a knife.

5. Place the slices on prepared baking sheets, allowing 2 in. (5 cm) between cookies.

Bar

This procedure is called the *bar* method because the dough is baked in long, narrow strips and later cut crosswise into bars. It should not be confused with sheet cookies (see next procedure), which are also called *bars* by many cooks.

1. Scale the dough into 1¾-lb (800-g) units. Units weighing 1 lb (450 g) may be used for smaller cookies.

2. Shape the pieces of dough into cylinders the length of the sheet pans. Place three strips on each greased pan, spacing them well apart.

3. Flatten the dough with the fingers into strips 3–4 in. (8–10 cm) wide.

4. If required, brush with egg wash.

5. Bake as directed in the formula.

6. After baking, while the cookies are still warm, cut each strip into bars about 1¾ in. (4.5 cm) wide.

7. In some cases, as with Italian-style *biscotti* (meaning "baked twice"), the strips are cut into thinner slices, placed on sheet pans, and baked a second time until dry and crisp. See page 508 for an example.

Sheet

Sheet cookies vary so much that it is nearly impossible to give a single procedure for all of them. Some are almost like sheet cakes, only denser and richer; they may even be iced like sheet cakes. Others consist of two or three layers that are added and baked in separate stages. The following procedure is only a general guide.

1. Spread cookie mixture into prepared sheet pans. Make sure the thickness is even.

2. If required, add topping or brush with an egg wash.

3. Bake as directed. Cool.

4. Apply icing or topping, if desired.

5. Cut into individual squares or rectangles. Best practice is to turn the sheet out onto a board (see p. 389 for unmolding sheet cakes) before cutting, to avoid damaging the sheet pans.

Stencil

The *stencil* method is a special technique used with a particular type of soft dough or batter. This batter is often called *stencil paste*. It is used not only for making this type of cookie but also for making ribbon sponge cake (p. 406) for decorative work. The recipe for Almond Tuiles (p. 502) illustrates the stencil method using a simple round stencil, but it is possible to cut a stencil in nearly any shape for making decorative pieces or special desserts.

1. Line a sheet pan with a silicone mat. If a mat is not available, use a sheet of parchment paper.

2. Use a ready-made stencil. Stencils in many shapes are available from equipment purveyors. Alternatively, make a stencil by cutting a hole of the desired pattern in a sheet of thick plastic or thin cardboard (the cardboard used for cake boxes is suitable, but you may need to use a double thickness).

3. Place the stencil on the silicone mat or parchment. With an offset palette knife, spread the batter across the stencil to make a thin layer that completely fills in the cutouts.

4. Lift off the stencil and repeat to make additional cookies.

PANNING, BAKING, AND COOLING

Preparing the Pans

1. Use clean, unwarped pans.

2. Lining the sheets with parchment or silicone paper is fast, and it eliminates the need to grease the pans.

3. A heavily greased pan increases the spread of the cookie. A greased and floured pan decreases spread.

4. Some high-fat cookies can be baked on ungreased pans.

Baking

1. Most cookies are baked at a relatively high temperature for a short time.

2. Too low a temperature increases spreading and may produce hard, dry, pale cookies.

3. Too high a temperature decreases spreading and may burn the edges or bottoms.

4. Even a single minute of overbaking can burn cookies, so watch them closely. Also, the heat of the pan will continue to bake the cookies if they are left on it after being removed from the oven.

5. Doneness is indicated by color. The edges and bottom should just be turning a light golden color.

6. Excessive browning is especially undesirable if the dough has been colored. The browning of the surface hides the color.

7. With some rich doughs, burned bottoms may be a problem. In these cases, *double-pan* the cookies by placing the sheet pan on a second pan of the same size.

Cooling

1. Most cookies baked without parchment paper must be removed from the pans while they are still warm, or they may stick.

2. If the cookies are very soft, do not remove them from the pans until they are cool enough and firm enough to handle. Some cookies are soft when hot but become crisp when cool.

3. Do not cool cookies too rapidly or in cold drafts, or they may crack.

4. Cool completely before storing.

After the cookies have been baked, check them for defects. Refer to the Cookie Faults and Their Causes table on page 484 to help correct problems.

PETITS FOURS SECS

In the previous chapter, we introduced the subject of petits fours in the discussion on petits fours glacés, or iced petits fours (p. 472). *Petits fours secs*, or dry petits fours, are, by contrast, more properly discussed in the context of cookies than cakes.

As you may recall, nearly any pastry or cake item small enough to be eaten in one or two bites can be considered a petit four. The term *sec*, French for "dry," means that these pastries are generally crisp rather than moist and soft; and they have no icing or cream filling, although they may be dipped in chocolate. In practice, small quantities of creams or jellies are sometimes used—for example, in sandwich-type cookies.

Petits fours secs are usually served with after-dinner coffee or as an accompaniment to such cold desserts as ice cream, mousses, and Bavarian creams.

The following items from this chapter may be served as petits fours secs, provided they are quite small. In addition, petits fours secs made from puff pastry and pâte à choux are presented in Chapter 14; madeleines can be found in Chapter 16.

Butter Tea Cookies

Almond Macaroons

Coconut Macaroons (Meringue Type)

Pistachio Macaroons

Shortbread and Short Dough Cookies

Fancy Icebox Cookies

Spritz Cookies

Langues de Chat

Almond Tuiles

Florentines

Almond Slices

Diamonds

STANDARDS OF QUALITY FOR COOKIES

ERRORS IN MIXING, scaling, baking, and cooling cookies result in many kinds of defects and failures. Many of these, along with their possible causes, are summarized, for easy reference, in the Cookie Faults and Their Causes table on the next page. If you examine the left column of the table, you will see that many of the faults are opposites of each other, such as "too tough" or "too crumbly"; "too browned" or "not browned enough"; "too much spread" or "not enough spread." Some of the faults are due to defects in the formula (or errors in scaling ingredients), and some are due to faulty mixing, makeup, or baking.

Remember, too, in order to correct a defect, it may not be enough to adjust one ingredient. For example, one possible cause of a cookie's being too crumbly is not enough eggs. But if you simply increase the quantity of eggs in the formula, you may find that the dough is too soft unless you also add more flour. In other words, your goal is a formula with all the ingredients in balance.

To judge the quality of a cookie, examine it for each of the defects listed in the table to see whether it avoids those defects.

COOKIE FAULTS AND THEIR CAUSES

FAULT	CAUSES
Too tough	Flour too strong
	Too much flour
	Not enough shortening
	Incorrect amount of sugar
	Mixed too long or improper mixing
Too crumbly	Improper mixing
	Too much sugar
	Too much shortening
	Too much leavening
	Not enough eggs
Too hard	Baked too long or baking temperature too low
	Too much flour
	Flour too strong
	Not enough shortening
	Not enough liquid
Too dry	Not enough liquid
	Not enough shortening
	Baked too long or baking temperature too low
	Too much flour
Not browned enough	Baking temperature too low
	Underbaked
	Not enough sugar
Too brown	Baking temperature too high
	Baked too long
	Too much sugar
Poor flavor	Poor-quality ingredients
	Flavoring ingredients left out
	Dirty baking pans
	Ingredients improperly measured
Sugary surface or crust	Improper mixing
	Too much sugar
Too much spread	Baking temperature too low
	Not enough flour
	Too much sugar
	Too much leavening (chemical leaveners or creaming)
	Too much liquid
	Pans greased too heavily
Not enough spread	Baking temperature too high
	Too much flour or flour too strong
	Not enough sugar
	Not enough leavening
	Not enough liquid
	Insufficient pan grease
Stick to pans	Pans improperly greased
	Too much sugar
	Improper mixing

KEY POINTS TO REVIEW

▮ What are the eight basic makeup methods for cookies? Describe how each of them is done.

▮ What guidelines should be followed for panning, baking, and cooling cookies?

▮ What are petits fours secs?

OATMEAL RAISIN COOKIES

Ingredients	U.S.		Metric	%
Butter or part butter and part shortening	8	oz	250 g	67
Brown sugar	1 lb		500 g	133
Salt	0.16 oz (¾ tsp)		5 g	1.5
Eggs	4	oz	125 g	33
Vanilla extract	0.33 oz (2 tsp)		10 g	3
Milk	1	oz	30 g	8
Pastry flour	12	oz	375 g	100
Baking powder	0.5	oz	15 g	4
Baking soda	0.25 oz		8 g	2
Cinnamon (optional)	0.12 oz (1¾ tsp)		4 g	1
Rolled oats (quick cooking)	10	oz	312 g	83
Raisins (see *Note*)	8	oz	250 g	67
Total weight:	**3 lb 12**	**oz**	**1884 g**	**502 %**

NOTE: If raisins are hard and dry, soak them in hot water until soft, then drain them and dry them well before adding them to the cookie batter.

PROCEDURE

MIXING

Creaming method (p. 478). Combine oats with other dry ingredients after they are sifted. Blend raisins in last.

MAKEUP

Drop method. Use greased or parchment-lined baking sheets.

BAKING

375°F (190°C) for 10–12 minutes, depending on size

CHOCOLATE CHIP COOKIES

Ingredients	U.S.		Metric	%
Butter or half butter and half shortening	5	oz	150 g	50
Granulated sugar	4	oz	120 g	40
Brown sugar	4	oz	120 g	40
Salt	0.12 oz (½ tsp)		4 g	1.25
Eggs	3	oz	90 g	30
Vanilla extract	0.16 oz (1 tsp)		5 g	1.5
Pastry flour	10	oz	300 g	100
Baking soda	0.12 oz (⅝ tsp)		4 g	1.25
Chocolate chips	10	oz	300 g	100
Walnuts or pecans, chopped	4	oz	120 g	40
Total weight:	**2 lb 8**	**oz**	**1213 g**	**404 %**

PROCEDURE

MIXING

Creaming method (p. 478). Blend in chocolate chips and nuts last.

MAKEUP

Drop method. Use greased or parchment-lined baking sheets.

BAKING

375°F (190°C) for 10–14 minutes, depending on size

VARIATION

BROWN SUGAR NUT COOKIES

Make the following ingredient adjustments:
Omit the granulated sugar and use 80% (8 oz/240 g) brown sugar.

Omit the chocolate chips and increase the nuts to 100% (10 oz/300 g).

TOLL HOUSE COOKIES

Chocolate chip cookies, in their many varieties, are the most popular cookies in North America. They owe their origin to the Toll House cookie, said to have been developed in the 1920s or 1930s by Ruth Wakefield, owner of the Toll House Inn in Whitman, Massachusetts. The original Toll House cookies are simple butter cookies with semisweet chocolate morsels mixed into the dough. Today's chocolate chip or chocolate chunk cookies are likely to contain any kind of chocolate plus other ingredients, especially nuts, such as pecans, walnuts, or macadamia nuts.

ICEBOX COOKIES

Ingredients	U.S.		Metric	%
Butter, or half butter and half shortening	1 lb		500 g	67
Granulated sugar	8	oz	250 g	33
Confectioners' sugar	8	oz	250 g	33
Salt	0.25 oz		8 g	1
Eggs	4	oz	125 g	17
Vanilla extract	0.25 oz		8 g	1
Pastry flour	1 lb 8	oz	750 g	100
Total weight:	**3 lb 12**	**oz**	**1891 g**	**252%**

PROCEDURE

MIXING

Creaming method (p. 478)

MAKEUP

Icebox method. Scale dough strips 1½ lb (750 g) each. Slice cookies ¼ in. (6 mm) thick. Bake on ungreased pans.

BAKING

375°F (190°C) for 10–12 minutes

VARIATIONS

To reduce spread, use all confectioners' sugar.

BUTTERSCOTCH ICEBOX COOKIES

Make the following ingredient adjustments:

In place of the sugars in the basic recipe, use 67% (1 lb/500 g) brown sugar.

Use only butter, no shortening.

Increase the eggs to 20% (5 oz/150 g).

Add ½ tsp (2 g) baking soda with the flour.

NUT ICEBOX COOKIES

Add 25% (6 oz/188 g) finely chopped nuts to the sifted flour in the basic recipe or the butterscotch cookie formula.

CHOCOLATE ICEBOX COOKIES

Add 17% (4 oz/125 g) melted, unsweetened chocolate to the creamed butter and sugar.

FANCY ICEBOX COOKIES

These are small cookies with designs in two colors. To make them, prepare white and chocolate icebox dough with only the 33% confectioners' sugar; omit the granulated sugar. This reduces the spread of the cookies and preserves the designs. Make the designs as follows:

PINWHEEL COOKIES

Roll out a sheet of white dough about ⅛ in. (3 mm) thick. Roll out a sheet of chocolate dough the same size and thickness. Brush the white sheet lightly and evenly with egg wash, being careful not to leave any puddles. Lay the chocolate sheet on top and brush with egg wash. Roll up like a jelly roll until the roll is 1 in. (2.5 cm) thick (a). Cut off the dough evenly. Continue making rolls with the rest of the sheet. Refrigerate the rolls. Slice and bake as in the basic procedure.

A

Pinwheel cookie dough.

— **VARIATIONS CONTINUED** —

CHECKERBOARD COOKIES

Roll out 1 sheet of white dough and 1 sheet of chocolate dough ¼ in. (6 mm) thick. Egg-wash one sheet lightly and lay the second sheet on top. Cut the double sheet of dough in half. Egg-wash one sheet and lay the second on top so you have four alternating colors. Chill until firm. Roll out another sheet of white dough very thin (less than ⅛ in.) and brush with egg wash. From the chilled four-layer sheet, cut off 4 slices ¼ in. (6 mm) thick (b). Lay one of these strips on the rolled-out sheet of dough along one edge. Egg-wash the top. Lay a second strip on top with the colors reversed, so chocolate dough is on top of white dough and white is on top of chocolate. Egg-wash the top. Repeat with the remaining two strips (c). Wrap in the thin sheet of dough (d). Chill, slice, and bake as in the basic procedure.

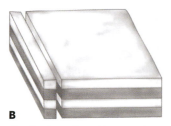

B
C
D

Checkerboard cookie dough.

BULL'S-EYE COOKIES

Roll out a cylinder of dough ½ in. (12 mm) thick. Roll out a sheet of contrasting-color dough ¼ in. (6 mm) thick. Egg-wash the top. Wrap the cylinder in the sheet of dough (e). Chill, slice, and bake as in the basic procedure.

E

Bull's-eye cookie dough.

SUGAR COOKIES

Ingredients	U.S.		Metric	%
Butter and/or shortening	8	oz	250 g	40
Sugar	10	oz	310 g	50
Salt	0.16	oz (¾ tsp)	5 g	0.8
Eggs	2	oz	60 g	10
Milk	2	oz	60 g	10
Vanilla extract	0.25	oz	8 g	1.25
Cake flour	1 lb 4	oz	625 g	100
Baking powder	0.625	oz	18 g	3
Total weight:	**2 lb 11**	**oz**	**1336 g**	**215 %**

PROCEDURE

MIXING

Creaming method (p. 478)

MAKEUP

Rolled method. Before cutting the rolled-out dough, wash it with milk and sprinkle with granulated sugar. Use greased or parchment-lined baking sheets.

BAKING

375°F (190°C) for 8–10 minutes

— **VARIATIONS** —

Lemon zest, extract, or emulsion may be used in place of vanilla.

BROWN SUGAR ROLLED COOKIES

Make the following ingredient adjustments:

Increase butter to 50% (10 oz/310 g).

Omit granulated sugar and use 60% (12 oz/375 g) brown sugar.

CHOCOLATE ROLLED COOKIES

Substitute 2 oz (60 g) cocoa for 2 oz (60 g) of the flour.

DOUBLE CHOCOLATE MACADAMIA CHUNK COOKIES

Ingredients	U.S.			Metric	%
Semisweet chocolate	1 lb	8	oz	750 g	200
Butter		8	oz	250 g	67
Sugar		4	oz	125 g	33
Eggs		5	oz	150 g	42
Salt		0.20 oz (⅞ tsp)		5 g	1.5
Bread flour		12	oz	375 g	100
Cocoa powder		1	oz	30 g	8
Baking powder		0.33 oz (2 tsp)		10 g	3
White chocolate, cut into small bits		8	oz	250 g	67
Macadamia nuts, coarsely chopped		4	oz	125 g	33
Total weight:	**4 lb**	**2**	**oz**	**2070 g**	**554 %**

PROCEDURE

MIXING

Modified sponge method:

1. Melt the semisweet chocolate and the butter together in a double boiler. Let the mixture cool to room temperature.

2. Mix the sugar, eggs, and salt together until well blended, but do not whip. Whipping to a foam creates more leavening, resulting in a more crumbly cookie. If the eggs are not at room temperature, stir the mixture over a hot-water bath just until the mixture is at a slightly warm room temperature.

3. Blend in the chocolate mixture.

4. Sift the flour, cocoa, and baking powder and fold in.

5. Fold in the white chocolate pieces and nuts.

MAKEUP

Dropped method. Use greased or parchment-lined baking sheets. Flatten to desired thickness; these cookies will not expand much.

Make up without delay, as the dough hardens as it sets. If it becomes too hard, let stand in a warm place for a few minutes to soften.

BAKING

350°F (175°C) for 10–15 minutes, depending on size

VARIATION

CHOCOLATE CHOCOLATE CHUNK COOKIES

Substitute dark chocolate for the white chocolate. Omit the macadamia nuts, or substitute pecans.

ALMOND SLICES

Ingredients	U.S.		Metric	%
Butter	6	oz	175 g	40
Brown sugar	12	oz	350 g	80
Cinnamon	0.07 oz (1 tsp)		2 g	0.5
Egg yolks	3	oz	90 g	20
Pastry flour	15	oz	440 g	100
Slivered almonds	6	oz	175 g	40
Total weight:	**2 lb 10**	**oz**	**1232 g**	**280 %**

PROCEDURE

MIXING

Creaming method (p. 478). Blend each stage of mixing until smooth, but do not cream until light.

MAKEUP

Icebox method. Scale the dough into 12-oz (350 g) units. Roll into round strips about 1½ in. (4 cm) in diameter, or into rectangular strips about 1¼ × 1¾ in. (3.5 × 4.5 cm). Chill until very firm. Using a sharp knife, slice about ⅛ in. (3 mm) thick. Take care to slice *through* the almonds and not pull them out of the dough. Place slices on greased or paper-lined sheets.

BAKING

375°F (190°C), about 10 minutes, until just starting to brown at edges, no longer. Do not overbake, or the cookies will be hard.

RICH SHORTBREAD

Ingredients	U.S.		Metric	%
Pastry flour	1 lb		500 g	100
Sugar	8	oz	250 g	50
Salt	0.12 oz (½ tsp)		4 g	0.75
Butter	12	oz	375 g	75
Egg yolks	4	oz	125 g	25
Optional flavoring (see *Note*)				
Total weight:	**2 lb 8**	**oz**	**1254 g**	**250 %**

PROCEDURE

MIXING

Sanding method (p. 478)

MAKEUP

Rolled method. Roll the dough ¼ in. (6 mm) thick (this is thicker than most rolled cookies). Use greased or parchment-lined pans.

BAKING

350°F (175°C), about 15 minutes

NOTE: Traditional Scottish shortbread is made with butter, flour, and sugar only—no eggs, flavoring, or liquid. Because this dough is very crumbly, it is usually not rolled out; rather, it is pressed into pans or molds and baked. For the formula given here, you may make the cookies without added flavoring, or flavor to taste with vanilla, almond, or lemon extract.

  You may also mix this formula by the creaming method.

BASIC SHORT DOUGH FOR COOKIES

Ingredients	U.S.		Metric	%
Butter or half butter and half shortening	1 lb		500 g	67
Sugar	8	oz	250 g	33
Salt	0.25 oz		8 g	1
Eggs	3	oz	95 g	12.5
Vanilla extract	0.25 oz		8 g	1
Pastry flour	1 lb 8	oz	750 g	100
Total weight:	**3 lb 3**	**oz**	**1611 g**	**214 %**

PROCEDURE

MIXING

Creaming method (p. 478)

MAKEUP

Rolled method. Roll out ⅛ in. (3 mm) thick and cut out with cutters of various shapes. See variations below.

BAKING

375°F (190°C), about 10 minutes

--- **VARIATIONS** ---

Short dough is a versatile mixture that can be made up in many ways to provide variety in the bakeshop. Some of the many possible variations are described here.

Flavoring the dough: During mixing, flavor the dough to taste with lemon, cinnamon, mace, maple, almond extract, or other flavoring. Fine coconut or chopped nuts also may be mixed with the dough.

Garnishing before baking: Decorate the tops with chopped or whole nuts, colored sugar, chocolate sprinkles, coconut, glacéed fruits, or an almond macaroon mixture. Tops may be egg-washed first to help the toppings stick.

Garnishing after baking: Examples of materials for garnishing cookies are fondant, royal icing, pecan halves on dabs of fudge or fondant icing, and melted chocolate (to coat completely or to drizzle on with a paper cone).

JAM TARTS

Cut out dough with large, round cutters. With a ½-in. (12-mm) cutter, cut out the centers of half the rounds. These will be the tops of the sandwiched cookies. When baked, cool completely. Dust the tops (the ones with the cut-out centers) with confectioners' sugar. Sandwich tops and bottoms together with a small dab of jam, so the jam shows through the hole on top.

ALMOND CRESCENTS

Cut crescent shapes from rolled-out dough. Spread tops with a layer of Almond Macaroon mixture (p. 498). Dip tops in chopped almonds. Bake at 350°F (175°C). When cooled, dip the tips of the crescents in melted chocolate.

PEANUT BUTTER COOKIES

Ingredients	U.S.		Metric	%
Butter or part butter and part shortening	12	oz	375 g	75
Brown sugar	8	oz	250 g	50
Granulated sugar	8	oz	250 g	50
Peanut butter (see *Note*)	12	oz	375 g	75
Eggs	4	oz	125 g	25
Vanilla extract	0.33 oz (2 tsp)		10 g	2
Pastry flour	1 lb		500 g	100
Baking soda	0.16 oz (⅞ tsp)		5 g	1
Total weight:	**3 lb 12**	**oz**	**1890 g**	**378%**

PROCEDURE

MIXING

Creaming method (p. 478). Cream the peanut butter with the fat and sugar.

MAKEUP

Molded method. Use a fork instead of a weight to flatten the cookies. Use greased or parchment-lined pans.

BAKING

375°F (190°C) for 11–14 minutes, depending on size

NOTE: This formula was developed with natural peanut butter, consisting of only ground peanuts and salt. You may need to add a little salt to the formula, depending on the salt content of the peanut butter you use. If you use unsalted peanut butter, add 1% (0.16 oz/ 5 g/ ¾ tsp) salt to the creaming stage.

SNICKERDOODLES

Ingredients	U.S.		Metric		%
Butter	15	oz	450	g	75
Sugar	1 lb		480	g	80
Eggs	4.5	oz	135	g	22.5
Vanilla extract	0.5	oz	15	g	2.5
Bread flour	1 lb 4	oz	600	g	100
Baking powder	0.2	oz	6	g	1
Salt	0.16	oz	4.8	g	0.8
Total dough weight	**3 lb 8**	**oz**	**1690**	**g**	**281 %**
For coating					
Cinnamon Sugar (p. 193)	as needed		as needed		

PROCEDURE

MIXING

Creaming method (p. 478)

MAKEUP

Molded method. For large cookies, roll dough into cylinders 1½ inches (4 cm) thick in parchment. Refrigerate until firm. Cut into 2-oz (60-g) portions. Roll each piece into a ball and then roll in cinnamon sugar. Pan on parchment-lined sheets. Flatten with a weight dipped in cinnamon sugar.

BAKING

375°F (175°C), about 10–12 minutes

Do not allow to brown.

MOLASSES COOKIES

Ingredients	U.S.		Metric	%
Butter	13	oz	405 g	54
Brown sugar	1 lb 3	oz	590 g	79
Eggs	2	oz	60 g	8
Molasses	10	oz	315 g	42
Bread flour	1 lb 8	oz	750 g	100
Baking soda	0.5	oz	15 g	2
Salt	0.33	oz	10 g	1.4
Ginger	0.2	oz	6 g	0.8
Cinnamon	0.2	oz	6 g	0.8
Ground cloves	0.1	oz	3 g	0.4
Total dough weight	**4 lb 5**	**oz**	**2160 g**	**288 %**

PROCEDURE

MIXING

Creaming method (p. 478)

MAKEUP

Molded method. For large cookies, roll dough into cylinders 1½ inches (4 cm) thick in parchment. Refrigerate until firm. Cut into 2-oz (60-g) portions. Roll each piece into a ball and then roll in sugar. Pan on parchment-lined sheets. Flatten slightly with a weight dipped in sugar.

BAKING

375°F (175°C), about 12–15 minutes

CINNAMON COOKIES

Ingredients	U.S.		Metric	%
Butter or part butter and part shortening	1 lb		500 g	80
Granulated sugar	8	oz	250 g	40
Brown sugar	8	oz	250 g	40
Salt	0.17 oz (¾ tsp)		5 g	0.8
Cinnamon	0.33 oz (4½ tsp)		10 g	1.7
Eggs	3	oz	90 g	15
Milk	1	oz	30 g	5
Pastry flour	1 lb 4	oz	625 g	100
Total weight:	**3 lb 8**	**oz**	**1760 g**	**282 %**

PROCEDURE

MIXING

Creaming method (p. 478)

MAKEUP

Molded method. Roll pieces in cinnamon sugar before placing on greased baking sheets and pressing flat.

BAKING

375°F (190°C), about 10 minutes

--- VARIATION ---

CHOCOLATE CINNAMON COOKIES

Substitute 4 oz (125 g) cocoa for 4 oz (125 g) of the flour.

NUT COOKIES

Ingredients	U.S.		Metric	%
Butter	14	oz	440 g	87.5
Confectioners' sugar	5	oz	155 g	31
Brown sugar	2	oz	60 g	12.5
Salt	0.08 oz (⅓ tsp)		2 g	0.5
Vanilla extract	0.33 oz (2 tsp)		10 g	2
Bread flour	1 lb		500 g	100
Ground nuts (hazelnuts, pecans, walnuts, almonds, etc.)	12	oz	375 g	75
Total weight:	**3 lb 1**	**oz**	**1542 g**	**308 %**

PROCEDURE

MIXING

Creaming method (p. 478)

Note that there is no egg in this formula; the only moisture is from the water content of the butter and the vanilla. Thus, there is very little gluten development and the dough is crumbly and not suitable for large cookies.

MAKEUP

Molded method. Mold cookies by hand into desired shape, such as balls, fingers, or crescents.

BAKING

350°F (175°C), about 25 minutes

FINISH

Dust cooled cookies heavily with confectioners' sugar.

SPECULAAS

Ingredients	U.S.		Metric	%
Butter or half butter and half shortening	1 lb		500 g	67
Confectioners' sugar	13	oz	412 g	55
Fine granulated sugar	4	oz	125 g	17
Grated lemon zest	0.16 oz (2 tsp)		5 g	0.7
Cinnamon	0.25 oz (3½ tsp)		8 g	1
Cloves	0.05 oz (¾ tsp)		2 g	0.2
Cardamom	0.05 oz (¾ tsp)		2 g	0.2
Eggs	2.5	oz	75 g	10
Pastry flour	1 lb 8	oz	750 g	100
Total weight:	**3 lb 12**	**oz**	**1879 g**	**251** %

PROCEDURE

MIXING

Creaming method (p. 478). Blend at each stage until smooth, but do not cream until light.

MAKEUP

The classic way to make these cookies is by the molded method. The dough is pressed into special wooden speculaas molds, then removed and placed on baking sheets. Alternatively, it is stamped with special tools to emboss a design in the dough.

If these molds are not available, make up the cookies either as icebox cookies or as rolled cookies cut with cookie cutters. They can be made small or large, as desired. Large cookies should be about ¼ in. (6 mm) thick.

Optional: Press sliced or whole blanched almonds onto the cookies after makeup.

BAKING

375°F (190°C) for medium to large cookies; 400°F (200°C) for small, thin cookies

DIAMONDS

For large-quantity measurements, see page 729.

Ingredients	U.S.		Metric	%
Butter, cut into small pieces	5	oz	140 g	70
Cake flour	7	oz	200 g	100
Confectioners' sugar	2	oz	60 g	30
Salt	0.04 oz (⅛ tsp)		1 g	0.5
Grated orange zest	0.08 oz (1 tsp)		2 g	1
Vanilla extract	0.08 oz (½ tsp)		2 g	1
For rolling				
Crystal sugar	2	oz	50 g	25
Total dough weight:	**14**	**oz**	**405 g**	**202** %

PROCEDURE

MIXING

One-stage method (p. 477)

MAKEUP

1. Shape the dough into cylinders 1¼ in. (3 cm) in diameter, making sure the dough is very tight and there are no air pockets.
2. Refrigerate the dough for 30 minutes.
3. Brush the cylinders with water. Roll in crystal sugar.
4. Cut into rounds ½ in. (1 cm) thick.

BAKING

5. Bake on buttered sheet pans at 325°F (160°C) for 20 minutes.

BUTTER TEA COOKIES

Ingredients	U.S.		Metric	%
Butter or half butter and half shortening	12	oz	335 g	67
Granulated sugar	6	oz	165 g	33
Confectioners' sugar	3	oz	85 g	17
Eggs	4.5	oz	125 g	25
Vanilla extract	0.16 oz (1 tsp)		4 g	0.9
Cake flour	1 lb 2	oz	500 g	100
Total weight:	**2 lb 11**	**oz**	**1214 g**	**242 %**

PROCEDURE

MIXING

Creaming method (p. 478)

MAKEUP

Bagged method. Using a plain or star tube, make small cookies about the size of a quarter. Bag out onto ungreased or parchment-lined baking sheets.

BAKING

375°F (190°C), about 10 minutes

VARIATIONS

Flavor with almond extract instead of vanilla.

FANCY TEA COOKIES

Add 17% (3 oz/85 g) almond paste to the first mixing stage.

CHOCOLATE TEA COOKIES

Substitute 3 oz (85 g) cocoa for 3 oz (85 g) of the flour.

SANDWICH-TYPE COOKIES

Select cookies all of the same size and shape. Turn half of them over and dot the centers of the flat sides with a small amount of jam or fudge icing. Sandwich with the remaining cookies.

GINGERBREAD COOKIES

Ingredients	U.S.		Metric	%
Butter or part butter and part shortening	11	oz	340 g	45
Brown sugar	8	oz	250 g	33
Baking soda	0.16 oz (⅞ tsp)		5 g	0.7
Salt	0.12 oz (½ tsp)		4 g	0.5
Ginger	0.16 oz (2¼ tsp)		5 g	0.7
Cinnamon	0.12 oz (1¾ tsp)		2 g	0.25
Cloves, ground	0.03 oz (½ tsp)		1 g	0.12
Eggs	3.5	oz	110 g	15
Molasses	11	oz	340 g	45
Pastry flour	1 lb 8	oz	750 g	100
Total weight:	**3 lb 10**	**oz**	**1807 g**	**240 %**

PROCEDURE

MIXING

Creaming method (p. 478)

MAKEUP

Rolled method

For small cookies, roll out ⅛ in. (3 mm) thick.

For large cookies, roll out ¼ in. (6 mm) thick.

Cut out cookies and place them on paper-lined or greased and floured baking sheets.

BAKING

375°F (190°C) for small, thin cookies

360°F (180°C) for larger, thicker cookies

GINGERSNAPS

Ingredients	U.S.		Metric	%
Shortening	6	oz	190 g	38
Sugar	6	oz	190 g	38
Salt	0.08 oz (⅓ tsp)		2 g	0.5
Ginger	0.25 oz (3½ tsp)		8 g	1.5
Molasses	10	oz	315 g	63
Baking soda	0.25 oz (1⅓ tsp)		8 g	1.5
Water	2	oz	65 g	13
Pastry flour	1 lb		500 g	100
Total weight:	**2 lb 8**	**oz**	**1278 g**	**256 %**

PROCEDURE

MIXING

Creaming method (p. 478). Blend the molasses into the creamed fat-sugar mixture first. Then dissolve the soda in the water and blend in. Add the flour last.

MAKEUP

Bagged method. With a plain tube, bag out cookies the size of a quarter. Flatten lightly.

May also be chilled and made up by molded or rolled methods. Use paper-lined or greased and floured pans.

BAKING

375°F (190°C), about 12 minutes

SPRITZ COOKIES

Ingredients	U.S.		Metric	%
Almond paste	12	oz	375 g	100
Sugar	6	oz	190 g	50
Salt	0.12 oz (½ tsp)		4 g	1
Butter	12	oz	375 g	100
Eggs	4.5	oz	145 g	38
Vanilla extract	0.16 oz (1 tsp)		5 g	1.5
Cake flour	6	oz	190 g	50
Bread flour	6	oz	190 g	50
Total weight:	**2 lb 14**	**oz**	**1474 g**	**390 %**

PROCEDURE

MIXING

Creaming method (p. 478). Blend the almond paste to a smooth, soft paste with a little of the egg. Add the butter and sugar, and cream as in the basic procedure.

MAKEUP

Bagged method. Bag out with star tube to desired shapes (small) on parchment-lined sheets. If desired, garnish tops with pieces of fruit or nuts.

BAKING

375°F (190°C)

LANGUES DE CHAT

Ingredients	U.S.		Metric	%
Butter	14	oz	350 g	88
Extra-fine granulated sugar	7	oz	175 g	44
Confectioners' sugar	7	oz	175 g	44
Egg whites	10	oz	250 g	63
Vanilla extract	0.25 oz (1½ tsp)		6 g	1.6
Cake flour	12	oz	300 g	75
Bread flour	4	oz	100 g	25
Total weight:	**3 lb 6**	**oz**	**1356 g**	**340 %**

PROCEDURE

MIXING

Creaming method (p. 478)

MAKEUP

Bagged method. Using a ¼-in. (6-mm) plain tube, bag out onto silicone paper in the shape of small fingers, 2 in. (5 cm) long. Allow at least 1 in. (2.5 cm) between cookies to allow for spreading. Double-pan for more even baking.

BAKING

400°F (200°C), about 10 minutes

FINISHING

Langues de chat may be served plain as petits fours sec. They may be used as decorations for ice cream, Bavarian cream, or other desserts. They may also be sandwiched together with ganache, buttercream, fudge, or jam. Sandwich cookies may be partially dipped in melted chocolate.

RAISIN SPICE BARS

Ingredients	U.S.		Metric	%
Granulated sugar	1 lb 4	oz	580 g	83
Butter and/or shortening	8	oz	230 g	33
Eggs	8	oz	230 g	33
Molasses	4	oz	115 g	17
Pastry flour	1 lb 8	oz	700 g	100
Cinnamon	0.12 oz (1¾ tsp)		3 g	0.5
Cloves, ground	0.04 oz (½ tsp)		1 g	0.16
Ginger	0.07 oz (1 tsp)		2 g	0.3
Baking soda	0.12 oz (⅝ tsp)		3 g	0.5
Salt	0.17 oz		5 g	0.75
Raisins (see *Note*)	1 lb		470 g	67
Total weight:	**5 lb**		**2339 g**	**335 %**

PROCEDURE

MIXING

One-stage method (p. 477)

MAKEUP

Bar method. Egg-wash strips with whole egg or egg whites.

Note: This is a soft, sticky dough, difficult to handle. Do not worry if the units are not perfectly shaped. A homemade look is appropriate for this cookie.

BAKING

350°F (175°C), about 15 minutes

Cool partially and cut crosswise to make cookies of desired width.

NOTE: If the raisins are hard and dry, soak them in hot water until soft, then drain them and dry them well before adding them to the cookie batter.

LEMON WAFERS

Ingredients	U.S.		Metric	%
Butter	1 lb		500 g	67
Sugar	12	oz	375 g	50
Lemon zest, grated	0.75 oz (3 tbsp)		25 g	3
Salt	0.25 oz (1 tsp)		8 g	1
Baking soda	0.25 oz (1⅓ tsp)		8 g	1
Eggs	4	oz	125 g	17
Milk	2	oz	60 g	8
Lemon juice	1	oz	30 g	4
Pastry flour	1 lb 8	oz	750 g	100
Total weight:	**3 lb 12**	**oz**	**1881 g**	**251%**

PROCEDURE

MIXING

Creaming method (p. 478). Cream at each stage just until smooth; do not cream until light.

MAKEUP

Bagged method. With a plain tube, bag out small mounds the size of a quarter on paper-lined pans, leaving 3 in. (8 cm) between them to allow for spread. Flatten slightly.

BAKING

375°F (190°C)

--- **VARIATION** ---

LIME WAFERS

Substitute lime zest and juice for the lemon. This is an unusual and tasty cookie.

COCONUT MACAROONS (MERINGUE TYPE)

Ingredients	U.S.		Metric	Sugar at 100% %
Egg whites	8	oz	250 g	40
Cream of tartar	0.06 oz (¾ tsp)		2 g	0.3
Sugar	1 lb 4	oz	625 g	100
Vanilla extract	0.5	oz	15 g	2.5
Macaroon coconut (see *Note*)	1 lb		500 g	80
Total weight:	**2 lb 12 oz**		**1392 g**	**222 %**

NOTE: Macaroon coconut is finely ground or flaked, unsweetened, dried coconut.

PROCEDURE

MIXING

Sponge method

1. Whip the egg whites with the cream of tartar until they form soft peaks. Gradually whip in the sugar. Continue to whip until stiff and glossy.

2. Fold in the coconut.

MAKEUP

Bagged method. Bag out with a star tube to make round cookies of desired size (usually 1–1½ in. or 2.5-4 cm in diameter) onto parchment-lined baking sheets.

BAKING

300°F (150°C), about 30 minutes

ALMOND MACAROONS

Yield: enough for about 150 cookies, 1½-in. (4 cm) in diameter

Ingredients	U.S.	Metric	Almond paste at 100% %
Almond paste and/or macaroon paste	1 lb	500 g	100
Egg whites	6 oz	190 g	37.5
Granulated sugar	1 lb	500 g	100
Total weight:	**2 lb 6 oz**	**1190 g**	**237 %**

VARIATION

AMARETTI

Make the following ingredient adjustments:

Use kernel paste instead of almond paste for a stronger flavor (optional).

Reduce the granulated sugar to 85% (13.5 oz/425 g).

Add 85% (13.5 oz/425 g) brown sugar.

PROCEDURE

MIXING

One-stage method (p. 477). Blend the almond paste with a little of the egg whites to soften it, then blend together all ingredients. If the mixture is too stiff for a pastry bag, add a little extra egg white.

MAKEUP

Bagged method. Using a plain tube, deposit the mix on silicone paper in mounds the size of a quarter. Double-pan.

BAKING

350°F (175°C). Let cool before removing from the paper. To make it easier to remove the macaroons from the paper, turn the sheets over and brush the bottoms of the sheets lightly with water.

PROCEDURE: MACAROONS AND MACARONS

The name *macaroon* is applied to a wide variety of cookies or confections made primarily of egg whites and either coconut or almond powder, or sometimes both. Various types of coconut macaroons are familiar in North America, while almond macaroons are found in Italy, France, and other parts of Europe.

The Parisian style of macaroon has become popular in recent years. As the French word for macaroon is *macaron*, this spelling is typically used to distinguish this style of confection from other macaroons.

The macaron has a smooth, slightly domed top and a ruffled base known as the "foot." The foot develops during baking, as the batter expands. Experts insist that, in a perfect macaron, the foot should not extend outward beyond the dome of the cookie.

The macaron is notoriously finicky to make. The slightest variation in ingredient quantities or in mixing technique can make a large difference in the finished product. Especially important is the consistency of the batter. It must be moist enough so the macaron has a smooth surface and the piped batter doesn't stand up too high. On the other hand, if it is even a little too moist, it spreads and flattens too much. When you are working with any formula, you may have to adjust the quantity of egg whites to get the right texture. Some chefs describe the texture of good macaron batter as that of molten lava.

Countless macaron recipes exist, each with different ingredient quantities and mixing techniques. Most macarons are made with a common meringue, but some use Italian meringue, and some even call for mixing the egg whites directly with the other ingredients without whipping into a meringue.

Some formulas direct you to let the bagged-out batter stand for a period of time before baking, while others do not.

The formulas here were chosen to give you experience with two techniques: using common meringue and using Italian meringue.

PARISIAN MACARONS I

Ingredients	U.S.		Metric
Powdered almonds	5	oz	125 g
Confectioners' sugar	8	oz	200 g
Egg whites	4	oz	100 g
Granulated sugar	1.6 oz		40 g
Food coloring	as desired		as desired
Filling (see variations)	as desired		as desired
Batter weight (not including filling):	**1 lb 2**	**oz**	**465 g**

--- VARIATIONS ---

PISTACHIO MACARONS

Tint the macaron batter with a few drops of green food color. After bagging out the batter onto baking pans, sprinkle a little finely chopped pistachio across the edge of each macaron. After baking and cooling, sandwich two macarons together with Pistachio Filling (recipe follows).

Other varieties of Parisian macarons can be created by substituting different fillings for the pistachio. Depending on the filling chosen, substitute another color for the green in the formula. For example, tint the batter pink when using strawberry-flavored filling, yellow for mango-flavored filling.

CHOCOLATE MACARONS

Prepare as in the basic formula, using the following ingredients and quantities. Process the cocoa with the almonds and sugar in step 1. Sandwich the baked, cooled macarons together with ganache or another chocolate filling.

Ingredients	U.S.		Metric
Powdered almonds	5.2	oz	130 g
Confectioners' sugar	8.4	oz	210 g
Cocoa	0.67 oz		17 g
Egg whites	4	oz	100 g
Granulated sugar	1.6	oz	40 g

PROCEDURE

MIXING

1. Blend the confectioners' sugar and almonds in a food processor for 5 minutes. Sift into a bowl.

2. Whip the egg whites to soft peaks. Gradually whip in the sugar and continue whipping to firm peaks.

3. Fold the egg whites one-third at a time into the sugar mixture until smooth. Add any desired coloring as you are mixing together the meringue and the almond mixture.

MAKEUP

Bagged. Using a plain tip, deposit the mix on parchment paper or on a silicone mat in mounds about 1½ in. (4 cm) in diameter. Allow to stand 10–15 minutes.

BAKING

320°F (160°C), 15–25 minutes. Test for doneness by lightly touching the top of a macaron with your fingertip and pushing gently from side to side. If macaron is still quite soft, continue baking. If it just barely moves from side to side, remove from oven. Cool completely, then remove from the parchment.

Parisian Macarons are traditionally sandwiched together with a filling (see Variations).

PISTACHIO FILLING FOR MACARONS

Ingredients	U.S.	Metric
Heavy cream	3 oz	75 g
Butter	1 oz	25 g
Glucose	1 oz	25 g
Pistachio paste	3 oz	75 g
Vanilla extract	¼ tsp	1 g
Kirsch	1 oz	25 g
Marzipan	8 oz	200 g
Total weight:	**1 lb 1 oz**	**426 g**

PROCEDURE

1. Combine the cream, butter, and glucose. Bring to a boil. Remove from the heat and cool.

2. Mix in the pistachio paste, vanilla, and kirsch.

3. Using a mixer with the paddle attachment, soften the marzipan, then add the cooked ingredients gradually to make a smooth paste.

4. Fill the macaroons using a pastry bag fitted with a small plain tip.

PARISIAN MACARONS II

Yield: 1 lb 3 oz (475 g)

Ingredients	U.S.		Metric
Powdered almonds	5	oz	125 g
Confectioners' sugar	5	oz	125 g
Egg whites	2.4	oz	60 g
Coloring	as desired		as desired
Italian meringue:			
Water	2	oz	50 g
Granulated sugar	5	oz	125 g
Egg whites	2	oz	50 g

PROCEDURE

MIXING

1. Process the almonds and confectioners' sugar in a food processor for 5 minutes. Sift into a bowl.
2. Mix in the first quantity of egg whites until smooth.
3. If desired, tint the mixture with a few drops of food coloring.
4. Heat the water and granulated sugar in a saucepan until the sugar dissolves and the mixture boils. Boil until a candy thermometer placed in the syrup registers 243°F (117°C).
5. While the syrup is cooking, beat the egg whites in a mixing machine until they form soft peaks.
6. With the machine running, very slowly beat in the hot syrup.
7. Continue beating until the meringue is cool and forms firm peaks.
8. Fold the meringue into the powdered almond mixture.

MAKEUP

Bagged. Using a plain tip, deposit the mix on parchment paper or on a silicone mat in mounds about 1½ in. (4 cm) in diameter. Allow to stand 10-15 minutes.

BAKING

320°F (160°C), 15–25 minutes. Test for doneness by lightly touching the top of a macaron with your fingertip and pushing gently from side to side. If macaron is still quite soft, continue baking. If it just barely moves from side to side, remove from oven. Cool completely, then remove from the parchment.

CHOCOLATE MACAROONS I

Ingredients	U.S.		Metric	Almond paste at 100% %
Almond paste	12 oz		350 g	100
Sugar	1 lb	5 oz	600 g	175
Cocoa	2 oz		60 g	17
Macaroon coconut	3 oz		90 g	25
Egg whites	8 oz		225 g	67
Total weight:	**2 lb 14 oz**		**1325 g**	**384%**

— VARIATION —

Use ground nuts in place of the macaroon coconut.

PROCEDURE

MIXING

One-stage method (p. 477). Blend the almond paste with a little of the egg whites until smooth. Mix in the remaining ingredients. If the mixture is still too stiff for a pastry bag, add a little extra egg white.

MAKEUP

Bagged method. Using a plain tube, deposit the mix on silicone paper in mounds the size of a quarter. Double-pan.

BAKING

350°F (175°C). Let cool before removing from the paper. To make it easier to remove the macaroons from the paper, turn the sheets over and brush the bottoms of the sheets lightly with water.

COCONUT MACAROONS (CHEWY TYPE)

Ingredients	U.S.		Metric	Sugar at 100% %
Sugar	1 lb 8	oz	700 g	100
Macaroon coconut	1 lb 8	oz	700 g	100
Corn syrup	3	oz	90 g	13
Vanilla extract	0.33 oz (2 tsp)		10 g	1.5
Pastry flour	1.5	oz	42 g	6
Salt	0.12 oz (½ tsp)		4 g	0.5
Egg whites	11	oz	315 g	45
Total weight:	**3 lb 15**	**oz**	**1861 g**	**266** %

PROCEDURE

MIXING

One-stage method (p. 477). Blend all ingredients together. Place in a kettle or stainless steel bowl and set over a hot-water bath. Stir constantly until the mixture reaches 120°F (50°C).

MAKEUP

Using a star tube or plain tube, bag out onto paper-lined sheet pans. Make the cookies about 1 in. (2.5 cm) across.

BAKING

375°F (190°C)

--- VARIATION ---

CHOCOLATE MACAROONS II

Add 1½ oz (45 g) cocoa to the basic recipe. Thin with an additional ½–1 oz (15–30 g) egg white, if necessary.

SWISS LECKERLI

Ingredients	U.S.		Metric		%
Honey	10	oz	315	g	42
Sugar	6	oz	185	g	25
Baking soda	0.25	oz	8	g	1
Water	4	oz	125	g	17
Salt	0.17 oz (¾ tsp)		5	g	0.7
Cinnamon	0.25 oz (3½ tsp)		8	g	1
Mace	0.06 oz (⅞ tsp)		1.5	g	0.2
Cloves, ground	0.06 oz (⅞ tsp)		1.5	g	0.2
Candied lemon peel, finely chopped	2	oz	60	g	8
Candied orange peel, finely chopped	2	oz	60	g	8
Blanched almonds, chopped	4	oz	125	g	17
Bread flour	1 lb		500	g	67
Cake flour	8	oz	250	g	33
Total weight:	**3 lb 4**	**oz**	**1644**	**g**	**220** %

PROCEDURE

MIXING

1. Heat the honey and sugar together until the sugar is dissolved. Cool.
2. Dissolve the baking soda in the water. Add to the honey mixture.
3. Add the remaining ingredients. Mix to a smooth dough.

MAKEUP

Sheet method. Roll out dough ¼ in. (6 mm) thick. Place on a well-greased baking sheet. Cut into small squares, but do not separate the squares until after they are baked.

Alternative method: Rolled method. Roll out ¼ in. (6 mm) thick and cut out with cutters, or cut into small squares. Place on greased, floured baking sheets.

BAKING

375°F (190°C) for 15 minutes or more. Immediately after baking, while still hot, brush tops with flat icing.

ALMOND TUILES I

Yield: enough to make about 90 cookies, 2½ in. (6 cm) in diameter

For large-quantity measurements, see page 730.

Ingredients	U.S.		Metric	%
Butter	3	oz	90 g	86
Confectioners' sugar	4	oz	120 g	114
Egg whites	3	oz	90 g	86
Cake flour	3.5	oz	105 g	100
Garnish				
Sliced almonds	2.5	oz	75 g	70
Batter weight:	**13**	**oz**	**405 g**	**386%**

NOTE: This batter is also known as stencil paste. Instead of the simple round stencils used for tuiles, stencils of any shape or size may be cut and used for decorative effect. This stencil paste is interchangeable with the slightly different stencil paste included in the Ribbon Sponge recipe on page 406. It is not, however, interchangeable with Almond Tuiles II, below, which is a very different batter, even though the makeup is similar.

A

B

C

PROCEDURE

MIXING

Creaming method

1. Using the paddle attachment, soften the butter to a creamy consistency. Add the sugar and beat until thoroughly mixed.

2. Beat in the egg whites.

3. Sift the flour over the mixture and mix in well.

MAKEUP

Stencil method. Line a sheet pan with a silicone mat or, if a mat is not available, a sheet of parchment paper. Use a commercially made stencil, or make a stencil by cutting a round hole in a sheet of thick plastic or thin cardboard (such as the cardboard used for cake boxes). For petit-four-size tuiles, make the circle 2½ in. (6 cm) in diameter. Using an offset palette knife, spread the batter across the stencil, then lift off the stencil (a). Sprinkle with a few sliced almonds (b).

BAKING

350°F (175°C), 5–10 minutes, depending on thickness, or until lightly browned. Remove the baked cookies from the baking sheet and immediately curve over a rolling pin or tuile rack (c) and allow to cool.

--- **VARIATIONS** ---

In addition to round stencils, you may use stencils in any shape to create a wide variety of items for dessert garnish. Commercially made stencils are available in dozens of shapes, and of course you may cut stencils of your own design. Almond garnish may be omitted, as desired.

TULIPES

Omit the almonds in the basic recipe. Immediately after baking, shape the cookies by molding them around the upturned bottom of a small glass or similar mold. The result, cup-shaped tulipes, are used as edible containers for portions of ice cream and other desserts.

ALMOND TUILES II

Ingredients	U.S.		Metric	%
Sugar	8	oz	240 g	533
Sliced, blanched almonds	9	oz	270 g	600
Bread flour	1.5	oz	45 g	100
Egg whites, lightly beaten	4.5	oz	135 g	300
Butter, melted	1.5	oz	45 g	100
Total weight:	**1 lb 8**	**oz**	**735 g**	**1633%**

PROCEDURE

MIXING

1. Mix the sugar, almonds, and flour in a bowl.
2. Add the egg whites and melted butter. Stir until well mixed.

MAKEUP

Dropped method. Drop by the tablespoonful 2 in. (5 cm) apart onto a greased and floured baking sheet. Use about ⅓–½ oz (10–15 g) per cookie. Flatten with a fork dipped in water, spreading the mixture until it is thin and flat. The dough will not spread during baking, and the cookies must be thin.

BAKING

375°F (190°C) until browned. Immediately remove one by one from the baking sheet with a spatula and then drape over a rolling pin, to give a curved shape. The cookies will become crisp when cool. If they do not become crisp, it indicates they are underbaked, so return them to the oven for 1 minute. If, on the other hand, they become crisp before they can be curved, return them to the oven for a few moments to soften them.

SESAME TUILES

Ingredients	U.S.		Metric	%
Confectioners' sugar	7	oz	210 g	100
Cake flour	7	oz	210 g	100
Nutmeg	large pinch		large pinch	
Egg whites	5	oz	150 g	71
Butter, melted	5	oz	150 g	71
Lemon zest, grated	0.08 oz (1 tsp)		3 g	1.5
Sesame seeds	1	oz	30 g	15
Garnish				
Sesame seeds	0.5	oz	15 g	7
Total batter weight:	**1 lb 9**	**oz**	**753 g**	**358 %**

PROCEDURE

1. Sift the sugar, flour, and nutmeg into a bowl. Make a well in the center.
2. Lightly beat the egg whites and add to the well. Add the butter and lemon zest.
3. Mix to make a soft batter. Add the first quantity of sesame seeds and mix in. Chill.
4. Cut a triangle-shaped stencil and use it to spread the batter onto buttered, chilled sheet pans, using the procedure for making Almond Tuiles I (p. 502). Sprinkle with the remaining sesame seeds.
5. Bake at 375°F (190°C) until golden.
6. Remove from the pan and immediately curve into an S-shape.

CLASSIC BROWNIES

Ingredients	U.S.			Metric	%
Unsweetened chocolate	1 lb			450 g	100
Butter	1 lb	8	oz	675 g	150
Eggs	1 lb	8	oz	675 g	150
Sugar	3 lb			1350 g	300
Salt		0.25	oz	7 g	1.5
Vanilla		1	oz	30 g	6
Bread flour	1 lb			450 g	100
Walnuts or pecans, chopped	1 lb			450 g	100
Total weight:	**9 lb**	**1**	**oz**	**4087 g**	**907** **%**

PROCEDURE

MIXING

Modified sponge method

1. Melt the chocolate and butter together in a double boiler. Let the mixture cool to room temperature.
2. Mix the eggs, sugar, salt, and vanilla together until well blended, but do not whip. Whipping to a foam creates more leavening, resulting in a more crumbly, less fudgy brownie.
3. Blend in the chocolate mixture.
4. Sift the flour and fold in.
5. Fold in the nuts.

MAKEUP

Sheet method. Grease and flour the pans, or line them with parchment. One recipe fills one full sheet pan (18 × 26 in./46 × 66 cm), two half-sheet pans, four 9 × 13 in. (23 × 33 cm) pans, or six 9-in. (23-cm) square pans. If desired, sprinkle the batter with an additional 50% (8 oz/225 g) chopped nuts after panning.

BAKING

325°F (165°C) for 45 to 60 minutes

For 2-in. (5-cm) square brownies, cut sheet pan into 8 rows of 12, to yield 96 pieces.

RICH BROWNIES

For large-quantity measurements, see page 730.

Ingredients	U.S.		Metric	%
Unsweetened chocolate	2	oz	60 g	50
Bittersweet chocolate	5	oz	145 g	125
Butter	10	oz	290 g	250
Eggs	7	oz	200 g	175
Sugar	9	oz	260 g	225
Salt	0.06 oz (¼ tsp)		2 g	1.5
Vanilla extract	0.25 oz (1½ tsp)		7 mL	6
Bread flour	4	oz	115 g	100
Walnuts or pecans, chopped	4	oz	115 g	100
Total weight:	**2 lb 9**	**oz**	**1194 g**	**1032 %**

PROCEDURE

MIXING

Modified sponge method

1. Melt the unsweetened chocolate, the bittersweet chocolate, and the butter together in a double boiler. Let the mixture cool to room temperature.
2. Mix the eggs, sugar, salt, and vanilla together until well blended, but do not whip (a). Whipping to a foam creates more leavening, resulting in a more crumbly, less fudgy brownie. If the eggs are not at room temperature, stir the mixture over a hot-water bath just until the mixture is at slightly warm room temperature.
3. Blend in the chocolate mixture (b).
4. Sift the flour and fold in (c).
5. Fold in the nuts.

MAKEUP

Sheet method. For 2 lb 9 oz (1194 g) batter, use one 9 × 13 in. (23 × 33 cm) pan or two 8-in. (20-cm) square pans. Grease and flour the pans, or line them with parchment.

BAKING

325°F (190°C), about 45–50 minutes

For 2-in. (5-cm) square brownies, cut sheet pan into 4 rows of 6, to yield 24 pieces.

VARIATION

For large-quantity measurements, see page 730.

Ingredients	U.S.	Metric	%
Baking powder	0.1 oz (½ tsp plus ⅛ tsp)	3 g	2.5%

For a more cakelike brownie, sift the above quantity of baking powder with the flour in step 4.

A

B

C

CREAM CHEESE BROWNIES

Yield: 3 lb (1400 g) batter is enough for one 9 × 13 in. (23 × 33 cm) pan or two 8-in. (20-cm) square pans

For lage-quantity measurements, see page 730.

Ingredients	U.S.		Metric
Cream cheese	8	oz	225 g
Sugar	2	oz	55 g
Vanilla extract	½	tsp	2 mL
Egg yolks	0.67 oz (1 yolk)		20 g
Rich Brownie batter without walnuts (p. 505) (1 recipe)	2 lb 9	oz	1190 g
Total weight:	**3 lb 3**	**oz**	**1492 g**

PROCEDURE

MIXING

1. In a mixer with the paddle attachment, work the cream cheese at low speed until smooth and creamy.
2. Add the sugar and vanilla and mix in at low speed until smooth.
3. Add the egg yolks and blend in.
4. Prepare the brownie batter according to the recipe.

MAKEUP

Sheet method. Grease and flour the pans, or line them with parchment. Pour about half the brownie batter into the pans (a). Spread it evenly (b). Deposit half the cream cheese mixture in pools on top of the brownie batter (c). Pour in the remaining brownie batter (d). Spread evenly in the pan. Drop the remaining cream cheese mixture in pools on top (e). Swirl the two batters together slightly, using a palette knife or a spoon handle (f).

BAKING

325°F (190°C), about 45–50 minutes

Cut into 2-in. (5 cm) square brownies.

A

B

C

D

E

F

FLORENTINES

Ingredients	U.S.	Metric	%
Butter	7 oz	210 g	350
Sugar	10 oz	300 g	500
Honey	3 oz	90 g	150
Heavy cream	3 oz	90 g	150
Sliced almonds	12 oz	360 g	600
Ground almonds or hazelnuts	2 oz	60 g	100
Candied orange peel, chopped	4 oz	120 g	200
Bread flour	2 oz	60 g	100
For finishing			
Chocolate, melted	as needed	as needed	
Total weight:	**2 lb 11 oz**	**1290 g**	**2150%**

VARIATION

For a lacier cookie, substitute chopped, blanched almonds for the sliced almonds.

PROCEDURE

MIXING

1. Combine the butter, sugar, honey, and cream in a heavy saucepan. Bring to a strong boil, stirring constantly. Cook, stirring, until the mixture reaches 240°F (115°C).

2. Mix together the remaining ingredients and add to the sugar mixture. Mix well.

MAKEUP

Dropped method. Drop while the mixture is hot; it will get very stiff when cool. Drop ½ oz (15 g) mounds on baking sheets lined with silicone paper, or greased and floured. Allow at least 2 in. (5 cm) between cookies for spreading. Flatten the cookies with a fork.

BAKING

375°F (190°C) until browned. As soon as the pans are removed from the oven, use a round cookie cutter to pull the cookies back together into a round shape (see photo). Let cool.

FINISHING

Spread the flat sides of the cookies with melted chocolate. Mark grooves in the chocolate with an icing comb.

BISCOTTI

Ingredients	U.S.		Metric	%
Eggs	10	oz	300 g	35
Sugar	1 lb 2	oz	550 g	65
Salt	0.5	oz	15 g	2
Vanilla extract	0.3	oz (2 tsp)	8 g	1
Orange zest, grated	0.15	oz (2 tsp)	4 g	0.5
Pastry flour	1 lb 12	oz	850 g	100
Baking powder	0.7	oz	20 g	2.5
Blanched almonds	10	oz	300 g	35
Total weight:	**4 lb 3**	**oz**	**2047 g**	**241 %**

NOTE: These cookies are hard when cooled. They are traditionally dipped in a sweet wine when eaten.

--- VARIATION ---

Omit the orange zest and flavor to taste with anise extract.

PROCEDURE

MIXING

Sponge method

1. Combine the eggs, sugar, and salt. Stir over hot water to warm the mixture, then whip until thick and light.
2. Fold in the vanilla and orange zest.
3. Sift together the flour and baking powder. Fold into the egg mixture.
4. Mix in the almonds.

MAKEUP

Bar method. Scale at 1 lb (500 g). Shape into logs 2–2½ in. (6 cm) thick. Do not flatten the logs (the dough will be sticky and somewhat difficult to handle). Egg-wash.

BAKING

325°F (160°C), about 30–40 minutes, or until light golden

FINISHING

Let cool slightly. Slice diagonally ½ in. (12 mm) thick. Place cut side down on sheet pans. Bake at 275°F (135°C) until toasted and dry, about 30 minutes.

ESPRESSO BISCOTTI

For large-quantity measurements, see page 730.

Ingredients	U.S.		Metric	%
Butter	4	oz	120 g	40
Sugar	6	oz	180 g	60
Salt	0.2	oz (⅞ tsp)	6 g	2.0
Eggs	3.33	oz (2 eggs)	100 g (2 eggs)	33
Water, hot	0.5	oz	15 g	5
Instant espresso powder	0.2	oz (2 tbsp)	6 g	2
Pastry flour	10	oz	300 g	100
Baking powder	0.25	oz (1½ tsp)	8 g	2.5
Blanched almonds	3.5	oz	105 g	35
Total weight:	**1 lb 11**	**oz**	**840 g**	**279 %**

NOTE: See the discussion of biscotti on page 509.

PROCEDURE

MIXING

Creaming method (p. 478). Dissolve the espresso powder in the hot water before adding it to the creamed mixture. Mix in the almonds after adding the sifted dry ingredients.

MAKEUP, BAKING, AND FINISHING

Same as Biscotti (above).

TWICE-BAKED

The Italian word *biscotto* (plural, *biscotti*) means "twice cooked." The British name for cookies, *biscuit*, comes from the same root and likewise means "twice cooked." In earlier times, when ovens were more primitive, double cooking was one method of producing dry, crisp flour goods. Dryness was desirable for these items because the low moisture content meant they kept longer.

Italian-style biscotti, made by the bar method—baked, sliced, and baked again until crisp—have become popular in the rest of Europe and in North America. Many flavor variations made today are, however, recent innovations, not the classic Italian confections.

CHOCOLATE PECAN BISCOTTI

For large-quantity measurements, see page 730.

Ingredients	U.S.		Metric		%
Butter	4	oz	120	g	40
Sugar	6	oz	180	g	60
Salt	0.1	oz (½ tsp)	3	g	1
Orange zest, grated	0.1	oz (1½ tsp)	3	g	0.5
Eggs	3.33	oz (2 eggs)	100	g (2 eggs)	33
Water	2	oz	60	g	20
Vanilla extract	0.16	oz (1 tsp)	5	g	1.5
Pastry flour	10	oz	300	g	100
Cocoa powder	1.5	oz	45	g	15
Baking powder	0.25	oz (1½ tsp)	8	g	2.5
Baking soda	0.08	oz (½ tsp)	2.5	g	0.8
Pecan pieces	2	oz	60	g	20
Small chocolate chips	2	oz	60	g	20
Total weight:	**1 lb 15**	**oz**	**946**	**g**	**314** **%**

NOTE: See the discussion of biscotti above.

PROCEDURE

MIXING

Creaming method (p. 478). Mix in the nuts and chocolate chips after adding the sifted dry ingredients.

MAKEUP, BAKING, AND FINISHING

Same as Biscotti (p. 508)

TERMS FOR REVIEW

cookie	sponge method	icebox	double-panning
spread	bagged	bar	petits fours secs
one-stage method	dropped	sheet	macaroon
creaming method	rolled	stencil	macaron
sanding method	molded	stencil paste	

QUESTIONS FOR REVIEW

1. What makes cookies crisp? How can you keep them crisp after they are baked?

2. If you baked cookies that came out unintentionally chewy, how would you correct for that in the next batch?

3. Describe briefly the difference between the creaming method and the one-stage method.

4. Besides cost control, why is accurate scaling and uniform sizing important when making up cookies?

19

CUSTARDS, PUDDINGS, MOUSSES, AND SOUFFLÉS

AFTER READING THIS CHAPTER, YOU SHOULD BE ABLE TO:

1. Prepare boiled puddings and range-top custards.
2. Prepare baked and steamed puddings.
3. Prepare Bavarian creams, mousses, and cold charlottes.
4. Prepare hot dessert soufflés.

THIS CHAPTER DISCUSSES a variety of desserts not covered in earlier chapters. Most of these items are not baked goods, in the sense that breads, pastries, cakes, and cookies are, but they, too, are popular desserts important in food service. They include custards, puddings, creams, and frozen desserts. Most of the items and techniques described here are related to one another and to techniques introduced in earlier chapters. For example, many puddings, Bavarian creams, mousses, soufflés, and frozen desserts are based on two basic custards—crème anglaise and pastry cream—presented in Chapter 12. Also, Bavarians, mousses, and soufflés depend on meringues (discussed in Chapter 12), whipped cream, or both, for their texture.

511

As you know, the art and science of baking and dessert preparation rely on a coherent set of principles and techniques applied over and over to many kinds of product. The topics in this chapter are further illustration of that fact.

RANGE-TOP CUSTARDS AND PUDDINGS

IT IS DIFFICULT to come up with a definition of *pudding* that includes everything called by that name. The term is used for such different dishes as chocolate pudding, blood sausages (blood puddings), and steak-and-kidney pudding. In this chapter, however, we consider only popular North American dessert puddings.

Two kinds of puddings, starch-thickened and baked, are the most frequently prepared in food service kitchens. A third type, steamed pudding, is less often served, and then only in cold weather, because it is usually rather heavy and filling.

Custards are the basis of many puddings, so we begin the chapter with a general discussion of this type of preparation. A *custard* is a liquid thickened or set by the coagulation of egg protein. There are two basic kinds of custards: *stirred custard*, which is stirred as it cooks and remains pourable when cooked (except for pastry cream; see below), and *baked custard*, which is not stirred and sets firm. (Baked custards are discussed in the next section.)

One basic rule governs the preparation of both types of custard: *Do not heat custards higher than an internal temperature of 185°F (85°C).* This temperature is the point at which egg-liquid mixtures coagulate. If they are heated beyond this, they tend to curdle. An overbaked custard becomes watery because the moisture separates from the toughened protein.

Crème anglaise, or vanilla custard sauce, discussed in detail in Chapter 12 (p. 260), is a stirred custard. It consists of milk, sugar, and egg yolks stirred over very low heat until lightly thickened.

Pastry cream, also discussed in Chapter 12 (p. 262), is stirred custard that contains starch thickeners as well as eggs, resulting in a much thicker and more stable product. Because of the stabilizing effect of the starch, pastry cream is an exception to the rule just given not to heat custards over 185°F (85°C). In addition to its use as a component of many pastries and cakes, pastry cream is also the basis for cream puddings.

Most range-top puddings are thickened with starch, which means they must be boiled in order to cook or gelatinize the starch. The first two types of pudding in the following list are of this type. The third type is bound with gelatin, making heating or cooking necessary to dissolve the gelatin. This type of pudding may need to be heated only gently, rather than simmered or boiled. The fourth type is based on crème anglaise; it may or may not be bound with gelatin:

1. **Cornstarch pudding or blancmange.** *Cornstarch pudding* consists of milk, sugar, and flavorings and is thickened with cornstarch (or, sometimes, another starch). If enough cornstarch is used, the hot mixture may be poured into molds, chilled, and unmolded for service. (The term *blancmange*, pronounced, approximately, blaw MAWNGE), comes from the French words for "white" and "eat.")

2. **Cream puddings.** *Cream pudding*, as we have suggested, is the same as pastry cream. These puddings are usually made with less starch, however, and may contain any of several flavoring ingredients, such as coconut or chocolate. The flavor of butterscotch pudding comes from using brown sugar instead of white sugar.

   Because these puddings are basically the same as pastry cream, which in turn is used for cream pie fillings, it is not necessary to give separate recipes here. *To prepare any of the following puddings, simply prepare the corresponding cream pie filling (p. 300), but use only half the starch.* The following puddings can be made on this basis:

   - Vanilla pudding
   - Coconut cream pudding
   - Banana cream pudding (purée the bananas and mix with the pudding)
   - Chocolate pudding (two versions, using cocoa or melted chocolate)
   - Butterscotch pudding

3. **Puddings bound with gelatin.** A pudding not thickened with starch or eggs must be bound, or stabilized, using another ingredient. Gelatin is often used for this purpose. One of the simplest and most popular desserts of this type is *panna cotta*, which is Italian for "cooked cream." In its most basic form, panna cotta is made by heating cream and milk with sugar, adding vanilla and gelatin, and chilling in molds until set. It is often served with fruits or caramel sauce.

   Mousses and Bavarian creams, which owe their light texture to whipped cream or meringue, are often bound with gelatin. They are covered in detail later in this chapter.

4. **Crémeux.** *Crémeux* (pronounced, approximately, cray mooh) is the French word for "creamy," and it is applied to almost as many preparations as its English equivalent. One of the more important preparations called *crémeux* is built on a base of *crème anglaise*. After the crème anglaise is made, one or more of the following is added to thicken or bind it: gelatin, butter, chocolate.

   The basic steps for making crémeux are fairly simple:

   1. Prepare crème anglaise.

   2. If gelatin is used, bloom it and stir it into the hot crème anglaise until dissolved.

   3. If chocolate is used, pour the hot crème anglaise over the chocolate and mix until the chocolate is melted and blended in. (When you are making large quantities, the most efficient tool to use is an immersion blender.)

   4. Add other desired flavorings.

   5. If butter is used, cool the crème anglaise to about 90°F (32°C). Mix softened butter into the crème anglaise, preferably with an immersion blender.

   6. Pour into desired containers and chill.

   The most popular crèmeux is chocolate. A recipe for it is included on page 514. By experimenting with the basic procedure, you can create crèmeux of other flavors. Adjust the quantities of chocolate, gelatin, and butter to give the desired texture.

BLANCMANGE, ENGLISH-STYLE

Yield: about 2½ pt (1.25 L)

Ingredients	U.S.		Metric	Milk at 100% %
Milk	2 lb	(1 qt)	1000 mL	80
Sugar	6	oz	190 g	15
Salt	0.04 oz (¼ tsp)		1 g	0.1
Cornstarch	4	oz	125 g	10
Milk, cold	8	oz (½pt)	250 mL	20
Vanilla or almond extract	0.25 oz		8 mL	0.6

NOTE: French blancmange is very different from the English style. The French style is made from almonds or almond paste and gelatin.

--- **VARIATIONS** ---

Blancmange or cornstarch pudding may be flavored in the same ways as cream puddings. See the general discussion preceding this recipe.

For puddings to be served in dishes, rather than unmolded, reduce the cornstarch to 2 oz (60 g).

PROCEDURE

1. Combine the milk, sugar, and salt in a heavy saucepan and bring to a simmer.

2. Mix the cornstarch and milk until perfectly smooth.

3. Pouring it in a thin stream, add about 1 cup (2.5 dL) of the hot milk to the cornstarch mixture. Stir this mixture back into the hot milk.

4. Stir over low heat until the mixture thickens and comes to a boil.

5. Remove from the heat and add desired flavoring.

6. Pour into ½-cup (125-mL) molds. Cool and then chill. Unmold for service.

PANNA COTTA

Ingredients	U.S.		Metric
Milk	10	oz	300 g
Heavy cream	10	oz	300 g
Sugar	4	oz	125 g
Gelatin (see *Note*)	1½ tsp–2¼ tsp		5–7 g (2½–3½ sheets)
Vanilla extract	1	tsp	5 g
Total Weight:	**1 lb 8**	**oz**	**740 g**

NOTE: The lower quantity of gelatin makes a soft, delicate dessert. Use this quantity if the room temperature is cool. The larger quantity makes a firmer dessert that can withstand more handling when unmolded.

PROCEDURE

1. Heat the milk, cream, and sugar until the sugar is dissolved.
2. Soften the gelatin in cold water (see pp. 80–82). Add the softened gelatin to the hot milk mixture and stir until dissolved.
3. Stir in the vanilla.
4. Pour into 3- or 4-oz. (90- or 125-mL) molds. Chill until set.
5. Unmold to serve.

CHOCOLATE CRÉMEUX

Yield: 1 lb 6 oz (660 g)

Ingredients	U.S.	Metric
Bittersweet chocolate	5 oz	150 g
Egg yolks	3 oz	90 g
Sugar	4 oz	120 g
Milk	8 oz	240 g
Heavy cream	8 oz	240 g

VARIATIONS

For a thicker crémeux, one that can be used as a filling for chocolate tart, increase the chocolate to 7 oz (210 g).

MILK CHOCOLATE CRÉMEUX

Bloom 0.15 oz (4.2 g) gelatin in cold water. Add to the hot crème anglaise and dissolve. Substitute milk chocolate for the bittersweet chocolate.

PROCEDURE

1. Review the guidelines for preparing crème anglaise (p. 261).
2. If using block chocolate, chop it into small pieces and place in a stainless steel bowl. If using chocolate wafers, simply place them in the bowl; they do not need to be chopped. Set aside.
3. Combine the egg yolks and sugar in a stainless steel bowl. Whip until light.
4. Scald the milk and cream together in a boiling-water bath or over direct heat.
5. Very gradually pour the hot milk into the egg yolk mixture while stirring constantly with a wire whip.
6. Set the bowl in a pan of simmering water. Heat it, stirring constantly, until it thickens enough to coat the back of a spoon or until it reaches 180°F (82°C).
7. Strain the crème anglaise into the bowl containing the chocolate (a).
8. Mix at low speed until the chocolate is melted and blended with the crème anglaise. For small quantities, a wire whip is the most convenient mixing tool (b). Stir gently, taking care not to make bubbles. For large quantities, use an immersion blender. Blend at low speed, and keep the blade immersed, so as not to make bubbles.
9. Pour into desired containers (c). Chill until set.

Dark Chocolate Crémeux (background) and Milk Chocolate Crémeux (foreground).

BAKED CUSTARDS AND PUDDINGS AND STEAMED DESSERTS

SWEET BAKED CUSTARDS, like custard sauce, consist of milk, sugar, and eggs—usually whole eggs for their thickening power. Unlike the sauce, this type of custard is baked rather than stirred over heat, so it sets and becomes firm. Baked custard is used as a pie filling, as a dessert by itself, and as a basis for many baked puddings. Many, if not most, baked puddings are custards that contain additional ingredients, usually in large quantities. Bread pudding, for example, is made by pouring a custard mixture over slices or cubes of bread arranged in a baking pan and placing it in the oven to bake. Rice pudding, made of cooked rice and custard, is another popular item.

A good custard holds a clean, sharp edge when cut. The amount of egg in a custard determines its firmness. A custard to be unmolded requires more egg than one to be served in its baking dish. Also, egg yolks make a richer custard with a softer texture than do whole eggs.

When baking custards, note in particular these guidelines:

1. Scald the milk before beating it slowly into the eggs. This reduces cooking time and helps the product cook more evenly.

2. Remove any foam that would mar the appearance of the finished product.

3. Bake at 325°F (165°C) or lower. Higher temperatures increase the risk of overcooking and curdling.

4. Bake in a water bath so the outside edges do not overcook before the inside is set.

5. To test for doneness, insert a thin-bladed knife an inch or two from the center. If it comes out clean, the custard is done (see illustration). The center may not be completely set, but it will continue to cook in its own heat after removal from the oven.

The procedure for making many baked puddings, such as bread pudding, is the same as that for making plain baked custard. A water bath may not be necessary if the starch content of the pudding is high.

Soft pie fillings, such as pumpkin, may also be considered baked puddings and can be served as such. These preparations are, strictly speaking, custards, because they are liquids or semiliquids set by the coagulation of eggs. They may also contain small amounts of starch as a stabilizer.

This section also includes the popular baked custard called *crème brûlée*, which means "burnt cream." The *brûlée*, or "burnt," part of the name refers to the crunchy layer of sugar that is caramelized on the top of the dessert shortly before it is served. The custard portion of the dessert is especially rich because it is made with heavy cream. Some recipe books and food articles refer to the custard mixture as "the brûlée," which makes no sense when you consider the meaning of the term.

Testing a baked pudding for doneness.

BAKED CUSTARD

Yield: 12 portions, 5 oz (150 g) each

Ingredients	U.S.		Metric		Milk at 100% %
Eggs	1 lb		500	g	40
Sugar		8 oz	250	g	20
Salt	0.08 oz (½ tsp)		2.5	g	0.2
Vanilla extract	0.5 oz		15	g	1.25
Milk	2 lb 8	oz (2½ pt)	1250	mL	100

PROCEDURE

1. Combine the eggs, sugar, salt, and vanilla in a mixing bowl. Mix until thoroughly blended, but do not whip.

2. Scald the milk in a double boiler or in a saucepan over low heat.

3. Gradually pour the milk into the egg mixture, stirring constantly.

4. Skim all foam from the surface of the liquid.

5. Arrange custard cups in a shallow baking pan.

6. Carefully pour the custard mixture into the cups. If bubbles form during this step, skim them off.

7. Set the baking pan on the oven shelf. Pour enough hot water into the pan around the cups so the level of the water is about as high as that of the custard mixture.

8. Bake at 325°F (165°C) until set, about 45 minutes.

9. Carefully remove the custard from the oven and cool. Store, covered, in the refrigerator.

VARIATIONS

CRÈME CARAMEL

Cook 12 oz (375 g) sugar with 2 oz (60 mL) water until it caramelizes (see the section on sugar cooking on page 252). Line the bottoms of the custard cups with this hot caramel. (Be sure the cups are clean and dry.) Fill with custard and bake as in a basic recipe. When cooled, refrigerate for 24 hours, to allow some of the caramel to dissolve and form a sauce for the dessert when it is unmolded.

VANILLA POTS DE CRÈME

Pots de crème (pronounced poh duh KREM) are rich cup custards. Substitute 1 pt (500 mL) heavy cream for 1 pt (500 mL) of the milk in the basic recipe. Use 8 oz (250 g) whole eggs plus 4 oz (125 g) egg yolks.

CHOCOLATE POTS DE CRÈME

Follow the procedure for vanilla pots de crème above, but stir 12 oz (375 g) chopped semisweet chocolate into the hot milk until melted and evenly blended. Reduce the sugar to 4 oz (125 g).

CRÈME BRÛLÉE

Yield: 12 portions, about 5 oz (150 g) each

Ingredients	U.S.		Metric	
Egg yolks	8	oz (12 yolks)	250	g (12 yolks)
Granulated sugar	6	oz	180	g
Heavy cream, hot	3 pt		1.5	L
Vanilla extract	0.25	oz (1½ tsp)	8	mL
Salt	¾	tsp	3	g
Granulated sugar	8	oz	250	g

PROCEDURE

1. Mix together the egg yolks and granulated sugar until well combined.

2. Gradually stir in the hot cream. Add the vanilla and salt. Strain the mixture.

3. Set 12 shallow ramekins or gratin dishes, about 1 in. (2.5 cm) deep, on a towel in a sheet pan (the purpose of the towel is to insulate the bottoms of the ramekins from the strong heat). Divide the custard mixture equally among the dishes. Pour enough hot water into the sheet pan to reach about halfway up the sides of the ramekins.

4. Bake at 325°F (165°C) until the custard is just set, about 25 minutes.

5. Cool, then refrigerate.

6. To finish, first dab any moisture from the tops of the custards. Sprinkle with an even layer of sugar. Caramelize the sugar with a blowtorch. (Alternatively, caramelize the sugar under the broiler: place the custards very close to the heat so the sugar caramelizes quickly before the custard warms up too much). When it cools, the caramelized sugar will form a thin, hard crust. Serve within an hour or two. If the custards are held too long, the caramel tops will soften.

VARIATIONS

Brown sugar may be used instead of granulated sugar. Spread the sugar on a pan and dry out in the oven at low heat. Cool, crush, and sift.

For a deluxe version, flavor the custard with vanilla beans instead of extract. Split 2 vanilla beans in half lengthwise and scrape out the tiny seeds. Simmer the pods and seeds with the heavy cream. Remove the pods and continue with the basic recipe.

COFFEE CRÈME BRÛLÉE

Flavor the hot cream to taste with coffee extract or instant coffee powder.

CINNAMON CRÈME BRÛLÉE

Add 2 tsp (3.5 g) cinnamon to the hot cream.

CHOCOLATE CRÈME BRÛLÉE

Use half milk and half cream. Mix 8 oz (250 g) melted bittersweet chocolate with the hot cream and milk mixture.

RASPBERRY OR BLUEBERRY CRÈME BRÛLÉE

Place a few berries in the ramekins before adding the custard mixture.

RASPBERRY PASSION FRUIT CRÈME BRÛLÉE

Reduce the quantity of cream to 2¾ pt (1375 mL). Omit the vanilla. Add 4 oz (125 mL) strained passion fruit juice and pulp to the mixture just before straining. Continue as for Raspberry Crème Brûlée.

Carmelizing Crème Brûlée with a blowtorch.

BROILER OR BLOWTORCH?

Which tool is better for caramelizing the sugar on crème brûlée: a butane torch or a broiler/salamander? It's a matter of personal preference and equipment availability. When making individual desserts to order, chefs often find a torch is easiest and quickest. Besides, not every pastry department has a broiler, and the broiler in the hot kitchen may not be available. On the other hand, when you are preparing crèmes brûlées in quantity for a banquet, it may be easier to arrange the custards on sheet pans and pass them under a broiler.

BREAD AND BUTTER PUDDING

Yield: about 5 lb (2.5 kg)

Ingredients	U.S.		Metric
White bread, in thin slices (see *Note*)	1 lb		500 g
Butter, melted	4	oz	125 g
Eggs	1 lb		500 g
Sugar	8	oz	250 g
Salt	0.08 oz (½ tsp)		2 g
Vanilla extract	0.5	oz	15 mL
Milk	2 lb 8	oz (1¼ qt)	1250 mL
Cinnamon	as needed		as needed
Nutmeg	as needed		as needed

NOTE: You may use bread with crust on or trimmed off, as desired. If bread crusts are not too hard, leaving them on gives the pudding more textural interest.

VARIATIONS

For a richer pudding, substitute cream for up to half of the milk.

Add 4 oz (125 g) raisins to the pudding, sprinkling them between the layers of bread.

BRANDY OR WHISKEY BREAD PUDDING

Add 2 oz (60 mL) brandy or whiskey to the custard mixture.

CABINET PUDDING

Prepare in individual custard cups instead of a baking pan. Substitute diced sponge cake for the bread and omit the melted butter. Add about 1½ tsp (4 g) raisins to each cup before pouring in the custard mix.

DRIED CHERRY BREAD PUDDING

Add 4–6 oz (125–185 g) dried cherries to the bread pudding, sprinkling them between the layers of the bread. Substitute heavy cream for up to half of the milk.

PROCEDURE

1. Cut each slice of bread in half. Brush both sides of each piece with melted butter.

2. Arrange the bread slices so they overlap in a buttered 10 × 12 in. (25 × 30 cm) baking pan. (To use a full-size hotel pan, double the quantities.)

3. Mix together the eggs, sugar, salt, and vanilla until thoroughly combined. Add the milk.

4. Pour the egg mixture over the bread in the pan.

5. Let stand, refrigerated, for 1 hour or longer, until the bread absorbs the custard mixture. If necessary, push the bread down into the pan once or twice after the mixture has had time to stand.

6. Sprinkle the top lightly with cinnamon and nutmeg.

7. Set the pan in a larger pan containing about 1 in. (2.5 cm) hot water.

8. Place in an oven preheated to 350°F (175°C). Bake about 1 hour, until set.

9. Serve warm or cold with whipped cream or crème anglaise (p. 261), a fruit purée, or confectioners' sugar.

CHOCOLATE BREAD PUDDING

Yield: about 5 lb (2500 g)

Ingredients	U.S.	Metric
Heavy cream	1 lb 4 oz	625 g
Milk	1 lb 4 oz	625 g
Sugar	6 oz	180 g
Bittersweet chocolate, chopped	12 oz	350 g
Dark rum	2 oz	60 g
Vanilla extract	2 tsp	10 g
Eggs	14 oz (8 eggs)	400 g (8 eggs)
White bread, in thick slices, crusts trimmed (see *Note*)	1 lb	500 g

NOTE: A good-quality, rich white bread, such as Challah (p. 132), is recommended for this recipe.

PROCEDURE

1. Combine the cream, milk, and sugar in a heavy saucepan. Heat, stirring, until the sugar is dissolved.

2. Remove the pan from the heat and let cool 1 minute. Then add the chocolate and stir until it is melted and completely blended in.

3. Add the rum and vanilla.

4. Beat the eggs in a bowl, then gradually beat in the warm chocolate mixture.

5. Cut the bread into large dice and place in a buttered half-size hotel pan or baking pan (10 × 12 in. or 25 × 30 cm), or use two 8-in. (20-cm) square pans. Pour the chocolate mixture over the bread. If any bread is not coated with the chocolate mixture, push it down into the chocolate to coat it.

6. Let stand, refrigerated, for 1 hour or longer, until the bread absorbs the custard mixture. If necessary, push the bread down into the pan once or twice after the mixture has had time to stand.

7. Bake at 350°F (175°C) until set, about 30–45 minutes.

RICE PUDDING

Yield: about 4 lb 8 oz (2.25 kg)

Ingredients	U.S.		Metric
Rice, medium- or long-grain	8	oz	250 g
Milk	3 lb	(3 pt)	1500 mL
Vanilla extract	0.16 oz (1 tsp)		5 mL
Salt	0.04 oz (¼ tsp)		2 g
Egg yolks	3	oz	95 g
Sugar	8	oz	250 g
Light cream	8	oz (½ pt)	250 mL
Cinnamon	as needed		as needed

PROCEDURE

1. Wash the rice well. Drain. (See *Note*.)

2. Combine the rice, milk, vanilla, and salt in a heavy saucepan. Cover and simmer over low heat until the rice is tender, about 30 minutes. Stir occasionally to be sure the mixture doesn't scorch on the bottom. Remove from the heat when cooked.

3. Combine the egg yolks, sugar, and cream in a mixing bowl. Mix until evenly combined.

4. Ladle some of the hot milk from the cooked rice into this mixture and mix well. Then slowly stir the egg mixture back into the hot rice.

5. Pour into a buttered 10 × 12 in. (25 × 30 cm) baking pan. Sprinkle the top with cinnamon. (To use a full-size hotel pan, double the quantities.)

6. Bake in a water bath at 350°F (175°C) 30–40 minutes, or until set. Serve warm or chilled.

Note: In order to remove even more loose starch, some cooks prefer to blanch the rice in boiling water for 2 minutes, then drain and rinse it.

VARIATIONS

RAISIN RICE PUDDING

Add 4 oz (125 g) raisins to the cooked rice and milk mixture.

RICE CONDÉ

Make the following adjustments:

   Increase the rice to 10.5 oz (325 g).

   Increase the egg yolks to 5 oz (150 g).

   Omit the cinnamon.

As soon as the egg yolks have been incorporated, pour the rice mixture into shallow, individual, buttered molds. Bake as in the basic recipe, then chill until firm. Unmold onto serving dishes.

Rice Condé can be served plain or with whipped cream or fruit sauce, or used as a base for poached fruit. Arrange the fruit on top of the unmolded rice; brush with Apricot Glaze (p. 194). Dishes made in this way are named after their fruit, such as Apricot Condé or Pear Condé.

TAPIOCA PUDDING

This pudding is prepared like rice pudding through step 4 in the procedure. However, it is not baked. Instead, whipped egg whites are folded in and the mixture is chilled. To prepare, make the following adjustments in the recipe:

   Substitute 4 oz (125 g) tapioca for the 8 oz (250 g) rice. Do not wash the tapioca. Cook it in the milk until tender.

   Reserve 2 oz (60 g) of the sugar (from step 3) for the meringue.

   After the egg yolks are incorporated, return the pudding to low heat for a few minutes to cook the yolks. Stir constantly. Do not let the mixture boil.

   Whip 4 oz (125 g) pasteurized egg whites with the reserved 2 oz (60 g) sugar to a soft meringue. Fold into the hot pudding. Chill.

CREAM CHEESECAKE

Yield: enough for two 10-in. (25-cm) cakes or three 8-in. (20-cm) cakes

Ingredients	U.S.		Metric	
Cream cheese	5 lb		2250	g
Sugar	1 lb 12	oz	790	g
Cornstarch	1.5	oz	45	g
Lemon zest, grated	0.25	oz	7.5	g
Vanilla extract	0.5	oz	15	g
Salt	0.75	oz	22	g
Eggs	1 lb		450	g
Egg yolks	6	oz	170	g
Heavy cream	8	oz	225	g
Milk	4	oz	112	g
Lemon juice	1	oz	30	g
Short Dough (p. 314) or sponge cake for lining pans				
Total Weight:	9 lb 2	oz	4115	g

VARIATIONS

CHEESECAKE WITH BAKER'S CHEESE

In place of the 5 lb (2250 g) cream cheese, use 3 lb 12 oz (1700 g) baker's cheese plus 1 lb 8 oz (675 g) butter. If desired, you may use all milk instead of part milk and part cream in step 5.

FRENCH CHEESECAKE

This cheesecake has a lighter texture achieved by incorporating whipped egg whites into the batter of either the cream cheese version or the baker's cheese version. To make French cheesecake, make the following adjustments in either recipe above:

Increase the cornstarch to 2.5 oz (75 g).

Reserve 8 oz (225 g) of the sugar and whip it with 1 lb 2 oz (520 g) egg whites, to make a soft meringue.

Fold the meringue into the cheese batter before filling the pans.

PROCEDURE

1. Prepare the pans by lining the bottoms with either a very thin layer of sponge cake or a thin layer of short dough. Bake the short dough until it begins to turn golden.

2. Put the cream cheese in the mixing bowl and, with the paddle attachment, mix at low speed until it is smooth and lump free.

3. Add the sugar, cornstarch, lemon zest, vanilla, and salt. Blend in until smooth and uniform, but do not whip. Scrape down the sides of the bowl and the beater.

4. Add the eggs and egg yolks, a little at a time, blending in thoroughly after each addition. Scrape down the bowl again to make sure the mixture is well blended.

5. With the machine running at low speed, gradually add the cream, milk, and lemon juice.

6. Fill the prepared pans. Scale as follows:

   10-in. pans: 4½ lb   25-cm pans: 2050 g
   8-in. pans: 3 lb   20-cm pans: 1350 g

7. Cheesecake may be baked with or without a water bath (see *Note*):

   To bake without a water bath, place the filled pans on sheet pans and set them in an oven preheated to 400°F (200°C). After 10 minutes, turn down the oven to 225°F (105°C) and continue baking until the mixture is set, about 1–1½ hours, depending on the size of the cake.

   To bake with a water bath, set the filled pans inside another, larger pan. Fill the outer pan with water and bake at 350°F (175°C) until set.

8. Cool the cakes completely before removing them from pans. To unmold a cake from a pan without removable sides, sprinkle the top of the cake with granulated sugar. Invert the cake onto a cardboard cake circle, then immediately place another circle over the bottom and turn it right side up.

Note: Baking in a water bath results in cakes with browned tops and unbrowned sides. Baking without a water bath results in browned sides and a lighter top. If you are not using a water bath, you may use either deep-layer cake pans or springform pans (pans with removable sides). However, if you are using a water bath, you must use deep cake pans, not springform pans.

CHEESECAKE

One meaning of the word *cake* is a baked, leavened confection made of flour, eggs, sugar, and other ingredients, usually made in a round or rectangular shape. This type of cake is covered in Chapter 16. Another meaning of *cake* is a shaped or molded mass of some substance, such as a cake of soap or a lump of snow caked on your boots. Many food preparations called cakes are closer to this second definition, and even some leavened flour goods, like pancakes, aren't normally discussed in the context of cake as described in Chapter 16.

In some baking discussions, cheesecakes are included along with flour-based cakes. Technically, however, cheesecake is the same type of preparation as baked custard or pumpkin pie filling. It is a liquid mixture of milk, sugar, eggs, and cream cheese that becomes firm when the eggs coagulate. The fact that it happens to be called a cake has nothing to do with its composition. Therefore, cheesecake does not belong in the cake chapter any more than do funnel cakes (a type of fritter) or crab cakes.

Cheesecakes in many styles are made around the world, using local cheese. In North America, most cheesecake is made with cream cheese. New York–style cheesecake is perhaps the richest of these, being made with heavy cream in addition to cream cheese. Cakes made with lower-fat baker's cheese are also found, but less often. In Italy, the dessert is made with ricotta cheese; and in Germany it is made with a fresh cheese called *quark*. Unbaked cheesecakes, which rely on gelatin rather than coagulated eggs to enable them to set firm, are a type of Bavarian cream (see p. 525) rather than a baked custard.

Steamed Desserts

Steamed puddings are primarily cold-weather fare. Their heavy, dense texture and richness make them warming, comforting desserts on winter nights. These same characteristics, however, make them inappropriate for year-round use.

The most famous steamed pudding is the English *Christmas pudding*, known in much of North America as *plum pudding*. A Christmas pudding, well made and with high-quality ingredients, offers an unforgettable combination of flavors. The long list of ingredients makes the recipe look difficult, but once the ingredients are assembled and scaled, the pudding is simple to produce.

In addition to Christmas pudding, recipes for less complex steamed puddings are included here to give you an idea of the range of possibilities. Many steamed puddings could be baked in a water bath, but steaming is more energy-efficient and helps keep the pudding moist during the long cooking time.

If a compartment steamer is available, simply set the filled, covered pudding molds in steamer pans and place them in the steamer. To steam on top of the stove, set the covered molds in large, deep pans and pour in enough hot water to come halfway up the sides of the molds. Bring the water to a boil, lower the heat to a gentle simmer, and cover the pan. Check the pan periodically and add more hot water as needed.

KEY POINTS TO REVIEW

▪ What is a custard? What are the two basic types of custard? Give an example of each.

▪ What are cream puddings? How are they made?

▪ What is panna cotta? How is it made?

▪ What is crémeux? How is it made?

▪ What is crème brûlée? How is it made?

CHRISTMAS PUDDING

For large-quantity measurements, see page 731.

Ingredients	U.S.		Metric	
Dark raisins	8	oz	250	g
Light raisins	8	oz	250	g
Currants	8	oz	250	g
Dates, diced	4	oz	125	g
Almonds, chopped	3	oz	90	g
Candied orange peel, finely chopped	2	oz	60	g
Candied lemon peel, finely chopped	2	oz	60	g
Brandy	6	oz	190	mL
Bread flour	4	oz	125	g
Cinnamon	½	tsp	2	mL
Nutmeg	⅛	tsp	0.5	mL
Mace	⅛	tsp	0.5	mL
Ginger	⅛	tsp	0.5	mL
Cloves, ground	⅛	tsp	0.5	mL
Salt	0.13 oz (⅝ tsp)		4	g
Beef suet, finely chopped	6	oz	190	g
Brown sugar	4	oz	125	g
Eggs	4	oz	125	g
Fresh bread crumbs	2	oz	60	g
Molasses	0.5	oz	15	g
Total Weight:	**3 lb 13**	**oz**	**1915**	**g**

PROCEDURE

1. Soak the fruits and almonds in the brandy for 24 hours.

2. Sift the flour with the spices.

3. Combine the flour mixture, suet, sugar, eggs, bread crumbs, and molasses. Add the fruit and brandy and mix well.

4. Fill greased pudding molds, allowing a little room for expansion. Cover the pudding mixture with rounds of greased parchment cut to fit inside the molds. Then cover the molds with foil and tie with string so steam cannot get inside.

5. Steam 4–6 hours, depending on size.

6. For storage, cool the puddings until just warm, then unmold. Wrap in cheesecloth and cool completely, then wrap again in plastic. The puddings will keep a year or more if sprinkled with brandy or rum every 7–10 days.

7. Christmas pudding must be served warm. To reheat it, place it in molds and steam 1–2 hours, or until heated through. Serve with Hard Sauce (p. 277).

STEAMED BLUEBERRY PUDDING

For large-quantity measurements, see page 731.

Ingredients	U.S.		Metric
Brown sugar	5	oz	150 g
Butter	2	oz	60 g
Salt	0.03 oz (⅛ tsp)		0.9 g (0.5 mL)
Cinnamon	0.05 oz (¾ tsp)		1.5 g (4 mL)
Eggs	2	oz	60 g
Bread flour	1	oz	30 g
Baking powder	0.18 oz (1 tsp)		6 g
Dry bread crumbs	5	oz	150 g
Milk	4	oz	125 g
Blueberries, fresh or frozen, without sugar	4	oz	125 g
Total Weight:	**1 lb 7**	**oz**	**708 g**

PROCEDURE

1. Cream together the sugar, butter, salt, and cinnamon.
2. Blend in the eggs, a little at a time. Cream until light.
3. Sift the flour with the baking powder, then mix with the bread crumbs.
4. Add the dry ingredients to the sugar mixture alternately with the milk. Blend to a smooth batter.
5. Carefully fold in the blueberries.
6. Fill well-greased molds about two-thirds full. Cover tightly and steam for 1½–2 hours, depending on the size of the molds.
7. Unmold and serve hot with Hard Sauce (p. 277) or Crème Anglaise (p. 261).

--- **VARIATION** ---

STEAMED RAISIN SPICE PUDDING

Add 1 oz (30 g) molasses, ¼ tsp (1 mL) ginger, and ⅛ tsp (0.5 mL) mace to the sugar mixture. In place of the blueberries, use 3 oz (90 g) raisins, soaked and drained, and 2 oz (60 g) chopped nuts. Serve hot with Hard Sauce (p. 277), Crème Anglaise (p. 261), or Lemon Sauce (p. 267).

STEAMED CHOCOLATE ALMOND PUDDING

Ingredients	U.S.		Metric
Butter	4	oz	125 g
Sugar	5	oz	150 g
Salt	0.04 oz (⅛ tsp)		1 g
Unsweetened chocolate, melted	1.5	oz	45 g
Egg yolks	3	oz	90 g
Milk or dark rum	1	oz	30 g
Powdered almonds	6	oz	190 g
Dry bread crumbs	1	oz	30 g
Egg whites	5	oz	150 g
Sugar	1.5	oz	45 g
Total Weight:	**1 lb 12**	**oz**	**856 g**

PROCEDURE

1. Cream the butter, sugar, and salt until light. Blend in the chocolate.
2. Add the egg yolks in two or three stages, then blend in the milk or rum. Scrape down the bowl to eliminate lumps.
3. Blend in the almond powder and bread crumbs.
4. Whip the egg whites and sugar to a soft meringue. Fold the meringue into the batter.
5. Butter the insides of molds and sprinkle with sugar. Fill three-fourths full with batter. Cover tightly and steam 1½ hours.
6. Unmold and serve hot with Chocolate Sauce (p. 267) or whipped cream.

BAVARIANS, MOUSSES, AND CHARLOTTES

BAVARIANS AND MOUSSES, along with soufflés and many other items discussed later in this chapter, have one thing in common: They all have a light, fluffy texture created by the addition of whipped cream, beaten egg whites, or both.

Bavarian creams are classic gelatin desserts containing custard and whipped cream. Chiffon pie fillings, covered in Chapter 13, are similar to Bavarians in that they are stabilized with gelatin and have a light, foamy texture. In the case of chiffons, however, this texture is due primarily to whipped egg whites; whipped cream may or may not be added. Chiffon pie fillings may also be served as puddings and chilled desserts.

Mousses may have a softer texture than Bavarians, although there is no precise dividing line between the two. Many desserts called *mousses* are made exactly like Bavarians. However, many mousses, especially chocolate mousses, are made without gelatin or with only a small amount. The light texture of mousses is created by adding whipped cream, meringue, or both.

Bavarians

A Bavarian, also known as *Bavarian cream*, and by its French name *Bavarois* (bah vahr WAH), is made of three basic elements: custard sauce or crème anglaise (flavored as desired), gelatin, and whipped cream. That's all there is to it. Gelatin is softened in cold liquid, stirred into hot custard sauce until dissolved, and chilled until almost set. Whipped cream is then folded in, and the mixture is poured into a mold until set. It is unmolded for service.

Accurate measurement of the gelatin is important. If not enough gelatin is used, the dessert will be too soft to hold its shape. If too much is used, the cream will be too firm and rubbery. The use of gelatin is described in detail in Chapter 4 (pp. 80–82) and in the section of Chapter 13 pertaining to chiffon pie fillings (p. 302).

Fruit Bavarians can be made like regular custard-based Bavarian creams by adding fruit purées and flavorings to the custard base. They can also be made without a custard base by adding gelatin to a sweetened fruit purée and then folding in whipped cream. A separate recipe is included in this section for basic fruit Bavarian creams, along with several recipes for modern specialty Bavarian creams.

Because they can be molded and decorated in many ways, Bavarian creams can be used to make elaborate, elegant desserts. They are the basis for a variety of desserts called *cold charlottes*, which are Bavarian creams molded in molds lined with various sponge cake products. Classic cold charlottes are usually decorated with whipped cream and fresh fruits, and are sometimes served with a fruit coulis. Procedures for assembling two famous charlottes from the classic pastry shop are included here, following the basic vanilla Bavarian recipe. (Note that although made in the same type of mold, hot charlottes are quite different from cold charlottes; see p. 583.)

Modern pastry chefs have created a new family of charlottes as a medium for displaying their decorative skills. This chapter includes several recipes of this type as examples of how flavorful and eye-appealing modern desserts can be developed using classic techniques. These charlottes are made in large ring molds— but please note they can also be made in single-portion sizes by using small ring molds 2¾ inches (7 cm) in diameter, just like several of the pastries in Chapter 15. See page 364 for an illustration of the technique.

This section also includes two other desserts made with the same techniques. *Rice impératrice* (p. 530), or empress rice, is an elegant molded rice pudding. The base is made somewhat like crème anglaise (which is the base for Bavarian cream), except the rice is cooked in the milk before the egg yolks and gelatin are added. Whipped cream is then folded in. (Another way of arriving at the same result is to combine equal parts Rice Condé mixture, found on p. 520, and Vanilla Bavarian Cream mixture, plus the candied fruit mixture indicated in the recipe on p. 530.)

CHARLOTTE

The first printed use of the word *charlotte* for a dessert dates to 1796 and refers to the baked apple dessert still made today (p. 583). This dessert consists of apples baked in a mold lined with buttered slices of bread. It may have been named for Queen Charlotte, wife of King George III of England.

Only a few years later, the great pastry chef Carême (see p. 6) borrowed the name charlotte for one of his own creations, a cold, gelatin-based creamy dessert made in a mold lined with ladyfingers or sponge cake. He invented the dessert while working in England, and called it Charlotte à la Parisienne. Although no one knows for sure, another similarly named dessert, Charlotte Russe, may have been adopted at a banquet in honor of the Russian Tsar Alexander I.

Cream cheese Bavarian is not made with a cooked custard base, but it does contain gelatin and whipped cream. Thus, it is similar in character and texture to other Bavarian creams. Similarly, three of the creams among the following recipes are based on pastry cream rather than crème anglaise like true Bavarian creams, although they belong in this section because of their gelatin and whipped cream content.

If a gelatin-based dessert is made in a bowl-shaped mold rather than a ring mold, unmold it by dipping the mold into hot water for 1 or 2 seconds. Quickly wipe the bottom of the mold and turn it over onto the serving plate (or invert the plate over the mold and flip the plate and mold over together). Alternatively, warm the mold carefully and briefly with a torch. If the dessert doesn't unmold after a gentle shake, repeat the warming procedure. Do not hold in the hot water for more than a few seconds or the gelatin will begin to melt.

PROCEDURE: Preparing Bavarian and Bavarian-Type Creams

1. Prepare the base—either Crème Anglaise (p. 261) or another base indicated in recipe.

2. Soften the gelatin in cold liquid and stir it into the hot base until dissolved (a). Or, if the base is not cooked, heat the gelatin and liquid until the gelatin is dissolved, then stir it into the base. Make sure the base isn't too cold, or the gelatin may congeal too quickly and form lumps.

3. If the recipe requires any flavorings, such as fruit purées, that were not included in the base (step 1), stir them in (b).

4. Cool the mixture until thick but not set. This is done most quickly by setting the bowl in an ice-water bath and stirring constantly.

5. Fold in the whipped cream (c).

6. Pour the mixture into prepared molds and chill until set.

Mousses

There are so many varieties of mousse that it is impossible to give a rule that applies to all of them. In general, we could define a *mousse* as any soft or creamy dessert made light and fluffy by the addition of whipped cream, beaten egg whites, or both. Note that Bavarians and chiffons fit this description. In fact, they are often served as mousses, but with the gelatin reduced or left out so the mousse is softer.

There are many kinds of bases for mousses. They may be nothing more than melted chocolate or puréed fresh fruit, or they may be more complex, like the bases for chiffons.

Some mousses contain both beaten egg whites and whipped cream. When this is the case, most chefs prefer to fold in the egg whites first, even though they may lose some volume. The reason is that if the cream is added first, there is more danger it will be overbeaten and turn to butter during the folding and mixing procedure.

If egg whites are folded into a *hot* base, they will cook or coagulate, making the mousse firmer and more stable. Whipped cream should never be folded into hot mixtures because it will melt and deflate.

In addition to the chocolate mousse recipes included in this section and the additional recipes in Chapter 12 (p. 273), you can also convert the chiffon pie filling recipes (pp. 304–306) and the Bavarian cream recipes (pp. 528–530) to mousses. Just reduce the quantity of gelatin to one-third or one-half the amount indicated in the recipe. For creamier mousses made from the chiffon recipes, substitute whipped cream for part of the meringue. (Some of the variations following the main recipes indicate this substitution.) By making these recipe adjustments, you can produce a number of popular mousses—including raspberry, strawberry, lemon, orange, and pumpkin—without needing separate recipes.

The Chocolate Terrine on page 539 could be said to be a chocolate mousse thick enough to be sliced. Compare this recipe to the recipe for Chocolate Mousse I on page 273. You will see that the procedures are almost the same, although the ingredient proportions are different.

VANILLA BAVARIAN CREAM

Yield: about 1½ qt (1.5 L)

Ingredients	U.S.		Metric
Gelatin	0.75 oz		22 g
Water, cold	5	oz	150 mL
Crème anglaise			
Egg yolks	4	oz	125 g
Sugar	4	oz	125 g
Milk	1 pt		500 mL
Vanilla	0.25 oz		8 mL
Heavy cream	1 pt		500 mL

PROCEDURE

1. Soak the gelatin in the cold water.
2. *Prepare the crème anglaise.* Whip the egg yolks and sugar until thick and light. Scald the milk and slowly stir it into the egg yolk mixture, beating constantly. Cook over a hot-water bath, stirring constantly, until it thickens slightly. Temperature should not exceed 180°F (82°C). (Review p. 260 for a detailed discussion of making crème anglaise.)
3. Remove from heat and stir in the vanilla.
4. Stir the gelatin mixture into the hot custard sauce until it is dissolved.
5. Cool the custard sauce in the refrigerator or over crushed ice, stirring occasionally to keep the mixture smooth.
6. Whip the cream until it forms soft peaks. Do not overwhip.
7. When the custard is very thick but not yet set, fold in the whipped cream.
8. Pour the mixture into molds or serving dishes.
9. Chill until completely set. If prepared in molds, unmold for service.

VARIATIONS

CHOCOLATE BAVARIAN CREAM
Add 6 oz (190 g) semisweet or bittersweet chocolate, chopped or grated, to the hot custard sauce. Stir until completely melted and blended in.

WHITE CHOCOLATE BAVARIAN CREAM
Add 8 oz (250 g) white chocolate, chopped or grated, to the hot custard sauce. Stir until completely melted and blended in.

COFFEE BAVARIAN CREAM
Add 1½ tbsp (6 g) instant coffee powder to the hot custard sauce.

STRAWBERRY BAVARIAN CREAM
Reduce the milk to 8 oz (250 mL) and the sugar to 3 oz (90 g). Mash 8 oz (250 g) strawberries with 3 oz sugar (90 g), or use 12 oz (375 g) frozen, sweetened strawberries. Stir this purée into the custard sauce before adding the whipped cream.

RASPBERRY BAVARIAN CREAM
Prepare like Strawberry Bavarian Cream, but use raspberries.

LIQUEUR BAVARIAN CREAM
Flavor to taste with a liqueur or spirit, such as orange, kirsch, maraschino, amaretto, or rum.

PRALINE BAVARIAN CREAM
Mix 3 oz (95 g) praline paste with the hot custard sauce.

DIPLOMAT BAVARIAN CREAM
Moisten diced sponge cake (about 4 oz/125 g) and diced candied fruit (about 4 oz/125 g) with kirsch (about 1½ oz/ 45 mL). Mix gently with vanilla Bavarian mixture.

ORANGE BAVARIAN CREAM
Proceed as in the basic recipe, except omit the vanilla and reduce the milk to 8 oz (250 mL). Flavor the custard sauce with the grated zest of 1 orange or with orange flavor. Before adding the whipped cream, stir 8 oz (250 mL) orange juice into the cold custard mixture.

CHARLOTTE RUSSE
Line the bottom and sides of a charlotte mold with ladyfingers (p. 407). For the bottom, cut the ladyfingers into triangles and fit them close together so the points meet in the center. (*Note:* The ladyfingers must fit tightly, with no space between them.) Fill the mold with Bavarian cream mixture and chill until set. Before unmolding, if necessary, trim the tops of the ladyfingers so they are level with the cream.

Another method for making Charlotte Russe, although not authentic, yields an attractive dessert. Mold some Bavarian cream mixture in an unlined charlotte mold. After unmolding, cover the top and sides with ladyfingers or Langues de Chat (p. 496), using a little melted Bavarian mixture to make them stick. Decorate with whipped cream.

CHARLOTTE ROYALE
Line a round mold with thin slices of a small jelly roll. Fit them close together so there is no space between them. Fill the mold with Bavarian mixture and chill until set. If desired, glaze the charlotte with Apricot Glaze (p. 194) after unmolding.

FRUIT BAVARIAN

Yield: about 2½ pt (1.25 L)

Ingredients	U.S.		Metric
Fruit purée (see *Note*)	8	oz	250 g
Extra-fine granulated sugar	4	oz	125 g
Lemon juice	1	oz	30 mL
Gelatin	0.5	oz	15 g
Water, cold	5	oz	150 mL
Heavy cream	12	oz	375 mL

Note: Use 8 oz (250 g) unsweetened or lightly sweetened fresh, frozen, or canned fruit, such as strawberries, raspberries, apricots, pineapple, peaches, or bananas. For heavily sweetened fruit, such as frozen, sweetened strawberries, use 10 oz (300 g) fruit and reduce the sugar to 2 oz (60 g).

PROCEDURE

1. Force the fruit purée through a fine sieve. Mix it with the sugar and lemon juice. Stir the mixture or let it stand until the sugar is completely dissolved.

2. Soften the gelatin in the cold water for 5 minutes. Heat the mixture gently until the gelatin is dissolved.

3. Stir the gelatin mixture into the fruit purée.

4. Chill the mixture until thickened but not set. *Note:* If the fruit purée is cold when the gelatin is added, it will start to set very quickly, so further chilling may not be needed.

5. Whip the cream until it forms soft peaks. Do not overwhip.

6. Fold the cream into the fruit mixture. Pour it into molds and chill.

RICE IMPÉRATRICE

Yield: 1 qt (1 L)

Ingredients	U.S.		Metric	
Rice, long-grain	3	oz	90	g
Milk	1 pt		0.5 L	
Vanilla	0.25 oz		8	mL
Egg yolks	2	oz	60	g
Sugar	3	oz	90	g
Gelatin	0.25 oz		8	g
Water, cold	2	oz	60	mL
Candied fruits, diced	3	oz	90	g
Kirsch	1	oz	30	mL
Heavy cream	6	oz	180	mL

NOTE: A traditional way of preparing this dish is to line the bottoms of the molds with about ¼ in. (6 mm) red fruit gelatin. For the quantity in this recipe, you will need about ¼ pt (125 mL) gelatin mixture. Use either 1 oz (30 g) flavored gelatin mix dissolved in 4 oz (125 mL) water or ¹⁄₁₆ oz (⅜ tsp/2 g) plain gelatin dissolved in 4 oz (125 mL) sweetened red fruit juice. Pour it into molds and chill until set.

PROCEDURE

1. Rinse and drain the rice. Simmer it slowly in the milk, covered, until tender. Add the vanilla.

2. Whip the egg yolks and sugar together. Stir in a little of the hot milk from the rice mixture. Then stir the egg yolk mixture into the rice mixture. Cook very slowly for a few minutes, stirring constantly, until it is lightly thickened.

3. Soften the gelatin in the water. Stir the gelatin mixture into the hot rice mixture until the gelatin is dissolved. (*Note:* For buffet service or in hot weather, increase the gelatin to 0.4 oz (11 g).

4. Stir in the candied fruits, which have been soaked in the kirsch at least one hour.

5. Chill the mixture until thick but not set.

6. Whip the heavy cream until it forms soft peaks. Fold it into the rice mixture.

7. Pour into molds (see Note). Chill until set. Unmold onto serving plates. Decorate with candied fruits and whipped cream, if desired. Serve with Melba Sauce (p. 270).

CREAM CHEESE BAVARIAN

Yield: about 1½ qt (1.6 L)

For large-quantity measurements, see page 731.

Ingredients	U.S.		Metric	
Cream cheese	12	oz	375	g
Sugar	4	oz	125	g
Salt	0.12 oz (⅝ tsp)		4	g
Lemon zest, grated	0.03 oz (⅜ tsp)		1	g
Orange zest, grated	0.02 oz (¼ tsp)		0.5	g
Vanilla extract	0.06 oz (⅜ tsp)		2	g
Lemon juice	1	oz	30	g
Gelatin	0.25 oz		8	g
Water, cold	2	oz	60	g
Heavy cream	1 pt		500	mL
Total weight:	**2 lb**	**3 oz**	**1105**	**g**

PROCEDURE

1. Place the cream cheese in the bowl of a mixer and mix at low speed to soften it. Add the sugar, salt, and flavorings and blend until smooth. Scrape down the sides of the bowl to eliminate lumps.

2. Blend in the lemon juice.

3. Soften the gelatin in the water, then heat the water gently until the gelatin is dissolved.

4. Whip the cream until it forms soft, not stiff, peaks. Do not overwhip.

5. Blend the warm gelatin mixture into the cream cheese mixture. Scrape down the bowl to make sure the gelatin is mixed in well.

6. Immediately fold in the cream. Do not let the cheese mixture stand after adding the gelatin, as it will set very quickly.

7. Pour the mixture into prepared molds or serving dishes. Chill until set.

--- **VARIATIONS** ---

ICEBOX CHEESECAKE

Use one of the following methods:

- Line the bottoms of cake pans or springform pans with thin sheets of sponge cake or with a crumb-crust mixture. Pour in the cream cheese Bavarian mixture and chill until set. Unmold.

- Follow the procedure for Bavarian Cream Torte (p. 458), using the cream cheese Bavarian mixture.

One full recipe is enough for one 9-in. (23-cm) cake.

THREE-CHOCOLATE BAVAROIS

Yield: three 7-in. (18-cm) Bavarians

Ingredients	U.S.		Metric
Chocolate Sponge layers (p. 410), 6 in. (15 cm) in diameter	3		3
Cocoa Vanilla Syrup (p. 254)	4	oz	125 g
Crème anglaise			
Milk	8	oz	250 g
Heavy cream	8	oz	250 g
Egg yolks	5.5	oz	160 g
Sugar	3	oz	85 g
Gelatin	0.4	oz	12 g
Semisweet chocolate, finely chopped	2.75	oz	80 g
Milk chocolate, finely chopped	2.75	oz	80 g
White chocolate, finely chopped	2.75	oz	80 g
Heavy cream	1 pt 5	oz	600 g
Cocoa Jelly (p. 429)	10	oz	300 g
White chocolate for piping (p. 637)	as needed		as needed

PROCEDURE

1. Line three 7½-in. (18-cm) charlotte rings with an acetate strip.

2. Place the rings on cake cards. Place a sponge layer in the base of each ring. (The sponge layers should be slightly smaller than the rings so there is a gap between the ring and sponge all the way around. If necessary, trim the sponge.)

3. Brush the sponge layers with the cocoa vanilla syrup.

4. Prepare the crème anglaise according to the basic procedure on page 261.

5. Soften the gelatin in cold water (see pp. 80–82). Add the gelatin to the hot crème anglaise and stir until dissolved.

6. Divide the crème anglaise into 3 equal portions. Add the dark chocolate to one bowl, the milk chocolate to the second, and the white chocolate to the third. Mix each thoroughly to melt the chocolate.

7. Whip the cream into soft peaks. Divide the whipped cream into 3 equal portions.

8. Cool the dark chocolate Bavarian over a cold-water bath until it is beginning to set. Fold in one-third of the whipped cream. Divide the chocolate Bavarian mixture among the 3 prepared charlotte rings, filling each about one-third full. Level the surfaces with an offset palette knife. Place in the refrigerator or freezer to set, approximately 20 minutes. The Bavarian should be firmly set before adding the next layer, or the layers will not be level.

9. Repeat step 8 with the milk chocolate, then with the white chocolate.

10. Place the finished layers in the freezer at least 1 hour.

11. Remove the charlottes from the freezer. Apply the cocoa jelly to the tops, running a palette knife across the top to smooth the glaze. Allow to set.

12. Decorate with piped white chocolate.

13. The ring molds may be removed at any time, but do not remove the acetate strips until ready to serve.

ALMOND CREAM

Ingredients	U.S.		Metric
Crème anglaise			
Milk	10	oz	300 g
Vanilla bean, split (see *Note*)	1		1
Sugar	2.5	oz	75 g
Egg yolks	2	oz	60 g
Marzipan	1.67	oz	50 g
Amaretto liqueur	1	oz	30 g
Gelatin	0.4	oz	12 g
Heavy cream	10	oz	300 g
Total weight:	**1 lb 11**	**oz**	**827 g**

NOTE: If vanilla beans are not available, instead add ½ tsp (2 mL) vanilla extract.

PROCEDURE

1. Make the crème anglaise: Heat the milk, vanilla bean, and half the sugar until simmering. Meanwhile, whip the egg yolks with the remaining sugar. Gradually beat in the hot milk, then return to the heat and cook until thickened just enough to coat a spoon.
2. Stir in the marzipan in small pieces until smooth.
3. Soften the gelatin in cold water (see pp. 80–82).
4. Mix in the amaretto and the softened gelatin. Stir until the gelatin is dissolved.
5. Cool the mixture over ice, stirring to make sure it stays smooth as it thickens.
6. Before the mixture sets, whip the cream to soft peaks and fold in. Pour the mixture into molds and chill until set.

PASSION FRUIT BAVARIAN

Ingredients	U.S.		Metric
Milk	7	oz	200 g
Sugar	3.5	oz	100 g
Egg yolks	4	oz (6 yolks)	120 g (6 yolks)
Sugar	3.5	oz	100 g
Gelatin	0.5	oz	14 g
Passion fruit purée or juice	7	oz	200 g
Heavy cream	14	oz	400 g
Total weight:	**2 lb 7**	**oz**	**1134 g**

PROCEDURE

1. Heat the milk and the first quantity of sugar in a pan.
2. Whip the yolks with the second quantity of sugar.
3. When the milk mixture comes to a boil, temper the yolks with one-fourth of this mix and return all to the pan. Cook to 185°F (85°C), being careful not to exceed this temperature.
4. Strain through a fine china cap.
5. Soften the gelatin in cold water (see pp. 80–82).
6. Bring the passion fruit pulp to a boil; add the gelatin and stir to dissolve. Stir over a cold-water bath until cooled to about 80°F (25°–28°C). Combine with the milk mixture.
7. Whip the cream into soft peaks. Carefully fold in the whipped cream, working quickly before the gelatin sets.
8. Pour into molds and chill.

CHARLOTTE AU CASSIS

Yield: one 7-in. (18-cm) round charlotte

Ingredients	U.S.	Metric
Plain Genoise sponge (p. 401)	Half-sheet pan, ¼ in. thick	Half-sheet pan, 0.5 cm thick
Raspberry jam	3.5 oz	100 g
Sugar	1.67 oz	50 g
Water	1.67 oz	50 g
Crème de cassis liqueur	1 oz	30 g
Mousse au Cassis (p. 534)	1 lb 4 oz	600 g
Fruit Glaçage (p. 428) made with blackcurrant (cassis) purée	2.5–3.5 oz	75–100 g
Berries and other soft fruits for decoration	as needed	as needed

PROCEDURE

1. Prepare the sponge for lining the mold. Cut one 6-in. (15-cm) circle from one end of the sponge sheet and reserve. Trim the remaining sponge to make a square about 12 in. (30 cm) on a side. Cut this square into 4 small squares of equal size. Spread 3 of the squares with raspberry jam and layer them. Top with the fourth sponge square. Press down lightly. Chill. (This makes enough for 2 charlottes; reserve the extra for later use.)

2. Line a 7-in. (18-cm) charlotte ring. (This is the same procedure as for baumkuchen, illustrated on p. 446.) Cut the sponge square into strips whose width is two-thirds to three-fourths the height of the ring molds. The exact width is not important, as long as all the strips are the same width. Cut each of these strips crosswise into strips ¼ in. (5 mm) thick. Place the ring molds on cake cards. Arrange the strips of sponge around the inside of the ring molds, pressing them into place, so the stripes of raspberry jam are vertical. Continue until the ring is compactly lined with sponge.

3. Make a syrup by boiling the sugar and water until dissolved. Remove from the heat and add the liqueur. (This small amount of syrup is enough for at least 2 or 3 charlottes.)

4. Place the sponge circle inside the ring to make a base. Brush with the syrup.

5. Fill the ring to the top with the mousse aux cassis. Level with a palette knife. Chill until set.

6. Spread the warm glaçage over the tops and level with a palette knife. Chill until set.

7. Remove the rings by warming them slightly with a blowtorch to release them, then lifting off.

8. Decorate as desired.

VARIATIONS

PASSION FRUIT CHARLOTTE

Make the following changes to the recipe:

Line the mold with yellow-striped Ribbon Sponge (p. 406), as illustrated on page 445.

In place of the cassis syrup for soaking the sponge, use a simple dessert syrup.

Substitute Passion Fruit Mousse (p. 534) for the Mousse au Cassis.

Use passion fruit purée for the glaçage. Add the seeds from one-half fresh passion fruit to the glaçage before applying to the charlotte.

The charlotte in the illustration at right is decorated with a bouquet of fruits and a free-form lattice made of piped choux pastry sprinkled with poppy seeds.

MOUSSE AU CASSIS (BLACKCURRANT MOUSSE)

Ingredients	U.S.		Metric
Gelatin	0.33 oz		10 g
Sugar	1.67 oz		50 g
Water	1 oz		30 g
Blackcurrant (cassis) purée	10 oz		300 g
Heavy cream	8 oz		250 g
Total weight:	**1 lb 5**	**oz**	**640 g**

PROCEDURE

1. Soften the gelatin in cold water (see pp. 80–82).
2. Heat the sugar and water until the sugar is dissolved. Remove from the heat and add the softened gelatin. Stir until dissolved.
3. Add the fruit purée to the gelatin mixture. Stir over ice until it begins to set.
4. Whip the cream to soft peaks and immediately fold into the fruit purée.
5. Fill molds and chill until set.

VARIATIONS

PASSION FRUIT MOUSSE

Substitute passion fruit purée for the blackcurrant purée in the main recipe. Omit the sugar and water syrup and instead use a syrup made of the following ingredients. Heat the water and sugar until dissolved. Remove from the heat and add the vodka.

Ingredients	U.S.	Metric
Sugar	1 oz	27 g
Water	1 oz	27 g
Vodka	0.5 oz	16 g

NOUGATINE CREAM

Ingredients	U.S.		Metric
Gelatin	0.25 oz		7.5 g
Pastry Cream (p. 263)	11 oz		320 g
Sugar	3 oz		85 g
Nougatine (p. 658), crushed	8.5 oz		250 g
Kirsch	1.25 oz		35 g
Heavy cream	2 lb 6 oz		1100 g
Total weight:	**3 lb 14**	**oz**	**1797 g**

PROCEDURE

1. Soften the gelatin in cold water (see pp. 80–82).
2. Heat the pastry cream just until hot.
3. Add the softened gelatin and sugar. Stir until dissolved.
4. Add the nougatine.
5. When the temperature has dropped to about 85°F (30°C), stir in the kirsch.
6. Whip the cream into soft peaks and fold it into the mixture.
7. Pour into the desired molds and chill.

PRALINE CREAM I

Ingredients	U.S.		Metric
Gelatin	0.12	oz	3 g
Pastry Cream (p. 263), freshly made and warm	10	oz	250 g
Praline paste	2	oz	50 g
Heavy cream	8	oz	200 g
Total weight:	**1 lb 4**	**oz**	**503 g**

PROCEDURE

1. Soften the gelatin in cold water (see pp. 80–82).
2. Add the gelatin to the pastry cream and stir until dissolved.
3. Add the praline paste and mix in.
4. Cool the mixture to about 75°–80°F (25°C). Whip the cream into soft peaks and mix about one-fourth of it into the mixture.
5. Fold in the remaining whipped cream.
6. Pour into desired molds and chill.

PRALINE CREAM II

Ingredients	U.S.		Metric
Pastry Cream (p. 263)	9	oz	225 g
Praline paste	3.5	oz	90 g
Gelatin	0.25	oz	6 g
Coffee liqueur	0.75	oz	20 g
Nougatine (p. 658), crushed	3	oz	75 g
Heavy cream	8	oz	200 g
Total weight:	**1 lb 8**	**oz**	**616 g**

PROCEDURE

1. Whip the pastry cream until smooth. Beat in the praline paste until well mixed in.
2. Soften the gelatin in cold water (see pp. 80–82).
3. Heat the coffee liqueur. Add the gelatin and stir until dissolved, rewarming as necessary.
4. Beat the gelatin mixture into the pastry cream. Chill.
5. Beat in the crushed nougatine.
6. Whip the cream until it forms soft peaks. Fold in.

BANANA MOUSSE

Ingredients	U.S.		Metric
Gelatin	0.33	oz	8 g
Banana pulp, fresh or frozen	12	oz	310 g
Lemon juice	1	oz	25 g
Sugar	1.33	oz	35 g
White rum	1	oz	25 g
Heavy cream	1 lb		420 g
Total weight:	**1 lb 15**	**oz**	**823 g**

PROCEDURE

1. Soften the gelatin in cold water (see pp. 80–82).
2. Heat one-third of the banana pulp to 140°F (60°C). Add the gelatin and stir until dissolved.
3. Mix in the lemon juice and sugar. Stir to dissolve the sugar.
4. Add this mixture to the remaining banana pulp and mix in the rum.
5. Once this mixture has cooled to about 75°F (25°F), fold in the whipped cream.
6. Fill molds and chill.

L'EXOTIQUE

Yield: one 6½-in. (16-cm) gâteau

Ingredients	U.S.	Metric
Ribbon Sponge (p. 406)	see step 1	see step 1
Hazelnut Coconut Sponge layers (p. 344) 6 in. (15 cm) in diameter	2	2
Coconut Mousse with Tropical Fruit (p. 537)	14 oz	400 g
Gelatin	0.13 oz	4 g
Mango pulp	4 oz	125 g
Sugar	0.4 oz (2¾ tsp)	12 g
Passion Fruit Ganache (p. 273), warm	6 oz	175 g
Decoration		
Chocolate for spraying	as needed	as needed
Mango wedges	as needed	as needed
Passion fruit seeds and pulp	as needed	as needed

PROCEDURE

1. Line a 6½-in. (16-cm) charlotte ring with a strip of acetate. Prepare a multicolored sheet of ribbon sponge with an abstract pattern, as shown on p. 406. Cut a strip and line the charlotte ring as on p. 445, making the strip slightly narrower than the height of the ring so some of the filling shows above it.

2. Place the ring on a cake card and put one of the sponge layers in the bottom.

3. Fill about one-third full with the coconut mousse. Smooth the top and chill until set.

4. Soften the gelatin in cold water (see pp. 80–82).

5. Heat about one-quarter of the mango pulp to 140°F (60°C), then stir in the gelatin and sugar until they are dissolved. Add the remaining mango pulp and stir.

6. Once the mousse has set, spread the jellied mango pulp on top of the coconut mousse. Place in the freezer to set.

7. Spread a thin layer of the coconut mousse (about ½ in./1 cm thick) on top of the mango.

8. Cover with the second layer of the sponge.

9. Finish with a third layer of the mousse, filling the mold to the top and leveling it. Place in the freezer to set.

10. Spread a layer of warm ganache ½ in. (1 cm) thick over the frozen cake. (This depth is necessary because so much ganache is removed by the cake comb.) Before the ganache sets, quickly pass a cake comb over the top to make a design.

11. Return to the freezer for 15 minutes to set.

12. Spray the top with a chocolate sprayer (see p. 637) to leave a velvety finish.

13. Remove the ring. Decorate the top with a few wedges of mango and a few passion fruit seeds.

COCONUT MOUSSE WITH TROPICAL FRUIT

Yield: about 1 lb 12 oz (800 g)

Ingredients	U.S.		Metric
Water	4	oz	120 g
Coconut milk, unsweetened	4	oz	120 g
Sugar	7	oz	200 g
Mango, diced	5	oz	150 g
Pineapple, diced	5	oz	150 g
Gelatin	0.2	oz	6 g
Milk	1.67	oz	50 g
Sugar	1	oz	30 g
Coconut, grated	1	oz	30 g
Coconut milk, unsweetened, chilled	4.5	oz	140 g
Coconut-flavored liqueur	4	tsp	20 g
Heavy cream	8	oz	250 g

PROCEDURE

1. For the fruit, heat together the water, coconut milk, and sugar to make a syrup. Add the diced mango and pineapple. Cover the surface with a round of parchment and poach the fruit for about 15 minutes, or until it is tender but still holding its shape. Do not overcook. Allow the fruit to cool in the syrup and then drain.
2. Soften the gelatin in cold water (see pp. 80–82).
3. Heat the milk, sugar, and coconut in a saucepan to about 175°F (80°C). Let stand a few minutes to allow the coconut to infuse.
4. Remove from the heat and add the gelatin, stirring to dissolve.
5. Add the second quantity of coconut milk. When the temperature has cooled to about 75°F (25°C), stir in the liqueur.
6. Whip the cream to soft peaks and fold in.
7. Fold in the drained fruit.
8. Pour into molds and chill.

CHOCOLATE MOUSSE III

Yield: about 2⅜ pt (1.12 L)

Ingredients	U.S.		Metric
Bittersweet chocolate	10	oz	300 g
Water	2.5	oz	75 g
Egg yolks, pasteurized	3	oz	90 g
Liqueur (see *Note*)	1	oz	30 g
Egg whites, pasteurized	4.5	oz	135 g
Sugar	2	oz	60 g
Heavy cream	8	oz	250 mL
Total weight:	**1 lb 15**	**oz**	**940 g**

NOTE: Any appropriate liqueur or spirit, such as orange liqueur, amaretto, rum, or brandy, may be used. If you don't wish to use a liqueur, use 1 oz (30 mL) strong coffee or 1½ tsp (8 mL) vanilla plus 1½ tbsp (22 mL) water.

PROCEDURE

1. In a saucepan, add the chocolate to the water and melt it over low heat, stirring constantly so the mixture is smooth.
2. Beat in the egg yolks. Whip the mixture over low heat for a few minutes until it thickens slightly.
3. Remove the mixture from the heat and stir in the liqueur or other liquid. Cool it completely.
4. Whip the egg whites with the sugar to form a firm meringue. Fold it into the chocolate mixture.
5. Whip the cream until it forms soft peaks. Fold it into the chocolate mixture.
6. Pour the mousse into serving bowls or individual dishes. Chill for several hours before serving.

CHOCOLATE MOUSSE IV

Yield: about 1¾ qt (1.75 L)

Ingredients	U.S.		Metric
Bittersweet chocolate	1 lb		500 g
Butter	4	oz	125 g
Egg yolks, pasteurized	6	oz	180 g
Egg whites, pasteurized	8	oz	250 g
Sugar	2.5	oz	75 g
Heavy cream	8	oz	250 mL
Total weight:	**2 lb 12**	**oz**	**1380 g**

PROCEDURE

1. Melt the chocolate in a dry pan over a hot-water bath.
2. Remove from the heat. Add the butter and stir until melted.
3. Add the egg yolks, mixing well.
4. Whip the egg whites with the sugar to form a soft meringue. Fold into the chocolate mixture.
5. Whip the cream until it forms soft peaks. Fold it into the chocolate mixture.
6. Transfer the mousse to serving bowls or individual dishes. Chill for several hours before serving.

— **VARIATIONS** —

The following variations are based on the above recipe. A few modifications are necessary to account for the different composition and handling properties of milk chocolate and white chocolate.

MILK CHOCOLATE MOUSSE

Substitute milk chocolate for the dark chocolate in the main recipe. Melt the chocolate with 4 oz (125 mL) water, stirring until smooth. Remove from the heat and proceed with step 2 of the procedure. Reduce the quantity of yolks to 2 oz (60 g). Reduce the quantity of sugar to 2 oz (60 g).

WHITE CHOCOLATE MOUSSE

Substitute white chocolate for milk chocolate in the preceding variation.

CHOCOLATE MOUSSE V (WITH GELATIN)

Ingredients	U.S.		Metric
Gelatin	0.2	oz	6 g
Sugar	1.67	oz	50 g
Water	1.67	oz	50 g
Glucose	0.33	oz	10 g
Egg yolks	2.67 oz (4 yolks)		80 g (4 yolks)
Bittersweet chocolate couverture, melted	7.25	oz	225 g
Heavy cream	1 lb		500 g
Italian Meringue (p. 259)	6	oz	180 g
Total weight:	**2 lb 3**	**oz**	**1100 g**

PROCEDURE

1. Soften the gelatin in cold water (see pp. 80–82).
2. Combine the sugar, water, and glucose and bring to a boil to make a syrup. Cook to 245°F (119°C).
3. Whip the egg yolks until thick and pale. Gradually beat in the hot syrup. Add the gelatin and beat until dissolved. Continue whipping until cold.
4. Fold the melted chocolate into the egg yolk mixture.
5. Whip the cream into soft peaks. Fold in.
6. Fold in the Italian meringue. Pour into molds and chill until set.

CHOCOLATE TERRINE

Ingredients	U.S.	Metric
Bittersweet chocolate	12 oz	375 g
Eggs whites, pasteurized	6 oz (6 whites)	175 g (6 whites)
Orange liqueur	2 oz	60 mL
Egg yolks, pasteurized	4 oz (6 yolks)	120 g (6 yolks)
Cocoa powder	as needed	as needed
Total weight:	**1 lb 8 oz**	**730 g**

--- VARIATION ---

Substitute 3 oz (90 g) strong espresso for the orange liqueur.

PROCEDURE

1. For each 12 oz (375 g) chocolate, prepare a 1-pt (500-mL) loaf pan by lining it with parchment. (For broader slices of the finished terrine, double the recipe and use a 1-qt/1-L loaf pan.)

2. Chop the chocolate into small pieces, then melt it over warm water. Do not allow any water to get into the chocolate.

3. Whip the egg whites until they form soft peaks. Set aside. (It is necessary to whip the egg whites before beginning to mix the chocolate because once you add the first liquid to the chocolate, you must continue the procedure without interruption.)

4. Add the orange liqueur to the chocolate and beat in. The chocolate will become very thick.

5. Beat the yolks into the chocolate, 1 or 2 at a time, until well blended.

6. Using a stiff whip, beat the egg whites into the chocolate mixture. Do not try to fold them in gently, as the mixture is too stiff.

7. To create the necessary smooth texture, force the mixture through a sieve to remove lumps of unblended chocolate or egg.

8. Pour some of the chocolate into the prepared pan(s), filling them to about halfway. Rap the pans on the bench sharply to remove air bubbles. Fill with the remaining chocolate, and again remove air bubbles.

9. Cover and refrigerate overnight.

10. Unmold onto a platter. Dust the top and sides lightly with cocoa powder. Slice about ¼ in. (6 mm) thick using a sharp, thin-bladed knife dipped into hot water and wiped dry before each slice. Serve small portions, as this dessert is very rich.

CHOCOLATE INDULGENCE

Yield: 2 gâteaux, 7 in. (18 cm) in diameter

Ingredients	U.S.	Metric
To line mold		
Joconde Sponge Cake (p. 405)	1 half-sheet pan	1 half-sheet pan
Ganache I (p. 541)	as needed	as needed
Ganache II (p. 541)	as needed	as needed
Syrup		
Water	2 oz	60 g
Sugar	2 oz	60 g
Orange liqueur, such as Cointreau	2 oz	60 g
Chocolate Mousse V (p. 538)	about 2 lb	900–1000 g
Ganache Icing (p. 427)	7 oz	200 g
Suggested decoration		
Chocolate fans (p. 635)	as needed	as needed
Cocoa powder	as needed	as needed
Fresh berries	as needed	as needed
Chocolate cigarettes (p. 635)	as needed	as needed

PROCEDURE

1. Prepare the joconde sponge cake for lining the mold. Cut two 6-in. (15-cm) circles from one end of the sponge sheet and reserve. Trim the remaining sponge to make a square about 12 in. (30 cm) on a side. Cut this square into 4 small squares of equal size. Spread one with a thin layer of Ganache I. Top with a second square and spread with a layer of Ganache II. Top with a third square and spread with a layer of Ganache I. Top with the fourth sponge square. Press down lightly. Chill. (To simplify production, omit the Ganache II and use Ganache I for all 3 layers.)

2. Line two 7-in. (18-cm) charlotte rings. (This is the same procedure as for baumkuchen, illustrated on p. 446.) Cut the sponge square into strips whose width is two-thirds to three-fourths the height of the ring molds. The exact width is not important, as long as all the strips are the same width. Cut each of these strips crosswise into strips ¼ in. (5 mm) thick. Place the ring molds on cake cards. Arrange the strips of sponge around the inside of the ring molds, pressing them into place, so the stripes of ganache are vertical. Continue until both rings are compactly lined with sponge.

3. Make a syrup by boiling the sugar and water until dissolved. Remove from the heat and add the liqueur.

4. Place one of the sponge circles inside each ring to make a base. Brush with the syrup.

5. Prepare the chocolate mousse and fill the rings to the top with the mousse. Level with a palette knife. Chill until set.

6. Spread the warm ganache icing over the tops and level with a palette knife. Chill until set.

7. Remove the rings by warming them slightly with a blowtorch to release them, then lift off.

8. Decorate as desired.

GANACHE I

Yield: 1 lb (450 g)

Ingredients	U.S.	Metric	PROCEDURE
Dark chocolate, chopped	7 oz	200 g	1. Melt the chocolate in a water bath. 2. Heat the cream and mix into the chocolate. 3. Chill.
Heavy cream	9 oz	250 g	

GANACHE II

Yield: 1 lb 4 oz (575 g)

Ingredients	U.S.	Metric	PROCEDURE
White couverture, chopped	1 lb	450 g	1. Melt the white couverture in a water bath. 2. Heat the cream and mix in. Add a little red coloring to give a pale pink color. 3. Chill.
Heavy cream	4.5 oz	125 g	
Red coloring	few drops	few drops	

DESSERT SOUFFLÉS

SOUFFLÉS ARE LIGHTENED with beaten egg whites and then baked. Baking causes the *soufflé* to rise like a cake because the air in the egg foam expands when heated. Toward the end of the baking time the egg whites coagulate, or become firm. However, soufflés are not as stable as cakes; in fact, they fall shortly after they are removed from the oven. For this reason, they should be served immediately.

A standard soufflé consists of three elements:

1. **Base.** Many kinds of bases are used for dessert soufflés; most are heavy, starch-thickened preparations, such as pastry creams or sweetened white sauces. If egg yolks are used, they are added to the base.

2. **Flavoring ingredients.** These are added to the base and mixed in well. Popular flavorings include melted chocolate, lemon, and liqueurs. Small quantities of solid ingredients such as dried candied fruits or finely chopped nuts may also be added. The base and flavor mixture may be prepared ahead of time and kept refrigerated. Portions can then be scaled to order and mixed with egg whites.

3. **Egg whites.** Whenever possible, egg whites should be whipped with some of the sugar. This makes dessert soufflés more stable.

Butter soufflé dishes well and coat them with sugar. Fill dishes to the rim and level off with a spatula. When baked, the soufflé should rise 1–1½ in. (2.5–4 cm) above the rim.

KEY POINTS TO REVIEW

- What are the steps in the procedure for preparing Bavarian cream?
- What is a cold charlotte?
- What is a mousse? Which ingredient or ingredients give a mousse its light, airy texture?
- What are the three basic components of a hot dessert soufflé?

VANILLA SOUFFLÉ

Yield: 10–12 portions

Ingredients	U.S.		Metric
Bread flour	3	oz	90 g
Butter	3	oz	90 g
Milk	1 pt		500 mL
Sugar	4	oz	120 g
Egg yolks	6	oz (8–9 yolks)	180 g (8–9 yolks)
Vanilla extract		0.33 oz (2 tsp)	10 mL
Egg whites	10	oz (10 whites)	300 g (10 whites)
Sugar	2	oz	60 g

VARIATIONS

CHOCOLATE SOUFFLÉ

Melt together 3 oz (90 g) unsweetened chocolate and 1 oz (30 g) semisweet chocolate. Add to the base after step 5.

LEMON SOUFFLÉ

Instead of vanilla, use the grated zest of 2 lemons for flavoring.

LIQUEUR SOUFFLÉ

Flavor with 2–3 oz (60–90 mL) desired liqueur, such as kirsch or orange liqueur, added after step 5.

COFFEE SOUFFLÉ

Flavor with 2 tbsp (15 g) instant coffee powder, or to taste, added to the milk in step 2.

PRALINE SOUFFLÉ

Blend 4–5 oz (125–150 g) praline paste with the base after step 5.

PROCEDURE

1. Work the flour and butter together to form a paste.
2. Dissolve the sugar in the milk and bring to a boil. Remove from the heat.
3. With a wire whip, beat in the flour paste. Beat vigorously to remove all lumps.
4. Return the mixture to the heat and bring it to a boil, beating constantly. Simmer for several minutes until the mixture is very thick and no starchy taste remains (a).
5. Transfer the mixture to a mixing bowl. Cover and let cool 5–10 minutes.
6. Beat in the egg yolks and vanilla (b).
7. Soufflés may be prepared ahead of time up to this point. Chill the mixture and scale portions of the base to order. Proceed with the following steps.
8. Prepare soufflé dishes by buttering the insides well and then coating with granulated sugar. The butter and sugar coating should come all the way to the top and slightly over the rim (c). This recipe will fill 10–12 single-portion dishes or two 7-in. (18-cm) dishes.
9. Whip the egg whites until they form soft peaks. Add the sugar and whip until the mixture forms firm, moist peaks.
10. Fold the egg whites into the soufflé base (d).
11. Pour the mixture into the prepared baking dishes and smooth the tops.
12. Bake at 375°F (190°C). Approximate baking times are 30 minutes for large dishes, 15 minutes for single-portion dishes.
13. *Optional step:* 3–4 minutes before soufflés are done, dust the tops generously with confectioners' sugar.
14. Serve as soon as removed from the oven.

A

B

C

D

TERMS FOR REVIEW

custard	cornstarch pudding	pot de crème	cold charlotte
stirred custard	cream pudding	Christmas pudding	rice impératrice
baked custard	panna cotta	Bavarian cream	mousse
crème anglaise	crémeux	Bavarois	soufflé
pastry cream			

QUESTIONS FOR REVIEW

1. What is the internal temperature at which the eggs in custard mixtures become cooked or coagulated? What happens to stirred custards and baked custards if they are cooked beyond this point?

2. The basic techniques used to make crème anglaise and baked custard are also used for some of the following preparations. Identify which of the following desserts are made using a stirred custard (custard sauce) technique, which are made using a baked custard technique, and which are made without any custard.

Bread pudding	Apple cobbler
Christmas pudding	Charlotte russe
Chocolate Bavarian	Chocolate pots de crème
Baked cheesecake	Apple charlotte

3. What is the main difference between cornstarch pudding and cream pudding?

4. In the production of Bavarian creams and other desserts stabilized with gelatin, why is it important to measure the gelatin carefully?

5. When making a Bavarian or chiffon pie filling, what difficulty would you encounter if you chilled the gelatin mixture too long before folding in the whipped cream or egg whites?

6. When making dessert soufflés, what is the advantage of adding part of the sugar to the whipped egg whites?

20

FROZEN DESSERTS

AFTER READING THIS CHAPTER, YOU SHOULD BE ABLE TO:

1. Judge the quality of ice creams and sorbets and common ice cream and sorbet desserts.
2. Prepare ice creams and sorbets.
3. Prepare still-frozen desserts, including bombes, frozen mousses, and frozen soufflés.

THE POPULARITY OF ice cream needs no explanation. Whether it is a plain scoop of vanilla ice cream in a dish or an elaborate assemblage of fruits, syrups, toppings, and numerous flavors of ice cream and sherbet, a frozen dessert appeals to everyone.

Until recently, few establishments made their own ice cream because of the labor involved, the equipment required, and the sanitation regulations and health codes that had to be followed. Furthermore, the wide availability of high-quality commercially produced ice creams made it unnecessary for operations to prepare their own. But today, many restaurants find that offering their own homemade sorbets and ice creams is appealing to customers. In fact, in the finest restaurants, customers may expect the pastry chef to produce frozen desserts as well as pastries. Thus, learning to make ice cream has become an important skill.

You will find that much of this chapter seems familiar. The base for ice cream, for example, is the same crème anglaise you have used in many other preparations. Other techniques, too, in this chapter, such as preparing syrups and whipping meringues, are used in many areas of the bakeshop.

IDENTIFYING QUALITY ICE CREAM AND SORBET DESSERTS

ICE CREAM AND sherbet are churn-frozen, meaning they are mixed constantly while being frozen. If they were not churned, they would freeze into solid blocks of ice. The churning keeps the ice crystals small and incorporates air into the dessert.

In this section we identify ice cream and sorbet products, learn how to judge the quality of frozen desserts, and look at some traditional frozen dessert combinations. This discussion applies to both commercially made and home-made ice creams and sorbets.

Types of Frozen Dessert Products

Ice cream is a smooth, frozen mixture of milk, cream, sugar, flavorings, and, sometimes, eggs. *Philadelphia-style ice cream* contains no eggs, and *French-style ice cream* contains egg yolks. The eggs add richness and help make a smoother product because of the emulsifying properties of the yolks.

Ice milk is like ice cream, but with a lower butterfat content. *Frozen yogurt* contains yogurt in addition to the normal ingredients for ice cream or ice milk.

Sherbets and *ices* are usually made from fruit juices, water, and sugar. American sherbets usually contain milk or cream and, sometimes, egg whites. The egg whites increase smoothness and volume. Ices, also called *water ices,* contain only fruit juice, water, sugar, and, sometimes, egg whites; they do not contain milk products. The French word *sorbet* (pronounced sor BAY) is sometimes used for these products. *Granité* (pronounced grah nee TAY) is coarse, crystalline ice, made without egg whites.

Italian versions of ice cream, sorbet, and granité are called *gelato* (plural, *gelati*), *sorbetto* (plural, *sorbetti*), and *granita* (plural in Italian, *granite*; or, in common English usage, *granitas*). Traditional Italian gelato (which means, basically, "frozen") is usually lower in fat than other ice creams. Gelato flavors such as vanilla and chocolate are often made with milk only, and no cream. Fruit gelati often contain cream, but because they are mostly fruit purée, they are still low in fat. In addition, many gelati are made without egg yolks, and most are made without other emulsifiers and stabilizers. Thus, they melt quickly and have a light texture and flavor in the mouth. On the other hand, they are mixed less than ice creams and have low *overrun* (defined below), contributing to a rich *mouth feel* (also defined on the next page).

Production and Quality

A basic French- or custard-style ice cream mix is simply a crème anglaise or custard sauce mixed with 1 or 2 parts heavy cream for every 4 parts milk used in the sauce. This base is flavored, as desired, with vanilla, melted chocolate, instant coffee, sweetened crushed strawberries, and so on, chilled thoroughly, and then frozen according to the instructions for the particular equipment in use.

When the mix has frozen, it is transferred to containers and placed in a deep freeze at below 0°F (−18°C) to harden. (Soft-frozen or soft-serve ice creams and gelati are served directly as they come from the churn freezer, without being hardened.)

Whether you make ice cream or buy it, you should be aware of three quality factors:

1. **Smoothness** is related to the size of the ice crystals in the product. Ice cream should be frozen rapidly and churned well during freezing so large crystals don't have a chance to form.

    Rapid hardening helps keep crystals small, as do eggs and emulsifiers or stabilizers added to the mix.

    Large crystals may form if ice cream is not stored at a low-enough temperature (below 0°F/−18°C).

2. *Overrun* is the increase in volume due to incorporation of air when freezing ice cream. It is expressed as a percentage of the original volume of the mix. For example, if the mixture

doubles in volume, then the amount of increase is equal to the original volume, and the overrun is 100%.

Some overrun is necessary to give a smooth, light texture. If ice cream has too much overrun, it is airy and foamy and lacks flavor. It was once thought that ice cream should have from 80 to 100% overrun, and that less would make it heavy and pasty. This may be true for ice creams containing gums and other stabilizers, but some high-quality manufacturers produce rich (and expensive) ice cream with as little as 20% overrun.

Overrun is affected by many factors, including the type of freezing equipment, the length of churning time, the fat content of the mix, the percentage of solids in the mix, and how full the freezer is.

3. **Mouth feel**, or body, depends, in part, on smoothness and overrun, as well as other qualities. Good ice cream melts in the mouth to a smooth, not too heavy liquid. Some ice creams have so many stabilizers they never melt to a liquid. Unfortunately, many people are so accustomed to these products that an ice cream that actually does melt in the mouth strikes them as "not rich enough."

Butterfat from cream contributes to a rich mouth feel. However, too high a fat content can detract from the texture. This is because, when fat content is especially high, some of the fat may congeal into tiny lumps of butter during churn-freezing, producing a grainy texture.

A good gelato has a light, smooth mouth feel, attributable to low fat content and lack of emulsifiers, combined with low overrun.

Storage and Service

Five guidelines are essential to the proper storage and service of churn-frozen desserts:

1. Store ice creams and sherbets below 0°F (–18°C). This low temperature helps prevent the formation of large ice crystals.

2. To prepare for serving, temper frozen desserts at 8° to 15°F (–13° to –9°C) for 24 hours so they will be soft enough to serve.

3. When serving, avoid packing the ice cream. The best method is to draw the scoop across the surface of the product so the product rolls into a ball in the scoop.

4. Use standard scoops for portioning ice cream. Normal portions for popular desserts are as follows:

Parfait	Three No. 30 scoops
Banana split	Three No. 30 scoops
À la mode topping for pie or cake	One No. 20 scoop
Sundae	Two No. 20 scoops
Plain dish of ice cream	One No. 10, 12, or 16 scoop

5. Measure syrups, toppings, and garnishes for portion control. For syrups, use pumps that dispense measured quantities, or use standard ladles.

Popular Ice Cream Desserts

Parfaits are made by alternating layers of ice cream and fruit or syrup in tall, narrow glasses. They are usually named after the syrup or topping. For example, a chocolate parfait has three scoops of vanilla or chocolate ice cream alternating with layers of chocolate syrup, and topped with whipped cream and shaved chocolate. (This is the most common meaning of the term *parfait* in North America. See page 558 for the original parfait.)

Sundaes or *coupes* consist of one or two scoops of ice cream or sherbet placed in a dish or glass and topped with any of a number of syrups, fruits, toppings, and garnishes. They are quick to prepare, unlimited in variety, and as simple or as elegant as you wish—served in an ordinary soda fountain glass or in a silver cup or crystal champagne glass.

Coupes are often elegant, attractively decorated desserts. Many types have been handed down from the classic cuisine of years ago. The following are classic coupes and similar desserts that still may be made today, but often with different names (the classical names are given as a point of interest, but with the exception of Peach Melba, Pear Belle Hélène, and Coupe au Marrons, they aren't often used today).

ICE CREAM STABILIZERS

Recall from earlier discussions of emulsions (pp. 67, 375) that fat and water, normally unmixable, can be combined into a stable mixture called an emulsion. Emulsions are essential for the smooth texture of ice cream, which contain water and butterfat.

A problem faced by commercially produced ice creams is that as temperatures change during shipping and storage, some of the water in ice cream can melt and refreeze, damaging the emulsion and, therefore, the texture of the product.

Ice cream manufacturers minimize this problem by adding a variety of stabilizers not generally found in high-quality homemade or artisan ice creams. Commonly used stabilizers include agar, carrageenan, guar gum, gelatin, pectin, and sodium alginate. These ingredients, when used in tiny quantities (from 0.15 to 0.5% of the mix), help prevent ice crystal formation when storage temperature fluctuates.

Coupe Arlesienne. In the bottom of the cup, place a spoonful of diced candied fruits that have been soaked in kirsch. Add a scoop of vanilla ice cream, top with a poached pear half, and coat with apricot sauce.

Coupe Black Forest. Place a scoop of chocolate ice cream in the cup and add sweet, dark cherries flavored with a little cherry brandy. Decorate with rosettes of whipped cream and shaved chocolate.

Coupe Edna May. Top vanilla ice cream with sweet cherries. Decorate with whipped cream mixed with enough raspberry purée to color it pink.

Coupe Gressac. Top vanilla ice cream with three small almond macaroons moistened with kirsch. Top with a small poached peach half, cut side up, and fill the center of the peach with red currant jelly. Decorate with a border of whipped cream.

Coupe Jacques. Place a scoop each of lemon sherbet and strawberry ice cream in a cup. Top with a mixture of diced, fresh fruit flavored with kirsch.

Coupe aux Marrons. Top vanilla ice cream with candied chestnuts (marrons glacés) and whipped cream.

Coupe Orientale. Place diced pineapple in the bottom of the cup and add pineapple sherbet. Top with apricot sauce and toasted almonds.

Peach Melba. Top vanilla ice cream with a poached peach half covered with Melba Sauce (p. 270) and topped with slivered almonds.

Pear Belle Hélène. Top vanilla ice cream with a poached pear half covered with chocolate sauce and garnished with toasted, sliced almonds.

Among other popular ice cream desserts mentioned earlier in this book are Meringues Glacèes (p. 346) and Frozen Éclairs and Profiteroles (p. 331). The popular festive dessert called *baked Alaska* is discussed in the Procedure for Making Baked Alaska. Although no one is surprised by it anymore, one of the classic names for this dessert is Soufflè Surprise, so called because it looks like baked whipped eggs on the outside but is frozen inside.

PROCEDURE: Making Baked Alaska

1. Pack softened ice cream into a dome-shaped mold of the desired size. Freeze solid.
2. Prepare a layer of sponge cake the same size as the flat side of the mold and about ½ in. (12 mm) thick.
3. Unmold the frozen ice cream onto the cake layer so the cake forms the base for the ice cream.
4. With a spatula, cover the entire dessert with a thick layer of meringue. If desired, decorate with more meringue forced from a pastry bag.
5. Bake at 450°F (230°C) until the raised edges of the meringue decorations turn golden brown.
6. Serve immediately.

KEY POINTS TO REVIEW

▪ What do the following terms mean as related to frozen desserts: Smoothness? Overrun? Mouth feel?

▪ How should frozen desserts be stored and served?

▪ What are sundaes? How are they prepared?

▪ What is baked Alaska? How is it prepared?

PREPARING ICE CREAMS AND SORBETS

THE SAME QUALITY factors that apply to commercially made frozen desserts, described above, apply to those you make yourself.

The first two recipes that follow illustrate the basic procedures for making ice cream and sorbet. Using the procedures in these two recipes, you can make an unlimited variety of frozen desserts, as exemplified by the many variations that follow each main recipe. Following these basic recipes are additional recipes for specialty ice creams and sorbets.

Ice Cream Production

As in other areas in the bakeshop, accurate measurement of ingredients is important. In the case of frozen desserts, proper measurement is important to ensure the mix freezes properly. This is because the ratio of sugar weight to total weight has a strong effect on freezing. If an ice cream or sorbet mix contains too much sugar, it will not freeze enough to become firm. On the other hand, an ice cream with too little sugar will not be as smooth as one with the correct amount.

For a basic vanilla ice cream, the weight of the sugar is usually 16 to 20% of the total weight. Adding other ingredients makes the calculation more complicated because many ingredients, such as fruits, contain sugar. When you are developing new recipes, test a small batch of the mixture to see how hard it freezes, and increase or decrease the quantity of sugar as necessary.

Ice creams have a better texture when the finished mix is refrigerated for about 12 hours before freezing. This maturing time enables the proteins of the eggs and milk to bond with more of the water molecules in the mixture. This bonding leaves fewer water molecules available to form ice crystals, which can give ice cream a grainy texture.

Careful sanitation procedures are critical to ice cream production because the ice cream mix is a good breeding ground for bacteria. Use equipment made of stainless steel or other nonporous and noncorrosive material, and properly clean and sanitize it after every use.

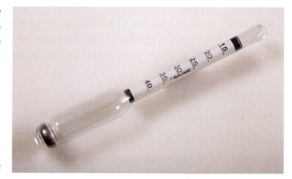

Hydrometer.

Sorbet Production

A basic sorbet mixture is simply a sugar syrup mixed with flavoring ingredients. For sorbets, the proportion of sugar in the mix is even more crucial to the texture of the final product than it is for ice cream, because sorbets do not contain the cream or egg yolks that contribute to the smooth texture of ice cream. Rather, the size of the ice crystals is the most important factor in texture.

The sugar content of fruit varies with its ripeness and other factors. Therefore, testing the sugar concentration of sorbet mix is the surest way to achieve proper texture. Sugar concentration can be measured with a hydrometer, also called a *saccharometer* (see photo, top right). Basic measurement of sugar concentration, using the Brix and Baumé scales, is discussed on page 252. For best freezing, sorbet mixtures should be at a concentration of 30° to 32.5° Brix or 16° to 18° Baumé (see photo, lower right). If the sugar density is too high, dilute with a little water. If it is too low, add a little sugar syrup to increase the sugar content.

Rapid freezing produces smaller ice crystals, and thus smoother texture, than slow freezing. For sorbets as well as for ice creams, chill the mixture well before freezing so it freezes in the shortest possible time.

Using a little corn syrup in place of some of the sugar for the syrup may also contribute slightly to smoothness in some sorbets. Classic sorbets, however, are based on a syrup made only with regular granulated sugar. Using corn syrup in a syrup for sorbets darkens it somewhat, because of increased browning of the sugars and starches in the corn syrup. This may be a disadvantage for some white or light-colored sorbets.

For granitas, unlike for sorbets, large crystals are characteristic of the product and are desirable. Classic granitas are made with sorbetlike mixes, but with two differences: First, the sugar content is slightly lower, so the ice crystals are larger. Second, rather than being churn-frozen, the mixture is still-frozen in a pan and stirred periodically as it freezes. This freezing method gives granitas their typical icy texture.

Testing a sorbet mix with a hydrometer.

VANILLA ICE CREAM

Yield: about 2 qt (2 L), depending on overrun

Ingredients	U.S.	Metric
Egg yolks	8 oz (12 yolks)	250 g (12 yolks)
Sugar	12 oz	375 g
Milk	2 pt	1 L
Heavy cream	1 pt	500 mL
Vanilla extract	2 tsp	10 mL
Salt	pinch	pinch

PROCEDURE

1. Vanilla ice cream mix is basically a custard sauce or crème anglaise with the addition of heavy cream. Review the guidelines for preparing crème anglaise on page 260.

2. Combine the egg yolks and sugar in a bowl. Whip until thick and light.

3. Scald the milk and gradually beat it into the egg mixture.

4. Heat the mixture over a hot-water bath or in a double boiler, stirring constantly, until it thickens enough to coat the back of a spoon. Immediately remove from the heat.

5. Stir in the cold cream to stop the cooking. Add the vanilla and salt. (Note: If you are not using freshly opened, pasteurized cream, it is best to scald and cool the cream, or else to heat it with the milk in step 3. In this case, set the cooked custard in an ice-water bath as soon as it is cooked, to stop the cooking.)

6. Chill the mixture thoroughly. Refrigerate overnight to mature the mix (see p. 549).

7. Freeze in an ice cream freezer according to the manufacturer's directions.

VARIATIONS

For a less rich ice cream, substitute milk for part of the cream. In addition, the quantity of egg yolks may be decreased to 4 oz (125 g).

VANILLA BEAN ICE CREAM

Split 1 or 2 vanilla beans, scrape out the seeds, and simmer the seeds and pods with the cream. Cool. Remove and discard the pods. Omit the vanilla extract from the basic recipe.

CHOCOLATE ICE CREAM

Reduce the sugar to 9 oz (280 g). Melt together 4 oz (125 g) unsweetened chocolate and 4 oz (125 g) bittersweet chocolate. When the custard has cooled to tepid, carefully stir it into the melted chocolate. Reduce the cream to 12 oz (375 mL).

CINNAMON ICE CREAM

Add 1 tbsp (5 g) cinnamon to the egg mixture before cooking.

COFFEE ICE CREAM

Flavor the hot custard mix to taste with instant coffee powder or instant espresso powder.

CAROB ICE CREAM

After adding the scalded milk to the egg mixture, beat in 3 oz (90 g) roasted carob powder. Proceed as in basic recipe.

COCONUT ICE CREAM

Reduce the number of egg yolks to 4 oz (125 g). Reduce the sugar to 4 oz (125 g). Add 12 fl oz (375 mL) canned, sweetened coconut cream to the yolks and sugar. Omit the heavy cream and vanilla. Stir the cooked mix over ice until cold, to prevent the coconut fat from separating.

CARAMEL ICE CREAM

Omit the vanilla. Caramelize the sugar, following the procedure in the recipe for Caramel Sauce (p. 271) but omitting the lemon. Add the 1 pt (500 mL) heavy cream from the basic recipe and simmer until the caramel is dissolved, again following the procedure in the caramel sauce recipe, steps 2–4. Beat the eggs, add the hot milk and caramel cream, make the custard, and finish the ice cream as in the basic recipe.

ALMOND, HAZELNUT, OR MACADAMIA PRALINE ICE CREAM

Make a praline with any of these nuts, following the recipe for Nougatine (p. 658). Crush 6 oz (185 g) praline and add it to chilled vanilla or caramel ice cream mix before freezing.

CHEESECAKE ICE CREAM

Prepare the basic vanilla ice cream mix, but use only 4 oz (125 g) egg yolks, and substitute milk for half of the cream. In a mixer with the paddle attachment, blend 2 lb (1 kg) cream cheese, 7 oz (200 g) sugar, 1 tsp (3 g) each grated lemon zest and orange zest, and 1½ oz (50 mL) lemon juice until light and free of lumps. Gradually add the chilled custard and mix until smooth. Chill well. Freeze.

STRAWBERRY ICE CREAM

Reduce the number of yolks to 4 oz (125 g). Mash 1½ lb (750 g) fresh or frozen (unsweetened) strawberries with 6 oz (185 g) sugar and refrigerate at least 2 hours. Mix the strawberries with the cold ice cream mix before freezing.

(continues)

— **VARIATIONS CONTINUED** —

RASPBERRY SWIRL ICE CREAM

Reduce the number of yolks to 4 oz (125 g). Mash 1 lb (500 g) fresh or frozen (unsweetened) raspberries with 4 oz (125 g) sugar. Refrigerate at least 2 hours. Make vanilla ice cream and freeze in an ice cream freezer. After the churn-freezing is finished but before hardening the ice cream, fold in the raspberries, but do not mix in completely; leave it in swirls.

MANGO ICE CREAM

Reduce the number of yolks to 4 oz (125 g). Combine 1½ lb (750 g) sieved mango purée, 3 oz (90 mL) lime juice, and 3 oz (90 g) sugar. Refrigerate at least 2 hours. Combine with cold custard mix and freeze.

PEACH ICE CREAM

Mash 2 lb (1 kg) sliced fresh peaches, 4 oz (125 g) sugar, and 1 oz (30 mL) lemon juice. Reduce the number of egg yolks to 4 oz (125 g). Omit the milk, increase the cream to 2 pt (1 L), and make the custard with the cream. Mix the peaches with the cold custard and freeze.

GINGERBREAD-SPICE ICE CREAM

Ingredients	U.S.	Metric
Ginger	1½ tsp	2.8 g (7 mL)
Cinnamon	1 tsp	1.7 g (5 mL)
Cloves, ground	½ tsp	1 g (2 mL)
Nutmeg	¼ tsp	0.5 g (1 mL)
Molasses	2 oz	60 g

Add the spices to the egg mixture before cooking. Add the molasses to the mixture after cooking.

LEMON ICE CREAM

Reduce the quantity of milk to 1 pt (500 mL) and the sugar to 8 oz (250 g). Scald the milk and cream together. Omit the vanilla. With these exceptions, make the ice cream mix as in the basic recipe.

Separately, combine 2 tbsp (15 g) grated lemon zest and 1 oz (30 g) sugar. Work the zest and sugar together with the back of a spoon or with a mortar and pestle to make a coarse paste. Beat this lemon sugar with 3 egg yolks (2 oz/60 g). Add 12 oz (375 mL) lemon juice and beat over hot water until thick and creamy, as for making crème anglaise. Cool over ice. Refrigerate the lemon mixture and the custard mixture separately until ready to freeze. Combine the mixtures and freeze.

LIME ICE CREAM

Substitute lime zest and juice for the lemon in the preceding recipe.

ICE CREAM FREEZERS

Modern commercial ice cream freezers operate on the same principle as old-fashioned hand-cranked freezers. In those home devices, refrigeration is provided by a mixture of ice, water, and salt. The salt lowers the temperature of the melting ice below the freezing point of water to enable it to freeze the ice cream mix. The ice cream mix is placed in a cylinder surrounded by the ice and salt. A paddle, or *dasher*, continuously scrapes the freezing ice cream mixture off the walls of the cylinder, and at the same time incorporates air into the mix.

Modern batch freezers work the same way, except an electric refrigeration unit does the freezing, instead of salt and ice. In vertical batch freezers, the cylinder is upright, just as in the old-style hand-cranked machines. This type of freezer incorporates the least amount of air into the mix, resulting in low overrun. Horizontal batch freezers, with a horizontal cylinder, incorporate more air and produce ice cream with overrun up to 100%. Depending on the model, horizontal machines freeze ice cream quickly, finishing a batch of 6 quarts (6 L) or more in about five minutes.

Continuous ice cream freezers are used by high-volume operations. Instead of producing one batch at a time, the mix flows continuously into one end of the cylinder, while the frozen product is extruded at the other end. Such machines can produce 150 to as much as 3000 quarts (liters) or more of ice cream in an hour. Continuous ice cream freezers also incorporate the most air, resulting in ice cream with overrun from 60 to 140%.

SORBET

Yield: variable

Ingredients	U.S.	Metric
Sugar (see *Note*)	12 oz	375 g
Water	8 fl oz	250 mL
Fruit juice or pulp or other flavor ingredients	(see variations)	(see variations)
Water	(see variations)	(see variations)

NOTE: Including corn syrup as part of the sugar may slightly increase smoothness in some sorbets, although traditional sorbets are made with only granulated sugar. To include corn syrup, decrease the sugar to 11.5 oz (360 g) and add 2 oz (60 g) corn syrup to the syrup ingredients.

— VARIATIONS —

The following sorbet variations indicate the quantities of flavor ingredients and additional water to be used in the basic recipe (the third and fourth ingredients in the ingredient table). If the ingredients require special preparation instructions, they are indicated. If no special directions are given, simply follow the basic procedure above. Note that most fruit sorbets require strained fruit purée for the smoothest texture. This means fruit pulp that has been puréed and then forced through a sieve.

PROCEDURE

1. Make a syrup by heating the sugar and first quantity of water to dissolve the sugar. Cool.

2. Prepare the desired flavor ingredients as indicated in the variations that follow. If additional water is required, mix it with the flavor ingredient.

3. Mix the syrup with the remaining ingredients.

4. If possible, test the sugar concentration with a hydrometer (saccharometer). The mixture should be between 16° and 18° Baumé, or between 30° and 32.5° Brix. If the concentration is too low, add a little more syrup. If it is high, dilute with a little water.

5. Chill the mixture well, then freeze in an ice cream freezer according to the manufacturer's instructions.

LEMON OR LIME SORBET

Ingredients	U.S.	Metric
Lemon or lime zest, grated	1 tbsp	8 g
Lemon or lime juice	8 fl oz	250 mL
Water	12 fl oz	375 mL

Boil the zest with the syrup. Cool and strain.

ORANGE OR TANGERINE SORBET

Ingredients	U.S.	Metric
Orange or tangerine juice	20 fl oz	625 mL
Water	4 fl oz	125 mL

RASPBERRY, STRAWBERRY, MELON, OR KIWI SORBET

Ingredients	U.S.	Metric
Strained fruit purée	1 lb 12 oz	875 g
Water	none	none

Taste the mix before freezing. Some fruit is low in acidity, so a little lemon juice may improve the flavor of the mix.

MANGO SORBET

Ingredients	U.S.	Metric
Strained mango purée	1 lb 12 oz	875 g
Lemon juice	1.5 fl oz	60 mL
Water	8 fl oz	250 mL

PINEAPPLE SORBET

Ingredients	U.S.	Metric
Fresh pineapple chunks	1 lb 8 oz	750 g
Water	12 fl oz	375 mL

Poach the pineapple in the syrup. Cool. Purée and force through a sieve. Add the water. Freeze.

BLUEBERRY SORBET

Ingredients	U.S.	Metric
Blueberries	2 lb 4 oz	1125.0 g
Lemon juice	2 fl oz	60.0 mL
Cinnamon	¼ tsp	0.4 g (1 mL)
Water	none	none

Simmer the blueberries, lemon juice, and cinnamon in the syrup until the berries are tender. Strain through a fine sieve.

BANANA PASSION FRUIT SORBET

Ingredients	U.S.	Metric
Banana pulp, strained	12 oz	375 g
Passion fruit pulp or juice, strained	1 lb	500 g
Water	none	none

(continues)

─────────────────── **VARIATIONS CONTINUED** ───────────────────

RHUBARB SORBET

Ingredients	U.S.	Metric
Rhubarb	2 lb	1000 g
Water	1 pt	500 mL

Cut the rhubarb into 1-in. (2.5-cm) slices. Combine the syrup, rhubarb, and water in a stainless steel saucepan. Bring to a simmer and cook until the rhubarb is tender, about 10 minutes. Let the mixture cool, then strain through a fine strainer. Do not press down on the rhubarb solids, but let the rhubarb stand in the strainer about 30 minutes to let all the flavored syrup drain off. This will keep the syrup clear. Measure the syrup and add enough cold water to bring the volume to 20 oz (625 mL). Freeze the syrup. Reserve the rhubarb for another use (for example, add sugar to taste to make a simple rhubarb compote).

WHITE WINE OR CHAMPAGNE SORBET

Ingredients	U.S.	Metric
White wine or champagne	2.5 pt	1.25 L
Water	4 fl oz	125 mL

CHOCOLATE SORBET

Ingredients	U.S.	Metric
Cocoa powder	1 oz	30 g
Bittersweet or semisweet chocolate	6 oz	185 g

Reduce the quantity of sugar in the syrup to 6 oz (185 g). Increase the water in the syrup to 1 pt (500 mL). Add the cocoa powder to the syrup ingredients. When the sugar has dissolved, remove the syrup from the heat and let it cool slightly. Melt the chocolate. Carefully stir the syrup into the melted chocolate. Bring to a simmer, stirring constantly, and simmer 1–2 minutes, until slightly thickened. Chill and freeze.

MASCARPONE SORBET

Ingredients	U.S.	Metric
Mascarpone (soft Italian cream cheese)	1 lb 8 oz	750 g
Lemon juice	1.5 fl oz	45 mL
Water	10 fl oz	300 mL

Be sure to chill the mixture thoroughly, and do not leave in the ice cream freezer too long. Overmixing in the churn-freezer may cause some milk fat to separate and form chunks of butter.

HONEY ICE CREAM

Yield: about 1 qt (1 L), depending on overrun

Ingredients	U.S.	Metric	PROCEDURE
Milk	8 oz	250 g	1. Heat the milk and the vanilla bean to the scalding point.
Vanilla bean, split	1	1	
Honey	4.33 oz	130 g	2. Whip the honey and egg yolks until light. Slowly beat in the hot milk.
Egg yolks	4 oz (6 yolks)	120 g (6 yolks)	3. Return the mixture to the pan. Cook over low heat, stirring constantly, until thick enough to coat the back of a spoon. Remove from the heat and cool. Scrape the seeds from the vanilla bean and add them to the mixture. Chill.
Heavy cream	8 oz	250 g	4. Add the heavy cream. Freeze in an ice cream freezer.

DULCE DE LECHE ICE CREAM

Yield: about 3½ pt (1750 mL), depending on overrun

Ingredients	U.S.	Metric
Milk	1 pt 8 fl oz	750 g
Dulce de Leche (p. 276)	1 lb 2 oz (about 14 fl oz)	560 g (about 425 mL)
Heavy cream	6 oz	185 g
Vanilla extract	¼ tsp	1 g
Salt	pinch	pinch

PROCEDURE

1. Heat the milk and the dulce de leche together until the dulce de leche is completely dissolved.
2. Remove from the heat and add the remaining ingredients.
3. Chill well. Refrigerate 12 hours to mature the mix (see p. 549).
4. Freeze in an ice cream freezer.

BITTER CHOCOLATE ICE CREAM

Yield: about 3 qt (3 L), depending on overrun

Ingredients	U.S.	Metric
Egg yolks	8 oz (12 yolks)	250 g (12 yolks)
Sugar	6 oz	190 g
Milk	2 pt 8 oz	1250 mL
Sugar	12 oz	375 g
Bittersweet chocolate	8 oz	250 g
Cocoa powder, sifted	8 oz	250 g
Heavy cream	1 pt	500 mL

PROCEDURE

1. Combine the egg yolks and the first quantity of sugar in a bowl. Whip until thick and light.
2. Combine the milk and the second quantity of sugar in a heavy saucepan. Bring to a simmer, stirring to dissolve the sugar.
3. Gradually beat the milk into the egg yolk mixture. Set over a hot-water bath and heat, stirring constantly, until the mixture thickens enough to coat the back of a spoon. Immediately remove from the heat. Let cool until lukewarm.
4. Melt the chocolate and let cool slightly.
5. Gradually stir in the custard mixture.
6. Add the cocoa and beat with a whip until it is thoroughly mixed in.
7. Stir in the heavy cream.
8. Chill the mixture. Refrigerate 12 hours to mature the mix (p. 549).
9. Freeze in an ice cream freezer.

RASPBERRY FROZEN YOGURT

Yield: about 3 pt (1.5 L), depending on overrun

Ingredients	U.S.	Metric
Raspberries, fresh or frozen, unsweetened	1 lb	500 g
Granulated sugar	8 oz	250 g
Water	4 oz	125 g
Plain low-fat or whole milk yogurt	12 oz	375 g

PROCEDURE

1. Combine the raspberries, sugar, and water in a food processor. Process until the raspberries are puréed and the sugar is dissolved.

2. Force the mixture through a fine sieve to remove the seeds.

3. Combine with the yogurt and mix until evenly blended.

4. Chill the mixture well.

5. Freeze in an ice cream freezer.

PISTACHIO GELATO

Yield: about 2½ pt (1250 mL), depending on overrun.

Ingredients	U.S.	Metric
Shelled, unsalted pistachios	8 oz	250 g
Whole milk	2 pt	1 L
Sugar	7 oz	220 g

PROCEDURE

1. Grind the pistachios in a food processor until fine. Transfer to a bowl.

2. Combine the milk and sugar in a saucepan. Bring to a boil. Stir to dissolve the sugar.

3. Pour the milk over the ground pistachios and stir.

4. Cover and refrigerate overnight.

5. Strain the pistachio mixture in a chinois or other fine strainer lined with several layers of cheesecloth (a). Gather up the corners of the cheesecloth, to make a bag, and squeeze gently to force the remaining liquid from the ground nuts (b).

6. Chill the liquid again, if necessary, and then freeze in an ice cream freezer (c).

A

B

C

COCONUT SORBET

Yield: about 1¾ pt (850 mL), depending on overrun

Ingredients	U.S.	Metric
Frozen coconut purée, thawed (see variation)	1 lb	480 g
Confectioners' sugar	3.5 oz	100 g
Lime juice, fresh	1.75 oz	50 g
Coconut-flavored rum	2 oz	60 g

PROCEDURE

1. Mix together all ingredients.
2. Freeze in an ice cream freezer.

VARIATION

The coconut purée used in this recipe contains 20% sugar. If this product is not available, use canned, unsweetened coconut milk and adjust the quantities as follows:

Ingredients	U.S.	Metric
Canned, unsweetened coconut milk	14 oz	400 g
Confectioners' sugar	6 oz	180 g
Lime juice	1.75 oz	50 g
Coconut-flavored rum	2 oz	60 g

CIDER APPLE SORBET

Yield: about 1½ pt (700 mL)

Ingredients	U.S.	Metric
Sugar	4.5 oz	135 g
Water	4 oz	120 g
Cooking apples	7 oz	200 g
Fermented cider	5.5 oz	165 g

PROCEDURE

1. Heat the sugar and water until the sugar is dissolved.
2. Peel, core, and chop the apples. Add to the syrup and cook until tender.
3. Add the cider. Place in a blender and blend until smooth. Pass through a fine strainer.
4. Cool, then freeze in an ice cream freezer.

COFFEE OR ESPRESSO GRANITA

Yield: about 2 pt 4 fl oz (1125 mL)

Ingredients	U.S.	Metric
Sugar	4 oz	125 g
Very strong coffee or espresso, freshly brewed	2 pt	1 L

PROCEDURE

1. Dissolve the sugar in the coffee.
2. Pour the coffee into a hotel pan or similar pan and place in the freezer.
3. When the coffee begins to freeze around the edges, stir with a spoon, fork, or whip. Return to the freezer.
4. Repeat step 3 every 15 or 20 minutes, until the mixture resembles crushed ice. When finished, it should be completely frozen but loose, or else it will freeze into a block when stored.
5. Cover and store in the freezer.

CASSATA ITALIENNE

Ingredients	U.S.	Metric
Common Meringue (p. 258)	3 oz	90 g
Vanilla Ice Cream (p. 550), softened	7 oz	200 g
Raspberry jam	1.5–2 oz	50 g
Raspberry Sorbet (p. 552), softened	7 oz	200 g
Total weight:	**1 lb 2 oz**	**540 g**

NOTE: This procedure is for rectangular (loaf) molds approximately 6½ × 3½ in. (17 × 9 cm). It can be modified for any size or shape mold.

PROCEDURE

1. Using a pastry bag with a plain tip, pipe the meringue onto a parchment-lined sheet pan in a rectangle the same size as the top of the mold. Bake at 250°F (120°C) for 1 hour. Cool.

2. Line the mold with plastic film.

3. Using a pastry bag with a plain tip, pipe the ice cream into the bottom of the mold and smooth the surface (using a pastry bag makes it easier to avoid air bubbles). Freeze until firm.

4. Spread the raspberry jam onto the ice cream in an even layer. Freeze until firm.

5. Pipe the raspberry sorbet into the mold and smooth the surface.

6. Place the baked, cooled meringue on top of the sorbet and press down gently. Freeze until firm.

7. Unmold, remove the plastic film, and slice to serve.

PREPARING STILL-FROZEN DESSERTS

THE AIR MIXED into ice cream by churn-freezing is important to its texture. Without this air, the ice cream would be hard and heavy rather than smooth and creamy. Desserts that are still-frozen—that is, frozen in a container without mixing—also must have air mixed into them in order to be soft enough to eat. In this case, the air is incorporated before freezing, by mixing in whipped cream, whipped egg whites, or both.

Thus, still-frozen desserts are closely related to products such as Bavarians, mousses, and hot soufflés. These products are all given lightness and volume by adding whipped cream or an egg foam. In fact, many of the same mixtures used for these products are also used for frozen desserts. However, because freezing serves to stabilize or solidify frozen desserts, they don't depend as much on gelatin or other stabilizers.

Still-frozen desserts include bombes, frozen soufflés, and frozen mousses. In classical theory, each type is made with a different mix; but in actual practice today, many of these mixes are interchangeable.

A note on the use of alcohol in frozen desserts: Liqueurs and spirits are often used to flavor these items. However, even a small amount of alcohol lowers the freezing point considerably. If you find that liqueur-flavored parfaits, bombes, and mousses aren't freezing hard enough, add more whipped cream. This will raise the freezing point. In future batches, you might try using less alcohol.

A high sugar concentration also inhibits freezing. It is important to avoid using too much sugar in these items to ensure they freeze properly.

Parfaits and Bombes

As noted earlier in the chapter, in North America, the term *parfait* usually refers to an ice cream dessert consisting of layers of ice cream and topping in a tall, thin glass. The original parfait, however, is a dessert still-frozen in a tall, thin mold and unmolded for service. (No doubt the ice cream parfait is so named because the glass it is served in is similar in shape to a parfait mold.)

The mixture for parfaits consists of three elements: a thick, sweet egg yolk foam, an equal volume of whipped cream, and flavorings. The parfait mixture is also called a *bombe mixture* because it is used in the production of a dessert called a *bombe*. The bombe is one of the most elegant frozen desserts, often elaborately decorated with fruits, whipped cream, petits fours secs, and other items after unmolding. It is made by lining a chilled mold (usually spherical or dome-shaped) with a layer of ice cream or sherbet and freezing it hard. The center is filled with a bombe mixture of compatible flavor and then frozen again. Mixtures for frozen mousses can also be used to fill bombes, as can regular ice cream or sherbet, but a special bombe mixture is the most common choice.

Two recipes are given below for bombe mixtures. The ingredients and final results are nearly the same, but the techniques differ. Note that the technique for the first mixture is the same as that used to make French Buttercream (p. 421). The second recipe requires a sugar syrup of a specific strength; the recipe for this syrup is also provided.

A procedure for assembling bombes is given, followed by descriptions of a number of classic bombes.

BASIC BOMBE MIXTURE I

Yield: 1½ qt (1.4 L)

Ingredients	U.S.	Metric
Sugar	6 oz	1800 g
Water	2 oz	60 g
Egg yolks	4 oz (6 yolks)	120 g (6 yolks)
Flavoring (see variations following recipe for Basic Bombe Mixture II)		
Heavy cream	1 pt	480 mL

PROCEDURE

1. Dissolve the sugar in the water over high heat and boil the mixture until it reaches 240°F (115°C). (See pp. 252–253 for information on boiling sugar.)

2. While the syrup is boiling, whip the egg yolks (using the whip attachment of the mixing machine) until light and foamy.

3. With the machine running, slowly pour the hot syrup into the egg yolks. Continue whipping until the mixture is cool. It should be very thick and foamy.

4. This mixture will keep, covered and refrigerated, up to 1 week. When you are ready to assemble a dessert, proceed with the next steps.

5. Stir the desired flavorings into the egg yolk mixture.

6. Whip the cream until it forms soft, not stiff, peaks. Do not overwhip.

7. Fold the cream into the base mixture. Pour the result into prepared molds or other containers and freeze it until firm.

SYRUP FOR BOMBES

Yield: about 1½ qt (1.5 L)

Ingredients	U.S.	Metric
Sugar	3 lb	1.5 kg
Water	2 lb	1 kg

NOTE: Simple syrup of this concentration is used in the Basic Bombe Mixture II (p. 560) and Frozen Mousse II (p. 563).

PROCEDURE

1. Combine the water and sugar in a saucepan. Bring the mixture to a boil, stirring until the sugar is completely dissolved.

2. Remove the syrup from the heat and let it cool. Store it in a covered container in the refrigerator.

BASIC BOMBE MIXTURE II

Yield: 1½ qt (1.4 L)

Ingredients	U.S.	Metric
Egg yolks	6 oz (9 yolks)	180 g (9 yolks)
Syrup for Bombes (see p. 559)	6 fl oz	180 mL
Flavoring (see variations below)		
Heavy cream	12 fl oz	360 mL

PROCEDURE

1. Whip the egg yolks lightly in a stainless steel bowl, then gradually beat in the syrup.

2. Set the bowl over hot water and whip the mixture with a wire whip until it is thick and creamy, about the consistency of a thick hollandaise sauce.

3. Remove the mixture from the heat, set it over ice, and continue whipping until it is cold.

4. Add the desired flavoring.

5. Whip the cream until it forms soft peaks. Do not overwhip. Fold it into the egg yolk mixture.

6. Pour the mixture into molds or other containers. Freeze until firm.

VARIATIONS

To create bombes of different flavors, add the suggested flavorings to either of the egg yolk mixtures in the two preceding recipes before folding in the whipped cream.

VANILLA

Add ½–¾ oz (15–22 mL) vanilla extract.

CHOCOLATE

Melt 2 oz (60 g) unsweetened chocolate. Stir in a little simple syrup to make a thick sauce. Then fold this into the yolk mixture. (For a stronger chocolate flavor, melt 1–1½ oz (30–45 g) semisweet chocolate with the 2 oz (60 g) unsweetened chocolate.)

LIQUEUR

Add 1–1½ oz (30–45 mL), or to taste, desired liqueur or spirit, such as orange liqueur, kirsch, or rum.

COFFEE

Add ¼ oz (8 g) instant coffee dissolved in ½ oz (15 mL) water.

PRALINE

Add 2½ oz (75 g) praline paste, softened with a little water, to the yolk mixture.

FRUIT (RASPBERRY, STRAWBERRY, APRICOT, PEACH, ETC.)

Add up to 8 oz (250 g) fruit purée.

BOMBE OR PARFAIT WITH FRUIT

Instead of flavoring the bombe mixture with a fruit purée, add solid fruits cut in small dice to plain or liqueur-flavored bombe mixture.

BOMBE OR PARFAIT WITH NUTS, SPONGE CAKE, OR OTHER INGREDIENTS

Solid ingredients besides fruit may be mixed with a plain or flavored bombe mixture, including chopped nuts, crumbled almond macaroons, marrons glacés (candied chestnuts), and diced sponge cake or ladyfingers moistened with liqueur.

PROCEDURE: Making Bombes

1. Place the bombe mold in the freezer until very cold.

2. Line the mold with a layer of slightly softened ice cream, using your hand to press it against the sides and smooth it. The ice cream layer should be about 1 in. (2 cm) thick for small molds and up to 1½ in. (4 cm) for large molds.

   If the ice cream becomes too soft to stick to the sides, place it in the freezer to harden it, then try again.

3. Freeze the mold until the ice cream layer is hard.

4. Fill the mold with bombe mixture, cover, and freeze until firm.

5. To unmold, dip the mold in warm water for a second, wipe the water from the outside of the mold, and turn out the bombe onto a cold serving plate. (Note: To keep the bombe from sliding around on the plate, turn it out onto a thin sheet of genoise, which acts as a base.)

6. Decorate with whipped cream and appropriate fruits or other items.

7. Serve immediately. Cut into wedges or slices so all portions are uniform.

A Selection of Classic Bombes

BOMBE AFRICAINE

Coating: chocolate ice cream

Filling: apricot bombe mixture

BOMBE AIDA

Coating: strawberry ice cream

Filling: kirsch-flavored bombe mixture

BOMBE BRESILIENNE

Coating: pineapple sherbet

Filling: bombe mixture flavored with vanilla and rum and mixed with diced pineapple

BOMBE CARDINALE

Coating: raspberry sherbet

Filling: praline vanilla bombe mixture

BOMBE CEYLON

Coating: coffee ice cream

Filling: rum-flavored bombe mixture

BOMBE COPPELIA

Coating: coffee ice cream

Filling: praline bombe mixture

BOMBE DIPLOMAT

Coating: vanilla ice cream

Filling: bombe mixture flavored with maraschino liqueur and mixed with candied fruit

BOMBE FLORENTINE

Coating: raspberry sherbet

Filling: praline bombe mixture

BOMBE FORMOSA

Coating: vanilla ice cream

Filling: bombe mixture flavored with strawberry purée and mixed with whole strawberries

BOMBE MOLDAVE

Coating: pineapple sherbet

Filling: bombe mixture flavored with orange liqueur

BOMBE SULTANE

Coating: chocolate ice cream

Filling: praline bombe mixture

BOMBE TUTTI-FRUTTI

Coating: strawberry ice cream or sherbet

Filling: lemon bombe mixture mixed with candied fruits

CASSATA NAPOLETANA

Cassatas are Italian-style bombes lined with three layers of different ice creams and filled with Italian meringue mixed with various ingredients. The most popular, Cassata Napoletana, is made as follows:

1. Line the mold first with vanilla, then with chocolate, and finally with strawberry ice cream.

2. Fill with Italian Meringue (p. 259) flavored with vanilla, kirsch, or maraschino and mixed with an equal weight of diced candied fruits. A little whipped cream may be added to the meringue, if desired.

Frozen Mousses and Frozen Soufflés

Frozen mousses are light frozen desserts containing whipped cream. Although they are all similar in character because of their whipped cream content, the bases for them are made in several ways. Three types of preparation are included here:

- Mousse with Italian meringue base.
- Mousse with syrup and fruit base.
- Mousse with custard base.

The mixture for bombes and parfaits can also be used for mousses.

The simplest method for serving mousse is to pour the mixture into individual serving dishes and freeze them. The mixture can also be poured into larger molds of various shapes. After unmolding, cut the mousse into portions and decorate it with whipped cream and appropriate fruits, cookies, or other items.

Frozen soufflés are simply mousse or bombe mixtures frozen in soufflé dishes or other straight-sided dishes. A band of heavy paper or foil, called a collar, is tied around the mold so it extends 2 inches (5 cm) or more above the rim of the dish. The mousse or bombe mixture is poured in until it reaches within ½ inch (12 mm) of the top of this band. After the dessert is frozen, the band is removed. The dessert thus looks like a hot soufflé that has risen above its baking dish.

Other items may be incorporated in the frozen soufflé, such as sponge cake, ladyfingers, baked meringue, fruits, and so forth. For example, you might pour one-third of the mousse mixture into the prepared dish, place a japonaise disk (p. 342) on top, pour in another layer of mousse, add a second japonaise disk, then fill with the mousse mixture. This technique can also be used with thin sponge cake layers. For further variety, arrange a layer of fruit on top of each genoise layer before adding more mousse.

KEY POINTS TO REVIEW

- ■ How is a basic (French-style) vanilla ice cream made?
- ■ How is sorbet made?
- ■ What are still-frozen desserts? Give examples and explain in general terms how they are made.
- ■ What is a bombe? How is it made?

FROZEN MOUSSE I (MERINGUE BASE)

Yield: 1½ qt (1.5 L)

Ingredients	U.S.	Metric
Italian meringue		
Sugar	8 oz	250 g
Water	2 oz	60 mL
Egg whites	4 oz	125 g
Flavoring (see *Note*)		
Heavy cream	12 oz	375 mL

NOTE: Possible flavorings include fruit purées, liqueurs, and chocolate. Use up to 3 oz (90 mL) strong spirits (brandy or dark rum, for example) or 4 oz (125 mL) sweet liqueur. Use 4 oz (125 g) melted unsweetened chocolate or up to 8 oz (250 g) thick fruit purée. Specific flavors are suggested in the variations following the basic procedure.

PROCEDURE

1. For the Italian meringue: In a saucepan, dissolve the sugar in the water and boil the syrup until it reaches 250°F (120°C). Meanwhile, whip the egg whites until they form soft peaks. Whipping constantly, slowly pour the hot syrup into the egg whites. Continue to whip the meringue until it is completely cool (unless you are flavoring it with liqueur—see next step).

2. Stir or fold in flavoring ingredients. If you are using melted chocolate or a thick fruit purée, stir a little of the meringue into the flavoring, then fold this into the rest of the meringue. If you are using a liqueur or spirit, add it while the meringue is still warm so most of the alcohol evaporates.

3. Whip the cream until it forms soft peaks. Fold it into the meringue mixture. Freeze.

--- **VARIATIONS** ---

The following are a few of many possible flavors for frozen mousse.

LIQUEUR MOUSSE

Flavor with 3 oz (90 mL) brandy, dark rum, or Calvados, or with 4 oz (125 mL) sweet liqueur.

CHOCOLATE MOUSSE

Melt 4 oz (125 g) unsweetened chocolate. Stir in a little Syrup for Bombes (p. 559) to make a thick sauce. Stir some of the meringue into this mixture, then fold the chocolate mixture into the rest of the meringue.

(continues)

─────────────────── **VARIATIONS CONTINUED** ───────────────────

APRICOT MOUSSE

Soak 6 oz (188 g) dried apricots in water overnight, then simmer until tender. Drain and purée in a food mill. Fold into the meringue. If desired, add ½ oz (15 mL) rum or kirsch.

BANANA MOUSSE

Purée 8 oz (250 g) very ripe bananas with ½ oz (15 mL) lemon juice. Add to meringue.

LEMON MOUSSE

Add 3 oz (90 mL) lemon juice and the grated zest of 1 lemon to the meringue.

CHESTNUT MOUSSE

Soften 7 oz (220 g) chestnut purée by blending it with 1 oz (30 mL) dark rum until smooth. Add it to the meringue.

RASPBERRY OR STRAWBERRY MOUSSE

Force 8 oz (250 g) fresh or frozen (unsweetened) raspberries or strawberries through a sieve. Add to the meringue.

FROZEN MOUSSE II (SYRUP AND FRUIT BASE)

Yield: about 2½ pt (1.25 L)

Ingredients	U.S.	Metric
Syrup for Bombes (p. 559)	8 oz	250 mL
Fruit purée	8 oz	250 mL
Heavy cream	1 pt	500 mL

PROCEDURE

1. Mix the syrup and fruit purée until uniformly blended.
2. Whip the cream until it forms soft peaks.
3. Fold the cream into the syrup mixture.
4. Pour the mixture into molds or dishes and freeze.

FROZEN MOUSSE III (CUSTARD BASE)

Yield: about 1½ qt (1.5 L)

Ingredients	U.S.	Metric
Egg yolks	5 oz (7–8 yolks)	150 g (7–8 yolks)
Sugar	8 oz	250 g
Milk	8 oz	250 mL
Flavoring (see step 6)		
Heavy cream	1 pt	500 mL

PROCEDURE

1. Whip the egg yolks with half the sugar until they are light and foamy.
2. Meanwhile, bring the milk to a boil with the rest of the sugar.
3. Pour the milk over the yolks, whipping constantly.
4. Set the milk and egg mixture over a hot-water bath and cook, stirring constantly, until the mixture thickens like crème anglaise (p. 261). Do not overcook, or the custard will curdle.
5. Cool the mixture, then chill it in the refrigerator or over ice.
6. Add the desired flavoring. The same flavorings and quantities may be used as in Frozen Mousse I (p. 562).
7. Whip the cream and fold it into the custard mixture.
8. Pour the mousse into molds or dishes and freeze.

WHITE CHOCOLATE PARFAIT WITH FLAMBÉED CHERRIES

Yield: 10 parfaits, 3 oz (95 g) each

Ingredients	U.S.		Metric
Flambéed cherries			
Fresh cherries (see *Note*)	10	oz	300 g
Sugar	2	oz	60 g
Vanilla extract	½	tsp	2 g
Port wine	5	oz	150 g
Baked disks of Chocolate Meringue (p. 341), 2½ in. (6 cm) in diameter	10		10
Sabayon			
Sugar	3.67	oz	110 g
Water	2.5	oz	75 g
Egg yolks	4	oz	120 g
White chocolate, chopped	5	oz	150 g
Heavy cream	12	oz	375 g
Decoration			
Chocolate curls	as needed		as needed
Pistachios	as needed		as needed
Total weight of parfait mix:	**1 lb 9**	**oz**	**775 g**

NOTE: Cherries packed in syrup may also be used. Morello cherries (griottes) are especially good in this preparation. Drain the cherries and proceed as in the basic recipe.

PROCEDURE

1. Prepare the cherries: Pit the cherries and place them and the sugar in a saucepan. Heat gently until liquid begins to cook out of the cherries. Continue to heat until the liquid is almost evaporated. Add the vanilla and the port. Place over high heat and flambé to burn off the alcohol. Continue to cook, lightly covered, over low heat until the juices are thick and syrupy. Drain the cherries for use in step 7. Reserve the syrup.

2. Set 2¾-in. (7-cm) ring molds on a tray. Place a disk of baked chocolate meringue in the base of each.

3. For the parfait, dissolve the sugar in the water and bring to a boil.

4. Whip the egg yolks until light and then gradually whip in the hot syrup. Continue whipping until cool.

5. Melt the white chocolate over a hot-water bath.

6. Quickly mix the chocolate into the egg yolk sabayon. Do not overmix, or the sabayon may fall.

7. Whip the cream and quickly fold it in.

8. Without delay, fill the molds about two-thirds full. Place 6–8 cherries in each one, pushing some of them down into the mix. (Reserve the remaining cherries and syrup to serve with the parfaits.) Fill to the top with parfait mix and level the tops. Freeze for at least 1 hour or until firm.

9. To serve, unmold by lightly warming the mold and lifting it off. Top with chocolate curls and pistachios and a few cherries. Spoon some of the cherry syrup and a few more cherries onto the plate.

ICED LOW-FAT RASPBERRY PARFAIT

Yield: about 3 pt (1.5 L)

Ingredients	U.S.		Metric		PROCEDURE
Italian Meringue					
Sugar	3.5	oz	100 g		
Water	2.25	oz	65 g		
Egg whites	3	oz	90 g		
Raspberries, fresh or frozen	7	oz	200 g		
Plain low-fat yogurt	7	oz	200 g		

PROCEDURE

1. Make an Italian meringue: Dissolve the sugar in the water and boil to 250°F (120°C). Whip the egg whites to soft peaks. While whipping constantly, slowly pour in the hot syrup. Continue whipping until the meringue is cool.

2. Purée the raspberries and force the purée through a sieve to remove the seeds.

3. Whip the yogurt until smooth and mix in the raspberry purée.

4. Fold the cold meringue, one-third at a time, into the yogurt mixture.

5. Pour into molds and freeze.

VARIATIONS

Other fruit purées may be substituted for the raspberries.

See page 612 for a serving suggestion.

TERMS FOR REVIEW

ice cream	sherbet	granita	parfait
Philadelphia-style ice cream	ice	overrun	bombe
French-style ice cream	granité	sundae	frozen mousse
ice milk	gelato	coupe	frozen soufflé
frozen yogurt	sorbetto	baked Alaska	

QUESTIONS FOR REVIEW

1. Why do ice cream and sherbet have to be frozen in a special freezer that mixes the product while it is being frozen? Why is it possible to freeze frozen mousses and similar desserts without this kind of freezer?

2. How does sugar affect the freezing properties of frozen desserts?

3. How does alcohol affect the freezing properties of frozen desserts?

4. How are still-frozen desserts similar to Bavarians?

5. Describe the procedure for making a baked Alaska or Soufflé Surprise.

6. Describe the basic procedure for making bombes.

21

FRUIT DESSERTS

AFTER READING THIS CHAPTER, YOU SHOULD BE ABLE TO:

1. **Work with fresh fruits, from selection to preparation, for use in desserts and calculation of fresh fruit yields.**

2. **Prepare various fruit desserts, including poached fruits and fruit compotes.**

INTEREST IN DESSERTS with less fat and fewer calories has stimulated interest in fruit desserts as alternatives to richer pastries and cakes. Fruits are, of course, important components of many pastries, cakes, and sauces, and many fruit desserts contain significant amounts of fat and sugar, including some in this chapter. Nevertheless, customers often perceive such desserts as more healthful, and this may account, in part, for their popularity. Another factor is the fresh, stimulating flavors of many fruit desserts.

In earlier chapters, we discussed fruit pies, fritters, pastries, tarts, cakes, and sauces. Many other types of fruit-based desserts, however, do not fit neatly into these categories. A representative sampling of recipes is included here, although, of course, they are only a small fraction of the many hundreds of recipes to be found elsewhere.

HANDLING FRESH FRUITS

ADVANCES IN TRANSPORTATION and refrigeration have made fresh fruits widely available year-round. Even exotic tropical fruits are increasingly common in the market. Not long ago, most fresh fruits were available during limited seasons only. For example, strawberries were usually available for a short time in the spring, when they were in season. Now, however, almost everything is in season somewhere in the world, and it is easy to ship that crop to any market.

Unlimited availability is a mixed blessing, however. Shipped-in, out-of-season fruits may not be at the peak of quality. Many fruit varieties, in addition, are bred for shipping rather than for flavor. Thus, it is important to be able to evaluate the quality of fresh fruit.

FRUIT VERSUS VEGETABLE

In culinary terms, a vegetable is a plant part used primarily in savory dishes. Plant parts include roots, tubers, stems, leaves, and fruits. Yes, fruits. A fruit is, in botanical terms, the part of the plant that bears the seeds. Cucumbers, squash, green beans, eggplant, okra, pea pods, tree nuts such as walnuts, avocados, and chiles are all fruits. And they are all vegetables. There is no contradiction in this statement any more than in saying that carrots, parsnips, and turnips are all roots and all vegetables.

In culinary terms, a fruit is the part of a plant that bears the seeds and is used primarily in sweet dishes. In most cases, the fruits used are those high in natural sugar content. In nature, however, most fruits are not sweet—think of milkweed pods and prickly burdock, for example. Similarly, many fruits used in the kitchen are not sweet—that is, they are vegetables.

Ripening

Part of evaluating the quality of fruits is judging their ripeness. As explained in the Maturity and Ripeness sidebar, some fruits continue to ripen after they are harvested, and the chef must be able to judge their degree of ripeness. Other fruits are harvested ripe and must be used quickly, before they deteriorate.

Ripening is a complex phenomenon. Some fruits change more than others. There are four main kinds of changes:

- **Aroma.** Bitter or unpleasant aromas fade, and attractive aromas develop. With few exceptions, this happens only before harvest.
- **Sweetness.** Sugar content increases. Some sugar comes from the plant before harvest, and some results as stored starches in the fruit break down.
- **Juiciness and texture.** Cell walls break down. This releases juices and makes the fruit softer.
- **Color.** Many fruits are green when immature, and then turn red, orange, purple, or another color when they ripen.

In general, do not refrigerate fruits until they have ripened. The exception is pears, which can be refrigerated before they ripen completely, to avoid mushiness. After fruits have ripened, refrigerate them to slow deterioration. Fruits that are picked fully ripe should be refrigerated upon receipt.

Familiarize yourself with the information in the following table, which specifies the changes undergone by common fruits.

MATURITY AND RIPENESS

A mature fruit is one that has completed its development and is physiologically capable of continuing the ripening process. A ripe fruit is one that is at its peak for texture and flavor and is ready to be consumed. In other words, maturity refers to biological development and ripeness refers to eating quality. Fruit that is harvested before it is mature will not soften and develop good eating quality. On the other hand, the riper a fruit is at harvest, the shorter its potential storage life. Therefore, growers, when possible, harvest fruit that is mature but not yet ripe. As indicated in the table, however, not all fruits are capable of ripening after they have been picked.

These fruits undergo changes in aroma, sweetness, juiciness and texture, and color when they ripen after picking.	Avocado (usually used as a vegetable, not in the bakeshop) Banana
These fruits become sweeter, juicier, and softer, and their color changes when they ripen after picking.	Apple (still crisp, unless overripe, but not as hard as unripe apples) Kiwi Mango Papaya Pear
These fruits do not become sweeter, but they do become juicier and softer, and their color changes when they ripen after picking.	Apricot Blueberry Fig Melon (hollow types) Nectarine Passion fruit Peach Persimmon Plum
These fruits are harvested fully ripe and do not ripen further after picking.	Berries (except blueberries) Citrus fruits (grapefruit, orange, tangerine, lemon, lime, kumquat) Cherries Grapes Pineapple Watermelon

Trimming Loss: Calculating Yields and Amounts Needed

All fresh fruits must be washed before being used. Following washing, nearly all fruits require further preparation and trimming. Sometimes prep is simple—pulling grapes from their stems or picking over blueberries to remove bits of stem and leaf. In other cases, further trimming, peeling, and cutting may be required. The next section describes basic preparation for individual fruits.

Because parts of a fruit may be removed and discarded, the amount purchased is not the same as the amount served. The percentage yield of a fruit indicates, on the average, how much of the *AP weight* (as-purchased weight) is left after pre-prep to produce the ready-to-cook item, or *EP weight* (edible portion weight). You can use this figure to do two basic calculations.

1. **Calculating yield.** Example: You have 10 lb AP kiwi fruit. Yield after trimming is 80 percent. What will your EP weight be?

    First, change the percentage to a decimal number by moving the decimal point two places to the left.

    $$80\% = 0.80$$

    Multiply the decimal by your AP weight to get EP yield.

    $$10 \text{ lb} \times 0.80 = 8 \text{ lb}$$

2. **Calculating amount needed.** Example: You need 10 lb EP kiwi fruit. What amount of untrimmed fruit do you need?

    Change the percentage to a decimal number.

    $$80\% = 0.80$$

    Divide the EP weight needed by this number to get the AP weight.

    $$\frac{10 \text{ lb}}{0.80} = 12.5 \text{ lb}$$

Evaluating and Preparing

This section summarizes the most commonly available fresh fruits. Emphasis is on which qualities to look for when purchasing them, and on how to trim and prepare them for use. In addition, identification information is included for certain exotic items. Nearly everyone knows what apples, bananas, and strawberries are, but not everyone can identify a persimmon or a passion fruit. Trimming yields are also given.

Apples

Granny Smith apple.

Golden Delicious apple.

Mature apples have a fruity aroma, brown seeds, and a slightly softer texture than unripe fruit. Overripe or old apples are soft and sometimes shriveled. Avoid apples with bruises, blemishes, decay, or mealy texture. Summer varieties (sold until fall) do not keep well. Fall and winter varieties keep well and are available for a longer period. Apples with a good acid content are usually better for cooking than bland eating varieties like Red Delicious. Granny Smith and Golden Delicious are widely used for cooking. See also the Apples for Pies sidebar on page 294.

To prepare, wash; pare if desired. Quarter and remove the core, or leave whole and core with a special coring tool. Use a stainless steel knife for cutting, to avoid discoloring the fruit. After paring, dip apples in a solution of lemon juice (or other tart fruit juice) or ascorbic acid to prevent browning.

Percentage yield: 75%

Rome apple.

Gala apple.

Macintosh apple.

Apricots

Only tree-ripened apricots have sufficient flavor, and they keep for only a week or less under refrigeration. They should be golden yellow, firm, and plump, not mushy. Avoid fruit that is too soft, blemished, or decayed.

To prepare, wash, split in half, and remove pit. Peeling is not necessary for most purposes.

Percentage yield: 94%

Apricots.

Courtesy iStockphoto.com.

Bananas

Look for plump, smooth bananas without bruises or signs of spoilage. All bananas are picked green, so you don't need to avoid unripe fruit. Avoid overripe fruit, however.

Ripen at room temperature for three to five days; fully ripe fruit is all yellow with small brown flecks and no green. Refrigerating the ripe fruit will darken the skin but not the flesh. Peel and dip in fruit juice to prevent browning.

Percentage yield: 70%

Bananas.

Berries

This category includes blackberries, blueberries, cranberries, blackcurrants (cassis), red currants, white currants, lingonberries, raspberries, and strawberries. Berries should be full, plump, and clean, with bright, fully ripe color. Watch for moldy or spoiled fruits. Wet spots on the carton indicate damaged fruit.

Refrigerate in the original container until ready to use in order to reduce handling. Except for cranberries, berries do not keep well. Sort out spoiled berries and foreign materials. Wash with gentle spray and drain well. Remove the stems and hulls from strawberries. Red currants for garnishing are often left on the stem. Handle berries carefully to avoid bruising.

Percentage yield: 92–95%

Blackberries.

Blueberries.　　Cranberries.

White currants.

Raspberries.

Strawberries.

Cherries

Look for plump, firm, sweet, juicy cherries. Bing or black cherries should be uniform dark red to almost black.

Refrigerate in the original container until ready to use. Just before use, remove stems and sort out damaged fruit. Rinse and drain well. Pit with a special pitting tool.

Percentage yield: 82% (pitted)

Cherries.

Coconut

Shake to hear liquid inside; fruits with no liquid are dried out. Avoid cracked fruits and fruits with wet "eyes."

To prepare, pierce an eye with an ice pick or nail and drain the liquid. Crack the coconut with a hammer and remove the meat from the shell (this job is easier if the shell is placed in a 350°F/175°C oven 10–15 minutes). Peel the brown skin with a paring knife or vegetable peeler.

Percentage yield: 50%

Coconut.

Figs

Calimyrna figs, also called Smyrna figs, are light green; Black Mission figs and Black Spanish (also called Brown Turkey) figs are purple. All figs are sweet when ripe, and soft and delicate in texture. They should be plump and soft, without signs of spoilage or sour odor.

Keep refrigerated (although firm, unripe figs can be left at room temperature, spread in one layer, for a few days to ripen slightly). Rinse and drain, handling carefully. Trim off hard stem ends.

Percentage yield: 95% (80–85% when peeled)

Calimyrna figs.

Grapefruit

Select fruit that is heavy for its size and has a firm, smooth skin. Avoid puffy, soft fruits and those with pointed ends, which have low yield and a lot of rind. Cut and taste for sweetness.

For sections and slices, peel with a chef's knife, removing all white pith. Separate sections from membrane with a small knife.

Percentage yield: 45–50% (flesh without membrane); 40–45% (juiced)

Black Mission figs.

Grapefruit.

Peeling a grapefruit.

A

Cut off the ends of the grapefruit and turn it on a flat end so it is stable. Slice off a section of the peel, following the contour of the grapefruit.

B

Make sure the cut is deep enough to remove the peel but not so deep as to waste the product.

C

Continue making slices around the grapefruit until all the peel is removed.

D

Slice or section the fruit. (Squeeze the remaining pulp for juice.)

Grapes

Look for firm, ripe, good-colored fruits in full bunches. Grapes should be firmly attached to stems and should not fall off when shaken. Watch for rotting or shriveling at stem ends.

Refrigerate in the original container. Wash and drain. Except for seedless varieties, cut in half and remove seeds with the point of a paring knife.

Percentage yield: 90%

Grapes.

Guava

There are many varieties of these small, tropical fruits. They may be round, oval, or pear-shaped, with aromatic flesh that may be green, pink, yellow, red, or white. Some are full of seeds and others are nearly seedless. The flavor is complex, ranging from sweet to sour. Select tender fruits with a full aroma.

To prepare, cut in half and scoop out the flesh. For many uses the flesh is puréed in a food processor or blender, seeds and all. Alternatively, cut into dice or other shapes, as desired.

Percentage Yield: 80%

Guava.

Kiwi Fruit

Kiwis are firm when unripe; they become slightly softer when ripe but do not change color significantly. Allow them to ripen at room temperature. Avoid fruits with bruises or soft spots.

To prepare, pare the thin outer skin. Cut crosswise into slices. Alternative method for slices with smooth, round edges: Cut off ends. Insert spoon into end, sliding it just beneath the skin; twist the spoon to completely free the flesh from the skin.

Percentage yield: 80%

Kiwi fruit.

Kumquats

These look like tiny, elongated oranges, about the size of a medium olive. The skin and even the seeds can be eaten. The skin is sweet, while the flesh and juice are tart. Avoid soft or shriveled fruit. Kumquats keep well and are usually in good condition in the market.

To prepare, wash, drain well, and cut as desired.

Percentage yield: 95–100%

Kumquats.

Lemons and Limes

Look for firm, smooth skins. Colors may vary: Limes may be yellow and lemons may have some green on skin. The most commonly used limes are called Persian limes, usually with a deep green rind. Key limes are much smaller and may be green or yellow. A special variety of lemon, called Meyer lemon, has a higher sugar concentration than regular lemons and thus has a sweeter taste. Once rare, Meyer lemons have become more widely available.

To prepare, cut in wedges, slices, or other shapes for garnish, or cut in half crosswise for juicing.

Percentage yield: 40–45% (juiced)

Lemons.

Limes.

Lychees (or Litchis)

This Chinese fruit is about the size of a walnut or ping-pong ball. Its rough, leathery outer skin, which ranges from reddish to brown, is easily peeled away to reveal aromatic, juicy white flesh that surrounds an inedible pit. Look for heavy, plump fruit with good color.

To prepare, peel, cut in half, and remove the seed.

Percentage yield: 50%

Lychees.

Mangoes

There are two main types of this tropical fruit: oval, with a skin that ranges from green to orange to red, and kidney-shaped, with skin that is a more uniform yellow when ripe. Mangoes have a thin but tough skin and yellow to yellow-orange flesh that is juicy and aromatic. Fruit should be plump and firm, with clear color and no blemishes. Avoid rock-hard fruit, which may not ripen properly.

Mangoes.

Let ripen at room temperature until slightly soft. Peel and cut away the flesh from the center stone; or cut in half before peeling, working a thin-bladed knife around both sides of the flat stone.

Percentage yield: 75%

Melons

Cantaloupe.

Look for the following characteristics when selecting melons:

Cantaloupes. Smooth scar on stem end, with no trace of stem (called *full slip*, meaning the melon was picked ripe). Yellow rind, with little or no green. Heavy, with good aroma.

Honeydew. Good aroma; slightly soft, heavy, creamy white to yellowish rind, not too green. Large sizes have best quality.

Crenshaw, Casaba, Persian, Canary, Santa Claus. Heavy, with a rich aroma and slightly soft blossom end.

Watermelon. Yellow underside; not white. Firm and symmetrical. Large sizes have best yield. Velvety surface; not too shiny. When cut, look for hard dark brown seeds and no white heart (hard white streak running through center).

Honeydew.

Crenshaw melon.

Canary melon.

Piel de sapo melon.

Watermelon.

Oranges.

To prepare hollow melons, wash, cut in half, and remove seeds and fibers. Cut into wedges and cut flesh from rind, or cut balls with ball cutter. Alternatively, cut the rind from the whole melon with a heavy knife, using the same technique as illustrated for grapefruit, above. Then cut in half, remove the seeds, and cut the flesh as desired. To prepare watermelon, wash, cut in half or into pieces, and cut balls with ball cutter, or cut flesh from rind and remove seeds.

Percentage yield: Watermelons, 45%; others, 50–55%

Nectarines

See peaches and nectarines.

Nectarines.

Tangerines.

Oranges and Mandarins (including Tangerines)

To select high-quality oranges, use the same guidelines as for grapefruit. Mandarins may feel puffy, but they should be heavy for their size. Unusual varieties include blood oranges, with dark red flesh and juice and intense flavor, and Seville oranges, with tart rather than sweet flesh. Seville oranges are prized for making marmalade.

Peel mandarins by hand and separate the sections. For juicing, cut oranges in half crosswise; for sections, see grapefruit.

Percentage yield: 60–65% (sections with no membranes); 50% (juiced)

Mandarins.

Blood oranges.

Courtesy iStockphoto.com.

Papaya.

Papayas

Papayas are pear-shaped tropical fruits with a mild, sweet flavor and slightly floral aroma. The flesh is yellow or pinkish, depending on the variety, and the center cavity holds a mass of round, black seeds. Papayas may weigh from less than 1 pound to several pounds (less than 500 g to more than 1 kg) each. Their skin is green when unripe, becoming yellow as they ripen. For best quality, select fruits that are firm and symmetrical, without bruises or rotten spots. Avoid dark green papayas, which may not ripen properly.

Let ripen at room temperature until slightly soft and nearly all yellow, with only a little green. Wash. Cut in half lengthwise and scrape out the seeds. Peel, if desired, or serve the seeded halves as they are, like small melon halves.

Percentage yield: 65%

Passion fruit.

Passion Fruit

These are tropical fruits about the size of eggs, with a brownish purple skin that becomes wrinkled when ripe. (There is also a yellow-skinned variety.) They are mostly hollow when ripe, with juice, seeds, and a little flesh inside. The tart juice has an intense, exotic flavor and an aroma that is greatly prized by pastry chefs. Select fruits that are large and heavy for their size. If they are smooth, let ripen at room temperature until the skin is wrinkled.

To use, cut in half, taking care not to lose any juice. Scrape out the seeds, juice, and pulp. The seeds can be eaten, so do not discard them. If you need only the juice, it is much more economical to buy the frozen juice, as fresh fruits are expensive.

Percentage yield: 40–45%

Peaches.

Peaches and Nectarines

Peaches should be plump and firm, without bruises or blemishes. Avoid dark green fruits, which are immature and will not ripen well. Avoid fruits that have been refrigerated before ripening, as they may be mealy. Select freestone varieties of peaches. Clingstone varieties require too much labor (they are used primarily for canning).

Let ripen at room temperature, then refrigerate. Peel peaches by blanching in boiling water 10 to 20 seconds, until the skin slips off easily, and cool in ice water. (Nectarines do not need to be peeled unless desired.) Cut in half, remove the pit, and drop into fruit juice, sugar syrup, or ascorbic acid solution to prevent darkening.

Percentage yield: 75%

Pears.

Pears

Pears should be clean, firm, and bright, with no blemishes or bruises. Pears for eating raw should be fully ripe and aromatic. However, once they have ripened, pears are likely to become mushy within a day, so refrigerate immediately upon ripening. For cooking, they are better if slightly underripe, as fully ripe pears are too soft when cooked.

To prepare, wash, pare, cut in halves or quarters, and remove core. To prevent browning, dip in fruit juice.

Percentage yield: 75% (peeled and cored)

Butter French pear.

Courtesy of the California Pear Advisory Board.

Forelle pear.

Courtesy of the California Pear Advisory Board.

Starcrimson pear.

Courtesy of the California Pear Advisory Board.

Comice pear.

Courtesy of the California Pear Advisory Board.

Seckel pear.

Courtesy of the California Pear Advisory Board.

Taylor gold pear.

Courtesy of the California Pear Advisory Board

Persimmons

Persimmons are orange-red fruits available in two varieties. The most common is Hachiya, which is shaped somewhat like a large acorn (about 8 oz/250 g each). It is extremely tannic when unripe, nearly inedible, but it ripens to a soft, jellylike mass. Ripe persimmons are sweet, juicy, and mild, but rich in flavor. The other variety, Fuyu, is smaller and more squat in shape. It lacks the tannin content of Hachiya persimmons and can be eaten even when not fully ripe. Select plump persimmons with a good red color and stem cap attached.

Ripen at room temperature until very soft, then refrigerate. Remove stem cap, cut as desired, and remove seeds, if there are any.

Percentage yield: 80%

Persimmons.

Pineapple

Pineapples should be plump and fresh-looking, with an orange-yellow color and abundant fragrance. Avoid soft spots, bruises, and dark, watery spots.

Store at room temperature for a day or two to allow some tartness to disappear, then refrigerate. Pineapples may be cut in many ways. For slices, chunks, and dice, cut off the top and bottom and pare the rough skin from the sides, using a stainless steel knife. Remove all "eyes." Cut into quarters lengthwise and cut out the hard center core. Slice or cut as desired.

Percentage yield: 50%

Pineapple.

Plums

Look for plump, firm, but not hard plums, with no bruises or blemishes.

To prepare, wash, cut in half, and remove pits.

Percentage yield: 95% (pitted only)

Prune plums.

Red plums.

Pomegranates

The pomegranate is a subtropical fruit about the size of a large apple. It has a dry red skin or shell enclosing a mass of seeds. Each seed is surrounded by a small sphere of juicy, bright red pulp. Pomegranates are used mostly for their red, tart-sweet juice. The seeds with their surrounding pulp can also be used as an attractive garnish for desserts and even meat dishes. Look for heavy fruits without bruises. When squeezed, they should yield to gentle pressure; if they are too hard, they may be dried out.

To prepare, lightly score the skin without cutting into the seeds and carefully break the fruit into sections. Separate the seeds from the membranes. Juicing is difficult. Some methods crush the seeds, which makes the juice bitter. To make a better juice, use this method: Roll the whole pomegranate on the countertop under the palm of the hand, to break the juice sacs. Then pierce a hole in the side of the fruit and squeeze out the juice.

Percentage yield: 55%

Black freestone plums.

Santa Rosa plums.

Pomegranate.

Prickly Pears or Cactus Pears

These are barrel-shaped fruits about the size of a large egg. Their skin color ranges from magenta to greenish red, and they have a bright pinkish-red, spongy interior with black seeds. The pulp is sweet and aromatic, but with a mild flavor. Good-quality fruits are tender but not mushy, with a good skin color, not faded. Avoid fruits with rotten spots.

If the fruit is firm, allow to ripen at room temperature, then refrigerate. Keep in mind these are the fruits of cacti, and thorns grow on the skin. These are removed before shipping, but small, hard-to-see thorns may remain. To avoid getting stung, hold the fruit with a fork while you slice off the top and bottom. Still holding it with a fork, pare the sides with a knife and discard the peels without touching them. Cut or slice the pulp as desired, or force it through a sieve to purée it and remove the seeds.

Percentage yield: 70%

Prickly pears.

Quince.

Quinces

Quinces grow in temperate climates and were once very popular in Europe and North America. Many old, neglected quince trees remain in New England and elsewhere. The fruit resembles a large, yellow, lumpy pear, with either a smooth or slightly downy skin. The raw fruit is never eaten, as it is dry and hard. When cooked (usually stewed or poached in a sugar syrup), it becomes aromatic, flavorful, and sweet, and the flesh turns slightly pink. The fruit keeps well. Select fruit with good color and free of bruises or blemishes.

Cut, pare, and core like apples or pears, then cook.

Percentage yield: 75%

Rhubarb

Rhubarb is a stem, not a fruit, but it is used like a fruit. Buy firm, crisp, tender rhubarb with thick stalks, not thin and shriveled.

To prepare, cut off all traces of leaf, which is poisonous. Trim the root end, if necessary. Peel with a vegetable peeler, if desired; you can omit this step if the skin is tender. Cut into desired lengths.

Percentage yield: 85–90% (if purchased without leaves)

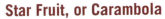

Rhubarb.

Star fruit.

Star Fruit, or Carambola

The star fruit is a shiny, yellow, oblong fruit with five ridges running its length, so it forms stars when sliced crosswise. It is fragrant, ranging from tart to sweet, with a crisp texture. Look for full, firm fruits. Avoid fruits with ribs that have browned and shrunk.

Wash and slice crosswise.

Percentage yield: 99%

FRUIT LIQUEURS AND ALCOHOLS

A variety of alcoholic beverages are distilled from or flavored with fruits. Many of these are useful as flavoring ingredients in the bakeshop. Most of the alcohols we use in the bakeshop fall into two categories: white alcohols and liqueurs.

White alcohols, also known as *eaux-de-vie* (oh duh VEE; singular, *eau-de-vie*), French for "water of life," are true brandies, meaning they are distilled from fruit. They are not aged in wood barrels, so they are clear and colorless. White alcohols have no sweetness and have a fresh, fruity aroma. The most common of this type found in the bakeshop is kirsch (made from cherries). Other white alcohols include poire (pear), mirabelle (yellow plum), and framboise (raspberry).

Liqueurs, also called *cordials*, are sweet alcoholic beverages flavored with fruit, herbs, or other ingredients. Orange-flavored liqueurs, such as curaçao, Cointreau, and Grand Marnier, are the most commonly used in the bakeshop.

PREPARING FRUIT DESSERTS

Simple Fruit Salads and Cooked Fruits

After a rich meal, a piece of fresh fruit can be a light and refreshing dessert. Most diners, however, are happier with something that requires a little more effort from the kitchen. Serving fresh fruit, such as berries, with cream or a sauce such as sabayon, crème anglaise, or coulis often satisfies these desires. (See Chapter 12 for a selection of dessert sauces.) A simple fruit salad can be an attractive alternative. Marinating fresh fruit in a flavored syrup adds a new dimension to the fruit and also allows the pastry chef to make an attractive mixture of colorful, carefully cut seasonal items.

A simple and versatile category of fruit dessert is the *compote*, which may be defined as cooked fruit, usually small fruits or cut fruit, served in its cooking liquid. Mixed-fruit compotes are versatile because they can be seasoned and sweetened as desired, and the combination of fruits is infinitely variable. Cooking media range from light syrups to concentrated spiced caramel, honey, or liqueur mixtures.

There is no clear dividing line between fresh fruit salads and lightly cooked fruit compotes. If a boiling syrup is poured over a mixture of fruit, and the fruit is marinated without additional cooking, it could be called either a compote or a fresh fruit salad.

Hard fruits and mixtures of dried fruits are usually cooked longer, until they are tender. Larger, whole fruits cooked in syrup are not usually called compotes, though the cooking procedure is the same. A pear poached in wine is a classic dessert that remains popular.

This chapter presents two types of compotes. The first part of the recipe section includes light mixtures of fresh fruit in syrup that are served as desserts. Later in the chapter you will find sweeter, more intensely flavored compotes that are not served by themselves but are used as sauces, condiments, and ingredients in pastries and other preparations.

Many fruits can also be sautéed for serving as desserts. This procedure is similar to sautéing vegetables, except that sugar is added to the fruit and butter in the pan. The sugar caramelizes and forms a rich sauce as it combines with the juices that are drawn out of the fruit. Apples, apricots, bananas, pears, peaches, pineapples, plums, and cherries are especially suited to this style of preparation. For examples of this type of preparation, see the recipe for Caramelized Pears (p. 581) and the variations that follow.

Traditional and Specialty Fruit Desserts

This chapter also includes a selection of recipes ranging from the old-fashioned and rustic to the stylishly modern. Traditional North American favorites include the *cobbler*, which is like a fruit pie made in large baking pans, but without a bottom crust; the *crisp*, which is like a cobbler but with streusel topping instead of a pastry crust; and the *betty*, which has alternating layers of rich cake crumbs and fruit. These homey desserts are, for the most part, easy to prepare.

More difficult to prepare is the Caramelized Pear Charlotte (p. 588), perhaps the most complex recipe in this chapter. Before attempting this dessert, you may need to review the information on Bavarians, mousses, and charlottes in Chapter 19.

Fruit Preserves, Condiments, and Garnishes

Finally, at the end of the chapter you will find a variety of preparations that are not served as desserts, but rather used as elements or ingredients in other dishes. These include jams and marmalades, sweet compotes used as sauces or garnishes, and specialty items such as fruit crisps, pâte de fruits, and candied citrus zests that add appeal to plated desserts and petit four trays.

KEY POINTS TO REVIEW

▐ What changes in aroma, sweetness, juiciness and texture, and color take place as a fruit ripens?

▐ Which of these changes can occur after fruit is picked? How does your answer depend on the particular fruit?

▐ If you know the percentage yield of a fruit, how do you perform calculations of yield and amount needed (EP and AP weights)?

▐ What is a compote?

▐ What are the following traditional North American fruit desserts: cobbler, crisp, and betty?

POACHED FRUIT (FRUIT COMPOTE)

Yield: about 3 lb (1.5 kg), plus syrup

Ingredients	U.S.	Metric
Water	1 qt	1 L
Sugar (see *Note*)	1–2 lb	0.5–0.75 kg
Vanilla extract (see *Note*)	2 tsp	10 mL
Prepared fruit (see individual variations)	3 lb	1.5 kg

NOTE: The amount of sugar used depends on the desired sweetness of the dessert and the natural sweetness of the fruit. Other flavoring may be used in place of the vanilla. A popular alternative is to add 2 or 3 strips lemon peel and 1 oz (30 mL) lemon juice to the syrup.

PROCEDURE

1. Combine the water and sugar in a saucepan. Bring to a boil, stirring until the sugar is dissolved.
2. Add the vanilla.
3. Add the prepared fruit to the syrup or, if using tender fruit, place the fruit in a shallow pan and pour the syrup over it.
4. Cook very slowly, just below a simmer, until the fruit is just tender.
5. Let the fruit cool in the syrup. When cool, refrigerate in the syrup until needed.

VARIATIONS

POACHED APPLES, PEARS, OR PINEAPPLE

Peel, quarter, and core the fruit. For pineapple, cut into small wedges. Poach as in basic recipe.

PEARS IN WINE

Substitute red or white table wine for the water. Omit the vanilla. Add ½ sliced lemon to the syrup. Peel the pears, but leave them whole.

POACHED PEACHES

Peel the peaches by blanching them in boiling water for a few seconds and slipping off the skins. Cut in half and remove the stones. Poach as in the basic recipe.

PEACHES IN WINE

Prepare the peaches as above. Poach as for Pears in Wine, flavoring the syrup with lemon.

POACHED APRICOTS, PLUMS, OR NECTARINES

Cut the fruits in half and remove the stones. (Nectarines may be peeled like peaches, if desired.) Poach as in the basic recipe.

POACHED CHERRIES

Pit the cherries with a cherry pitter. Poach as in the basic recipe.

POACHED DRIED FRUIT

Soak dried fruit in water overnight. Use the soaking liquid for making the syrup. Poach as in the basic recipe, adding 1 oz (30 mL) lemon juice to the syrup.

TROPICAL FRUIT COMPOTE

Prepare the syrup as in the basic recipe, flavoring it with lemon and orange zest in addition to the vanilla and substituting white wine for half the water. Prepare a mixture of kiwi fruit, peeled and sliced crosswise; papayas, peeled, seeded, and cut into thin wedges or slices; mangoes, peeled, pitted, and sliced; orange wedges; and strawberries, trimmed and halved. While the syrup is still hot, pour it over the fruit. Cool, cover, and refrigerate overnight. If desired, top each portion with toasted or untoasted shredded coconut.

FRESH FRUIT SALAD

This is an uncooked version of fruit compote. Prepare the syrup as in the basic recipe. Cool it completely. Prepare a mixture of fresh fruits; dice large fruits or cut them into bite-size pieces. Combine the fruits and cold syrup and let them stand several hours or overnight in the refrigerator.

FRUIT SALAD

Yield: about 2 lb 8 oz (1100 g), including syrup

Ingredients	U.S.	Metric
Apple	1	1
Pear	1	1
Orange	1	1
Peach	1	1
Strawberries	10	10
Raspberries	10	10
Red plum	1	1
Passion fruit	1	1
Sugar	11 oz	300 g
Water	14 oz	400 g
Cinnamon sticks	2	2
Vanilla bean	1	1
Bay leaves	2	2

PROCEDURE

1. Prepare all the fruit as necessary (wash, peel, pit, core, and so on, depending on the fruit). Cut all the fruit, except the passion fruit, into large, bite-size pieces and place in a bowl. Add the pulp, juice, and seeds from the passion fruit to the bowl.

2. Heat the sugar, water, cinnamon sticks, vanilla bean, and bay leaves gently until the sugar has dissolved. Bring to a boil. Remove from the heat and pour over the prepared fruit.

3. Let the mixture steep and infuse 2–3 hours.

4. Drain or serve with a slotted spoon. Reserve the syrup for other uses, if desired.

MARINATED TROPICAL FRUITS

Yield: about 4 lb (2 kg), including syrup

Ingredients	U.S.	Metric
Mangoes	3	3
Large pineapple	1	1
Kiwi fruits	5	5
Water	7 oz	200 g
Sugar	7 oz	200 g
Cinnamon stick	1	1
Orange rind, in strips	0.3 oz	8 g
Lemon	½	½
Cloves, whole	4	4
Mint sprig	1	1
Vanilla bean	1	1

PROCEDURE

1. Peel the fruit. Core the pineapple and remove the pit from the mangoes. Cut into large cubes (about 1 in./2.5 cm). Place the fruit in a saucepan.

2. Combine the remaining ingredients and bring to a boil, stirring to dissolve the sugar. (If desired, tie the spices in a cheesecloth bag so they can be removed easily before serving.)

3. Pour the boiling syrup over the fruit, cover with a round of parchment, and simmer 5 minutes. Cool and then chill the fruit in the syrup.

CHILLED SUMMER FRUIT SOUP

Yield: approximately 3 pt (1.5 L)

Ingredients	U.S.			Metric
Water	2 pt	8	oz	1250 mL
Sugar	1 lb	8	oz	750 g
Lime juice		5	oz	150 mL
Lime zest, grated		0.25	oz	8 g
Strawberries, sliced		8	oz	250 g
Bananas, sliced		12	oz	375 g
Gelatin		0.25	oz	8 g
Cold water		4	oz	125 g
Garnish: assorted fresh fruit, such as strawberries, raspberries, blackberries, plums, red currants, blueberries, kiwi fruit	as desired			as desired

PROCEDURE

1. Combine the sugar and water in a saucepan. Bring to a boil and stir to dissolve the sugar.

2. Add the lime juice and zest, the strawberries, and the bananas. Remove from the heat, cover, and let stand until cooled to room temperature.

3. Pass the soup through a fine sieve. Let the liquid drain, but do not press down on the solids, which would make the soup cloudy.

4. Soften the gelatin in the cold water. Reheat the soup until just below the simmering point and add the gelatin. Stir until dissolved.

5. Cool and then chill the soup. The quantity of gelatin is just enough to give the soup a little body without gelling it.

6. Prepare the desired fruit for garnish. Leave small berries whole, and cut larger fruit as desired.

7. To serve, ladle the soup into soup plates and add the desired garnish.

CARAMELIZED PEARS

Yield: 8 portions

Ingredients	U.S.	Metric
Pears, ripe	8	8
Butter	2 oz	60 g
Granulated sugar	4 oz	125 g

VARIATIONS

Cut the pears into halves instead of quarters. To serve, place them cut side down on a plate, slice crosswise, and fan or shingle the slices. For a more caramelized surface, sprinkle the top of the fruit with sugar and then caramelize under a salamander or broiler, being careful not to let the sugar scorch.

The following fruits can be prepared using the same basic method. Adjust the quantities of butter and sugar according to taste and the sweetness of the fruit.

CARAMELIZED APPLES

Peel, core, and slice the apples. Use white or brown sugar, depending on the desired flavor. If desired, season with cinnamon and nutmeg, vanilla, or lemon zest.

CARAMELIZED PEACHES

Blanch and skin the peaches. Cut in half and remove the pits. Slice or cut into wedges.

CARAMELIZED PINEAPPLE

Peel, slice crosswise, and remove the core from each slice using a small, round cutter. Use white or brown sugar, as desired.

CARAMELIZED BANANAS

Peel; quarter by cutting in half crosswise and then lengthwise. Use brown sugar. Because bananas release little juice, you may add a little orange juice or pineapple juice. Flavor with cinnamon and nutmeg or mace.

PROCEDURE

1. Peel, core, and quarter the pears.

2. Heat the butter in a sauté pan. Add the pears and sugar. Cook over moderately high heat. The pears will give off juice, which will combine with the sugar to form a syrup. Continue to cook, turning and basting the pears, until the syrup reduces and thickens and the pears are lightly caramelized. The syrup will become light brown; do not try for a dark brown color or the fruit will overcook.

3. Serve warm. A small scoop of vanilla ice cream is a good accompaniment. Caramelized fruits are most often used as components of other desserts, and are also used as garnish for savory items such as pork and duck.

APPLE CRISP

Yield: 1 pan, 12 × 20 in. (30 × 50 cm); 48 portions, 4 oz (120 g) each

Ingredients	U.S.		Metric
Peeled, sliced apples	8 lb		4000 g
Sugar	4	oz	125 g
Lemon juice	2	oz	60 mL
Butter	1 lb		500 g
Brown sugar	1 lb 8	oz	750 g
Cinnamon	0.12 oz (2 tsp)		4 g
Pastry flour	1 lb 8	oz	750 g

PROCEDURE

1. Toss the apples gently with the sugar and lemon juice. Spread evenly in a 12 × 20-in. (30 × 50 cm) baking pan.

2. Rub the butter, sugar, cinnamon, and flour together until well blended and crumbly.

3. Sprinkle evenly over the apples.

4. Bake at 350°F (175°C) for about 45 minutes, until the top is browned and the apples are tender.

--- **VARIATION** ---

PEACH, CHERRY, OR RHUBARB CRISP

Substitute peaches, cherries, or rhubarb for the apples. If rhubarb is used, increase the sugar in step 1 to 12 oz (375 g).

FRUIT COBBLER

Yield: 1 pan, 12 × 20 in. (30 × 50 cm); 48 portions, 5 oz (150 g) each

Ingredients	U.S.	Metric
Fruit pie filling	12–15 lb	5.5–7 kg
Flaky Pie Dough (p. 283)	2 lb	1 kg

--- **VARIATION** ---

In place of the pie pastry, use biscuit dough (p. 216). Roll out the dough ¼ in. (6 mm) thick and cut it into 1½-in. (4-cm) rounds. Place the rounds on top of the fruit filling.

PROCEDURE

1. Place the fruit filling in a 12 × 20-in. (30 × 50 cm) baking pan.

2. Roll out the pastry to fit the top of the pan. Place on top of the filling and seal the edges to the pan. Pierce small holes in the pastry to allow steam to escape.

3. Bake at 425°F (220°C) for about 30 minutes, until the top is browned.

4. Cut the dessert in 6 rows of 8, or 48 portions. Serve warm or cold.

APPLE BETTY

Yield: 1 pan, 12 × 20 in. (30 × 50 cm); 48 portions, 4 oz (120 g) each

Ingredients	U.S.		Metric
Peeled, sliced apples	8 lb		4000 g
Sugar	1 lb 8	oz	750 g
Salt	0.25 oz (1 tsp)		7 g
Nutmeg	0.08 oz (1 tsp)		2 g
Lemon zest, grated	0.12 oz (1½ tsp)		3 g
Lemon juice	2	oz	60 mL
Yellow or white cake crumbs	2 lb		1000 g
Butter, melted	8	oz	250 g

PROCEDURE

1. Combine the apples, sugar, salt, nutmeg, zest, and lemon juice in a bowl. Toss gently until well mixed.

2. Place one-third of the apple mixture in an even layer in a well-buttered 12 × 20-in. (30 × 50 cm) baking pan.

3. Top with one-third of the cake crumbs.

4. Continue until all the apples and crumbs have been used. You will have 3 layers of fruit and 3 layers of crumbs.

5. Pour the butter evenly over the top.

6. Bake at 350°F (175°C) for about 1 hour, until the fruit is tender.

APPLE CHARLOTTE

Yield: one 1-qt (1-L) mold

Ingredients	U.S.		Metric	
Tart cooking apples	2 lb		900	g
Butter	1	oz	30	g
Lemon zest, grated	0.08 oz (1 tsp)		2	g
Cinnamon	0.01 oz (¼ tsp)		0.4	g
Puréed apricot jam	2	oz	60	g
Sugar	1–2	oz	30–60	g
Firm white bread, trimmed of crusts	12 slices		12 slices	
Butter, melted	4	oz	110	g

NOTE: Apple charlottes should normally not be made in sizes larger than 1 qt (1 L), or they are likely to collapse after unmolding. To help avoid collapse, cook the apple mixture until it is quite thick. Make sure the bread is firm; and bake the charlotte long enough to brown the bread well. (See the Charlotte sidebar on p. 525 for a history of the *apple charlotte*.)

PROCEDURE

1. Peel, core, and slice the apples. Combine them with the butter, zest, and cinnamon in a broad, shallow pan. Cook over moderate heat until soft. Mash the apples lightly with a spoon and continue to cook until they form a thick purée (a few remaining lumps of apple are acceptable).

2. Stir in the apricot jam. Add sugar to taste, depending on the sweetness of the apples.

3. Line a 1-qt (1-L) charlotte mold, or two 1-pt (500-mL) charlotte molds, or other straight-sided molds in the following manner: Dip the bread slices in the melted butter and line the mold with the buttered side against the inside of the mold. The bottom may be lined with one round slice or with wedges of bread cut to fit. Line the sides with half-slices of bread overlapping shingle-fashion.

4. Fill with the apple purée and top with the remaining bread.

5. Bake at 400°F (200°C) 30–40 minutes.

6. Cool for 20 minutes, then carefully unmold. Serve warm or cold.

STRAWBERRIES ROMANOFF

Yield: 8–12 portions

Ingredients	U.S.		Metric
Strawberries, fresh	2 qt		2 L
Orange juice	4	fl oz	125 mL
Confectioners' sugar	2	oz	60 g
Orange liqueur, such as curaçao	2	fl oz	60 mL
Heavy cream	12	oz	400 mL
Confectioners' sugar	0.75 oz (3 tbsp)		20 g
Orange liqueur, such as curaçao	0.75 fl oz (1½ tbsp)		20 mL

PROCEDURE

1. Trim the stems and hulls from the strawberries. Cut the berries in half if they are large.

2. Combine the berries with the orange juice and the first quantities of sugar and liqueur. Let stand for 1 hour, refrigerated.

3. Prepare whipped cream flavored with orange liqueur, following the procedure on pages 255–256.

4. To serve, put the berries and juices in a serving bowl or individual dessert dishes. Fill a pastry bag fitted with a star tube with the whipped cream. Pipe the cream decoratively over the berries, covering them completely.

VARIATION

Place a small scoop of orange sorbet in each dessert dish and cover it with the marinated berries. Cover with whipped cream as in the basic recipe.

GRATIN DE FRUITS ROUGES (BERRY GRATIN)

Yield: 5 portions, 5 oz (150 g) each

Ingredients	U.S.	Metric
Sponge layers (see step 1)	5	5
Dessert syrup flavored with kirsch (p. 254)	as needed	as needed
Strawberries	7 oz	200 g
Blackberries	3.5 oz	100 g
Raspberries	3.5 oz	100 g
Red currants	2.5 oz	75 g
Sabayon I (p. 274)	5 oz	150 g
	(about 15 fl oz)	(about 450 mL)
Raspberry Sauce (p. 270)	3.5 oz	100 g
Additional fruit for garnish	as needed	as needed

PROCEDURE

1. Cut 5-in. (12-cm) circles of sponge ¼ in. (6 mm) thick. (Sponge Roll II, p. 402, is recommended, but Genoise, p. 401, or other sponges may be used.)

2. Place the circles of sponge on serving plates. Brush with the syrup.

3. Clean the fruit as necessary, and cut the strawberries into halves or quarters, depending on size. Arrange the fruit on top of the sponge.

4. With a spoon, cover the fruit with a layer of sabayon at least ⅛ in. (3 mm) thick.

5. Place under a hot salamander or broiler until lightly browned.

6. Pour a ribbon of raspberry sauce around each gratin and serve immediately.

RASPBERRY OR CHERRY GRATIN

Ingredients per Portion	U.S.		Metric
Genoise layer (p. 401; see step 2)			
Raspberries or sweet, pitted cherries	3	oz	90 g
Pastry Cream (p. 263)	2	oz	60 g
Whipped cream	1	oz	30 g
Kirsch, orange liqueur, or raspberry or cherry brandy	to taste		to taste
Sliced almonds	0.25 oz		7 g
Butter, melted	0.25 oz		7 g
Confectioners' sugar			

PROCEDURE

1. Select a shallow gratin dish or other heatproof dish large enough to hold the fruit in a shallow layer.

2. Cut a thin slice of genoise (about ⅜ in./ 1 cm thick) to cover the bottom of the dish.

3. Arrange the fruit on top of the genoise. (If desired, marinate the fruit ahead of time in fruit brandy or liqueur and a little sugar. Drain and use the liquid in step 4.)

4. Combine the pastry cream, whipped cream, and flavoring. Spread the mixture over the fruit, covering completely.

5. Mix the almonds and butter and sprinkle over the pastry cream. Dredge the top heavily with confectioners' sugar.

6. Place under a broiler or in the top of a hot oven for a few minutes to brown the top. Serve hot or warm.

BAKED APPLES TATIN-STYLE

Yield: 6 apples, about 4½ oz (130 g) each

Ingredients	U.S.		Metric
Puff pastry	6	oz	150 g
Stuffing			
Brown sugar	2	oz	50 g
Butter	2	oz	50 g
Almonds, chopped	2	oz	50 g
Pecans, chopped	1	oz	25 g
Raisins	2	oz	50 g
Prunes, chopped	2	oz	50 g
Armagnac or brandy	0.5	oz	15 g
Cinnamon	1	tsp	2 g
Topping			
Sugar	5	oz	150 g
Vanilla bean (see *Note*)	½		½
Butter	3	oz	70 g
Sliced almonds, toasted	0.75	oz	20 g
Pecans, chopped	0.75	oz	20 g
Pine nuts	0.75	oz	20 g
Raisins	0.75	oz	20 g
Pistachios	0.75	oz	20 g
Granny Smith apples	6		6
Butter, melted	2	oz	50 g
Crème Anglaise (p. 261)	12	oz	300 g
Calvados	2	oz	50 g

NOTE: If vanilla beans are not available, add ¼ tsp (1 g) vanilla extract to the caramel in step 4.

PROCEDURE

1. Roll out the pastry until it is very thin. Dock and chill. Cut 6 circles 4½ in. (11 cm) in diameter. Return to the refrigerator until needed.

2. Butter 6 pudding molds about 3 in. (7–8 cm) in diameter on top, or large enough to hold an apple. Set aside.

3. Prepare the stuffing: Cream the butter and sugar. Mix in the remaining stuffing ingredients.

4. Prepare the topping: Cook the sugar to the caramel stage. Keeping the pan over moderate heat, add the vanilla and butter and stir constantly until the butter is incorporated into the caramel (see p. 271 for information on butter caramel). Pour a little of the caramel into the bottoms of the pudding molds, using about one-fourth of the caramel in all. Add the remaining topping ingredients to the remaining caramel and keep warm.

5. Peel and core the apples. Brush with melted butter.

6. Place the apples in the pudding molds and fill the cores with the stuffing mixture. Press down well.

7. Cover with foil and bake at 350°F (180°C) until the apples start to soften, about 15 minutes. Remove from the oven and allow to cool slightly.

8. Place a disk of puff pastry on top of each apple and tuck in the sides.

9. Bake at 400°F (200°C) until the pastry is browned.

10. Mix the crème anglaise with the Calvados. Ladle pools of this sauce onto serving plates. Turn out the apples onto the pools with the puff pastry on the bottom. Spoon a little of the topping over the apples.

CRÈME BRÛLÉE SOPHIA

Yield: 6 portions

Ingredients	U.S.		Metric
Grapefruits	2		2
Peaches, fresh or canned, drained and chopped	8	oz	250 g
Sugar	1.75	oz	50 g
Milk	9	oz	280 g
Heavy cream	3	oz	90 g
Whole eggs	5	oz	150 g
Egg yolks	1.33	oz	40 g
Sugar	3.5	oz	100 g
Vanilla extract	½	tsp	2 g
Peach schnapps	2	oz	60 g
Extra-fine granulated sugar	3.5	oz	100 g

PROCEDURE

1. Segment the grapefruits. If any segments are thick, cut them in half horizontally to make thinner segments. Drain on absorbent paper until thoroughly dry to the touch.

2. Cook the peach flesh with the sugar over low heat until soft, then purée. Divide the purée among 6 shallow 5-oz (150-mL) ramekins, spreading it evenly on the bottom.

3. Bring the milk and cream to scalding point.

4. Whip the eggs, yolks, and sugar until light. Temper with half of the hot milk, then stir this back into the remaining milk mixture. Add the vanilla.

5. Strain through a fine china cap.

6. Add the peach schnapps. Pour carefully into the ramekins so as not to stir the peach purée.

7. Place in a hot-water bath and bake at 215°F (100°C) until just set.

8. Cool completely.

9. Arrange the grapefruit wedges on top in a pinwheel pattern. Just before serving, dust with sugar and caramelize the tops with a blowtorch.

FIGS IN PORT WINE

Yield: about 1 lb 4 oz (600 g) figs in sauce, depending on size of figs

Ingredients	U.S.		Metric
Sugar	3.75	oz	100 g
Butter	1.5	oz	40 g
Red wine	3	oz	80 g
Port wine	3	oz	80 g
Vanilla extract	½	tsp	2 g
Blackcurrant purée	2	oz	50 g
Figs, fresh, whole	8		8

PROCEDURE

1. Cook the sugar to a golden caramel.

2. Keeping the pan over moderate heat, add the butter, and stir constantly until the butter is incorporated into the caramel (see p. 271 for information on butter caramel).

3. Add the red wine, port, and vanilla extract. Simmer until the caramelized sugar is dissolved.

4. Add the blackcurrant purée and reduce by one-third.

5. Trim the hard stem ends of the figs and cut the figs in half lengthwise.

6. Place the figs in a baking dish and pour the caramel-wine syrup over them.

7. Bake at 350°F (180°C) until the figs are slightly puffed, 10–20 minutes—longer if the figs are not ripe.

8. Serve the figs with the sauce.

CARAMELIZED PEAR CHARLOTTE

Yield: 3 cakes, 7 in. (18 cm) each

Ingredients	U.S.		Metric
Caramelized pears			
Sugar	10	oz	270 g
Water	4	oz	110 g
Heavy cream	11	oz	310 g
Vanilla bean, split (see *Note*)	1		1
Pears, peeled, cored, and quartered	6		6
Syrup			
Sugar	2	oz	60 g
Water	2	oz	60 g
Poire Williams	3.33 oz		100 g
Assembly			
Baumkuchen (p. 409)	see step 3		see step 3
Genoise layer (p. 401)	see step 3		see step 3
Mousse			
Milk	7.5	oz	220 g
Egg yolks	3	oz	90 g
Sugar	0.6	oz (4 tsp)	20 g
Gelatin, softened in water	0.5	oz	14 g
Caramel from the pears	8	oz	240 g
Heavy cream	1 lb 7	oz	650 g
Glaçage			
Gelatin	0.25	oz	6 g
Caramel from the pears	4	oz	120 g
Glucose	1	oz	30 g
Poire Williams	1	oz	30 g
Decoration			
Italian Meringue (p. 259)	as needed		as needed
Chocolate cigarettes (p. 635)	as needed		as needed
Red currants or other berries	as needed		as needed
Mint leaves	as needed		as needed

NOTE: If vanilla beans are not available, add ½ tsp (2 g) vanilla extract to the caramel in step 1.

PROCEDURE

1. For the pears: Make a syrup with the sugar and water and cook to a golden caramel. Carefully add the cream and vanilla bean. Stir and simmer until the caramel is dissolved. Add the pears. Cover with a round of parchment and simmer until tender. Drain and reserve both the caramel and the pears. Scrape the seeds from the vanilla bean and add them to the caramel. There should be about 12 oz (360 g) caramel.

2. For the syrup: Heat the water and sugar until the sugar is dissolved. Remove from the heat and add the Poire Williams.

3. Line three 7-in. (18-cm) charlotte rings with baumkuchen, as shown on page 446. Place the rings on cake cards. Cut 6 thin layers from the genoise and place one in the bottom of each ring. (Reserve the other 3 layers for step 8.) Brush the genoise with the syrup.

4. Reserve 3 pear quarters for decorating the charlottes and chop the remaining pears into bite-size pieces, retaining any juices they release when cut. Add these juices to the caramel. Place the chopped pears on top of the genoise layers.

5. For the mousse: Heat the milk to scalding point. Whip the egg yolks and sugar until light, then whip in half the milk. Return this mixture to the pan with the remaining milk and heat until thick enough to coat the back of a spoon.

6. Add the gelatin and two-thirds of the reserved caramel from the pears. Stir until the gelatin is dissolved.

7. Cool the mixture by stirring over ice. Before it sets, whip the cream to soft peaks and fold in.

8. Fill the rings three-fourths full with the mousse mixture and level the tops. Place a layer of genoise on top and press down gently. Brush with syrup.

9. Fill the rings to the top with the remaining mousse and level the tops with a palette knife. Chill until set.

10. For the glaçage: Soften the gelatin in cold water (see pp. 80–82). Heat the remaining caramel with the glucose. Stir in the gelatin until dissolved. Add the Poire Williams. Cool slightly.

11. Spoon the glaçage over the mousse. Smooth with a palette knife and chill.

12. Remove the charlotte rings by warming them slightly with a blowtorch and lifting them off.

13. Decorate the tops with a few scrolls of Italian meringue, piped with a star or plain tip, a fanned quartered pear, some chocolate cigarettes, berries, and mint leaves.

SPICED PINEAPPLE

Yield: about 2 lb (950 g) pineapple and sauce

Ingredients	U.S.		Metric
Baby pineapples (see *Note*)	4		4
Sugar	7	oz	200 g
Butter	3.5 oz		100 g
Star anise, whole	2		2
Cloves, whole	2		2
Cinnamon sticks	2		2
Rum	1.5 oz		40 g
Vanilla extract	½	tsp	2 g
Heavy cream	3.5 oz		100 g

NOTE: Baby pineapples weigh about 8 oz (250 g) each and yield about 5 oz (150 g) flesh. If they are not available, substitute 20 oz (600 g) peeled, cored fresh pineapple, in large pieces.

PROCEDURE

1. Peel, core, and eye the pineapples.
2. Cook the sugar to a golden caramel. Keeping the pan over moderate heat, add the butter and spices. Stir constantly until the butter is incorporated into the caramel (see p. 271 for information on butter caramel).
3. Roll the pineapple in the caramel and transfer the fruit to a baking dish.
4. Add the rum and vanilla to the caramel and flambé. Pour this mixture over the pineapple.
5. Bake at 350°F (180°C), basting regularly, until the pineapple is tender, about 35 minutes.
6. Slice the pineapples and serve warm. Heat the caramel sauce, add the cream, and strain. Pour the sauce over the pineapple. See page 620 for a serving suggestion.

RASPBERRY JAM

Yield: 15 oz (480 g)

For large-quantity measurements, see page 731.

Ingredients	U.S.		Metric	Fruit at 100% %
Sugar	6	oz	188 g	75
Water	2	oz	60 g	25
Raspberries, fresh	8	oz	250 g	100
Glucose	0.8	oz	24 g	10
Sugar	1.2	oz	36 g	15
Pectin	0.67 oz		20 g	8

PROCEDURE

1. Place the first quantity of sugar and water in a saucepan and bring to a boil, dissolving the sugar.
2. Add the raspberries and glucose. Boil until the fruit has broken down and the consistency is thick.
3. Mix together the pectin and the remaining sugar. Add to the cooked fruit. Mix well and simmer another 3 minutes.
4. Pour into a clean glass jar and seal. Keep refrigerated.

— VARIATION —

Other soft fruits may be prepared in the same way.

APPLE MARMALADE

Yield: 2 lb 2 oz (1060 g)

For large-quantity measurements, see page 731.

Ingredients	U.S.	Metric	Fruit at 100% %
Apples, peeled and cored	2 lb	1000 g	100
Water	4 oz	125 g	12.5
Sugar	10 oz	300 g	30

PROCEDURE

1. Chop the apples.
2. Place all ingredients in a saucepan and cook over low heat until very soft and of a purée consistency.
3. Force through a sieve or food mill.
4. Pour into clean glass jars. Refrigerate.

STRAWBERRY MARMALADE

Yield: 13 oz (400 g)

For large-quantity measurements, see page 731.

Ingredients	U.S.		Metric	Fruit at 100% %
Strawberries	8	oz	250 g	100
Sugar	8	oz	250 g	100
Pectin	0.17	oz	5 g	2
Lemon juice	0.5	oz	15 g	3

PROCEDURE

1. If the strawberries are large, cut them into halves or quarters. Otherwise, leave them whole.
2. Mix the berries with the sugar. Refrigerate overnight.
3. Bring the sugared fruit to a simmer and cook until at a purée consistency.
4. Remove from the heat. Sprinkle the pectin over the fruit and stir in. Return to the heat and cook 3–4 minutes.
5. Add the lemon juice and mix in.
6. Pour into clean glass jars and seal. Refrigerate.

CARAMELIZED APRICOTS

Yield: 12 oz (300 g)

For large-quantity measurements, see page 732.

Ingredients	U.S.	Metric
Sugar	4 oz	100 g
Water	1 oz	25 g
Honey	2 oz	50 g
Butter	1 oz	25 g
Canned apricots, drained	12 oz	300 g

PROCEDURE

1. Combine the sugar, water, and honey, and cook to the caramel stage.
2. Keeping the pan over moderate heat, add the butter and stir constantly until the butter is incorporated into the caramel (see p. 271 for information on butter caramel).
3. Add the apricots to the caramel mixture. Heat until the apricots are well coated with the caramel.
4. Remove the apricots from the caramel mixture and place on a tray or sheet pan. Cover with plastic film and cool.

PLUM COMPOTE

Yield: 2 lb 4 oz (1000 g)

Ingredients	U.S.	Metric
Sugar	7 oz	200 g
Butter	2 oz	50 g
Star anise, whole	2	2
Vanilla bean (see *Note*)	1	1
Red or black plums, stoned and diced or quartered	2 lb 4 oz	1000 g
Lemon juice	1 oz	30 g
Lemon zest, grated	1 tsp	2 g
Port wine, warmed	2 oz	50 g

NOTE: If desired, omit the vanilla bean and add 1 tsp (5 mL) vanilla extract to the simmering fruit in step 4.

PROCEDURE

1. Melt the sugar in a heavy saucepan. Cook to a pale caramel.
2. Remove from heat; cool slightly.
3. Add the butter, star anise, plums, lemon juice, zest, wine, and vanilla.
4. Bring to a boil, then reduce to a simmer. Cook until the fruit is tender but the pieces remain intact. Cool.

APRICOT COMPOTE

Yield: 9.5 oz (240 g)

For large-quantity measurements, see page 732.

Ingredients	U.S.	Metric
Sugar	4.5 oz	112 g
Water	0.6 oz	15 g
Apricots, fresh or canned, halved and pitted	5 oz	125 g
Pectin	0.4 oz	10 g
Glucose	0.5 oz	12 g

— VARIATION —

APRICOT AND ALMOND COMPOTE

For large-quantity measurements, see page 732.

Ingredients	U.S.	Metric
Whole blanched almonds	2 oz	50 g

Add the almonds to the apricots at the same time as the pectin and glucose.

PROCEDURE

1. Combine the sugar and water in a saucepan and bring to a boil to dissolve the sugar and make a syrup. Cook to 221°F (105°C).
2. Cut the apricot halves into halves or thirds, depending on size. Add to the syrup. Cook an additional 15–17 minutes if the apricots are fresh, about 3 minutes if canned.
3. Add the pectin and glucose and mix in well. Cook an additional 3 minutes.

PINEAPPLE KUMQUAT COMPOTE

Yield: 11 oz (270 g)

For large-quantity measurements, see page 732.

Ingredients	U.S.	Metric
Sugar	4.5 oz	112 g
Water	0.6 oz	15
Vanilla bean (see *Note*)	½	½
Glucose	0.5 oz	12 g
Canned pineapple, drained and diced	5 oz	125 g
Kumquats, sliced and blanched	2 oz	50 g
Pistachios	0.4 oz	10 g

NOTE: If vanilla beans are not available, flavor the finished compote with vanilla extract to taste.

PROCEDURE

1. Place the sugar, water, and vanilla bean in a saucepan. Bring to a boil. Cook to 238°F (120°C).
2. Add the fruit and nuts to the syrup.
3. Cook over high heat 2–3 minutes. Remove the vanilla bean.
4. Pour into clean glass jars and seal. Refrigerate.

--- VARIATION ---

KUMQUAT COMPOTE

For large-quantity measurements, see page 732.

Ingredients	U.S.	Metric
Sugar	4.5 oz	112 g
Water	0.6 oz	15 g
Glucose	0.5 oz	12 g
Kumquats, halved or sliced, blanched	5 oz	125 g
Pistachios	0.75 oz	20 g

Follow the procedure in the basic recipe, but omit the pineapple and vanilla and adjust the quantities as listed above.

CANDIED ORANGE OR LEMON ZEST

Yield: variable

Ingredients	U.S.	Metric
Oranges or lemons	4	4
Water	as needed	as needed
Sugar	7 oz	200 g
Water	7 oz	200 g

PROCEDURE

1. Peel the zest from the oranges in strips, using a vegetable peeler. Using a small, sharp knife, remove the white pith. Square off the strips and then cut them into julienne.
2. Boil the zest in a generous quantity of water until tender. Drain and discard the water.
3. Boil the sugar and water to make a syrup.
4. Poach the zest in the syrup until tender and translucent. Cool.
5. The zest may be stored in the syrup and drained as needed. Alternatively, drain and pat off excess syrup with absorbent paper. Then roll in extra-fine granulated sugar and shake in a sieve to remove excess sugar.

APPLE CRISPS

Yield: variable, depending on size of apple and thickness of cuts

Ingredients	U.S.	Metric
Sugar	7 oz	200 g
Water	7 oz	200 g
Green apple, peeled	2	2

VARIATION

Other fruits, such as oranges, pineapple, pears, and large strawberries, may be prepared in the same way.

PROCEDURE

1. Heat the sugar and water until the sugar is dissolved.

2. Cut the apple crosswise into paper-thin slices, preferably using a slicing machine or a mandoline. Immediately drop the slices into the syrup and heat gently for 2 minutes.

3. Allow the fruit to cool in the syrup.

4. Carefully remove the slices from the syrup and arrange on a silicone mat laid on a sheet pan. Dry in an oven at 175°F (80°C) until dry and crisp.

5. Use as a garnish for fruit desserts (see, for example, p. 612).

APPLESAUCE

Yield: about 1 qt (1 L)

Ingredients	U.S.	Metric
Apples	4 lb	2 kg
Sugar	as needed	as needed
Flavoring (see step 5)		
Lemon juice	to taste	to taste

PROCEDURE

1. Cut the apples into quarters and remove the cores. Skins may be left on because they will be strained out later. (Red peels will color the applesauce pink.) Coarsely dice the apples.

2. Place the apples in a heavy saucepan with about 2 oz (60 mL) water. Cover.

3. Set the pan over a low heat and cook the apples until very soft. Stir occasionally.

4. Remove the cover. Add sugar to taste. The amount depends on the desired sweetness of the sauce and the sweetness of the apples.

5. Add desired flavoring to taste, such as grated lemon zest, vanilla, or cinnamon. Add lemon juice to taste, especially if the apples lack tartness. Simmer for a few minutes to blend in flavors.

6. Pass the sauce through a food mill.

7. If the sauce is too thin or watery, let it simmer uncovered until thickened.

APRICOT JELLIES (PÂTE DE FRUITS)

Yield: about 1 lb 8 oz (720 g)

Ingredients	U.S.		Metric
Apricot purée	1 lb		480 g
Sugar	2	oz	60 g
Pectin	0.4	oz	12 g
Sugar	1 lb		480 g
Glucose syrup	3	oz	90 g
Lemon juice	0.33	oz	10 g
Sugar for coating	as needed		as needed

VARIATION

Other fruits, or mixtures of fruits, may be substituted for the apricot.

PROCEDURE

1. Line a half sheet pan with a silicone mat or parchment paper.
2. Bring the apricot purée to a boil in a heavy saucepan.
3. Mix the pectin with the first quantity of sugar. Add to the fruit purée.
4. Bring to a boil, stirring frequently.
5. Add *half* the remaining sugar. Return to a boil, stirring constantly.
6. Add the remaining sugar and the glucose. Return to a boil. Continue to boil, stirring constantly, until a candy thermometer inserted in the mixture reads 225°F (107°C). (*Note:* Wearing gloves while stirring helps protect your hand from hot spatters.)
7. Stir in the lemon juice. Remove the pan from the heat and let stand until the bubbling stops.
8. Pour the mixture into the prepared half sheet pan.
9. Let stand overnight, until firm.
10. Sprinkle the top with sugar and turn the jelly out onto a cutting surface. Cut into 1-in. (2.5-cm) squares, or whatever size is desired.
11. Roll the cut pieces in sugar.

TERMS FOR REVIEW

compote	crisp	apple charlotte
cobbler	betty	

QUESTIONS FOR REVIEW

1. Briefly describe each of the following fruits:

kumquat	persimmon
lychee	pomegranate
mango	prickly pear
papaya	quince
passion fruit	

2. True or false: Berries should be removed from their containers and washed as soon as possible after delivery or purchase. Explain.

3. For the following fruits, describe how to select produce of good quality.

apples	grapefruit
apricots	grapes
bananas	peaches
coconuts	pineapples

4. Describe in general terms how to sauté a fruit for a dessert.

5. Describe the procedure for preparing pears poached in red wine.

22

DESSERT PRESENTATION

1. **Describe the concepts behind planning attractive plated desserts.**
2. **Plate attractive presentations of desserts with appropriate sauces and garnishes, and judge the quality of plated desserts.**

IN RECENT YEARS, chefs have devoted more of their creativity to the arrangement of food on the plate. This is something of a change from earlier decades, when much of the plating of foods in elegant restaurants was done by the dining room staff at tableside. This trend has extended to the service of desserts as well. A piece of pastry or a wedge of cake that was at one time served by itself on a small dessert plate is now likely to be served on a large plate with a sauce and one or more items of garnish.

A pastry chef may devote as much attention to the appearance of a plated dessert as he or she gives to the decoration of a cake or the assembly of a large pastry for the display case or retail counter. The purpose of this chapter is to present guidelines and general suggestions for the presentation of individual desserts. The discussion concludes with a list of specific suggestions that employ recipes from throughout this book.

OVERVIEW OF DESSERT PLATING

THE ART OF the plated dessert is a fairly new aspect of the pastry chef's craft. As noted in the introduction, until recently, desserts in fine restaurants were presented on a pastry cart and plated by the dining room staff, or else they were plated very simply in the kitchen, again by the dining room staff or, sometimes, a pantry cook. Hot desserts such as soufflés may have been prepared by a line cook. The head chef or one of the cooks, perhaps a pantry cook, often prepared the other desserts, or they were purchased from an outside vendor. If the restaurant employed a pastry chef, she or he was simply an anonymous member of the cooking staff.

Today, the situation is very different. Many restaurants—not just the finest establishments, but even casual neighborhood spots—proudly display the names of their pastry chefs on their menus. Dessert menus are likely to be printed separately, as opposed to appearing at the bottom of the main menus. Desserts, prepared by a high-profile pastry chef, are seen as products that not only will increase the check average but also draw public attention to the restaurant and to the creativity of the kitchen, thus bringing in more customers.

Plating styles have changed noticeably in a few short years. Many of the pastry chefs who were pioneers in this area created complex architectural assemblies that were impressive and beautiful to look at but difficult to eat. Diners were fascinated but found they had to take the construction apart in order to begin to eat it. Often, chefs added to the complexity by decorating the rims of the plates with squirts of sauce or sprinklings of cocoa powder or 10X sugar, which was likely to end up on the sleeves of diners' clothing. Gradually, pastry chefs began to shift their focus back to flavor, discovering that they could make great-looking and great-tasting desserts without building towering constructions.

An important factor in the development of plating styles is the way pastry chefs and kitchen chefs work together as a team to shape the culinary identity of the restaurant. Dessert menus are treated as continuations of the dining experience, not simply as an unrelated sweet course tacked on at the end. The pastry chef's work complements and harmonizes with the hot food in plating styles as well as in ingredients and flavors.

Dessert plating styles are constantly changing and evolving, thanks to today's creative pastry chefs. There are many opinions on what makes a successful presentation, and chefs have thought and discussed and written a great deal about this subject. There is much disagreement, of course. When chefs try to develop an individual style to showcase their talents, the result is more variety to attract and satisfy customers.

Because pastry chefs do not always agree on how best to present a dessert, it is impossible to set down a list of hard-and-fast rules to follow. But we can discuss a number of ideas that influence chefs in their decisions and some of the factors pastry chefs consider when planning a dessert menu.

Three Essentials of Dessert Presentation

Making desserts look good requires that the pastry chef pay careful attention to all of his or her tasks. To create attractive plated desserts, the chef should observe three basic principles. Note that only the third one concerns the actual design of the plating.

1. **Good basic baking and pastry skills.** A pastry chef cannot make superior plated desserts without having mastered basic skills and techniques. Individual components must be properly prepared. If puff pastry doesn't rise evenly and well because the chef hasn't mastered correct rolling-in techniques, if cake layers have poor texture because of incorrect mixing methods, if a slice of cake is poorly cut, if sauces have poor texture, or if whipped cream is overwhipped and curdled, then no fancy plate design will correct those faults.

2. **Professional work habits.** Plating attractive and appealing desserts is partly a matter of being neat and careful and using common sense. Professionals take pride in their work and in the food they serve. Pride in workmanship means that chefs care about the quality of their work, and do not serve a dessert they aren't proud of.

3. **Visual sense.** Beyond being neat, effective dessert presentation depends on a thorough understanding of the techniques involving balance of colors, shapes, textures, and flavors, and learning how to arrange the dessert, garnish, and sauce on a plate to achieve this balance. This is the subject of the next sections.

Flavor First

"Too much presentation and not enough flavor." That is an often-expressed opinion of some of the complicated towering constructions that were common on dessert plates not long ago. It is true that you can be more structural with dessert presentations than with hot food. It is also true, as the saying goes, that "the eye eats first." But it is important to remember that food is still food. After the customers have dismantled the structure on the plate and finished eating the dessert, it is the flavor—or lack of it—they will remember. The presentation should enhance the flavor experience, not cover up a lack of flavor.

Flavor, as you know, begins with ingredients. In baking as well as in cooking, there is no substitute for using the best ingredients available. To get maximum flavor from fruits and other perishable ingredients, look for the freshest, locally grown products in season. This means the dessert menu changes as certain high-quality items go out of season and become unavailable. Chefs take their inspiration from the best in the market. A new crop of fresh summer berries, for example, gets chefs thinking about how best to feature them on the menu. In the fall, local apples and pears show up on menus in many forms.

Simplicity and Complexity

Offering the best and freshest flavors on the plate frequently means knowing when to stop. It is often harder to leave a presentation alone than to keep adding to it. One pastry expert has written that a good chef can take a great peach and make something original and inventive out of it, but a great chef will know when to let the peach speak for itself. When you are using the best ingredients, often a simple presentation is the best, and the more complexity you add, the more it distracts from the flavors.

This doesn't mean there is no place for complex presentations on dessert menus. It is good practice to offer customers variety. Furthermore, elaborate presentations often draw attention in the dining room and stimulate additional sales and so raise check averages. But you should always consider the function and importance of each additional element you place on a plate. Does it harmonize with the rest of the presentation? Does it serve a purpose, or did you add it just because you could? Even a simple garnish, such as the mint sprigs that seem to appear on every dessert plate in some restaurants, should not be added without thought. What is the mint for? If only to add color, is the color necessary? Some chefs argue that nothing should be put on the plate that isn't intended to be eaten. You may or may not agree, but at least have a reason for what you include on your dessert presentations.

One argument for elaborate dessert presentations is that customers should be offered desserts they can't, or probably wouldn't, prepare at home. For some people this may be true, but many others are attracted most of all to familiar comfort foods. The creative pastry chef can find ways to satisfy both types of customers with a varied dessert menu. Even when presenting home-style desserts, chefs can add a distinctive touch in the form of garnish or sauces, while keeping the base of the dessert recognizable. Even more important, they can make the base dessert so well that even the familiar is lifted to a new level of excellence.

Which dessert do you think is more successful: one the customer thinks is too beautiful to eat, or one the customer can't wait to start eating?

Another factor to consider when designing your presentations concerns kitchen capabilities. A pastry chef's hours vary from establishment to establishment, but in many cases he or she starts early, finishes all the baking, and goes home before dinner service begins. Desserts are then plated by the kitchen staff, or even the dining room staff. If the pastry chef's artful designs are too complex for these other staff members to construct properly, simpler presentations are probably advisable.

Plating for the Customer

Customers love desserts. However, not all customers order them. What should the pastry chef do to create and present desserts that more customers will order? Variety is the key—offering something for everyone.

A sizable number of diners are simply too full after a satisfying restaurant meal to order a large, rich dessert; but they would welcome a little sweet. In the average restaurant, perhaps two-thirds, at most, of the diners order dessert. Of the remaining third, some undoubtedly would order dessert if something light and refreshing were on the menu. Therefore, when planning for variety, don't neglect to include lighter, simpler presentations to appeal to diners with smaller appetites.

Here are other guidelines to keep in mind:

- If most of your dessert presentations are elaborate or complex, include at least one or two simple comfort foods.
- Think of the convenience of the diner. Don't make the dessert into a presentation that is difficult or awkward to eat.
- For each presentation, select plates large enough to hold the arrangement without over-crowding (but not so large that the dessert looks sparse on the plate). Besides looking sloppy and unprofessional, desserts falling over the rims of plates risk spilling onto the customer.

Meeting Expectations

Pastry chefs designing dessert menus must face the fact that their ideas may be more creative than their customers are ready for. Chefs love to experiment and to showcase their new ideas, while customers are often less fond of experimentation and happier with familiar foods. Classic, familiar desserts sell well, but chefs sometimes get bored making their best sellers over and over again. On the other hand, ultra-modern dessert styles appeal to chefs but may be less well received by some customers.

You can avoid some of these problems by serving what customers expect but personalizing the desserts in your own style, with a special plate arrangement, an unusual sauce, or signature garnishes and accompaniments.

Be honest on the menu so people know what to expect. Don't take such liberties with menu terminology in an effort to be creative that you confuse or disappoint your customers. For example, a chef might like to reinvent the classic Tarte Tatin (p. 356), by presenting the basic flavors—crisp pastry and caramelized apples—in a modern way, perhaps by topping a rectangle of crisp short pastry with a rectangle of a gelée of caramelized apples, topped in turn by a quenelle of green apple sorbet, the plate accented with an artful brush stroke of caramel sauce and a sprinkling of diced raw apples. This may be a wonderful dessert, but it's not Tarte Tatin. If you call it that on the menu, some of your customers are sure to be unhappy, no matter how good it is.

> ### KEY POINTS TO REVIEW
>
> - What are the three essentials of dessert presentation?
> - What is the role of flavor in plate design?
> - When designing a dessert, what factors should be kept in mind to enhance the comfort and meet the expectations of the customer?

PRACTICAL PLATING GUIDELINES

THE BAKER'S ART consists of two stages: first, cooking and baking doughs, batters, fillings, creams, and sauces; and second, assembling these components into finished desserts and pastries. In Chapter 17, for example, you learned how to take an assortment of baked cake and pastry layers, icings, mousses, fruits, and fillings, and build them into attractive and sometimes complex cakes and tortes.

The same principle is applied to plating dessert presentations. A plated dessert is an arrangement of one or more components. For most desserts, all the components are prepared well in advance. The plated dessert itself, however, is assembled at the last minute. All the components discussed throughout this book—including meringues, mousses, ice creams and sorbets, cookies, puff pastry, sponge and other cake layers, pastry cream, and dessert sauces—are used to make a presentation that is more than the sum of its parts. Of course, this means that in order to make successful plated desserts, you first have to learn how to prepare the components.

Balancing Dessert Components

The basic elements of a plated dessert are the following:

- Main item
- Secondary items and décor
- Sauce

In classical cuisine, secondary items or supporting items are called *garnish*. Many of today's pastry chefs, however, avoid that term because it suggests simple add-ons, like mint sprigs. In modern platings, the supporting items serve more important roles.

The term *décor* is used to refer to small food items whose main purpose is decoration. However, carefully selected décor items have other functions as well: They add important flavor and texture accents to the dessert plating.

In its simplest form, a dessert can be a portion of a single main item, such as a slice of cake or a wedge of pie, served unadorned on a plate. More often, other items are added to enhance flavor, texture, and eye appeal. In some cases, a presentation may have two or more main items. Secondary items enhance and add contrast to the main item (or items).

When deciding what to put on the plate, you should consider five characteristics of each component of the dessert. The first three of these characteristics are related to taste and mouth feel and are the most important:

- Flavor
- Texture
- Temperature

The other two are visual elements:

- Color
- Shape

Flavors should enhance or complement each other, such as a caramel sauce with a caramelized fruit gratin, or offer a pleasing contrast, such as a soothing crème anglaise with a slightly tart fruit. To ensure you achieve this, taste the components alone and then together to evaluate the flavors and make sure they work as a combination.

Look for pleasing varieties of texture and temperature. If the main item is soft, such as a mousse or ice cream, add a crisp or crunchy item such as small cookies or caramelized nuts, for texture contrast. Temperature contrasts are also pleasing, such as a spoonful of ice cream with a warm fruit tart.

Visually, a variety of colors and shapes can be attractive, but be careful not to include too much, or the result will come across as a jumble. And don't feel compelled to add color to every plate. Brown is a good color, too, and a well-prepared dessert in a few shades of brown can look very appetizing. A lusciously caramelized tarte tatin, for example, needs little or no garnish to make it appealing.

Shapes, too, can be varied in many ways, such as by using different shapes of molds for molded desserts, different cutters for cakes and similar items, and a variety of stencils for tuile garnishes. In addition, plates in various shapes can enhance the overall presentation of your desserts.

Secondary Items and Décor

Many if not most dessert presentations are improved with one or more items added to enhance them. But before you add anything, take a moment to consider whether serving the dessert alone wouldn't be effective. A simple, ungarnished plating is usually all that's needed for home-style desserts and, at the opposite extreme, for elegant pastries or gâteaux that are beautiful on their own and need no added elements.

Fruit is a good complement for many pastries, cakes, and other desserts. Nearly any fresh or cooked fruit can be used. Depending on size and shape, they can be used whole (such as berries) or cut into slices, wedges, or other shapes (such as apples, pears, pineapple, mango, kiwi, and peaches).

Ice creams and *sorbets* can provide both temperature and texture contrasts in a dessert presentation. For home-style desserts such as pies, the ice cream is usually served with a standard scoop. For more elegant presentations, the ice cream is often shaped into a small, oval *quenelle*. To shape a quenelle, first make sure the ice cream or sorbet is tempered to a soft, workable consistency. With a tablespoon dipped in water, scoop a portion of the frozen dessert. With a second spoon, scoop the ice cream out of the first spoon. This forms the ice cream into a neat, oval shape about the size of the bowl of the spoon. Repeat the scooping action with the first spoon, if necessary, to make the oval neater. Alternatively, using an oval scoop or spoon, simply draw the scoop across the surface of the ice cream. If the ice cream is at the proper serving temperature, it should curl into a perfect quenelle.

Whipped cream, applied with a pastry bag or spoon, is a classic garnish for many desserts. (Whipped cream could also be considered a sauce rather than a garnish.)

A small *cookie (petit four sec)* or two gives textural contrast to soft desserts such as mousses, Bavarians, and ice creams.

Fruit crisps or *chips* (p. 593) are used to decorate fruit desserts of a corresponding flavor. Not only do they give a textural contrast but they also add flavor interest by providing a variation on the flavor of the main item. For example, one or more apple crisps can enhance a plating of baked apple with apple sorbet.

Chocolate decorations of many types, including curls, cigarettes, cutouts, and piped lacework, go well with many kinds of dessert, not only chocolate desserts. (Decorative chocolate work is discussed in Chapter 23.)

A *choux lattice* is used in the photo of a decorated slice of Passion Fruit Charlotte (p. 533). This decoration is made as follows: Draw lattice designs on a sheet of parchment, then turn the parchment over (the drawing should show through). Using a paper cone (p. 436), pipe pâte à choux over the design outlines. Use the point of a small knife to make the joints neat, as necessary. Sprinkle with poppy seeds, if you like, and bake at 375°F (190°C) until golden. Choux paste can be used to make décor not just in lattice shapes but in many others as well.

Stencil paste or *tuile batter* (pp. 406 and 502) can be piped in design forms the same way choux paste is, then baked until crisp. Alternatively, use the stencil method of cookie makeup (p. 482) to make wafers in decorative shapes for dressing up dessert presentations. Remember that tuile batter items can be bent into decorative curves while they are still hot.

Sugar spirals, spun sugar, and other forms of decorative *sugar work*, as well as caramelized or toasted nuts, are other items used to garnish appropriate desserts. Sugar work is discussed in Chapter 25.

These are only some of the simplest and most commonly used décor items. For more ambitious plating styles, you can also add to the plate small portions of pastries and confections that, in a larger portion size, could stand on their own as main items—for example, a frozen pineapple mousse cake garnished with pineapple fritters, or a chocolate tart accompanied by a small raspberry crème brûlée. In such presentation it can be difficult to determine which is the main item and which are the secondary items. Usually, however, one of the items dominates and the others play supporting roles. The possible combinations are limitless.

In summary, always keep in mind these general concepts when planning dessert presentations:

- Every component should have a purpose. Don't add elements merely to make the plate fuller. Limit the items added primarily for decoration.

- Components or elements can work together by complementing or by contrasting.

- When elements contrast, be sure they balance. For example, when you balance a rich mousse with a tart fruit sauce, be sure the sauce isn't so tart or strong-flavored that it overwhelms the mousse.

One final point: It is possible to get carried away with the concept of balance. It is not necessary to garnish every soft dessert with something crisp or every hot dessert with something cold. Sometimes customers prefer just a plain, unadorned dish of ice cream or a simple slice of warm apple pie.

Sauce

Dessert sauces enhance desserts both by their flavor and their appearance, just as savory sauces enhance meats, fish, and vegetables. The most popular and useful dessert sauces are discussed in Chapter 12. Crème anglaise variations, chocolate sauce, caramel sauce, and the many fruit sauces or sweetened fruit purées are the most versatile. One or another of these complements nearly every dessert.

Except in the case of some home-style desserts and frozen desserts, sauces are usually not ladled over a dessert because this would mar its appearance by covering it up. Decorative lines of sauce can be applied to the top of a dessert with a pastry bag or squeeze bottle without covering it up. In most cases, however, the sauce is applied in a decorative fashion to the plate rather than the dessert. Many different styles of plate saucing are available.

Pouring a pool of sauce onto plate is known as *flooding*. Although plate flooding often looks old-fashioned today, it can still be a useful technique for some traditional desserts. Flooded plates can be made more attractive by applying a contrasting sauce and then blending or feathering the two sauces decoratively with a pick or the point of a knife. For this technique to work, the two sauces should be of about the same weight and consistency.

Rather than flooding the entire plate, it's more appropriate for many desserts to apply a smaller pool of sauce to the plate, as this avoids overwhelming the dessert with too much sauce.

A variation on the flooding technique is *outlining*, whereby a design is piped onto the plate in chocolate and allowed to set. The spaces can then be flooded with colorful sauces.

A squeeze bottle is useful for making dots, lines, curves, and streaks of sauce in many patterns. A pastry bag can be used in the same way, but the squeeze bottle works better with more liquid sauces. Nothing more than a spoon is needed to drizzle random patterns of sauce onto a plate. Other techniques for saucing a plate include applying a small amount of sauce and streaking it with a brush, an offset spatula, or the back of a spoon.

In addition to the illustrations here, you will see other saucing techniques in the photos of individual desserts in the next section.

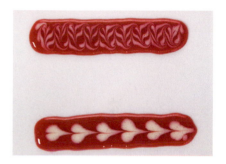

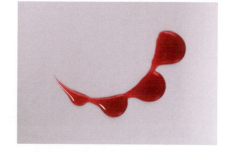

Adapting Plating Styles

By carefully designing a plate arrangement, the chef can adapt nearly any dessert idea to a range of plating styles suitable to almost any restaurant and to the expectations of its customers. Guests at a casual neighborhood restaurant are most likely to expect casual or even homey desserts, while at high-end restaurants noted for their creative, modern cuisine, guests will expect more creative and refined presentations.

Let's look at an example of how the same item can be presented in different styles.

One Dessert, Four Plate Designs

Bread pudding is a normally casual dessert that is popular in many restaurants. Adding chocolate to bread pudding, as in the recipe on page 519, adds richness and another flavor dimension to this classic item. A series of "plating maps" or diagrams shows how this item can be designed for different venues. In addition, photos show the actual platings created with the help of the plating maps

CHOCOLATE BREAD PUDDING, VERSION 1

If you made this dish at home, you might simply scoop out a portion with a spoon, place it in a bowl, and serve it as is. Even in the most casual diner, however, a little more thought to presentation enhances the dessert. One suggestion is to cut a square of the pudding, place it in the middle of a small dessert plate or shallow bowl, top it with a dollop of whipped cream or a small scoop of ice cream, and spoon a little crème anglaise or chocolate sauce around the base (see the illustration).

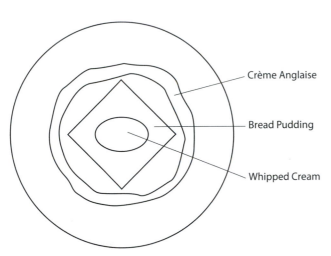

Chocolate bread pudding, version 1.

Note that there is little textural contrast in this plating. Similarly, because all the flavors are either chocolaty or creamy, there is not much flavor contrast, either. Nevertheless, such a presentation is well suited to many casual restaurants and is likely to be appealing to customers, and it is simple enough to be within the capabilities of less-experienced kitchen staff.

CHOCOLATE BREAD PUDDING, VERSION 2

Today's restaurants include a growing number that are both casual and somewhat more upscale. Typical of these is the high-end specialty hamburger restaurant, appealing to customers looking for hearty portions and top quality. In such a restaurant, we might want to increase the portion size of the pudding and add some interesting secondary items to it, while keeping it casual.

For example, caramelize three banana quarters in butter and brown sugar and arrange them on a square plate (see the illustration on the following page). To contrast with the square plate, cut a generous portion of pudding with a round cutter and set it on top of the bananas. Top the pudding with a scoop of vanilla or cinnamon ice cream. Send the dessert to the table with a small pitcher of chocolate sauce or crème anglaise (or a pitcher of each), to be poured around the pudding by the customer or the server.

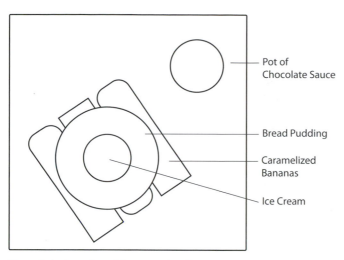

Pot of
Chocolate Sauce

Bread Pudding

Caramelized
Bananas

Ice Cream

Chocolate bread pudding, version 2.

A hearty presentation like this may not be suitable for an elegant restaurant, but it has great appeal in the kind of restaurant described here.

CHOCOLATE BREAD PUDDING, VERSION 3

A chef can take the same ingredients and give them a more elegant yet still somewhat traditional presentation. Place a square of the chocolate bread pudding slightly off-center on a round plate. Top the pudding with a crisp spiral of baked tuile batter (made by piping the batter in lines, baking them, and twisting them into curls while still hot). Next to the pudding, arrange a small mound of crushed nougatine, and then place a quenelle of vanilla ice cream on the crumbs, as in the illustration. The nougatine gives textural contrast while also anchoring the ice cream so that it doesn't slide around on the plate. In the remaining space, place a decorative series of dots of raspberry coulis. Raspberry sauce is chosen, rather than a chocolate sauce or crème anglaise, to lighten the dish and provide tartness, for a pleasing contrast to the rich chocolate.

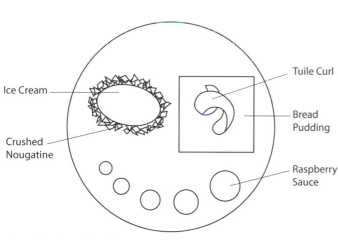

Ice Cream

Crushed
Nougatine

Tuile Curl

Bread
Pudding

Raspberry
Sauce

Chocolate bread pudding, version 3.

CHOCOLATE BREAD PUDDING, VERSION 4

The components can be given a more modern flair in the fourth version. Bake individual portions of chocolate bread pudding in attractive ramekins. Choose a rectangular plate and arrange the basic components in a diagonal line across the plate (see the illustration). Toward one corner, place a ramekin of the pudding. Top the pudding with a small piece of nougatine. In the center of the plate, place a mound of chocolate cookie crumbs and a quenelle of vanilla ice cream. In the opposite corner apply a streak of chocolate sauce with a pastry brush or an offset spatula.

Place two quarters of caramelized banana, one diagonally across the other, on the chocolate sauce. Alongside the line of these three components, pipe a narrow streak of raspberry sauce, using a squeeze bottle.

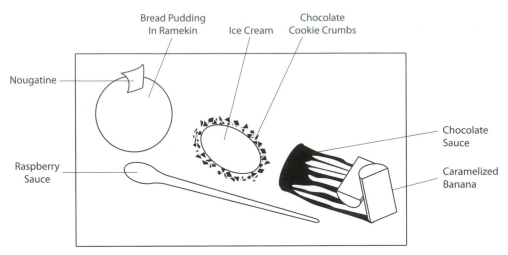

Chocolate bread pudding, version 4.

Additional Examples of Dessert Presentations

KEY POINTS TO REVIEW

▍ What are the three main components of a plated dessert?

▍ Which five characteristics of each of these components should you consider to achieve a balanced dessert presentation?

▍ What are the foods most commonly used as secondary items or decorative items on dessert plates?

▍ What methods are used to apply sauce to a dessert plate?

As the preceding examples show, plating styles can be adapted in countless ways. Moreover, styles continue to change, as inventive chefs look for new ways to display their creativity. Some styles that are modern and cutting-edge this year may appear dated the next. But if you have mastered the basic skills of your trade, you should be able to adapt easily as styles evolve.

The techniques and recipes presented in other chapters of this book and in the first part of this chapter give you the tools you need to prepare an unlimited variety of desserts for many styles of service.

This section follows a format similar to the one used to explain the procedures for preparing gâteaux and torten (beginning on p. 451). In other words, no new recipes are required; individual components—as prepared from recipes elsewhere in this book—are assembled and arranged as indicated.

The presentations described here are intended merely as suggestions, selected to provide a sampling of ideas using different types of desserts and a variety of arrangement styles. Presentations include traditional styles, simple, casual platings, and more complex, modern designs. Each procedure begins with a list of the components required for the presentation. Page numbers refer to recipes or procedures elsewhere in this book. Where no page number is given, there may be two or more recipes, any of which is suitable; refer to the index for page numbers. Photos or plating diagrams help you visualize the suggested arrangements.

CHOCOLATE CRÉMEUX AND RASPBERRIES

Components

Fresh raspberries

Chocolate Crémeux
 (p. 514)

Raspberry Coulis (p. 267)

Whipped cream

Chocolate cigarette
 (p. 635) and shavings

Streusel (p. 195), baked
 on a sheet pan and
 cooled

Raspberry Sorbet (p. 552)

PROCEDURE

1. Place 3 raspberries in a small glass.

2. Prepare the crémeux and fill the glass about two-thirds full. Chill until set.

3. Add about ⅛ in. (3 mm) raspberry coulis to the glass on top of the crémeux. Top with a rosette of whipped cream and a raspberry and decorate with chocolate décor.

4. Place the glass on the left side of a rectangular plate.

5. On the right side of the plate, sprinkle streusel in a line from left to right.

6. Place a quenelle or a small scoop of sorbet on top of the streusel.

PEACH NAPOLEON

Components

3 phyllo layers for napoleons, one of which is caramelized (p. 338)

Pastry Cream (p. 263) flavored with amaretto

Caramelized peach slices (p. 581)

Clear Caramel Sauce (p. 271)

Peach Ice Cream (p. 551)

PROCEDURE

1. Place a plain phyllo layer just to one side of the center of a plate. Cover with caramelized peach slices.
2. With a pastry bag filled with a star tube, pipe pastry cream over the peaches. Alternatively, place a small spoonful of pastry cream on the peaches and spread gently over the center with the back of a spoon.
3. Top with another phyllo layer and additional peaches and pastry cream.
4. Top with the caramelized phyllo layer.
5. Drizzle caramel sauce onto the plate around the napoleon.
6. Place a quenelle of ice cream next to the napoleon. Serve at once.

VARIATION

Instead of the peach ice cream, use Caramel Ice Cream (p. 550), Cinnamon Ice Cream (p. 550), or whipped cream flavored with amaretto.

CRÈME BRÛLÉE WITH MELON

Components

Crème Brûlée (p. 517), made in a shallow square dish

Langues de Chat (p. 496), or similar long, thin, crisp cookies

Assorted tiny melon balls

PROCEDURE

1. Place the dish of crème brûlée on a plate, setting it at a 45-degree angle.
2. Set 2 cookies in the crème brûlée dish resting against the back corner.
3. Arrange a few melon balls in front of the cookies.

APPLE-FILLED BRIOCHE WITH BERRIES

Components

Brioche (p. 188)

Applesauce (p. 593; see procedure)

Pastry Cream Mousseline (p. 263)

Crème Anglaise (p. 261)

Assorted fresh berries

Candied Orange Zest (p. 592)

PROCEDURE

1. Slice off the top of the brioche. Hollow out the brioche and toast the resulting case lightly in the oven.

2. Prepare an applesauce that is sweet, not too tart, and well flavored with vanilla. Leave it slightly chunky; do not force it through a food mill.

3. Spoon a little pastry cream mousseline into the bottom of the brioche case. Fill almost to the top with the applesauce. Place a little more pastry cream on top, using a pastry bag with a star tip, and replace the top of the brioche.

4. Place the filled brioche on the left side of a square or round plate.

5. Arrange fresh berries on the right side of the brioche.

6. Spoon a small pool of crème anglaise in front of the berries and brioche.

7. Drape a few thin strips of candied orange zest over the brioche.

CHILLED SUMMER FRUIT SOUP WITH STRAWBERRY SORBET

Components

Tuile batter (p. 502)

Chilled Summer Fruit Soup
  (p. 580)

Grated lime zest

Strawberry Sorbet (p. 552)

PROCEDURE

1. With the tuile batter, make wafers about 1 in. (2.5 cm) wide and long enough to place across the rim of the soup plates in which you intend to serve the soup.

2. Plate the soup in shallow soup plates.

3. Sprinkle the soup lightly with grated lime zest.

4. Lay a wafer across the top of the plate with the ends resting on opposite rims.

5. Place a small scoop or quenelle of sorbet on the center of the wafer, above the soup.

6. Serve immediately.

— **VARIATION** —

In place of the strawberry sorbet, use another sorbet appropriate to the fruit used in the soup garnish, such as raspberry, mango, or pineapple.

RUSSIAN CAKE WITH HONEY ICE CREAM

Components	**PROCEDURE**

Components

Russian Cake (p. 463), without décor

Chocolate sauce

Honey Ice Cream (p. 553)

Curled strip of baked tuile batter (p. 502)

Toasted sliced almonds

Confectioners' sugar

PROCEDURE

1. Prepare Russian cake without the piped buttercream and almonds on top. Cut a strip of the cake ¾ in. (2 cm) wide and 6 in. (15 cm) long.

2. Place two streaks of chocolate sauce diagonally from front to rear on a square plate.

3. Place the slice of cake across the lines of chocolate sauce just to the rear of center on the plate.

4. Place a quenelle of ice cream on the cake at the left. Lean the tuile strip against the ice cream.

5. Arrange some toasted almonds on the front of the plate at the right and dredge lightly with confectioners' sugar.

PASSION FRUIT CHARLOTTE

Components

Passion Fruit Charlotte (p. 533)

Kumquat Compote (p. 592)

Red currants

Choux Pastry Lattice (p. 332)

Crème Anglaise (p. 261)

Confectioners' sugar

PROCEDURE

1. Place a wedge of the charlotte toward the back of a plate.

2. Place a spoonful of kumquat compote in front of the charlotte wedge and garnish with a few red currants or other small red berries to add color.

3. Prop a piece of choux pastry lattice in front of the compote so it leans against the wedge of charlotte.

4. Spoon a little crème anglaise on the plate in a decorative fashion.

5. Dust the pastry lattice lightly with confectioners' sugar.

SPICE CAKE WITH CARAMELIZED APPLES

Components

Brown Sugar Spice
  Cake (p. 393), baked
  as a sheet cake

Caramelized Apples
  (p. 581), apples cut
  into medium dice
  before caramelizing

Crème Anglaise
  (p. 261), made
  with half milk
  and half heavy
  cream

Apple Crisps (p. 593)

PROCEDURE

1. Place a square of spice cake in the center of a dessert plate.
2. Top with caramelized apples.
3. Ladle a generous pool of crème anglaise around the cake. If desired, drizzle a little over the cake as well.
4. Dot the pool of sauce with a few additional dice of caramelized apple.
5. Insert an apple crisp into the mound of apples on top of the cake so it stands upright.

ICED LOW-FAT RASPBERRY PARFAIT WITH ALMOND MACARONS

Components

Iced Low-Fat Raspberry
  Parfait (p. 565)

Italian Meringue
  (p. 259)

Raspberry Sauce
  (p. 270)

Fresh raspberries and
  other berries

Macarons (p. 499)

PROCEDURE

1. Freeze the parfait in a gutter mold (see photo for shape) lined with plastic film.
2. Unmold the parfait onto a tray and remove the plastic film. Using a pastry bag fitted with a star tip, coat the top and sides of the parfait with Italian meringue. Brown lightly with a blowtorch.
3. For each portion, cut a slice of the parfait 1¼–1½ in. (3–4 cm) thick and stand it on one side of a plate. Spoon a crescent of raspberry sauce on the other side of the plate. Top the pool of sauce with a bouquet of fruit and 2 or 3 macarons.

SAVARIN WITH BERRIES

Components

Savarin (p. 186), small, single-portion size

Fresh berries

Sabayon (p. 274)

Pistachios

Florentine (p. 507; use variation made with chopped almonds only)

PROCEDURE

1. Place a savarin on the left side of a round plate.

2. Spoon sabayon in a small pool to the right of the savarin.

3. Fill the center of the savarin with berries.

4. Place additional berries on the right side of the plate and sprinkle with pistachios.

5. Break the florentine into a wedge and insert it in the savarin.

BROWNIE CHERRY CHEESECAKE ICE CREAM SANDWICH

Components

Two 2-in. (5-cm) Cream
  Cheese Brownies
  (p. 506)

1½–2 oz (45–60 g)
  Cheesecake Ice Cream
  (p. 550)

1 oz (30 g) Cherry Pie
  Filling (p. 292)

Whipped cream

Chocolate shavings
  or other chocolate
  decorations

PROCEDURE

1. Place one brownie slightly off-center on a plate. Top with the ice cream, which has been flattened slightly.
2. Place the second brownie on top.
3. Spoon the cherry pie filling onto the plate next to the brownie sandwich.
4. Decorate with whipped cream and chocolate decorations.

STEAMED CHOCOLATE ALMOND PUDDING WITH PRALINE ICE CREAM

Components

Steamed Chocolate
  Almond Pudding (p. 524)

Chocolate sauce

Crushed Nougatine
  (p. 658)

Praline Ice Cream (p. 550)

PROCEDURE

1. Unmold the pudding and place it just to the right of center on a round plate.
2. Place chocolate sauce in a decorative curve across the front of the plate.
3. Place a small mound of crushed nougatine to the left of the pudding. Top the nougatine with a quenelle of ice cream.

TRIO OF FRUIT SORBETS

Components

Three fruit purée sauces
(p. 267) of contrasting
colors, such as
raspberry, kiwi, and
mango

Tuile batter (p. 502),
baked in long, thin strips

Three fruit sorbets (p. 552)
of contrasting colors,
such as blueberry,
lemon, and raspberry

PROCEDURE

1. Place a small pool of one of the sauces on the left side of a rectangular plate. Using a brush or a small offset spatula, spread it in a streak to the opposite side of the plate.

2. Place two narrow strips of tuile on top of the sauce, about ½ in. (1 cm) apart and slightly offset.

3. With a squeeze bottle, pipe a row of dots of a second sauce on the front, right of the plate, parallel to the tuiles.

4. Pipe dots of the third sauce on the rear, left of the plate in the same way.

5. Arrange 1 quenelle of each of the three sorbets on top of the tuiles.

APPLE FRITTERS WITH MASCARPONE SORBET

Components

Apple Fritters (p. 235), made with halved apple slices

Raspberry Sauce (p. 270)

Apple Crisp (p. 593)

Mascarpone Sorbet (p. 553)

Raw green apple, in small dice, dipped in water mixed with lemon juice and drained (to prevent browning)

PROCEDURE

1. Place a small pool of raspberry sauce on the right side of a rectangular plate. With the back of a spoon, streak the sauce slightly to the left, leaving most of the pool in place.

2. Place four fritters on top of the pool of sauce.

3. On the left side of the plate, place one apple crisp and top it with a scoop of sorbet.

4. Sprinkle diced apple in a line in front of the sorbet and fritters.

ANGEL FOOD CAKE WITH PLUM COMPOTE AND MASCARPONE SORBET

Components

Angel Food Cake batter (p. 403)

Plum Compote (p. 591)

Florentines (p. 507) without chocolate, or Almond Tuiles (p. 502), made in 2½-in. (6-cm) rounds and left flat

Mascarpone Sorbet (p. 553)

PROCEDURE

1. Bake the cake batter in 2½-in. (6-cm) ring molds. Cool and remove from the molds.
2. Spoon the plum compote onto a dessert plate.
3. Place a cake round on top of the plums in the center of the plate.
4. Top with a florentine or almond tuile.
5. Place a small scoop of sorbet on top of the cookie.

PANNA COTTA WITH CARAMEL AND FRESH BERRIES

Components

Caramel for Cages (p. 666)

Panna Cotta (p. 514)

Clear Caramel Sauce (p. 271)

Assorted fresh berries

PROCEDURE

1. Prepare the caramel decorations: Drizzle the caramel onto a silicone mat or an oiled sheet pan into desired shapes or patterns. Allow to cool and harden.
2. Unmold a portion of panna cotta onto a broad soup plate or other suitable plate.
3. Ladle a little caramel sauce around the panna cotta.
4. Distribute the mixed berries around the panna cotta on top of the caramel sauce.
5. Top with the caramel decoration immediately before serving. Do not let it stand, or the caramel decoration may begin to dissolve in the moisture from the dessert.

RASPBERRY MILLEFEUILLE

Components

Almond Tuile batter (p. 502)

Fresh raspberries

Whipped cream flavored with orange liqueur

Confectioners' sugar (optional)

Raspberry Sauce (p. 270)

Cream Sauce for Piping (p. 277) (optional)

PROCEDURE

1. Bake tuile wafers about 3 in. (7 cm) in diameter, but leave them flat; do not bend or mold them.
2. Place 1 wafer in the center of a plate. Arrange a ring of berries on the wafer lining the outside edge. Using a pastry bag, fill the space in the center of the berry ring with the flavored whipped cream.
3. Top with a second wafer and repeat with the berries and cream.
4. Dredge a third wafer generously with confectioners' sugar, if desired. Carefully place it on top of the dessert.
5. Spoon a ring of raspberry sauce onto the plate around the pastry. If desired, marble the raspberry sauce with the cream sauce for piping. Serve at once, while the wafers are crisp.

VARIATION

Garnish with a spoonful of Raspberry or Orange Sorbet (p. 552)

FRENCH DOUGHNUTS WITH PINEAPPLE

Components

2 French Doughnuts, fried by method 2 (p. 236)

Confectioners' sugar

2 oz (60 g) Coconut Sorbet (p. 556)

Toasted coconut

Blanched pineapple leaves (optional)

2½–3 oz (80 g) Pineapple Kumquat Compote (p. 592)

Pistachios

Red currants

PROCEDURE

1. Dust the doughnuts lightly with confectioners' sugar.
2. Place 1 doughnut on one side of a plate. Top with a scoop of sorbet and then with the second doughnut.
3. Sprinkle a little toasted coconut around the doughnuts and, if desired, decorate with blanched pineapple leaves.
4. Place the pineapple kumquat compote on the other side of the plate and decorate with a few pistachios and red currants.

FRENCH-TOASTED CHALLAH WITH CHEESECAKE ICE CREAM

Components

Challah (p. 132), baked in a loaf pan rather than braided

Batter for French toast (mixture of beaten eggs, milk, a little sugar, cinnamon)

Whipped cream

Melba Sauce (p. 270)

Cheesecake Ice Cream (p. 550)

Chopped, toasted almonds

PROCEDURE

1. Slice the bread. Soak it in the egg batter and pan-fry it in butter to make French toast. Cut into neat triangles.

2. On the front right corner of a square plate, place a small pool of melba sauce. With a brush or small offset spatula, streak the sauce toward opposite corner.

3. Stand three triangles of French toast along the back of the plate.

4. Using a pastry bag with a star tip, pipe a row of whipped cream behind the French toast.

5. Sprinkle a few chopped, toasted almonds onto the melba sauce at the bottom right of the plate (to anchor the ice cream in place), and place a scoop of ice cream on top of them.

6. Sprinkle a line of chopped, toasted almonds in a line across the bottom left quadrant of the plate, parallel to the line of sauce.

SPICED PINEAPPLE WITH COCONUT SORBET

Components
Tuile batter (p. 502)
Fine coconut
Spiced Pineapple (p. 589)
Coconut Sorbet (p. 556)
Pistachios
Pine nuts
Pomegranate seeds
Toasted coconut

PROCEDURE

1. Bake tuiles in the shape of long, narrow triangles. Sprinkle the batter with coconut before baking. After baking, bend into a curve.

2. Rewarm the pineapple if it was prepared in advance, and finish the sauce with the cream as in the basic recipe. Strain it, reserving the spices. Slice the pineapple and cut into quarters.

3. On the left side of a round plate, spoon a rectangular pool of the sauce from front to back.

4. Overlap five slices of pineapple in a mound on top of the sauce.

5. Place a coconut tuile on the right side of the plate, resting on its broad end. (If necessary, place a dab of sauce under the base of the tuile to keep it from sliding.)

6. Place a quenelle of sorbet on top of the base of the tuile.

7. Sprinkle a few pistachios, pine nuts, and pomegranate seeds on the plate.

8. Finish the plate by sprinkling with a little toasted coconut.

FINANCIERS WITH CHOCOLATE SAUCE AND FROZEN "CAPPUCCINO"

Components

Coffee Bombe Mixture
  (p. 560)

Whipped cream

Cinnamon

Chocolate sauce

Financiers au Café (p. 368)

PROCEDURE

1. Prepare the bombe mixture and freeze in a small glass cup, filling the cup to within ½ in. (12 mm) of the top.

2. At service time, fill the cup to the top with whipped cream and dust the top with a light dash of cinnamon.

3. On a square plate, place a small pool of chocolate sauce on the front left corner and, with the back of a spoon, spread it in an arc across the front of the plate.

4. Arrange three financiers on the right side of the plate.

5. Place the cup of frozen coffee bombe on the left side of the plate behind the chocolate sauce.

CHARLOTTE AU CASSIS

Components

Charlotte au Cassis
  (p. 533)

Chocolate fan (p. 636)

Fresh berries

Candied Orange Zest
  (p. 592)

Mint

Crème Chantilly (p. 257)

Sauces (see step 4)

PROCEDURE

1. Place a wedge of charlotte toward the back of a plate.

2. In front of the charlotte, place a chocolate fan and fill it with berries. Garnish with a few pieces of candied orange zest and a sprig of mint.

3. Make a quenelle of crème chantilly and place it next to the chocolate fan. Alternatively, pipe a rosette of the cream using a star tip.

4. Spoon a band of sauce around the plate and marble it with a sauce of a contrasting color. (The sauces in the photograph are syrup from kumquat compote and raspberry coulis.)

LINZER "SHORTCAKE" WITH BERRIES

Components

Linzer Dough (p. 315)

Fresh raspberries or a
  mixture of raspberries,
  blackberries, and
  strawberries

Simple syrup

Confectioners' sugar

Crème Chantilly (p. 257)

Grated lime zest

Crushed Nougatine
  (p. 658)

PROCEDURE

1. Make small shortbread cookies with the Linzer dough. Roll it out thin, cut into squares 1½ in. (4 cm) across, and bake until crisp. (*Note:* The dough is very soft and difficult to roll thin, so be sure it is not too warm, and use plenty of flour for dusting; or else roll out between two sheets of parchment.) Cool completely.

2. If you are using strawberries, cut them into quarters or wedges. Place all the berries in a bowl and add enough simple syrup to cover. Refrigerate several hours or overnight.

3. Dust the cookies very lightly with confectioners' sugar.

4. On a dessert plate or in shallow soup bowl, ladle some berries and a little of the syrup.

5. Place 1 shortbread cookie in the center of the berries. Place a dollop of crème chantilly on top of the cookie, using either a pastry bag or a spoon. Repeat with 2 more cookies and additional cream. Either stack the cookies vertically, like a napoleon, or lean them against the first one, like a stack that has tipped on its side. Top with a fourth cookie, but do not top this one with cream.

6. If desired, dust the dessert very lightly with confectioners' sugar by holding a sieve over the plate and giving it one or two light taps, taking care not to get the sugar on the rim of the plate.

7. Sprinkle the berries lightly with lime zest.

8. Finish with a light sprinkle of crushed nougatine.

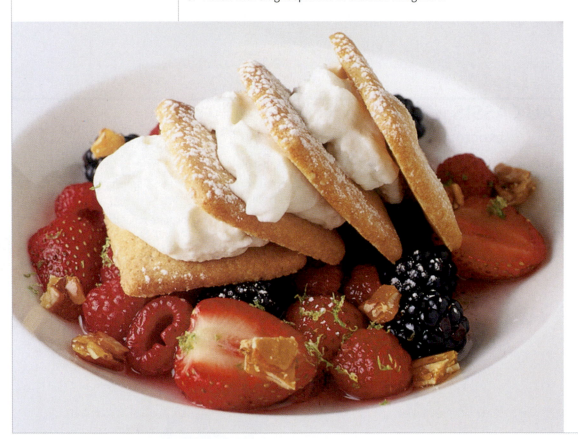

POACHED PEAR WITH BAKLAVA AND MASCARPONE CREAM

Components	PROCEDURE
Whole pear poached in white wine (p. 578), with some of the poaching syrup Mascarpone Crème fraîche Confectioners' sugar Baklava (p. 340) Pistachios or walnuts, coarsely chopped Cinnamon	1. With a melon baller, remove the core of the pear through the blossom end, taking care to leave the pear whole. Cut a thin slice off the bottom of the pear so it stands upright. 2. Reduce the poaching syrup until it is thickened and syrupy. 3. Mix together equal parts mascarpone and crème fraîche. Sweeten lightly with confectioners' sugar. Whip until stiff. 4. Using a pastry bag, fill the pear with the whipped mascarpone cream. 5. Stand the pear on a dessert plate. 6. Lean a triangle of baklava against the pear, taking care that the pastry layers don't fall apart. Alternatively, simply place the baklava on the plate next to the pear. 7. Drizzle a little crème fraîche and a little of the pear syrup around the pear. 8. Sprinkle with chopped nuts and just a dash of cinnamon.

TERMS FOR REVIEW

garnish

décor

quenelle

flooding

outlining

QUESTIONS FOR REVIEW

1. Discuss how the quality of ingredients affects dessert plating presentations.

2. Explain the advantages and disadvantages of simple presentations versus elaborate or complex presentations.

3. What are the three basic elements of a plated dessert? Is it necessary to have all three of these elements in each presentation?

4. Each component of a dessert can be said to have five characteristics. What are they? Which are visual characteristics and which are flavor or mouth-feel characteristics? Suggest examples of how to balance each of these characteristics when designing a plated dessert.

5. What is a quenelle of ice cream? Describe how to make it.

6. Name four types of items that can be used as secondary items or garnishes for a dessert.

7. Describe techniques for applying sauce to a plate.

23

CHOCOLATE

AFTER READING THIS CHAPTER, YOU SHOULD BE ABLE TO:

1. **Temper chocolate couverture.**
2. **Use tempered chocolate for molding.**
3. **Produce a variety of chocolate decorations.**
4. **Make chocolate truffles and other chocolate confections, including dipped chocolates.**

NOT ONLY IS chocolate one of the world's most popular confections, it is also a wonderful medium for decorative work, ranging from simple garnishes for desserts to elaborate showpieces. Many pastry chefs make a specialty of chocolate work and become well known for their imaginative and skillful pieces.

Because of its composition, chocolate is difficult to work with. It is sensitive to temperature and moisture. Proper melting and cooling require accurate temperature control. Unless a liquid is to be added, chocolate must be protected from moisture. A single drop of water will ruin its texture and make it unusable for dipping or molding.

This chapter provides an introduction to fine chocolate work. The fundamentals of handling chocolate are discussed, followed by procedures for simple decorative work and molding. A brief look at chocolate confections closes the chapter.

625

PRODUCTION AND TEMPERING OF CHOCOLATE

Chocolate is produced from the seeds of a tropical tree called the *cocoa* or, more properly, *cacao* tree. As with coffee, the quality of cocoa is sensitive to growing conditions, so cocoa from the best growing regions commands the highest prices. Cocoa trees produce large pods full of seeds called *cocoa beans*. After the pods are harvested, the beans are quickly removed and allowed to ferment until they lose most of their moisture. There are several ways of doing this, but the traditional method is to spread them between layers of banana leaves and leave them for several days, turning them often so they ferment evenly.

CHOCOLATE HISTORY

The cacao tree originated in the western hemisphere, where it grows in tropical climates from northern South America to southern Mexico. Long before the European discovery of the Americas, native peoples, including the Mayans and Aztecs, brewed a bitter, unsweetened beverage from the beans, which they had learned to ferment and dry. The beverages, probably enjoyed hot, were often flavored with chiles, vanilla, and other ingredients.

The cacao tree grew in limited areas, so the pods were prized and became objects of trade. They were even used for currency. In addition, they were important in religious ceremonies.

Spanish conquerors at first disliked the bitter, black beverage the natives brewed from cacao, but they soon learned to appreciate it and began carrying cocoa beans back to Europe in the 1500s. Availability was limited at first, but by 1700 cocoa had spread through much of Europe. Its use was still mostly as a beverage, although Europeans found they enjoyed the drink more when it was sweetened. Cocoa was also used as a medicine and as a cooking spice.

In the early 1800s, a Dutch chemist and chocolate maker named Coenraad Johannes van Houten developed a process for removing much of the cocoa butter from raw cocoa, using a powerful press. He also discovered that processing the cocoa with an alkali yielded a milder product with a darker color. This "dutching" process is still used today for some cocoa.

Van Houten's inventions enabled the development of modern chocolate manufacturing and expanded the use of chocolate beyond beverages, for confections. Manufacturers discovered that by adding cocoa butter back to ground cocoa, they could make a smooth paste that hardened into blocks. In 1842, the Cadbury brothers (George and Richard) began selling block chocolate in England. In the 1880s, the Swiss Rudolphe Lindt invented the conching process (described in the text) to make a smoother product. Around the same time, another Swiss, Daniel Peter, created milk chocolate by adding dried milk to the paste. (Dried milk had been invented by Henri Nestlé.)

The chemical changes that take place during fermentation turn the beans from yellowish to brown and begin to develop the flavor. The fermented beans are next dried in the open air, because they still contain a great deal of moisture. The dried beans are then ready to be shipped to processors. A single tree yields only 1 to 2 pounds (500 g to 1 kg) dried beans.

Cocoa processors clean the dried beans thoroughly and then roast them. The true flavor of the cocoa develops during roasting, making the temperature and degree of roasting important factors in the quality of the finished chocolate. After roasting, the beans are cracked and the shells are removed. The broken particles of cocoa that result are called *nibs*. Nibs contain more than 50 percent fat, in the form of *cocoa butter*, and very little moisture.

Grinding the nibs produces a paste and releases the cocoa butter from inside the cell walls. This paste is called *chocolate liquor* or *cocoa mass* and is the basis of chocolate production. When chocolate liquor cools, it sets into a hard block. (Chocolate liquor contains no alcohol, in spite of its slightly misleading name.)

The next stage of manufacturing is to separate the cocoa powder from the cocoa butter. This is done with powerful hydraulic presses that squeeze out the melted fat, leaving hard cakes that are then ground into cocoa powder. Meanwhile, the cocoa butter is purified to remove odor and color.

To manufacture chocolate, the cocoa powder is mixed with sugar and, in the case of milk chocolate, milk solids. These ingredients are ground and blended together. At this point comes the critical procedure called *conching*. This is a two-stage process that first removes additional moisture and refines the flavor. During the second stage of conching, cocoa butter is added back and the liquid mass is ground and mixed for hours or even days to develop a fine, smooth texture. Conching also plays an important role in reducing the viscosity of the chocolate. In general, higher-quality, more expensive chocolates derive their superior texture from longer conching. Finally, the liquid chocolate is tempered, as explained below, and molded into blocks for sale as couverture.

Couverture

The basic types of chocolate are introduced in Chapter 4. Please review pages 84–88 and, in particular, note the difference between *couverture* and *coating chocolate* or *baking chocolate*. Genuine couverture contains cocoa butter and no other fat. Coating chocolate is chocolate that has part or most of the cocoa butter replaced with other fats in order to make it easier to handle and reduce the cost. In this chapter, we are concerned entirely with couverture, also known as *confectioners' chocolate*.

Dark couverture consists of these components:

- Total cocoa solids:
  - Nonfat cocoa solids
  - Cocoa butter
- Sugar

In addition, it may also contain small quantities of vanilla (a flavoring) and lecithin (an emulsifier). On the packaging of a block of professional couverture, you may see a series of numbers such as the following: 65/35/38. The first two numbers refer to the ratio of total cocoa solids to sugar—in this case, 65% cocoa solids to 35% sugar. The last number is the total fat content (38% in the

example) and is a factor in determining the viscosity, or thickness, of the chocolate. The higher the fat content, the thinner the chocolate will be when melted. Couverture must contain at least 31% cocoa butter.

The quantities of cocoa solids and sugar determine whether dark couverture is referred to as *semisweet, bittersweet,* or *extra-bittersweet.* The higher the percentage of total cocoa solids, the lower the sugar content will be. Semisweet chocolate couverture contains 50 to 60% cocoa solids. Chocolates with more cocoa solids (and, therefore, less sugar) are called bittersweet and extra-bittersweet. The highest practical percentage of cocoa content is around 85%.

Milk chocolate couverture contains milk solids in addition to cocoa solids and sugar. It usually contains about 36% cocoa solids and no more than 55% sugar. *White couverture* technically cannot be called chocolate because it contains no nonfat cocoa solids, only cocoa butter, sugar, milk solids, and flavoring.

In this chapter, the term *couverture,* when used by itself, always refers to *dark chocolate.* Milk chocolate couverture or white couverture is specified where those types are intended.

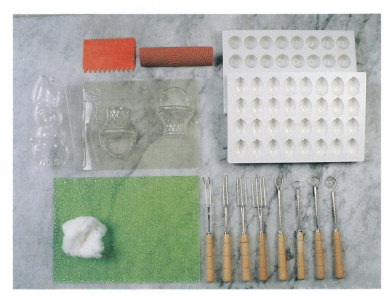

Tools for chocolate. Clockwise from top left: grooved scraper, wood-grain tool, molds for truffles and small chocolates, dipping forks, plastic mat for textured cutouts, cotton wool for polishing molds and acetate, and inexpensive molds for larger pieces.

Tempering

For most chocolate work, couverture will not handle properly when simply melted. It will take too long to set, and when it does set, it will not have the desired shine or the proper texture. The process of preparing couverture for dipping, coating, molding, and other purposes is called *tempering*.

The reason for tempering can be explained as follows: When melted cocoa butter cools and solidifies, it is able to form six different kinds of crystals. Some of these crystals melt at a low temperature and some at a high temperature (see the Cocoa Butter Crystal Melt Points sidebar). The two forms with the highest melting point, known as V and VI crystals, are considered stable, while the other four (I through IV) are unstable because they melt too easily. Fine chocolate work depends on having chocolate with many stable crystals. These high-melt-point crystals give high-quality chocolate its shine and its "snap" (high-quality chocolate that has been properly tempered and cooled breaks with a clean, sharp snap).

COCOA BUTTER CRYSTAL MELT POINTS

CRYSTAL FORM	MELTING POINT (U.S.)	MELTING POINT (METRIC)
I	63°F	17°C
II	70°F	21°C
III	79°F	26°C
IV	82°F	28°C
V	94°F	34°C
VI	97°F	36°C

The object of tempering is to get the melted chocolate to form many of the stable crystals (mostly form V) and few of the unstable ones. When chocolate is tempered, stable crystals begin to form first. Stirring the chocolate mixes these crystals through the mass of chocolate, causing more stable crystals form. In melted chocolate that has been properly tempered, many high-melt-point stable crystals are well distributed throughout the chocolate mass. Therefore, the chocolate solidifies quickly when cooled and has a good crystal structure.

BETA 6 CRYSTALS

Technology has simplified the tricky process of tempering chocolate. Now available commercially, beta 6 crystals are crystals of cocoa butter in their most stable form. Simply by adding the crystals to melted couverture, the pastry chef can quickly and easily temper the chocolate. The basic procedure for tempering with beta 6 crystals consists of three steps:

1. Bring melted couverture to 95°F (35°C).

2. Add beta 6 crystals equal to 1% of the weight of the chocolate. (For example, for 6 lb of chocolate, you need only 1 ounce of crystals; for 3 kg of chocolate, 30 g crystals.) Stir well to make sure they are blended in thoroughly.

3. Wait 10 minutes. The couverture is now tempered.

If the chocolate contains too many of the unstable crystals, it will set slowly, have a dull surface showing streaks of cocoa butter, and have a poor, crumbly texture. The whitish coating on poorly tempered or untempered chocolate is called *bloom*.

The actual process of melting and tempering chocolate consists of three steps. The proper temperatures for each of these three stages depend on the type of chocolate and its exact composition. The Critical Temperatures for Tempering Chocolate table below indicates the range of temperatures appropriate to the basic chocolate types. The manufacturer or the supplier should be able to indicate the exact temperatures that are best for each of its products.

1. **Melting.** The chocolate is placed in a pan or bowl and set over hot water to melt. It should not be set over direct heat because the chocolate is easily damaged by heat, which destroys both the texture and the flavor. Stir constantly while the chocolate is melting. The chocolate must be brought to a temperature high enough to completely melt all the fats, including the high-melt-point fats. Refer to the table below.

2. **Cooling or precrystallizing.** When the chocolate is melted, it is removed from the heat. All or part of the chocolate is then cooled until it is thick and pasty. At this point, many stable fat crystals have formed. The chocolate is stirred during this process so that the crystals are well distributed throughout the chocolate.

3. **Rewarming.** The chocolate is too thick at this point for dipping, molding, or most other uses, and must be warmed slightly before it can be worked with. Set it over warm water and stir it until it is the proper temperature and thickness for use. Correct rewarming raises the temperature above the melting point of form IV crystals. At this point, all unstable crystals have melted and the chocolate contains only stable crystals.

Rewarming must be done carefully. Do not let the chocolate get warmer than the recommended temperature. If this happens, too many of the stable form V crystals melt and the chocolate is no longer tempered, making it necessary to repeat the whole procedure. If the chocolate is too thick at the proper temperature, thin it with a little melted cocoa butter. Do not thin it by heating it.

Manufacturers and large processors use precise thermostatically controlled equipment to automatically temper the chocolate to the exact temperatures required. In the pastry shop, however, two other methods are used for tempering small quantities of couverture. The first method, *tablage*, is quick to do and is, perhaps, the most popular. The second method is *seeding*. Both methods are described in the Procedures for Tempering Chocolate.

CRITICAL TEMPERATURES FOR TEMPERING CHOCOLATE			
PROCESS	DARK CHOCOLATE COUVERTURE	MILK CHOCOLATE COUVERTURE	WHITE COUVERTURE
Melting	115°–120°F (46°–49°C)	110°–115°F (43°–46°C)	110°–115°F (43°–46°C)
Precrystallizing (cooling)	80°–84°F (27°–29°C)	78°–82°F (26°–28°C)	78°–82°F (26°–28°C)
Rewarming	88°–90°F (31°–32°C)	86°–88°F (30°–31°C)	84°–86°F (29°–30°C)

Once the chocolate is tempered, it is ready for molding, dipping, and other uses. The following sections outline procedures for a variety of chocolate work.

Before beginning to work with tempered chocolate, make sure the work area is at a temperature between 65° and 77°F (18° and 25°C). If it is colder, the chocolate will set up too quickly and be difficult to handle. If warmer, the chocolate will take too long to set; in addition, the marble slab used for tablage and much other chocolate work will be too warm for some techniques to work.

PROCEDURE: Tempering Chocolate

Method 1: Tablage

Caution: In all stages of this procedure, do not let even a trace of moisture come in contact with the chocolate.

1. With a heavy knife, chop the chocolate into small pieces. (If you are working with chocolate wafers instead of block chocolate, this step is not necessary.) Place the pieces in a dry stainless steel bowl.

2. Set the bowl in a pan of warm water. Stir the chocolate constantly so it melts uniformly.

3. Continue stirring until the chocolate is completely melted and reaches the proper temperature, as indicated in the Critical Temperatures for Tempering Chocolate table.

4. Remove the bowl from the water bath. Wipe all traces of moisture from the bottom of the bowl, to avoid contaminating the chocolate.

5. Pour about two-thirds of the chocolate onto a marble slab (a). With a metal scraper and a spatula, spread the chocolate and quickly scrape it back together, continuing to mix the chocolate so it cools uniformly (b).

6. When the chocolate cools to the proper temperature (78°–84°F/26°–29°C, as indicated in the table on page 628), it will become thick and pasty. Quickly scrape it back into the bowl with the remaining melted chocolate (c).

7. Mix and reheat the chocolate over hot water to the proper rewarming temperature (84°–90°F/29°–32°C, depending on the chocolate). Do not warm it above the recommended temperature. The chocolate is now ready for use.

Procedure Variation

Instead of working the chocolate on a marble slab as indicated in step 5, some chefs prefer to set the entire bowl over cold water and stir until the chocolate cools to the proper temperature. Then they rewarm the chocolate as in step 7. This method may not produce chocolate with as good a temper, and it raises the risk of getting water in the chocolate. However, it has the advantage of speed.

Method 2: Seeding or Injection

1. Chop the chocolate to be melted into small pieces, as in method 1.

2. Cut fine shreds or shavings from a block of tempered chocolate and set them aside.

3. Melt the chopped chocolate as in method 1.

4. Remove the melted chocolate from the water bath. Stir in some of the shaved chocolate.

5. When these shavings are nearly all melted, add a few more shavings. Continue adding and stirring until the melted chocolate is cooled to the proper tempering point. Do not add the shavings too fast, or they may not all melt.

6. Rewarm the chocolate as in method 1.

KEY POINTS TO REVIEW

▌ What is the composition of dark couverture? Of milk chocolate couverture? Of white couverture?

▌ What is tempering, and why is it necessary?

▌ What are the steps in the two procedures for tempering chocolate?

MOLDING CHOCOLATE

MOLDING CHOCOLATE IS possible because it contracts when it sets. Thus, it pulls away from the mold and can be easily removed. Molds for chocolate are made of metal or plastic. They must be kept clean and dry, and the insides must be shiny and free of scratches. If they are scratched, chocolate will stick to them.

To be sure the molds are completely clean and smooth, polish the inside surfaces with clean cheesecloth or cotton wool. Be sure they are completely dry before proceeding to mold the chocolate.

This section describes molding procedures for hollow chocolates. Large hollow molds are used for display pieces, while smaller molds are used for decorative work as well as for confections (such as chocolate rabbits for Easter). Procedures for molding chocolate truffles and other filled candies are covered in the last part of this chapter.

Molding chocolate eggs is one of the simpler molding procedures. It also serves to illustrate the techniques used in other types of molds. The Procedure for Molding Chocolate Eggs details two methods. Next is a more general description of other types of molds and how to use them.

These procedures explain molding single-color chocolates. You can also use contrasting colors of chocolate for decorative effects. This is done by decorating the inside of the mold with one color and then coating it with another color, as illustrated on page 639. Use the same techniques as described in the discussion of chocolate cutouts, below.

Two-part molds are used to make hollow chocolate items. There are two kinds: completely enclosed molds and molds with open bottoms. The first step for using either kind of mold is to paint the inside surfaces with a thin layer of tempered chocolate, using a soft brush. This step is frequently omitted, but it is recommended because it eliminates small air bubbles that might otherwise mar the surface of the chocolate. When the chocolate is set but not hard, continue with one of the following procedures.

To use two-part molds with open bottoms, clip the two parts together. Pour tempered chocolate into the opening until the mold is nearly full. Tap the mold with a wooden stick to release air bubbles. After a few moments, invert the mold over the chocolate pot and pour out the chocolate, leaving a layer of chocolate coating the mold. Set the mold, open end down, on a sheet of parchment. Additional melted chocolate will run down the inside and seal the open end. Leave the filled mold in a cool place until set, then open it and remove the chocolate.

If you are using plastic molds, you can easily see when the chocolate has set and pulled away from the mold. With metal molds, however, you just have to let the molds stand long enough until you are certain the chocolate is set.

To use enclosed molds, pour enough tempered chocolate into one half of the mold to completely coat the insides of both halves. Place the second half of the mold on top and clip it in place. Turn the mold over and over so the inside is completely coated with chocolate. Tap the mold several times while rotating it in order to release air bubbles. Let the chocolate stand until set, then unmold.

PROCEDURE: Molding Chocolate Eggs

Method 1

1. Polish the insides of the mold with cheesecloth or cotton wool.

2. Using a clean, dry brush, brush the inside of the mold with tempered chocolate. Be sure to cover the inside of the mold completely with an even layer.

3. Let the mold stand until the chocolate is partially set. It should be firm but not hard.

4. Using a metal scraper, scrape the excess chocolate from the top of the mold so the half-egg has a smooth, sharp edge.

5. Let the mold stand in a cool place until the chocolate is completely set and hard.

6. Turn the mold over and tap it gently to unmold the egg. To avoid getting fingerprints on the shiny surface of the unmolded chocolate, handle it with disposable plastic gloves.

7. To glue two halves together to make a whole hollow egg, use one of two methods:

   - Using a paper cone filled with tempered chocolate, pipe a fine line of chocolate onto the edge of one of the halves, then press the two halves together.

   - Place one of the halves open side down on a warm baking sheet for just an instant to melt the edge slightly, then fasten the two halves together.

8. Use the point of a small knife to trim excess chocolate from the seam.

Method 2

1. Polish the inside of the mold with cheesecloth or cotton wool.

2. Fill the mold with tempered chocolate until it runs over the top.

3. Invert the chocolate over the container of tempered chocolate to dump out the chocolate, leaving just a coating on the insides of the molds.

4. Prop the molds upside down over two sticks set on a sheet of parchment or clean sheet pan to allow the excess to drip out.

5. Continue with step 3 of method 1.

CHOCOLATE DECORATIONS

TEMPERED CHOCOLATE CAN be used to make a variety of decorations for cakes, pastries, and other items. The most popular of these are described here.

Chocolate Cutouts

To make chocolate cutouts, begin by polishing a sheet of acetate with cheesecloth or cotton wool. Pour tempered chocolate onto the acetate and spread into a thin layer with a palette knife. Let the chocolate stand until it clouds over and becomes firm but not hard. Cut with a small, sharp knife, cutting straight through to the acetate; or use a metal cutter, slightly warmed, to cut out desired shapes. Do not attempt to remove the cutouts at this point. Let stand until the chocolate is hard and the acetate peels away easily from the chocolate.

For decorative effects, you can coat the acetate with two colors of chocolate, making attractive patterns. The following are some of the easiest and most popular techniques:

- Flick or spatter streaks of one color of chocolate—for example, white couverture. Let the chocolate set, and then coat the acetate with a contrasting color of chocolate.

- With a paper cone, pipe a latticework design of fine stripes with one color of chocolate. Let the chocolate set, and then coat the acetate with a contrasting color.

- With a paper cone, pipe large dots of chocolate at regular intervals. Let the chocolate set, and then coat the acetate with a contrasting color.

- Spread with one color of chocolate, then scrape with a comb scraper, using the same technique as for ribbon sponge (p. 406). Then cover with another color.

- Use *chocolate transfer sheets*, which are commercially made acetate sheets with designs on them. Use as you would a plain acetate sheet, making sure the raised or textured side—the side that has the design on it—is facing up. After the chocolate has set and the acetate is peeled off, the design remains on the chocolate. Custom-made transfer sheets, embossed with a company's name or logo, for example, are available. (A transfer sheet is used to illustrate the procedure in the next section.)

- To marble chocolate, add a little tempered white couverture to tempered dark couverture and mix just until the white shows streaks against the dark (see the illustration). Then coat the acetate.

Mix dark and white couverture very lightly to marble.

Pour some of the chocolate onto a sheet of acetate.

Lift the acetate and tilt it from side to side so the chocolate coats the entire sheet.

When the chocolate clouds over and is set but not hard, cut out desired shapes with a sharp knife or cutter.

Broken pieces of dark chocolate streaked with white and cutouts of marbled white and milk chocolate.

Curled Cutouts

The previous section explained regular flat chocolate cutouts. By curling the cutouts, you can make chocolate décor that has even more visual impact. Following is the procedure.

1. Place a transfer sheet, rough side up, on a work surface, preferably a marble slab.

2. Spread with a layer of tempered chocolate (a).

3. When the chocolate is set but not hard, cut into triangles or other desired shapes (b).

4. Lay a sheet of parchment over the chocolate and roll up diagonally (c).

5. Set the roll in a curved mold to secure it while it hardens (d).

6. When the chocolate has hardened, peel off the acetate (e) and carefully separate the cutouts (f).

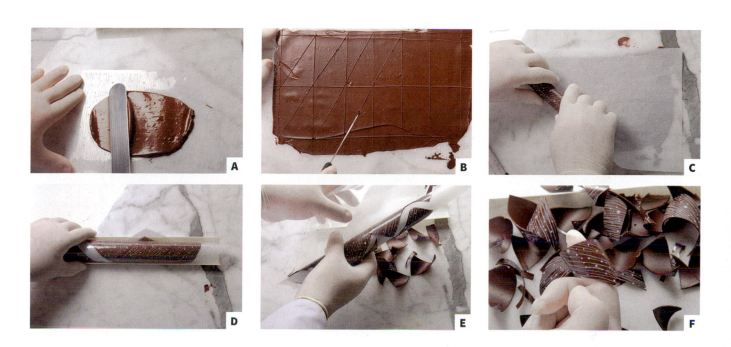

Chocolate Strips

Strips of acetate can be coated with decorative chocolate in the same way as sheets. Strips have many uses, such as ribbons and bows for showpieces (p. 634) and liners for charlotte molds. The procedure for coating a strip of acetate with tempered chocolate is similar to coating a large sheet, as described above:

1. Use a palette knife to spread the chocolate in an even layer to cover the strip.

2. Then carefully lift the strip and run your fingers along its edges to remove excess chocolate and make a neat, straight edge.

Chocolate strips may be decorated with patterns of chocolate in two colors, using the same techniques as on the previous page. An additional technique, which creates a pattern with the appearance of wood grain, requires a special tool, shown on page 627.

1. Drizzle a little tempered dark chocolate onto an acetate strip (a) and, with a palette knife, spread it into a thin layer covering the strip (b).

2. Scrape the wood-grain tool down the length of the strip, rocking it back and forth to make the grain pattern (c). Let stand a few minutes to allow the chocolate to set.

3. Spread the strip with a layer of tempered white couverture (d).

4. Lift the acetate strip and run your fingers along both edges to remove excess chocolate (e). The acetate side of the strip shows the pattern (f).

5. Fit the strip into a ring mold and allow it to set (g). The mold shown here is used to make a Julianna cake (p. 466). For a freestanding chocolate ring, such as the one used for the candy box on page 631, spread the chocolate more thickly so the ring will be sturdier.

A

B

C

D

E

F

G

Chocolate Bows

A

For chocolate bows, cut strips of acetate to the desired size. Spread with tempered chocolate, either in a single color or in a pattern of two colors. Allow the chocolate to cloud and partially set, then bend into a teardrop shape and fasten the ends together with a paper clip. If necessary, pipe a little tempered chocolate with a paper cone into the joint between the ends of the chocolate to strengthen the seam. Let set until hardened.

Peel the acetate from the bows after they are completely set (a). Cut the ends to points so they will fit together on the box (b). To hold the bows in place, pipe a little tempered chocolate with a paper cone (c). Fit the bow in place. Hold steady until the chocolate sets (d).

B

C

D

Chocolate strips made into teardrops (like bows, but larger) are used for plating presentations of desserts such as chocolate mousse. Place the teardrop on the plate and use a pastry bag to fill it with mousse.

Curled Strips

The chocolate strips in the previous sections are the basis for the following more advanced technique. This procedure begins with a strip of acetate coated with tempered chocolate, just as in the above technique, but uses an icing comb to create a lacy strip that is twisted into a decorative curl.

1. Spread a layer of chocolate onto an acetate strip (a).
2. Scrape along the length of the strip with an icing comb (b).
3. Using a paper cone filled with tempered chocolate, connect the lines of chocolate with small dots as shown (c).

4. Carefully lift the acetate strip and twist it into a spiral (d). Set it into a curved mold to hold it securely while the chocolate hardens.
5. When the chocolate is hard, peel off the acetate (e).
6. Trim off any excess to make the finished curl (f).

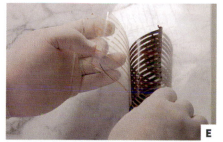

Chocolate Cigarettes and Shavings

Melted chocolate can be used for these decorations. Tempered chocolate may also be used but is not necessary. For cigarettes, spread the chocolate in a long strip on a slab of marble. Allow the chocolate to set. It should be completely set but not hard and brittle. If it becomes too hard, warm it slightly by rubbing it with the palm of your hand. Hold a metal scraper and push it forward so the chocolate curls up ahead of the metal edge (a).

For curls and shavings, score the strip of chocolate with the point of a knife (b) and then scrape up the curls with the knife (c).

Soft Strips and Fans

The chocolate strips described in this section are used for wrapping around cakes and pastries (see Pralinette, p. 369, and Feuille d'Automne, p. 459). Chocolate fans are used as decorations for various cakes and pastries. As in the case of chocolate strips, chocolate does not have to be tempered for this procedure. Melted, untempered chocolate may be used, resulting in softer chocolate.

Heat a clean half-sheet pan at 325°F (160°C) for 4 minutes. Use a clean, unwarped pan, preferably one reserved for chocolate work only. The tray should be warm but not too hot to handle. (The purpose of warming the pan is to enable you to spread a thinner coat of chocolate; be careful, however, not to get the pan too hot. Some chefs prefer to use cold trays.) Turn the sheet upside down and spread melted chocolate in a thin, even layer on the bottom of the pan. Let stand until the chocolate looks cloudy, then refrigerate until set. Remove from the refrigerator and let warm to room temperature.

To make chocolate strips, push the scraper against the tray and, with the other hand, lift off the strip of chocolate as it is released by the scraper (a). Handle the strip of chocolate very lightly (b). After coating the sides of the cake (c), make more strips for the top (d). Arrange the strips on the top (e). Finish the cake with coiled strips (f), touching them as little as possible to prevent melting (g). (The cake pictured here is a Feuille d'Automne.)

A

A

B

C

D

E

F

G

To make chocolate fans, scrape the chocolate as for strips, except hold your thumb against one corner of the scraper so the strip bunches or gathers on one side (a). Carefully neaten the ruffles or folds of the fan as necessary (b).

A

B

Chocolate Petals

Like soft strips and fans, chocolate petals are made by scraping chocolate off a flat surface. In this case, however, the scraping tool is a round cutter. Following is the procedure:

1. Spread a thin layer of chocolate on a marble slab or other flat surface (a).

2. When the chocolate is set but not yet hard and brittle, hold the bottom edge of a round cutter as shown (b) and scrape up curled petals by pulling the cutter toward you.

3. The resulting cup-shaped petals (c) can be used for a variety of decorative purposes (see, for example, the Harlequin Roll on page 470).

Piping Chocolate

With the use of a paper cone, as described in Chapter 17, tempered chocolate can be made into decorations for cakes, pastries, and other desserts. It can be piped directly onto the dessert or onto parchment paper in small designs and left to harden. After they are set, the decorations can be removed from the paper and placed on the desserts. In this way, decorations can be made during slack hours and stored until needed.

Ordinary tempered chocolate is adequate for small, fine decorations, such as those for petits fours (see p. 472), but it is too thin for most other piped decorations. To make piping chocolate, add a very little warm simple syrup to the tempered chocolate. This will thicken the chocolate immediately. Stirring constantly, add more syrup, very slowly, until the chocolate is thinned to piping consistency.

Modeling Chocolate

Modeling chocolate is a thick paste that can be molded by hand to make a variety of shapes, just as you might use marzipan. Simply combine melted chocolate with half its weight of glucose (corn syrup) that has been warmed to the temperature of the chocolate. Mix them together well. Place them in an airtight container and let stand for an hour or more. Knead the mixture until it forms a workable paste.

Spraying Chocolate

You can use a standard paint sprayer to spray liquid chocolate. The sprayed chocolate creates a velvety coating on cakes, pastries, and showpieces.

To enable the chocolate to pass through the sprayer, thin it with melted cocoa butter. The usual ratio is two parts couverture to one part cocoa butter by weight.

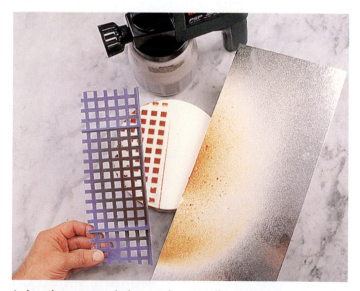

A chocolate sprayer being used to stencil a pattern on a dessert.

CHOCOLATE TRUFFLES AND CONFECTIONS

CHOCOLATE TRUFFLES ARE named for their resemblance to black truffles, the aromatic underground fungus prized by gourmets.

In their simplest form, *chocolate truffles* are simply balls of chocolate ganache, the thick mixture of chocolate and cream introduced in Chapter 12. Ganache can be made with not only dark chocolate but also milk chocolate and white couverture. Many flavorings and other ingredients can be added to create a variety of confections. (Review the discussion of ganache on page 268.)

The simplest way of finishing truffles, and one of the most popular, is simply to coat the balls of ganache with cocoa powder. This technique is used in the first recipe in this section, Dark Chocolate Truffles.

For more elaborate presentations, the truffles may be coated with chocolate by dipping or molding.

Dipping Chocolates

For candy makers, the techniques for dipping and molding candies are basic. There are two basic procedures for dipping small items such as truffles, other candy centers, and nuts.

For the first method, place the items one at a time on the surface of the tempered chocolate. With a dipping fork, turn them over to cover them completely, then lift them out. Tap the fork holding the chocolate on the edge of the bowl to even the coating. Draw the fork holding the coated chocolate over the edge of the bowl to wipe off excess chocolate from the bottom of the fork, then set the item on a sheet of parchment. To mark the chocolate, touch the top of the item lightly with the dipping fork. Each kind of fork will leave its own distinctive pattern, so you can mark different flavors with different patterns. Let stand until hardened.

The second method is hand-dipping. To hand-dip plain truffles, pipe bulbs of ganache onto a parchment sheet (a). Using plastic gloves, hand-roll the truffles with a little cornstarch to round them (b). Still wearing plastic gloves, coat the truffles with a thin layer of tempered chocolate by hand-rolling them in tempered chocolate (c). Drop into a bowl of cocoa powder (d). Remove from the cocoa with a dipping fork and drop into a sieve to remove excess cocoa (e).

A

B

C

D

E

Molding Filled Chocolates

Small molds for individual candies are lined with chocolate using the same techniques as for larger molds, as discussed on page 630. Either of the two methods described there may be used for small candy molds, as well: (1) brush tempered chocolate onto the inside of the molds to coat them in an even layer; or (2) pour tempered chocolate into the molds to fill, then pour the chocolate out, leaving a layer coating the molds.

The procedure described in this section is an example of the second technique.

Before filling the molds, you can decorate them using any of several techniques. For example:

- Spray the inside of the molds with colored cocoa butter (illustrated in the following procedure).

- Spatter streaks of a contrasting color of tempered chocolate into the molds. Let set before coating the molds.

- With a paper cone, pipe fine lines of a contrasting color of tempered chocolate into the molds and let set.

- Brush the insides of the molds very lightly with a contrasting color of tempered chocolate to create a marbled or stippled effect. Let set.

Brushing the inside of the mold.

After each of these techniques, you must scrape or wipe any residue chocolate from the flat surface of the mold before continuing with the next steps.

The entire procedure is as follows:

1. Carefully wipe the insides of the molds with cheesecloth or cotton wool to make sure they are clean and smooth.

2. Spray the insides of the molds lightly with colored cocoa butter (a).

3. Wipe off the flat surface of the mold with a warm, dry towel to remove all cocoa butter that is not inside the molds.

4. Fill the molds with tempered chocolate (b). Using an offset palette knife, spread the chocolate to make sure all molds are filled (c).

5. Scrape off excess chocolate from the flat surface of the mold (d).

6. Tap the mold sharply with the handle of the scraper to remove any air bubbles that might mar the appearance of the finished chocolates (e).

7. Turn the mold over and pour out the chocolate into your bowl of tempered chocolate, leaving a thin layer coating the molds (f).

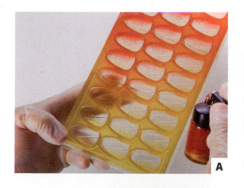

A

B

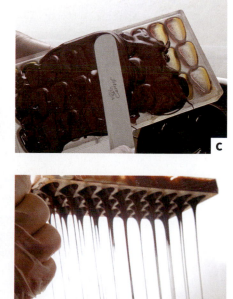

C

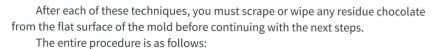

D

E

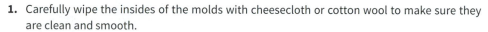

F

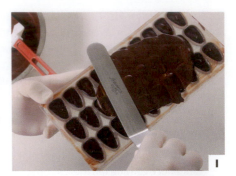

8. With a scraper, once again scrape off excess chocolate from the surface of the mold (g).

9. Place a piece of parchment on a flat work surface and place the mold upside down on the parchment. This allows any excess chocolate to run out rather than settle in the bottoms of the molds. Before the chocolate sets, lift the mold off the parchment and again scrape off the flat surface.

10. Let the mold stand in a cool place until the chocolate has hardened.

11. Using a paper cone or a pastry bag with a fine tip, fill the molds with ganache or other desired filling (h). Do not fill too full, but leave room for a final cap of chocolate. Filling too full makes it impossible to seal the chocolates properly.

12. Let stand until the ganache has firmed up. Depending on the filling, this may take as long as 24 hours. If necessary, cover the molds lightly with a sheet of parchment to protect them from contamination. Do not wrap tightly.

13. Spread tempered chocolate over the filling to seal the chocolates (i).

14. Place a piece of acetate on the mold (j).

15. Pass over the acetate with a rolling pin to flatten the bottoms of the chocolates and to remove excess chocolate from the base (k).

16. Allow to harden completely. (Unless the work area is very cool, you may need to chill the chocolates to harden them.) Unmold the finished chocolates (l) by turning the molds over onto a piece of parchment and tapping gently. The chocolates should fall out easily.

KEY POINTS TO REVIEW

▪ What techniques are used to mold chocolate?

▪ What procedures are used to make simple chocolate decorations: cutouts, strips, cigarettes, curls, and fans?

▪ What techniques are used to make chocolate truffles and to coat them with chocolate by dipping or molding?

DARK CHOCOLATE TRUFFLES

Yield: about 75 truffles, ⅓ oz (10 g) each

Ingredients	U.S.	Metric
Ganache		
Heavy cream	7 oz	225 g
Vanilla extract	½ tsp	2.5 g
Dark chocolate couverture, chopped	1 lb	500 g
Butter	2 oz	60 g
Coating		
Cocoa powder	as needed	as needed

PROCEDURE

1. Heat the cream and vanilla to a simmer.
2. Pour over the chopped chocolate in a bowl. Stir until the chocolate is completely melted and blended in. Cool the mixture until it is just slightly warm to the touch.
3. Stir in the butter until it is melted and completely blended in.
4. Let the mixture stand until it starts to thicken, then put it in a pastry bag fitted with a medium plain tip.
5. Pipe the mixture into small mounds, about 2 tsp (10 mL) each, on sheets of parchment paper. Chill until firm.
6. Wearing disposable gloves, one by one, roll the mounds between the palms of the hands to round the pieces of ganache; drop them into a bowl of cocoa powder.
7. Remove the truffles from the cocoa and shake in a sieve to remove excess cocoa.

BANANA TRUFFLES

Yield: about 120 truffles, ⅓ oz (9 g) each

Ingredients	U.S.		Metric
Ganache centers			
Banana pulp	5	oz	150 g
Rum	4	tsp	20 g
Heavy cream	3.33 oz		100 g
Butter	4	tsp	20 g
Honey	3.33 oz		100 g
Milk chocolate couverture	4	oz	125 g
Dark chocolate	3.33 oz		100 g
Coating (see *Note*)			
Dark chocolate couverture, tempered	7	oz	200 g
White couverture, tempered	1 lb 5	oz	600 g

NOTE: The quantity of chocolate needed for the coating is approximate. Because you need enough for the molding procedure, you must temper more chocolate than you will use.

PROCEDURE

1. Mash the bananas with the rum until smooth.
2. Heat the cream, butter, and honey to the boiling point. Remove from heat.
3. Melt the milk and dark chocolates and stir into the cream mixture.
4. Mix in the bananas. Let stand until completely cold.
5. Prepare hard (polycarbonate) chocolate molds by polishing them with cheesecloth or cotton wool.
6. Brush the inside of the molds very lightly with tempered dark chocolate to create a marbled effect. Allow to set.
7. Coat the molds with tempered white couverture, as described in the procedure on pages 639–640, steps 4–10.
8. Put the ganache mixture into a piping bag fitted with a small plain tip and fill the molds three-quarters full.
9. Seal and finish the molds as described in the procedure on page 640, steps 13–16.

ORANGE TRUFFLES

Yield: about 120 truffles, ⅓ oz (9 g) each

Ingredients	U.S.		Metric
Heavy cream	4	oz	120 g
Orange juice, strained to remove all pulp	1	oz	30 g
Orange liqueur	3	oz	90 g
Butter	2	oz	60 g
Egg yolks	1.67 oz		50 g
Sugar	1.67 oz		50 g
Dark chocolate, chopped	7	oz	215 g
Coating (see *Note*)			
Dark chocolate couverture, tempered	1 lb 4	oz	600 g

NOTE: The quantity of chocolate needed for the coating is approximate. Because you need enough for the molding procedure, you must temper more chocolate than you will use.

PROCEDURE

1. Combine the cream, juice, liqueur, and butter in a saucepan and bring to a boil.

2. Whip the egg yolks with the sugar until light.

3. Gradually beat the hot liquid into the egg mixture.

4. Return this mixture to the heat and bring quickly to a simmer, then remove from heat.

5. Strain the liquid over the chopped chocolate in a bowl. Stir until all the chocolate is melted and the mixture is evenly blended.

6. Let the mixture stand until it starts to thicken. This may take an hour or longer, depending on the room temperature. If necessary, the mixture can be chilled briefly, but do not let it become too hard. Then put it in a pastry bag fitted with a medium plain tip.

7. Pipe the mixture into small mounds, about 2 tsp (10 mL) each, on sheets of parchment paper. Chill until firm.

8. One by one, roll the pieces of ganache between the palms of the hands, to round them. Place them back onto the parchment.

9. Coat the truffles in one of two ways:

   • Drop them a few at a time into a bowl of tempered chocolate, then remove with a dipping fork and place on a parchment-lined tray.

   • Wearing disposable plastic gloves, roll in tempered chocolate in the palms of the hands, as shown on page 638, then place on a parchment-lined tray.

   Let stand until the chocolate is completely set.

ROCHER WITH ALMONDS

For large-quantity measurements, see page 732.

Ingredients	U.S.	Metric
Dark chocolate	4 oz	100 g
Praline paste	6 oz	150 g
Ice cream wafers (pailletine), finely crushed	2 oz	50 g
Dark chocolate	6 oz	150 g
Almonds, toasted and chopped	1 oz	25 g
Total weight:	**1 lb 3 oz**	**475 g**

PROCEDURE

1. Melt the first quantity of dark chocolate over a hot-water bath.

2. Add the praline paste and mix quickly.

3. Add the crushed wafers and mix.

4. As soon as the mixture starts to thicken but before it starts to solidify, use a spoon to drop 1-tbsp (12-g) pieces onto a parchment-lined sheet pan. If desired, roll between palms to shape into balls.

5. Allow to set at room temperature, 2–3 hours.

6. Temper the remaining dark chocolate and add the chopped almonds.

7. Dip each ball into the tempered chocolate and retrieve using a chocolate fork.

8. Place onto a parchment-lined baking sheet and allow to harden.

LEMON TRUFFLES

Yield: about 110 truffles, ½ oz (14 g) each

Ingredients	U.S.		Metric
Ganache centers			
Milk	4	oz	125 g
Heavy cream	4	oz	125 g
Glucose	1.67	oz	50 g
White couverture, chopped	1 lb		500 g
Lemon juice	3.25	oz	100 g
Coating (see *Note*)			
White couverture, tempered	1 lb 10	oz	800 g

NOTE: The quantity of chocolate needed for the coating is approximate. Because you need enough for the molding and dipping procedure, you must temper more chocolate than you will use.

PROCEDURE

1. Heat the milk, cream, and glucose until the mixture is warm and the glucose is dissolved.

2. Add the white couverture and stir until it is melted and uniformly blended with the cream mixture.

3. Stir in the lemon juice.

4. Let the mixture cool completely. Place the ganache in a pastry bag fitted with a small, plain tip.

5. Prepare hemispherical polycarbonate truffle molds by polishing them with cheesecloth or cotton wool.

6. Coat the insides of the molds with tempered white chocolate as described in the procedure on pages 639–640, steps 4–10.

7. Fill to the top with the ganache filling. Unmold. For each truffle, press 2 half-spheres together to make a round ball.

8. Dip in tempered white chocolate, remove with a dipping fork, and place on a wire rack. To create a textured surface, allow to set a few moments, then roll along the rack to give a spiked coating to the truffle. Allow to harden completely before removing from the rack.

ALTERNATIVE PROCEDURE

Use ready-made chocolate shells. Fill them using a pastry bag with a small plain tip and seal the opening by covering it with tempered couverture using a paper cone. Dip as in the basic procedure above.

MUSCADINES

Yield: about 45 truffles, ⅓ oz (10 g) each

Ingredients	U.S.		Metric
Ganache			
Milk chocolate couverture	6.75	oz	200 g
Praline paste	1	oz	30 g
Water, boiling	1	oz	30 g
Butter, softened	4	tsp	20 g
Orange liqueur, such as Cointreau	1	oz	30 g
Coating (see *Note*)			
Confectioners' sugar	as needed		as needed
Milk chocolate couverture	8	oz	250 g
Cocoa butter, melted	3.25	oz	100 g

NOTE: The quantity of chocolate needed for the coating is approximate. Because you need enough for the molding and dipping procedure, you must temper more chocolate than you will use.

PROCEDURE

1. Melt the first quantity of chocolate and stir in the praline paste.

2. Add the water and stir until evenly mixed.

3. Mix in the butter and liqueur. Chill over an ice-water bath until the mixture is thick enough to hold its shape.

4. Place in a piping bag fitted with a large star tip (approximately ½ in./1 cm wide at the opening). Pipe long logs of the mixture onto a baking sheet lined with parchment paper. Cut the logs into 1½-in. (4-cm) lengths. Chill.

5. Sift confectioners' sugar onto a tray or sheet pan until it is about ½ in. (1 cm) deep.

6. Temper the milk chocolate and stir in the cocoa butter.

7. Dip each piece of chilled ganache into the chocolate, remove with a dipping fork, and tap off the excess chocolate. Place in the confectioners' sugar. Shake the tray to cover the chocolates in sugar. Allow to set before removing.

TERMS FOR REVIEW

chocolate	conching	dark couverture	bloom
cocoa bean	couverture	milk chocolate couverture	tablage
cocoa butter	coating chocolate	white couverture	seeding
chocolate liquor	baking chocolate	dark chocolate	chocolate truffle
cocoa mass	confectioners' chocolate	tempering	

QUESTIONS FOR REVIEW

1. Why is it necessary to temper chocolate for making chocolate molds?

2. Briefly explain two methods for tempering chocolate.

3. If tempered chocolate is at the correct temperature for molding but is too thick, how should you thin it?

4. Why is *white chocolate* an inaccurate term?

5. Why are chocolate molds polished with cotton wool before use?

6. Describe one procedure for molding chocolate eggs.

7. Describe five techniques for making decorative patterns using two colors of chocolate for cutouts.

8. Describe the procedure for making chocolate fans, starting with melted chocolate.

9. What are chocolate truffles? Give as complete an answer as you can, describing various types and forms.

24

MARZIPAN, PASTILLAGE, AND NOUGATINE

1. **Handle marzipan, from making it to molding decorative items from it.**
2. **Prepare pastillage and make decorative items with it.**
3. **Prepare nougatine and make simple decorative items with it.**

THIS CHAPTER AND the next are an introduction to the pastry chef's art of making decorative items out of sugar and other materials. Although all the ingredients used for these pieces are edible, and many of these items are used to decorate cakes and other desserts, they are, in many cases, made as showpieces, such as centerpieces for dessert buffet tables, and are not intended to be eaten.

In hotels and other food service and retail operations, such showpieces can be useful, and even profitable. They serve to draw the customers' attention to the skill and artistry of the pastry chef and, thus, indirectly lead to higher sales of desserts. Perhaps even more important, from a pastry chef's point of view, they are an enjoyable outlet for creative skills.

647

Some of the items in these two chapters are comparatively easy to make, while others, such as pulled sugar, require a great deal of practice before you can expect to achieve good results. The text and the many photographs that illustrate the techniques provide an introduction but, for the most part, the only effective way to learn these skills is with the guidance of an instructor.

MARZIPAN

Marzipan is a paste made of almonds and sugar that is worked to a plastic consistency. Its texture allows it to be rolled out with a rolling pin, like dough, or modeled into the shapes of fruits, animals, flowers, and other designs.

Pastry chefs and confectioners once had to grind almonds to make marzipan, but today the ready availability of almond paste makes the job much easier. As you can see in the accompanying formula, making marzipan involves moistening the almond paste and blending it with confectioners' sugar. Formulas may vary slightly—calling for more or less sugar, or using different moistening agents, such as fondant or egg whites—but the principle behind them is the same.

Here are important guidelines for working with marzipan:

- To preserve the color of the marzipan, be sure that all equipment, including bowls, mixer attachments, and work surfaces, is very clean. Use stainless steel rather than aluminum mixing bowls, because aluminum discolors marzipan.

- Marzipan dries quickly when exposed to air, and forms a crust on the surface. To avoid this when you are working with marzipan, keep unused portions in a bowl covered with a damp cloth. To store marzipan, keep it wrapped or covered in an airtight container. It keeps indefinitely when protected from air. If left uncovered, it eventually becomes hard as a rock.

- When marzipan is kneaded and worked, the oil content (from the almonds) comes to the surface and makes the marzipan sticky. To avoid this, dust the work surface lightly with confectioners' sugar. Keep a pan of confectioners' sugar handy for this purpose.

Marzipan Sheets and Cutouts

Marzipan can be rolled out into sheets with a rolling pin in the same way that you roll out short dough. Confectioners' sugar, rather than flour, is used for dusting the workbench and rolling pin. Make sure the bench and the pin are completely clean.

Marzipan sheets are useful for covering cakes and petits fours, as explained in Chapter 17. They may be left smooth or textured with a ribbed roller or basketweave roller (see p. 448).

Colored patterns, such as stripes or polka dots, can be made on marzipan sheets as follows: Roll out a sheet of marzipan partway, so it is about twice as thick as desired. Roll out another small piece of marzipan in a contrasting color until it is ⅛ inch (3 mm) thick. Cut out small circles or strips and arrange them carefully on top of the thick sheet. Now continue to roll out this sheet to the desired thickness. Be careful to roll it evenly in all directions, to keep the design uniform.

Using round or fancy cutters, cut out small shapes from the marzipan sheets and use them to decorate cakes and desserts. For additional effect, spread the sheet of marzipan with tempered chocolate and texture it with an icing comb. Make cutouts before the chocolate hardens completely. Create another variation by texturing the marzipan with ribbed rollers and then spinning fine lines of chocolate over the sheet, using a paper cone with a very small opening. (Note that the Easter plaque on the chocolate egg pictured on p. 631 is made of a textured marzipan sheet.)

Marzipan petits fours can be made to look like fancy icebox cookies. Using two colors of marzipan instead of icebox cookie dough, make checkerboard or pinwheel slices using the procedures for Icebox Cookies (p. 486). (Do not bake the slices.)

MARZIPAN

Ingredients	U.S.	Metric
Almond paste	1 lb	500 g
Glucose or corn syrup	3 oz	90 g
Confectioners' sugar, sifted	1 lb	500 g
Total weight:	**2 lb 3 oz**	**1090 g**

PROCEDURE

1. In a clean stainless steel bowl, blend the almond paste and glucose, using the paddle attachment, until smooth.

2. Add the sifted sugar, a little at a time, just as fast as it is absorbed. Stop adding sugar when the desired consistency is reached. The marzipan should be stiff but workable and not too dry.

3. If colored marzipan is desired, add a small amount of food coloring and work it in.

Modeling with Marzipan

Fruits, vegetables, animals, flowers, and many other shapes can be molded with marzipan. Small marzipan fruits, served as petits fours or candies, are perhaps the most popular items.

Fruits and Flowers

To make small fruits, first divide the paste into equal portions. For example, to make ¾-ounce (22-g) pieces, flatten 1½ pound (700 g) marzipan into a fairly thick rectangle of uniform thickness. With a knife, carefully cut the rectangle into 4 rows of 8 to make 32 equal pieces.

Begin by rolling each piece between the palms of your hands into a round ball that is perfectly smooth and free of seams and cracks. (Bananas are an exception. In this case, begin by rolling the pieces into smooth sausage shapes.) Then start modeling the balls with your fingers into the shapes of pears, apples, and other fruits. The best way to make realistic-looking fruits is to use real fruits as models. Imitate the shapes of the real fruits as closely as possible.

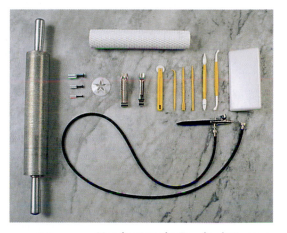

Marzipan tools. Top: basketweave roller. Middle row: metal rolling pin, small cutters with release plungers, strawberry leaf cutter, nippers, modeling tools, smoother for covering cakes with sheets of marzipan. Bottom: color sprayer.

Marzipan rose, carnation, strawberry, and oranges.

You can add special effects using ordinary tools or special modeling tools. For example, to make the crease on the sides of peaches, apricots, plums, and cherries, use the back of a knife. Texture the surfaces of strawberries by poking them lightly with a toothpick. Imitate the rough surface of lemons and oranges by rolling them lightly over a cheese grater.

Let the fruits dry overnight before coloring. Coloring can be done in two ways:

- Start with tinted marzipan—green for apples and pears, yellow for bananas, peaches, and lemons, and so on. Apply food coloring with a brush to add highlights and markings, such as the brown streaks and dots on bananas, the red blush on apples and peaches, and so on.

- Start with untinted marzipan. Tint the finished fruits with background colors, using either a brush or a sprayer. Let the color dry, then add the highlights.

Flowers such as carnations and roses are useful items to make because they can be used to decorate cakes as well as display pieces.

PROCEDURE: Making a Marzipan Strawberry

1. Roll the ball of marzipan into a strawberry shape with the palms of your hands (a).
2. Indent the stem end of the strawberry with an appropriate modeling tool (b).

3. Roll the strawberry in sugar to simulate the textured surface of the real berry (c).
4. Cut out a leaf shape for the stem end and fasten it in place using an appropriate modeling tool (d).

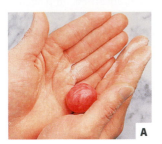

PROCEDURE: Making a Marzipan Orange

1. Roll a piece of marzipan into a round ball (a).
2. Using a marzipan modeling tool, make an indentation in the ball to resemble the stem end of the orange (b).

PROCEDURE: Making a Marzipan Carnation

1. Flatten a strip of marzipan on the workbench until the edges are paper thin. Feather the edge with the point of a knife (a).
2. Release the strip of marzipan by sliding a knife under it. Gather it together into a carnation shape (b).

PROCEDURE: Making a Marzipan Rose

1. Taper a ball of marzipan to serve as the base of the rose.

2. Mold the ball with the tapered end pointing up, to serve as the center of the flower.

3. For the petals, roll a log of marzipan and cut pieces of equal size. Flatten these pieces into small disks.

4. With the back of a spoon, flatten the disks, using a circular motion to taper the edges to paper thinness.

5. Wrap the petal around the base, leaving one edge free so the second petal can be inserted under it.

6. Attach the second petal.

7. Continue adding petals in the same fashion until the rose is the desired size. With a sharp knife, cut the rose from the base.

Other Items

The variety of objects that can be modeled from marzipan is limited only by the imagination and talent of the pastry cook. Vegetables such as carrots, asparagus, potatoes, and peas in the pod can be made in the same way as fruits. Marzipan snowmen and holly leaves are often used to decorate the Bûche de Noël (p. 470). Animals such as dogs, pigs, and frogs are also popular subjects. Features such as eyes, noses, and tongues can be applied with royal icing, chocolate, or fondant.

Frames for chocolate paintings on pastillage (p. 653) are generally made of marzipan. Roll marzipan into long, round strips of perfectly uniform thickness and fasten them around the pastillage plaque. With assorted marzipan nippers and modeling tools, texture the marzipan to look like a carved frame. Highlight the raised details by very carefully browning them with a blowtorch.

PASTILLAGE

Pastillage (pronounced PAHS tee yahzh) is a sugar paste used for modeling decorative items. Unlike marzipan and other modeling pastes, it is rarely, if ever, intended to be eaten. Although it is made entirely of edible items, pastillage is as hard and brittle as plaster of Paris when it dries, and nearly as tasteless. It is used primarily for making display pieces, such as centerpieces for dessert buffet tables, or small baskets or boxes to hold petits fours and candies. Pastillage is normally left pure white, although it may be colored in pastel shades.

The formula given here is a simple and popular one using readily available ingredients: confectioners' sugar, cornstarch (as a drying agent), water, cream of tartar (to help preserve whiteness), and gelatin (as a stiffening and stabilizing agent). Pastillage is sometimes called *gum paste*, although that term is more correctly used when a vegetable gum (usually gum tragacanth) is used instead of gelatin (see the Gum Paste sidebar).

Pastillage tools: Ribbed roller, molds, and cutters.

Making and Handling Pastillage

Many of the same precautions must be taken in the production of pastillage as in the production of marzipan. Great care is essential to preserve the pure white color. Make sure all equipment is scrupulously clean, and use a stainless-steel bowl, not aluminum, for mixing (aluminum imparts a grayish color to the paste). Likewise, the work surface, rolling pin, and molds must be clean and dry.

Pastillage dries and crusts over even faster than marzipan, so it must be kept covered at all times. While working with pastillage, keep unused portions in a bowl covered with a damp cloth. Work quickly and without pause until your products are formed and ready for drying.

Most pastillage pieces are made of thin sheets of the paste cut to shape with the aid of paper patterns. The pieces are left flat, or curved around molds, and allowed to dry, then assembled by gluing them together with royal icing. A marble slab is ideal for rolling out pastillage because it gives the paste a smooth surface. Use cornstarch to dust the work surface. Be careful not to use more starch than is necessary to keep the paste from sticking. Excessive starch dries the surface of the paste quickly and causes it to crust over and crack.

For the most attractive, delicate pieces, the pastillage sheets should be rolled thin (about ⅛ in./3 mm thick). Thick sheets make heavy, clumsy-looking pieces. Have paper patterns handy, so that as soon as the pastillage is rolled out you can place the patterns on it. Then cut cleanly and accurately with a sharp knife or cutter.

For pieces that are to be molded, have the molds clean, dry, and dusted with cornstarch. For example, to make a pastillage bowl, you can use the outside of another bowl, placed upside down on the workbench, as your mold. Carefully fit the sheet of paste to the mold, gently fitting it to the shape of the mold with your hands.

When the pastillage is partially dry and firm, turn it over to allow the bottom to dry. Continue turning it over from time to time to dry it evenly. Pastillage that does not dry evenly tends to curl or distort out of shape. Drying time depends on the size and thickness of the pieces and may take from 12 hours to several days.

Dried pastillage may be lightly sanded with extra-fine sandpaper until it is very smooth. This also helps smooth the cut edges, which may be rough or sharp. Finally, assemble the pieces using royal icing as glue. Use as little icing as necessary; any excess is likely to squeeze out at the seams, which spoils the appearance of the piece.

The Techniques for Creating a Showpiece from Pastillage procedure on the next two pages illustrates most of the steps discussed here. In the accompanying photos, the pastry chef is making and assembling the display piece pictured below. The flowers are tinted with food colors using the sprayer depicted on page 649.

Another advantage of the pure-white, smooth surface of pastillage is that it makes an ideal canvas for chocolate painting. To use it in this way, begin by making a round, oval, or rectangular plaque of pastillage; let it dry and then sand it smooth. Using an artist's brush, draw a picture on it using melted unsweetened chocolate. Create light and dark shades by diluting the chocolate with varying proportions of melted cocoa butter. For fine detail, etch lines in the chocolate with a sharp wooden pick. After the chocolate has set, the painting can be finished off with a marzipan frame (p. 652).

GUM PASTE

Although the terms *gum paste* and *pastillage* are sometimes used interchangeably, they are slightly different products in spite of their similar appearance. Gum paste is made with a vegetable gum called *gum tragacanth* (see p. 82). Because this gum is somewhat expensive, gum paste is less practical than pastillage for large pieces or high-volume work. Also, gum paste dries more slowly than pastillage, making it inconvenient when time is an important factor in finishing a display piece.

The slow-drying property of gum paste is sometimes an important advantage as well. Because it doesn't dry or crust as quickly as pastillage, it is a good choice when you are doing a detailed, intricate piece that takes a long time to shape. And because it is more pliable, it can be rolled thinner and used to make more delicate items.

For those interested in comparing gum paste and pastillage, a formula is included on page 732.

PASTILLAGE

Ingredients	U.S.			Metric	Sugar at 100% %
Gelatin		0.5	oz	12 g	1.25
Water, cold		5.5	oz	140 g	14
Confectioners' sugar (10X)	2 lb 8		oz	1000 g	100
Cornstarch		5	oz	125 g	12.5
Cream of tartar		0.04 oz (½ tsp)		1 g	0.1
Total weight:	**3 lb 3**		**oz**	**1278 g**	**127** %

PROCEDURE

1. Stir the gelatin into the water. Let stand 5 minutes, then heat until the gelatin is dissolved.

2. Sift together the sugar, starch, and cream of tartar.

3. Place the gelatin mixture in a stainless steel mixer bowl. Fit the mixing machine with the dough hook.

4. With the machine running at low speed, add most of the sugar mixture just as fast as it is absorbed, keeping back a little of the sugar in case the texture must be adjusted. Mix to a smooth, pliable paste. It should have the consistency of a firm dough. If it is too moist, add some or all of the remaining sugar.

5. Keep the paste covered at all times.

Techniques for creating this pastillage showpiece are illustrated on pages 654–655.

TECHNIQUES: Creating a Showpiece from Pastillage

The techniques shown here are used to create the showpiece pictured on page 653.

1. Roll out the pastillage on a work surface, preferably marble, dusted lightly with cornstarch.

2. Check the thickness.

3. Lift the rolled-out pastillage from the workbench by first draping it over a rolling pin. Always dust off excess cornstarch.

4. Create a textured surface with a ribbed roller.

5. Cut out desired shapes. Working on a tray allows you to remove the pieces from the workbench for drying without disturbing them. Be sure to dust the tray with cornstarch.

6. You can cut some shapes freehand with a knife.

7. Use small cutters to cut additional pieces.

8. Use a ring mold to measure the width of a strip to form the sides of the box.

9. Cut a strip of pastillage and fit it inside the ring mold. Trim the ends so the joint fits smoothly.

10. Trim excess from the top.

11. For leaves and petals, cut appropriate shapes.

12. Press the cutout shapes in a leaf mold.

13. Fit the petals into a mold lined with a little square of parchment, to prevent sticking.

14. To make the center of the flower, press a ball of pastillage into a sieve.

15. Set the center of the flower in place.

16. To use this type of cutter/ molder, stamp out a piece of pastillage, press it in to mold it, and then push it out with the spring-loaded plunger.

17. For the feet of the box, press balls of pastillage into a chocolate mold. Pass a scraper over the top of the mold to remove excess and flatten the tops.

18. Once the pastillage has dried, sand it with fine sandpaper to achieve a smooth surface.

19. Fasten pieces together with royal icing.

20. Fasten the dried top of the box, which has been textured with a ribbed roller, in place.

21. Fasten the side pieces in place.

22. Make the decorative lacework by coloring royal icing and piping it using a paper cone.

NOUGATINE

Nougatine is a candy made of caramelized sugar and almonds. (Almonds are traditional, but other sliced nuts are sometimes used as well.) It looks somewhat like peanut brittle but is more attractive because of the sliced almonds. The caramelized sugar should be a clear amber color, not cloudy. The sugar is soft and pliable when it is hot, so it can be cut and molded into shapes to make decorative pieces.

Production and Shaping

As can be seen in the following formula, cooking nougatine involves two fairly simple steps: caramelizing the sugar and adding the almonds. The glucose inverts some of the sugar (see p. 64), thus preventing unwanted crystallization. Cream of tartar or lemon juice is sometimes used instead of glucose.

Nougatine can be cut into many shapes, and is often cut freehand. If your display piece requires precise shapes, however, it is best to cut patterns out of sheets of parchment. Have all your patterns ready before starting to make the nougatine. Then lay the patterns on top of the sheet of nougatine to guide your work.

When the nougatine is ready, pour it onto a silicone mat or an oiled tray or marble slab. It will cool quickly, so you must work fast. When the sheet has begun to set, flip it over with a spatula to cool it evenly. Have your paper pattern ready. Flatten the sheet with an oiled rolling pin to even the thickness. Place the patterns on the sheet and quickly cut out shapes with a heavy oiled knife. The oiled surface should prevent the patterns from sticking, but don't press them down or leave them on the nougatine too long.

Prepare the molds ahead of time by oiling them lightly. For example, to make a nougatine bowl, you can use the bottom of a stainless steel bowl placed upside down on the bench and rubbed with oil. Lay the soft, cut nougatine over the bowl and carefully press it into shape.

If the nougatine cools and hardens before you can shape it, place it on an oiled baking sheet and place it in a hot oven for a moment to soften it. You can even join two sheets together by laying them next to each other and heating them. Just keep in mind that every time you reheat nougatine it darkens a little more. Too many shades of nougatine in a display piece detract from its appearance.

When the molded nougatine pieces have cooled and hardened, cement them together as necessary, using either royal icing or a hot sugar syrup boiled to 310°F (190°C). Nougatine pieces can also be decorated with royal icing.

Other Uses of Nougatine

Unlike some decorative materials, such as pastillage, nougatine is a tasty confection. Thin nougatine sheets can be cut into fancy shapes and used to decorate cakes and other desserts.

Hard nougatine can be crushed and used like chopped nuts for masking the sides of cakes. Finely ground and sifted, or ground to a paste, it makes an excellent flavoring for creams and icings. This product is similar to praline paste, except that praline generally contains hazelnuts.

KEY POINTS TO REVIEW

■ What is pastillage, and how is it made?

■ What guidelines should be followed when making and handling pastillage?

■ What is nougatine, and how is it made and handled?

TECHNIQUES: Working with Nougatine

1. Pour out the hot nougatine mixture onto a silicone mat.

2. With a spatula or your hands (wear rubber gloves), fold the mass over on itself as it cools, to cool it evenly.

3. While it is still hot and soft, roll out the nougatine with a rolling pin to the desired thickness.

4. The nougatine shown here is to be used as the base of a centerpiece. It is molded to shape in a lightly oiled cake tin.

5. Trim off excess with a chef's knife.

6. Cut thinly rolled nougatine into shapes for decorating cakes (such as the top layer of Brasilia, p. 462) and pastries.

7. Bend the cutout to the desired shape while still hot, or rewarm until pliable.

NOUGATINE

Yield: about 2 lb 8 oz (1220 g)

Ingredients	U.S.		Metric	Sugar at 100% %
Sliced almonds	12	oz	375 g	50
Sugar	1 lb 8	oz	750 g	100
Glucose	9.5 oz		300 g	40
Water	6.5 oz		200 g	27

PROCEDURE

1. Place the almonds on a heated baking sheet in a 320°F (160°C) oven, mixing occasionally until light golden in color.

2. Cook the water, sugar, and glucose to a blond caramel.

3. Add the almonds to the caramel all at once and mix in carefully. Do not overmix, or the almonds will break into small pieces.

4. Pour the mixture onto an oiled baking sheet or silicone mat.

5. Spread the nougatine in small quantities and use a metal rolling pin to make an even layer.

6. Work the nougatine near the opening of the oven, as this will keep it pliable much longer. The nougatine should not stick to the rolling pin or table. If it does, allow the nougatine to cool a little before continuing, returning it to the oven to achieve the correct consistency.

7. Trimmings may be used again after gentle reheating, but be careful not to use nougatine once it has become dark in color and the almonds are broken to a fine powder.

TERMS FOR REVIEW

marzipan   gum paste

pastillage   nougatine

QUESTIONS FOR REVIEW

1. What precaution must be taken when mixing marzipan in order to preserve its color?

2. Suppose you wanted to cover a strawberry-filled Swiss roll with white marzipan decorated with pink polka dots. How would you make the marzipan sheet?

3. Describe the procedure for making a marzipan carnation.

4. What procedure is used to make sure pastillage dries properly?

5. How are dried pieces of pastillage fastened together?

6. Describe the procedure for making, cutting, and molding nougatine.

7. What are some uses for leftover nougatine trimmings?

25

SUGAR TECHNIQUES

AFTER READING THIS CHAPTER, YOU SHOULD BE ABLE TO:

1. Boil sugar syrups correctly for decorative sugar work.

2. Make spun sugar, sugar cages, and poured sugar.

3. Prepare pulled sugar and make simple pulled- and blown-sugar decorative items.

4. Prepare basic boiled-sugar confections.

MANY PASTRY CHEFS consider sugar work the pinnacle of their decorative art. One reason is surely the sheer beauty of skillfully made pulled- and blown-sugar pieces, which can be elaborate constructions of multicolored sugar flowers in blown-sugar vases, large sprays of sugar flowers cascading down the sides of a wedding cake, or sugar baskets filled with sugar fruit and set on sugar pedestals wrapped with sugar ribbons and bows.

Another reason, no doubt, is the difficulty of decorative sugar work. Becoming proficient at this art requires dedication and hours, even years, of practice and study, and chefs who have mastered it well deserve the respect their accomplishment brings them. Students are often irresistibly drawn to the challenge of learning these techniques when they see the results that are possible.

This chapter is an introduction to sugar work, beginning with the simpler techniques for making spun sugar and sugar cages, and proceeding to the more difficult procedures for preparing pulled and blown sugar. Later in the chapter, isomalt, a modern alternative to sugar for decorative work, is introduced. The chapter concludes with an introduction to confections based on boiled sugar.

BOILING SYRUPS FOR SUGAR WORK

IN CHAPTER 12, we explained the process of boiling sugar syrups for use in various desserts. When syrups are boiled until nearly all the water has evaporated, the sugar becomes solid when it cools. This process enables us to make decorative pieces out of sugar that is boiled to 300°F (149°C) or more and shaped while still hot.

As you learned in Chapter 4 (p. 64), sugar that is boiled in a syrup containing an acid undergoes a chemical change called *inversion*, in which a molecule of double sugar (sucrose) combines with a molecule of water and changes into two molecules of simple sugar (dextrose and levulose). Invert sugar, you remember, resists crystallization, and plain sucrose (granulated sugar) crystallizes easily. The amount of sugar that is inverted depends on the amount of acid present. This principle is used in the production of fondant icing (p. 417): Just enough cream of tartar or glucose is added to the syrup to create a mass of extremely fine sugar crystals that give fondant its pure white color.

This technique is also used for the sugar work discussed in this section, especially in pulled sugar. If too much cream of tartar or glucose is used, too much sugar is inverted, resulting in sugar that is too soft and sticky to work and that doesn't harden enough when cool. If not enough cream of tartar or glucose is used, too little sugar is inverted and the sugar is hard, making it difficult to work and easily broken.

As long as it is kept within limits, the exact amount of tartar or glucose to be used depends largely on the preferences of the pastry chef or confectioner. Some artists prefer to work with a harder sugar, while others prefer a softer one. Consequently, you will see many formula variations. Your instructor may have his or her own favorite to substitute for those in this book.

The temperature to which syrup is boiled is also important. The higher the temperature, the harder the sugar will be. The temperature range recommended in this book is 311° to 320°F (155° to 160°C), and the actual temperature used for the pulled and blown sugar items shown in the illustrations was 320°F (160°C). Nevertheless, you may see slightly different temperatures used in other books, because all chefs have their own preferred procedures.

Cooking the sugar to a higher temperature makes it harder and more brittle and thus more difficult to work. Cooking to a lower temperature makes a softer sugar that is easier to work, but the pieces may not hold up as well, especially in a humid climate. Inexperienced cooks may want to start with temperatures at the lower end of the range, and not worry about the keeping qualities of their pieces until they develop greater proficiency with sugar work.

Two more precautions are necessary regarding temperature and the addition of tartaric acid (cream of tartar). First, boiled invert sugar discolors more rapidly than pure sucrose. Therefore, the acid should not be added until near the end of the boiling process. In the recipes in this book, the tartaric acid is not added to the syrup until it has reached 275°F (135°C). Second, the syrup should be boiled rapidly over moderately high heat. Boiling slowly gives the syrup more time to discolor, and it will not be clear white.

If color is added to the syrup during boiling (for poured or pulled sugar), it should be added partway through the cooking, at about 260°F (125°C). If it is added earlier, it has more time to discolor, but it must be added early enough to allow the alcohol or water to cook off.

Slightly different syrups are used for each of the techniques in this chapter. Follow the specific recipes in each section, keeping these guidelines in mind:

1. Use pure white granulated cane sugar. Sift the sugar to remove any impurities that may have fallen into it during storage.

2. Place the sugar and water in a clean, heavy pan. Set the mixture over low heat and stir gently until the sugar is dissolved.

3. When the sugar is dissolved, raise the heat to moderately high and do not stir any more. To prevent crystallization, use a clean pastry brush dipped in hot water to wash any sugar crystals down the side of the pan. *Do not let the brush touch the syrup.*

4. Always use a sugar thermometer.

5. Add coloring and tartaric acid solution at the temperatures specified in the recipes.

6. Do not use liquid colors in an acid solution. For best results, use powdered colors and dissolve them in a little water or alcohol. Good-quality paste colors may also be used.

SPUN SUGAR, CARAMEL DECORATIONS, AND POURED SUGAR

Spun Sugar

Spun sugar is a mass of threadlike or hairlike strands of sugar used to decorate cakes and showpieces. Gâteau St-Honoré (p. 360) is often decorated with spun sugar.

Spun sugar should be made just before it is needed because it does not keep well. It gradually absorbs moisture from the atmosphere and becomes sticky. Eventually, this absorbed moisture causes the sugar to dissolve.

Prepare a workstation by propping a lightly oiled wooden rod or rolling pin on the edge of a table so it projects horizontally beyond the edge of the table by 1 to 2 feet (30–60 cm). Spread plenty of paper on the floor below to catch drippings. To spin the sugar, you will need a wire whip with the ends cut off.

Tools for sugar work. Top: sugar lamp. Bottom, left to right: sugar thermometer, rubber gloves, leaf molds, blowpipe, cutoff wire whip for spun sugar.

PROCEDURE: Making Spun Sugar

1. Prepare the syrup as in the formula on page 666. When the correct temperature is reached, remove the pan from the heat and allow the syrup to stand for a few minutes until it is slightly cooled and thickened.

2. Dip the cutoff wire whip in the syrup and tap lightly to remove excess. Wave or flick the whip vigorously over the wooden rod so the sugar is thrown off in fine, long threads.

3. Repeat until the desired amount of spun sugar is hanging from the rod. Carefully lift the mass from the rod.

4. Coil the sugar, or shape as desired for decoration.

5. If the syrup cools too much to spin, simply rewarm it over low heat.

Caramel Cages and Other Shapes

Sugar cages are delicate, lacy sugar domes made of caramelized sugar. Their decorative effect can be impressive and elegant. Sugar cages can be made large enough to cover whole cakes, bombes, Bavarian creams, and other desserts, or small enough to decorate individual portions.

Bowls of the desired size can be used as molds for large cages. Ladles are usually used for small, single-portion cages. Lightly oil the bottom of the ladle or other mold so the sugar can be removed when it is hard.

PROCEDURE: Making Caramel Cages

1. Prepare a syrup as in the formula on page 666. Testing with a sugar thermometer is the most accurate way to determine the stage of the boiled syrup.

2. Cool the syrup slightly. Holding the mold in one hand, dip a spoon in the sugar and drizzle it in a random, lacy pattern over the mold, turning the mold so all sides receive some of the syrup.

3. Trim off excess, let the sugar cool until hard, and carefully lift off.

Other shapes can be made by piping or drizzling the sugar onto a silicone mat or oiled work surface. To create fine, even lines of sugar, use a paper cone, as described in the formula procedure. Wear rubber gloves to protect your hands from the heat. For a rougher or more casual look, dip a spoon in the sugar and drizzle it onto the mat. The caramel shape decorating the panna cotta dessert pictured on page 617 was made this way.

Sugar spirals make elegant garnishes for some plated desserts. These are made using the Procedure for Making a Sugar Spiral.

PROCEDURE: Making a Sugar Spiral

1. Prepare a syrup as for making caramel cages (p. 666).

2. Wind a strand of hot syrup around a lightly oiled pencil or thin wooden rod.

3. Slip the spiral off the pencil when the sugar has hardened.

SPUN SUGAR

Yield: about 12 oz (360 g)

Ingredients	U.S.	Metric	Sugar at 100% %
Sugar	10 oz	300 g	100
Water	5 oz	150 g	50
Glucose	2 oz	60 g	20
Coloring, if desired			

PROCEDURE

1. Make a syrup of the sugar, water, and glucose. See page 252 for guidelines on cooking sugar syrups.

2. Boil to 255°F (125°C); add coloring, if desired.

3. Continue to boil to 320°F (160°C), and then stop the cooking immediately by plunging the base of the pan into cold water. Remove from the cold water and allow to stand 2–3 minutes to thicken slightly.

4. Lightly oil a rolling pin or metal pole and suspend it horizontally. Place sheets of paper on the floor under the pole to catch drips.

5. Dip a cutoff wire whip in the syrup and flick it over the pole, as in the illustrations. Continue until the desired quantity is made.

6. Lift the spun sugar from the pole and shape as desired.

CARNIVAL TREAT

Cotton candy, the popular circus and carnival treat, is nothing more than spun sugar made from a flavored, colored syrup. The syrup is forced through tiny holes in a spinning head that flings the fine threads of sugar against the sides of a bowl, where it is wound around a paper cone. The amount of sugar in an entire portion of cotton candy is usually less than 1 ounce (30 g).

CARAMEL FOR CAGES AND OTHER SHAPES

Yield: about 10 oz (300 g)

Ingredients	U.S.		Metric	Sugar at 100% %
Sugar	10	oz	300 g	100
Water	10	oz	300 g	100
Glucose	1.33 oz		40 g	13

PROCEDURE

1. Make a syrup of the sugar, water, and glucose. See page 252 for guidelines on cooking sugar syrups.

2. Boil to 320°F (160°C), then stop the cooking immediately by plunging the base of the pan into cold water. Remove from the cold water and allow to stand 2–3 minutes to thicken slightly.

3. Wear rubber gloves to protect your hands from the hot syrup. Pour the syrup into a paper cone. Snip off the tip and pipe desired shapes onto a silicone mat or oiled work surface. Allow to cool. Remove and store in an airtight container until use.

4. For cages, lightly oil the bottom of a ladle. Dip a spoon in the syrup (or, for more delicate sugar, dip the point of a knife in the syrup) and drizzle it in a lace pattern over the bottom of the ladle. Trim off excess with scissors. Let stand 2 minutes then carefully lift off.

Poured Sugar

Poured sugar, also called *cast sugar*, is boiled sugar that is allowed to harden in various shapes. Usually it is cast in flat sheets like glass, although, like nougatine, it can be bent and shaped while it is hot and pliable. The syrup can also be colored before it finishes cooking.

There are several ways of preparing molds for casting the sugar. For round shapes, simply use a flan ring or charlotte ring. Metal molds in other shapes (like large cookie cutters) can also be used. For other shapes, bend a strip of metal into the desired shape. An easy way to make a mold of any shape is to roll heat-resistant plasticine (a type of modeling clay) into a rope and work it to the desired shape on an oiled marble slab or silicone mat. Whatever mold you use, it should be lightly oiled to prevent the sugar from sticking.

Once the edges of the sugar shape have hardened enough, remove the mold. When the entire shape has hardened enough, slide a palette knife under it to detach it from the work surface. (This is not necessary if you are using a silicone mat, which will peel away easily.)

To bend cast sugar, remove it from the work surface while it is still soft enough to be pliable. If it gets too hard, simply place it on an oiled baking sheet and heat it in an oven just until it is pliable. Then bend as desired, or use an oiled mold to shape it as you would nougatine (p. 656).

Another item that can be made simply by pouring sugar onto a surface is sugar lace. Sugar lace can be seen in the display piece pictured on page 674. The base of this piece is made with poured sugar.

PROCEDURE: Pouring Sugar

1. Prepare the syrup as in the formula on page 668. Color the syrup as desired, as indicated in the formula.

2. When the syrup reaches the proper temperature, briefly plunge the base of the saucepan into cold water to stop the cooking. Let stand for a moment.

3. Place a lightly oiled mold on a sheet of parchment. Pour the hot syrup—in this case, colored black—into the mold to the desired thickness.

4. Before the sugar cools, you can marble it with another color—here, a little white coloring.

PROCEDURE: Making Sugar Lace

1. Pour a small pool of boiled sugar onto a square of silicone paper.

2. With a palette knife, quickly spread it to a thin layer.

3. Before the sugar hardens, crinkle the paper to shape the sugar.

ISOMALT

Isomalt is a sugar substitute chemically derived from regular sugar (sucrose). It can be melted or boiled and worked in many of the same ways as regular sugar. Although it is significantly more expensive than sugar, many pastry chefs prefer it for certain kinds of decorative work. (More information on working with isomalt is on page 676).

KEY POINTS TO REVIEW

- What steps are taken to boil syrups correctly and avoid crystallization?
- What is the procedure for making spun sugar?
- What is the procedure for making caramel cages?
- What is the procedure for making poured or cast sugar?

POURED SUGAR

Yield: about 2 lb 6 oz (1200 g)

Ingredients	U.S.	Metric	Sugar at 100% %
Sugar	2 lb	1000 g	100
Water	1 lb	500 g	50
Glucose	6.5 oz	200 g	20
Coloring, as desired			

PROCEDURE

1. Prepare molds of the desired shape: Brush metal rings with oil, or roll heat-resistant plasticine to the desired shape, then brush it with oil. Place the molds on a silicone mat or an oiled or parchment-covered marble slab.
2. Make a syrup of the sugar, water, and glucose. See page 252 for guidelines on cooking sugar syrups.
3. Boil to 255°F (125°C); add coloring, if desired.
4. Continue to boil to 330°F (165°C). If desired, add a few drops of another color at this point without mixing to create a marbled effect.
5. Stop the cooking immediately by plunging the base of the pan into cold water. Remove from the cold water and allow to stand 2–3 minutes to thicken slightly.
6. Pour into desired mold until approximately ¼ in. (5 mm) thick.
7. Once the edges have set enough, remove the rings. Score lightly with an oiled knife, if desired.
8. Use a little reheated sugar as glue to attach pieces together.

PULLED SUGAR AND BLOWN SUGAR

Pulled sugar and *blown sugar* are, perhaps, the most difficult of the pastry chef's decorative art forms. This section outlines the basic procedure for making pulled sugar. Several techniques for making ribbons, flowers, leaves, and blown fruits are illustrated in detail, and a number of other techniques are explained in the text.

Before beginning work, assemble your equipment. The following tools are the most important items you will need, depending on which pieces you are making:

- Sugar thermometer, for accurate control of the temperature of the boiling syrup.
- Sugar lamp or other warmer, to keep the stock of sugar warm and soft. (See the Sugar Lamp sidebar on page 671.)
- Scissors and knife, lightly oiled, for cutting the sugar.
- Alcohol lamp, for melting sugar to fasten pieces together.
- Blowpipe, for blowing sugar. A pipe with a bulb for inflating is easier to use than one that is blown with the mouth.
- Silicone mat or oiled marble slab, for pouring out the cooked syrup.
- Fan or hair dryer, for cooling sugar items.
- Rubber gloves, to protect from burns when handling hot sugar (some experienced chefs prefer to work without gloves).

Prepare the syrup according to the formula on page 670. Note the need for liquid tartaric acid, which is a solution of equal weights of cream of tartar and water, prepared as indicated in the recipe.

Once the pulled sugar is prepared, it can be used at once or cooled and stored in an airtight container for later use. To use stored sugar for pulled or blown items, first reheat it under a sugar lamp (warming lamp) or in an oven preheated to 170°F (75°C). Turn the lumps of sugar over from time to time so they warm evenly. This is particularly important when using a sugar lamp and should be done regularly the entire time you are working with the sugar, because the heat comes only from above.

After it has been heated to the proper temperature, the sugar must again be pulled and folded as in step 7 of the formula on page 670 until it is cooled to a workable temperature and is even in texture. Test the sugar by pulling a bit from the edge of the ball with your thumb and forefinger and attempting to break it off. If it breaks off cleanly, the sugar is ready. This pulling and folding procedure is sometimes called *pearling* because of the pearl-like appearance it gives the sugar. This appearance is caused by the incorporation of air in the sugar structure during the pulling. For this reason, another common name for pearling is *aerating*. If this process is not followed, it will not be possible to work the sugar properly.

GOING TO THE NEXT LEVEL

Success at advanced decorative work requires not only good instruction but also a great deal of practice and repetition. Many of the most commonly used sugar techniques are explained and illustrated in this chapter. Doing these procedures only once or twice, however, will not make you an accomplished *décorateur* (a pastry chef specializing in or skilled at decorative work). To develop your sugar skills, it is suggested that you practice the techniques in this chapter repeatedly until you are comfortable with them.

Once you have gained some mastery over the basic techniques, you will have skills that will enable you to produce a wide variety of décor. At that point, you might want to consult books on more advanced decorative work, some of which are listed in the Bibliography (p. 748). As you will see, the variety of shapes you can make with sugar is limited only by your own imagination and skill.

PULLED SUGAR AND BLOWN SUGAR

Yield: about 2 lb 6 oz (1200 g)

Ingredients	U.S.	Metric	Sugar at 100% %
Sugar	2 lb	1000 g	100
Water	9.5 oz	300 g	30
Glucose	6.5 oz	200 g	20
Color	as desired	as desired	
Tartaric acid solution (see *Note*)	8 drops	8 drops	

NOTE: To prepare tartaric acid solution, use equal weights of cream of tartar and water. Bring the water to a boil, remove from the heat, and add the cream of tartar. Let cool.

PROCEDURE

1. Make a syrup of the sugar, water, and glucose. See page 252 for guidelines on cooking sugar syrups.

2. Boil to 255°F (125°C); add coloring, if desired. (Color can also be added when the sugar is poured out in step 5.)

3. Continue to boil to 275°F (135°C) and add the tartaric acid.

4. Continue boiling. When the temperature reaches 320°F (160°C), or whatever final temperature is desired (see p. 662), stop the cooking immediately by plunging the base of the pan into cold water. Remove from the cold water and allow to stand 2–3 minutes to thicken slightly.

5. Pour out onto a silicone mat or oiled marble slab. If color was not added in step 2, you can add it now, as on page 671.

6. Let cool slightly; but before the sugar begins to harden around the outside edges, fold the edges into the center. Repeat until the sugar mass can be picked up off the table.

7. Begin stretching the sugar and folding it back onto itself. Repeat until the mixture is cooler and makes a faint crackling or clicking sound when pulled. Do not attempt to pull the sugar when it becomes too cool, as it could start to crystallize. Cut the sugar into smaller pieces with scissors and then place the pieces under a sugar lamp to keep them at workable temperature. Pull and fold the pieces one at a time so they will have a uniform texture and temperature. The sugar will take on a silky or pearled appearance after about 12 to 20 folds. Do not pull too much, or the sugar will lose this pearled appearance and become less shiny.

8. The sugar is now ready to be shaped into blown or pulled sugar decorations.

Ribbons

A sugar ribbon of a single color is made simply by pulling a piece of sugar out into a thin ribbon shape. This sounds easy, but making a thin, delicate strip of perfectly even thickness and width takes a great deal of practice and skill. Be sure the piece of sugar is uniformly warm and that all parts of the strip stretch the same amount.

To make a two-colored ribbon, start with two pieces of sugar in contrasting colors. Shape them into strips of the same size and shape. Press them together side by side, then stretch them into a ribbon. For multiple stripes, cut the two-colored strip in half when it is partly stretched. Lay the two pieces side by side so you have four alternating stripes. Finish stretching them into a ribbon shape. (You can produce a ribbon of three or more colors with the same technique.)

To make a bow, cut off a length of ribbon with scissors and bend it into a loop. Cool the loop in front of a fan so it holds its shape. Make as many loops as desired. Fasten them into a bow by heating one end of each loop over a gas flame to soften the sugar, and then pressing the heated ends together.

PROCEDURE: Making Pulled Sugar

1. Pour the cooked sugar onto a silicone mat.

2. If a color is desired and was not added during cooking, add the color now with an eyedropper.

3. As the sugar cools, fold the edges toward the center so it cools evenly.

4. When the color is blended in, pick up the mass of sugar and begin to stretch and fold it.

5. Pull and fold the sugar until it has a silky or pearly appearance and makes a faint clicking sound when stretched.

6. Store the lumps of sugar under the sugar lamp as you work them in order to keep them at the proper temperature.

SUGAR LAMP

A sugar lamp is simply a fixture for an infrared heat bulb, usually 250 watts. The bulb housing is on a long, flexible neck, which enables the pastry chef to adjust the distance between the heat source and the sugar when it is on a silicone mat.

To be workable, sugar for pulling or blowing must be warm enough to be pliable, generally around 100° to 130°F (38° to 55°C) for pulling, and as high as 175°F (80°C) for blowing, depending in part on the preference of the chef. Because the heat lamp warms the sugar mostly from the top, the sugar must be turned and folded to warm it uniformly.

Let the lump of sugar rest under the lamp until the surface is shiny and almost liquid in appearance. Then pull the sugar gently into an oblong shape and fold the ends over so they meet in the middle. (Alternatively, simply fold it in half.) Take care not to trap air bubbles between the layers of sugar. Repeat several times until the sugar is uniformly warmed and soft.

As you work with one piece of sugar to create decorative items, repeatedly turn over the remaining lumps of sugar under the lamp so they stay uniformly heated and soft.

PROCEDURE: Making Pulled Sugar Ribbons

1. Make equal-size ropes of the selected colors and place them side by side under the sugar lamp.

2. Pull or stretch to begin to form the ribbon.

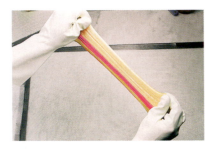

3. Fold the ribbon so the two ends are side by side; snip in half with oiled scissors.

4. Repeat this pulling and doubling procedure until you have a ribbon of the desired pattern and width.

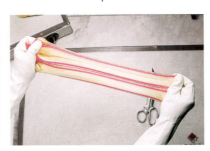

5. Before the sugar hardens, bend it into folds to resemble a slightly crinkled ribbon.

6. Snip the ribbon into desired lengths with lightly oiled scissors.

Flowers and Leaves

The basic techniques for making simple flowers are detailed in the Procedure for Making a Pulled Sugar Lily (p. 673), which illustrates the production of both a lily and a leaf. Note the mold used to mark the veins in the leaf. If such a mold is not available, you can mark the pattern of veins using the back of a knife.

Another popular flower to make with pulled sugar is, of course, the rose. Rose petals are made by following the same basic technique as for lily petals, except the petal is pulled into a round shape, rather than stretched into a long form. Roll the first petal into a tight cone shape. Then curl additional petals around the center cone, just as you would for a marzipan rose (p. 651). Make the outer petals a little larger than the inner ones, and curl back the edges to resemble real rose petals.

An alternative method is to make all the petals first without assembling them. Then heat the bottom edges of the petals over the flame of an alcohol lamp so they stick together, and assemble them to make the flower.

To make a stem that will support the weight of a flower, draw a strong piece of wire through warm pulled sugar until it is completely coated. While the sugar is still soft, bend the covered wire to the desired shape.

PROCEDURE: Making a Pulled Sugar Lily

1. Stretch one side of a ball of pulled sugar to make a thin edge.

2. Grasp this thin edge and pull outward to make a pointed petal.

3. Snip off the petal with oiled scissors. Repeat to make additional petals.

4. Attach the petals together into the shape of a lily.

5. For the inside of the flower, stretch pulled sugar into thin strands.

6. Fold two pieces of these sugar strands, as shown, and insert in the flower.

7. To make leaves, pull sugar as for the petals, but make the pieces wider to resemble leaves.

8. Lay the leaf pieces on one half of a leaf mold.

9. Press the piece of sugar with the other half of the mold to give it the texture of a leaf. The finished flowers are shown on page 674.

Simple Baskets

To create a simple basket, roll out a piece of pulled sugar with a rolling pin into a thin sheet. Mold it over an oiled bowl or large tin can, just as you would shape nougatine. You can also attach a handle.

Woven Baskets

A woven pulled-sugar basket filled with pulled-sugar flowers or fruit is one of the most impressive of all display pieces. To make the basket, you need a base board into which an uneven number of holes has been drilled. The holes should be evenly spaced and should form a circle, oval, or square. In addition, you need wooden pegs that fit loosely into these holes. The holes should be drilled at an angle so the pegs tilt outward. This makes the basket wider at the top than at the bottom.

Before weaving the basket, oil the pegs and board lightly. Then take a ball of soft pulled sugar and start to pull a rope or cord of sugar from the ball. Starting at the inside edge of one of the pegs, weave the sugar cords in and out around the pegs, pulling out more of the sugar as you go. Be careful to keep the thickness of the cord uniform. Continue weaving the sugar around the pegs until the basket is as high as desired.

Now make pulled sugar rods the same size and number as the wooden pegs. One by one, pull out the pegs and replace them with the pulled sugar rods. If necessary, trim the tops of the rods with a hot knife or scissors.

Next, shape a base for the basket using poured sugar (p. 668) or pulled sugar rolled out with a rolling pin. Attach it to the basket with hot boiled syrup.

To finish off the top and bottom edges, twist two cords of pulled sugar together to make a rope. Coil the rope around the top and bottom edges of the basket and seal the ends together. Make a handle for the basket by shaping heavy wire and then weaving a rope of sugar around it.

Parts of the sugar display piece before assembly.

Blown Sugar

Hollow sugar fruits and other items are blown from pulled sugar in much the same way glass is blown. Traditionally, sugar was blown with the mouth, using a length of tube, and many chefs still prefer this method. Today, however, the use of a blowpipe inflated with a squeeze bulb (see p. 663) has become common and makes the work a little easier. Especially for the beginner, this type of blowpipe is easier to control than a tube blown with the mouth.

The shape of the sugar piece depends on how it is manipulated and supported with the hands and on how it is cooled or warmed. To make round objects, such as apples, hold the blowpipe and sugar upward at an angle, so the weight of the sugar does not cause it to elongate. For long, thin objects such as bananas, stretch the sugar gently as you blow.

If the sugar on one side becomes too thin, cool that side slightly with a fan until it hardens. By watching demonstrations and practicing, you can learn to control the temperature of the piece on all sides in order to shape it as you want. The best sugar pieces have a thin, delicate wall of sugar that is of even thickness all around.

More complex pieces, such as animals, birds, and fish, can be made with practice. For example, to make a long-necked bird, first blow the sugar into the shape of a vase and then stretch out the neck to form the long neck of the bird. An animal's head and body may be blown separately and attached. Parts such as wings and fins are made separately from pulled sugar.

When the blown sugar has hardened, add more coloring to make fruit look more realistic. If the pieces were blown from colored pulled sugar, you may need to add only a few highlights and markings with an artist's brush. An alternative method is to use uncolored sugar for blowing and then a sprayer for adding layers of color to give a more blended effect. When done skillfully, this can give the fruit a more natural look. For spraying, dissolve powdered color in alcohol. If a dull rather than a shiny surface is appropriate for the item, dust the finished piece with cornstarch.

The Procedure for Blowing Sugar illustrates the major steps in making blown-sugar fruits.

Finished sugar display piece.

PROCEDURE: Blowing Sugar

1. Make a depression in a lump of hot pulled sugar and insert the end of the blowpipe.

2. Press the sugar firmly around the pipe to seal.

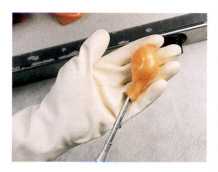

3. For a pear, inflate the bulb of sugar slowly, shaping the fruit as it is blown up.

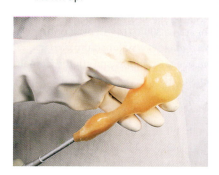

4. Continue to inflate the sugar, shaping it with the fingers. When the desired shape and size are achieved, harden the sugar by cooling it with a fan.

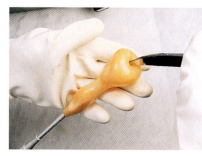

5. Heat the neck of the pipe over a flame and detach the pear from the pipe. Mold the stem end with the fingers.

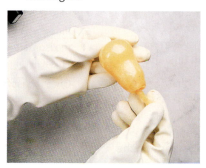

6. Mold other fruit in a similar fashion, such as bananas . . .

7. . . . and apples.

8. These finished fruits have been colored with a sprayer (see p. 649) and highlighted with a small paintbrush.

KEY POINTS TO REVIEW

- What is the procedure for making pulled sugar and preparing it for use in making pulled- and blown-sugar items?
- What techniques are used to make ribbons, flowers, and leaves from pulled sugar?
- What is the basic procedure for blowing sugar?

Working with Isomalt

As noted in the Isomalt sidebar (p. 668), this product has become popular with pastry chefs as a substitute for sugar in poured, pulled, and blown sugar pieces. Isomalt has less of a tendency to absorb moisture from the air, so finished work made with it lasts longer and stays drier. In addition, it is less likely to crystallize, so it stays clearer than sugar. Cast sugar pieces made with isomalt can be as clear as glass. In fact, when using isomalt it is not necessary to add glucose or tartaric acid to prevent crystallization, as it is for sugar.

A disadvantage of isomalt (besides its higher cost) is that its working temperature (the temperature that the sugar must be when you are pulling or blowing it) is somewhat higher than sugar, so it may not be the best material for beginners. Other than the temperature difference, however, isomalt is handled much like sugar, so many instructors recommend that those pulling sugar for the first time work with sugar first, until they get comfortable with the techniques. They can then transfer these skills to working with isomalt.

The Guidelines for Preparing Isomalt will help you prepare isomalt for use in decorative work. After the isomalt is ready, it can be poured out onto a silicone mat and handled like sugar for pulling. Alternatively, it can be poured into molds, like poured or cast sugar.

GUIDELINES: Preparing Isomalt

1. Isomalt can be melted dry, but its working temperature will be higher than isomalt cooked with water. That is why many pastry chefs prefer to mix it with water. For each 1 lb of isomalt, add 2 oz water (125 g water per 1 kg isomalt). Mix in a heavy stainless steel pot until the mixture resembles wet sand.

2. Distilled water is recommended, because it is less likely to discolor the isomalt.

3. Cook the mixture until it reaches a temperature of 335°F (168°C). During the first stage of cooking, wash down the sides of the pot with a brush dipped in water, just as for cooking sugar.

4. As soon as the desired temperature is reached, immediately plunge the bottom of the pot into cold water for about 5 seconds to stop the cooking and to keep the temperature from rising more.

5. Add any desired color when the isomalt has cooled to about 310°F (154°C). Drop the color onto the top of the hot isomalt and swirl it lightly until the bubbling stops, to cook off moisture. Then stir in the color thoroughly.

6. Place the pot in an oven preheated to 300°F (149°F) until the isomalt is perfectly clear and contains no bubbles. This will take about 15 minutes.

7. Once the isomalt is clear, pour it into molds until hardened, or pour it out onto a silicone mat and proceed as for pulled sugar.

8. Store cooked isomalt in an airtight container to prevent it from absorbing moisture. For long-term storage, it is helpful to put packets of food-grade silica gel in the container to absorb any moisture.

9. Remelt stored, cooked isomalt by placing it in a stainless steel pot and setting it in a 300°F (149°C) oven until melted. Or melt it in a microwave at medium power. Stop the microwave every 5 minutes and stir the isomalt so that it heats evenly.

BOILED SUGAR CONFECTIONS

EXCEPT FOR CHOCOLATES, a large proportion of old-fashioned candies are based on a boiled sugar solution. The background material in Chapter 12 and this chapter prepare you to make the recipes that follow. In particular, review the information on boiling sugar syrups, including the steps to avoid crystallization, explained in Chapter 12.

Hard candies are simply a flavored syrup boiled to the hard-crack stage. Note that the recipe on page 677 is the same as for pulled sugar, with the addition of flavoring. Fancy candies, such as multicolored ribbon, can be made using the procedures for pulled sugar. Alternatively, simple candies can be made by preparing the candy through step 6 in the recipe procedure. Then roll the sugar to a uniform thickness with an oiled rolling pin and cut it into small squares with an oiled knife.

Toffee is essentially the same as the butter caramel introduced in Chapter 12 (p. 271), with the addition of flavorings and other ingredients that transform it into a delectable candy. Note that the core of the toffee recipe, the sugar and butter, are the same as in the butter caramel recipe. Peanut brittle is a similar confection, but with less butter and with the addition of a large quantity of peanuts. Soft caramels, too, are made in a similar fashion, except the syrup is made with cream or milk instead of water, and the candy is cooked to a lower temperature so less moisture is cooked away, resulting in confections that are soft rather than hard.

Finally, classic, old-fashioned fudge also should be understood as a boiled sugar confection rather than as a chocolate candy. Although chocolate is often used as a flavoring, other flavorings may be used as well. The basic procedure for fudge is similar to that for making fondant icing: The boiled syrup is cooled to the proper temperature and then agitated to create extremely fine crystals. Review the poured fondant recipe (p. 417) and compare with the fudge recipe given here. A critical point in both procedures is the temperature to which the syrup is cooled. If it is stirred or agitated while it is still too warm, the crystals will be too large and the texture will be grainy.

> ### KEY POINTS TO REVIEW
>
> ■ What guidelines should be followed when working with isomalt to make pulled sugar items?
>
> ■ In what ways are toffee, peanut brittle, and soft caramels similar? In what ways are they different?
>
> ■ Why is fudge considered basically a boiled sugar confection rather than a chocolate confection?

HARD CANDIES

Yield: about 2 lb 6 oz (1200 g)

Ingredients	U.S.	Metric	Sugar at 100% %
Sugar	2 lb	1000 g	100
Water	9.5 oz	300 g	30
Glucose or corn syrup	6.5 oz	200 g	20
Tartaric acid solution (see p. 670)	8 drops	8 drops	
Coloring	as desired	as desired	
Flavoring, such as peppermint, lemon or other citrus, cinnamon	few drops	few drops	

PROCEDURE

1. Make a syrup of the sugar, water, and glucose. See page 252 for guidelines on cooking sugar syrups.

2. Boil to 255°F (125°C) and add coloring, if desired. (Color may also be added when the sugar is poured out, in step 5.)

3. Continue to boil to 275°F (135°C) and then add the tartaric acid.

4. Continue boiling. When the temperature reaches 320°F (160°C), or whatever final temperature is desired (see p. 662), stop the cooking immediately by plunging the base of the pan into cold water. Remove from the cold water and allow to stand 2–3 minutes to thicken slightly.

5. Pour out onto a silicone mat or an oiled marble slab. If color was not added in step 2, you can add it now, as on page 671.

6. Let cool slightly and add the flavoring to the top of the sugar. Before the sugar begins to harden around the outside edges, fold the edges into the center. Repeat until the sugar mass can be picked up off the table.

7. Begin stretching the sugar and folding it back onto itself. Repeat until the mixture is cooler and makes a faint crackling or clicking sound when pulled. Do not attempt to pull when the sugar becomes too cool, as it could start to crystallize. Cut the sugar into smaller pieces with scissors and place under a sugar lamp to keep them at workable temperature. Pull and fold the pieces one at a time so they will have a uniform texture and temperature. The sugar will take on a silky or pearled appearance after about 12 to 20 folds. Do not pull too much, or the sugar will lose this pearled appearance and become less shiny.

8. Pull each lump of sugar into a rope about ½ in. (12 mm) thick. With scissors, snip off pieces ½ in. (12 mm) long.

9. Let cool. Store in an airtight container.

TOFFEE

Yield: about 3 lb 6 oz (1650 g)

Ingredients	U.S.		Metric	Sugar at 100% %
Granulated sugar	2 lb		1000 g	100
Water	8	oz	250 g	25
Glucose or corn syrup	5	oz	160 g	16
Butter	1 lb		500 g	50
Salt	0.2 oz (1 tsp)		6 g	0.6
Almonds, chopped fine	3	oz	90 g	9
Vanilla extract	0.2 oz (1 tsp)		6 g	0.6

VARIATION

After scoring the toffee, allow it to cool until just warm, and spread it with a thin layer of melted chocolate. Sprinkle with finely chopped almonds. Cool and break into pieces.

PROCEDURE

1. Lightly oil a marble slab and arrange oiled caramel rulers (see the Caramel Rulers and Caramel Cutters sidebar) on the slab to make a rectangle about 15 × 16 in. (38 × 40 cm).

2. Make a syrup of the sugar, water, and glucose. See page 252 for guidelines on cooking sugar syrups.

3. Boil to 280°F (138°C).

4. Add the butter and salt and stir in. Continue to boil to 315°F (157°C).

5. Stir in the almonds and vanilla. Continue to boil to 320°F (160°C).

6. Pour the syrup onto the prepared marble slab.

7. When the syrup has begun to firm up but is still soft and hot, score or mark the toffee into 1-in. (2.5-cm) squares using a knife, a wheel knife, or a caramel cutter.

8. When the toffee has cooled and hardened, break apart into squares.

CARAMEL RULERS AND CARAMEL CUTTERS

Caramel rulers are heavy steel bars used to contain hot syrups when poured out onto a marble slab or other flat surface. They are useful in many boiled-sugar preparations, especially in the production of soft caramels, toffee, and similar confections.

A caramel cutter, also called a *toffee cutter*, consists of a row of wheel cutters spaced along a steel rod, with handles on both ends, like a rolling pin. Spacers of various lengths enable the worker to adjust the tool to cut multiple rows of the desired width. Using a caramel cutter, you can cut or score a sheet of caramel into uniform squares with one pass of the cutter lengthwise and one pass crosswise.

PEANUT BRITTLE

Yield: 4 lb 4 oz (2125 g)

Ingredients	U.S.		Metric	Sugar at 100% %
Granulate sugar	2 lb		1000 g	100
Glucose or corn syrup	1 lb 7	oz	720 g	72
Water	12	oz	380 g	38
Raw peanuts (see *Note*)	1 lb 8	oz	750 g	75
Butter	1.75 oz		55 g	5.5
Vanilla extract	0.33 oz (2 tsp)		10 g	1
Salt	0.2 oz (1 tsp)		6 g	0.6
Baking soda	0.33 oz (2 tsp)		10 g	1

NOTE: If raw peanuts are not available, use unsalted, roasted peanuts and add them just before pouring out onto marble.

PROCEDURE

1. Lightly oil a marble slab.
2. Combine the sugar, corn syrup, and water in a heavy saucepan. Bring to a boil to dissolve the sugar and make a syrup. See page 252 for guidelines on cooking sugar syrups.
3. Boil the syrup until the temperature reaches 250°F (121°C).
4. Add the peanuts and butter.
5. Continue to boil until the mixture reaches 312°F (155°C). Stir constantly and gently, to prevent burning on the bottom.
6. Remove the pan from the heat. Stir in the vanilla, salt, and baking soda. Use caution, as the hot syrup will foam up for a moment.
7. Pour the mixture onto the marble slab.
8. The syrup will flow outward more than the peanuts. To ensure an even distribution of nuts, use an oiled palette knife to carefully spread some of the peanuts toward the edges of the slab of syrup.
9. *Optional step to make a thinner, finer-textured candy:* Put on a pair of latex gloves to protect your hands during this step. As soon as the syrup has cooled enough so the edges can be lifted with the palette knife, carefully raise the edges with your gloved hands and pull outward to stretch the candy so it becomes thinner between the nuts. This is easiest to do with two or more workers on opposite sides of the slab, as it cools and hardens quickly. Be careful not to touch any part of the sugar that is still molten. As the candy hardens, break off pieces from the edge, and continue stretching the rest of the brittle.
10. Cool completely and store in airtight containers.

SOFT CARAMELS

Yield: 3 lb (1.5 kg)

Ingredients	U.S.		Metric		Sugar at 100% %
Heavy cream	3 pt		1.5 L		200
Granulated sugar	1 lb 8	oz	750	g	100
Glucose or corn syrup	6.5	oz	200	g	27
Salt	0.15 oz (¾ tsp)		4	g	0.6
Butter	6.5	oz	200	g	27
Vanilla extract	0.5	oz (1 tbsp)	15	mL	2

VARIATIONS

CHOCOLATE CARAMELS

Add 3.5 oz (100 g) melted unsweetened chocolate after the butter has been stirred in.

NUT CARAMELS

Before pouring out the cooked mixture onto the parchment, stir in 10 oz (300 g) finely chopped walnuts or pecans.

PROCEDURE

1. Place a sheet of parchment on a marble slab or other work surface. Arrange oiled caramel rulers on the parchment in a rectangle about 12 × 16 in. (30 × 40 cm).

2. Combine the cream, sugar, and glucose in a heavy saucepan. Bring to a boil, stirring to dissolve the sugar.

3. Turn the heat to low and cook, stirring, until the mixture reaches 230°F (110°C).

4. Add the butter and vanilla. Continue to cook slowly, stirring constantly, until the mixture reaches 245°F (118°C).

5. Pour the mixture onto the prepared parchment. Allow to cool completely.

6. When completely cool, cut into 1-in. (2.5-cm) squares or other desired shape.

7. If desired, dip cooled caramels in tempered chocolate (p. 638).

CARAMEL TEXTURE

Within a narrow range, the texture of soft caramels may vary from soft to fairly firm but still chewy. To test the texture as you are cooking, drop a small amount into a bowl of cold water and examine the texture of the cooled caramel. It should form a ball that is soft but firm enough to hold its shape. If it is too soft, cook the mixture a little longer. If it is too firm, stir a little water into the mixture and test again.

CHOCOLATE FUDGE

Yield: 2 lb 12 oz (1375 g) without walnuts

Ingredients	U.S.		Metric	Sugar at 100% %
Granulated sugar	2 lb		1000 g	100
Milk	12	oz	375 g	37.5
Glucose or corn syrup	4	oz	125 g	12.5
Butter	4	oz	125 g	12.5
Unsweetened chocolate, chopped fine	5	oz	155 g	15.5
Salt	0.1 oz (½ tsp)		3 g	0.3
Vanilla extract	0.5 oz (1 tbsp)		15 g	1.5
Walnuts, chopped (optional)	6	oz	200 g	20

PROCEDURE

1. Prepare a 9-in. (23-cm) square pan by lining it with aluminum foil.
2. Combine the sugar, milk, and glucose in a heavy saucepan. Bring to a boil, stirring constantly, until the sugar is dissolved. See page 252 for guidelines on cooking sugar syrups.
3. Continue to cook the mixture over moderate heat until the temperature reaches 230°F (110°C). Stir gently and slowly as the mixture cooks, to prevent scorching on the bottom of the pan.
4. Add the butter and stir gently until it is blended in.
5. Add the chocolate, salt, and vanilla. Stir until the chocolate is melted and blended in.
6. Continue to boil, stirring very gently, until the mixture reaches 236°F (113°C).
7. Pour onto a marble slab. Let cool, undisturbed, until the temperature reaches 110°F (43°C).
8. When the fudge has reached the proper temperature, mix it with a bench scraper or metal spatula until it thickens and becomes less shiny. If using nuts, add them at this time.
9. Quickly, while the mixture is still quite soft, transfer the fudge to the prepared pan to cool completely.
10. When cool, cover tightly and let stand at room temperature overnight. This maturing or ripening period improves the texture.
11. Cut into squares of desired size.

VARIATIONS

VANILLA FUDGE

Omit the chocolate.

BROWN SUGAR FUDGE

Use brown sugar instead of white sugar. The acidity of the sugar will curdle the milk during the first stages of cooking, but this will not harm the finished product.

PEANUT BUTTER FUDGE

Omit the chocolate and instead add 25% (8 oz/250 g) peanut butter in step 5.

TERMS FOR REVIEW

inversion	sugar cage	cast sugar	pulled sugar
spun sugar	poured sugar	isomalt	blown sugar

QUESTIONS FOR REVIEW

1. When boiling sugar for pulled sugar, why is it important to boil it rapidly?
2. Describe the procedure for making spun sugar (assuming you have already boiled the syrup).
3. Explain the importance of the final cooking temperature when cooking a syrup for pulled sugar.
4. Discuss the effect of tartaric acid in the production of pulled sugar. Include in your discussion the time it is added and the total quantity used.
5. Describe the procedure for making a pulled-sugar ribbon using two alternating colors of sugar.
6. If pulled sugar is made in advance and stored, what must be done to make it workable?

26

BAKING FOR SPECIAL DIETS

AFTER READING THIS CHAPTER, YOU SHOULD BE ABLE TO:

1. Describe nutritional concerns associated with baked goods and desserts.
2. Describe allergy and food intolerance concerns associated with baked goods and desserts.
3. Using a knowledge of ingredient functions, describe how to reduce or eliminate fat, sugar, gluten, dairy products, and eggs in baking formulas.

WHAT IS "HEALTHFUL" food? First, of course, the food must not cause harm. In light of our increasing awareness of food allergies, certain foods that are perfectly safe for some people are anything but healthful for those who are allergic to one or more of their ingredients. Second, to be healthful, a food must contribute to our well-being. It might be argued that even a rich dessert that has no nutritional value and is high in fat and sugar can contribute to our emotional well-being simply because it is delicious and satisfying. Most pastry chefs would probably agree with that statement. However, what we usually mean when we say a food is healthful is that it is high in nutrients and low in calories from fat and sugar.

It is sometimes said that bakers are in the "fat business" because the products they make are high in fat. This is not completely true, or at best it is misleading. Many of the most important products of the bakeshop are low in fat or are fat-free, from French breads to fruit compotes and meringues. Still, it is true that other products, such as pastries and cookies, are high in fat and low in nutrients other than calories. To address this, many pastry chefs today are trying to develop more healthful versions of popular items. More importantly—because allergic reactions can be fatal—cooks, bakers, and pastry chefs alike are responding to the very real problem posed by food allergies by producing foods that are both delicious and safe for their customers.

NUTRITIONAL CONCERNS

DIET AND HEALTH are increasingly in the news. Rising obesity rates are regularly in the headlines. Increasing numbers of people suffer from food allergies. Health problems caused by diet are increasing the costs of medical care. Often, it seems, people are too afraid of food to enjoy it. At the same time, our love affair with restaurants and bakeries continues to grow. People want food they can enjoy and that is also healthful.

Dietary concerns can be divided into two broad areas: those about nutrition, and those about food allergies and intolerances. Having good nutrition means consuming a varied diet that includes essential vitamins, minerals, proteins, and other nutrients. At the same time, it means limiting the intake of foods that can be harmful in large quantities. Managing weight gain requires limiting calories, especially calories from fats and sugar. The term *empty calories* refers to foods that provide few nutrients per calorie. Foods of high *nutrient density* are those that have a high level of nutrients per calorie. Fruits, vegetables, and whole grains are examples of foods with high nutrient density, while refined sugar and flour have low nutrient density.

For the customer, choosing nutritious foods is optional. Even people who usually choose nutritious foods can enjoy a rich pastry or choose a piece of white bread over whole grain. Enjoying limited sweets as part of a balanced diet provides enjoyment without necessarily having ill effects. For those with food allergies, however, choosing the right foods can be a matter of life or death. Allergic reactions can range from discomfort to severe illness and even death, so addressing these concerns is of great importance to all food service workers.

In this chapter, we approach nutrition concerns and allergies in separate sections because they require somewhat different approaches to finding alternatives in the bakeshop. After exploring the main dietary issues, we examine ways to modify formulas for special needs. The chapter concludes with a selection of formulas that give examples of ways to satisfy special dietary needs. These formulas were developed using the techniques outlined in this chapter.

Dietary baking is a large and complex subject, one that encompasses many subtopics, such as gluten-free baking and baking with sugar substitutes. Many books have been written about each of these subtopics, so this chapter is intended to serve only as an introduction to them, to familiarize you with the main issues and the general procedures for devising formulas suitable for restricted diets. Consult the Bibliography (p. 748) for books that delve more deeply into the topics touched on here. In particular, you will find collections of formulas for many different dietary purposes.

Nutrition in the Bakeshop

The role of the baker or pastry chef in preparing nutritious foods varies greatly, depending on the part of the industry in which he or she works. Food services in schools, hospitals, and nursing homes must, of course, plan menus to meet basic nutritional needs. A qualified dietitian is usually required in such establishments. On the other hand, retail bakers and restaurant pastry chefs have a primary responsibility to prepare a variety of attractive and flavorful items that will sell. For them, it is often good business to include more healthful preparations among the items they offer, but many customers will still prefer chocolate mousse over fruit compote.

Satisfying nutritional concerns has two aspects: providing desirable nutrients and avoiding undesirable nutrients. A *nutrient* is a substance that is essential for the functioning or growth of an organism. For this discussion, we divide nutrients into two categories:

1. Nutrients that provide energy: fats, carbohydrates, and proteins. (Note that proteins can be used by the body for energy, but their more important function is to provide the building blocks of all cells. See Basic Nutrients Reviewed sidebar.)
2. Nutrients that are needed for metabolism, or basic body functioning, including all the chemical processes that take place within cells: vitamins, minerals, and water.

A healthful, balanced diet is one that includes all the nutrients in just the right amounts, not too much or too little of any of them. For many people, balancing the diet means consuming foods with more vitamins and minerals—the metabolism nutrients—and less fat and carbohydrates—the energy nutrients.

Increasing Desirable Nutrients

In our culture, foods from the bakeshop form a relatively small part of the normal diet. Thus, we don't normally look to these foods—desserts, pastries, and breads—to give us more than a small part of our essential nutrients each day.

Nevertheless, bakers can take some steps to give customers the option of choosing items with more vitamins, minerals, and fiber (see the Fiber sidebar). The most significant sources of valuable vitamins and minerals among bakeshop ingredients are whole grains, fruits, and nuts. Bakers have ways of incorporating these ingredients to give customers the option of choosing more nutritious breads and desserts. For example:

- Replace part of the white flour in doughs and batters with whole wheat flour. Replacing up to 2 ounces per pound (125 g per kg) usually has only a small effect on dough formation. Replacing more than this can be done, but the bread or other product is likely to be heavier.

FIBER

The term *fiber* refers to a group of complex carbohydrates that can't be absorbed and used by the body. Thus, fiber supplies no calories or nutrients. However, fiber is important for the proper functioning of the intestinal tract and the elimination of body waste. In addition, there is evidence that sufficient dietary fiber helps prevent some kinds of cancers and helps lower cholesterol in the blood. Fruits and vegetables, especially raw, and whole grains supply dietary fiber.

BASIC NUTRIENTS REVIEWED

Carbohydrates are the body's most important sources of food energy. These compounds consist of long chains of carbon atoms with oxygen and hydrogen atoms attached to the sides. Starches and sugars are the most important dietary carbohydrates.

Fats supply energy to the body in highly concentrated form. Also, some fatty acids are necessary for regulating certain body functions. Third, fats act as carriers of fat-soluble vitamins.

Proteins are essential for growth, for building body tissue, and for basic body functions. They can also be used for energy if the diet doesn't contain enough carbohydrates and fats.

Vitamins are present in foods in extremely small quantities, but they are essential for regulating body functions. Unlike proteins, fats, and carbohydrates, they supply no energy, but some of them must be present in order for energy to be utilized in the body. Water-soluble vitamins (the B vitamins and vitamin C) are not stored in the body, so they must be consumed every day. Fat-soluble vitamins (A, D, E, and K) can be stored in the body, but the total amount eaten over time must be sufficient.

Minerals, like vitamins, are also consumed in small quantities and are essential for regulating certain body functions. Major minerals include calcium, chloride, magnesium, phosphorus, sulfur, sodium, and potassium. Trace minerals, eaten in even smaller amounts, include chromium, copper, iron, zinc, and iodine. Of all these, sodium, the major mineral in table salt, can contribute to high blood pressure if eaten in large quantities, as it too often is.

Water supplies no energy, but the body can't function without it. The adult human body is 50 to 60 percent water by weight.

- Replace part of the white flour with whole-grain flour from another grain, such as oats, barley, amaranth, buckwheat, soy, or millet, or a grain product such as wheat germ, wheat bran, or oat bran. For yeast breads, you may need to use a wheat flour with higher gluten to compensate for the lack of gluten in these other grains.
- Add a small amount of flaxseed meal to doughs to provide beneficial fiber and fatty acids.
- Use flaxseeds, rolled oats, sunflower seeds, and other grains and seeds as toppings for breads, rolls, and quick breads.
- Seek out more whole-grain and mixed-grain bread formulas. There are several in this book, and many more are available in bookstores, libraries, and online.
- Add ground nuts in small quantities to dough formulas, and add chopped nuts to muffins and pastries.
- Add raisins and other dried fruits to breads and other baked goods. (See, for example, the Fig Hazelnut Bread on page 177.)
- Offer more desserts made with fruits, such as fruit compotes and fruit coulis.

Reducing Undesirable Nutrients

The idea of reducing nutrients to be more nutritious may seem a contradiction, but the fact is that many people consume far too many energy-producing nutrients in the form of fats, sugars, and starches. As a result, many people suffer from obesity, heart disease, diabetes, and other ailments related to diet. For the baker, this is a difficult problem to address because these components, especially starches, are the baker's stock in trade. For the consumer, one of the best ways to cut down on consumption of fats, starches, and sugars is simply to avoid breads and desserts, or at least reduce consumption of them. Nevertheless, the baker can take some measures to make choices easier for health-conscious consumers. To understand how to approach the problem, a short review of these energy nutrients and issues concerning them is needed.

Calories and Weight Gain

The *calorie* (or, more correctly, the kilocalorie; see the Calories and Kilocalories sidebar) is a unit of energy measurement. It is defined as the amount of heat needed to raise the temperature of 1 kilogram of water by 1°C.

The calorie is used to measure how much of the energy the body needs to function is supplied by certain foods. Carbohydrates, proteins, and fats can be used by the body to supply energy.

- 1 gram of carbohydrate supplies 4 calories.
- 1 gram of protein supplies 4 calories.
- 1 gram of fat supplies 9 calories.

There is a direct connection between calorie intake, physical activity, and weight gain or loss. Simply put, if you consume more calories than you burn, you gain weight. If you consume fewer calories than you burn, you lose weight. All the diet schemes and fashions in the world—at least those that are medically sound—can be reduced to this. In other words, losing weight is possible only by eating fewer calories, burning more calories through exercise, or both.

Fat

As the above list shows, fats are a concentrated form of energy, supplying more than twice as many calories per gram as do carbohydrates and proteins. This suggests that reducing fats in the diet is an effective dietary method of weight loss. Always keep in mind, however, that some fat is necessary in the diet, both for regulating certain body functions and for carrying fat-soluble vitamins.

Fats may be classified as saturated, monounsaturated, or polyunsaturated. *Saturated fats* are solid at room temperature. Animal products—eggs and dairy products, as well as meats, poultry, and fish—and solid shortenings are the major source of saturated fats. Tropical oils such as coconut oil and palm kernel oil are also rich in saturated fats. Health experts believe eating high levels of these fats contribute significantly to heart disease and other health problems.

CALORIES AND KILOCALORIES

In scientific terminology, the amount of heat needed to raise the temperature of 1 kilogram of water by 1°C is called a *kilocalorie*, sometimes written *Calorie* (with a capital "C") and abbreviated *kcal*. When written with a small "c," the term *calorie* refers to a unit of energy measurement that is only 1,000th as large—the amount of heat needed to raise the temperature of 1 gram of water by 1°C.

Nevertheless, in discussions of nutrition, the word *calorie* is commonly substituted for *kilocalorie*. Just remember that when you see *calorie* in connection with food, the real meaning is *Calorie* (or *kilocalorie*).

Polyunsaturated fats and monounsaturated fats are liquid at room temperature. Although consuming too much of any kind of fat is unhealthy, these fats are considered more healthful than saturated fats. *Polyunsaturated fats* are found in vegetable oils such as corn oil, safflower oil, sunflower oil, and cottonseed oil. High levels of *monounsaturated fats* are found in olive oil and canola oil. Recent research has suggested that monounsaturated fat may actually lower the levels of the most harmful kinds of cholesterol in the body. Both kinds of unsaturated fats are also found in other plant products as well, including whole grains, nuts, and some fruits and vegetables.

One group of saturated fats of special concern is *trans fats*. These fats occur only in small amounts in nature. Most of the trans fats in our diets come from manufactured fats subjected to a process called *hydrogenation*. Hydrogenated fats are fats that are changed from liquid to solid by adding hydrogen atoms to the fat molecules. This is the process used to make products such as solid shortening and margarine. Trans fats are of concern because they limit the body's ability to rid itself of cholesterol that builds up on the walls of arteries.

Fats are members of a group of compounds called *lipids*. Another lipid found in the body is *cholesterol*, a fatty substance that has been closely linked with heart disease because it collects on the walls of arteries and blocks the flow of blood to the heart and other vital organs. It is found only in animal products and is especially high in egg yolks, butterfat, and organ meats such as liver and brains. The human body can manufacture its own cholesterol, so not all the cholesterol in the blood is necessarily from foods. Although some cholesterol is necessary for body functions, it is not considered a nutrient because the body is able to manufacture all the cholesterol it needs. Experts generally agree it is best to keep the cholesterol in the diet as low as possible.

Sugars and Starches

Sugars are simple carbohydrates. Simple sugars, such as glucose, are small compounds containing 6 carbon atoms. Table sugar, or sucrose, is a larger sugar molecule with 12 carbon atoms. Sugars are found in sweets and, to a lesser extent, in fruits and vegetables.

Starches are complex carbohydrates consisting of long chains of simple sugars bound together. They are found in such foods as grains, bread, peas and beans, and many vegetables and fruits.

Most authorities believe that complex carbohydrates, especially those from whole grains and unrefined foods, are better for you than simple carbohydrates. This is partly because starchy foods also have many other nutrients, while sweets have few other nutrients. Also, there is some evidence that a lot of sugar in the diet may contribute to heart and circulatory diseases. Simple sugars and refined starches are primary sources of empty calories.

Many consumers believe that honey, raw sugar, and some other sweeteners are more nutritious than refined white sugar. It is true that these products have some beneficial minerals and other nutrients, but only in tiny amounts. They are still mostly sugar. Substituting one of these for white sugar does not reduce the amount of carbohydrate in a formula.

Sodium

As explained above, excess sodium in the diet has been linked to high blood pressure, so people with this ailment are generally advised to reduce their sodium intake. Salt is the primary source of sodium in the diet. Most of a person's salt intake, however, does not come from baked goods and desserts but rather from main courses, side dishes, and salty snacks. For people on salt-free diets, reducing or eliminating salt in desserts and pastries may be advisable, and this can be done with only a small effect on flavor. For most people, however, this change will have only a small effect on their total sodium intake. Be careful, also, when reducing the salt content of yeast breads, as one of the functions of salt is to regulate yeast activity (see p. 88).

Vegetarian Diets

A vegetarian diet is one consisting entirely or mostly of foods derived from plants. People follow vegetarian diets for a variety of reasons: concerns about nutrition and health, ethical standards, or moral, religious, or cultural beliefs.

There are several types of vegetarian diets. The *vegan* diet is the most restrictive. It includes plant products only. All animal products, including dairy and eggs, are off-limits.

Lacto-vegetarians eat dairy products in addition to plant products, but they will not eat other animal products. *Ovo-vegetarians* eat eggs in addition to plant products. *Lacto-ovo-vegetarians* eat dairy and egg products as well as plant products.

For the baker or pastry chef, the main ingredients of concern to vegetarians are the following:

- *Dairy products*, including milk, cream, butter, and cheese, must not be included in products intended for vegans. They are acceptable for lacto-vegetarians and lacto-ovo-vegetarians.

- *Eggs* must not be included in products intended for vegans, although they are permitted for ovo-vegetarians and lacto-ovo-vegetarians.

- *Honey* should not be used in baked goods and desserts for vegans, because it is an animal product.

- *Refined sugar* poses problems for vegans. Because some cane sugar is refined with the use of animal bone char, many vegans avoid all refined sugar, to be on the safe side. If you can assure the customer that the sugar is made from sugar beets and not refined with bone char, some vegans may be willing to eat it. A safer approach is to substitute a product like date sugar or maple sugar. These products impart a distinctive flavor, however, and are also more expensive than refined white sugar. In addition, avoid using any prepared ingredient that contains sugar, because you can't be sure of the source of that sugar.

- *Gelatin* is an animal product, so it must be avoided in vegetarian products. Agar-agar, a gelatinlike product made from seaweed, can be substituted (see p. 82).

KEY POINTS TO REVIEW

▪ What do the terms *empty calorie* and *nutrient density* mean, and how are they related?

▪ What are the six basic nutrients, and what are their functions?

▪ What techniques can be used to add desirable nutrients to baked goods?

▪ What nutrients can be reduced to create a more healthy diet?

▪ What are the main types of vegetarian diet?

FOOD ALLERGIES AND INTOLERANCES

AN ALLERGEN IS any substance that triggers an allergic reaction. Many foods, including many ingredients used in the bakeshop, are potential *allergens*. Health agencies report that more and more people are being diagnosed with food allergies each year, so this is a growing problem worldwide.

A food allergy is an abnormal response to a food triggered by the immune system. In other words, the body's immune system mistakenly believes a food item is harmful and reacts to protect the body. This reaction may include the production of chemicals that are actually harmful to the body, sometimes even fatal. A sudden, severe, allergic reaction of the immune system is called *anaphylaxis*.

The foods that most commonly spur allergic reactions are peanuts, tree nuts, eggs, fish, shellfish, milk, soybeans, and wheat. Note that, with the exception of fish and shellfish, all of these products may be found in the bakeshop. Wheat, milk, and eggs are among the baker's main ingredients.

A food allergy is not the same as a *food intolerance*. A person may develop gas and bloating after eating a particular food, but this reaction does not involve the immune system. For example, people with lactose intolerance lack an enzyme that enables them to digest milk sugar, or lactose. These individuals may develop gas and abdominal pain when they consume dairy products. For the purpose of this discussion, we treat allergies and intolerances together because they both involve foods that must be avoided by the affected customer.

In food service operations and retail bakeries, precautions must be taken both in the preparation of food and in service to customers. The following are just a few of the steps you should take.

Food Preparation

1. Train staff to be aware of ingredients that can cause allergic reactions.
2. Read the ingredient labels on all prepared food items used in the kitchen.
3. Don't make casual or unannounced ingredient substitutions.
4. Avoid cross-contamination. For example, a "safe" food could become dangerously allergenic if it is prepared on an inadequately cleaned prep table containing dust from peanuts used in prepping an earlier item. Ideally, set up a separate prep area for preparing foods for allergy sufferers.

Food Service

1. Service and sales personnel should be aware of the ingredients in all menu items and should be prepared to answer questions about ingredients or to consult someone on staff who knows the answers.
2. Be sensitive to customers' questions; if someone asks whether an ingredient is used, find out if that customer has an allergy. If a customer's questions cannot be answered with confidence, admit it and be prepared to suggest alternative choices.

Among bakeshop ingredients, nuts, gluten, dairy products, soy products, and eggs are the primary culprits for sufferers of food allergies and intolerances. To this list we add alcohol, which is not an allergen but which must be completely avoided by some people.

Nuts

Peanuts and tree nuts—such as walnuts, almonds, Brazil nuts, and pecans—are among the most potent allergens. They are responsible for many of the 150 to 200 deaths from food allergies each year in the United States. (*Note:* Peanuts are not true nuts but legumes, like peas and beans, so the allergies are somewhat different.) Even trace amounts of these nuts, such as dust from peanuts left on a work surface, can trigger an allergic reaction. The only safe measure to take is complete avoidance. It is not enough, for example, to leave the nuts out of a baked item or dessert. The surest way to guarantee a product is nut-free is to make it in a separate prep area using equipment that is reserved strictly for use in preparing goods that do not contain nuts.

Fortunately for the baker or pastry chef, nuts are not critical ingredients in most baked goods. Most formulas do not call for nuts, and it is not difficult to eliminate them from those that do, or to substitute similar preparations—for example, substitute a plain meringue disk for japonaise (p. 342), or use plain short dough instead of linzer dough (p. 314).

Gluten

Celiac disease is a genetic (inherited) disorder in which the intestine is unable to process gluten proteins (see the "Celiac Disease" sidebar). Symptoms may be severe, and there is no cure. The only remedy is to avoid gluten completely.

The difficulty for the baker is that gluten is the backbone of breads and many other baked goods, and is a component of wheat flour, the baker's main ingredient. In addition, gluten proteins are found in rye, barley, spelt, and oats.

Nevertheless, it is possible to bake a variety of products using gluten-free flours, such as rice, millet, buckwheat, amaranth, and quinoa flours; potato starch, cornstarch, and cornmeal; and flours from chickpeas and other legumes. The structure-building properties of gluten proteins must be supplied by other ingredients, such as egg proteins and vegetable gums. These ingredients don't work the same way as gluten, however, so the texture of the products will differ. Doughs will be less elastic, and baked items are likely to be more crumbly than similar items baked with wheat flour.

CELIAC DISEASE

Celiac (pronounced SEE lee ak) is a disease of the immune system, like other food allergies. When gluten is ingested by someone with this disease, the gluten proteins damage the lining of the small intestine. As a result, the body is less able to absorb other nutrients. The disease has many, and varied, symptoms—including anemia, fatigue, intestinal pain, and malnutrition—making it difficult for doctors to diagnose. Only recently has the scope of the problem become more widely recognized. There are still probably many people who suffer from the disease without knowing what it is.

Lactose Intolerance and Milk Allergies

Lactose, also called *milk sugar*, is a form of simple sugar found in dairy products. Some people are unable to digest lactose, and drinking milk or eating products containing lactose results in intestinal discomfort, gas, bloating, and other symptoms. Because lactose is not an important component of baked goods, lactose-free milk and other lactose-free dairy products can easily be substituted in most formulas. Other milk replacers, such as soy milk, can also be used.

Milk allergies are immune reactions to milk proteins, rather than to lactose. This allergy is fairly common in infants, but most children grow out of it. The allergy is uncommon in adults. Those who suffer from it must usually avoid all dairy products.

Soy

Soy products contain at least 15 proteins, and it is not clear whether allergic reactions are caused by one or more of these proteins or by other components of soybeans. A great many prepared foods contain soy products, so it is necessary to read ingredient labels carefully. The emulsifier *lecithin*, for one, is used in many products, including chocolate, and may not be identified as derived from soybeans. As with lactose, soy products are not essential ingredients in most bake-shop formulas, so avoiding them is relatively easy, as long as bakers are attentive to ingredient labels.

Eggs

Like milk allergy, egg allergy affects primarily infants and children, and most people outgrow it by the time they are about five years old. Nevertheless, it does affect some adults, who may react with stomach cramps, skin rashes, coughing and wheezing, or, in some cases, severe anaphylaxis (see page 688). The allergic reactions are triggered by one or more of the proteins in the egg. Some people are allergic to egg white proteins, while others have a reaction to the yolks.

Because many common egg substitutes are made with egg whites, these products can't be used as baking ingredients for allergy sufferers. *Eggless egg substitutes*, on the other hand, contain no egg products. They are made of flour or other starches, plus vegetable gums and stabilizers, and, sometimes, soy protein. They are intended for use in baked goods only—that is, in doughs and batters—and are not suitable for use in custards or breakfast egg preparations.

Alcohol

Unlike the other food items discussed so far, alcohol is not an allergen, but it must be avoided by people suffering from the disease alcoholism. Trace quantities of alcohol are present in a number of products of the bakeshop or pastry department. Alcohol is a byproduct of yeast fermentation and so is present in freshly baked bread, but the amount is so small it doesn't generally pose a problem. By the time the bread cools and is stored, nearly all the alcohol has evaporated.

Small quantities of liqueurs may be used to flavor dessert syrups used to moisten cakes, but here, too, the amount per portion is usually minute. Be prepared to advise customers, however, if a dessert contains significant amounts of alcohol. In some cases, merely the flavor of the alcoholic beverage, even if the alcohol has been burned away, can trigger an undesirable reaction.

KEY POINTS TO REVIEW

▌ What is the difference between food allergy and food intolerance?

▌ What are the most important food allergies and intolerances?

MODIFYING FORMULAS FOR SPECIAL NEEDS

SO FAR IN this chapter we've focused on the ingredients or components of baking formulas and desserts that may have to be modified to accommodate special diets, and why some customers may need or desire to avoid those ingredients. It should be clear from this information that there is no single solution to dietary baking. For example, the discussion of increasing vitamins and minerals suggests adding nuts to baked goods to increase nutrients. However, the discussion of allergens indicates that nuts must be completely avoided by some customers. Similarly, for people with lactose intolerance, soy milk may be substituted for dairy milk as an ingredient, but that substitution would then make the product unsuitable for people with soy allergy.

In other words, there are many approaches to baking for special needs, but each is directed at a specific problem. No one of them is suitable for every problem or every customer.

Ingredient Functions

Whether you want to modify an ingredient of a baking formula to reduce fat or calories or to eliminate an allergen, you must first understand the functions of that ingredient in the formula.

Three ways to modify an ingredient are to *eliminate* it, *reduce* it, or *substitute* another ingredient for it.

Eliminating an ingredient may be the best method if that ingredient does not have a major structural or flavor function in a formula. For example, eliminating the chopped nuts in a brownie or cookie formula does not affect the dough or batter, so this step can be easily taken.

Reducing the amount of an ingredient may be successful, even if the reduction makes a slight change in the finished product. For example, some quick bread formulas are high in fat. Perhaps in those formulas the fat could be reduced to make a more healthful product, one that is still appealing even if the texture is slightly drier.

Substituting other ingredients is the only option when the ingredient has a critical structural function in the baked item. Wheat flour is the main example. The gluten in wheat flour is important for the structure of many baked goods. Eliminating it would make the formula unworkable. The only option is to substitute other ingredients that can take on those structure-building functions.

The explanations of basic ingredients in Chapter 4 include lists of the primary functions of the principal ingredients. Review these sections so the functions are fresh in your mind for the following discussion. In addition, reread the discussion on cake formula balance on pages 385–386. The basic principles explained there apply to all doughs and batters:

- Tougheners or structure builders include flour and eggs.
- Tenderizers have the opposite function of structure builders. They include fats, sugars, and leaveners.
- Moisteners include water, liquid milk, syrups, and eggs.
- Dryers include flours, other starches, milk solids, and cocoa powder.

Apply the principle of formula balance when you are modifying a formula for dietary purposes. When an ingredient is eliminated or reduced, you must balance the formula by doing one or both of the following:

1. Replace the ingredient with another that performs the same functions. For example, when reducing fat, which is a tenderizer, add or increase other tenderizers, such as sugars.
2. Reduce the amount of ingredients that have the opposite effect. For example, if you are eliminating gluten, a toughener or structure builder, also reduce the tenderizers to maintain structure.

The next section applies these principles to ingredients that bakers may want to eliminate or reduce for health or dietary reasons.

Ingredient Substitutions

The ingredients or components discussed in this section are those that may have to be reduced or omitted for dietary reasons. However, these components perform important functions in baking formulas. When one of them is reduced or eliminated, its functions must be performed by other ingredients.

Fat

Modifying the fat content of a formula usually involves one of the following goals:

1. Replacing saturated fats and trans fats with more healthful unsaturated fats
2. Reducing the total amount of fat

REPLACING SATURATED FATS AND TRANS-FATS WITH MORE HEALTHFUL UNSATURATED FATS

Recall that saturated fats are solid at room temperature. Saturated fats include the most important fats in the bakeshop: butter, shortening, and margarine. Unsaturated fats are liquid oils.

Fats in doughs and batters function as tenderizers, and they improve the mouth feel of cakes and quick breads by giving the feel of moistness. When an oil is used in place of a solid fat, the oil still performs these tenderizing and moisturizing functions. In fact, because the oil doesn't solidify at room temperature, a muffin made with oil may seem even moister than one made with solid fat.

Another important function of solid fats is to form and retain air cells when creamed with sugar. Some creaming-method batters depend entirely on these air cells for leavening. Oils cannot be creamed with sugar to form air cells. Therefore, oil cannot be substituted for solid fats when creaming is essential to leavening. However, sometimes it is possible to substitute oil for *part* of the fat. When trying this substitution, make a test batch and compare the quality of the resulting product with the regular formula. In most cases, the best procedure is to cream the solid fat with the sugar and add the oil to the batter with other liquids.

To make up for lost leavening power, increase the baking powder, or fold in whipped egg whites.

Liquid fats work better when incorporated using the muffin method, rather than the creaming method. Try reworking creaming-method formulas to convert them to the muffin method.

When the fat is butter, flavor is also another important factor. If butter is a primary flavor in the product, substituting other fats for it is likely to decrease quality. The substitution works better for products with other dominant flavors, such as chocolate cake, spice cake, and many quick breads.

There is no substitute for solid fat in laminated doughs. The rolled-in fat in some formulas may be reduced slightly, but the resulting product may not rise as well or be as flaky.

Finally, remember that oil has as much fat and calories per gram as solid fat—even more, in the case of butter—so substituting oil for solid fat does not reduce total fat or calories. It reduces unhealthful saturated fats only.

REDUCING THE TOTAL AMOUNT OF FAT

Reducing the fat in a formula means reducing the total amount of tenderizers. To maintain the desired texture of the baked item, then, you must either substitute other tenderizers, reduce the tougheners, or both.

Use the following techniques when reducing total fat:

To Reduce Tougheners

- Use a softer flour. For example, substitute cake flour for pastry flour, or substitute pastry flour for part of the bread flour.
- Substitute whole-grain flours, especially of a gluten-free grain, for part of the wheat flour.
- Reduce the quantity of egg. You will probably have to increase other liquids to make up for the lost moisture of the egg.
- Avoid overmixing, which develops gluten.
- Avoid overbaking, which dries the product and also toughens protein.

To Increase Tenderizers in the Formula or Add Other Tenderizers or Moisteners in Place of the Fat

- Increase sugars. Liquid sweeteners such as honey, molasses, corn syrup, and maple syrup are useful for this purpose.

- Add a fruit or vegetable purée. Many purées can substitute for fats to increase the tenderness and moistness of a baked item, such as applesauce, prune purée, date purée, squash or pumpkin purée, fruit jelly or jam, banana purée, and fruit juice concentrates. Select a flavor that blends well with the flavors of the baked item.

- Add a dairy fat substitute. Fat-free buttermilk, sour cream, and yogurt can be substituted for part of the fat. They increase moistness, and their acidity tenderizes the gluten. Unlike fruit or vegetable purées, they don't change the flavor significantly.

- Use reduced-fat margarine or butter. These products contain less fat and more water and milk protein than regular margarine and butter. They can be substituted in many quick breads and cakes.

Finally, remember that there are many low-fat items already in the baker's standard repertory. For example:

- Use a low-fat icing, such as fondant or boiled icing, instead of buttercreams on cakes.
- Use angel food or sponge cakes instead of high-fat creaming-method and high-ratio cakes.
- Use baked meringues instead of short doughs in pastries and tarts.
- Use fruit fillings instead of high-fat fillings such as frangipane and cream cheese.

Sugar

In addition to adding sweetness and flavor, sugars perform the following functions in baked goods:

- They create tenderness and fineness of texture.
- They retain moisture, thus improving texture and keeping qualities.
- They act as creaming agents with fats, to provide leavening.
- They give crust color because of their browning properties.

When sugar in a formula is reduced, these functions must be performed by other ingredients.

Some customers who want to reduce or eliminate refined white sugar in their diets have no objection to natural sugars like honey, even though they may have the same number of calories. Another granular sugar, such as date sugar or maple sugar, can be substituted for white sugar in equal weights without other changes to the formula. If a liquid sugar is used, such as honey, brown rice syrup, molasses, or maple syrup, the following adjustments to the formula may be necessary:

- Liquid sugars have no creaming ability, so other forms of leavening must be substituted. You may be able to mix the batter by the muffin method rather than the creaming method, as long as you increase the quantity of baking powder.

- If a large quantity of liquid sugar is used, reduce the other liquids in the formula.

- Not all liquid sugars have the same sweetening power, so you may have to adjust quantities. Brown rice syrup, for example, is only 30 to 60 percent as sweet as white sugar, whereas honey is sweeter than white sugar.

Sugar substitutes are used when it is necessary to reduce the total quantity of sugar in a formula. Sugar substitutes are chemicals that have a sweet taste, usually much sweeter than sugar, but no or little nutritional value. Aspartame and saccharin are intensely sweet chemicals often used as beverage sweeteners, but they have little use in baking because they don't perform any of the functions of sugar listed above, other than providing sweetness. Also, aspartame is destroyed by heat, so it is of no use in baked goods. Furthermore, these sweeteners leave aftertastes that are unpleasant to many people, and there are also questions about their safety.

Granular sucralose.

Sucralose is the most useful sugar substitute in baked goods. It is sold under the brand name Splenda. Pure sucralose is 600 times sweeter than sugar. For baking, it is mixed with a bulking agent called *maltodextrin* to give it the same sweetening power and texture as an equal volume of sugar. This product is called *granular sucralose*. In pies, cookies, quick breads, dessert sauces, and custards, substitute an equal volume of granular sucralose for the sugar in the formula. (Granular sucralose has 96 calories per cup/240 mL, primarily from the bulking agents, while granulated sugar has 770 calories for the same volume.)

Granular sucralose, however, does not have good creaming abilities, it does not contribute to browning, it doesn't contribute to texture, and it does not improve keeping quality as sugar does. When these functions are important, the usual technique is to substitute granular sucralose for *half* of the sugar in the formula, thus reducing the number of calories from sugar by half. A so-called baker's blend, consisting of half granular sucralose mixed with half sugar, is available, but it is more cost-effective to make the blend yourself.

Please note that when you are substituting granular sucralose for sugar, you must substitute an *equal volume*, not an equal *weight*, because the granular sucralose is much lighter than sugar. One cup (240 mL) granular sucralose weighs about 25 grams, slightly less than 1 ounce.

When baking with sucralose, monitor the products carefully for doneness. You can't rely on the usual amount of crust browning as a doneness indicator because the product won't brown as well.

Isomalt is another sugar substitute, discussed in Chapter 25 in connection with decorative sugar work (p. 676). It is white and granular in appearance and can be substituted for an equal weight of regular sugar. Isomalt has only half the calories of sugar, but it also has only half the sweetness, so it is not a suitable substitute in all formulas. Also, it is not easily digested and can cause intestinal discomfort and bloating when eaten by some people.

Gluten

Perhaps the biggest challenge for a baker is making baked goods without gluten. Gluten is a component of wheat flour and is a major structural component of most baked goods.

Wheat flour supplies the bulk of most baked goods. This bulk-forming function can be duplicated simply by substituting other flours and starches for wheat flour. The structure-building functions of gluten proteins, however, are more difficult to duplicate (see pages 95–98 to review gluten formation and functions). Gluten-free baked goods must contain other ingredients that help build structure, or the item will be excessively crumbly, will not hold together, or will not rise. For some items, such as certain quick breads, egg protein can provide the necessary structure.

Vegetable gums, including pectin, are also used to provide necessary structure. Pectin is a component of fruit jellies, preserves, and purées. Adding these to gluten-free quick breads and other batters may improve the structure and texture. Powdered vegetable gums (see p. 82) can be used for the same purpose without adding the sweetness and flavor of fruit products. Xanthan gum is perhaps the most useful gum in gluten-free baking.

Xanthan gum.

Some starches, such as cornstarch, can also partly compensate for an absence of gluten. Gelatinized cornstarch, for example, forms a firm gel that can improve the structure of some baked goods.

The following flours and starches can be used to make gluten-free baked goods. Usually, a mixture of several performs better than any single one. Keep in mind that each of these absorbs a different quantity of water, which means you will have to do some experimenting and adjusting of liquids when making substitutions in formulas.

Amaranth flour*

Arrowroot

Buckwheat flour

Chickpea (garbanzo) flour

Fava bean flour

Garfava flour (blend of garbanzo and fava flours)

Cornmeal

Corn flour (like cornmeal but finer in texture)

Cornstarch

Millet flour*

Nut flours (not suitable, obviously, when nut allergies are a concern)

Potato starch

Quinoa flour*

Rice flour

Sorghum flour

Soy flour

Tapioca flour and starch

*These items are sometimes contaminated with wheat during processing and shipping, so caution is necessary.

Of these ingredients, rice flour, potato starch, tapioca starch, and cornstarch are especially useful because they have relatively little flavor of their own and thus most closely approximate white wheat flour.

Commercial gluten-free mixes also are available for various purposes. For example, one commercial pizza dough mix contains rice flour, potato starch, cornstarch, crystallized honey, guar gum, and salt.

The grains and other ingredients listed next contain gluten proteins and so are *not suitable* for gluten-free diets:

Barley

Kamut

Malt (made from barley)

Oats

Puffed rice cereal (may be processed in a facility that also processes wheat)

Rye

Semolina

Spelt (farro)

Triticale

Wheat

Gluten-free items, even with structure-building ingredients added, always have a markedly different texture from similar items made with wheat flour. The strength and elasticity of gluten can't be duplicated by other ingredients. In general, gluten-free baked goods have a more crumbly or grainy texture.

Dairy

Dairy ingredients in baking formulas are modified to achieve either of two goals: to reduce the fat and calories from full-fat dairy products, or to make the product lactose- and allergen-free.

In many formulas, full-fat milk can be replaced with low-fat or nonfat milk without significantly changing the characteristics of the finished product. If, however, the fat from the milk is an important structural component of the baked item, you may have to compensate by making some of the adjustments discussed in the section on fat. Low-fat and fat-free sour cream can be substituted for regular sour cream in some formulas, and fat-free yogurt often works in place of sour cream, as does whole-milk yogurt.

Lactose intolerance and milk allergies require a different approach, usually the complete elimination of all dairy ingredients. Recall that lactose, which some people can't digest, is a form of sugar present in milk. Milk allergies, on the other hand, involve the proteins in milk products. Many lactose-free dairy products, including fluid milk, are available and can be consumed by people who are lactose intolerant. Lactose-free, however, is not the same as dairy-free. People with milk allergies cannot consume lactose-free milk.

Many types of milk substitutes are available. These can replace milk in most formulas to make the product suitable for anyone with a milk allergy or lactose intolerance. Soy milk is perhaps the most familiar, although this of course is not suitable for people with soy allergies. Other commercially available milk substitutes are made from rice, almonds, quinoa, potatoes, sesame seeds, and coconut. (Coconut milk, unlike the other products, is high in fat—17% or more.) Some of these are available in powdered as well as liquid form.

Dairy-free margarines can be substituted for butter in almost any formula. Read the label carefully, however, as many margarines contain milk protein. Margarines labeled *parve* or *pareve* are dairy-free.

Eggs

Egg yolks contain fat and cholesterol, while egg whites are fat-free. If the goal is to reduce fat and cholesterol, use egg whites in place of an equal weight of whole eggs in doughs and batters when the egg is used as a binder.

When egg foams are used for leavening, egg-white foams can often be substituted for whole-egg foams. Of course, when the eggs are also a main structural component of a baked item, using egg-white foams in place of whole eggs causes too great a change in the product. For example, if you substitute egg whites in a genoise sponge cake formula, the product will no longer be a genoise but something more like an angel food cake.

For egg allergies, substituting egg whites is not acceptable. All egg products must be eliminated. Commercial baking egg substitutes (described on p. 690) containing starches and gums are designed to be used in place of eggs in doughs and batter.

Other starches, gums, and proteins can substitute for eggs to replace their binding power. Flaxseed meal is rich in gums and soluble fiber and is a useful egg replacement. To use, mix 1 tablespoon (15 mL) flaxseed meal with each 4 ounces (120 g) flour in the formula. Tapioca flour and arrowroot can be used in the same way. Alternatively, try substituting an equal weight of puréed tofu or puréed banana for the eggs in batter formulas. (Tofu, a soy product, can't be used for people with soy allergies.)

Sample Formulas

As writers, publishers, dieticians, and chefs have become aware of dietary issues related to baking and desserts, many books have become available that contain collections of recipes specialized for all sorts of diets, from low-fat and sugar-free to gluten-free, lactose-free, and other allergen-free diets. A few of these books are listed in the Bibliography (p. 748). More recipes can be found online and at any bookstore.

The purpose of this chapter is to explain the dietary reasons for modifying baking formulas and to outline the techniques you can use to adapt formulas to meet these dietary needs. It is not intended to be a comprehensive collection of dietary recipes. Nevertheless, it is useful to examine a few formulas that have been developed by applying the principles discussed in the first part of this chapter. Included are examples of gluten-free formulas, low-fat versions of high-fat baked goods, sugar-free formulas, and lactose-free formulas.

KEY POINTS TO REVIEW

▐ What are the four categories of baking ingredients based on their structural functions? What are the most important ingredients in each category?

▐ What techniques can be used to reduce fat in a formula?

▐ What techniques can be used to reduce sugar in a formula?

▐ What techniques can be used to eliminate gluten from a formula?

▐ What techniques can be used to eliminate dairy and eggs from formulas?

LOW-FAT APPLE HONEY MUFFINS

Ingredient	U.S.		Metric	%
Whole wheat flour	12	oz	340 g	75
Oat flour	4	oz	110 g	25
Baking powder	1	oz	30 g	6
Cinnamon	0.1	oz (1½ tsp)	3 g	0.6
Cardamom	0.03	oz (½ tsp)	1 g (2 mL)	0.2
Applesauce, unsweetened	1 lb 4	oz	560 g	125
Honey	10	oz	280 g	62.5
Egg whites, beaten	4	oz	110 g	25
Raisins	6	oz	170 g	38
Total weight:	**3 lb 9**	**oz**	**1604 g**	**357** %

PROCEDURE

MIXING

Muffin method (p. 213):

1. Sift together the flours, baking powder, and cardamom.

2. Mix together the applesauce, honey, and egg whites.

3. Add the liquid ingredients to the dry ingredients and mix just until combined.

4. Mix in the raisins.

PANNING

Use paper muffin cups to line muffin pans, or spray the pan with a nonstick spray. Fill tins one-half to two-thirds full. Exact weight depends on pan size. Average sizes are 2 oz (60 g) for small muffins, 4 oz (110 g) for medium muffins, and 5–6 oz (140–170 g) for large muffins.

BAKING

375°F (190°C) for approximately 20 minutes, depending on size

LOW-FAT MULTIGRAIN BROWN BREAD

Ingredient	U.S.		Metric		%
Whole wheat flour	7	oz	200	g	44
Cornmeal	4	oz	110	g	25
Rye flour	3	oz	85	g	19
Oat flour	2	oz	55	g	12
Baking soda	0.7	oz (3½ tsp)	18	g	4
Ginger	0.14	oz (2 tsp)	4	g (10 mL)	0.9
Nutmeg	0.07	oz (1 tsp)	2	g (5 mL)	0.45
Cinnamon	0.06	oz (1 tsp)	1.8	g (5 mL)	0.4
Low-fat buttermilk	1 lb		450	g	100
Molasses	6	oz	170	g	38
Prune purée (see *Note*)	8	oz	225	g	50
Egg whites, lightly beaten	3	oz	85	g	19
Total weight:	**3 lb 1**	**oz**	**1405**	**g**	**313** **%**

NOTE: If prune purée is not available, soak pitted prunes in just enough warm water to cover, then purée the prunes and water in a food processor.

PROCEDURE

MIXING

Muffin method (p. 213):

1. Sift together the flours, baking soda, and spices.

2. Mix together the buttermilk, molasses, prune purée, and egg whites.

3. Stir the liquids into the dry ingredients just until combined.

PANNING

Spray the insides of 8½ × 4½ in. (22 × 11 cm) loaf pans with nonstick spray. Scale 1 lb 8 oz (700 g) batter per pan.

BAKING

375°F (190°C), about 50 minutes

LOW-FAT CHOCOLATE PIE

Yield: one 9-in. (23-cm) pie

Ingredient	U.S.		Metric
Skim milk	1 pt		500 mL
Sugar	2	oz	60 g
Cornstarch	2	oz	60 g
Sugar	2.5	oz	75 g
Cocoa powder	1	oz	30 g
Skim milk	8	fl oz	250 mL
Vanilla extract	0.25 fl oz (1½ tsp)		7 mL
9-in. (23-cm) low-fat graham cracker pie shell (below)	1		1

PROCEDURE

1. Combine the first quantities of milk and sugar in a heavy saucepan. Heat to dissolve the sugar, and bring the liquid just to a boil.

2. Sift the cornstarch, sugar, and cocoa powder into a bowl. Gradually stir in the second quantity of (cold) milk, making a smooth, lump-free mixture.

3. Gradually stir in the hot milk from step 1.

4. Return the mixture to the saucepan and set over moderate heat. Bring to a boil, stirring constantly.

5. When the mixture comes to a boil, remove it from the heat and set the pan in an ice-water bath. Stir constantly to cool the mixture to lukewarm.

6. Stir in the vanilla.

7. Pour the mixture into the prepared pie shell.

8. Chill until cold and set.

─── **VARIATION** ───

LOW-FAT CHOCOLATE PUDDING

Reduce the cornstarch to 1.5 oz (45 g). Prepare as in basic recipe, omitting pie shell.

LOW-FAT GRAHAM CRACKER PIE SHELL

Yield: one 9-in. (23-cm) pie shell

Ingredient	U.S.		Metric
Graham cracker crumbs	4.5 oz		125 g
Raspberry jam	2	oz	55 g

PROCEDURE

1. In a food processor or a mixer with the paddle attachment, mix together the crumbs and jam until evenly blended and crumbly.

2. Spray the inside of a 9-in. (23-cm) pie tin with nonstick spray.

3. Put the crumbs in the pie tin. Pack them evenly against the bottom and sides of the tin. The mixture is sticky, so you may want to use a disposable glove. Alternatively, use the back of a kitchen spoon and dip it in sugar as needed to keep the crumbs from sticking to it.

4. Bake at 350°F (175°C) for 10 minutes.

5. Cool thoroughly before filling.

NO-SUGAR-ADDED LEMON COOKIES

Ingredient	U.S.		Metric		%
Butter, soft	8	oz	225	g	50
Sucralose, granular	1.3	oz (12 fl oz)	36	g	8
Salt	0.12	oz (½ tsp)	3.5	g	0.8
Grated lemon zest	0.5	oz	14	g	3
Eggs	3	oz	85	g	19
Vanilla	0.33	oz (2 tsp)	10	g	2.4
Pastry flour	1 lb		450	g	100
Baking powder	0.4	oz (2½ tsp)	11	g	2.5
Total weight:	**1 lb 13**	**oz**	**834**	**g**	**185** **%**

--- VARIATION ---

NO-SUGAR-ADDED CINNAMON COOKIES

Omit the lemon zest. Add 1% (0.16 oz/4.5 g; about 1 tsp/5 mL) cinnamon.

PROCEDURE

MIXING

Creaming method (p. 478):

1. Combine the butter, sucralose, salt, and zest in the bowl of a mixer fitted with the paddle attachment. Cream until light, scraping down the bowl as necessary to make sure all ingredients are evenly blended. (*Note:* The mixture will not cream as well as butter and sugar.)

2. Add the eggs a little at a time; mix until each addition is completely absorbed before adding more.

3. Blend in the vanilla.

4. Sift together the flour and baking powder. Add to the mixing bowl and mix at low speed until evenly blended and smooth.

MAKEUP

Icebox method:

1. Divide the dough into approximately 8-oz (230-g) parts.

2. Roll each into a cylinder 1 in (2.5 cm) thick. Wrap each tightly in plastic film and refrigerate for several hours or overnight.

3. Slice ¼ in. (6 mm) thick. Bake on parchment-lined sheet pans.

BAKING

350°F (160°C), about 10 minutes

REDUCED-SUGAR APPLE SPICE CAKE

Ingredient	U.S.		Metric		%
Pastry flour	1 lb		500	g	100
Sucralose, granular		1.25 oz	40	g	8
Baking soda		0.5 oz	15	g	3
Baking powder		0.16 oz (1 tsp)	5	g	1
Salt		0.16 oz (¾ tsp)	5	g	1
Cinnamon		0.08 oz (1 tsp)	2.5	g	0.5
Ginger		0.05 oz (¾ tsp)	1.5	g	0.3
Ground cloves		0.05 oz (¾ tsp)	1.5	g	0.3
Nutmeg		0.03 oz (⅜ tsp)	1	g	0.2
Applesauce, unsweetened	1 lb 4	oz	625	g	125
Molasses		11.5 oz	360	g	72
Vegetable oil	3	oz	95	g	19
Eggs, beaten (or liquid egg substitute)	6	oz	190	g	38
Total weight:	**3 lb 10**	**oz**	**1841**	**g**	**368 %**

PROCEDURE

MIXING

Muffin method:

1. Sift together the dry ingredients.
2. Mix together the applesauce, molasses, oil, and eggs until well blended.
3. Add the dry ingredients to the liquids and mix just until smooth.

SCALING AND BAKING

Refer to the weights for high-fat cakes in the table on page 388. When a weight range is given, use the lower end of the range. Use the temperatures indicated in the table.

NOTE: This formula is called "reduced-sugar" rather than "no-sugar-added" because of the sugar content of the molasses. No other sugar is added.

GLUTEN-FREE CHOCOLATE CAKE

Ingredient	U.S.		Metric		%
Butter	8	oz	240	g	80
Sugar	14	oz	420	g	140
Bittersweet chocolate, melted	4	oz	120	g	40
Eggs	6.7	oz	200	g	67
Rice flour	6.5	oz	195	g	65
Potato starch	2.5	oz	75	g	25
Tapioca flour	1	oz	30	g	10
Xanthan gum		0.16 oz (1¼ tsp)	4.8	g	1.6
Baking soda		0.25 oz (1¼ tsp)	7.8	g	2.5
Baking powder		0.18 oz (1 tsp)	5.4	g	1.8
Salt		0.18 oz (½ tsp)	5.4	g	1.8
Buttermilk	8	oz	240	g	80
Water	4	oz	120	g	40
Vanilla		0.17 oz (1 tsp)	5	g	1.7
Total weight	**3 lb 7**	**oz**	**0**		**556 %**

PROCEDURE

MIXING

Creaming method (p. 377)

SCALING AND BAKING

See the table on page 388. Butter and flour the pans heavily (using flour from a gluten-free grain, such as rice), or line with parchment. The cake is very tender, even when cooled, and may break if it doesn't release easily from the pan. Handle cake layers carefully when assembling and icing.

GLUTEN-FREE YEAST BREAD

Ingredient	U.S.		Metric	%
Rice flour	1 lb		500 g	67
Potato starch	3	oz	95 g	12.5
Cornstarch	2	oz	60 g	8
Tapioca flour	3	oz	95 g	12.5
Sugar	1	oz	30 g	4
Nonfat milk solids (or powdered milk replacer)	2.5	oz	75 g	10
Xanthan gum	0.5	oz (5 tsp)	15 g	2
Salt	0.5	oz	15 g	2
Instant yeast	0.5	oz	15 g	2
Butter or margarine, melted	2	oz	60 g	8
Water, warm	1 lb 12	oz	875 g	117
Distilled white vinegar	0.33	oz (2 tsp)	10 g	1.4
Egg whites, lightly beaten	6	oz	190 g	25
Total weight:	**4 lb 1**	**oz**	**2035 g**	**271 %**

PROCEDURE

MIXING

1. Sift all the dry ingredients (a) into the bowl of a mixer fitted with the paddle attachment. Mix on low speed until the ingredients are uniformly blended.

2. With the machine running on low speed, slowly add the melted butter (b), water (c), and vinegar. Blend the ingredients together.

3. Add the egg whites. Turn the machine to high speed and mix for 3 minutes. Note that the mixture forms a batter, not a dough (d).

PANNING, PROOFING, AND BAKING

Note that this batter does not have a fermentation period like regular yeast doughs.

1. Grease loaf pans and dust with rice flour.

2. Fill pans half full of the batter.

3. Proof until double in bulk.

4. Bake at 400°F (200°C) for about 50 minutes, depending on the size of the loaves.

GLUTEN-FREE CHOCOLATE CHIP COOKIES

Ingredient	U.S.		Metric		%
Butter or margarine	5	oz	150	g	50
Granulated sugar	4	oz	120	g	40
Brown sugar	4	oz	120	g	40
Salt	0.12 oz (½ tsp)		4	g	1.25
Eggs	3	oz	90	g	30
Vanilla extract	0.16 oz (1 tsp)		5	g	1.6
Cornstarch	3.5	oz	105	g	35
Tapioca flour	3.5	oz	105	g	35
Chickpea (garbanzo) flour	2	oz	60	g	20
Rice flour	1	oz	30	g	10
Baking soda	0.12 oz (¾ tsp)		4	g	1.25
Xanthan gum	0.05 oz (½ tsp)		1.5 g		0.5
Chocolate chips	7	oz	210	g	70
Total weight:	**2 lb 1**	**oz**	**1004**	**g**	**334** **%**

NOTE: This formula is adapted from the formula on p. 485.

PROCEDURE

MIXING

Creaming method:

1. Cream together the butter, sugars, and salt until light.
2. Add the eggs a little at a time, waiting before each addition is absorbed before adding the next.
3. Add the vanilla.
4. Sift or mix together the dry ingredients and blend them into the creamed mixture.
5. Stir in the chocolate chips.

MAKEUP

Drop method: Drop ¾ oz (22 g) portions onto parchment-lined sheet pans.

BAKING

Bake at 350°F (175°C), about 12 minutes

GLUTEN-FREE BROWNIES

Ingredient	U.S.			Metric	%
Unsweetened chocolate		12	oz	338 g	75
Butter	1 lb	8	oz	675 g	150
Eggs	1 lb	3	oz	525 g	117
Sugar	2 lb	5	oz	1050 g	233
Salt		0.25	oz	7 g	1.5
Vanilla extract		1	oz	30 g	6
Rice flour		10	oz	284 g	63
Potato starch		4	oz	112 g	25
Tapioca flour		2	oz	54 g	12
Xanthan gum		0.25	oz	7 g	1.5
Walnuts or pecans, chopped (optional)		12	oz	338 g	75
Total weight	**7 lb**	**9**	**oz**	**3420 g**	**759 %**

PROCEDURE

MIXING

1. Melt the chocolate and butter together in a double boiler. Let the mixture cool to room temperature.
2. Mix the eggs, sugar, salt, and vanilla together until well blended, but do not whip to a foam.
3. Blend in the chocolate mixture.
4. Sift together the dry ingredients. Fold them into the chocolate mixture.
5. Fold in the nuts, if desired. Leave them out, of course, if nut allergies are a concern.

PANNING

Grease sheet pans or other baking pans and dust them with rice flour. Pour the batter into the pans. One recipe is enough for one full-size sheet pan, two half-sheet pans, four 9 × 13-in. (23 × 33 cm) pans, or six 9-in. (23-cm) or 8-in. (20-cm) square pans.

BAKING

325°F (165°C) for 45–50 minutes.

LACTOSE-FREE CRÈME CARAMEL

Yield: 12 portions, 5 oz (150 g) each

Ingredient	U.S.	Metric	
Sugar	12 oz	375	g
Water	2 fl oz	60	mL
Eggs	1 lb	500	g
Sugar	8 oz	250	g
Salt	½ tsp	2.5	g
Vanilla extract	1 tbsp	15	mL
Soy milk (see *Note*)	2½ pt	1250	mL

NOTE: For soy allergies, use another of the milk substitutes listed on pages 695–696 in place of the soy milk.

PROCEDURE

1. Cook the first quantity of sugar with the water until it caramelizes. (See the section on sugar cooking, p. 252.)

2. Line the bottoms of twelve 6-oz (180-mL) custard ramekins with the hot caramel. (Be sure the cups are clean and dry before adding the caramel.) Let cool.

3. Combine the eggs, sugar, salt, and vanilla in a mixing bowl. Mix thoroughly but do not whip.

4. Scald the soy milk in a double boiler or in a saucepan over low heat.

5. Gradually pour the milk into the egg mixture, stirring constantly.

6. Skim off all foam from the surface of the liquid.

7. Arrange the caramel-lined custard ramekins in a shallow baking pan.

8. Carefully pour the custard mixture into the ramekins.

9. Set the baking pan on the oven shelf. Pour enough hot water into the pan around the cups to reach about as high as the level of the custard mixture.

10. Bake at 325°F (165°C) until set, about 45 minutes.

11. Carefully remove the custard from the oven and cool. Cover and refrigerate at least 12 hours to allow the caramel time to partly dissolve and form a sauce.

12. Before serving, carefully unmold onto a serving dish.

LACTOSE-FREE MANGO COCONUT ICE CREAM

Yield: about 3 qt (3 L), depending on overrun

Ingredient	U.S.		Metric
Egg yolks	4 oz (6 yolks)		125 g (6 yolks)
Sugar	12 oz		375 g
Coconut milk	8 fl oz		250 mL
Coconut milk	2 pt	8 fl oz	1250 mL
Mango purée	1 lb	8 oz	750 g
Lime juice	3 fl oz		90 mL
Sugar	3 oz		90 g

PROCEDURE

1. Combine the egg yolks, sugar, and first quantity of coconut milk in a bowl. Whip until smooth and evenly mixed.

2. Scald the remaining coconut milk and gradually beat it into the egg mixture.

3. Heat in a hot-water bath or a double boiler, stirring constantly, until the mixture thickens enough to coat the back of a spoon. Immediately remove from the heat and set in an ice-water bath to stop the cooking. (See p. 260 for guidelines on preparing crème anglaise.)

4. Chill the mixture thoroughly. Refrigerate overnight.

5. Mix the mango purée, lime juice, and sugar until evenly blended. Chill for several hours or overnight.

6. Combine the custard mixture and the mango purée. Freeze in an ice cream freezer.

TERMS FOR REVIEW

empty calorie	vitamin	lipid	anaphylaxis
nutrient density	mineral	cholesterol	food intolerance
nutrient	calorie	vegan	celiac disease
fiber	saturated fat	lacto-vegetarian	lactose
carbohydrate	polyunsaturated fat	ovo-vegetarian	lecithin
fat	monounsaturated fat	lacto-ovo-vegetarian	sucralose
protein	trans fat	allergen	

QUESTIONS FOR REVIEW

1. Describe five ways to increase the vitamin, mineral, and fiber content of yeast breads.

2. True or false: Replacing the sugar in a muffin formula with honey makes the muffins more nutritious. Explain your answer.

3. A guest at a catered banquet tells the waiter she is allergic to nuts and can't eat the cake that is being served for dessert, a white cake with chocolate icing decorated with walnut halves. The waiter removes the nuts from the cake and serves it to the customer. Is this the proper response? Explain your answer.

4. Which of the following ingredients can be used to make cookies for people with celiac disease: barley flour, rye flour, whole wheat flour, spelt flour, oat flour?

5. Name and describe the three basic ways to modify an ingredient or ingredient quantity in a formula to make the formula suitable for special dietary needs.

6. Explain why it is important to understand the function of an ingredient in a baking formula when you want to eliminate that ingredient for customers who are allergic to it.

7. Why is it especially important to avoid overmixing if you reduce the butter content of a muffin formula?

Large-Quantity Measurements

HARD ROLLS (P. 126)

Ingredients	U.S.			Metric
Bread flour	5 lb	8	oz	2500 g
Water	3 lb	4	oz	1480 g
Yeast, instant		1.6	oz	45 g
Salt		2	oz	55 g
Sugar		2	oz	55 g
Shortening		2	oz	55 g
Egg whites		2	oz	55 g
Total weight:	**9 lb**	**5**	**oz**	**4245 g**

VIENNA BREAD (P. 126)

Ingredients	U.S.			Metric
Bread flour	5 lb	8	oz	2500 g
Water	3 lb	4	oz	1480 g
Yeast, instant		1.6	oz	45 g
Salt		2	oz	55 g
Sugar		2.5	oz	75 g
Malt syrup		1	oz	25 g
Oil		2.5	oz	75 g
Eggs		3.5	oz	100 g
Total weight:	**9 lb**	**9**	**oz**	**4355 g**

ITALIAN BREAD (P. 127)

Ingredients	U.S.			Metric
Bread flour	7 lb			3000 g
Water	4 lb	4	oz	1840 g
Yeast, instant		1.3	oz	36 g
Salt		2	oz	60 g
Malt syrup		0.5	oz	15 g
Total weight:	**11 lb**	**7**	**oz**	**4951 g**

--- VARIATION ---

WHOLE WHEAT ITALIAN BREAD

Use the following proportions of flour in the above formula.

Ingredients	U.S.	Metric
Whole wheat flour	3 lb	1300 g
Bread flour	4 lb	1700 g

Increase the water to 63–65% to allow for the extra absorption by the bran. Mix 8 minutes.

BAGUETTE (P. 129)

Ingredients	U.S.			Metric
Bread flour	6 lb	6	oz	3000 g
Salt		2	oz	60 g
Yeast, instant		0.75	oz	24 g
Water	4 lb	2	oz	1950 g
Total weight:	**10 lb**	**10**	**oz**	**5034 g**

FRENCH BREAD (STRAIGHT DOUGH) (P. 128)

Ingredients	U.S.			Metric
Bread flour	7 lb			3000 g
Water	4 lb	8	oz	1920 g
Yeast, instant		1	oz	27 g
Salt		2	oz	60 g
Malt syrup		0.5 oz		15 g
Sugar		2	oz	50 g
Shortening		2	oz	50 g
Total weight:	**11 lb**	**15**	**oz**	**5122 g**

VARIATION

WHOLE WHEAT FRENCH BREAD

Use the following proportions of flour in the above formula.

Ingredients	U.S.	Metric
Whole wheat flour	3 lb	1300 g
Bread flour	4 lb	1700 g

Increase the water to 63–64% to allow for the extra absorption by the bran. Mix 8 minutes.

FRENCH BREAD (SPONGE) (P. 164)

Ingredients	U.S.			Metric
Sponge				
Bread flour	2 lb			1000 g
Water	2 lb			1000 g
Yeast, instant		0.67 oz		20 g
Malt syrup		1	oz	30 g
Dough				
Bread flour	4 lb			2000 g
Water	2 lb			1000 g
Salt		1.75 oz		52 g
Total weight:	**10 lb**	**3**	**oz**	**5102 g**

VARIATION

COUNTRY-STYLE FRENCH BREAD

Use the following proportions of flour and water in the dough stage of the above formula.

Ingredients	U.S.	Metric
Clear or bread flour	1 lb 8 oz	740 g
Whole wheat flour	2 lb 8 oz	1260 g
Water	2 lb 2 oz	1040 g

Make up the dough into round loaves.

CUBAN BREAD (P. 129)

Ingredients	U.S.			Metric
Bread flour	6 lb			3000 g
Water	3 lb	12	oz	1860 g
Yeast, instant		1.5 oz		45 g
Salt		2	oz	60 g
Sugar		4	oz	120 g
Total weight:	**10 lb**	**3**	**oz**	**5085 g**

CIABATTA (P. 165)

Ingredients	U.S.			Metric
Sponge				
Bread flour	4 lb			1800 g
Water	4 lb	4	oz	1920 g
Yeast, instant		1.33 oz		37 g
Virgin olive oil		3	oz	80 g
Dough				
Salt		2	oz	60 g
Bread flour	2 lb			880 g
Total weight:	**10 lb**	**10**	**oz**	**4777 g**

WHITE PAN BREAD (P. 130)

Ingredients	U.S.			Metric
Bread flour	5 lb			2000 g
Water	3 lb			1200 g
Yeast, instant		1.6 oz		40 g
Salt		2	oz	50 g
Sugar		3	oz	75 g
Nonfat milk solids		4	oz	100 g
Shortening		3	oz	75 g
Total weight:	**8 lb**	**13**	**oz**	**3540 g**

VARIATION

WHOLE WHEAT BREAD

Use the following proportions of flour in the above formula.

Ingredients	U.S.	Metric
Bread flour	2 lb	800 g
Whole wheat flour	3 lb	1200 g

WHITE PAN BREAD (SPONGE) (P. 166)

Ingredients	U.S.			Metric
Sponge				
Flour	4 lb			2000 g
Water	2 lb	12	oz	1350 g
Yeast, instant		0.75	oz	24 g
Malt syrup		0.5	oz	15 g
Dough				
Flour	2 lb			1000 g
Water		14	oz	450 g
Salt		2	oz	60 g
Nonfat milk solids		3	oz	90 g
Sugar		5	oz	150 g
Shortening		3	oz	90 g
Total weight:	**10 lb**	**8**	**oz**	**5229 g**

SOFT ROLLS (P. 131)

Ingredients	U.S.			Metric
Bread flour	5 lb	4	oz	2500 g
Water	3 lb	2	oz	1500 g
Yeast, instant		1.6	oz	48 g
Salt		1.5	oz	50 g
Sugar		8	oz	240 g
Nonfat milk solids		4	oz	120 g
Shortening		4	oz	120 g
Butter		4	oz	120 g
Total weight:	**9 lb**	**13**	**oz**	**4698 g**

EGG BREAD AND ROLLS (P. 130)

Ingredients	U.S.			Metric
Bread flour	5 lb	4	oz	2500 g
Water	2 lb	10	oz	1250 g
Yeast, instant		1.6	oz	48 g
Salt		1.5	oz	50 g
Sugar		8	oz	240 g
Nonfat milk solids		4	oz	120 g
Shortening		4	oz	120 g
Butter		4	oz	120 g
Eggs		8	oz	240 g
Total weight:	**9 lb**	**13**	**oz**	**4688 g**

100% WHOLE WHEAT BREAD (P. 131)

Ingredients	U.S.			Metric
Whole wheat flour	6 lb	8	oz	3000 g
Water	4 lb	8	oz	2070 g
Yeast, instant		1.6	oz	45 g
Sugar		2	oz	60 g
Malt syrup		2	oz	60 g
Nonfat milk solids		3	oz	90 g
Shortening		4	oz	120 g
Salt		2	oz	60 g
Total weight:	**11 lb**	**14**	**oz**	**5505 g**

CHALLAH (P. 132)

Ingredients	U.S.			Metric
Bread flour	5 lb			2000 g
Water	2 lb			800 g
Yeast, instant		1.6	oz	40 g
Egg yolks	1 lb			400 g
Sugar		6	oz	150 g
Malt syrup		0.5	oz	10 g
Salt		1.5	oz	38 g
Vegetable oil		8	oz	250 g
Total weight:	**9 lb**	**1**	**oz**	**3688 g**

MILK BREAD (PAIN AU LAIT) (P. 132)

Ingredients	U.S.			Metric
Bread flour	6 lb	12	oz	3000 g
Sugar		10	oz	300 g
Salt		2.25	oz	60 g
Yeast, instant		1	oz	30 g
Eggs		10	oz	300 g
Milk	3 lb	6	oz	1500 g
Butter or margarine		15	oz	450 g
Malt syrup		1	oz	30 g
Total weight:	**12 lb**	**9**	**oz**	**5670 g**

LIGHT AMERICAN RYE BREAD AND ROLLS (P. 133)

Ingredients	U.S.		Metric
Light rye flour	2 lb		1000 g
Bread flour or clear flour	3 lb		1500 g
Water	3 lb		1500 g
Yeast, instant	1	oz	30 g
Salt	1.5	oz	45 g
Shortening	2	oz	60 g
Molasses or malt syrup	2	oz	60 g
Caraway seeds (optional)	1	oz	30 g
Rye flavor	1	oz	30 g
Total weight:	**8 lb 8**	**oz**	**4255 g**

ONION RYE (P. 133)

Ingredients	U.S.		Metric
Light rye flour	1 lb 12	oz	700 g
Clear flour	3 lb 4	oz	1300 g
Water	3 lb		1200 g
Yeast, instant	1	oz	25 g
Dried onions, scaled, soaked in water, and well drained	4	oz	100 g
Salt	1.5	oz	40 g
Caraway seeds	1	oz	25 g
Rye flavor	1	oz	25 g
Malt syrup	2	oz	50 g
Total weight:	**8 lb 10**	**oz**	**3465 g**

VARIATION

ONION PUMPERNICKEL (NONSOUR)

Use the following proportions of flour in the above formula.

Ingredients	U.S.	Metric
Rye meal (pumpernickel flour)	1 lb	400 g
Medium rye flour	12 oz	300 g
Clear flour	3 lb 4 oz	1300 g

Dough may be colored with caramel color or cocoa powder.

BASIC YEAST STARTER (BIGA) (P. 168)

Ingredients	U.S.		Metric
Bread flour	3 lb 12	oz	1800 g
Water	2 lb 4	oz	1080 g
Yeast, instant	0.06	oz	2 g
Total weight:	**6 lb**		**2882 g**

RYE STARTER I (P. 168)

Ingredients	U.S.		Metric
Rye flour	5 lb		2000 g
Water	3 lb 12	oz	1500 g
Yeast, instant	0.4 oz		10 g
Onion, halved (optional)	1		1
Total weight:	**8 lb 12**	**oz**	**3510 g**

RYE STARTER II (P. 168)

Ingredients	U.S.		Metric
Rye flour	4 lb		2000 g
Water, warm (85°–90°F/30°–35°C)	4 lb		2000 g
Yeast, instant	0.32 oz		10 g
Total weight:	**8 lb**		**4010 g**

OLD-FASHIONED RYE BREAD (P. 169)

Ingredients	U.S.		Metric	
Water	3 lb		1200	g
Fermented Rye Starter I or II	3 lb 8	oz	1440	g
Clear flour	6 lb		2400	g
Yeast, instant	0.33	oz	8.5	g
Salt	2	oz	50	g
Total weight:	**12 lb 10**	**oz**	**5098**	**g**

Optional

Caraway seeds	up to 1.5	oz	up to 35	g
Molasses or malt syrup	up to 3	oz	up to 70	g
Caramel color	up to 1.5	oz	up to 35	g

PUMPERNICKEL BREAD (P. 169)

Ingredients	U.S.			Metric
Water	3 lb			1500 g
Fermented Rye Starter I or II (p. 168)	2 lb	8	oz	1260 g
Rye meal (pumpernickel)	1 lb	4	oz	600 g
Clear flour	4 lb	12	oz	2400 g
Yeast, instant		0.5	oz	15 g
Salt		2	oz	60 g
Malt syrup		1	oz	30 g
Molasses		2	oz	60 g
Caramel color (optional)		1.5	oz	45 g
Total weight:	**11 lb**	**15**	**oz**	**5970 g**

FRENCH RYE (P. 170)

Ingredients	U.S.			Metric
Rye Starter II (p. 168)	6 lb			3000 g
Bread flour	1 lb			500 g
Salt		1.25	oz	40 g
Total weight:	**7 lb**	**1**	**oz**	**3540 g**

PAIN DE CAMPAGNE (COUNTRY-STYLE BREAD) (P. 170)

Ingredients	U.S.			Metric
Rye Starter II (p. 168)	1 lb	2	oz	600 g
Bread flour	4 lb	8	oz	2400 g
Rye flour	1 lb	2	oz	600 g
Salt		1.75	oz	60 g
Yeast, instant		0.5	oz	15 g
Water	3 lb	12	oz	1950 g
Lard or goose fat (optional)		1.75	oz	60 g
Total weight:	**10 lb**	**12**	**oz**	**5685 g**

ENGLISH MUFFINS (P. 135)

Ingredients	U.S.			Metric
Bread flour	4 lb			2000 g
Yeast, instant		0.33	oz	10 g
Water	3 lb			1500 g
Salt		1	oz	30 g
Sugar		1	oz	30 g
Nonfat milk solids		1.5	oz	45 g
Shortening		1	oz	30 g
Total weight:	**7 lb**	**4**	**oz**	**3645 g**

BAGELS (P. 136)

Ingredients	U.S.			Metric
High-gluten flour	4 lb			2000 g
Water	2 lb	4	oz	1120 g
Yeast, instant		0.64	oz	20 g
Diastatic malt powder		0.4	oz	12 g
Salt		1.3	oz	40 g
Total weight:	**6 lb**	**6**	**oz**	**3192 g**

OLIVE FOCACCIA (P. 137)

Ingredients	U.S.			Metric
Bread flour	6 lb			3000 g
Water	3 lb	12	oz	1875 g
Yeast, instant		0.7	oz	20 g
Salt		2	oz	60 g
Olive oil		3.5	oz	100 g
Chopped, pitted oil-cured black olives	2 lb			1000 g
Total weight:	**12 lb**	**2**	**oz**	**6055 g**

HERB FOCACCIA (SPONGE METHOD) (P. 167)

Ingredients	U.S.			Metric
Sponge				
Flour	2 lb			925 g
Water	1 lb	8	oz	675 g
Yeast, instant		0.25	oz	7 g
Flour	5 lb			2275 g
Water	3 lb	8	oz	1600 g
Yeast, instant		0.25	oz	7 g
Salt		2	oz	60 g
Olive oil		4	oz	125 g
Rosemary and salt (see Makeup)				
Total weight	**12 lb**	**6**	**oz**	**5674 g**

CHESTNUT BREAD (P. 137)

Ingredients	U.S.			Metric
High-gluten flour	2 lb	13	oz	1350 g
Chestnut flour		15	oz	450 g
Water	2 lb	4	oz	1080 g
Yeast, instant		1.2	oz	36 g
Salt		1.5	oz	45 g
Butter		1.75	oz	54 g
Total weight:	**6 lb**	**4**	**oz**	**3015 g**

PROSCIUTTO BREAD (P. 171)

Ingredients	U.S.			Metric
Bread flour	3 lb			1500 g
Water	1 lb	11	oz	855 g
Yeast, instant		0.33	oz	10 g
Salt		1	oz	30 g
Rendered lard or prosciutto fat		3	oz	90 g
Basic Yeast Starter (p. 168) or fermented dough		10	oz	300 g
Prosciutto, chopped or diced into small pieces		10	oz	300 g
Total weight:	**6 lb**	**3**	**oz**	**3085 g**

OLIVE BREAD (P. 172)

Ingredients	U.S.			Metric
Bread flour	3 lb	12	oz	1800 g
Whole wheat flour		8	oz	240 g
Rye flour		12	oz	360 g
Yeast, instant		0.4	oz	12 g
Water	3 lb	2	oz	1480 g
Salt		1.5	oz	50 g
Olive oil		4	oz	120 g
Basic Yeast Starter (p. 168) or fermented dough		8	oz	240 g
Pitted black olives, whole or halved	1 lb	8	oz	720 g
Total weight:	**10 lb**	**7**	**oz**	**5022 g**

CRUMPETS (P. 138)

Ingredients	U.S.			Metric
Water, warm	3 lb	12	oz	1650 g
Yeast, instant		1	oz	30 g
Bread flour	3 lb	6	oz	1500 g
Salt		1	oz	30 g
Sugar		0.4	oz	10 g
Baking soda		0.16	oz	4.5 g
Water, cold		15	oz	420 g
Total weight:	**8 lb**	**3**	**oz**	**3644 g**

SWEET ROLL DOUGH (P. 183)

Ingredients	U.S.			Metric
Butter, margarine, or shortening	1 lb			400 g
Sugar	1 lb			400 g
Salt		1.5	oz	40 g
Nonfat milk solids		4	oz	100 g
Eggs		12	oz	300 g
Bread flour	4 lb			1600 g
Cake flour	1 lb			400 g
Yeast, instant osmotolerant		1.6	oz	40 g
Water	2 lb			800 g
Total weight:	**10 lb**	**3**	**oz**	**4080 g**

RICH SWEET DOUGH (P. 184)

Ingredients	U.S.	Metric
Milk, scalded and cooled	2 lb	800 g
Yeast, instant osmotolerant	1.6 oz	40 g
Bread flour	2 lb 8 oz	1000 g
Butter	2 lb	800 g
Sugar	1 lb	400 g
Salt	1.5 oz	40 g
Eggs	1 lb 4 oz	500 g
Bread flour	2 lb 8 oz	1000 g
Total weight:	**11 lb 7 oz**	**4580 g**

VARIATIONS

STOLLEN

Ingredients	U.S.	Metric
Almond extract	0.5 oz	10 g
Lemon rind, grated	0.5 oz	10 g
Vanilla extract	0.5 oz	10 g
Raisins (light, dark, or a mixture)	1 lb	600 g
Mixed glacéed fruit	1 lb 12 oz	700 g

Add almond extract, lemon rind, and vanilla extract to the butter and sugar during the blending stage. Knead the raisins and mixed glacéed fruit into the dough.

BABKA

Ingredients	U.S.	Metric
Vanilla extract	0.5 oz	10 g
Cardamom	0.25 oz	5 g
Raisins	1 lb	400 g

Add the vanilla and cardamom to the butter during blending. Knead the raisins into the dough.

HOT CROSS BUNS (P. 186)

Ingredients	U.S.	Metric
Sweet Roll Dough (p. 183)	10 lb	5000 g
Dried currants	1 lb	1250 g
Golden raisins	8 oz	625 g
Mixed candied peel, diced	4 oz	300 g
Ground allspice	4 tsp	10 g
Total weight:	**11 lb 12 oz**	**7185 g**

BABA/SAVARIN DOUGH (P. 186)

Ingredients	U.S.	Metric
Milk, scalded and cooled	1 lb	480 g
Yeast, instant	1 oz	30 g
Bread flour	10 oz	300 g
Eggs	1 lb 4 oz	600 g
Bread flour	1 lb 14 oz	900 g
Sugar	1 oz	30 g
Salt	0.8 oz	24 g
Butter, melted	1 lb	500 g
Total weight:	**5 lb 14 oz**	**2864 g**

BRIOCHE (P. 188)

Ingredients	U.S.	Metric
Milk, scalded and cooled	8 oz	250 g
Yeast, instant osmotolerant	0.65 oz	20 g
Bread flour	8 oz	250 g
Eggs	1 lb 4 oz	600 g
Bread flour	2 lb	950 g
Sugar	2 oz	60 g
Salt	0.84 oz	24 g
Butter, softened	1 lb 8 oz	720 g
Total weight:	**5 lb 15 oz**	**2874 g**

DANISH PASTRY DOUGH (BRIOCHE-STYLE) (P. 191)

Ingredients	U.S.	Metric
Milk	1 lb 6 oz	675 g
Yeast, fresh	4 oz	120 g
Bread flour	4 lb 14 oz	2400 g
Eggs	10 oz	300 g
Butter, melted	4.5 oz	150 g
Salt	1 oz	30 g
Sugar	4.5 oz	150 g
Milk	7.5 oz	225 g
Butter, softened	3 lb	1500 g
Total weight:	**11 lb 3 oz**	**5550 g**

CROISSANTS (P. 192)

Ingredients	U.S.		Metric
Milk	2 lb		900 g
Sugar	2	oz	60 g
Salt	1	oz	30 g
Butter, softened	6	oz	160 g
Bread flour	3 lb 8	oz	1600 g
Yeast, instant	0.8	oz	22 g
Butter	2 lb		900 g
Total weight:	**8 lb 1**	**oz**	**3672 g**

DANISH PASTRY (P. 193)

Ingredients	U.S.		Metric
Butter	10	oz	250 g
Sugar	12	oz	300 g
Nonfat milk solids	4	oz	100 g
Salt	1.5	oz	40 g
Cardamom or mace (optional)	0.16 oz (2 tsp)		4 g
Whole eggs	1 lb		400 g
Egg yolks	4	oz	100 g
Bread flour	4 lb		1600 g
Cake flour	1 lb		400 g
Yeast, instant osmotolerant	1.6	oz	40 g
Water	2 lb		800 g
Butter (for rolling in)	2 lb 8	oz	1000 g
Total weight:	**12 lb 9**	**oz**	**5034 g**

CINNAMON SUGAR

(P. 193)

Ingredients	U.S.	Metric
Sugar	2 lb	1000 g
Cinnamon	2 oz	60 g
Total weight:	**2 lb 2 oz**	**1060 g**

STREUSEL OR CRUMB TOPPING (P. 195)

Ingredients	U.S.		Metric
Butter and/or shortening	1 lb		500 g
Granulated sugar	10	oz	300 g
Brown sugar	8	oz	250 g
Salt	0.16 oz (1 tsp)		5 g
Cinnamon or mace	0.08–0.16 oz (1–2 tsp)		2.5–5 g
Pastry flour	2 lb		1000 g
Total weight:	**4 lb 2**	**oz**	**2060 g**

APRICOT GLAZE I (P. 194)

Yield: 3 lb 4 oz (3760 g)

Ingredients	U.S.		Metric
Apricots, canned	2 lb		1000 g
Apples	2 lb		1000 g
Sugar	3 lb 12	oz	1900 g
Water	2	oz	50 g
Sugar	4	oz	100 g
Pectin	1.33 oz		40 g

APRICOT GLAZE II (P. 194)

Yield: 1 lb 12 oz (880 g)

Ingredients	U.S.	Metric
Apricot preserves	2 lb	1000 g
Water	8 oz	250 g

LEMON CHEESE FILLING (P. 195)

Ingredients	U.S.		Metric
Cream cheese	1 lb 4	oz	600 g
Sugar	4	oz	120 g
Grated lemon zest	0.4 oz (5 tsp)		12 g
Total weight:	**1 lb 8**	**oz**	**732 g**

DATE, PRUNE, OR APRICOT FILLING (P. 195)

Yield: about 6 lb (3000 g)

Ingredients	U.S.		Metric
Dates, prunes (pitted), or dried apricots	4 lb		2000 g
Sugar		12 oz	400 g
Water	2 lb		1000 g

ALMOND FILLING I (FRANGIPANE) (P. 196)

Ingredients	U.S.	Metric
Almond paste	2 lb	1000 g
Sugar	2 lb	1000 g
Butter and/or shortening	1 lb	500 g
Pastry or cake flour	8 oz	250 g
Eggs	8 oz	250 g
Total weight:	**6 lb**	**3000 g**

ALMOND CREAM (CRÈME D'AMANDE) (P. 196)

Ingredients	U.S.		Metric
Butter	12 oz		360 g
Fine granulated sugar	12 oz		360 g
Grated lemon zest	0.12 oz (1½ tsp)		4 g
Whole eggs	6.67 oz (4 eggs)		200 g
Egg yolks	2.67 oz (4 yolks)		80 g
Vanilla extract	8 drops		8 drops
Powdered almonds	12 oz		360 g
Cake flour	4 oz		120 g
Total weight:	**3 lb 1 oz**		**1484 g**

APPLE COMPOTE FILLING (P. 197)

Yield: about 4 lb (2 kg), or 2 lb 4 oz (1100 g) drained

Ingredients	U.S.	Metric
Apples, peeled and cored	2 lb 4 oz	1100 g
Butter	10 oz	300 g
Sugar	1 lb	480 g
Water	8 oz	240 g

CINNAMON RAISIN FILLING (P. 197)

Ingredients	U.S.		Metric
Powdered almonds	14	oz	400 g
Sugar	8	oz	240 g
Maple syrup	4	oz	120 g
Egg whites	8	oz	240 g
Cinnamon	1.33	oz	40 g
Raisins, golden	7	oz	200 g
Total weight:	**2 lb 10**	**oz**	**1240 g**

PECAN MAPLE FILLING (P. 198)

Ingredients	U.S.	Metric
Powdered hazelnuts	14 oz	400 g
Sugar	8 oz	240 g
Egg whites	8 oz	240 g
Maple syrup	4 oz	120 g
Pecans, finely sliced or chopped	8 oz	240 g
Total weight:	**2 lb 10 oz**	**1240 g**

HAZELNUT FILLING (P. 198)

Ingredients	U.S.		Metric
Hazelnuts, toasted and ground	1 lb		500 g
Sugar	2 lb		1000 g
Cinnamon		0.5 oz	15 g
Eggs		6 oz	190 g
Cake crumbs	2 lb		1000 g
Milk	1–2 lb		500–1000 g
Total weight:	**6 lb 6 oz to**		**3205 g to**
	7 lb 6 oz		**3705 g**

CHOCOLATE FILLING (P. 199)

Ingredients	U.S.	Metric
Sugar	1 lb	400 g
Cocoa	6 oz	150 g
Cake crumbs	3 lb	1200 g
Eggs	4 oz	100 g
Butter, melted	6 oz	150 g
Vanilla	1 oz	25 g
Water (as needed)	12 oz	300 g
Total weight:	**5 lb 13 oz**	**2425 g**

HONEY PAN GLAZE (FOR CARAMEL ROLLS) (P. 199)

Ingredients	U.S.		Metric
Brown sugar	2 lb 8 oz		1000 g
Butter, margarine, or shortening	1 lb		400 g
Honey	10 oz		250 g
Corn syrup or malt syrup	10 oz		250 g
Water (as needed)	4 oz		100 g
Total weight:	**5 lb**		**2000 g**

CRANBERRY DROP SCONES (P. 221)

Ingredients	U.S.			Metric
Butter	1 lb	2	oz	560 g
Sugar		15	oz	470 g
Salt		0.75	oz	22 g
Egg yolks		4	oz (6 yolks)	120 g
Pastry flour	4 lb	8	oz	2250 g
Baking powder		3.75	oz	112 g
Milk	2 lb	10	oz	1300 g
Dried cranberries		12	oz	380 g
Total weight:	**10 lb**	**7**	**oz**	**5214 g**

CHOCOLATE CAKE DOUGHNUTS (P. 233)

Ingredients	U.S.			Metric
Shortening		6	oz	180 g
Sugar	1 lb			500 g
Salt		0.5	oz	15 g
Nonfat milk solids		3	oz	90 g
Vanilla extract		1	oz	30 g
Whole eggs		6	oz	180 g
Egg yolks		2	oz	60 g
Cake flour	2 lb	8	oz	1500 g
Bread flour	1 lb	8	oz	500 g
Cocoa powder		5	oz	155 g
Baking powder		2	oz	60 g
Baking soda		0.4	oz (2⅔ tsp)	13 g
Water	2 lb	2	oz	1060 g
Total weight:	**8 lb 11**		**oz**	**4343 g**

RICH VANILLA SPICE DOUGHNUTS (P. 234)

Ingredients	U.S.			Metric
Bread flour	1 lb	8	oz	750 g
Cake flour	1 lb	8	oz	750 g
Baking powder		1.5	oz	45 g
Nutmeg		0.4	oz (2 tbsp)	12 g
Cinnamon		0.12	oz (2 tsp)	4 g
Salt		0.6	oz (1 tbsp)	18 g
Whole eggs		10	oz	310 g
Egg yolks		2	oz	60 g
Sugar	1 lb	4	oz	630 g
Milk	1 lb	3	oz	600 g
Vanilla extract		1.5	oz	45 g
Butter, melted		6	oz	190 g
Total weight:	**6 lb 13**		**oz**	**3414 g**

FRITTER BATTER I (P. 235)

Ingredients	U.S.			Metric
Pastry flour	2 lb	4	oz	1000 g
Sugar		2	oz	60 g
Salt		0.5	oz	15 g
Baking powder		0.5	oz	15 g
Eggs, beaten	1 lb	2	oz	500 g
Milk	2 lb			900 g
Oil		2	oz	60 g
Vanilla extract		0.33	oz (2 tsp)	10 g
Total weight:	**5 lb 11**		**oz**	**2560 g**

FRITTER BATTER II (P. 236)

Ingredients	U.S.			Metric
Bread flour	1 lb	8	oz	750 g
Cake flour		8	oz	250 g
Salt		0.5	oz	15 g
Sugar		1	oz	30 g
Milk	2 lb	4	oz	1125 g
Egg yolks, beaten		4	oz	125 g
Oil		4	oz	125 g
Egg whites		8	oz	250 g
Total weight:	**5 lb 5**		**oz**	**2670 g**

FRENCH DOUGHNUTS (BEIGNETS SOUFFLÉS) (P. 236)

Ingredients	U.S.		Metric
Milk	1 lb 14	oz	750 g
Butter	12	oz	300 g
Salt	0.5	oz	15 g
Sugar	0.5	oz	15 g
Bread flour	1 lb 2	oz	450 g
Eggs	1 lb 8	oz	600 g
Total weight:	**5 lb 5**	**oz**	**2130 g**

BEIGNETS DE CARNIVAL (P. 237)

Ingredients	U.S.		Metric
Bread flour	1 lb 5	oz	600 g
Sugar	1.5	oz	45 g
Salt	0.5	oz	15 g
Egg yolks	6	oz	180 g
Light cream	6	oz	180 g
Kirsch	1.5	oz	45 g
Rose water	1	oz	30 g
Total weight:	**2 lb 5**	**oz**	**1095 g**

VIENNOISE (P. 238)

Ingredients	U.S.	Metric
Brioche dough (p. 188)	5 lb	2400 g
Egg wash	as needed	as needed
Red currant jelly	14 oz	400 g

CANNOLI SHELLS (P. 239)

Ingredients	U.S.		Metric
Bread flour	1 lb 8	oz	700 g
Pastry flour	1 lb 8	oz	700 g
Sugar	4	oz	120 g
Salt	0.15 oz (⅔ tsp)		4 g
Butter	8	oz	240 g
Egg, beaten	6.5	oz	200 g
Dry white wine or Marsala	1 lb		500 g
Total weight:	**5 lb 2**	**oz**	**2464 g**

RICOTTA CANNOLI FILLING (P. 239)

Ingredients	U.S.	Metric
Ricotta impastata (see p. 72)	4 lb	2000 g
Confectioners' sugar	2 lb	1000 g
Cinnamon extract	1 oz	30 g
Candied citron, candied citrus peel, or candied pumpkin, finely diced	6 oz	180 g
Sweet chocolate, finely chopped, or tiny chocolate bits	4 oz	120 g
Total weight:	**6 lb 11 oz**	**3530 g**

VANILLA SYRUP (P. 254)

Ingredients	U.S.	Metric
Water	1 lb 12 oz	800 g
Sugar	1 lb 8 oz	720 g
Vanilla bean, split	2	2
Total weight:	**3 lb 4 oz** (about 2¼ pt)	**1520 g** (about 1300 mL)

COCOA VANILLA SYRUP (P. 254)

Ingredients	U.S.	Metric
Water	1 lb	500 g
Sugar	1 lb	500 g
Vanilla bean	2	2
Cocoa powder	4 oz	125 g
Total weight:	**2 lb 4 oz** (about 30 fl oz)	**1125 g** (about 1 L)

COFFEE RUM SYRUP (P. 255)

Ingredients	U.S.		Metric
Sugar	10	oz	260 g
Water	10	oz	260 g
Ground coffee	0.67	oz	20 g
Rum	14	oz	360 g
Total weight:	**2 lb 2**	**oz**	**900 g**
	(29–31 fl oz)		**(770–800 mL)**

VARIATIONS

COFFEE SYRUP

Ingredients	U.S.	Metric
Coffee liqueur	6.5 oz	160 g

Omit the rum in the basic formula and add the coffee-flavored liqueur.

RUM SYRUP

Ingredients	U.S.	Metric
Water	12 oz	300 g
Sugar	10.5 oz	260 g
Dark rum	2 oz	60 g

Omit the coffee in the basic formula and adjust the ingredient quantities as listed above.

CRÈME CHANTILLY (P. 257)

Ingredients	U.S.	Metric
Heavy cream or crème fraîche	2 pt	1000 g
Confectioners' sugar	5 oz	155 g
Vanilla extract	2 tsp	10 mL
Total weight:	**2 lb 5 oz**	**1165 g**

PASSION FRUIT GANACHE

(P. 273)

Ingredients	U.S.	Metric
Heavy cream	12 oz	360 g
Passion fruit juice	12 oz	360 g
Butter	6 oz	180 g
Egg yolks	5 oz	150 g
Sugar	6 oz	180 g
Bittersweet or semisweet chocolate, chopped	1 lb 5 oz	645 g
Total weight:	**3 lb 14 oz**	**1875 g**

VANILLA CRÈME DIPLOMAT

(P. 266)

Ingredients	U.S.		Metric
Milk	1 pt 8	oz	750 g
Vanilla bean, split	1		1
Egg yolks	4	oz	120 g
Fine granulated sugar	3	oz	90 g
Cake flour	2	oz	60 g
Cornstarch	1.5	oz	45 g
Orange liqueur, such as Grand Marnier	3	oz	90 g
Crème Chantilly (p. 257)	1 lb 4	oz	600 g
Total weight:	**3 lb 9**	**oz**	**1755 g**

VARIATION

CHOCOLATE CRÈME DIPLOMAT

Ingredients	U.S.	Metric
Bittersweet chocolate, finely chopped	7 oz	210 g

Omit the orange liqueur from the basic formula. Stir the dark chocolate into the hot pastry cream in step 4. Stir until the chocolate is completely melted and well mixed.

CARAMEL SAUCE (P. 271)

Yield: 1½ qt (1.5 L)

Ingredients	U.S.		Metric
Sugar	2	lb	1 kg
Water		8 fl oz	250 mL
Lemon juice		1 tbsp	15 mL
Heavy cream	1.5 pt		750 mL
Milk or additional cream	1.5 pt		500 mL

PIE DOUGH (P. 283)

Ingredients	Flaky Pie Dough		Mealy Pie Dough	
	U.S.	Metric	U.S.	Metric
Pastry flour	5 lb	2000 g	5 lb	2000 g
Shortening, regular	3 lb 8 oz	1400 g	3 lb 4 oz	1300 g
Water, cold	1 lb 8 oz	600 g	1 lb 4 oz	500 g
Salt	1.5 oz	40 g	1.5 oz	40 g
Sugar (optional)	4 oz	100 g	4 oz	100 g
Total weight:	**10 lb 5 oz**	**4140 g**	**9 lb 13 oz**	**3940 g**

ENRICHED PIE PASTRY (P. 283)

Ingredients	U.S.	Metric
Pastry flour	3 lb	1500 g
Sugar	8 oz	250 g
Butter	1 lb 8 oz	750 g
Egg yolks	4 oz	120 g
Water, cold	12 oz	375 g
Salt	0.5 oz	15 g
Total weight:	**6 lb**	**3010 g**

RAISIN PIE FILLING (P. 293)

Yield: about 10½ lb (4.8 kg)
Six 8-in. (20-cm) pies   Five 9-in. (23-cm) pies
Four 10-in. (25-cm) pies

Ingredients	U.S.	Metric
Raisins	4 lb	1800 g
Water	4 pt	2000 mL
Water, cold	8 oz	250 mL
Cornstarch	2.5 oz	75 g
or		
Modified starch (waxy maize)	2 oz	60 g
Sugar	1 lb 4 oz	570 g
Salt	0.33 oz (2 tsp)	10 g
Lemon juice	3 oz	90 mL
Grated lemon zest	0.1 oz (1 tbsp)	3 g
Cinnamon	0.06 oz (1 tsp)	2 g
Butter	3 oz	90 g

PEACH SOUR CREAM PIE FILLING (P. 295)

Yield: 5 lb (4500 g)
Five 8-in. (20-cm) pies   Four 9-in. (23-cm) pies
Three 10-in. (25-cm) pies

Ingredients	U.S.	Metric
Sour cream	2 lb	1000 g
Sugar	1 lb	500 g
Cornstarch	2 oz	60 g
Eggs, beaten	13 oz	400 g
Vanilla extract	2 tsp	8 mL
Nutmeg	½ tsp	2 mL
Fresh peaches, sliced	4 lb	2000 g
Streusel (p. 195)	1 lb 8 oz	720 g

CUSTARD PIE FILLING (P. 297)

Yield: 8 lb (3.7 kg)
Five 8-in. (20-cm) pies
Four 9-in. (23-cm) pies
Three 10-in. (25-cm) pies

Ingredients	U.S.	Metric
Eggs	2 lb	900 g
Sugar	1 lb	450 g
Salt	0.17 oz (1 tsp)	5 g
Vanilla extract	1 oz	30 mL
Milk	5 pt	2400 mL
Nutmeg	0.07–0.14 oz (1–2 tsp)	2–3 g

FRESH APPLE PIE FILLING I

(P. 294)

Yield: about 12 lb (5300 g)
Six 8-in. (20-cm) pies   Five 9-in. (23-cm) pies
Four 10-in. (25-cm) pies

Ingredients	U.S.		Metric	
Apples, peeled and sliced	10 lb		4500	g
Butter	5	oz	150	g
Sugar	15	oz	450	g
Water, cold	10	oz	300	g
Cornstarch	3.75	oz	120	g
or				
Modified starch (waxy maize)	2.5	oz	75	g
Sugar	1 lb		500	g
Salt	0.3	oz (1 tsp)	5	g
Cinnamon	0.3	oz (5 tsp)	5	g
Nutmeg	0.1	oz (1¼ tsp)	2.5	g
Lemon juice	1.67	oz	50	g
Butter	1.25	oz	35	g

─── VARIATIONS ───

FRESH APPLE PIE FILLING II

Ingredients	U.S.	Metric
Water	1 lb	500 g

Omit the first quantity of butter. Instead, simmer the apples in water and the first quantity of sugar as in the basic cooked fruit method, using the quantity of water listed above.

APPLE GINGER PIE FILLING

Ingredients	U.S.	Metric
Ground ginger	0.15 oz (1¼ tsp)	2.5 g
Candied ginger, finely chopped	3.5 oz	100 g

Prepare as for Fresh Apple Pie Filling I or II, but omit the cinnamon and instead add ground and candied ginger.

APPLE WALNUT PIE FILLING

Ingredients	U.S.	Metric
Chopped walnuts	12 oz	375 g

Mix the walnuts into Fresh Apple Pie Filling I or II.

RHUBARB PIE FILLING

Ingredients	U.S.	Metric
Fresh rhubarb	7 lb	3200 g

Substitute the rhubarb, cut into 1-in. (2.5-cm) pieces, for the apples. Omit the cinnamon, nutmeg, and lemon juice.

PECAN PIE FILLING (P. 297)

Yield: 7 lb (3.3 kg) filling plus 1 lb 4 oz (570 g) pecans
Five 8-in. (20-cm) pies   Four 9-in. (23-cm) pies
Three 10-in. (25-cm) pies

Ingredients	U.S.		Metric
Granulated sugar	1 lb 12	oz	800 g
Butter	8	oz	230 g
Salt	0.2	oz	6 g
Eggs	1 lb 12	oz	800 g
Dark corn syrup	3 lb (about 34 fl oz)		1400 g
Vanilla extract	1	oz	30 g
Pecans	1 lb 4	oz	570 g

PUMPKIN PIE FILLING (P. 298)

Yield: about 17 lb (8 kg)
Ten 8-in. (20-cm) pies   Eight 9-in. (23-cm) pies
Six 10-in. (25-cm) pies

Ingredients	U.S.		Metric
Pumpkin purée	6 lb 10 (1 No. 10 can or 4 No. 2½ cans)	oz	3000 g
Pastry flour	4	oz	120 g
Cinnamon	0.5	oz	15 g
Nutmeg	0.08	oz (1 tsp)	2 g
Ginger	0.08	oz (1 tsp)	2 g
Cloves	0.04	oz (½ tsp)	1 g
Salt	0.5	oz	15 g
Brown sugar	2 lb 8	oz	1150 g
Eggs	2 lb 8	oz	1200 g
Corn syrup or half corn syrup and half molasses	8	oz	240 g
Milk	5 pt		2400 mL

KEY LIME PIE FILLING (P. 299)

Yield: 5 lb 6 oz (2520 g)
Five 8-in. (20-cm) pies   Four 9-in. (23-cm) pies
Three 10-in. (25-cm) pies

Ingredients	U.S.		Metric
Egg yolks, pasteurized	10	oz	320 g
Sweetened condensed milk	3 lb 8	oz	1600 g
Freshly squeezed key lime juice	1 lb 4	oz	600 g

VANILLA CREAM PIE FILLING

(P. 300)

Yield: about 2¼ qt (2.25 L) or 6 lb 4 oz (3.1 kg)

Five 8-in. (20-cm) pies   Four 9-in. (23-cm) pies
Three 10-in. (25-cm) pies

Ingredients	U.S.	Metric
Milk	4 pt	2000 mL
Sugar	8 oz	250 g
Egg yolks	6 oz	180 g
Whole eggs	8 oz	240 g
Cornstarch	5 oz	150 g
Sugar	8 oz	250 g
Butter	4 oz	125 g
Vanilla extract	1 oz	30 mL

VARIATIONS

CHOCOLATE CREAM PIE FILLING I

Ingredients	U.S.	Metric
Unsweetened chocolate	4 oz	125 g
Semisweet chocolate	4 oz	125 g

Melt together the unsweetened and sweet chocolate and mix into the hot vanilla cream filling.

CHOCOLATE CREAM PIE FILLING II

Ingredients	U.S.		Metric
Milk	3 lb	8 oz (3½ pt)	1750 mL
Sugar		8 oz	250 g
Egg yolks		6 oz	180 g
Whole eggs		8 oz	240 g
Cold milk		8 oz	250 g
Cornstarch		5 oz	150 g
Cocoa		3 oz	90 g
Sugar		8 oz	250 g
Butter		4 oz	125 g
Vanilla extract		1 fl oz	30 mL

This variation uses cocoa instead of chocolate. The cocoa is sifted with the starch. Some of the milk must be included with the eggs to provide enough liquid to make a paste with the starch and cocoa. Follow the procedure in the basic formula, but use the above ingredients.

BUTTERSCOTCH CREAM PIE FILLING

Ingredients	U.S.	Metric
Brown sugar	2 lb	1000 g
Butter	10 oz	300 g

Combine the brown sugar and butter in a saucepan. Heat over low heat, stirring, until the butter is melted and the ingredients are blended. Prepare the basic vanilla cream filling formula, but omit all the sugar and increase the starch to 6 oz (180 g). As the mixture comes to a boil in step 5, gradually stir in the brown sugar mixture. Finish as in the basic formula.

LEMON PIE FILLING

Ingredients	U.S.			Metric
Water	3 lb	8	oz (3½ pt)	1750 mL
Sugar	1 lb 12		oz	800 g
Egg yolks		10	oz	300 g
Cornstarch		6	oz	180 g
Sugar		8	oz	250 g
Salt		0.1	oz (½ tsp)	2 g
Lemon zest, grated		0.65 oz		20 g
Butter		4	oz	125 g
Lemon juice		12	fl oz	360 mL

Follow the procedure for vanilla cream filling, but use the above ingredients. Note the lemon juice is added after the filling is thickened.

PUMPKIN CHIFFON PIE FILLING (P. 305)

Yield: 7 lb 12 oz (3.4 kg)

Six 8-in. (20-cm) pies   Five 9-in. (23-cm) pies
Four 10-in. (25-cm) pies

Ingredients	U.S.		Metric
Pumpkin purée	2 lb	8 oz	1200 g
Brown sugar	1 lb	4 oz	600 g
Milk		12 oz	350 g
Egg yolks		12 oz	350 g
Salt		0.2 oz (1 tsp)	5 g
Cinnamon		0.25 oz (3½ tsp)	7 g
Nutmeg		0.16 oz (2 tsp)	4 g
Ginger		0.08 oz (1 tsp)	2 g
Gelatin		1 oz	30 g
Water, cold		8 oz	240 mL
Egg whites, pasteurized	1 lb		450 g
Sugar	1 lb		450 g

VARIATION

PUMPKIN CREAM CHIFFON PIE FILLING

For a creamier filling, reduce the egg whites to 12 oz (350 g). Whip 1 pt (500 mL) heavy cream and fold it in after the meringue.

STRAWBERRY RHUBARB PIE FILLING (P. 301)

Yield: 7 lb (3360 g)

Five 8-in. (20-cm) pies Four 9-in. (23-cm) pies
Three 10-in. (25-cm) pies

Ingredients	U.S.			Metric
Rhubarb, fresh or frozen, in 1-in. (2.5-cm) pieces	2 lb	8	oz	1200 g
Sugar	1 lb	8	oz	720 g
Water		8	oz	240 g
Egg yolks		5.33	oz	160 g
Heavy cream		8	oz	240 g
Cornstarch		3	oz	90 g
Fresh strawberries, hulled and quartered	2 lb			1000 g

STRAWBERRY CHIFFON PIE FILLING (P. 304)

Yield: 6 lb 8 oz (3 kg)

Six 8-in. (20-cm) pies Five 9-in. (23-cm) pies
Four 10-in. (25-cm) pies

Ingredients	U.S.		Metric
Frozen sweetened strawberries	4 lb		1800 g
Salt	0.2 oz (1 tsp)		5 g
Cornstarch	1	oz	30 g
Water, cold	4	oz	120 mL
Gelatin	1	oz	30 g
Cold water	8	oz	240 mL
Lemon juice	1	oz	30 mL
Egg whites, pasteurized	1 lb		450 g
Sugar	12	oz	350 g

──── **VARIATIONS** ────

STRAWBERRY CREAM CHIFFON PIE FILLING

For a creamier filling, reduce the egg whites to 12 oz (350 g). Whip 1 pt (500 mL) heavy cream and fold it in after the meringue.

RASPBERRY CHIFFON PIE FILLING

Substitute raspberries for strawberries in the basic recipe.

PINEAPPLE CHIFFON PIE FILLING

Use 3 lb (1.4 kg) crushed pineapple. Mix the drained juice with an additional 1 pt (500 mL) pineapple juice and add 8 oz (240 g) sugar.

CHOCOLATE CHIFFON PIE FILLING (P. 305)

Yield: 7 lb (3.2 kg)

Six 8-in. (20-cm) pies Five 9-in. (23-cm) pies
Four 10-in. (25-cm) pies

Ingredients	U.S.			Metric
Unsweetened chocolate		10	oz	300 g
Water	1 pt	8	oz	750 mL
Egg yolks	1 lb			450 g
Sugar	1 lb			450 g
Gelatin		1	oz	30 g
Water, cold		8	oz	240 mL
Egg whites, pasteurized	1 lb	4	oz	580 g
Sugar	1 lb	8	oz	700 g

──── **VARIATION** ────

CHOCOLATE CREAM CHIFFON PIE FILLING

For a creamier filling, reduce the egg white to 1 lb (450 g). Whip 1 pt (500 mL) heavy cream and fold it in after the meringue.

LEMON CHIFFON PIE FILLING (P. 306)

Yield: 7 lb (3.2 kg)

Six 8-in. (20-cm) pies Five 9-in. (23-cm) pies
Four 10-in. (25-cm) pies

Ingredients	U.S.			Metric
Water	1 pt	8	oz	750 mL
Sugar		8	oz	240 g
Egg yolks		12	oz	350 g
Water, cold		4	oz	120 mL
Cornstarch		3	oz	90 g
Sugar		8	oz	240 g
Lemon zest, grated		0.5	oz	15 g
Gelatin		1	oz	30 g
Water, cold		8	oz	250 mL
Lemon juice		12	oz	350 mL
Egg whites, pasteurized	1 lb			450 g
Sugar	1 lb			450 g

──── **VARIATIONS** ────

LIME CHIFFON PIE FILLING

Substitute lime juice and zest for the lemon juice and zest.

ORANGE CHIFFON PIE FILLING

Make the following ingredient adjustments: Use orange juice instead of water in step 1. Omit the first 8 oz (240 g) sugar. Substitute orange zest for the lemon zest. Reduce the lemon juice to 4 oz (120 mL).

PÂTE BRISÉE (P. 313)

Ingredients	U.S.			Metric
Pastry flour	1 lb	8	oz	800 g
Salt		0.6	oz	20 g
Sugar		0.6	oz	20 g
Butter, chilled		12	oz	400 g
Eggs		8	oz	260 g
Water		1.2	oz	40 g
Vanilla extract		8 drops		8 drops
Lemon zest, grated		0.25 oz		8 g
Total weight:	**2 lb 14**		**oz**	**1548 g**

PÂTE SABLÉE (P. 313)

Ingredients	U.S.			Metric
Butter, softened	1 lb	8	oz	600 g
Confectioners' sugar		12	oz	300 g
Salt		0.12 oz (½ tsp)		3 g
Lemon zest, grated		0.16 oz (2 tsp)		4 g
Vanilla extract		8 drops		8 drops
Egg, beaten		4	oz	100 g
Pastry flour	2 lb	4	oz	900 g
Total weight:	**4 lb 12**		**oz**	**1907 g**

─── VARIATION ───

CHOCOLATE PÂTE SABLÉE

Ingredients	U.S.			Metric
Butter	1 lb	8	oz	600 g
Confectioners' sugar		12	oz	300 g
Grated orange zest		0.33 oz		8 g
Eggs, beaten		8	oz	200 g
Pastry flour	1 lb	12	oz	700 g
Cocoa powder		4	oz	120 g

Substitute the above ingredients and follow the basic procedure. Sift the flour with the cocoa.

PÂTE SUCRÉE (P. 314)

Ingredients	U.S.			Metric
Butter, softened		13	oz	432 g
Confectioners' sugar		8	oz	264 g
Salt		0.12 oz (¾ tsp)		4 g
Lemon zest, grated		0.12 oz (1½ tsp)		4 g
Vanilla extract		8 drops		8 drops
Eggs, beaten		6	oz	200 g
Pastry flour	1 lb	8	oz	800 g
Total weight:	**3 lb 3**		**oz**	**1704 g**

SHORT DOUGH I (P. 314)

Ingredients	U.S.			Metric
Butter or butter and shortening	2 lb			1000 g
Sugar		12	oz	375 g
Salt		0.25 oz		8 g
Eggs		9	oz	280 g
Pastry flour	3 lb			1500 g
Total weight:	**6 lb 5**		**oz**	**3163 g**

ALMOND SHORT DOUGH (P. 315)

Ingredients	U.S.			Metric
Butter	2 lb			800 g
Sugar	1 lb	8	oz	600 g
Salt		0.4 oz (2½ tsp)		10 g
Powdered almonds	1 lb	4	oz	500 g
Eggs		6.5 oz		165 g
Vanilla extract		0.2 oz (1¼ tsp)		5 g
Pastry flour	2 lb	8	oz	1000 g
Total weight:	**7 lb 11**		**oz**	**3080 g**

─── VARIATION ───

LINZER DOUGH I

Ingredients	U.S.		Metric
Cinnamon	0.25 oz (4 ½ tsp)		6 g
Nutmeg	0.04 oz (½ tsp)		1 g

Use ground hazelnuts, ground almonds, or a mixture of the two. Mix in the cinnamon and nutmeg with the salt in step 1.

SHORT DOUGH II (P. 314)

Ingredients	U.S.			Metric
Butter	1 lb	4	oz	600 g
Sugar		14	oz	400 g
Salt		0.25	oz	8 g
Vanilla powder		0.25	oz	8 g
Powdered almonds		4	oz	120 g
Eggs		7	oz	200 g
Pastry flour	2 lb	2	oz	1000 g
Total weight:	**4 lb 15**		**oz**	**2336 g**

CLASSIC PUFF PASTRY (PÂTE FEUILLETÉE CLASSIQUE) (P. 318)

Ingredients	U.S.		Metric
Bread flour	3 lb		1500 g
Salt		1 oz	30 g
Butter, melted		8 oz	225 g
Water	1 lb	8 oz	750 g
Butter, for rolling in	1 lb	12 oz	900 g
Total weight:	**6 lb 13 oz**		**3405 g**

ORDINARY PUFF PASTRY (P. 319)

Ingredients	U.S.		Metric
Bread flour	3 lb		1500 g
Cake flour	1 lb		500 g
Butter, softened		8 oz	250 g
Salt		1 oz	30 g
Water, cold	2 lb	4 oz	1125 g
Butter	4 lb		2000 g
Bread flour		8 oz	250 g
Total weight:	**11 lb 5 oz**		**5655 g**

ALMOND MERINGUES (P. 342)

Ingredients	U.S.	Metric
Egg whites	1 lb	500 g
Fine granulated sugar	1 lb	500 g
Powdered almonds	1 lb	500 g
Total weight:	**3 lb**	**1500 g**

SUCCÈS (P. 344)

Ingredients	U.S.		Metric
Egg whites	1 lb	2 oz	540 g
Granulated sugar		12 oz	360 g
Powdered almonds		12 oz	360 g
Confectioners' sugar		12 oz	360 g
Cake flour		3 oz	90 g
Total weight:	**3 lb**	**9 oz**	**1710 g**

YELLOW BUTTER CAKE (P. 392)

Ingredients	U.S.			Metric
Butter	3 lb			1440 g
Sugar	3 lb	4	oz	1566 g
Salt		0.5	oz	14 g
Eggs	1 lb	14	oz	900 g
Cake flour	3 lb	12	oz	1800 g
Baking powder		2.5	oz	72 g
Milk	3 lb	12	oz	1800 g
Vanilla extract		1	oz	30 g
Total weight:	**15 lb 14**		**oz**	**7622 g**

— VARIATION —

PAN SPREAD

For one sheet pan:

Ingredients	U.S.		Metric
Brown sugar	1 lb		450 g
Granulated sugar		6 oz	170 g
Corn syrup or honey		4 oz	120 g
Water (as needed)			

Cream together the first three ingredients. Thin with water to spreading consistency.

CHOCOLATE BUTTER CAKE
(P. 392)

Ingredients	U.S.			Metric
Butter	2 lb	4	oz	1125 g
Sugar	3 lb	12	oz	1875 g
Salt		0.75	oz	22 g
Unsweetened chocolate, melted	1 lb	8	oz	750 g
Eggs	2 lb			1000 g
Cake flour	3 lb			1500 g
Baking powder		2	oz	60 g
Milk	3 lb	7	oz	1725 g
Vanilla extract		1	oz	30 g
Total weight:	**16 lb**	**2**	**oz**	**8087 g**

DEVIL'S FOOD CAKE (P. 399)

Ingredients	U.S.			Metric
Cake flour	3 lb			1500 g
Cocoa		8	oz	250 g
Salt		1	oz	30 g
Baking powder		1.5	oz	45 g
Baking soda		1	oz	30 g
Emulsified shortening	1 lb	12	oz	870 g
Sugar	4 lb			2000 g
Skim milk	2 lb			1000 g
Vanilla extract		0.75 oz (4½ tsp)		20 g
Skim milk	1 lb	8	oz	750 g
Eggs	2 lb			1000 g
Total weight:	**15 lb**			**7495 g**

SACHER MIX II (P. 396)

Ingredients	U.S.			Metric
Butter, softened		13.5 oz		400 g
Fine granulated sugar		11	oz	330 g
Egg yolks		12	oz	360 g
Egg whites	1 lb	2	oz	540 g
Fine granulated sugar		6	oz	180 g
Cake flour		4	oz	120 g
Cocoa powder		4	oz	120 g
Powdered almonds, toasted		5.5 oz		165 g
Total weight:	**4 lb**	**10**	**oz**	**2215 g**

GENOISE MOUSSELINE
(P. 401)

Ingredients	U.S.	Metric
Whole eggs	1 lb 14 oz	900 g
Egg yolks	4 oz (6 yolks)	120 g (6 yolks)
Sugar	1 lb 2 oz	540 g
Cake flour, sifted	1 lb 2 oz	540 g
Total weight:	**4 lb 6 oz**	**2100 g**

WHITE CAKE (P. 398)

Ingredients	U.S.			Metric
Cake flour	3 lb			1500 g
Baking powder		3	oz	90 g
Salt		1	oz	30 g
Emulsified shortening	1 lb	8	oz	750 g
Sugar	3 lb	12	oz	1875 g
Skim milk	1 lb	8	oz	750 g
Vanilla extract		0.75 oz (4½ tsp)		20 g
Almond extract		0.36 oz (2¼ tsp)		10 g
Skim milk	1 lb	8	oz	750 g
Egg whites	2 lb			1000 g
Total weight:	**13 lb**	**9**	**oz**	**6775 g**

MILK AND BUTTER SPONGE
(P. 403)

Ingredients	U.S.			Metric
Sugar	2 lb	8	oz	1250 g
Whole eggs	1 lb	8	oz	750 g
Egg yolks		8	oz	250 g
Salt		0.5	oz	15 g
Cake flour	2 lb			1000 g
Baking powder		1	oz	30 g
Skim milk	1 lb			500 g
Butter		8	oz	250 g
Vanilla extract		1	oz	30 g
Total weight:	**8 lb**	**2**	**oz**	**4075 g**

JOCONDE SPONGE CAKE (BISCUIT JOCONDE) (P. 405)

Ingredients	U.S.		Metric
Powdered almonds	14	oz	340 g
Confectioners' sugar	12	oz	300 g
Cake flour	4	oz	100 g
Whole eggs	1 lb 3	oz	480 g
Egg whites	13	oz	320 g
Sugar	1.6	oz	40 g
Butter, melted	5	oz	120 g
Total weight:	**4 lb 4**	**oz**	**1700 g**

ALMOND CHOCOLATE SPONGE (P. 410)

Ingredients	U.S.	Metric
Marzipan	13 oz	390 g
Egg yolks	8 oz	240 g
Egg whites	12 oz	360 g
Sugar	5 oz	150 g
Cake flour	4 oz	120 g
Cocoa powder	4 oz	120 g
Butter, melted	4 oz	120 g
Total weight:	**3 lb 2 oz**	**1500 g**

MARJOLAINE SPONGE CAKE

(P. 407)

Ingredients	U.S.	Metric
Confectioners' sugar	12 oz	360 g
Powdered almonds	12 oz	360 g
Egg yolks	10 oz	300 g
Egg whites	6 oz	180 g
Egg whites	15 oz	450 g
Sugar	9 oz	270 g
Pastry flour, sifted	9 oz	270 g
Total weight:	**4 lb 9 oz**	**2190 g**

CHOCOLATE SPONGE LAYERS

(P. 410)

Ingredients	U.S.	Metric
Egg whites	1 lb 4 oz	600 g
Sugar	1 lb	480 g
Egg yolks	14 oz	400 g
Cake flour	14 oz	400 g
Cocoa powder	4 oz	120 g
Total weight:	**4 lb 4 oz**	**2000 g**

HAZELNUT SPONGE CAKE

(P. 408)

Ingredients	U.S.		Metric
Butter, softened	14	oz	400 g
Sugar	11	oz	330 g
Egg yolks	12	oz	360 g
Egg whites	1 lb 2	oz	540 g
Sugar	6	oz	180 g
Cake flour	4	oz	120 g
Cocoa powder	4	oz	120 g
Ground hazelnuts, toasted	5.5	oz	165 g
Total weight:	**4 lb 10**	**oz**	**2215 g**

CHOCOLATE VELVET CAKE (MOELLEUX) (P. 411)

Ingredients	U.S.		Metric
Almond paste	7.5	oz	225 g
Confectioners' sugar	5	oz	150 g
Egg yolks	6	oz	180 g
Egg whites	6	oz	180 g
Sugar	2.5	oz	75 g
Cake flour	4	oz	120 g
Cocoa powder	1	oz	30 g
Butter, melted	2	oz	60 g
For baking			
Almonds, chopped	3	oz	90 g
Total batter weight:	**2 lb 2**	**oz**	**1020 g**

LEMON MADELEINES (P. 412)

Ingredients	U.S.		Metric	
Butter	15	oz	450	g
Sugar	13	oz	420	g
Honey	2.4	oz	72	g
Salt	0.03	oz	1.2	g
Grated lemon zest	0.7	oz	30	g
Eggs	1 lb 0.5	oz	495	g
Pastry flour	15	oz	450	g
Baking powder	0.4	oz	11.5	g
Total weight:	**3 lb 15**	**oz**	**1929**	**g**

── VARIATION ──

CHOCOLATE AND ORANGE MADELEINES

Ingredients	U.S.		Metric	
Butter	15	oz	495	g
Sugar	13	oz	420	g
Honey	2.4	oz	72	g
Salt	0.03	oz	1.2	g
Grated orange zest	1	oz	30	g
Eggs	1 lb 0.5	oz	495	g
Pastry flour	3.5	oz	315	g
Cocoa powder	3.6	oz	105	g
Baking powder	0.54	oz	15	g

Follow the basic procedure, but change the ingredients as listed above.

SIMPLE BUTTERCREAM

(P. 419)

Ingredients	U.S.		Metric
Butter	2 lb		1000 g
Shortening	1 lb		500 g
Confectioners' sugar	5 lb		2500 g
Egg whites, pasteurized	5		160 g
Lemon juice	0.33 oz (2 tsp)		10 g
Vanilla extract	0.5	oz	15 g
Water (optional)	4	oz	125 g
Total weight:	**8 lb 9**	**oz**	**4310 g**

ITALIAN BUTTERCREAM (P. 420)

Yield: 6 lb 12 oz (3400 g)

Ingredients	U.S.		Metric
Italian meringue			
Sugar	2 lb		1000 g
Water	8	oz	250 mL
Egg whites	1 lb		500 g
Butter	3 lb		1500 g
Emulsified shortening	8	oz	250 g
Lemon juice	0.33 oz (2 tsp)		10 mL
Vanilla extract	0.5	oz	15 mL

FRENCH BUTTERCREAM (P. 421)

Yield: 5 lb 8 oz (2750 g)

Ingredients	U.S.		Metric
Sugar	2 lb		1000 g
Water	8	oz	250 mL
Egg yolks	12	oz	375 g
Butter, softened	2 lb 8	oz	1250 g
Vanilla extract	0.5 oz		15 mL

PRALINE BUTTERCREAM (P. 421)

Yield: 3 lb 6 oz (1650 g)

Ingredients	U.S.	Metric
Water	4 oz	120 g
Sugar	12 oz	360 g
Egg yolks	10 oz	300 g
Butter, softened	1 lb 2 oz	540 g
Praline paste	15 oz	450 g

LIGHT PRALINE CREAM (P. 422)

Ingredients	U.S.		Metric
Butter, softened	2 lb		1000 g
Praline paste	1 lb		500 g
Cognac	6	oz	200 g
Italian Meringue (p. 259)	3 lb 6	oz	1700 g
Total weight:	**6 lb 12 oz**		**3400 g**

CARAMEL BUTTERCREAM
(P. 422)

Yield: 4 lb (2000 g)

Ingredients	U.S.		Metric
Water	4	oz	100 g
Sugar	1 lb 10	oz	740 g
Water	7	oz	200 g
Heavy cream	5	oz	140 g
Coffee extract	0.75	oz	20 g
Egg yolks	8	oz	240 g
Butter, softened	1 lb 11	oz	760 g

VANILLA CREAM (P. 422)

Ingredients	U.S.		Metric
Pastry Cream (p. 263)	2 lb 8	oz	1125 g
Gelatin	0.5	oz	15 g
Rum	1.75	oz	50 g
Butter, softened	1 lb 2	oz	500 g
Total weight:	**3 lb 12**	**oz**	**1690 g**

FLAT ICING (P. 425)

Ingredients	U.S.		Metric
Confectioners' sugar	4 lb		2000 g
Water, hot	12	oz	375 mL
Corn syrup	4	oz	125 g
Vanilla extract	0.5	oz	15 g
Total weight:	**5 lb**		**2500 g**

COCOA JELLY (P. 429)

Ingredients	U.S.		Metric
Water	1 lb		450 g
Fondant	1 lb 8	oz	675 g
Glucose	8	oz	225 g
Gelatin	1	oz	30 g
Cocoa powder	4.75	oz	135 g
Total weight:	**3 lb 5**	**oz**	**1515 g**

OPERA GLAZE (P. 428)

Ingredients	U.S.		Metric
Coating chocolate (p. 86)	1 lb 8	oz	750 g
Semisweet or bittersweet chocolate couverture	10.5	oz	300 g
Peanut oil	4	oz	120 g
Total weight:	**2 lb 6**	**oz**	**1170 g**

VARIATION

If couverture is used alone instead of part coating chocolate and part couverture, increase the quantity of oil so the icing has the proper texture and can be cut easily with a cake knife.

Ingredients	U.S.		Metric
Dark chocolate couverture	2 lb 2.5	oz	1050 g
Peanut oil	6	oz	180 g

COFFEE MARBLE GLAZE
(P. 429)

Yield: 2 lb (1000 g)

Ingredients	U.S.		Metric
Gelatin	1	oz	24 g
Water	1 lb 8	oz	750 g
Sugar	4	oz	120 g
Glucose	4	oz	120 g
Vanilla bean, split	2		2
Coffee liqueur	2	oz	60 g
Coffee extract	1	oz	30 g

DIAMONDS (P. 493)

Ingredients	U.S.		Metric
Butter, cut in small pieces	1 lb 4	oz	560 g
Cake flour	1 lb 12	oz	800 g
Confectioners' sugar	8	oz	240 g
Salt	0.16 oz (2¾ tsp)		4 g
Orange zest, grated	0.3 oz (4 tsp)		8 g
Vanilla extract	0.3 oz (2 tsp)		8 g
For rolling			
Crystal sugar	7	oz	200 g
Total dough weight:	**3 lb 15**	**oz**	**1620 g**

ALMOND TUILES I (P. 502)

Ingredients	U.S.	Metric
Butter	12 oz	360 g
Confectioners' sugar	1 lb	480 g
Egg whites	12 oz	360 g
Cake flour	14 oz	420 g
Garnish		
Sliced almonds	10 oz	300 g
Batter weight:	**3 lb 6 oz**	**1620 g**

ESPRESSO BISCOTTI (P. 508)

Ingredients	U.S.	Metric
Butter	12 oz	360 g
Sugar	1 lb 2 oz	540 g
Salt	0.6 oz	18 g
Eggs	10 oz	300 g
Water, hot	1.5 oz	45 g
Instant espresso powder	0.6 oz	18 g
Pastry flour	1 lb 14 oz	900 g
Baking powder	0.75 oz	24 g
Blanched almonds	11 oz	315 g
Total weight:	**5 lb 4 oz**	**2520 g**

CHOCOLATE PECAN BISCOTTI (P. 509)

Ingredients	U.S.	Metric
Butter	12 oz	360 g
Sugar	1 lb	540 g
Salt	0.3 oz	9 g
Orange zest, grated	0.3 oz	9 g
Eggs	10 oz	300 g
Water	6 oz	180 g
Vanilla extract	0.5 oz	15 g
Pastry flour	1 lb 14 oz	900 g
Cocoa powder	4.5 oz	135 g
Baking powder	0.75 oz	24 g
Baking soda	0.25 oz	8 g
Pecan pieces	6 oz	180 g
Small chocolate chips	6 oz	180 g
Total weight:	**5 lb 12 oz**	**2840 g**

RICH BROWNIES (P. 505)

Yield: one large formula (about 10 lb 5 oz/4652 g)
Fills one full-size sheet pan (18 × 26 in./46 × 66 cm), two half-size sheet pans, four 9 × 13 in. (23 × 33 cm) pans, or six 9-in. (23-cm) square pans.

Ingredients	U.S.		Metric
Unsweetened chocolate	8	oz	225 g
Bittersweet chocolate	1 lb 4	oz	560 g
Butter	2 lb 8	oz	1125 g
Eggs	1 lb 12	oz	790 g
Sugar	2 lb 4	oz	1015 g
Salt	0.25	oz	7 g
Vanilla extract	1	oz	30 mL
Bread flour	1 lb		450 g
Walnuts or pecans, chopped	1 lb		450 g
Total weight:	**10 lb 5**	**oz**	**4652 g**

VARIATION

Ingredients	U.S.	Metric
Baking powder	0.4 oz	11 g

For a more cakelike brownie, sift the above quantity of baking powder with the flour in step 4.

CREAM CHEESE BROWNIES (P. 506)

Yield: one large formula (about 12 lb/5600 g)
Fills one full-size sheet pan (18 × 26 in./46 × 66 cm), two half-size sheet pans, four 9 × 13 in. (23 × 33 cm) pans, or six 9-in. (23-cm) square pans.

Ingredients	U.S.		Metric
Cream cheese	2 lb		900 g
Sugar	8	oz	225 g
Vanilla extract	2	tsp	7 mL
Egg yolks	2.7 oz (4 yolks)		80 g
Rich Brownies batter (above) without walnuts (1 recipe)	10 lb 5	oz	4650 g
Total weight:	**12 lb 15**	**oz**	**5862 g**

CHRISTMAS PUDDING (P. 523)

Ingredients	U.S.			Metric	
Dark raisins	2 lb			1000 g	
Light raisins	2 lb			1000 g	
Currants	2 lb			1000 g	
Dates, diced	1 lb			500 g	
Almonds, chopped		12	oz	375 g	
Candied orange peel, finely chopped		8	oz	250 g	
Candied lemon peel, finely chopped		8	oz	250 g	
Brandy	1 pt	8	oz	750 mL	
Bread flour	1 lb			500 g	
Cinnamon		0.12 oz (1¾ tsp)		4 g	
Nutmeg		0.03 oz (½ tsp)		1 g	
Mace		0.03 oz (½ tsp)		1 g	
Ginger		0.03 oz (½ tsp)		1 g	
Cloves, ground		0.03 oz (½ tsp)		1 g	
Salt		0.5 oz		15 g	
Beef suet, finely chopped	1 lb	8	oz	750 g	
Brown sugar	1 lb			500 g	
Eggs	1 lb			500 g	
Fresh bread crumbs		8	oz	250 g	
Molasses		2	oz	60 g	
Total weight:	**15 lb**	**7**	**oz**	**7700 g**	

STEAMED BLUEBERRY PUDDING (P. 524)

Ingredients	U.S.			Metric
Brown sugar	1 lb	4	oz	625 g
Butter		8	oz	250 g
Salt		0.08 oz (½ tsp)		3 g
Cinnamon		0.17 oz (1 tbsp)		5 g
Eggs		8	oz	250 g
Bread flour		4	oz	125 g
Baking powder		0.75 oz		22 g
Dry bread crumbs	1 lb	4	oz	625 g
Milk	1 lb			500 g
Blueberries, fresh or frozen, without sugar	1 lb			500 g
Total weight:	**5 lb**	**13**	**oz**	**2905 g**

CREAM CHEESE BAVARIAN (P. 530)

Yield: about 6 qt (6.5 L)

Ingredients	U.S.			Metric	
Cream cheese	3 lb			1500	g
Sugar	1 lb			500	g
Salt		0.5	oz	15	g
Lemon zest, grated		0.12 oz (1½ tsp)		4	g
Orange zest, grated		0.08 oz (1 tsp)		2.5	g
Vanilla extract		0.25 oz (1½ tsp)		8	g
Lemon juice		4	oz	125	g
Gelatin		1	oz	30	g
Water, cold		8	oz	250	g
Heavy cream	4 pt			2000	mL
Total weight:	**8 lb 13**		**oz**	**4434**	**g**

RASPBERRY JAM (P. 589)

Yield: 3 lb 12 oz (1900 g)

Ingredients	U.S.			Metric
Sugar	1 lb	8	oz	750 g
Water		8	oz	250 g
Raspberries, fresh	2 lb			1000 g
Glucose		3.2	oz	100 g
Sugar		5	oz	150 g
Pectin		2.67 oz		80 g

APPLE MARMALADE (P. 589)

Yield: 8 lb 8 oz (4240 g)

Ingredients	U.S.	Metric
Apples, peeled and cored	8 lb	4000 g
Water	1 lb	500 g
Sugar	2 lb 8 oz	1200 g

STRAWBERRY MARMALADE (P. 590)

Yield: 3 lb 4 oz (1600 g)

Ingredients	U.S.			Metric
Strawberries	2 lb			1000 g
Sugar	2 lb			1000 g
Pectin		0.67 oz		20 g
Lemon juice		2	oz	30 g

CARAMELIZED APRICOTS

(P. 590)

Yield: 3 lb (1200 g)

Ingredients	U.S.		Metric
Sugar	1 lb		400 g
Water		4 oz	100 g
Honey		8 oz	200 g
Butter		4 oz	100 g
Canned apricots, drained	3 lb		1200 g

APRICOT COMPOTE (P. 591)

Yield: 2 lb 6 oz (960 g)

Ingredients	U.S.		Metric
Sugar	1 lb	2 oz	450 g
Water		2.5 oz	60 g
Apricots, fresh or canned, halved and pitted	1 lb	4 oz	500 g
Pectin		1.5 oz	40 g
Glucose		2 oz	50 g

VARIATION

APRICOT AND ALMOND COMPOTE

Ingredients	U.S.	Metric
Whole blanched almonds	8 oz	200 g

Add the almonds to the apricots at the same time as the pectin and glucose.

ROCHER WITH ALMONDS

(P. 642)

Ingredients	U.S.		Metric
Dark chocolate	1 lb		450 g
Praline paste	1 lb	8 oz	675 g
Ice cream wafers (pailletine), finely crushed		8 oz	225 g
Dark chocolate	1 lb	8 oz	675 g
Almonds, toasted and chopped		4 oz	112 g
Total weight:	**4 lb 12 oz**		**2137 g**

PINEAPPLE KUMQUAT COMPOTE (P. 592)

Yield: 2 lb 12 oz (1080 g)

Ingredients	U.S.		Metric
Sugar	1 lb	2 oz	450 g
Water		2.5 oz	60 g
Vanilla bean		1	1
Glucose		2 oz	48 g
Canned pineapple, drained and diced	1 lb	4 oz	500 g
Kumquats, sliced and blanched		8 oz	200 g
Pistachios		1.5 oz	40 g

VARIATION

KUMQUAT COMPOTE

Ingredients	U.S.		Metric
Sugar	1 lb	2 oz	450 g
Water		2.5 oz	60 g
Glucose		2 oz	48 g
Kumquats, halved or sliced, blanched	1 lb	4 oz	500 g
Pistachios		3 oz	80 g

Follow the procedure in the basic recipe, but omit the pineapple and vanilla and adjust the quantities as listed above.

GUM PASTE (P. 653)

Ingredient	U.S.	Metric
Confectioners' sugar	2 lb 8 oz	1250 g
Gum tragacanth	1 oz (3 tbsp)	30 g
Water	6 fl oz	190 mL
Glucose syrup	2 oz	60 g
Confectioners' sugar	8 oz or as needed	250 g
Total weight:	**3 lb 9 oz**	**1780 g**

PROCEDURE

1. Sift the confectioners' sugar into a bowl.
2. Add the gum tragacanth and mix in.
3. Add the water and glucose. Mix until smooth.
4. Transfer the mixture to a work surface. Knead in the remaining sugar, or enough to make a smooth, firm dough.
5. Roll the gum paste into a cylinder. Coat it with a light film of shortening (to prevent drying) and wrap tightly in plastic film. Let stand overnight.

Metric Conversion Factors

Weight

1 ounce equals 28.35 grams

1 gram equals 0.035 ounce

1 pound equals 454 grams

1 kilogram equals 2.2 pounds

Volume

1 fluid ounce equals 29.57 milliliters

1 milliliter equals 0.034 fluid ounce

1 cup equals 237 milliliters

1 quart equals 946 milliliters

1 liter equals 33.8 fluid ounces

Length

1 inch equals 25.4 millimeters

1 centimeter equals 0.39 inch

1 meter equals 39.4 inches

Temperature

To convert Fahrenheit to Celsius: Subtract 32, then multiply by $\frac{5}{9}$.

Example: Convert 140°F to Celsius.

$$140 - 32 = 108$$

$$108 \times \tfrac{5}{9} = 60°C$$

To convert Celsius to Fahrenheit: Multiply by $\frac{9}{5}$ then add 32.

Example: Convert 150°C to Fahrenheit.

$$150 \times \tfrac{9}{5} = 270$$

$$270 + 32 = 302°F$$

Note: The metric measurements in the recipes in this book are not equivalent to the corresponding U.S. measurements. See page 21 for a complete explanation.

Decimal Equivalents of Common Fractions

FRACTION	ROUNDED TO 3 PLACES	ROUNDED TO 2 PLACES
⅚	0.833	0.83
⅘	0.8	0.8
¾	**0.75**	**0.75**
⅔	**0.667**	**0.67**
⅝	0.625	0.63
⅗	0.6	0.6
½	**0.5**	**0.5**
⅓	**0.333**	**0.33**
¼	**0.25**	**0.25**
⅕	0.2	0.2
⅙	0.167	0.17
⅛	**0.125**	**0.13**
1⁄10	0.1	0.1
1⁄12	0.083	0.08
1⁄16	0.063	0.06
1⁄25	0.04	0.04

Approximate Volume Equivalents of Dry Foods

The following equivalents are rough averages only. Actual weight varies considerably. For accurate measurement, weigh all ingredients.

Following common practice, volume measures in this chart are represented as common fractions rather than as decimals.

Bread flour, sifted

    1 lb = 4 cups

    1 cup = 4 oz

Bread flour, unsifted

    1 lb = 3⅓ cups

    1 cup = 4.75 oz

Cake flour, sifted

    1 lb = 4¼ cups

    1 cup = 3.75 oz

Cake flour, unsifted

    1 lb = 3½ cups

    1 cup = 4.5 oz

Granulated sugar

    1 lb = 2¼ cups

    1 cup = 7 oz

Confectioners' sugar, sifted

    1 lb = 4 cups

    1 cup = 4 oz

Confectioners' sugar, unsifted

    1 lb = 3½ cups

    1 cup = 4.5 oz

Cornstarch, sifted

    1 lb = 4 cups

    1 cup = 4 oz

    1 oz = 4 tbsp = ¼ cup

    1 tbsp = 0.25 oz

Cornstarch, unsifted

    1 lb = 3½ cups

    1 cup = 4.5 oz

    1 oz = 3½ tbsp

    1 tbsp = 0.29 oz

Cocoa, unsifted

    1 lb = 5 cups

    1 cup = 3.2 oz

    1 oz = 5 tbsp

    1 tbsp = 0.2 oz

Gelatin, unflavored

    1 oz = 3 tbsp

    0.25 oz = 2¼ tsp

    1 tbsp = 0.33 oz

    1 tsp = 0.11 oz

Baking soda

    1 oz = 5¼ tsp

    0.25 oz = 1⅓ tsp

    1 tbsp = 0.57 oz

    1 tsp = 0.19 oz

Baking powder (phosphate type and sodium aluminum sulfate type)

    1 oz = 2 tbsp

    0.25 oz = 1½ tsp

    1 tbsp = 0.5 oz

    1 tsp = 0.17 oz

Cream of tartar

    1 oz = 4 tbsp

    0.25 oz = 1 tbsp

    1 tsp = 0.08 oz

Salt

    1 oz = 4½ tsp

    0.25 oz = 1¼ tsp

    1 tsp = 0.2 oz

Ground spices

    1 oz = 14 tsp

    0.25 oz = 3½ tsp

    1 tsp = 0.07 oz

Grated lemon zest

    1 oz = 4 tbsp

    1 tsp = 0.08 oz

Temperature Calculations for Yeast Doughs

In Chapter 7 (p. 123), a simple formula is presented to enable you to calculate the correct water temperature for a mixed dough of a specified temperature. This formula is sufficient for most straight doughs made in small batches. However, other calculations may sometimes be required. These are detailed here.

Machine Friction

Machine friction depends on many factors, including the type of mixer, amount of dough, stiffness of dough, and mixing time. This friction may be determined for each dough prepared, assuming a constant batch size.

Ice Calculation

If your tap water is warmer than the water temperature you need for a batch of dough, you can cool the water with crushed ice.

A simple formula can be used to calculate how much crushed ice to use.

This formula is based on the fact that it requires 144 BTUs of heat energy to melt 1 pound ice. A BTU (British thermal unit) is the amount of heat needed to raise the temperature of 1 pound water 1°F. Therefore, it takes 144 BTUs to melt 1 pound ice, but only 1 more BTU to heat that pound of melted ice from 32° to 33°F.

You can use the following formula without understanding how it is derived. For those who wish to know where the formula comes from, however, an explanation follows the formula and sample calculation. Please note that this formula is more accurate than many of those you will see elsewhere. Many other formulas allow for the heat energy needed to melt the ice, but don't account for the fact that the melted ice is also warmed up to the final water temperature.

Also, please remember that the ice counts as part of the water for the dough.

PROCEDURE: Determining Machine Friction

1. Prepare a batch of dough, first measuring the room temperature, flour temperature, and water temperature. Add these three figures.

2. Measure the temperature of the dough as it comes from the mixer. Multiply this figure by 3.

3. Subtract the result of step 1 from the result of step 2. This is the machine friction.

4. Use this factor when calculating the water temperature required for subsequent batches of this particular dough, as explained on page 123.

Example:

Room temperature = 72°F
Flour temperature = 65°F
Water temperature = 75°F
Dough temperature = 77°F

1. $72 + 65 + 75 = 212$
2. $77 \times 3 = 231$
3. $231 - 212 = 19$

Machine friction = 19°F

PROCEDURE: Determining Ice Requirement

1. Measure the temperature of the tap water. Subtract the water temperature needed for your dough from the tap water temperature. This number is the temperature decrease needed.

$$\text{Tap water temperature} - \text{Desired water temperature} = \text{Temperature decrease}$$

2. Calculate the weight of ice needed by using the following formula.

$$\text{Ice weight} = \frac{\text{Total water} \times \text{Temperature decrease}}{\text{Tap water temperature} + 112}$$

Total water is the weight of water needed for the dough recipe.

3. Subtract the ice weight from the total water needed to get the weight of the tap water needed.

$$\text{Total water} - \text{Ice} = \text{Tap water}$$

Example: For a batch of bread, you need 16 lb water at 58°F. Your tap water is 65°F. How much tap water, and how much ice should you use?

$$\text{Ice} = \frac{16\text{ lb} \times (65 - 58)}{65 + 112} = \frac{16\text{ lb} \times 7}{177}$$

$$= \frac{112\text{ lb}}{177} = 0.63\text{ lb} = 10\text{ oz}$$

$$\text{Tap water} = 16\text{ lb} - 10\text{ oz} = 15\text{ lb } 6\text{ oz}$$

You need 10 oz ice plus 15 lb 6 oz tap water.

The formula in the Procedure for Determining Ice Requirement is based on the fact that the number of BTUs needed to raise the ice to the desired water temperature equals the number of BTUs lost by the tap water when it is cooled to the desired temperature.

This can be expressed as follows:

$$\left.\begin{array}{l}\text{BTUs to melt ice } plus \\ \text{BTUs to heat melted ice to} \\ \text{desired temperature}\end{array}\right\} = \text{BTUs lost by tap water}$$

Remember, as explained earlier, that 144 BTUs are needed to melt 1 pound ice and that 1 BTU is needed to heat 1 pound water 1°F.

Therefore, the three BTU values in the above equation can each be expressed mathematically:

$$\text{BTUs to melt ice} = \text{Ice weight (in pounds)} \times 144$$

$$\begin{array}{l}\text{BTUs to heat melted ice} \\ \text{to temperature}\end{array} = \begin{array}{l}\text{Ice weight} \times \text{Degrees of} \\ \text{temperature rise}\end{array}$$

or

$$\begin{array}{l}\text{Ice weight} \times (\text{Desired} \\ \text{temperature} - 32°F)\end{array}$$

$$\text{BTUs lost by tap water} = \begin{array}{l}\text{Weight of tap water} \times \text{Degrees of} \\ \text{temperature drop}\end{array}$$

or

$$\begin{array}{l}(\text{Total water} - \text{Ice}) \times (\text{Tap water} \\ \text{temperature} - \text{Desired temperature}\end{array}$$

To make the calculations easier to read, we adopt the following abbreviations. Then we substitute them in our basic equation and proceed to simplify it mathematically.

$$I = \text{Ice weight}$$
$$W = \text{Tap water weight}$$
$$W + I = \text{Total water required in recipe}$$
$$T = \text{Tap water temperature}$$
$$D = \text{Desired temperature}$$

$$\left.\begin{array}{l}\text{BTUs to melt ice } plus \\ \text{BTUs to heat melted ice to} \\ \text{desired temperature}\end{array}\right\} = \text{BTUs lost by tap water}$$

$$(I \times 144) + (I \times (D - 32)) = ((W + I) - I) \times (T - D)$$

$$I \times (144 + D - 32) = ((W + I) \times (T - D)) - (I \times (T - D))$$

$$(I \times (144 + D - 32)) + (I \times (T - D)) = (W + I) \times (T - D)$$

$$I \times (144 + D - 32 + T - D) = (W + I) \times (T - D)$$

$$I \times (112 + T) = (W + I) \times (T - D)$$

$$I = \frac{(W + I) \times (T - D)}{112 + T}$$

$$\text{Ice} = \frac{\text{Total water} \times \text{Temperature decrease}}{\text{Tap water temperature} + 112}$$

Egg Safety

Egg products, including whole, clean, uncracked shell eggs, are sometimes contaminated with *Salmonella enteritidis,* and thus are a potential source of foodborne disease. Egg products should be handled, stored, cooked, and cooled according to the guidelines for potentially hazardous foods, as explained in Chapter 2.

The following guidelines apply primarily to fresh shell eggs. Note in particular that, to be safe, fresh eggs must be cooked until the yolk and white are completely firm. For dishes that include raw or undercooked eggs, always use pasteurized egg products.

Storage

- Per USDA/FSIS, store shell eggs and liquid eggs (eggs removed from their shell) at 40°F (4.4°C) or below, do not freeze.
- Store shell eggs in their case.
- Store away from foods with strong odors (such as fish, apples, cabbage, or onions).
- Rotate—First in/First out.

Handling

- Always wash hands with soap and warm water.
- Take out only as many eggs as are needed for immediate use. Do not stack egg flats (trays) near the grill or stove.
- Use only clean, uncracked eggs.
- Eggs should not be washed before using; they are washed and sanitized before they are packed.
- Use clean, sanitized utensils and equipment.
- Never mix the shell with internal contents of the egg.
- Do not reuse a container (blender, bowl, mixer) after it has had raw egg mixture in it. Clean and sanitize the container thoroughly before using again.
- Never leave egg dishes at room temperature more than one hour (including preparation and service time).

Preparation Guidelines

To ensure food safety, whole eggs should be cooked until the white and yolk are firm. Egg-containing dishes, including quiches and casseroles, should be cooked to an internal temperature of 160°F. Scrambled eggs need to be cooked until firm throughout with no visible liquid egg remaining. Egg white coagulates between 144°F and 149°F and the yolk between 149°F and 158°F. Therefore, it is not necessary to cook eggs until rubbery in order to kill any bacteria that may be present.

- A good rule of thumb is that whole eggs should be cooked until the white and yolk are completely coagulated (set).
- Cook scrambled eggs in small batches no larger than 3 quarts according to rate of service, until firm throughout and there is no visible liquid egg remaining.
- Pooling eggs, the practice of breaking large quantities of eggs together and holding before or after cooking, greatly increases the risk of bacterial growth and contamination.
- Never leave egg or egg-containing dishes at room temperature for more than one hour (including preparation and service time).
- Egg dishes for those who are pregnant, elderly, very young, or ill should be thoroughly cooked. These groups at highest risk should avoid consuming raw or undercooked eggs. Pasteurized egg products are a low-risk alternative for these groups.
- Hold cold egg dishes below 40°F.
- Hold hot egg dishes above 140°F. Do not hold hot foods on buffet line for longer than one hour.
- Always cook eggs and egg dishes before placing on steam table.
- Do not combine eggs that have been held in a steam table pan with a fresh batch of eggs. Always use a fresh steam table pan.
- Do not add raw egg mixture to a batch of cooked scrambled eggs held on a steam table.
- When refrigerating a large quantity of a hot egg-rich dish or leftovers, divide into several shallow containers so it will cool quickly.

Source: Website of the American Egg Board (http://www.aeb.org/foodservice/egg-safety-handling)

Glossary

Many culinary terms in common use are taken from the French. Phonetic guides for difficult-to-pronounce words are included here, using English sounds. However, exact renderings are impossible in many cases because the French language has a number of sounds that do not exist in English.

1-2-3 dough: A pastry dough made of one part sugar, two parts fat, and three parts flour, by weight.

Absorption: The amount of water a flour can take up and hold while being made into a simple dough. Absorption is based on a predetermined standard dough consistency or stiffness; expressed as a percentage of the weight of flour.

Active dry yeast: A dry, granular form of yeast that must normally be rehydrated before using.

Aerobic: Requiring oxygen to live and grow; said of some bacteria.

Air cell: A tiny bubble of air, created by creaming or foaming, that assists in leavening a dough or batter.

Allergen: A substance that triggers an allergic reaction.

All-purpose flour: Flour formulated to be slightly weaker than bread flour so it also can be used for pastries.

Allumette: French for "matchstick"; any puff pastry item made in thin sticks or strips.

Almond paste: A mixture of finely ground almonds and sugar.

Amylase: An enzyme in flour that breaks down starches into simple sugars.

Anaerobic: Requiring an absence of oxygen to live and grow; said of some bacteria.

Anaphylaxis: A sudden and severe allergic reaction of the immune system.

Angel food cake: A type of cake made of meringue (egg whites and sugar) and flour.

Angel food method: A cake-mixing method that involves folding a mixture of flour and sugar into a meringue.

Apple charlotte: A dessert of apples cut up and baked in a mold lined with bread slices.

AP weight: As purchased; the weight of an item before trimming.

Artisan bread: Bread made by a skilled manual worker; usually refers to handmade breads made using traditional methods and with natural ingredients only.

Ash: The mineral content of flour; expressed as a percentage of the total weight.

Autolyse: A resting period early in the mixing procedure of yeast doughs during which the flour fully absorbs the water.

Baba: A type of yeast bread or cake that is soaked in syrup.

Babka: A type of sweet yeast bread or coffee cake.

Bagel: A ring-shaped lean yeast dough product made from a very stiff dough.

Bagged: A cookie makeup method in which the dough is shaped and deposited on the pan or sheet using a pastry bag.

Baked Alaska: A dessert consisting of ice cream on a sponge cake base, covered with meringue and browned in the oven.

Baked custard: A custard that is baked undisturbed so it sets into a solid.

Baked meringue: Any meringue mixture that is baked until dry.

Baker's cheese: A soft, unaged cheese used to make pastry fillings, cheesecake, and similar products.

Baker's percentage: A method of expressing ratios of ingredients in a baking formula in which the weight of each ingredient is expressed as a percentage of the weight of the flour.

Baking ammonia: A leavening ingredient that releases ammonia gas and carbon dioxide.

Baking chocolate: A chocolate product in which another fat is substituted for part of the cocoa butter.

Baklava: A Greek or Middle Eastern dessert made of nuts and phyllo dough and soaked with syrup.

Bar: A cookie makeup method in which the dough is shaped into flattened cylinders, baked, and sliced crosswise into individual cookies; also, a cookie made by this method.

Barm: A thin or batter-like sourdough starter.

Batter: A semiliquid mixture containing flour or other starch, used for the production of such products as cakes and breads and for coating products to be deep fried.

Baumé: A unit of measure indicating the specific gravity of a solution, often used to indicate sugar concentration.

Baumkuchen (BOWM koo khen): A cake made by adding one thin layer of batter at a time to a pan and browning lightly under a broiler after each addition, repeating until the cake is the desired thickness.

Bavarian cream: A light, cold dessert made of gelatin, whipped cream, and custard sauce or fruit.

Bavarois (bah var WAH): French for Bavarian cream.

Beignet soufflé (ben YAY soo FLAY): A type of fritter made with éclair paste, which puffs up greatly when fried.

Benching: An intermediate fermentation and resting period for yeast doughs, after folding and before rounding or preshaping.

Betty: A baked dessert consisting of layers of fruit and cake crumbs.

Biga: A yeast pre-ferment made as a stiff dough.

Biscuit method: A mixing method in which the fat is mixed with the dry ingredients before the liquid ingredients are added.

Black Forest torte: A chocolate sponge layer cake filled with whipped cream and cherries.

Blancmange (blaw MAWNGE): (1) An English pudding made of milk, sugar, and cornstarch. (2) A French dessert made of milk, cream, almonds, and gelatin.

Blitz puff pastry: A type of pastry mixed like a very flaky pie dough, then rolled and folded like puff pastry.

Bloom: (1) A whitish coating on chocolate caused by separated cocoa butter. (2) To hydrate gelatin. (3) The relative strength or gelling power of a grade of gelatin.

Blown sugar: Pulled sugar made into thin-walled, hollow shapes by being blown up like a balloon.

Boiled icing: Italian meringue used as a cake icing.

Bolting: The process of sifting flour, primarily to separate the bran.

Bombe: A type of frozen dessert made in a dome-shaped mold.

Boston cream pie: Not a pie, but a sponge cake or other yellow cake filled with pastry cream and topped with chocolate fondant or confectioners' sugar.

Boulanger (boo lawn ZHAY): The bread baker, who prepares breads and other yeast goods, including such breakfast items as brioche, croissants, and Danish pastry.

Boulanger, A.: An eighteenth-century Parisian credited with starting the first restaurant.

Bran: The hard outer covering of kernels of wheat and other grains.

Bran flour: Flour to which bran flakes have been added.

Bread flour: Strong flour, such as patent flour, used for breads.

Break system: A milling system to produce various grades of flour by repeatedly breaking the grains between rollers, and sifting.

Brioche: Rich yeast dough containing large amounts of eggs and butter; a product made from this dough.

Brix: A unit of measure indicating the sugar concentration of a solution.

Brown sugar: Regular granulated sucrose containing impurities that give it a distinctive flavor and color.

Buttercream: An icing made of butter and/or shortening blended with confectioners' sugar or sugar syrup and, sometimes, other ingredients.

Butterfat: The fat in dairy products. Also called *milk fat*.

Buttermilk: (1) The milky liquid drained off after cream is churned to make butter. Rarely sold. (2) Milk, usually low-fat or fat-free, that has been cultured by bacteria to resemble the original buttermilk (definition 1).

Cabinet pudding: A baked custard containing sponge cake and fruit.

Cake flour: A fine white flour made from soft wheat.

Calorie: The amount of heat needed to raise the temperature of 1 kilogram of water 1 degree Celsius.

Cannoli: Fried Italian pastries made in tube shapes, generally with a sweet cream or cheese filling (singular form: *cannolo*).

Caramelization: The browning of sugars caused by heat.

Caramelize: To change sugar into caramel by means of heat.

Carbohydrate: Any of a group of compounds composed of carbon, hydrogen, and oxygen atoms, including starches and sugars, that supply energy to the body.

Carême, Marie-Antoine: Important and influential nineteenth-century cook and pastry chef.

Carotenoid: An orange-yellow pigments present in many plant products, including unbleached flour; responsible for the creamy color of flour.

Cassata: An Italian-style bombe, usually with three layers of different ice creams, plus a filling of Italian meringue.

Cast sugar: Sugar boiled to the hard-crack stage and then poured into molds to harden. Also called *poured sugar*.

Celiac disease: A reaction to gluten in which the lining of the intestine is damaged.

Celsius scale: The metric system of temperature measurement, with 0°C at the freezing point of water and 100°C at the boiling point of water.

Centi-: Prefix in the metric system meaning *one-hundredth*.

Challah: A rich egg bread, often made as a braided loaf.

Charlotte: (1) A cold dessert made of Bavarian cream or other cream in a special mold, usually lined with ladyfingers or other sponge products. (2) A hot dessert made of cooked fruit and baked in a special mold lined with strips of bread.

Charlotte ring: A metal ring used as a mold for charlottes and other desserts.

Chef de cuisine: The head of a kitchen.

Chef garde manger: Pantry chef.

Chemical leavener: A leavener such as baking soda, baking powder, or baking ammonia, which releases gases produced by chemical reactions.

Chiffon cake: A light cake made by the chiffon method.

Chiffon method: A cake-mixing method that involves the folding of whipped egg whites into a batter made of flour, egg yolks, and oil.

Chiffon pie: A pie with a light, fluffy filling containing egg whites and, usually, gelatin.

Chocolate: Any of a number of products made from fermented, roasted, ground cocoa (or cacao) beans. Often with the addition of sugar, flavorings, and other ingredients.

Chocolate liquor: Unsweetened chocolate, consisting of cocoa solids and cocoa butter. Also called *cocoa mass*.

Chocolate truffle: A small ball of chocolate ganache, served as a confection.

Cholesterol: A fatty substance found in foods derived from animal products and in the human body; a high level of cholesterol has been linked to heart disease.

Christmas pudding: A dark, heavy steamed pudding made of dried and candied fruits, spices, beef suet, and crumbs.

Ciabatta: A type of Italian bread made from a very slack dough deposited on pans with minimal shaping.

Cleanup stage: A stage of yeast dough mixing in which the ingredients become fully incorporated into a dough; so-called because the formed dough "cleans up" formerly unmixed ingredients from the mixing bowl.

Clear flour: A tan-colored wheat flour made from the outer portion of the endosperm.

Coagulation: The process by which proteins become firm, usually when heated.

Coating chocolate: A sweetened chocolate similar in appearance to couverture but with other fats substituted for part of the cocoa butter.

Cobbler: A fruit dessert similar to a pie, but without a bottom crust.

Cocoa: The dry powder that remains after cocoa butter is pressed out of chocolate liquor.

Cocoa bean: Seed of the cacao tree. Fermented, roasted, and ground to make cocoa and chocolate products.

Cocoa butter: A white or yellowish fat found in natural chocolate.

Cocoa mass: Unsweetened chocolate, consisting of cocoa solids and cocoa butter. Also called *chocolate liquor*.

Cold charlotte: A dessert consisting of Bavarian cream made in a mold lined with a sponge-cake product.

Common meringue: Egg whites and sugar whipped to a foam. Also called *French meringue*.

Complex presentation: A dessert plating style consisting of an arrangement of two or more desserts plus sauces and garnishes.

Complex sugar: A large sugar molecule containing at least 12 carbon atoms. Sucrose or table sugar is a complex sugar. *See also* Simple sugar.

Compote: Cooked fruit served in its cooking liquid, usually a sugar syrup.

Compressed yeast: Live, moist yeast, made into dense cakes. Also called *Fresh yeast*.

Conching: A step in the manufacturing of chocolate, the purpose of which is to create a fine, smooth texture.

Condensed milk: Heavily sweetened milk that has had 60% of the water content removed.

Confectioners' chocolate: *See* Couverture.

Confectioners' sugar: Sucrose ground to a fine powder and mixed with a little cornstarch to prevent caking.

Confiseur (cone fee SUR): A confectioner, or candy maker.

Contact method: A decorating technique in which the tip of a paper cone of icing stays in contact with the decorated surface.

Contaminated: Containing a harmful substance not originally present in the food.

Cooked fruit method: A method for making pie fillings in which the fruit is cooked and thickened before being placed in the pie crust.

Cooked juice method: A method for making pie fillings in which the fruit juices are cooked, thickened, and mixed with the fruit.

Cookie: North American name for a small, flat, baked treat, usually containing fat, flour, eggs, and sugar. Known in England and other English-speaking countries as "biscuit."

Cornstarch pudding: A sweetened liquid, usually milk and flavorings, boiled with cornstarch to thicken it.

Corn syrup: A syrup made from corn, consisting mostly of glucose.

Corrective action: In the HACCP system, a procedure that must be followed whenever a critical limit is not met.

Coulis (koo LEE): A sweetened fruit purée, used as a sauce.

Coupe: A dessert consisting of one or two scoops of ice cream or sherbet placed in a dish or glass and topped with any of a number of syrups, fruits, toppings, and garnishes; a sundae.

Couverture: Natural, sweet chocolate containing no added fats other than natural cocoa butter; used for dipping, molding, coating, and similar purposes. Also called *Confectioners chocolate*.

Cracked wheat: A type of wheat meal in which the grains are broken into coarse pieces.

Cream cheese: A soft, fresh cheese with a high milk fat content.

Cream pie: An unbaked pie containing a pastry cream-type filling.

Cream pudding: A boiled pudding made of milk, sugar, eggs, and starch.

Creaming: The process of beating fat and sugar together to blend them uniformly and to incorporate air.

Creaming method: A mixing method that begins with the blending of fat and sugar; used for cakes, cookies, and similar items.

Crème anglaise (krem awn GLEZZ): A light vanilla-flavored custard sauce made of milk, sugar, and egg yolks.

Crème brûlée: French for "burnt cream"; a rich custard with a brittle top crust of caramelized sugar.

Crème caramel: A custard baked in a mold lined with caramelized sugar, then unmolded.

Crème chantilly (krem shawn tee YEE): Sweetened whipped cream flavored with vanilla.

Crème Chiboust (krem shee BOO): A cream filling made of pastry cream, gelatin, meringue, and flavorings.

Crème fraîche (krem fresh): A slightly aged, cultured heavy cream with a slightly tangy flavor.

Crémeux: A type of cream or pudding consisting of crème anglaise plus one or more thickeners or binders, such as chocolate, gelatin, or butter.

Crêpe (krep): A very thin French pancake, often served rolled around a filling.

Crêpes Suzette: French pancakes served in a sweet sauce flavored with orange.

Crisp: (1) A baked fruit dessert with a streusel topping. (2) A confection or garnish consisting of a very thin slice of fruit that has been dried.

Critical control point (CCP): An action that can be taken to eliminate or minimize a food safety hazard.

Croissant (krwa SAWN): A flaky, buttery yeast roll shaped like a crescent and made from a rolled-in dough.

Cross-contamination: The transfer of pathogens to food from another food or from work surfaces or equipment.

Crumb: The interior of a baked item, distinct from the crust.

Crumb crust: A piecrust made of cookie crumbs, butter, and sugar.

Crystallize: To form crystals, as in the case of dissolved sugar.

Cuisinier (kwee zeen YAY): A cook; the head of a kitchen.

Custard: A liquid thickened or set by the coagulation of egg protein.

Dark chocolate: Sweetened chocolate that consists of chocolate liquor and sugar.

Dark couverture: Couverture consisting of chocolate liquor and sugar; contains no milk solids.

Deci-: Prefix in the metric system meaning *one-tenth*.

Décor: Small food items whose primary purpose is decoration.

Décorateur: A pastry chef who specializes or is skilled in decorative work, such as showpieces, sugar work, and fancy cakes.

Degree Celsius: Unit of measure of temperature in the metric system. One degree Celsius is 1/100 of the temperature range between the freezing point and the boiling point of water.

Demerara sugar: A type of crystalline brown sucrose.

Dessert syrup: A flavored sugar syrup used to flavor and moisten cakes and other desserts.

Devil's food cake: A chocolate cake made with a high percentage of baking soda, which gives the cake a reddish color.

Diastase: Various enzymes found in flour and in diastatic malt that convert starch into sugar.

Disaccharide: A complex or double sugar, such as sucrose.

Dobos torte: A Hungarian cake made of seven thin layers, filled with chocolate buttercream, and topped with caramelized sugar.

Docking: Piercing or perforating pastry dough before baking in order to allow steam to escape and to avoid blistering.

Double-acting baking powder: Baking powder that releases some of its gases when it is mixed with water and the remaining gases when it is heated.

Double-panning: Placing a baking sheet or pan on or in a second pan to prevent scorching the bottom of the product being baked.

Dough conditioner: Any of a variety of ingredients added by the baker during production of yeast products to improve gluten development, aid yeast fermentation, and delay staling. Also called *dough improver*.

Dough relaxation: A period of rest in the production of yeast dough during which gluten strands become adjusted to their new length and become less tight.

Dough strength: An indication of the texture and gluten development of a yeast dough; a combination of elasticity, tenacity, and extensibility.

Drained weight: The weight of solid canned fruit after draining off the juice.

Dredge: To sprinkle or coat thoroughly with sugar or another dry powder.

Dried whole milk: A powdered form of whole milk with the water content removed.

Drop batter: A batter that is too thick to pour but will drop from a spoon in lumps.

Dropped: A cookie makeup method in which portions of dough are measured with a scoop or spoon and dropped onto a baking pan.

Drop-string method: A decorating technique in which the tip of a paper cone of icing stays above the decorated surface and the icing drops as a string onto the surface. Also used to suspend strings of icing between two points.

Durum flour: Flour made from durum wheat, a high-gluten wheat, and used primarily to make spaghetti and other dried pasta.

Dutch process cocoa or dutched cocoa: Cocoa processed with an alkali to reduce its acidity.

Éclair: A cylindrical piece of baked éclair paste with a pastry cream filling.

Éclair paste: A paste or dough made of boiling water or milk, butter, flour, and eggs; used to make éclairs, cream puffs, and similar products.

Egg-foam cake: A cake leavened primarily by whipped eggs; it usually has a low percentage of fat.

Elasticity: The ability of a dough to spring back when it is stretched.

Empty calorie: A food that provides few nutrients per calorie.

Emulsified shortening: Shortening containing emulsifiers and used for high-ratio cakes.

Emulsion: A uniform mixture of two or more normally unmixable substances.

Endosperm: The starchy inner portion of grain kernels.

English muffin: A yeast dough product made in the shape of a disk and cooked on a griddle.

Enriched flour: Flour to which vitamins and minerals are added to compensate for the nutrients lost when the bran and germ are removed.

EP weight: Edible portion; the weight of an item after trimming.

Escoffier, Georges-August: Most important chef of late nineteenth and early twentieth century; organized cooking principles and kitchen hierarchy.

Evaporated milk: Milk, either whole or skim, that has had 60% of the water removed.

Extensibility: The ability of a dough to be stretched.

Extract: A flavoring ingredient consisting of flavorful oils or other substances dissolved in alcohol.

Extraction: The portion of the grain kernel separated into a particular grade of flour. Usually expressed as a percentage.

Facultative: Able to live and grow with or without the presence of oxygen; said of some bacteria.

Fat: Any of a group of compounds consisting of chains of fatty acids that supply energy to the body in a concentrated form.

Fermentation: The process by which yeast changes carbohydrates into carbon dioxide gas and alcohol.

Fiber: A type of complex carbohydrate that is not absorbed by the body but is necessary for the proper functioning of the digestive system.

Final development stage: The stage of yeast dough mixing in which gluten becomes smooth and elastic.

Flaky piecrust: A piecrust that has a flaky texture due to layers of fat sandwiched between layers of dough.

Flaky pie dough: A pie dough that has a flaky texture when baked. *See* Flaky piecrust.

Flat icing: A simple icing made of confectioners' sugar and water, usually used for Danish pastries and sweet rolls.

Flooding: Covering a plate, or a portion of a plate, with sauce.

Flour-batter method: A cake-mixing method in which the flour is first mixed with the fat.

Flow of food: The path food travels in a food service operation, from receiving to serving.

Foaming: The process of whipping eggs, with or without sugar, to incorporate air.

Focaccia: A flat Italian bread similar to a thick pizza dough.

Fondant: A type of icing made of boiled sugar syrup that is agitated so it crystallizes into a mass of extremely small white crystals.

Food Danger Zone: The temperature range of 40° to 140°F (4.5° to 60°C), in which bacteria grow rapidly.

Food intolerance: A nonallergic reaction to a food that may be characterized by any of a variety of undesirable symptoms.

Formula: A set of ingredients and quantities and, usually, instructions for preparing a bakery product; a baker's recipe.

Fortified nonfat or low-fat milk: Milk that has had all or part of the fat removed and that contains added substances, such as vitamins A and D, that increase its nutritional value.

Fougasse: A regional French bread made in the shape of a trellis or ladder.

Four-fold: A technique used to increase the number of layers in puff pastry or Danish pastry by folding the dough in fourths.

Frangipane: A type of almond-flavored cream.

French bread: Any of a variety of crisp-crusted yeast breads usually consisting only of flour, water, yeast, and salt.

French doughnut: A fried pastry made of choux paste.

French meringue: Egg whites and sugar whipped to a foam; also called *common meringue.*

French pastry: Any of a variety of small fancy cakes and other pastries, usually in single-portion sizes.

French-style ice cream: Ice cream containing egg yolks.

Fresh yeast: *See* Compressed yeast.

Fritter: A deep-fried item made of or coated with a batter or dough.

Frozen mousse: A still-frozen dessert containing whipped cream.

Frozen soufflé: A frozen mousse served in a soufflé dish or ramekin so that it resembles a baked soufflé.

Frozen yogurt: A frozen dessert similar to ice cream but made with yogurt instead of or in addition to milk.

Fruit cake: A loaf cake containing a high percentage of dried and candied fruits and, usually, nuts.

Fruit gratin: A dessert consisting of fruit plus a topping, browned under a broiler.

Fruit pie: A baked single- or double-crust pie with a fruit filling.

Fruit torte: A layer cake topped with a decorative arrangement of fruit.

Fungus: A class of organisms that includes yeasts, molds, and mushrooms.

Fusion cuisine: The use of techniques and ingredients from more than one regional cuisine in a single dish.

Ganache (gah NAHSH): A rich cream made of sweet chocolate and heavy cream.

Garnish: An edible item added to another food as a decoration or accompaniment.

Gâteau (gah tow): French word for "cake."

Gâteau St-Honoré: A pastry consisting of a base made of short pastry and pâte à choux and a cream filling, usually crème Chiboust or crème diplomat.

Gaufre (GO fr): French for "waffle."

Gelatin: A water-soluble protein extracted from animal tissue; used as a jelling agent.

Gelatinization: The process by which starch granules absorb water and swell in size.

Gelato: Italian ice cream.

Gelée (zhuh LAY): (1) A liquid thickened with gelatin. (2) Any other kind of jelly, especially one set with pectin.

Genoise: A sponge cake made by whipping whole eggs with sugar and folding in flour and, sometimes, melted butter.

Germ: The plant embryo portion of a grain kernel.

Glacé (glah SAY): (1) Glazed; coated with icing; (2) frozen.

Glacier (glah see YAY): A chef whose specialty is ice cream.

Glaze: (1) n. A shiny coating, such as a syrup, applied to a food. (2) v. To make a food shiny or glossy by coating it with a glaze or by browning it under a broiler or in a hot oven.

Gliadin: A protein in wheat flour that combines with another protein, glutenin, to form gluten.

Glucose: A simple sugar available in the form of a clear, colorless, tasteless syrup.

Gluten: An elastic substance formed from proteins present in wheat flours that gives structure and strength to baked goods.

Glutenin: *See* Gliadin.

Gluten window: A thin membrane of yeast dough made in order to test gluten development.

Gram: The basic unit of weight in the metric system; equal to about one-thirtieth of an ounce.

Granita: Italian equivalent of the French term Granité.

Granité (grah nee TAY): A coarse, crystalline frozen dessert made of water, sugar, and fruit juice or another flavoring.

Granulated sugar: Sucrose in a fine crystalline form.

Gum paste: A type of sugar paste or pastillage made with vegetable gum.

HACCP: Hazard Analysis Critical Control Points. HACCP is a food safety system of self-inspection designed to highlight hazardous foods and to ensure proper food handling, by identifying, monitoring, and controlling dangers of food contamination.

Half-and-half: A kind of high-fat milk or low-fat cream containing 10 to 18% milk fat.

Hard meringue: A meringue baked until crisp.

Hard sauce: A flavored mixture of confectioners' sugar and butter; often served with steamed puddings.

Hard wheat: Wheat high in protein.

Hazard: A potentially dangerous food condition caused by contamination, growth of pathogens, survival of pathogens, or presence of toxins.

Head baker: The professional in charge of staff and production in a bakery.

Hearth bread: A bread baked directly on the bottom of the oven, not in a pan.

Heavy pack: A type of canned fruit or vegetable with very little added water or juice.

High-fat cake: A cake with a high percentage of fat; distinguished from a sponge or egg-foam cake.

High-ratio method: *See* Two-stage method.

High-ratio: (1) Term referring to cakes and cake formulas mixed by a special method and containing more sugar than flour. (2) The mixing method used for these cakes. (3) Term referring to certain specially formulated ingredients used in these cakes, such as shortening.

Homogenized milk: Milk processed so the cream does not separate out.

Hot milk and butter sponge: A sponge cake batter in which a mixture of warm milk and melted butter is mixed into the batter.

Hydration: The process of absorbing water.

Hydrogenation: A process that converts liquid oils to solid fats (shortenings) by chemically bonding hydrogen to the fat molecules.

Ice cream: A churn-frozen mixture of milk, cream, sugar, flavorings, and, sometimes, eggs.

Ice milk: A frozen dessert similar to ice cream, but with a lower fat content.

Icebox: A cookie makeup method in which the dough is shaped into cylinders, refrigerated until firm, and then sliced.

Ice: A frozen dessert made of water, sugar, and fruit juice.

Icing comb: A plastic triangle with toothed or serrated edges; used for texturing icings.

Icing screen: A screen on which cakes are set when iced or glazed, allowing excess to run off.

Improved mix: A yeast dough mixing technique that combines a medium mixing period with a medium fermentation period.

Initial development stage: The first part of the development stage of mixing yeast doughs, in which the dough still appears rough and undermixed.

Instant dry yeast: A dry, granular yeast product that does not require hydration before being added to doughs.

Instant starch: A starch that thickens a liquid without cooking because it has been precooked.

Intensive mix: A yeast dough mixing technique that combines a long mixing period with a short fermentation period.

Inversion: A chemical process in which a double sugar splits into two simple sugars.

Invert sugar: A mixture of two simple sugars, dextrose and levulose, resulting from the breakdown of sucrose.

Isomalt: A compound derived from sucrose, used as a dietary sugar substitute and as an alternative to sugar in decorative sugar work.

Italian meringue: A meringue made by whipping a boiling syrup into egg whites.

Jalebi: A type of Indian dessert made of deep-fried batter soaked in syrup.

Japonaise (zhah po nez): A baked meringue flavored with nuts.

Kernel paste: A nut paste, similar to almond paste, made of apricot kernels and sugar.

Kilo-: Prefix in the metric system meaning *one thousand*.

Kirsch: A clear alcoholic beverage distilled from cherries.

Kirsch torte: A torte made of genoise, meringue disks, and buttercream, and flavored with kirsch.

Kugelhopf: A type of rich, sweet bread or coffee cake, usually made in a tube-type pan.

Lactobacilli: A group of bacteria primarily responsible for producing the acidity in sourdough starters.

Lacto-ovo-vegetarian: A vegetarian diet that allows dairy products and eggs.

Lactose: A form of sugar naturally present in milk.

Lacto-vegetarian: A vegetarian diet that allows milk and other dairy products.

Ladyfinger: A small, dry, finger-shaped sponge cake or cookie.

Lag phase: A period after bacteria have been introduced to a new environment and before they begin to grow and reproduce.

Laminated dough: A dough consisting of many alternating layers of dough and butter or other fat.

Langue de chat (lawng duh SHAH): A thin, crisp cookie. The French name means "cat's tongue," referring to the shape of the cookie.

Lattice crust: A top crust for a pie made of strips of pastry in a crisscross pattern.

Lean dough: A dough low in fat and sugar.

Leavening: The production or incorporation of gases in a baked product to increase volume and to produce shape and texture.

Lecithin: An emulsifier usually derived from soybeans.

Levain: Sourdough starter.

Levain-levure: French for yeast pre-ferment.

Levure: Commercial yeast.

Light cream: Cream with a fat content of 18 to 30%.

Linzertorte: A tart made of raspberry jam and a short dough containing nuts and spices.

Lipid: Any of a group of compounds containing fats and cholesterol.

Liquid levain: A thin or batter-like sourdough starter.

Liter: The basic unit of volume in the metric system; equal to slightly more than 1 quart.

Long-fermentation dough: A yeast dough that requires a long fermentation period.

Low-fat milk: Milk with a fat content of 0.5 to 2%.

Macaron: French spelling for macaroon, usually referring to a particular style of almond-paste cookie.

Macaroon: A cookie made of eggs (usually whites) and almond powder, almond paste, or coconut.

Maillard reaction: A chemical reaction that causes the browning of proteins and sugars together when subjected to heat.

Malt syrup: A type of syrup containing maltose sugar, extracted from sprouted barley.

Marble: To partly mix two colors of cake batter or icing so the colors are in decorative swirls.

Margarine: An artificial butter product made of hydrogenated fats and flavorings.

Marron: French for "chestnut."

Marshmallow: A light confection, icing, or filling made of meringue and gelatin (or other stabilizers).

Marshmallow icing: Boiled icing with the addition of gelatin.

Marzipan: A paste or confection made of almonds and sugar and often used for decorative work.

Mature (dough): The ideal stage of development for a yeast dough.

Mature (fruit): Fruit that has completed its development and is physiologically capable of continuing the ripening process, even after removal from the plant.

Maza: An early type of bread; cakes of grain paste baked by the ancient Greeks.

Meal: Coarsely ground grain.

Mealy piecrust: A piecrust in which the fat has been mixed in thoroughly enough so the dough does not have a flaky texture.

Mealy pie dough: A pie dough that has a mealy texture when baked. *See* Mealy piecrust.

Melba sauce: A sweet sauce made of puréed raspberries and, sometimes, red currants.

Meringue: A thick, white foam made of whipped egg whites and sugar.

Meringue chantilly (shawn tee YEE): Baked meringue filled with whipped cream.

Meringue glacée: Baked meringue filled with ice cream.

Meter: The basic unit of length in the metric system; slightly longer than 1 yard.

Metric system: A measurement system based entirely on decimals.

Microorganism: A life form, such as bacteria, too small to be seen without a microscope.

Milk chocolate: Sweetened chocolate containing milk solids.

Milk chocolate couverture: Couverture consisting of chocolate liquor, sugar, and milk solids.

Milk fat: The fat content of milk; also called *butterfat*.

Millefeuille (mee foy): French term for napoleon; literally, "thousand leaves." Also used for various layered desserts.

Milli-: Prefix in the metric system meaning *one-thousandth*.

Mineral: An inorganic element, such as calcium, iron, potassium, sodium, or zinc, that is essential to nutrition.

Mixed fermentation: A type of yeast dough fermentation utilizing both a pre-ferment or sour starter and a commercial yeast.

Modeling chocolate: A thick paste made of chocolate and glucose that can be molded by hand into decorative shapes.

Modified straight dough method: A mixing method similar to the straight dough method, except the fat and sugar are mixed together first to ensure uniform distribution. Used for rich doughs.

Molasses: A heavy brown syrup made from sugarcane.

Molded: A cookie makeup method in which the dough is shaped into cylinders, cut into equal portions, and shaped as desired.

Monosaccharide: A simple or single sugar such as glucose and fructose.

Monounsaturated fat: A type of fat, normally liquid at room temperature, that contains one double bond in its carbon chain.

Mousse: A soft or creamy dessert made light by the addition of whipped cream, egg whites, or both.

Muffin method: A mixing method in which the mixed dry ingredients are combined with the mixed liquid ingredients.

Napoleon: A dessert made of layers of puff pastry filled with pastry cream.

Natural sour: *See* Sourdough starter.

Natural starter: *See* Sourdough starter.

Net weight: The weight of the total contents of a can or package.

Nonfat milk: Milk with all the fat removed.

Nonfat dried milk: Fat-free milk with all the moisture removed.

No-time dough: A bread dough made with a large quantity of yeast and given no fermentation time, except for a short rest after mixing.

Nougatine: A mixture of caramelized sugar and almonds or other nuts, used in decorative work and as a confection and flavoring.

Nouvelle cuisine: Important cooking style of the 1960s and 1970s, known for lighter flavors and elaborate plating styles.

Nutrient: A substance essential for the functioning or growth of an organism.

Nutrient density: The quantity of nutrients per calorie.

Oil: A liquid fat.

Old dough: A dough that is overfermented.

One-stage method: (1) A cookie-mixing method in which all ingredients are added to the bowl at once. (2) A cake-mixing method in which all the ingredients, including high-ratio liquid shortening, are mixed together at once.

Opera cake: A layer cake made of thin sponge layers, coffee-flavored buttercream, and chocolate ganache.

Opson: In ancient Greece, any food eaten with bread.

Osmotolerant yeast: A type of yeast that can remain active even in a high concentration of sugar. Used for sweet doughs.

Outlining: Drawing shapes on a plate with chocolate or a thick sauce prior to filling in the spaces in those shapes with one or more sauces.

Oven spring: The rapid rise of yeast goods in the oven due to the production and expansion of trapped gases caused by the oven heat.

Overrun: The increase in volume of ice cream or frozen desserts caused by the incorporation of air while freezing.

Ovo-vegetarian: Referring to a vegetarian diet that allows eggs.

Oxidation: The process that occurs when oxygen reacts with other compounds or elements. In the bakeshop, it usually refers to oxidation of components of flour during mixing.

Pain d'épice (pan day peece): French for "spice bread." A type of gingerbread.

Pain de campagne: French country-style bread.

Palmier (palm yay): A small pastry or petit four sec made of rolled, sugared puff pastry cut into slices and baked.

Panettone: An Italian sweet bread made in a large loaf, generally containing dried and candied fruits.

Panna cotta: An Italian pudding made of cream, gelatin, and flavorings; literally, "cooked cream."

Paper cone: A tool made of parchment paper formed into a cone and filled with icing, sauce, or other semi-liquid. Used for decorative work.

Parasite: An organism that can survive only by living on, with, or inside another organism.

Parfait: (1) A type of sundae served in a tall, thin glass. (2) A still-frozen dessert made of egg yolks, syrup, and heavy cream.

Paris-Brest: A dessert consisting of a ring of baked éclair paste filled with cream.

Pasteurize: To heat-treat substances, such as milk, to kill bacteria that might cause disease or spoilage.

Pastillage (pahs tee yahzh): A sugar paste used for decorative work, which becomes very hard when dry.

Pastry cream: A thick custard sauce containing eggs and starch.

Pastry flour: A weak flour used for pastries and cookies.

Pastry method: A mixing method in which the fat is mixed with the dry ingredients before the liquid ingredients are added. Also called *Biscuit method*.

Pâte à choux (paht ah shoo): Éclair paste.

Pâte brisée: A type of rich pastry dough used primarily for tarts.

Pâte fermentée: Fermented dough, used as a starter for yeast breads.

Pâte feuilleté (PAHT fuh yuh TAY): French name for puff pastry.

Pâte sablée: A rich, crumbly pastry dough high in fat. Also called *short dough*.

Pâte sucrée: A type of pastry dough similar to pâte brisée but higher in sugar.

Patent flour: A fine grade of wheat flour milled from the inner portions of the kernel.

Pathogen: A disease-causing microorganism.

Pâtissier (pah tis YAY): A pastry chef.

Peasant tart: A baked tart with a custard filling containing prunes.

Pectin: A soluble plant fiber, used primarily as a jelling agent for fruit preserves and jams.

Peel: A flat wooden shovel used to place hearth breads in an oven and to remove them.

Pentosan: A category of carbohydrate gums present in wheat flour and having strong water absorption capability.

Petit four (p'tee foor): A delicate cake, pastry, cookie, or confection small enough to be eaten in one or two bites.

Petit four glacé: An iced or cream-filled petit four.

Petit four sec: An un-iced or unfilled petit four (*sec* means "dry"), such as a small butter cookie or palmier.

pH: A measure of the acidity or alkalinity of a substance.

Philadelphia-style ice cream: Ice cream containing no eggs.

Phyllo (FEE lo) dough: A paper-thin dough or pastry used to make strudels and various Middle Eastern and Greek desserts. Also spelled *filo* or *fillo*.

Pickup stage: The first stage of yeast dough mixing, in which the loose dry ingredients are gradually picked up and incorporated into the developing dough.

Piping jelly: A transparent, sweet jelly used for decorating cakes.

Pithiviers (pee tee vyay): A cake made of puff pastry filled with almond cream.

Plant toxin: Any poison naturally present in plants.

Poissonier: The station chef in charge of fish preparation.

Polyunsaturated fat: A type of fat, normally liquid at room temperature, that contains more than one double bond in its carbon chain.

Poolish: A thin yeast starter made with equal parts flour and water, plus commercial yeast.

Pot de crème (poh duh krem): A rich baked custard.

Pound cake: (1) A cake made of equal weights of flour, butter, sugar, and eggs; (2) any cake resembling this.

Pour batter: A batter thin or liquid enough to pour. *See also* Drop batter.

Poured fondant: *See* Fondant.

Poured sugar: Sugar boiled to the hard-crack stage and then poured into molds to harden. Also called *cast sugar*.

Praline: A confection or flavoring made of nuts and caramelized sugar.

Pre-ferment: A fermented dough or batter used to provide leavening for a larger batch of dough.

Press: A scaled piece of dough divided into small, equal units in a dough divider.

Profiterole: A small puff made of éclair paste. Often filled with ice cream and served with chocolate sauce.

Proofing: Fermenting made-up yeast products to increase their volume and lighten their texture before baking.

Protein: Any of a group of nutrients essential for growth, building body tissue, and basic body functions, and that can also be used for energy if the diet does not contain enough carbohydrates and fats.

Puff pastry: A very light, flaky pastry made from a rolled-in dough and leavened by steam.

Pulled sugar: Sugar boiled to the hard-crack stage, allowed to harden slightly, then pulled or stretched until it develops a pearly sheen.

Pullman loaf: A long, rectangular loaf of bread.

Pumpernickel flour: A coarse, flaky meal made from whole rye grains.

Punching: A method of expelling gases from fermented dough.

Purée: A food made into a smooth pulp, usually by being ground or forced through a sieve.

Quenelle (kuh NELL): A small oval portion of food.

Recipe: A set of instructions, including ingredients and quantities, for preparing a certain dish. *See also* Formula.

Regular shortening: Any basic shortening without emulsifiers, used for creaming methods and for icings.

Retarder-proofer: An automated, timer-controlled combination of retarder/freezer and proofer, used for holding and proofing yeast products.

Retarding: Refrigerating a yeast dough to slow its fermentation.

Reversed puff pastry: A type of puff pastry made with the dough enclosed between layers of butter.

Ribbon sponge: A thin sponge cake layer with a decorative design made of stencil paste.

Rice condé: A thick, molded rice pudding, usually topped with fruit.

Rice impératrice: A rich rice pudding containing whipped cream, candied fruits, and gelatin.

Rich dough: A dough high in fat, sugar, and/or eggs.

Ripe (fruit): Fruit that is at its peak of texture, flavor, and sweetness, and ready to be consumed.

Rolled: A cookie makeup method in which the dough is rolled out into a sheet and cut into shapes with cookie cutters.

Rolled fondant: A dough-like sugar product with the texture of a stiff dough. Rolled into thin sheets and used to cover cakes.

Rolled-in dough: Dough in which a fat has been incorporated in many layers using a rolling and folding procedure.

Roller milling: A process of milling wheat into flour that involves repeatedly cracking and sifting the grain.

Rôtisseur (ro tee sur): Roast cook or meat cook.

Rounding: A method of molding a piece of dough into a round ball with a smooth surface or skin.

Royal icing: A form of icing made of confectioners' sugar and egg whites; used for decorating.

Rye blend: A mixture of rye flour and hard wheat flour.

Rye flour: Rye grain milled into a flour.

Rye meal: Coarse rye flour.

Sabayon: A foamy dessert or sauce made of egg yolks whipped with wine or liqueur.

Sablage: *See* Sanding method.

Sachertorte: A rich chocolate cake from Vienna.

Sacristain (sak ree stan): A small pastry made of a twisted strip of puff paste coated with nuts and sugar.

Sanding method: A pastry- and cookie-mixing method involving blending the fat with the dry ingredients and then adding in egg.

Saturated fat: A fat that is normally solid at room temperature.

Saucier: The station chef who prepares sauces and stews and sautés foods to order.

Savarin: A type of yeast bread or cake soaked in syrup.

Scaling: Weighing, usually ingredients, doughs, or batters.

Scone: A type of biscuit or biscuitlike bread.

Scone flour: A mixture of flour and baking powder used when very small quantities of baking powder are needed.

Seeding: A technique for tempering chocolate by adding grated tempered chocolate to melted chocolate to cool it.

Self-rising flour: White flour to which baking powder and, sometimes, salt has been added.

Sfogliatelle (SFO lee ah TELL eh): A southern Italian flaky turnover pastry with a sweet cheese filling.

Sheet: A cookie makeup method in which the dough is baked in sheets and then cut into portions.

Sherbet: A frozen dessert made of water, sugar, fruit juice, and, sometimes, milk or cream.

Short: Having a high fat content, which makes the product (such as a cookie or pastry) very crumbly and tender.

Shortbread: A crisp cookie made of butter, sugar, and flour.

Short dough: A pastry dough, similar to a basic cookie dough, made of flour, sugar, and fat. *See also* Short.

Shortening: (1) Any fat used in baking to tenderize the product by shortening gluten strands. (2) A white, tasteless, solid fat formulated for baking or deep frying.

Short-fermentation straight dough: A yeast dough, usually with a high percentage of yeast, that is fermented for only a short time before being made up and baked.

Short mix: A yeast dough mixing technique combining a short mixing period with long fermentation.

Simple fold: One part of the procedure for making Danish and croissant dough, which requires folding the dough in thirds. Also called *three-fold*.

Simple presentation: A style of plating a dessert consisting of a portion of one dessert plus optional sauces and garnishes.

Simple sugar: A sugar with the simplest or smallest possible molecule, containing 6 carbon atoms. Glucose is a simple sugar.

Simple syrup: A syrup consisting of sucrose and water in varying proportions.

Single-acting baking powder: Baking powder that releases gases as soon as it is mixed with water.

Skim milk: Milk with all the fat removed.

Sodium bicarbonate: Baking soda; a chemical that releases carbon dioxide gas when combined with an acid.

Soft meringue: The type of meringue traditionally used for pie toppings; usually with a low percentage of sugar.

Soft pie: A single-crust pie with a custard-type filling—that is, a filling that sets or coagulates due to its egg content.

Soft wheat: Wheat low in protein.

Solid pack: A type of canned fruit or vegetable with no water added.

Sorbet (sor BAY): French for "sherbet."

Sorbetto: Italian for "sherbet."

Soufflé: (1) A baked dish containing whipped egg whites, which cause the dish to rise during baking. (2) A still-frozen dessert made in a soufflé dish so it resembles a baked soufflé.

Sour: Sourdough starter.

Sour cream: A cream, usually with about 18% milk fat, that has been fermented by bacteria until thick.

Sourdough: A dough leavened by a sourdough starter.

Sourdough starter: A dough or batter that contains wild yeasts and bacteria, has a noticeable acidity as a result of fermentation by these organisms, and is used to leaven other doughs.

Sous chef: The station chef who assists the executive chef and is directly in charge of the cooking during production.

Sponge: A batter or dough of yeast, flour, and water that is allowed to ferment and is then mixed with more flour and other ingredients to make a bread dough.

Sponge cake: A type of cake made by whipping eggs and sugar to a foam, then folding in flour.

Sponge method: A cake- and cookie-mixing method based on whipped eggs and sugar.

Sponge roll: *See* Swiss roll.

Spread: The tendency of a cookie to expand and flatten out when baked.

Spun sugar: Boiled sugar made into long, thin threads by dipping wires into the sugar syrup and waving them so the sugar falls off in fine streams.

Staling: The change in texture and aroma of baked goods due to the loss of moisture by the starch granules.

Standardized formula: A set of instructions describing the way a particular establishment prepares a certain baked item.

Starch retrogradation: A chemical change of starch molecules that is responsible for staling.

Stencil: A pattern or design cut from plastic or cardboard, used for depositing batter for thin cookies made in decorative shapes.

Stencil paste: A type of thin cookie or wafer dough used to make cookies in decorative shapes; also used to make decorative patterns in ribbon sponge.

St-Honoré: (1) A dessert made of a ring of cream puffs set on a short dough base and filled with a type of pastry cream; (2) the cream used to fill this dessert, made of pastry cream and whipped egg whites.

Stirred custard: A custard stirred while it is cooked so it thickens but does not set.

Stollen: A type of sweet yeast bread with fruit.

Straight dough method: A mixing method for yeast goods in which all ingredients are mixed together at once.

Straight flour: Flour made from the entire wheat kernel minus the bran and germ.

Stream: The portion of flour that is separated in any one of the stages in the roller-milling of grain.

Streusel (STROY sel): A crumbly topping for baked goods, consisting of fat, sugar, and flour rubbed together.

String work: The production of decorative icing designs using a paper cone; *see* drop-string method.

Strong flour: Flour with a high protein content.

Strudel: A baked item consisting of a filling rolled up in a sheet of strudel dough or phyllo dough.

Strudel dough: A type of dough that is stretched until paper-thin.

Sucralose: A type of synthetic sweetener derived from sucrose.

Sucrose: The chemical name for regular granulated sugar and confectioners' sugar.

Sugar cage: A lacy dome of hard or caramelized sugar.

Sundae: A dessert consisting of ice cream in a dish, with various sauces and toppings.

Swiss meringue: Egg whites and sugar warmed, usually over hot water, and then whipped to a foam.

Swiss roll: A thin sponge cake layer spread with a filling and rolled up.

Syrup: One or more types of sugar dissolved in water, often with small amounts of other compounds or impurities that give the syrup flavor.

Syrup pack: A type of canned fruit containing sugar syrup.

Tablage: A technique for tempering chocolate by cooling it on a marble slab.

Tart: A flat, baked item consisting of a pastry and a sweet or savory topping or filling; similar to a pie but usually thinner.

Tarte Tatin: An upside-down apple tart.

Tempering: The process of melting and cooling chocolate to a specific temperature to prepare it for dipping, coating, or molding.

Tenacity: The resistance of a dough to being stretched.

Three-fold: A technique used to increase the number of layers in puff pastry or Danish pastry by folding the dough in thirds.

Tiramisù: An Italian dessert made of ladyfinger sponge, flavored with espresso coffee and a creamy cheese filling.

Torte: German for various types of cakes, usually layer cakes.

Trans fat: A solid fat, usually manufactured by hydrogenation, that limits the body's ability to rid itself of cholesterol.

Tulipe: A thin, crisp cookie molded into a cup shape.

Tunneling: A condition of muffin products characterized by large, elongated holes; caused by overmixing.

Turntable: A pedestal with a flat, rotating top, used for holding cakes while they are being decorated.

Two-stage method: A cake-mixing method that begins with the blending of flour and high-ratio shortening and is followed by the addition of liquids. Also called the *high-ratio method*.

UHT pasteurization: Ultra Heat Treated or Ultra High Temperature pasteurization. Subjection to a relatively high heat for a defined period in order to kill microorganisms and extend shelf life.

Ultrapasteurized: *See* UHT pasteurization.

Unsaturated fat: A fat that is normally liquid at room temperature.

Vacherin (vahsh er ran): A crisp meringue shell filled with cream, fruits, or other items.

Vegan: A vegetarian diet that excludes all animal products, including dairy products and eggs.

Virus: An extremely small microorganism, smaller than bacteria, responsible for a variety of diseases.

Vital wheat gluten: Wheat gluten in a concentrated form, usually about 75% by weight, added to flour to improve the quality of yeast-raised doughs.

Vitamin: Any of a group of compounds that are present in foods in very small quantities and are necessary for regulating body functions.

Wash: (1) n. A liquid brushed onto the surface of a product, usually before baking. (2) v. To apply such a liquid.

Water hardness: The mineral content of water.

Water pack: A type of canned fruit or vegetable containing the water used to process the item.

Weak flour: Flour with a low protein content.

Whipping cream: Cream with a high enough fat content, usually above 30%, to enable it to be whipped into a foam.

White couverture: A confection consisting of cocoa butter, milk solids, and sugar. Sometimes erroneously called white chocolate.

Whole milk: Milk with 3.5% fat content.

Whole wheat flour: Flour made by grinding the entire wheat kernel, including the bran and germ.

Yeast pre-ferment: A dough or batter fermented with commercial yeast and used to provide leavening for a larger batch of dough.

Yeast starter: Another name for yeast pre-ferment.

Yogurt: Milk cultured with special bacteria until thick.

Young dough: A dough that is underfermented.

Zabaglione: An Italian dessert or sauce made of whipped egg yolks and Marsala wine.

Zest: The colored outer portion of the peel of citrus fruits.

Bibliography

Amendola, Joseph, and Nicole Rees. *The Baker's Manual*, 5th ed. Hoboken, NJ: John Wiley & Sons, 2003.

——. *Understanding Baking,* 3rd ed. Hoboken, NJ: John Wiley & Sons, 2003.

Bilheux, Roland, et al. *Special and Decorative Breads*. 2 vols. New York: John Wiley & Sons, 1989.

Bilheux, Roland, and Alain Escoffier. *Professional French Pastry Series*. 4 vols. New York: John Wiley & Sons, 1988.

Boyle, Peter T. *Sugar Work*. New York: John Wiley & Sons, 1988.

Boyle, Tish, and Timothy Moriarty. *Grand Finales: The Art of the Plated Dessert*. New York: John Wiley & Sons, 1997.

——. *Grand Finales: A Neoclassic View of Plated Desserts*. New York: John Wiley & Sons, 2000.

Bundy, Ariana. *Sweet Alternative*. North Vancouver, BC: Whitecap Books, 2005.

Clayton, Bernard. *The Breads of France*. Indianapolis: Bobbs-Merrill, 1978.

——. *Bernard Clayton's New Complete Book of Breads*. New York: Fireside, 1995.

Coppedge, Richard J. Jr. *Baking for Special Diets*. Hoboken, NJ: John Wiley & Sons, 2017.

Culinary Institute of America. *Baking and Pastry*, 3rd ed. Hoboken, NJ: John Wiley & Sons, 2016.

Daley, Regan. *In the Sweet Kitchen*. New York: Artisan, 2001.

DiMuzio, Daniel T. *Bread Baking: An Artisan's Perspective*. Hoboken, NJ: John Wiley & Sons, 2010.

Duchene, Laurent, and Bridget Jones. *Le Cordon Bleu Dessert Techniques*. New York: William Morrow, 1999.

Eagan, Maureen, and Susan Davis Allen. *Healthful Quantity Baking*. New York: John Wiley & Sons, 1992.

Escoffier, A. *The Escoffier Cook Book*. New York: Crown, 1969.

Fance, Wilfred J., ed. *The New International Confectioner*, 5th ed. London: Virtue & Co., 1981.

Felder, Amy. *Savory Sweets: From Ingredients to Plated Desserts*. Hoboken, NJ: John Wiley & Sons, 2008.

Figoni, Paula. *How Baking Works*, 3rd ed. Hoboken, NJ: John Wiley & Sons, 2011.

Fleming, Claudia. *The Last Course*. New York: Random House, 2001.

French Culinary Institute. *The Fundamental Techniques of Classic Bread Baking*. New York: Stewart, Tabori, and Chang, 2011.

——. *The Fundamental Techniques of Classic Pastry Arts*. New York: Stewart, Tabori, and Chang, 2009.

Friberg, Bo. *The Professional Pastry Chef*, 4th ed. New York: John Wiley & Sons, 2002.

——. *The Advanced Professional Pastry Chef*. Hoboken, NJ: John Wiley & Sons, 2003.

Garrett, Toba M. *Professional Cake Decorating,* 2nd ed. Hoboken, NJ: John Wiley & Sons, 2012.

Gioannini, Marilyn. *The Complete Food Allergy Cookbook*. Roseville, CA: Prima, 1997.

Glezer, Maggie. *Artisan Baking Across America*. New York: Artisan, 2000.

Hagman, Bette. *The Gluten-Free Gourmet: Living Well Without Wheat*. New York: Henry Holt, 2000.

Hamelman, Jeffrey. *Bread: A Baker's Book of Techniques and Recipes,* 2nd ed. Hoboken, NJ: John Wiley & Sons, 2013.

Hermé, Pierre. *Desserts by Pierre Hermé Pastries*. New York: Stewart, Tabori, and Chang, 2012.

Labensky, Sarah R., Priscilla Martel, *and Eddy van Damme*. *On Baking*, 3rd ed. Upper Saddle River, NJ: Prentice Hall, 2016.

Leach, Richard. *Sweet Seasons*. New York: John Wiley & Sons, 2001.

Matz, S. A. *Bakery Technology and Engineering*, 3rd ed. McAllen, TX: Pan-Tech International, 1999.

MacLauchlan, Andrew. *New Classic Desserts*. New York: John Wiley & Sons, 1995.

——. *The Making of a Pastry Chef*. New York: John Wiley & Sons, 1999.

National Restaurant Association Educational Foundation. *ServSafe Coursebook*, 6th ed., Upper Saddle River, NJ: Prentice Hall, 2014.

Notter, Ewald. *The Art of the Chocolatier*. Hoboken, NJ: John Wiley & Sons, 2011.

——. *The Art of the Confectioner: Sugarwork and Pastillage*. Hoboken, NJ: John Wiley & Sons, 2012.

Payard, François, and Tish Boyle. *Payard Desserts*. Boston: Houghton Mifflin Harcourt, 2013.

Pyler, E. J., and Gorton L. A. *Baking Science and Technology*, 4th ed. 2 vols. Kansas City, MO: Sosland, 2010.

Reinhart, Peter. *The Bread Baker's Apprentice*. Berkeley, CA: Ten Speed Press, 2001.

Roux, Michel. *Desserts*. Boston: Houghton Mifflin Harcourt, 2011.

Schünemann, Claus, and Günter Treu. *Baking: The Art and Science*. Calgary, Alberta: Baker Tech, 1986.

Suas, Michel. *Advanced Bread and Pastry: A Professional Approach*. Clifton Park, NY: Delmar Cengage Learning, 2009.

Sultan, William J. *Practical Baking*, 5th ed. New York: John Wiley & Sons, 1989.

Teubner, Christian. *The Chocolate Bible*. New York: Penguin, 1997.

Trotter, Charlie. *Charlie Trotter's Desserts*. Berkeley, CA: Ten Speed Press, 1998.

Welker, Hans. *Professional Bread Baking*. Hoboken, NJ: John Wiley & Sons, 2017.

Woodruff, Sandra. *Secrets of Fat-Free Baking*. Garden City Park, NY: Avery, 1995.

Recipe Index

Subject Index